SOCIALIZATION

THOMAS RHYS WILLIAMS

Research Professor of Anthropology

George Mason University
Fairfax, Virginia

PRENTICE-HALL, INC., Englewood Cliffs, New Jersey 07632

Library of Congress Cataloging in Publication Data

WILLIAMS, THOMAS RHYS.
  Socialization.

  Bibliography: p.
  Includes index.
  1. Socialization. !. Title.
HQ783.W54   303.3'2   82-577
ISBN 0-13-815597-6   AACR2

A child is a person who is going to carry on what you have started. He is going to sit where you are sitting, and when you are gone, attend to those things which you may think are important. You may adopt all the policies you please, but how they are carried out depends on him. He will assume control of your cities, states and nations. He is going to move in and take over your churches, schools, universities and corporations—the fate of humanity is in his hands.

ABRAHAM LINCOLN

Editorial/production supervision by Fred Bernardi
Cover design by Miriam Recio
Manufacturing buyer: Edmund W. Leone

© 1983 by Prentice-Hall, Inc., Englewood Cliffs, New Jersey 07632

Printed in the United States of America

10 9 8 7 6 5 4 3 2 1

ISBN 0-13-815597-6

Prentice-Hall International, Inc., *London*
Prentice-Hall of Australia Pty. Limited, *Sydney*
Prentice-Hall of Canada, Ltd., *Toronto*
Prentice-Hall of India Private Limited, *New Delhi*
Prentice-Hall of Japan, Inc., *Tokyo*
Prentice-Hall of Southeast Asia Pte. Ltd., *Singapore*
Whitehall Books Limited, *Wellington, New Zealand*

CONTENTS

CHAPTER 6   KINSHIP, KIN GROUPS, AND SOCIALIZATION   195

Subsystems and Patterns of Culture   195; Ethnographic Examples—Arunta and Ashanti   197; Contextual and Holocultural Studies of Socialization   228; Conclusions   242; Summary   243; References Cited and Suggested Readings   244

CHAPTER 7   STATUS-ROLE, CLASS, AND SOCIALIZATION   254

Status-Role and Socialization   254; Class and Socialization   289; Caste and Socialization   297; Conclusions   299; Summary   300; References Cited and Suggested Readings   300

CHAPTER 8   TECHNOLOGY, IDEOLOGY, AND SOCIALIZATION   309

Technology and Socialization   309; Ideology and Socialization   328; Conclusions   345; Summary   347; References Cited and Suggested Readings   336

CHAPTER 9   LANGUAGE AND SOCIALIZATION   353

Language Origins and Evolution   353; Human and Animal Communication   358; Thought and Language   361; Learning Language   370; Language and Socialization   382; Conclusions   386; Summary   386; References Cited and Suggested Readings   387

CHAPTER 10   A SOCIALIZATION CONCEPTUAL SCHEME   397

Theory and Concept in Socialization Research   397; Structure of the Socialization Process   399; Functions of the Socialization Process   405; Discussion: A Socialization Conceptual Scheme   410; Alternate Socialization Conceptual Schemes   415; Further Development of a Socialization Conceptual Scheme   419; Applications of a Socialization Conceptual Scheme   419; Conclusions   420; Summary   421; References Cited and Suggested Readings   421

FOREWORD*

Margaret Mead

Socialization, the process by which human children born potentially human become human, able to function within the societies in which they are born, has been a subject of increasing interest during the last fifty years. Each decade has added new material, as we began to learn something about child development, something about the kinds of character formation which Freud described, something about the different ways in which children were reared in different cultures, something about learning, and more recently something about the interlocking of instinctive and learned behavior in many animal species and a little about the functioning of the brain. It has been a field that no discipline has been adequate to tackle alone, so anthropologists have relied on the work of psychiatrists and clinical psychologists; sociologists have used the work of anthropologists. Each advance in the field has relied on several different approaches. Of the various approaches it has been said that any one of them left alone long enough might have developed an adequate theory. But in actuality no one of them has been left alone, nor has any of them remained closely enough in touch with what the others have done. The field has steadily become more fragmented.

This textbook is an attempt to bring together within an evolutionary framework evidence from cultural anthropology, experimental psychology, and studies of social behavior within the industrialized world—three areas each of which has developed a rationale of its own. As no one has com-

*Author's Note: A year prior to her death in December, 1978, I asked Dr. Mead to rewrite this foreword, first published in 1972.[1] It was her intention to provide some indications of her present thinking concerning the study of the cultural transmission process. Dr. Mead urged me to concentrate on revision of my 1972 work and noted that she would rewrite her foreword. However, the rapid progress of her fatal illness precluded my requesting her attention to that task. But, during the last year of her life Dr. Mead continued an active and searching interest in the questions that were being phrased in the writing of this work. We spent a period together at my home in Columbus, Ohio, on April 21 and 22, 1978, reviewing a draft manuscript of the present work in detail, with Dr. Mead outlining the possible major directions to be taken in future research and theory in study of the cultural transmission process. My writing and later revision of this work was informed significantly by the insights provided by Margaret Mead as she neared the close of more than a half century of concentrated effort in seeking to understand cultural transmission, learning and the personal behavior consequences of such learning and transmission. My work has proceeded from the scientific legacy of Margaret Mead.

[1]T. R. Williams, *Introduction to Socialization: Human Culture Transmitted* (St. Louis: C. V. Mosby, 1972), pp. ix–xi.

manded all three of these fields, no one is in a position to fully introduce this book. It represents an enormous undertaking on the part of the author to start to organize a coherent theory from such diverse materials. I am competent to write only about the anthropological section, and no one of those who have been asked to read and criticize it is competent to judge the whole book. This is inevitable in a new field, a field in which there have been courses long before there were even the beginnings of a text.

The book represents the kind of problem that faces every teacher of university classes in the human sciences, whether that teacher be anthropologist or sociologist or psychologist. In his or her own area, based on experience, he or she can teach from first hand knowledge; for the rest there is dependence upon written reports, films, and tapes, from which the teacher tries to wring a sense of first hand experience. So when Dr. Williams speaks of the Papago and the Dusun among whom he has done field work, they come to life in vivid and concrete detail. For the other fields, he must summarize studies and experiments. But every teacher who has had the same experience should find it congenial to work with these same problems, and, in his or her own turn, contrast what he knows first hand with what is known from the literature, as he as a college teacher struggles, often on some very isolated campus, with articles in some two dozen journals, using half a dozen vocabularies and striking differences in methods and style.

Dr. Williams has also done what I believe every good textbook should do; he has stopped a little short of the present. The book attempts to summarize areas of consensus from which the explorers and innovators of today took off. The student is not presented with the latest controversial results, just hot off the press. At the same time, and this I find most interesting and I believe students will also, the phrasing of the book has been done carefully in the light of what has just been published and may later turn out to be very important.

I have known Tom Williams since 1958. I met him just before his first field trip to Borneo, and we had a long discussion about methods. I have been in close touch with his work ever since. He had entered the field of culture and personality advisedly, after his first field work among the Papago Indians, and finished his graduate work at Syracuse under Douglas Haring, who had worked with Boas and Ruth Benedict and myself at Columbia University. It was through Haring that Williams became the inheritor of the whole line of thinking which had led Franz Boas to designate the field of development of the individual in culture as of next importance. In 1922, Boas had said that he realized that the study of diffusion was finished. It had been demonstrated that human cultures could borrow from each other; that each did not have to go through an evolutionary sequence. Now we had to tackle the question of which aspects of human behavior were biologically given and which were due to having been born into one culture rather than another, in a technologically more advanced or technologically simpler culture, on one continent rather than on another. On his first field trip to Borneo Tom Williams took with him this long tradition, which required careful ethnography, that is, study of the whole culture, and then a study of the way in which children learned that culture. He also brought to his work an interest in the new techniques of adequate photographic documentation, of detailed studies of perception, of careful recording of gesture. He knew the importance of keeping track of his own responses to the field experience. All this he has described elsewhere in his books, *The Dusun: A North Borneo Society,* 1965; *Field Methods in the Study of Culture,* 1967; and *A Borneo Childhood: Enculturation in Dusun Society,* 1969.

I have followed each of these books, and the manuscript which preceded this text, with great interest, and I have learned a great deal thinking about some of the problems the text raises. To me one of the most important contributions is the way in which he has brought some of the very controversial findings of operant conditioning into line with much of what we knew about the kind of cultural learning which Boas used to call automatic behavior, or cultural behavior that in a sense the child teaches himself. Where so much of the emphasis in the controversy between B. F. Skinner and his critics has turned on manipulation—when looked at from the side of the experimenter—it is refreshing to have a discussion like this, which emphasizes instead what is done by the learning creature. When it was said, some thirty years ago that man is a maze learning animal, the emphasis was on the constructed maze. The pictures that Williams draws here of children who learn without either reward or punishment, who are given the responsibility for learning things themselves, many things which no one bothers to teach them, is congruent with much of our new thinking about education, where the emphasis is shifting from teaching to learning and it is the teacher as well as the pupil who learns.

Dr. Williams came into the field late enough to have the benefit of what had been learned from the cross-disciplinary concept of cybernetics, so that instead of representing the adults as doing something to a more or less ready child, he emphasizes the interrelationships between what the child has already learned on the basis of which the adult takes the next step in response. Nor does he have to waste time on sterile discussion of nature and nurture. Gone are the days, I hope, when students would rebel when I talked in one lecture about innate capacities and individual differences and in the next about the different way in which character is formed in different cultures systematically and how different the results were. Someone was sure to go away muttering: "She can't have it both ways." But, of course, we can. Inborn capacities become capabilities only when experience makes it possible for them to manifest themselves, and attention to the differences between individuals and between cultures is what makes it possible, in the long run, to identify the similarities also.

Dr. Williams has followed the route that is familiar to anthropologists. He has approached his problem through intensive study of particular cultures, but equipped with many of the ways in which we have learned to look cross-culturally at the whole experience of learning. Initially, like a student well versed in making phonetic transcripts, he learned a particular language; then, informed and transformed by the experience of studying the Tambunan Dusun of Borneo in detail, he has used this experience to work toward a cross-cultural vocabulary at another level.

This text reflects seven years of hard work, combining forays into the extensive and scattered and contradictory literature, with teaching. Each teacher who uses this book will be able to reenact these same struggles—in his own terms—and students who want to go further will have a platform from which to take off.

MARGARET MEAD
New York, January, 1972

PREFACE

The purpose of this text is to provide a discussion of the nature and major features of the socialization process. This work has been written in a manner that will provide for understanding of socialization whether or not readers have an expert in the field for a teacher and without regard to their level of study. There has been no effort to avoid unsettled problems in the book, since the contemporary study of socialization is a dynamic effort involving diverse theoretical views, ways of research and conflicting assumptions.

Many things said in this work rest upon large amounts of complex literature in anthropology, sociology, psychology, biology, medicine, and education. I am responsible for interpreting the ideas and research of other persons. I do not believe that in a brief work I can present completely all the theoretical ideas, concepts and factual detail involved in the study of socialization.

This text is not intended to serve as a basic research source. Hence, so far as possible, consistent with the highest standards of accuracy and fairness in giving credit for specific ideas, exhaustive citations to the socialization research literature have not been provided.

The scope of the study of the socialization process is far too broad to be comprehended from within the confines of only one research discipline. I have presented an approach that includes many of the ways an anthropologist would discuss socialization. But not all anthropologists, or other specialists concerned with socialization research, would take the approach used here. That is as it should be in a field just beginning to give sustained attention to the complex problems found in the study of the socialization process.

There have been two major theoretical approaches in modern studies of culture. First, there is the position based in the nineteenth century intellectual traditions of naturalism, positivism, and evolution, which depicts culture as an autonomous, superpsychical and superorganic entity, subject only to its own laws, stages of development, and internal dynamics. Then there is the theoretical position that has its roots in the humanistic traditions of the European Renaissance and the rationalism of the eighteenth century philosophers of the Enlightenment which depicts culture as the product of human discovery and creativity and therefore fully subject to human control and direction. The central problem in contemporary cultural theory is the definition of the nature of culture.[1]

---

[1]Goodenough (1974) has discussed ways these two theoretical positions are expressed by contemporary cultural theorists. See also Goodenough, 1981; Manners and Kaplan, 1968; Kaplan and Manners, 1972; Sahlins, 1976; Harris, 1968.

This text is not concerned with defining the nature of culture. However, it does use the concept of culture consistently in a way that emphasizes the role of human intelligence and freedom and the actions of individuals in forming and determining their own cultural destiny as well as the conditions of their society. The text also proceeds with the assumption that there is substantial merit in trying to understand the natural origins and the internal logic of an evolving tradition of learned, patterned, transmitted and widely shared human behavior.

Too, I must say that I am not unmindful of the place and value of the concepts of social system and society in studies of human behavior. I have tried to follow the distinctions between the concepts of culture and social system made by Alfred Kroeber and Talcott Parsons without necessarily accepting all of the theoretical definitions used in their work.[2] However, I have also assumed that the possibility of fully understanding the concepts of culture, social system, and society increases in relation to the degree to which the analytic distinctions between the concepts are recognized and followed.

It should be noted that this text is characterized by *transcultural, transtemporal,* and *holistic* orientations, that is, by a specific concern that general statements about socialization are inclusive of all cultures, through the very long time of the existence of culture, and are based on understandings gained from study of all of culture rather than some selected parts.

The organization and writing of this work required a careful selection of diverse materials. Those finally included appear to be the works useful in gaining a basic understanding of the socialization process. This text does not include citations to all the socialization publications in the several years immediately preceding its publication. However, key ideas and the persons associated with them have been noted, where possible, to allow readers to anticipate major future developments in the study of socialization.

Some research will undoubtedly alter the ways in which the socialization process is considered. For instance, Margaret Mead, in *Culture and Commitment* (1970), has offered the hypothesis that the present generation of young humans are participating in a fundamental change in cultural transmission, so that for the first time, some young people know more than their parents, and now are informing their elders in ways that parents traditionally have enculturated children. Similarly, the research of Eliot Chapple, Ray Birdwhistell, Edward T. Hall, Alan Lomax, and others in the area of what may be termed as "microcultural" studies of human communication and cultural transmission may lead to significant changes in theory and method in socialization research.[3] This new field is still developing. Hence, while this research has been noted, it has not been discussed in detail. This same procedure of selection has been followed in the instances of other major advances in socialization research. For example, the quite substantial and original theory of cultural transmission developed by

---

[2]See Kroeber and Parsons, 1958.

[3]See Chapple, 1970; Birdwhistell, 1970; Hall, 1966; Lomax, 1968. See also Hinde, 1972; Goffman, 1967; Kendon, 1976; Kendon, Harris & Key, 1975; and Williams, 1975.

John and Beatrice Whiting and their associates, has led to a whole range of new ideas, many being formed and tested at present.[4] This work is noted in several places in the text.

This book owes much to the pioneering research of Margaret Mead, especially her long-term field studies concerned with cultural transmission, learning, human development, and nutrition, and her theoretical development of these topics.[5] It has been said that it is difficult to discuss personality theory without reference to the research of Sigmund Freud, Henry Murray and Gordon Allport. It is similarly difficult to describe our present understanding of the process of cultural transmission without explicitly acknowledging the great debt owed Margaret Mead for informing us of the possibilities of a scientific understanding of cultural transmission.

This text is based on a work first published in 1972.[6] The present work has been substantially revised and written with attention to basic research between 1972 and 1981. It contains a new final chapter as well as other altered chapters and suggested readings. Readers familiar with the earlier work will find changes in the text are based on recent research and my rethinking of parts of the earlier work and certain theoretical issues.

My wife Peggy has provided continuing support, encouragement and insight in the course of my work. I have learned with her about cultural transmission from our sons, Rhys, Ian and Tom. This work is dedicated to my wife and our sons for their loving understanding over very many years. It also is dedicated to my parents, Dorothy and Harold Williams, for their care and love through my enculturation.

THOMAS RHYS WILLIAMS
Reston, Virginia

[4]See B. Whiting and J.W.M. Whiting, 1975. See also Barry & Schlegel, 1980; Shweder, 1979.

[5]See Schwartz, 1976; Lindzey, 1974; Gordan, 1976; Mead, 1976.

[6]See Williams, 1972.

REFERENCES

BARRY, H. III and A. SCHLEGEL (eds.) 1980.   *Cross-Cultural Samples and Codes.* Pittsburgh: University of Pittsburgh Press.

BIRDWHISTELL, R. 1970.   *Kinesics and Context; Essays on Body Motion Communication.* Philadelphia: University of Pennsylvania Press.

CHAPPLE, E. 1970.   *Culture and Biological Man; Explorations in Behavioral Anthropology.* New York: Holt, Rinehart and Winston.

GOFFMAN, E. 1967.   *Interaction Ritual.* New York: Anchor Books.

———. 1971.   *Relations in Public.* New York: Basic Books.

GORDAN, J. (ed.) 1976.   *Margaret Mead, The Complete Bibliography 1925-1975.* The Hague; Mouton.

GOODENOUGH, W. 1974.   "On Cultural Theory." *Science* 186: 435–436.

———. 1981.   *Culture, Language and Society.* Menlo Park, Calif.: Benjamin/Cummings.

HALL, E. T. 1966.   *The Hidden Dimension.* New York: Doubleday.

HARRIS, M. 1968.   *The Rise of Anthropological Theory.* New York: Crowell.

HINDE, R. (ed.) 1972. *Non-Verbal Communication*. Cambridge: Cambridge University Press.
————. 1973. "Toward a Grammar of Dyadic Conversation." *Semiotica* 9: 29–46.
KAPLAN, D. and R. MANNERS, 1972. *Culture Theory*. Englewood Cliffs, N.J.: Prentice-Hall.
KENDON, A. 1976. *Studies in the Behavior of Social Interaction*. Bloomington, Ind.: Indiana University Research Center, Studies in Semiotics, Number 6.
KENDON, A., R. HARRIS and M. KEY (eds.) 1975. *The Organization of Behavior in Face-to-Face Interaction*. The Hague: Mouton.
KROEBER, A.L. and T. PARSONS. 1958. "The Concepts of Culture and Social System." *American Sociological Review* 23: 582–583.
LINDZEY, G. (ed.) 1974. "Margaret Mead," in *A History of Psychology in Autobiography*. New York: Prentice-Hall, pp. 293-326.
LOMAX, A. 1968. *Folk Song Style and Culture*. Washington, D.C.: American Association for the Advancement of Science.
MANNERS, R. and D. KAPLAN (eds.) 1968. *Theory in Anthropology*. Oxford: Clarendon Press.
MEAD, M. 1970. *Culture and Commitment; A Study of the Generation Gap*. New York: Natural History Press and Doubleday.
————. 1976. "Towards a Human Science." *Science* 191: 903–909.
SAHLINS, M. 1976. *Culture and Practical Reason*. Chicago: University of Chicago Press.
SCHWARTZ, T. (ed.) 1976. *Socialization as Cultural Communication; Development of a Theme in the Work of Margaret Mead*. Berkeley: University of California Press.
SHWEDER, R. 1979. "Rethinking Culture and Personality." *Ethos* 7: 255–278; 279–311.
WHITING, B. and J.W.M. WHITING. 1975. *Children of Six Cultures; A Psycho-Cultural Analysis*. Cambridge, Mass.: Harvard University Press.
WILLIAMS, T.R. 1972. *Introduction to Socialization: Human Culture Transmitted*. St. Louis: C.V. Mosby.
————. (ed.) 1975. *Socialization and Communication in Primary Groups*. The Hague: Mouton.

INTRODUCTION

If we could safely transport human embryos to some distant planet or galaxy and mechanically provide all the physical conditions necessary for their "birth" and maturation, the question would arise, "Would the embryos become human beings as we know them?" The answer is quite clear; unless a way could be found to provide the embryos with culture, they would lack many of the attributes implied by the word human.[1] A way would have to be found to transmit the complex whole of knowledge and habits that characteristically are associated with being human.

This text is concerned with abstract statements of empirical reference concerning the transmission of culture. The text distinguishes conceptually between *socialization*, the process of transmitting human culture, and *enculturation*, the process of transmitting a particular culture.[2] Eskimo infants and children are enculturated in Eskimo culture; all human infants and children are socialized in human culture.[3] It is necessary to note this conceptual difference to maintain a clear distinction between statements regarding transmission of human culture ("It would appear that, on the whole, adult *Homo sapiens* has rarely taken it for granted that children could or would just naturally learn by spontaneous imitation." Henry, 1960:304) and statements regarding transmission of one culture ("Although there were customs of kindness and tolerance toward children, the society [Nunivak Eskimo] centered in the adult males." Lantis, 1960:167). The confounding of statements concerning socialization and enculturation has led to different conceptual uses and definitions of the term socialization. Thus Elkin (1960:4) says:

> We may define socialization as the process by which someone learns the ways of a given society or social group so that he can function within it.

---

[1] In this work the concept of culture will be used generally as it has been defined by Kroeber and Kluckhohn (1952:181): "Culture consists of patterns, explicit and implicit, of and for behavior acquired and transmitted by symbols, constituting the distinctive achievement of human groups, including their embodiments in artifacts; the essential core of culture consists of traditional (i.e., historically derived and selected) ideas and especially their attached values; culture systems may, on the one hand, be considered as products of action, and on the other hand as conditioning elements of further action."

[2] The term *process* refers to a series of continuous, regular and interrelated events with certain defined and recognizable entities or properties. Mead (1963) has commented on the confounding of the terms, socialization and enculturation, and has noted the confusion resulting in general statements about the historical particulars of learning one culture (enculturation) being taken to be statements concerning the process of learning culture (socialization) true of all humans.

[3] I do not mean to imply that Eskimos are not human.

In a review of socialization research, Child (1954:655) notes:

> Socialization is used here as a broad term for the whole process by which an individual born with behavioral potentialities of enormously wide range, is led to develop actual behavior which is confined within a much narrower range—the range of what is customary and acceptable for him according to the standards of his group.

Brim (1966:3) has defined socialization as:

> The process by which individuals acquire the knowledge, skills and dispositions that enable them to participate as more or less effective members of groups and the society.

In a text containing a series of essays reviewing research and theory in socialization, Clausen comments accurately that the term socialization has a history of varied use. He also says:

> To large degree, childhood socialization is the social orientation of the child and his enculturation, first within the small social world of family and neighborhood and then in relation to the larger society and culture. (Clausen, 1968:4).

Although Clausen notes a distinction between socialization and enculturation (c.f., Clausen, 1968:47), he chooses to use the term socialization to refer generally to the transmission and acquisition of one culture, rather than human culture. Cohen (1971:387) also defines socialization as a process within a particular society when he says:

> Socialization—the inculcation of basic psychological patterns through spontaneous interaction with parents, siblings, and others—is the predominant mode of shaping the mind in social systems in which kinship is the primary principle in the organization of economic, political and other social relations.

In contrast, Kimball (1974:160) has defined the socialization process as a variable relationship between a ". . . social and cultural environment, which prescribes the method and content of education, and the individual in whom experience is organized and internalized." Gearing and Tindall (1973:96) take a similar approach to the one used by Kimball, when they define socialization as

> . . . constituted in regularly occurring patterns of encounter, wherein are transacted various equivalences of meaning, which equivalences together form a network and are a cultural system of the community in question.

And, Tindall (1976:199) offers a similar definition of socialization when he notes

. . . cultural transmission is constituted in two interrelated processes; the inter-psychic process which is concerned with who (actors) does what (interactive form or mode including setting or circumstance) about what topics (content of communication and complexity of information), and the intra-psychic process of cognition wherein people organize the stimuli which are made available to them in their social and cultural environment.

In other words Kimball, Gearing and Tindall define socialization as a human process which is focused and operates on the level of one culture or community.

This text is based on the idea that the systematic study of cultural transmission requires concepts and generalizations not limited to the unique history or ecological conditions of one culture, or a group of related cultures, and their particular ethnocentrisms, xenophobias, and special views of the "proper" social relations between humans, or of their place in the universe.

It is only because of historic accident that we happen to know a great deal more about the ways some kinds of American and Western European children have their local variations of human culture transmitted to them than we do about the transmission of other cultures. The fact that we have a body of literature concerning the ways European and American cultures are transmitted is very seductive because it leads to the false assumption that Western European and American enculturation processes really represent the prototype of human culture transmission.

The often prevailing tendency of scholars concerned with study of socialization to narrowly focus study and theory upon the facts of transmitting a particular culture, rather than on the transmission of human culture, is a transient state. It is very easy to be *culture-bound*, that is, limited to study of one culture, particularly when the tools of research are written questionnaires, interviews conducted in carefully selected "sample" neighborhoods, a library containing the broad range of journals and texts needed, or the teaching, clinical, or experimental laboratory, readily available and often well supplied with children amenable to being talked to and observed. The problem is that, until recently, many students of socialization have not been trained to think about and to conduct their research in transcultural, or universally human, terms.

It is important to note that the term cultural transmission is meant to be defined here to include the concept of acquisition as well as the transmission of culture. In considering the discussion in this text, it will be helpful to remember that the phrase, "cultural transmission" directly implies the process of acquiring culture, while the expression "acquisition of culture" directly implies the process of cultural transmission. There is no dichotomy, or a conceptual division into two subordinate and separate parts implied in the term, "cultural transmission." In this text, acquisition of culture and cultural transmission are considered as necessary conceptual reciprocals of one another.

Furthermore, it should be noted that the phrase, "acquisition of culture" also carries with it the corollary idea of the consequences of acquiring culture for the individual. The understanding of the precise ways in which personality traits and patterns leading to individual acts are produced through the socialization process is a highly desirable goal in basic research. However, this text concentrates upon discussing the essential nature of cultural transmission. This work is not primarily concerned with consequences of cultural transmission for individuals.

The study of the consequences of cultural transmission for individuals is a separate area of specialized research. In the field of anthropology this area of research is termed *culture-personality* studies, or more recently, *psychological anthropology*. In the field of psychology this area of research often is termed *social psychology*, or sometimes is included as part of studies in *child psychology, developmental psychology, motivation,* or *personality*. In sociology this area of research is designated by the name *social psychology*, or the term, "socialization." There are a number of texts that provide detailed introductions to the study of the consequences of the cultural transmission process.[4] Readers should not expect this work to be a psychological anthropology, social psychology, or personality development text, or a work concerned primarily with the transcultural study of human development.[5]

An analogy is useful in trying to make clear the reason for the focus of this work upon the origin and nature rather than the consequences of the socialization process. Suppose that a space pioneer transporting human embryos to a distant planet somehow had lost a wristwatch before returning to earth. Then, imagine one of the embryos, left behind to be mechanically nurtured to adult form but lacking human culture, picking up the wristwatch from the extraterrestrial surface. Unless this being was equipped with culture for understanding the watch, it would be presented with the puzzle of trying to explain the purposes and origins of the unknown object.

Through the use of modern scientific procedures, which are cultural inventions, humans have come to possess detailed information concerning the objects and events they see and "pick up" in the natural world. We now have acquired a very great store of descriptive knowledge about "how" natural objects and events occur and are constructed. But so far modern science has not provided many answers to the "why" of natural objects and events. For example, it has been demonstrated that ribonucleic acid (RNA) accelerates learning when introduced into the cerebral cortex of some animals; yet we do not know why this occurs. The working of the genetic code contained in deoxyribonucleic acid (DNA) molecules has been described in detail, but we still do not know why DNA operates as it does in hereditary transmission. We know that foreign protein substances introduced into the bodies of many animals produce an outpouring of antibodies that destroy

[4]See Honigman, 1954, 1967; Kaplan, 1961; Endleman, 1967; Hunt, 1967; Goodman, 1967; McNeil, 1969; Wallace, 1970; Edgerton, 1971; Elkin and Handel, 1978; Levine, 1973; Zigler and Child, 1973; Price-Williams, 1975; Maller, Pine and Bergman, 1975; Thompson, 1975; Hewitt, 1976; Sepell, 1976; White, 1977; Barnouw, 1979; Bock, 1980.

[5]For an account of human development in a transcultural perspective see Munroe and Munroe, 1975. See also, Freeman, 1974.

the intruding matter. However, we still do not know why the antibodies do not also destroy their host body as the antigen-antibody process occurs.

Similarly, through the use of scientific procedures, we have come to know more about humans than ever before. We know from descriptions of how humans live and behave that much of human behavior is learned, rather than genetically transmitted, and that a substantial amount of such learning occurs in a socialization process. We are aware that socialization is profoundly important in human affairs, yet we still have to determine why this process came into existence, gained its basic nature and why its origins and nature are related to its consequences for human life and behavior. In some respects, contemporary humans are similar to a wristwatch that somehow has come to be possessed of the capacity to pick itself up from the ground and speculate upon its own origins and functions while it marvels at its precise measurement of time, a concept it does not comprehend.

There have been a number of scientific approaches to searching out the "why" of the socialization process. One method has been a comparison of careful description and analysis of the details of enculturation, or cultural transmission in specific societies. A second approach has been to describe and analyze the personalities and behavior of individuals who have been enculturated in a society. Another approach has been description and analysis of different whole cultural and social systems, seeking through this procedure to abstract some basic explanations for the socialization process. A fourth approach has been to describe and analyze the various social positions, or statuses, and behaviors associated with specific statuses, or roles, and the ways these are organized into social classes to determine how the socialization process operates and changes through time. Each of these approaches has produced a large amount of descriptive, or "how" material. However, so far all have been unsuccessful in providing insight as to the nature of the socialization process.

The discussion in this work will be concerned with examining a number of topics that appear to bear upon an understanding of the origin and nature of the socialization process.[6] It will draw upon all the different approaches to study of socialization and will use relevant data and theory from a wide range of scientific disciplines.

The text begins with four chapters discussing the evolutionary origins and human biological bases of the socialization process. Chapter One presents some of the major details of the possible beginnings of socialization. Chapter Two describes specific human biological features developed in the course of evolution that appear to serve as organic bridgeheads, or key transition points, between human biology and culture in socialization. Chapter Three briefly reviews four major models of learning, which then are contrasted to case study data of enculturation in a native North American society, noting some of the ways human reflective and symbolic processes enter into and are integral to cultural transmission. Chapter Four is

---

[6]For discussions of the nature and possible origins and evolutionary development of cultural transmission, see Williams, 1972, 1975.

a discussion of some of the specific ways that culture and biology may become interrelated in cultural transmission.

Chapter Five discusses research data from studies of isolated individuals and twins that can aid in illustrating some of the ways human biology and culture become interrelated in socialization. This chapter also is concerned with a key hypothesis, termed the "critical periods hypothesis," that has been used often in studies of socialization.

The next four chapters are concerned with the relationship between the socialization process and specific patterns and forms of culture. Chapter Six discusses some possible interrelationships between socialization and the cultural patterns of kinship and kin groups. Chapter Seven notes some possible relations between socialization and patterns of status-role, and social class behavior. Chapter Eight discusses the ways cultural patterns of technology and ideology may be related to socialization. Chapter Nine is concerned with the ways socialization and language may be related. Chapter Ten presents a conceptual scheme for study of socialization. The text concludes with a brief Epilogue. The Epilogue is followed by an Appendix containing a bibliography of suggested readings on enculturation in 128 societies. A Glossary of Terms is included at the close of the text.

It should be noted that this text uses case studies illustrating features of enculturation in several societies and that all of these discussions have been written in the *ethnographic present*, that is, as if the people being described live today as they once did, before contact with the modern world. The case studies are written in the ethnographic present only because it is an effective way to present a brief discussion of a specific system of enculturation. It is important to say this because a great many changes have occurred in most previously isolated, nonliterate, and nonindustrial societies. No one reading the case study material should complete the text thinking that the peoples referred to in the case study examples are culturally backward folk surviving at the fringes of Western European and American civilization. Nothing could be further from the truth in this rapidly changing world.

REFERENCES CITED AND SUGGESTED READINGS

ABERLE, D.F. 1961. "Culture and Socialization." In F.L.K. Hsu (ed.), *Psychological Anthropology*. Homewood, Ill.: Dorsey, pp. 381–399.

BARNOUW, V. 1979. *Culture and Personality*. Homewood, Ill.: Dorsey. (3d. rev. ed.).

BOCK, P. 1980. *Continuities in Psychological Anthropology*. San Francisco: W.H. Freeman.

BRIM, O.G. Jr. 1966. "Socialization Through the Life Cycle." In O.G. Brim, Jr. and S. Wheeler (eds.), *Socialization After Childhood*. New York: Wiley, pp. 3–7.

———. 1968. "Socialization: Adult Socialization." In D.L. Sills (ed.), *International Encyclopedia of the Social Sciences* 14: 555–562. New York: Macmillan and the Free Press.

BRONFENBRENNER, U. 1970. *Two Worlds of Childhood*. New York: Russell Sage Foundation.

BURTON, R.V. 1968. "Socialization: Psychological Aspects." In D.L. Sills (ed.), *International Encyclopedia of the Social Sciences* 14: 534–545. New York: Macmillan and The Free Press.

CAMPBELL, E.Q. 1975. *Socialization: Culture and Personality*. DuBuque: W.C. Brown.

CHILD, I.L. 1954. "Socialization." In G. Lindzey (ed.), *Handbook of Social Psychology*, Vol. II. Reading, Mass.: Addison-Wesley, pp. 655–692.

CLAUSEN, J.A. (ed.) 1968.   *Socialization and Society.* Boston: Little, Brown.
COHEN, Y.A. 1971.   "The Shaping of Men's Minds: Adaptations to Imperatives of Culture."
In M. Wax, S. Diamond and F. Gearing (eds.), *Anthropological Perspectives on Education.*
New York: Basic Books, pp. 19–50.
DANZIGER, K. (ed.) 1970.   *Readings in Child Socialization.* Oxford: Pergamon.
DENNIS, J. 1973.   *Socialization to Politics: A Reader.* New York: Wiley.
DEVOS, G.A. 1973.   *Socialization for Achievement; Essays on the Cultural Psychology of the Japanese.*
Berkeley: University of California Press.
EDGERTON, R.B. 1971.   *The Individual in Cultural Adaptation.* Berkeley: University of California
Press.
ELKIN, F. 1960.   *The Child and Society: The Process of Socialization.* New York: Random House.
ELKIN, F. and G. HANDEL. 1978.   *The Child and Society.* New York: Random House (3d. ed.).
ELKIND, D. 1979.   *The Child and Society.* New York: Oxford University Press.
ENDLEMAN, R. (ed.) 1967.   *Personality and Social Life.* New York: Random House.
FREEMAN, I. 1974.   *Human Infancy: An Evolutionary Perspective.* Hillsdale, N.J.: Earlbaum As-
sociates.
GEARING, F. and B.A. TINDAL. 1973.   "Anthropological Studies of the Educational Process."
Annual Review of Anthropology. 2: 95–105.
GEARING, F. and L. SANGREE (eds.) 1978.   *Toward a Cultural Theory of Education and Schooling.*
The Hague: Mouton.
GOODMAN, M. E. 1967.   *The Individual and Culture.* Homewood, Ill.: Dorsey.
GOSLIN, D. (ed.) 1969.   *Handbook of Socialization Theory and Research.*
GREENBERG, E.S. 1970.   *Political Socialization.* New York: Atherton Press.
GREENSTEIN, R. I. 1968.   "Socialization: Political Socialization." In D.S. Sills (ed.), *International
Encyclopedia of the Social Sciences* 14: 551–555. New York: Macmillan and the Free Press.
Harvard Educational Review. 1968.   "Political Socialization." Volume 38, Number 3 (entire
issue).
HEMPEL, C.G. 1952.   *Fundamentals of Concept Formation in Empirical Science.* Chicago: University
of Chicago Press.
HENRY, J. 1960.   "A Cross-Cultural Outline of Education." *Current Anthropology.* 1: 267–305.
HEWITT, J.P. 1976.   *Self and Society.* Boston: Allyn and Bacon.
HONIGMANN, J.J. 1954.   *Culture and Personality.* New York: Harper.
———. 1967.   *Personality in Culture.* New York: Harper.
HOPPE, R., G. MILTON, and E. SIMMEL (eds.) 1970.   *Early Experiences and the Processes of So-
cialization.* New York: Academic Press.
HSU, F.L.K. (ed.) 1972.   *Psychological Anthropology.* Cambridge, Mass.: Schenkman.
HUNT, R. (ed.) 1967.   *Personalities and Cultures.* Garden City, N.J.: Natural History Press.
KAPLAN, B. (ed.) 1961.   *Studying Personality Cross-Culturally.* New York: Harper and Row.
KIMBALL, S.T. 1974.   *Culture and the Educative Process.* New York: Teachers College Press.
KOLLER, M.R. and O.W. RITCHIE. 1978.   *Sociology of Childhood.* Englewood Cliffs, N.J.: Pren-
tice-Hall (2d. ed.).
KROEBER, A.L., and C. KLUCKHOHN. 1952.   *Culture: A Critical Review of Concepts and Definitions.*
Papers of the Peabody Museum of American Archaeology and Ethnology, Harvard
University, XLVII, Number One.
LANTIS, M. 1960.   *Eskimo Childhood and Interpersonal Relationships.* Seattle: University of Wash-
ington Press.
LEIDERMAN, P.H., et al. (eds.) 1977.   *Culture and Infancy: Variations in Human Experience.* New
York: Academic Press.
LEVINE, R. 1973.   *Culture, Behavior and Personality.* Chicago: Aldine.
LINTON, R. 1936.   *The Study of Man.* New York: Appleton-Century.
MALLER, M., F. PINE and A. BERGMAN. 1975.   *The Psychological Birth of the Human Infant.* New
York: Basic Books.
MAYER, P. (ed.) 1970.   *Socialization: The Approach from Social Anthropology.* London, Tavistock.
MCNEIL, E. 1969.   *Human Socialization.* Belmont, California: Brooks/Cole.
MEAD, M. 1963.   "Socialization and Enculturation," *Current Anthropology* 4: 184–188.
———. 1971.   Review of P. Mayer (ed.) "Socialization: The Approach from Social Anthro-
pology." *American Anthropologist* 73: 327–328.
MUNROE, R.L. and R. MUNROE. 1975.   *Cross-Cultural Human Development.* Monterey, Califor-
nia: Brook/Cole.

NAGEL, E. 1961. *The Structure of Science; Problems in the Logic of Scientific Explanation.* New York: Harcourt, Brace and World.

PRICE-WILLIAMS, D. 1975. *Explorations in Cross-Cultural Psychology.* San Francisco: Chandler and Sharp.

ROSE, P.I. (ed.) 1979. *Socialization and the Life Cycle.* New York: St. Martin.

ROSOW, I. 1975. *Socialization to Old Age.* Berkeley: University of California Press.

SCARR-SALAPATEK, S. and P. SALAPATEK (eds.) 1973. *Socialization.* Columbus, Ohio: Merrill.

SCHWARTZ, T. (ed.) 1976. *Socialization as Cultural Communication; Development of a Theme in the Work of Margaret Mead.* Berkeley: University of California Press.

———. 1981. "The Acquisition of Culture." *Ethos* 9: 4–36.

SEPELL, R. 1976. *Culture's Influence on Behavior.* London: Methuen.

SHIMAHARA, N. 1970. "Enculturation—A Reconsideration." *Current Anthropology* 11: 143–154.

SHIPMAN, M. 1972. *Childhood: A Sociological Perspective.* New York: Humanities Press.

SMITH, B.O., and D.L. ORLOSKY, 1975. *Socialization and Schooling: The Basics of Reform.* Bloomington, Ind.: Phi Delta Kappa.

SPIRO, M.E. 1951. "Culture and Personality; The Natural History of a False Dichotomy." *Psychiatry* 14: 19–46.

THOMPSON, R.A. 1975. *Psychology and Culture.* Dubuque: William C. Brown Company.

TINDALL, B.A. 1976. "Theory in the Study of Cultural Transmission." *Annual Review of Anthropology* 5: 195–208.

WALLACE, A.F.C. 1970. *Culture and Personality.* New York: Random House.

WHITE, G. 1977. *Socialisation.* London: Longman.

WHITING, J.W.M. 1968. "Socialization: Anthropological Aspects." In D. L. Sills (ed.), *International Encyclopedia of the Social Sciences* 14: 545–551. New York: Macmillan and the Free Press.

WHITING, B.B., and J.W.M. WHITING. 1975. *Children of Six Cultures; A Psycho-Cultural Analysis.* Cambridge: Harvard University Press.

WILSON, R.W. 1974. *The Moral State: A Study of the Political Socialization of Chinese and American Children.* New York: Free Press.

WILLIAMS, T.R. 1969. *A Borneo Childhood: Enculturation in Dusun Society.* New York: Holt, Rinehart, and Winston.

———. 1972. "The Socialization Process: A Theoretical Perspective," in F. E. Poirier (ed.), *Primate Socialization.* New York: Random House, pp. 207–260.

———. 1975. "On the Origin of the Socialization Process." In T. R. Williams (ed.), *Socialization and Communication in Primary Groups.* The Hague: Mouton, pp. 233–249.

———. 1979. "Comment on a Cultural Theory of Education and Schooling." In F. Gearing and L. Sangree (eds.), *Toward a Cultural Theory of Education and Schooling.* The Hague: Mouton, pp. 151–166.

YARROW, M.R., et al. 1968. *Childrearing; An Inquiry into Research and Methods.* San Francisco: Jossey-Bass.

ZIGLER, E. and I.L. CHILD, 1973. *Socialization and Personality Development.* Reading, Mass.: Addison-Wesley Press.

CHAPTER ONE
BACKGROUND
OF SOCIALIZATION
Introduction

This chapter discusses some of the ways the cultural transmission process is based on and proceeds from the human evolutionary heritage.

POSTULATES FOR STUDY OF CULTURAL TRANSMISSION

There is abundant scientific evidence to confirm at least two postulates on which the study of cultural transmission may be based. These postulates are:

1. The human ability for transmitting and acquiring culture derives from a particular kind of anatomy and physiology.
2. Culture is the natural ecology of humans.

To understand these postulates it is necessary to examine briefly the main outline of human biological evolution and beginnings of culture. The following review provides some general ideas concerning the ways in which cultural transmission has developed from biological bases through natural evolutionary events and has come to be a significant aspect of human life.

Thinking About Human Evolution

Homo sapiens sapiens, or contemporary humans, are the product of a very long biological evolutionary process. This process began more than a billion years ago with the extremely complex transition on the earth from inorganic, nonliving substances to organic, living entities. One thing that was true of all of these first living forms, and has remained true of all living forms throughout the course of evolution, is that *living things act in characteristic ways*. Such characteristic behavior derives from the kinds of bodies living things possess, whether one is talking about the first fishes (ostracoderms) of the *Ordovician* period of 500 million years ago, the giant dinosaurs of the *Triassic* period of 200 million years ago, or *Homo sapiens sapiens*. Humans are living things and behave in characteristic ways that are determined by the structure of their bodies.

The human body is structurally organized on the basis of features that are the consequence of cumulative evolutionary adaptations through an immense span of time—that is, humans have inherited the evolutionary structural modifications that have occurred during more than a billion years. Although humans have characteristics of the phylum *Chordata*, they do not have all the physical characteristics of chordates. Humans do not have a skin with placoid scales, as do sharks and rays, nor do they possess skin with feathers, as is typical of birds, because the particular animal populations from which humans have evolved did not adapt to their environments through development of such special body structures. So the kind of body humans have is the product of cumulative evolutionary adaptations of the animals ancestral to humans. One major consequence of the concept of cumulative evolutionary adaptations is the avoidance of the "nothing-but" fallacy—that is, "humans are nothing but animals" and therefore have only the attributes of all other animals and can be studied through experimental procedures applied to laboratory animals. This is false reasoning, as applied to humans. It is very important to realize that, through the evolutionary process of cumulative adaptations, humans have come to possess a total set of body charactertistics not shared with any other animal form.

Primitive Mammals

On the basis of their physical traits, humans are classified as a member of the *primate order* of the animal class termed *mammals*. The first primitive animals of the mammal class appear in the fossil record in the *Triassic* period about 200 million years ago. By the end of the *Mesozoic* era, which occurred about 220 million to 60 million years ago, primitive mammals had adapted by evolutionary biological processes—for instance, natural selec-

TABLE 1-1 Geological Time Scale of Appearance of Various Forms of Life

Life forms	Millions of years since the beginnings of epochs and eras	Epochs, periods	Era
Homo sapiens	1/40*	Recent	
Homo erectus	2	Pleistocene	Present
Homo	12	Pliocene	
Anthropoid apes	25	Miocene	
Primitive apes	35	Oligocene	Cenozoic
Spread of modern mammals	55	Eocene	
Appearance of earliest primates	60	Paleocene	
Rise of mammals and birds	120	Cretaceous	
Spread of primitive mammals	180	Jurassic	Mesozoic
Appearance of primitive mammals	220	Triassic	
Spread of amphibians and insects	285	Permian	
Primitive reptiles, insects, spiders	350	Carboniferous	
Rise of fishes and amphibians	400	Devonian	
First land plants, rise of ostracoderms	450	Silurian	Paleozoic
First primitive fishes, the ostracoderms	500	Ordovician	
No land life in fossil record	600	Cambrian	
Sponges, protozoans, mollusks	925		Proterozoic
Simple one-celled sea forms	1,500		Archeozoic

*NOTE: The dates for appearance of forms of life and duration of epochs have been fixed by dating techniques of geology and geochemistry. There are disagreements between specialists concerning precise dates for epochs and eras.

tion, mutation, gene recombinations, and population isolation—to difficult environmental conditions and had separated into three quite distinct groups: egg-laying mammals (*Monotremata*), pouched mammals (*Marsupialia*), and placental mammals (*Eutheria*). Primates are placental mammals. The placental mammals first appear in the fossil record in the *Cretaceous* rocks of Mongolia, some 120 million years ago.

The fossil record indicates that the placental mammal population of the later *Cretaceous* period included many widely scattered populations of small, tree-living, insect-eating animals, which probably looked very much like today's tree shrew. These creatures probably were like the contemporary tree shrew in their behavior—that is, they were alert, active, and agile among the high branches of the *Cretaceous* forests. These creatures had to rely more on their visual sense and less on their sense of smell, which had been the ancestral placental mammal evolutionary adaptation to hunting along the ground. They also had to adapt to grasping for balance among the high tree branches. It is believed that these kinds of animals were possibly ancestral to the primate order.

Changes Toward Primate Structure

The first primate populations appear to have possessed the visual, sensory, and grasping structures of the primitive mammals. They probably had movable ears at the top of their heads, sensitive tactile vibrissa (hairlike structures) on their long muzzles, a highly developed sense of smell, and generally weak vision. A sense of smell is not as vital as a developed sense of vision in getting food in the trees. Animals living on the ground can easily sniff out food and pick it up with their jaws. In the trees, animals have to see food to catch it, especially if the diet is insect life. They have to catch flying and hopping insects by using the forelimbs while using the hind limbs for grasping, balance, and support on landing. Animals who pick food out from under tree bark by using their sharp nails also have to develop eye and forelimb movements not used in ground hunting of food. Such a sensory adaptation would mean that in time there would be a major structural change in the head, face, and brain form. The size of the external ear would be reduced, the ears would be moved to the sides of the head, the tactile snout vibrissa would become less essential and would be decreased in number and size, the eyes would be moved from the sides of the head to a more frontward location under the dome of the skull, the length of the snout would be reduced as sight hunting replaced smell hunting, and the brain structure would be changed as the area devoted to smell diminished in size, while the portion devoted to sight increased. With the need for greater coordination in moving swiftly in an arboreal environment, the brain would also be increased in size in the area controlling motor skills.

The first evolutionary adaptations that occurred among the earliest primates probably were quite similar to those just noted and are the foundation for the three vital aspects of the body structure of contemporary humans: (1) The evolutionary development freeing the forelimbs for the handling of objects in specialized hands led to the extremely fine and very complex motor skills needed for making and using tools and made possible a bipedal ground locomotion; (2) the increase in dependence on the use of sight, rather than smell, resulted in the full use of stereoscopic, color vision and made possible the extension of the "space of recognition" typical of humans—that is, it greatly developed early primate awareness of an environment well beyond the immediate vicinity; (3) a very early increase in brain size made possible further evolutionary adaptation in primate learning, reason, and reflection.

The Apes Appear

The fossil record appears to indicate that in the *Paleocene* period, between 60 and 57 million years ago, a number of ancestral primate populations existed that possessed the first two major evolutionary primate adaptations—that is, the *locomotor* adaptation of *grasping* and a *special sensory sight* adaptation. At the beginning of the *Eocene* period, about 55 million years ago, these ancestral primate populations had spread over most of the world. However, by the end of the late *Eocene* or the beginning of the early *Oligocene* period, some 35 million years ago, the majority of these ancestral primates had become extinct because of increasingly more severe climate changes; survivors seem to have been restricted to limited areas of western North America and northern Europe. It appears that at this time the earth's climate zones became considerably cooler on the average. In the early part of the *Oligocene* period, perhaps because of increasing cold weather, some primates in western North America moved into Central and South America. Here, during the late *Oligocene* and *Miocene* periods, "New World" (*platyrrhine*) primates evolved. It is probable that, at the same time ancestral

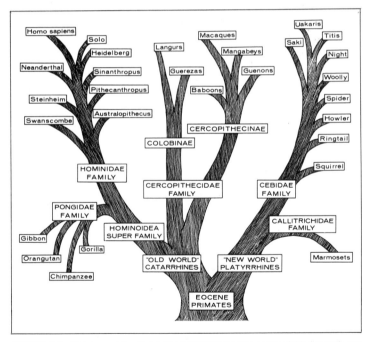

FIGURE 1-1 Divisions of the Suborder Anthropoidea. The levels of this figure do not correspond to the actual time of evolution, and the directions of the "branches" have no evolutionary meanings.

primates were moving south from western North America, groups from the same region migrated across one of the land bridges existing at the Bering Straits area and then moved into various regions of Asia, Africa, and Europe. These ancestral primate populations could have given rise to the "Old World" (*catarrhine*) monkeys and apes. It is in Old World primate populations that the further evolutionary adaptations occurred that made possible the kind of body humans now possess.

The ancestral primate groups that moved into the Old World regions of Asia, Africa, and Europe in the *Oligocene* period were the inheritors of the first two major structural adaptations—that is, *locomotion by grasping* and a *special sensory reorganization*.

The third major adaptation leading to the kind of body humans possess was also a locomotor, or motion, adaptation. This adaptation, termed *brachiation*, involved complex structural changes in the wrist, elbow, shoulder, and chest regions of the body and resulted from the abandoning of motion in the trees by grasping and short hopping to a motion form utilizing the arms, shoulders, and chest for leaping to, grasping, and then swinging to the next tree branch. Brachiation made it possible for evolving primates to further extend their "space of recognition" by making possible rapid movement over large areas. During the *Oligocene* period in parts of Asia and Africa, brachiation became the major means of locomotion of primate populations that were evolving from the Old World (*catarrhine*) forms.

Walking Upright

Some time in the early *Miocene* period, about 20 million years ago, a fourth major primate evolutionary adaptation began that also involved a change in locomotion. This adaptation, called *bipedalism*, involved complex structural changes in the pelvis, leg, and foot bones and muscles and became the basic adaptation for the appearance of humans. The discovery and approximate dating of fossil bones from a large group of bipedal *hominoids* in Pakistan and India shows that in the early *Miocene* period some populations of primates had moved from an entirely tree-dwelling, brachiating life to at least partial life on the ground.[1] Later members of these popu-

---

[1]The terms *Hominoid, Hominid, Homo,* and *Homo sapiens* have specific definitions in studies of evolution:
  a) *Hominoid (Hominidea)*: The *super family* including the *Hominidae* and *Pongidae*:
  b) *Hominid (Hominidae)*: The *family* including all species of *Homo* as well as the *Australopithecines*:
  c) *Homo*: The *genus* to which modern humans belong:
  d) *Homo sapiens*: The only living *species* of the genus *Homo*.

lations had skulls and brains that were similar to those now seen in modern apes such as the chimpanzee but also had pelvic, leg, and foot anatomy resembling those in modern humans.

During the *Miocene* and *Pliocene* periods the adaptation of *bipedal* locomotion proceeded until there were many populations of nearly erect primates regularly living on the ground. Bipedalism made possible an even greater extension of the primate "space of recognition" by making possible a form of locomotion that allowed the early ground-living *hominoids* to move about an area measured in miles rather than in fractions of miles, as did the *brachiators*, or in yards, as did the primates who had undergone only the first two adaptations of *grasping* and *special sensory reorganization*. The bipedal populations of the late *Miocene* and *Pliocene* periods could range about a territory that was expanded a thousandfold over the one covered by their primitive, smell hunting, preprimate ancestors. The significant increase in the primate awareness of the world that came with the bipedalism adaptation was one of the factors contributing to the appearance of culture, the fifth major evolutionary adaptation experienced by primates.

PRIMATE ADAPTATIONS:
A SUMMARY

Before turning to culture, the final major primate evolutionary adaptation, it would be useful to review and summarize the discussion to this point. It has been postulated that the human ability for transmitting and acquiring culture derives from the kind of body humans have—that is, a set of biological characteristics that lead to typical human behavior forms. If modern humans are examined carefully, they will be found to be a structural mosaic of the basic evolutionary adaptive characters of all primates, while also retaining some secondary features that accompanied each major adaptation. The first major adaptation of the primates, the *first locomotion adaptation of grasping*, shows in the structure of human hands, in long digits, sensitive tactile pads, and flattened fingernails. The second major adaptation, a *special sensory reorganization*, shows in the general head form, brain structure, and vision sense of humans. The third major adaptation, the *second locomotor adaptation of brachiation*, is seen in the muscle and bone structure of the human chest, shoulders, and arms. The fourth major adaptation, the *third locomotor adaptation* of bipedalism, is reflected in the bone and muscle structure of the human pelvis, leg, and foot.

The human body, and hence typical behavior, is shared in *part* with other primates but in *whole* with no other member of the primate order. All primates share the grasping adaptation. The special sensory reorgan-

TIME	ADAPTATION			FORM	ECOLOGY RELATIONS
50,000+ B.P.* 600,000+ B.P. 2 ± Million B.P.	Radiation	Adaptive Culture (2nd Sensory) ↑ 5th Major Adaptation	Radiation	Homo sapiens Homo	↑ Culture Transmission and Acquisition
5 ± Million B.P. 12 ± Million B.P.	Radiation	Adaptive Bipedalism (3rd Locomotor) ↑ 4th Major Adaptation	Radiation	Hominids	
25 ± Million B.P. 35 ± Million B.P.	Radiation	Adaptive Brachiation (2nd Locomotor) ↑ 3rd Major Adaptation	Radiation	Hominoids	
55 ± Million B.P.	Radiation	Adaptive Special Sensory Reorganization (1st Sensory) ↑ 2nd Major Adaptation	Radiation	Monkey Lemur-Tarsier	"Natural"
60 ± Million B.P.	Radiation	Adaptive Grasping (1st Locomotor) ↑ 1st Major Adaptation	Radiation	(Primates) Tree Shrew-like Insectivores	
200 ± Million B.P.	↑ Primitive Mammals			Primitive Mammals	

*B.P. means "before the present."

FIGURE 1-2 Major adaptations and population radiations in the primate order.

ization adaptation is shared only by the monkeys, apes, and humans. The second locomotor adaptation, brachiation, is shared among the apes.[2] The bipedal adaptation has been shared only among the members of the *hominid* group. However no primate other than *Homo* is possessed of all these physical characteristics.

[2]Some monkeys (*e.g.*, the "spider" monkey) also are brachiators. However such forms have not fully developed the muscle and bone structure typical of the brachiating apes.

8

A Transition to Human Form

Until the early 1970s specialists in the study of human physical evolution supposed that there had been only one type of bipedal, small-brained *hominid* evolving toward the form of contemporary humans. This type of *hominid*, termed *Australopithecine*, was believed to be intermediate between the late *Miocene*–early *Pliocene hominids* and much later forms of *Homo* whose fossil remains were dated in the middle and late *Pleistocene* period. The general sequence of human evolutionary development from at least the late *Pliocene* period onward was believed to be (1) *Australopithecines*, (2) *Homo*, and (3) *Homo sapiens*.[3] However work at Lake Rudolf and at Lake Turkana in Kenya, East Africa, in 1971 and in subsequent years by Richard Leakey, Glynn Isaac, and their associates that resulted in the discovery of human fossil material, some (Lake Turkana KNM-ER 1470) dated at 2.9 million years ago, has raised questions concerning the place of the *Australopithecines* in the evolutionary sequence leading to modern humans. Leakey and Isaac recovered parts of a skull which showed more fineness of structure than had been known, except among the much later appearing *Homo erectus* fossils of the Middle *Pleistocene* period. The 2.9-million-year-old human remains appear to be related to a brain capacity of approximately 800 cc., in contrast to the modern human average brain size of 1450 cc. and the *Australopithecine* average brain size of approximately 500 to 700 cc.[4] Because of structural characteristics, as well as some associated archaeological materials, particularly tools, this fossil form is said by Richard Leakey to have been a bipedal, toolmaking, early human. On the basis of this discovery and other fossil discoveries in the Lake Rudolf area of East Africa, Richard Leakey suggests that the *Australopithecines* be dropped from the main sequence of human evolution and be considered as a "sideline" of *hominid* evolutionary development.[5]

[3]It should be noted that the late Louis Leakey (see Leakey, Prost, & Prost, 1971) argued strongly against the view that *Australopithecines* were ancestral to *Homo*. Leakey's wife, Mary, and son, Richard, continue to hold the view of Louis Leakey that *Homo* is very old, dating back to more than 3 million years ago. For a nontechnical account of this argument by someone holding the view that *Homo* is derived from *Australopithecine* stock, see Johanson & Edey, 1981b; see also Leakey, 1981.

[4]The expression "cc" refers to cubic centimeters, a measure of capacity of the skull and an indication of brain size. The usual procedure of measurement on an intact skull is to fill the cranial cavity with mustard seed or small shot packed tightly by shaking the skull, then pouring the material into a cubic centimeter measuring glass. Mathematical estimates can also be made from skull fragments.

[5]Richard Leakey's argument for the antiquity of *Homo* is based on the dating of the Lake Turkana fossils at 2.9 million years old. However, Johanson and Edey (1981a, 55) point out that this date is in error by about one million years and really is 1.9 million years old. It should be noted that Leakey did not perform the dating studies which led to the 2.9 million years age for the Lake Turkana "KNM-ER 1470" fossil materials.

Richard Leakey's proposal to remove the *Australopithecines* from the main sequence of human evolution appears to be strongly opposed on the basis of fossil evidence from discoveries made in 1974 and subsequent years by D.C. Johanson and others at Hadar, in the Awash river basin of Ethiopia. These remains, which included the jaw parts of a number of individuals, have been dated by Johanson as being 4.1 million years old, or 1.2 to 2.2 million years older than the materials found by Leakey and Isaac, and appear to exhibit features which Johanson believes to be those of a fossil ancestral to both *Australopithecine* and *Homo* which he terms <u>*Australopithecus*</u>

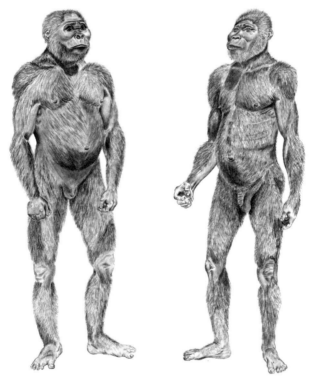

Conjectural drawings of Australopithecus. (Based on drawings by Jay Matternes. In Howell, F. C. (ed.) 1965. *Early Man.* New York: Time-Life. Especially prepared for this text by Priscilla Piros.)

afarenis. Johanson and others have also reported the discovery of fossil remains from the same area which include body parts of two children, between four and five years of age, and from three to five adults, dated as being from 3 to 3.5 million years old and said to be human. These fossil materials, which also include a number of bones of a hand structure strikingly similar in form to the hand of much later types of humans, are believed by Johanson to be the remains of a human family group trapped and drowned in a flash flood.[6]

[6]See Johanson & Edey, 1981b.

In 1977 David Pilbeam and others reported discovery on the Potwar plateau in Pakistan of the fossil remains of some 80 individuals, dated at between 8 and 13 million years old. Pilbeam notes that among these fossils there is a type of "pre-man"—that is, a common ancestor of all later humanlike forms, including the *Australopithecines*. The Potwar fossil remains are about three times older than the fossil humans reported by Richard Leakey and Carl Johanson and their associates. The Pilbeam discovery indicates that sufficient time existed, more than 5 million years, for the processes of biological evolution to affect a long transition from the "pre-men" of the late *Miocene* and early *Pliocene* periods through intermediary *hominid* types to the human forms found by both Leakey and Johanson and their colleagues. Until further clarification of these recent fossil discoveries is undertaken by other specialists in human evolution, it seems reasonable to assume that the general evolutionary sequence leading to contemporary humans from the middle *Miocene* period onward consisted of broad transitions from (1) various types of "pre-men," to (2) small-brained, bipedal *hominids*, including the *Australopithecines*, to (3) *Homo*, and to (4) *Homo sapiens*.[7]

Tools, Bigger Brains, and Changed Behavior

In the early 1950s Sherwood L. Washburn, a specialist in human evolutionary studies, suggested that a specific behavior pattern—the regular making and using of tools—was directly responsible for the appearance among late *Miocene* and *Pliocene hominids* of the anatomical features considered characteristically human. These features include a larger brain and a changed shape of the head, face, jaws, and hands. The bipedal *hominids* of the early *Pliocene*, including the *Australopithecines*, all appear to have been small-brained creatures with head, facial, and jaw features that are more "apelike" than human in their appearance. However at least by the close of the *Pliocene* period, according to the fossil evidence discovered in East Africa by both Richard Leakey and Carl Johanson and their associates, bipedal hominids had become increasingly much larger-brained creatures, including an estimated 800 cc. brain size in the instance of the fossil skull materials discovered by Leakey in 1971.

Prior to the 1959 discovery of an *Australopithecine* form termed *Zinjanthropus* (now classed as *Australopithecus boisei*) by L.S.B. Leakey and his wife, Mary, in Tanzania, East Africa, specialists in human evolution believed that bipedal *hominids* with cranial capacities of less than 750 cc. could not make or use tools. However, the tools directly associated with *Zinjanthropus*, with a brain size of 600 cc. and dated in the upper part of the lower *Pleistocene* period, or approximately 600,000 years ago, clearly indicate that

---

[7]For a discussion of one recent interpretation of these fossil *hominid* materials and their possible meanings, see White, 1980.

toolmaking and use as a form of behavior adaptation to a natural environment was possible for *hominids* with brain sizes less than half of the average 1450 cc. brain size of contemporary humans.

In 1971 east of Lake Rudolf in Kenya Richard Leakey and Glynn Isaac discovered tools, said to be in association with human skull parts, that are estimated by Leakey to have belonged to a skull with an 800 cc. brain size. The tools included chert pebble choppers and many chert flakes made in a style that appears to be similar to the earliest tools found in "Bed I" at a site in the Olduvai Gorge in East Africa, termed by L.S.B. Leakey and others as "Oldowan" chopper tools. The Oldowan Bed I tools at the Olduvai site have been dated as being from 1.8 to 1.65 million years old and are said to be associated with the fossil *hominid* types described by L.S.B. Leakey as *Australopithecus boisei* and *Homo habilis*. This would indicate that the stone tools made by the human form discovered in 1971 by Richard Leakey and others, which were similar in form to the Oldowan type tools at Olduvai Gorge, represent a basic development in toolmaking and use that appears to be directly associated with an increase in brain size among the evolving *hominids*.

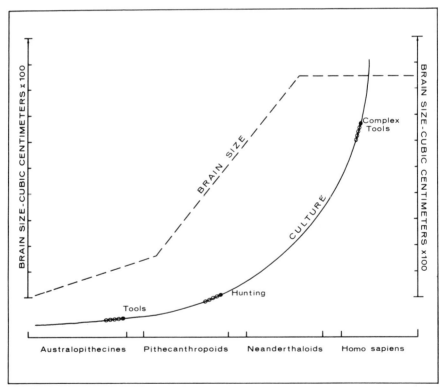

FIGURE 1–3 Possible relationships between change in brain size and cultural development. (Adapted from Brace, C.L., and M. F. A. Montagu. 1965. *Man's Evolution; An Introduction to Physical Anthropology.* New York: Macmillan.)

If, as it now seems clear, there are no scientific reasons for not assuming that behavioral changes can precede and produce structural changes in human evolution, then as Washburn proposed, it could be that tool use by small-brained bipedal *hominids* led during the *Pliocene* to a significant increase in *hominid* brain size and significant changes in the central nervous system, face, head, and hands. These structural changes in these *hominid* populations had profound consequences for the later course of the evolution of *Homo*, including making possible a cultural transmission process.[8]

Communication Among Tool-Using Hominids

Since language is such a vital part of cultural transmission among modern humans, an important question that should be examined concerns whether late *Pliocene* and *Pleistocene* bipedal, tool-using *hominids* communicated their experiences and ideas by sounds formed into a language. This question has been answered in several different ways. Montagu (1960) believes there were no anatomical reasons to prevent small-brained, bipedal *hominids* from using language. Washburn and Avis (1958) feel that intelligible speech probably occurred only in the large-brained humans of the Middle *Pleistocene* period. Broom and Schepers (1946) examined impressions made from the inside of *Australopithecine* skulls to see if these small-brained *hominids* would show evidence of the brain structure in the parts known to control speech in modern humans. They concluded that these bipedal *hominids* did have the brain centers for articulate speech. In reviewing then-available fossil skeletal evidence for speech (jaw, muscle attachment areas, and brain impressions on skull bones), Vallois (1961), however, concluded that the early bipedal *hominid* evidence is much too uncertain to support the conclusions offered by Broom and Schepers. The conclusion that bipedal small-brained *hominids* did not have the anatomy for articulate speech tends to be generally accepted among contemporary specialists in human evolution.

All contemporary apes, and many monkeys, have developed gestures for communication of emotion. The earliest bipedal *hominids* probably lived in very compact social groups where they usually were in sight of one another. They may have depended as much on gesture as on vocal sounds for communication. Among modern baboons much communication is by gesture and has no sound component. The presence of particular scalp and ear muscle attachment points in the fossil bipedal *hominids*, which usually are associated in modern apes with specific movements of the scalp

---

[8]White (1980) has challenged Washburn's tool-use hypothesis for humanization and has concluded that a striding, bipedal form of locomotion developed by early *hominids* probably served as the prime force of natural selection in the course of human evolution. White leaves unanswered the question of how a striding gait led to central nervous system changes, which led to increased brain size. It is possible that these hypotheses can be combined.

and ears to convey what human observers term *emotion*, and their great atrophy in *Homo sapiens sapiens* would also seem to point to the small role of articulate speech among the early, small-brained, bipedal *hominid* forms. Human language also appears dependent on a large brain. *Homo sapiens sapiens* individuals afflicted with microcephaly (an abnormally small brain and head) have limited linguistic abilities.

It seems reasonable to conclude that communication of ideas through speech probably came after the significant increase in size of the brain in the evolutionary changes between the Middle *Pliocene* populations of bipedal *hominids* and the Middle *Pleistocene* forms of *Homo*. This does not mean, however, that an interchange of complex, symbolic information by means of sign, gesture, or posture did not occur among bipedal *hominids* undergoing the major evolutionary adaptation of culture. Such acts would leave no records. A great amount of information and learning is passed between individuals, both among modern humans and in many animal groups, by unverbalized, inarticulate behavior forms that leave no artifacts or marks. As the senior female red deer leads the young of a herd, or adult chimpanzees lead young chimpanzees through the experiences of a variety of patterned behaviors that are specific to a given natural environment and characteristic of a particular animal species, so too the adults of a modern human group can and do regularly lead their children through similar patterned behaviors, specific to a cultural ecology but also characteristic of human cultural life, without any use of linguistic communication.[9]

A transmission of ideas by such *inarticulate experience* probably was a vital part of primate behavior for a very long time before the occurrence of the bipedal evolutionary adaptation and still is the basis for a speechless, yet clearly symbolic, interaction exchange that occurs regularly among modern monkeys and apes, as well as in some other social mammals, such as wolves. The question of whether toolmaking, small-brained bipedal *hominids* had intelligible speech communication is very important in the study of the cultural transmission process because a key part of the contemporary definition of culture is the presence of transmission from one generation to the next of a system of learned behavior that is patterned, or regular, in its form and is shared widely within a social group. Since language plays a key role in the process by which learned behavior is transmitted generationally and shared among contemporary humans, these data and conclusions are important for understanding the nature of cultural transmission.

The concept of transmitting culture from one generation to the next has implied use of language which is intelligible to its users and hearers, as in the case of *Homo sapiens sapiens*. If tool-using, small-brained bipedal *hominids* of the *Pliocene* period can be shown to have transmitted learned,

---

[9]See Chapter 9 for a discussion of this point.

shared, and patterned behavior forms either by "inarticulate experience" or some form of speechless "symbolic interaction," then it would be necessary to conclude that research on cultural transmission must be broadened significantly to account for transmission and acquisition of culture by means in addition to language. It is not correct, as Clark (1961) has argued, "Until *hominids* had developed words as symbols the possibility of transmitting, and so accumulating, culture hardly existed."

Homo Appears

By the early to middle part of the Middle *Pleistocene* period, about 375,000 to 230,000 years ago, large-brained, tool-using, bipedal human populations were dispersed widely over Africa, in the parts of Asia south and east of the Himalaya Mountains, and in the Asian continental offshore islands such as Java and Sumatra. The term *Homo erectus* now is used to describe these humans. In Asia, *Homo erectus* ranged from North China to Java. This variety of *Homo erectus,* which may be termed *Pithecanthropian*, were humans with a cranial capacity averaging 871 cc.[10]

Pithecanthropians made stone tools that could have been used to shape other tools, such as wood spears. *Pithecanthropian* remains have been found in direct association with the bones of elephants, rhinoceros, bison, water buffalo, horses, camels, wild boar, sabre-tooth tigers, cave bears, leopards, and a giant form of hyena, as well as deer, antelope, roebuck, and sheep. The major portion of their diet seemed to have been deer, but these forms of *Homo erectus* regularly killed large, much more powerful and agile animals. Thus equipped with only crude tools of stone and probably wood shaped with stone tools, the *Pithecanthropians* successfully faced a very dangerous natural world. Their success appears to have been because they seem to have possessed the greatest advantage in the natural order of their

[10]The *Pithecanthropians* are now usually classed in the genus *Homo* with a single species, *erectus*, and three subspecies, *erectus, pekinensis*, and *soloensis*. The *Neanderthals* are also classed in the genus *Homo*; there is some question concerning the number of species and subspecies of this form. The remains of more than one hundred of these fossil forms are usually classed as (1) *early Neanderthals*, or (2) *later ("classic") Neanderthals*. The early *Neanderthals* are associated with the third (Riss-Wurm) interglacial period of the European early Upper Pleistocene epoch, some 100,000 years ago, and are represented by such specimens as *Ehringsdorf, Krapina, Mount Carmel*, and *Galilee*. The later *Neanderthals* are associated with the fourth glacial (Wurm I) period of the European Upper Pleistocene epoch, between 100,000 and 50,000 years ago, and are represented by such specimens as *Gibraltar, Le Moustier, Monte Circeo, Neanderthal*, and *La Quina*. As noted, the status of the *Australopithecines* is not yet clear; unquestionably these forms are members of the family *Hominidae*. Whether they are all to be classed as members of a separate subfamily *Australopithecinae*, genus *Australopithecus*, and therefore quite distinct from the subfamily *Hominidae*, genus *Homo*, remains open. L.S.B. Leakey claims that a fossil he has termed *Homo habilis*, which he found at the site of the *Zinanthropus* fossil, is a form of human probably directly ancestral to *Homo sapiens*. Other scholars believe this form is similar to the Asian *Pithecanthropians*. The present tendency of most specialists in human evolution studies is to class *Homo habilis* as being in the evolutionary sequence of the *Australopithecines* until more evidence is available (Campbell, 1976).

time—the ability to regularly reflect on past and present acts and to learn from these acts in anticipating the future. The possession of a greater degree of *reflection*, or a capacity to anticipate future events on the basis of past or immediate experience, not only enabled the *Pithecanthropians* to survive but also appears to have set them off distinctly from earlier forms of bipedal, tool-using, small-brained *hominids*.

The evidence found at the living sites of the *Pithecanthropians* makes it clear that, because of their limited tools, this form of *Homo* must have hunted large and dangerous animals through use of a social system and some form of communication and transmission of reflective products, either by speech, inarticulate experience, or perhaps some combination of both. Courage alone could not have led these early *Homo* forms to the regular, successful conquest of larger, stronger, and more agile animals. Some type of social cooperation in driving, herding, and trapping large and dangerous animals must have been regularly used by this early form of *Homo*.

We know that in the late Middle *Pleistocene* epoch a more structurally advanced form of *Homo*, called *Neanderthal*, used primitive pit traps to kill large carnivores. We also know that both the *Neanderthals* and the *Pithecanthropians* used fire. From the evidence in living sites it has been inferred that fire was probably used by these two kinds of early humans as a tool to make wood weapons, to transform the energy in raw food into a more easily digested cooked form, to heat and light living shelters, and perhaps to frighten away dangerous animals. Fire, in the form of torches, could also have been used as a tool to herd and drive animals into areas where they could be attacked and killed.

Tools, Death, and Thinking

The regular making and using of tools over long periods would seem to imply reflection. The reuse of stone tools would show an even greater capacity for reflection, since reuse involves consideration of effort and time involved in the manufacture of a tool and the meaning of its subsequent discard after use on one or two occasions. Available evidence indicates that *Pithecanthropians* and *Neanderthals* regularly used the same stone tools repeatedly over long periods of time. This reuse of tools indicates a greater degree of reflectivity on the part of these forms of *Homo*. When compared to the *Australopithecines*, who appear to have abandoned their tools after limited use, both the *Pithecanthropians* and *Neanderthals* reused tools regularly. However, disposal of the dead by the *Pithecanthropians* shows no marked changes from the acts of earlier *hominids*. The ways in which the bones of the *Pithecanthropians* occur in archaeological sites indicate there was no practice of burial or even the rudiments of ceremonial interment of the dead. In all instances, bones of these forms were scattered about habitation sites in the same ways as other animal bones.

By the time of the appearance of the *Neanderthals*, in the Middle *Pleistocene* epoch, a concept of ritual interment of the dead had been introduced into the life of humans. The *Neanderthals* sometimes used mineral pigments to stain the bodies of their dead and buried them in graves with tools and other cultural objects. It can be inferred from this evidence that *Homo* forms following the *Pithecanthropians* in the evolutionary record had developed the capacity for reflection to an even greater degree than had earlier human forms.

A Screen of Culture

While the *Pithecanthropians* appear to have been advanced in their capacity for reflective behavior, especially when compared to the earlier *Australopithecines*, they failed to make the transition to the even greater degree of reflection clearly exhibited by the *Neanderthals* of a later era. Reflection is a vital prerequisite to the appearance of culture. If a key aspect of culture is the act of transmission of learned, shared, and patterned behavior, then regular reflection, or the ability to anticipate future consequences on the basis of past and present experiences, would also seem to be one of the conditions for culture. The capacity for knowing that knowledge and experience would be useful and meaningful to another generation, or even to the dead, as in the instance of the *Neanderthals*, must

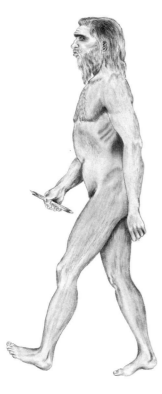

Conjectural drawing of early form of *Homo sapiens*. (Especially prepared for this text by Priscilla Piros.)

Artist's depiction of *Homo sapiens* family group. (Courtesy, British Museum, Natural History)

Artist's depiction of *Homo erectus* hunting group. (Courtesy, British Museum, Natural History)

be present in order for a generational transmission of learned, shared, and patterned behavior acts to occur.

The capacity for heightened reflection exhibited by the later "classic" *Neanderthals* of the Upper *Pleistocene* and their human contemporaries, such as *Cro-Magnon*, apparently continued to expand significantly through the last portion of that geological period. Substantial evidence for the expansion of human reflection is found in the increased inventory of the artifact products of the several forms of *Homo sapiens*. With regular use of artifacts, Upper *Pleistocene* humans brought about a gradual change in their general relations with their natural environment.[11]

The ecology, or the system of mutual relations between an organism and its environment, of humans in the *Pleistocene* period was a natural one. Early humans were born into and lived in a world over which they had little effective control. In the Lower *Pleistocene*, populations of humans responded to events in their natural world and only rarely could shape or alter the conditions that adversely affected them. With the gradual changes in head shape, brain size, and central nervous system functions that would have followed from the early attempts to control the natural world through regular tool use, human populations came to have an increase of the potential to more often anticipate natural events before they occurred, or recurred, and to prepare in some ways to deal with conditions that directly and often violently affected early humans. For example, early humans probably were the victims of large carnivores that were naturally equipped to outrun, outclimb, outswim, and outbite them. Until the advent of a regular use of the capacity for reflection, joined with the manufacture and use of tools, early humans had no effective means of defending themselves from attack by prowling carnivores. The invention of the spear, perhaps at first a long branch broken to a point, then later sharpened to a point with a crudely chipped stone adze or knife, gave early humans some means of at least delaying or sometimes turning aside the initial onslaught of large carnivores. While the spear would not protect its user, it could allow other members of the group to escape. Field observations of Asian tigers hunting game in the grasslands of India indicate that a solitary Bengal tiger often will not try a second chance to kill a deer or bullock if it misses on the initial rush, apparently because when lacking the vital element of surprise the

---

[11]The designation, *Cro-Magnon*, is now used to refer to the first modern humans, or *Homo sapiens sapiens*, everywhere they lived on earth after about 40,000 years ago. The term was first used to refer to human remains found in a rock shelter in southwestern France, dated from 35,000 to 10,000 years ago. However today it is recognized that *Cro-Magnon*–type humans were appearing in widely separated places 40,000 years ago in Hungary, the U.S.S.R., the Middle East, South Africa, China, Southeast Asia, Australia, and North and South America. Campbell (1976, 381) notes that he believes the *Cro-Magnon* people had the necessary physical equipment for constructing complex patterns of language similar to those used by contemporary humans and that human languages probably originated about the time of the *Cro-Magnons*.

tiger cannot cripple its prey by breaking the neck or back in one attack and so hold the animal stationary for further attacks to kill.

Today East African baboons protect their troops in a fashion that may be similar to one employed by the bipedal, small-brained *hominids* of the *Pliocene* period. The larger males of a baboon troop will attempt to turn aside the charges of a predator by lunging boldly at the animal to allow the female and younger members of a group time to flee to the safety of nearby trees. Baboons in southwest Africa have also been observed repeatedly dropping stones weighing more than a pound from the side of a steep canyon wall onto the human intruders below, while calling in the form identified by the human observers as the one used when predators threatened the baboon troop. Unlike humans, contemporary baboons are anatomically incapable of an overhand throw of an object, such as a stone, and cannot defend themselves by throwing well-aimed missiles.

Humans of the Middle *Pleistocene* period may have considerably improved on these defensive maneuvers by adding, through use of reflection on the situation, the aimed throwing of objects such as stones and the making of a sharpened stick to thrust out at, and so to further deflect, the charge of carnivores.

Adriaan Kortlandt, a Dutch zoologist, has observed and filmed the behavior of chimpanzees living on the open African grassland plains of northwest Guinea. When confronted with a stuffed, full-sized leopard animated by a mechanism that caused the head and tail to move, a group of about 30 chimpanzees made an organized attack on the dummy, with loud yelling and hooting. Kortlandt reports that the chimpanzees threw with accuracy everything they could pick up and that several chimpanzees broke branches off nearby trees, stripped off leaves and twigs and attacked the leopard dummy with great vigor, remaining upright and vigorously swinging their tree branch "clubs" at the intruder.

So the conditions were probably set among the upright, bipedal *hominids* and early, larger-brained humans in a similar fashion for further reflection and the tool improvement that could have followed: the cutting of longer and stronger shafts for spears and the shaping and attaching of stone or bone points to inflict pain and hurt on the attacking predators. Such improvements on the basic invention of the spear came very slowly, since it is not until very late in the Upper *Pleistocene* period that there are stone artifacts made in a fashion that would clearly indicate they were once attached to spear shafts.

As these cultural innovations were occurring, very slowly and probably at great cost in the lives of early humans, a *screen of culture* was being built between humans and the physical environments in which they lived. At first, and for a very long time, the culture screen was quite widely meshed; a wooden spear with a tip sharpened by a crudely shaped stone knife and hardened to a point in a fire is not more than a slight improvement on throwing stones at predators. It is likely that few *Pithecanthropian* or *Neanderthal* "spear bearers" survived many encounters with prowling cave bears and tigers. What is important was that each basic cultural invention improved the chances of survival for the population being defended.

Early humans also may have improved their chances of survival through application of concentrated heat to otherwise nonedible foods. Many plants, such as cassava, are inedible by humans in an uncooked form. The cooking of animal carcasses undoubtedly made the digestion and absorption of meat easier, since heat energy applied to meat makes the protein more easily digestible by humans.

More Than Stone and Bone It is important to note that the evidence for the evolution of culture as the natural ecology of humans continues to be limited, since the tools used probably were made of perishable plant materials such as wood or fiber. Contemporary hunting and gathering peoples have much of their technology in perishable artifacts. Only durable cultural objects such as stone, bone, or carbon from fires could possibly survive long periods of time. Durable artifacts are the only products of reflection that could be expected to have survived over the past three to four million years. In discussing the evolution of culture as the natural ecology of humans, it is also helpful to point out that the humans of the Upper *Pleistocene* quite probably had an extensive amount of culture transmitted to and acquired by infant and young members of these societies that left no traces in the evolutionary record. Contemporary native societies, such as those of the Arctic, New Guinea, or Borneo, possess a large and complex body of culture that rarely is manifested in their tools.

Breaking Out from the Limits By the middle of the Upper *Pleistocene* period, through invention of culture, humans had forever altered the relationships between themselves and the physical world. The transition to cultural life was a complex and lengthy one. There were hundreds of thousands of years in the *Pleistocene* when thousands of human individuals in hundreds of human populations lived and died largely in the same manner as their bipedal, small-brained *hominid* forebears. Eventually, however, the behavior changes brought about by reflection, invention of cultural forms, and more reflection led to the creation of a culture system that could be acquired and widely shared within a group and then transmitted to the next generation. In this way humans transcended the basic physical limitations imposed on other animals in a natural environment. Some, if not all, of each new generation of humans could come to know, through cultural transmission, ways to avoid the deadly mistakes of the preceding generations in dealing with natural events, whether these were the attack of a cave bear, a flood, a savannah grass fire, or a critical shortage of food.

Evolution and Cultural Transmission   The facts of human biological evolution and the appearance of culture are directly relevant to an understanding of the cultural transmission process. These data indicate that there was a time in the past when essentially human populations lived out their lives as did other animal forms. Then, as reflection, cognition, and understanding underwent gradual evolutionary development, perhaps because of tool using, the humans came to live more and more in a cultural as well as a natural environment. As the products of reflection began to be transmitted regularly to and acquired by succeeding generations, probably first through inarticulate experience, then through use of language, the process of acquiring culture as the natural ecology of humans had its beginning. There is presently no way of knowing exactly when the cultural transmission process began and no certainty as to what constitutes the empirical evidence to be used. However it seems reasonable to say that as early as the time of *Homo erectus*—that is, the *Pithecanthropians*—and most certainly by the time of the "classic" *Neanderthals,* learning by offspring of the patterned and widely shared products of adult reflection and life experiences must have been a regular feature of human life. It could be said that at least by time of the appearance of *Cro-Magnon* humans 40,000 years ago humans possessed a culture system and were teaching their young to act in cultural ways. If this is true, then it can be said that at least 40,000 years ago, and probably much earlier—between 300,000 and 600,000 years ago—a process of cultural transmission had come into existence.

Most studies of cultural transmission have paid little attention to the questions of the origin and development of this process. Research on the transmission and acquisition of culture and the consequences for an individual of acquiring culture usually begins with the fact of the existence of the cultural transmission process in its contemporary form. This has resulted in continuing inattention to a whole series of basic questions. Why and how did the cultural transmission process arise in the course of human evolutionary development? Has it persisted unchanged for the past hundred thousand or more years, or are there still significant evolutionary processes affecting it? What specific features are crucial to its appearance and continued existence, and why? Answers to these and similar questions are needed to illuminate and place in perspective some of the dilemmas of current research on cultural transmission. One of the major points these data of human evolution and the origin of cultural transmission suggest is that it is time that relevant data from human evolutionary biology and archaeology be incorporated into research on cultural transmission. This chapter, as well as Chapter 2, discusses a wide range of evolutionary products involved in cultural transmission that have been given little attention in basic research.

COMPETING THEORIES

Adaptations to Local Circumstances

It is very useful to know that at present there are two strongly competing evolutionary biology theories that may be used in studies of cultural transmission. One theory, as presented in the research and writing of S. L. Washburn and other physical anthropologists following the traditions of the "new physical anthropology" (c.f. Washburn, 1950), recognizes the validity of the concept of social facts, as first defined by the French sociologist Emile Durkheim, emphasizes the basic difference between human heredity and human learning, and stresses the importance of incorporating basic data of contemporary archaeology and history into statements concerning the origins and causes of human social and cultural behavior. This theoretical approach seeks to avoid the logical error of nineteenth-century evolutionary biologists who typically arranged data of evolution without attention to analysis of individual cases, some of which would have proved particular evolutionary schemes or interpretations to be incorrect. It is considered crucial in this theoretical approach that evolutionary biological interpretations of the origins and causes of human behavior be stated in terms of a general knowledge of contemporary human behavior as described by ethnographers, sociologists, psychologists, and other human scientists.

One vigorous critic of this theoretical approach has termed it ". . . the usual cerebral-anatomical-ecological run around with, for explanation of process, not much more than vague appeals to 'adaptation' " (Fox, 1977, 27). This comment points out the key conceptual difference between the two competing evolutionary biology theories—that is, in their ways of providing explanations for the origins and causes of human behavior.

In the theory used by Washburn and others, there is an underlying assumption that in human evolution, natural selection favored an increasing modifiability of learned behavior to the point where any major *differences* in the behavior of modern human populations simply are adaptations to local circumstances, including the physical environment, and are not at all associated with basic genetic, or inherited, variations between such populations. Thus in the Washburn et al. theoretical approach it is assumed that all contemporary humans belong to one species *(Homo sapiens sapiens)* and share to a large degree their genes and that significant behavior differences between local groups of humans are the product of their learned responses to specific situations and not their genetic inheritance. Hence, a Rarotongan avoids the bite of a shark and a Berber avoids the bite of a camel because there are no sharks in the North African Saharan desert and no camels on the Central Pacific island of Rarotonga, not because there are basic genetic differences between Rarotongans and Berbers.

Sociobiology Approach

A second evolutionary biology theory that could be used in research on the origins and development of cultural transmission has come to be termed *sociobiology* or *biosocial anthropology* and is described in the research and writing of evolutionary biologists such as George Williams (1957, 1966), W. D. Hamilton (c.f. 1963, 1964, 1971, 1972, 1975), E. O. Wilson (1975, 1978), and R. L. Trivers (1971, 1972) as well as in the recent work of anthropologists (c.f. Chagnon & Irons, 1979; Fox, 1975).[12] This theoretical approach employs the genetic concept of *inclusive fitness* and uses the assumption that under certain evolutionary conditions natural selection favors altruistic, or self-sacrificing, behavior among closely related individuals, a process termed as *kin selection*.[13] Particular genes are transmitted through successive generations because closely related individuals in a population automatically behave in ways that promote the survival and subsequent reproduction of kin possessing the same genes. In the view of sociobiologists, such behavior, which may lead to the death of the altruistic individual, is a primary means of protecting particular genes that promote a successful way of life in hostile environments.[14] In addition to altruism, sociobiologists have extended this type of genetic explanation to other human behavior forms such as male dominance, mate selection, aggression, xenophobia, neuroticism, depression, schizophrenia, and some psychomotor and sports activities. Sociobiologists seek to account for significant differences in forms of behavior among human populations by referring these differences to specific genes that are said to have been naturally selected through successive generations by individuals acting in ways that protect and promote such genes.[15]

[12]Sociobiological concepts also are employed in the works of some behavioral geneticists (see, Cavalli-Sforza & Feldman, 1973; Feldman & Cavalli-Sforza, 1980).

[13]The basic ideas of sociobiology are set forth in a technical manner in Wilson's work (1975) and explained in a more readable form in another work by Wilson (1978). Alexander (1979) has published an easily read account of the key ideas in sociobiology, while Harris and Wilson (1978) have exchanged views, *pro* and *con,* covering sociobiology. Sahlins (1976) and Montagu (1980) have examined the ideas of sociobiology from the perspectives and knowledge of anthropology. Barash (1977), Clutton-Brock and Harvey (1978), Daly and Wilson (1978), and Barkow and Silverberg (1980) have provided a variety of readings on the theory and concepts of sociobiology.

[14]Dawkins (1976) presents the view of some sociobiologists that humans are simply "containers" for their genes seeking expression.

[15]The concept of a *faculative genetic trait* has been introduced into recent sociobiological theory to cope with assertion that the theory rests on the assumption that all behavioral variation is associated with genetic variation.

Critics of the sociobiological theoretical approach have charged that it ignores entirely the mass of evidence indicating that most human behavior is learned. Sociobiologists have also been attacked for advocating the social and cultural status quo in emphases on female and racial inequality. Washburn has also been quoted as saying (MacPherson, 1976, 81) that sociobiological works ". . . read like a mixture of science fiction and the 19th century" because of a failure to provide any supporting evidence for a genetic basis in humans for kin selection, male dominance, aggression, or other claimed heritable forms of human behavior (see also Chapple, 1976). Marshall Sahlins (1976) has argued that the causes for human behavior cannot be reduced to human biology, since a cultural system is interposed between the human genes and human behavior. Sahlins also sees the basic sociobiological concept of kin selection to be in substantial error, since he believes ethnographic evidence of human behavior clearly indicates that humans define altruism in moral, rather than kin, terms. Thus when altruistic behavior occurs among humans, such behavior follows a culturally structured value code for proper conduct between individuals in a society and is a learned behavior form.

Wilson (1975, 1978) has met such criticisms by noting that sociobiological theory is not intended to promote racial, social, or sexual inequality and that whatever else may be said by advocates of either one of the competing evolutionary biological theories, human behavior, in all of its great variability, still falls within very definite limits. Wilson notes that there clearly are "species-wide characteristics," or "transcultural" traits, of human behavior. However Wilson and other sociobiologists have concluded that it logically follows from this assertion that there are specific genes directly controlling the expression of particular species-wide, or transcultural, behavior forms. Wilson (1978) has also noted that it would not be a great loss if the sociobiological concept of kin selection were shown to be in error, since the fact would remain that there still are some species-wide forms of human behavior which indicate a genetic basis for behavior forms.

It should be noted that cultural anthropologists have been concerned for nearly a half century with defining "universal categories of culture" (c.f. Kluckhohn, 1953) or transcultural behavior patterns. In general, universal categories of culture–language, family (including sexual and age-graded divisions of labor within the family unit), tool use, selective exploitation of an environment to provide food, shelter, and protection, the organization of family units into associated groups and communities, body ornamentation, and a system of ideas for related humans to the perceived universe—have been viewed by cultural anthropologists as arising from the human cultural system as it has evolved through a period of over three million years and is now shared among human groups. In this sense, only those cultural behavior forms presently shared among every group of humans may be termed *transcultural,* or *species-wide,* forms. In modern cultural anthropology such designations refer to irreversible patterns of human culture and not to the genetic basis for such patterns. Thus in discussions of universal categories of culture by contemporary cultural anthropologists, the term *species-wide* indicates a sharing of learned culture patterns by all human groups and does not denote a human gene, or genes, controlling expression of particular behavior forms. So while it may appear that Wilson and other sociobiologists share a common theoretical ground with cultural and social anthropologists in a concern with transcultural, or species-wide, forms of human behavior, there are fundamental conceptual differences between these two groups in their conceptions of such terms. This difference is now of an order sufficient to preclude most exchanges of basic ideas. Unlike sociobiologists, most cultural anthropologists continue to emphasize the basic differences between human heredity and learning and to treat human learning as being related to and dependent upon individual human beings. Another way to state this would be to note that, at present, cultural anthropologists usually consider most of human behavior to be essentially learned and not genetically transmitted.

ANOTHER WAY OF ANALYSIS

The theoretical approach in this text seeks to combine important features of the two evolutionary biology theoretical approaches, while avoiding the extreme positions taken by advocates of one theory or the other. It is quite clear that the most important theoretical question before anthropologists, as well as evolutionary biologists and behavioral geneticists, involves the nature of the specific interrelationships between culture and human biology.

In this chapter, data of human evolution and the possible beginnings of the cultural transmission process have been interpreted and arranged following the general outline of the evolutionary biology theoretical approach developed during the past three decades by Washburn and other anthropologists. It has been assumed in this chapter that this theoretical approach is more precise and useful than current sociobiological theory in terms of gaining understanding of the full scope of human evolution. However an approach is taken to understanding the nature of the cultural transmission process in Chapter 2 that accepts the probability, as it has been assumed in sociobiological theory, that there are forms of human behavior clearly associated with specific human gene complexes which function in accordance with known genetic laws.[16] Some of these behavior forms

[16]Kaufman (1975) offers similar ideas to those advanced here.

are clearly identified and briefly discussed in Chapter 2, but no claims are made concerning specific ways genetic mechanisms, such as Dawkins' (1976) concept of *meme*, are involved in these forms of human behavior. It seems too early in the study of cultural transmission to offer even preliminary statements on this topic.[17] Finally, Chapters 1 and 2 present the context of another theoretical approach to the nature and evolutionary origins and development of cultural transmission, which has been developed and presented elsewhere (Williams, 1972, 1975).

Beyond Nature vs. Nurture

In this theory scientific explanations for species-wide forms of human behavior, such as cultural transmission, are founded upon accurate interpretations of a complex cybernetic interaction process (see Chapter 4) between human culture (C) and human biology (B), [C ↔ B], operating in the human population through a long period of time, at least the past three to five million years, to produce typical forms of human behavior processes, as well as a human biological structure (e.g., the structure of *Homo sapiens sapiens*). As used in this text a cybernetic approach to data of human evolution and the origins of human behavior forms and processes incorporates some of the important features of the two evolutionary biology theoretical approaches presently competing for acceptance as the more scientifically valid and does not attempt to argue for the superiority of culture over biology, as Sahlins (1976) and others have done, or of biology over culture, as Hamilton (1964), and Wilson (1975, 1978), and others have in their works. In this cybernetic theory, culture and human biology are viewed, rather, as complexly interdependent, [C ↔ B] phenomena, with reciprocal consequences taking place in human culture when major changes occur in human biology, and vice versa. Thus in the long course of human evolution, changes occurring in human biology directly affected an evolving culture system, while changes occurring in a developing culture system directly affected evolving human biology.[18] The advantage of a cybernetic theoretical approach is that it provides a way to understand that, while it is true that most human behavior is learned, such learning proceeds directly from particular human biological features that are the products of the

[17]Dawkins (1976, 213) has proposed the concept of a *meme* as the basic unit of the cultural transmission process, which he believes to be involved in a natural selection-like competition where some *memes* are favored over others in exploiting the cultural environment to their own advantage.

[18]Bajema (1972) has described this cybernetic theory, while Dunham (1979) has discussed the ways that *coevolution* may proceed, following an essentially sociobiological approach. Williams (1972, 1975) has presented theoretical discussions of the nature, origins, and development of the process of cultural transmission using a cybernetic approach. Lumsden and Wilson (1981) have presented an essentially sociobiological interpretation and definition of *coevolution* in which genes and genetic processes are claimed to dominate culture. Singer (1981) examines this claim by considering the ways human values influence culture.

operation through millions of years of a mutually dependent interactive process in which human biology and culture have directly affected one another in profound ways, so that to speak of human heredity as being more important than culture, or vice versa, is to miss entirely the crucial point that human biology and culture exist, and have existed for a long time, in a dynamic state of complex interaction and dependence upon each other. Detailed scientific knowledge of this dynamic state will be of inestimable value in gaining a precise understanding of cultural transmission, for it is in this process that it is possible to see clearly, as in few other aspects of contemporary human experience, the evidence for the existence of a long-term cybernetic interdependence of human biology and culture.

SOME CONCLUSIONS

What does this mean for the study of cultural transmission? Among other things it suggests that individuals concerned with study of cultural transmission might undertake a thorough search of the scientific literature reporting studies of systematic naturalistic field observations of primates closest to humans in structure and behavior (chimpanzee, gorilla, orangutan, gibbon) to learn of some of the behavioral-biological cybernetic foreshadowings and precursors of cultural transmission that might help illuminate and broaden understanding of this process. Goodall's (1964) pioneering field studies of chimpanzees, the basic field work on baboon behavior by Washburn and his students (Washburn & Devore, 1961), Schaller's (1963) field study of the mountain gorilla, Carpenter's (1964) field studies, and a large number of recent experimental and field studies of many others concerning primate behavior may provide basic insights into some of the possible beginnings of cultural transmission that have generally been ignored by students of this process.[19] It is very important to remember that the behavior of living nonhuman primates does not represent the ways of early humans. However studies of nonhuman primates are useful for gaining some clues and ideas concerning the behavioral-biological cybernetic evolutionary process that might have been at work 5 to 15 million or more years ago among the *hominoids* and among evolving *hominids* of 1 to 4 million years ago. More detailed attention must also be given to data and conclusions of contemporary archaeological research, for these materials may contain evidence that can help understanding of the origins, development, and nature of the cultural transmission process. This is not to suggest that students of cultural transmission should focus their concern upon the artifacts that demonstrate sequences and phases of particular cultures. Rather, it may be possible to determine from data of cultural evolution in

---

[19]See, for instance, Lancaster, 1975; Menzel, 1972; and vonCranach & Vine, 1973.

the last three to four million years some of the ways the process of cultural transmission may have operated, changed, remained stable, and so on. Most specialists concerned with cultural transmission have given little attention to these data and have not yet begun to broaden their perspective of that process as a long-term, uniquely human adaptation to the natural world.

Finally, these data of human evolution and the beginnings of cultural transmission make it quite clear that this process is a human phenomenon—that is, a universally human process. This view of cultural transmission is helpful in evaluating the conclusions and basic principles derived from studies of cultural transmission that are limited to one culture or to specific subgroups within a culture, such as social classes, occupational specialties, educational levels, particular residential or geographic areas, or special conditions of human life, such as poverty, urban or rural settings, as well as various forms of discrimination, including sexual, racial, age, economic, or religious discrimination. Although conclusions taken from studies limited by such factors may be valid for a particular culture, subgroup, or set of individuals sharing conditions of life, such conclusions usually are restricted in their scientific usefulness since these statements do not seem to contribute, except in a circumscribed way, to understanding the basic nature of the cultural transmission process. On the other hand long-term, intensive, transcultural and holistic research, such as the detailed ethnographic work conducted in six different cultures by Beatrice and John W. M. Whiting (1975) and their associates, has moved the study of cultural transmission toward the basic scientific goals of understanding of the cultural transmission process as a human phenomenon.[20] The work by the Whitings has led to general principles and conclusions that apply transculturally and holistically and so should be considered an important scientific step in the study of cultural transmission as a universally human process.[21]

SUMMARY

This chapter has been concerned with presenting some of the major details and the main outline of the evolutionary origin and development of the cultural transmission process. The discussion began with some postulates and ideas necessary for thinking about cultural transmission in an

---

[20]It should be noted that Bock (1980) and Schweder (1979) have presented critical evaluations of the Whitings' theoretical and methodological approach and do not agree with the evaluation of that work presented in this text.

[21]For a list of 65 working hypotheses derived from transcultural study of socialization, see Williams, 1978, 156–161. See also Chapter 6, *Table 6–4.*

evolutionary perspective. Details were offered concerning four major primate evolutionary adaptations preceding and leading to the appearance of the human adaptation of culture. The discussion then turned to an examination of data concerning the development of culture, with suggestions concerning some possible ways the cultural transmission process began to function as succeeding generations of humans began to transmit reflective products and experiences to their offspring. The chapter concluded with a series of comments regarding the study of cultural transmission as a universally human process.

REFERENCES CITED AND SUGGESTED READINGS

ALEXANDER, R. D. 1974. "The Evolution of Social Behavior." *Annual Review of Ecology and Systematics*, 5, 325–383.
––––––. 1979. *Darwinism and Human Affairs*. Seattle: University of Washington Press.
ALTMANN, S. A. 1967. *Social Communication among Primates*. Chicago: University of Chicago Press.
ALTMANN, S. A., & J. ALTMANN. 1971. *Baboon Ecology*. Chicago: University of Chicago Press.
BAJEMA, C. 1972. "Transmission of Information about the Environment in the Human Species: A Cybernetic View of Genetic and Cultural Evolution." *Social Biology*, 19, 224–226.
BARASH, D. P. 1977. *Sociobiology and Behavior*. New York: Elsevier.
BARKOW. C. W., & J. SILVERBERG (eds.). 1980. *Sociobiology: Beyond Nature Nurture?* Boulder, Colo.: Westview Press, American Association for the Advancement of Science Select Symposium 35.
BISHOP, W. W., & J. A. MILLER (eds.). 1972. *Calibration of Hominoid Evolution*. Edinburgh: Scottish Academic Press.
BOCK, P. C. 1980. *Continuities in Psychological Anthropology*. San Francisco: W. H. Freeman & Company Publishers
BORDES, F. 1968. *The Old Stone Age*. New York: McGraw-Hill.
BRACE, C. L., H. NELSON & N. KORN. 1971. *Atlas of Fossil Man*. New York: Holt, Rinehart & Winston.
BROOM, R., & G. W. H. SCHEPERS. 1946. *The South African Fossil Ape-Men: The Australopithecinae*. Pretoria: Transvaal Museum Memoir, Number 2.
BUTZER, K.W., & G. K. ISAAC. 1975. *After the Australopithecines*. The Hague: Mouton.
CAMPBELL, B. G. 1976. *Humankind Emerging*. Boston: Little, Brown (2d ed.)
CARPENTER, C. R. 1964. *Naturalistic Behavior of Non-human Primates*. University Park: Pennsylvania State University Press.
CAVALLI-SFORZA, L. & M. W. FELDMAN. 1973. "Models for Cultural Inheritance, I: Group Mean and Within-Group Variation." *Theoretical Population Biology*, 4, 42–55.
CHAGNON, N. & W. IRONS (eds.). 1979. *Evolutionary Biology and Human Social Behavior: An Anthropological Approach*. Belmont, Calif.: Duxbury.
CHANCE, M., & C. JOLLY. 1970. *Social Groups of Monkeys, Apes and Men*. London: Jonathan Cape.

CHAPPLE, E. D. 1976. "Ethology Without Biology." *American Anthropologist*, 78, 590–593.

CLARK, G. 1961. *World Prehistory; An Outline.* Cambridge: Cambridge University Press.

CLUTTON-BROCK, T. H., & P. H. HARVEY. 1978. *Readings in Sociobiology.* San Francisco: W. H. Freeman & Company Publishers

DALY, M., & M. WILSON. 1978. *Sex, Evolution and Behavior.* North Scituate, Mass.: Duxbury Press.

DARLING, F. F. 1937. *A Herd of Red Deer, A Study of Animal Behavior.* London: Oxford University Press.

DAWKINS, R. 1976. *The Selfish Gene.* New York: Oxford University Press.

DEVORE, I. (ed.). 1965. *Primate Behavior: Field Studies of Monkeys and Apes.* New York: Holt, Rinehart & Wilson.

DOLHINOW, P. (ed.). 1972. *Primate Patterns.* New York: Holt, Rinehart & Winston.

DOLHINOW, P., & V. M. SARICH. 1971. *Background for Man.* Boston: Little, Brown.

DUNHAM, W.H. 1979. "Toward a Coevolutionary Theory of Human Biology and Culture." In N. Chagnon & W. Irons (eds.), *Evolutionary Biology and Human Social Behavior: An Anthropological Perspective.* Belmont, Calif.: Duxbury Press, pp. 39–59.

FELDMAN, L.M., L.L. CAVALLI-SFORZA, & K.H. CHEN. 1980. "Empirical Approaches to the Study of Cultural Transmission and Evolution." Paper presented to the 79th annual meeting, *American Anthropological Association*, December 5, 1980, Washington, D.C.

FOX, R. (ed.). 1975. *Biosocial Anthropology.* New York: Halsted/Wiley.

———. 1977. "Letter to the Editor." *Anthropology Newsletter*, 18 (No. 5), 27.

GARN, S.M. 1973. *On-Going Human Evolution.* Minneapolis, Minn.: Burgess.

GOODALL, J.V.L. 1964. "Tool-Using and Aimed Throwing in a Community of Free-Living Chimpanzees." *Nature.* 201, 1264, 1266.

HAMILTON, W.D. 1963. "The Evolution of Altruistic Behavior." *American Naturalist*, 97, 354–356.

———. 1964. "The Genetical Evolution of Social Behavior I, II." *Journal of Theoretical Biology*, 7, 1–52.

———. 1971. "Selection of Selfish and Altruistic Behavior in Some Extreme Models." In J.F. Eisenberg & W.S. Dillon (eds.), *Man and Beast; Comparative Social Behavior.* Washington, D.C.: Smithsonian Institution Press, pp. 57–91.

———. 1972. "Altruism and Related Phenomena: Mainly the Social Insects." *Annual Review of Ecology and Systematics*, 3, 193–323.

———. 1975. "Innate Social Aptitudes of Man: An Approach From Evolutionary Genetics." In R. Fox (ed.), *Biosocial Anthropology.* New York: John Wiley, pp. 133–155.

HARRIS, M., & E. O. WILSON. 1978. "Encounter: The Envelope and the Wig." *The Sciences*, 18, 9–15, 27–28.

HOWELLS, W. 1973. *Evolution of the Genus Homo.* Reading, Mass.: Addison-Wesley.

IRONS, W. 1977. "Letter to the Editor." *Anthropology Newsletter*, 18 (No. 5), 27.

ISAAC, G.L., R.E. LEAKEY, & A.K. BEHRENSMEYER. 1971. "Archaeological Traces of Early Hominid Activities, East of Lake Rudolf, Kenya." *Science*, 173, 1129–1134.

JOHANSON, D., & M.A. EDEY. 1981a. "Lucy: A 3.5 Million-Year-Old Woman Shakes Man's Family Tree." *Science-81*, 2, 44–55.

———. 1981b. *Lucy: The Beginnings of Humankind.* New York: Simon & Schuster.

JOHANSON, D., & T. WHITE. 1979. "A Systematic Assessment of Early African Hominids." *Science* 203: 321–330.

JOLLY, C.J. 1970. "The Seed-Eaters: A New Model of Hominid Behavioral Differentiation Based on a Baboon Analogy." *Man*, 5, 5–26.

JOLLY, A. 1972. *The Evolution of Primate Behavior*. New York: Macmillan.

KAUFMAN, I.C. 1975. "Learning What Comes Naturally: The Role of Life Experiences in the Establishment of Species Typical Behavior." *Ethos*, 3, 129–142.

KENNEDY, K.A.R. 1975. *Neanderthal Man*. Minneapolis, Minn.: Burgess.

KLUCKHOHN, C. 1953. "Universal Categories of Culture." In A.L. Kroeber (ed.), *Anthropology Today*. Chicago: University of Chicago Press, pp. 507–523.

LANCASTER, J. 1975. *Primate Behavior and the Emergence of Human Culture*. New York: Holt, Rinehart & Winston.

LEAKEY, L.S.B., J. PROST, & S. PROST. 1971. *Adam or Ape*. Cambridge, Mass.: Schenkman.

LEE, R.B., & I. DEVORE (eds.). 1968. *Man the Hunter*. Chicago: Aldine.

LEAKEY, R.B. 1981. *The Making of Mankind*. New York: Dutton.

LEHRMAN, D.S. 1976. "Semantic and Conceptual Issues in the Nature-Nurture Problem." In L.R. Arsonen *et al.* (eds.), *Development and Evolution of Behavior*. San Francisco: W.H. Freeman & Company Publishers, pp. 17–52.

LUMSDEN, C.J., & E.O. WILSON. 1981. *Genes, Mind and Culture: The Coevolutionary Process*. Cambridge, Mass.: Harvard University Press.

MACPHERSON, M. 1976. "Sociobiology; Scientists at Odds." *The Washington Post*, November 21, 1976, pp. 81, 84.

MAYR, E. 1958. "Behavior and Systematics." In A. Roe & G.G. Simpson (eds.), *Behavior and Evolution*. New Haven, Conn.: Yale University Press, pp. 341–362.

MENZEL, E.W., Jr. (ed.). 1972. *Precultural Primate Behavior*. Basel: S. Karger.

MONTAGU, M.F.A. 1960. *An Introduction to Physical Anthropology*. Springfield, Ill.: Thomas.

———. (ed.). 1980. *Sociobiology Examined*. New York: Oxford University Press.

NAPIER, J.R., & P.H. NAPIER. 1967. *A Handbook of Living Primates*. London: Academic Press.

OAKLEY, K.P. 1958. "Tools Maketh Man." Washington, D.C.: *Smithsonian Report*, 61, 431–445.

———. 1976. *Man the Tool Maker*. Chicago: University of Chicago Press (6th ed.).

PILBEAM, D. 1970. *The Evolution of Man*. London: Thames & Hudson.

———. 1972. *The Ascent of Man*. New York: Macmillan.

ROBINSON, J.T. 1973. *Early Hominid Posture and Locomotion*. Chicago: University of Chicago Press.

SAHLINS, M. 1976. *The Use and Abuse of Biology; An Anthropological Critique of Sociobiology*. Ann Arbor: University of Michigan Press.

SCHALLER, G.B. 1963. *The Mountain Gorilla: Ecology and Behavior*. Chicago: University of Chicago Press.

SCHULTZ, A.H. 1969. *The Life of Primates*. London: Weidenfield & Hicholson.

SCHWEDER, R.A. 1979. "Rethinking Culture and Personality, Part I, Part II." *Ethos*, 7, 255–311.

SEBEOK, T.A. (ed.). 1968. *Animal Communication: Techniques of Study and Results of Research*. Bloomington: University of Indiana Press.

SINGER, P. 1981. *The Expanding Circle: Ethics and Sociobiology*. New York: Farrar, Straus & Giroux.

TATTERSALL, I., & N. ELDREDGE. 1977 "Fact, Theory and Fantasy in Human Paleontology." *American Scientist*, 65, 204–211.

TOBIAS, P.V. 1971. *The Brain in Hominid Evolution*. New York: Columbia University Press.

TRIVERS, R.L. 1971. "The Evolution of Reciprocal Altruism." *Quarterly Review of Biology*, 46, 35–57.

———. 1972. "Parental Investment and Sexual Selection." In B. Campbell (ed.), *Sexual Selection and the Descent of Man*. Chicago: Aldine, pp. 136–179.

TRIVERS, R.L., & H. HARE. 1976. "Haplodiphoidy and the Evolution of Social Insects." *Science*, 191, 299–263.

TUNNELL, G. 1973. *Culture and Biology*. Minneapolis, Minn.: Burgess.

TUTTLE, R. (ed.). 1972. *The Functional and Evolutionary Biology of Primates*. Chicago: Aldine.

———(ed.). 1975a. *Socioecology and Psychology of Primates*. The Hague: Mouton.

———(ed.). 1975b. *Paleoanthropology: Morphology and Paleocology*. The Hague: Mouton.

———(ed.). 1975c. *Primate Functional Morphology and Evolution*. The Hague: Mouton

VALLOIS, H.V. 1961. "The Social Life of Early Man: The Evidence of Skeletons." In S.L. Washburn (ed.), *Social Life of Early Man*. Chicago: Aldine, pp. 214–235.

vonCRANACH, M., & I. VINE (eds.). 1973. *Social Communication and Movement: Studies of Interaction and Expression in Man and Chimpanzee*. New York: Academic Press.

WASHBURN, S.L. 1950. "The Analysis of Primate Evolution with Particular Reference to the Origin of Man." *Cold Spring Harbor Symposia on Quantitative Biology*, 15, 67–76.

———. 1960. "Tools and Human Evolution." *Scientific American*, 203, 62–87.

———. 1977. "Sociobiology." *Anthropology Newsletter*, 180 (No. 3), 15.

WASHBURN, S.L., & V. AVIS. 1958. "Evolution of Human Behavior." In A. Roe & G.G. Simpson (eds.), *Behavior and Evolution*. New Haven: Yale University Press, pp. 421–436.

WASHBURN, S.L., & I. DeVORE. 1961. "Social Behavior of Baboons and Early Man." In S.L. Washburn (ed.), *Social Life of Early Man*. Chicago: Aldine, pp. 91–105.

WASHBURN, S.L., & P.C. JAY (eds.). 1968. *Perspectives on Human Evolution*. New York: Holt, Rinehart & Winston.

——— (eds.). 1972. *Perspectives on Human Evolution II*. New York: Holt, Rinehart & Winston.

WASHBURN, S.L., & R. MOORE. 1974 *Ape into Man: A Study of Human Evolution*. Boston: Little, Brown.

WHITE, T.D. 1980. "Evolutionary Implications of Pliocene Hominid Footprints." *Science*, 208, 175–176.

WHITING, B.B. & J.W.M. 1975, *Children of Six Cultures: A Psycho-Cultural Analysis*. Cambridge, Mass.: Harvard University Press.

WILSON, E.O. 1975. *Sociobiology: The New Synthesis*. Cambridge, Mass.: Harvard University Press.

———. 1978 *On Human Nature*. Cambridge, Mass.: Harvard University Press.

WILLIAMS, G.C. 1957. "Pleiotrophy, Natural Selection and the Evolution of Senescence." *Evolution*, 11, 398–411.

———. 1966. *Adaptation and Natural Selection*. Princeton, N.J.: Princeton University Press.

WILLIAMS, G.C., & D.C. WILLIAMS. 1957. "Natural Selection of Individually Harmful Social Adaptations Among Sibs with Special Reference to Social Insects." *Evolution*, 11, 32–39.

WILLIAMS, T.R. 1972. "The Socialization Process: A Theoretical Perspective." In F.E. Poirier (ed.), *Primate Socialization*. New York: Random House, pp. 207–260.

————. 1975   "On the Origin of the Socialization Process." In T.R. Williams (ed.), *Socialization and Communication in Primary Groups*. The Hauge: Mouton, pp. 233–249.

————. 1978.   "Socialization Research: Planning for the Future." In D.B. Shimkin, S. Tax, & J.W. Morrison (eds.), *Anthropology for the Future*. Urbana-Champaign, Ill.: Department of Anthropology, University of Illinois, Research Report No. 4, pp. 142–161.

CHAPTER TWO
ORGANIC BRIDGEHEADS
TO SOCIALIZATION

This chapter discusses the kinds of biological equipment a newborn human possesses that provide specific links, or organic bridgeheads, between human biology and culture in the cultural transmission process. The point of this chapter is that some specific aspects of human biology, which are all evolutionary products, are involved in the process of cultural transmission.

The organic bridgeheads to cultural transmission consist of at least four very complexly interrelated classes of phenomena: (1) *species-characteristic behavior*, (2) *reflexes*, (3) *drives*, and (4) *capacities*. This chapter does not discuss the interrelations between these phenomena, since little is known concerning this topic.

SPECIES-CHARACTERISTIC BEHAVIOR

Instincts

Before 1920 students of human behavior, particularly psychologists and sociologists, had formulated a variety of theories based on the concept of *instinct*. This term was borrowed from biological studies of animal behavior. It was a vaguely defined term and at best was an explanation *ob-*

scurum per obscurius—that is, the term *instinct* explained an unknown phenomenon through use of another unknown phenomenon. In the 1920s instinct was widely supposed to be the cause of most human behavior. As descriptive accounts of human behavior in a wide variety of cultural settings began to accumulate, however, it became apparent that there was a fallacy in attributing highly variable, culturally structured phenomena to a constant biological factor such as instinct.

By the middle 1920s the term *instinct* had been demonstrated by anthropologists to be a less than useful basis for theories of human behavior. However the term tended to remain in the vocabulary of many social and behavioral scientists until about the time of World War II, when it ceased to be used generally as an explanation for human behavior. The term *instinct* remains in everyday use as a popular way of dealing with puzzling and frustrating facets of human behavior and because some specialists in the study of human behavior continue to employ the term in special ways in their explanations of complex human actions.

Another Explanation   In the past 40 years biologists concerned with systematic research on animal behavior, a field of study termed *ethology*, have devoted a considerable effort to the definition and identification of the physical and chemical basis of behavior.[1] At the close of the first 20 years of such study, ethologists generally defined an *instinct* as the complex unlearned activity characteristic of a species of animals and proposed four criteria for evaluation of any behavior of an animal as instinctive: (1) Is there a definite physiological basis for the supposedly instinctive action of the animal? (2) Is the instinctive action universal in the species of animals? (3) Does the physiologically based, universally functioning, biological entity clearly determine the behavior in question? (4) Is such behavior at all modifiable through learning and experience? By the early 1960s it had become increasingly clear to ethologists that the consistent application of these criteria for evaluating and establishing animal "instincts" had demonstrated that the concept of instinct was no longer scientifically useful. Students of animal behavior now have generally abandoned the use of the term *instinct* and, using the criteria listed above, have substituted the broader concept of *species-characteristic behavior.*

Ethologists have found that nearly every form of behavior in all animals studied is capable of being modified through experience and learning. Today *species-characteristic behavior* is defined by ethologists as including all those forms of action by an animal that are assumed to have a physical or chemical basis, are typical in members of a species, and are subject to some modification through experience.

---

[1]Ethology, the study of animal behavior, should not be confused with ethnology, the comparative study of human cultures. Discussions of the field of ethology are found in Hinde (1974), Klopfer and Hailman (1974), Eibl-Eibesfeldt (1975a), and Bateson and Hinde (1976).

And in Humans   A newborn human does not seem to possess any species-characteristic behavior forms comparable to the nest-building activity of the South African weaver bird or the honey dance of bees. Weaver birds clearly illustrate a species-characteristic behavior form; they usually construct nests of twigs with a foundation of coarse hair strands. In one study an experimental adult pair of weaver birds and their descendants were isolated completely from others of the species for six generations. During five generations the birds were not supplied with nest-building materials normally used by their wild ancestors. The sixth isolated generation of birds was provided with the normal, or "wild," nest-building materials, mixed with a variety of other materials. The isolated weaver birds proceeded to select the "proper" material and build their nests in the pattern typical of their wild ancestors. Thus a complex, typical, unlearned form of activity persisted in these creatures while they were isolated over six generations and then "reappeared" once again. Similarly bees isolated from other bees over many generations continue to collect honey and store it in the typical ways of wild bees and to even perform a complex "dance," which is believed by specialists in bee studies to show the general direction and amount of honey available.

Human infants do not appear, on casual observation, to exhibit similar forms of complex unlearned activity. This does not mean that species-characteristic behavior forms are not present in *Homo sapiens sapiens*. On the contrary a variety of particular activities exhibited by human infants could be termed species-characteristic behavior forms. For example, human infants are born possessing complex, unlearned tendencies toward gross random movements, including wiggling of the torso, waving of the arms, leg kicking, and noise making of a "babbling" type. These motor patterns cannot be identified as being related directly to any particular environmental or physiological stimulus and seem modifiable only by long and continued exposure to cultural and social learning situations. However these complex, unlearned movements appear to serve as a basis for the maturation of later, specific human motor activities, which become shaped and directed through the cultural transmission process, often through *inarticulate learning.* These movements appear to serve as a foundation for the whole range and style of the postures, gestures, gaits, and modes of locomotion typical of adults in a particular culture.

Additional Species Characteristic Forms

In addition to gross random movements, the human infant also exhibits other species-characteristic behavior forms: (1) *free soiling*, (2) *organic repression of smell*, (3) *organic emphasis of sight*, (4) *organic emphasis of hearing*, (5) *absolute nutritional dependence*, and (6) *infantilization*. These forms, which have been studied in detail through use of both experimental and naturalistic observations, are discussed in following paragraphs.

There also may be some other species-characteristic behavior forms that do not appear until the later periods of life, for example, nonseasonal sexuality.[2] The later-appearing species-characteristic behavior forms usually are expressed at the time and in particular levels of individual biological maturation. Thus a species-characteristic, human, nonseasonal (regular and continuous), sexual interest begins usually at about age 11 or 12 and may continue through adult life until a very old age. It is helpful to know that later-appearing species-characteristic behavior forms may be significantly shaped, or impeded, by the way individual biological maturation occurs and by other, still unknown, interactions between learning and development in specific human individuals.

There have also been suggestions that half a dozen other, and perhaps more, species-characteristic behavior forms exist in *Homo sapiens sapiens*. In discussing the incest taboo, Cohen (1964) has said that there is a significant factor in the human biological makeup that leads to establishing an incest taboo between parents and their children in the nuclear family. Cohen believes this taboo is an innate striving for a minimal degree of privacy or for freedom from extreme emotional and physical stimulation, especially from other closely related persons.[3]

Following Freud's original ideas, and on the basis of clinical observations made by a large number of specialists in different cultures, Róheim (1943) concluded that the *Oedipus complex* is a human species-characteristic behavior form. Freud's conception of the Oedipus complex was that it is innate, appears very early during human psychosexual development, and consists of sexual attraction by an individual to the parent of the opposite sex and a basic hostility toward the same-sex parent.

Ainsworth (1967) and Eibl-Eibesfeldt (1975a), as well as a number of other individuals studying the effects of infant-mother separation, have suggested that there is a human species-characteristic behavior form manifested by infants which involves a *"mediating social interaction"* (Ainsworth, 1967, 434) between parents and their offspring through which infants become indissolubly "attached," or socially and emotionally "bonded" with parents.

In addition, Washburn and Yahraes (1969) and Omark, Omark, and Edelman (1975) have proposed the existence of a human species-characteristic behavior form of *aggressive behavior* and the expression of aggression in infancy and childhood through repeated formation of social *dominance hierarchies*, which are used to shape and direct all personal relationships. Washburn and Yahraes note that during the long period in which evolving

[2]LaBarre (1954) presents a detailed account of these aspects of human biology.
[3]However, see the discussion by Brain and others, 1977. See also Barton, 1973.

humans were big-game hunters humankind became biologically "programmed" to enjoy killing and to glorify conflict leading to death. They note that while a hunting way of life provided the possibility of aggression as a human species-characteristic behavior form, during the same evolutionary period natural selection also took place for individuals who were able to control their killing "rage" to enable them to cooperate successfully with others in forming and maintaining human societies.[4] However Omark, Omark, and Edelman suggest that such cooperation is really based on dominance by some humans in all social activities.

Kendon (1972) has analyzed the relationships between the structure of human speech and the movement of body parts. He notes that during the utterance of any speech unit a speaker holds particular parts of the body in a constant position with *the length of time involved in the speech unit directly related to the length of time a body part is held motionless.* Kendon also notes that the more central the body part held motionless, the longer the speech unit used. McBride (1968, 1975) has proposed that the relationship between a body part being held motionless and the length of a speech unit is a human species-characteristic behavior form derived from the evolutionary development by *hominids* of the use of speech to control and direct vital social interactions.

Experimental studies reported by Karelitz and Fischelli (1962), Lind (1965), Condon and Sander (1974), Bullowa, Fidelholtz, and Kessler (1975), and others, including Cohen and Salapatek (1975a, 1975b) and Wohlwill (1973), have noted that a human infant cries in a pattern that can be interpreted as a species-characteristic behavior vocalization serving to communicate inner states of being prior to the development of a speech capacity. P. Lieberman and others (1967, 1972, 1975) have proposed that infant crying is a necessary precursor of human language since this vocalization pattern prepares infants to participate in an ongoing system of complex adult symbolic communication necessary to successful functioning as an adult. Lieberman (1975), with some others, also suggests that the evolutionary development of a *hominid* vocal symbolic communication system is reflected in contemporary humans in the infant cry pattern as a distinctive human species-characteristic behavior form.

In a discussion of the possibilities of a human science, Mead (1976) notes that, based on ethological studies of the behavior of newborn lambs and kids, Helen Blauvelt has concluded that newborn human infants appear to possess a species-characteristic behavior form which involves *propelling themselves unassisted up the human body* through use of a grasping-and-pull-type hand-over-hand climbing motion.

[4]It should be noted that the evolutionary origin of human aggression has been defined and accounted for as a species-characteristic behavior form in quite different ways by Tiger and Fox (1971) and others; see Fox, 1975.

Tambunan Dusun (Sensuron) girls seated in two typically adult female postures (back and right) during a game of "jacks." (T. R. Williams, 1959.)

In a series of texts Claude Levi-Strauss (1958; 1962) has also proposed that there is an inescapable *pattern underlying human intellectual operations* that, somewhat like the program of the high-speed computer, directs the work, actions, and shape of most of everything thought, perceived, or undertaken by humans. Levi-Strauss postulates that this pattern works as

Tambunan Dusun village of Sensuron, March, 1960. (T.R. Williams, 1960.)

the least common denominator of human thought. If such a pattern exists, it should be termed a human species-characteristic behavior.

Following the suggestions of Sigmund Freud, Bettelheim (1967) and Rapaport (1958), among others, have also suggested that all *humans are born with certain species-characteristic "apparatuses for relating to reality."* These scholars feel that individual personality will fail to unfold if these apparatuses are not permitted adequate development in infancy (see Chapter 5).

While important questions may be raised concerning each one of these ten possible human species-characteristic behavior forms, it may be said that a distinct possibility exists that in the near future there will be scientifically acceptable statements for understanding the role of such phenomena in human life. Until this time is reached, however, it may help to learn of some of the possible dimensions of the seven human species-characteristic behavior forms that now appear to be fairly well described in scientific terms. It is important to recall, however, that at present the range of human species-characteristic behavior forms is numbered from 7 to 17 of these vital organic bridgeheads in the cultural transmission process.

Free Soiling   The species-specific behavior form of free soiling involves disposal of body wastes. Waste disposal is as important for animals as food getting. This activity is particularly critical in nesting animals, such as birds, where the vulnerable young are kept in a very limited space. Several species-characteristic behavior forms are used in different bird groups to rid the nest of infant waste and prevent free soiling. Infants of some birds of prey eject body waste over the nest edge using specially developed muscles. In most perching songbirds fecal matter is encased in sacks of a gelatinous material secreted in the intestine. Parent birds dispose of the sacks after their elimination by the young in the nest. Nestlings of some bird species cannot defecate until a parent taps the cloaca with its beak. This species-characteristic form ceases when the infant birds leave their nest. This form of behavior appears to be a naturally selective, evolutionary adaptive mechanism designed to prevent contagion from nest soiling.

Free-ranging primates are usually born singly and carried regularly on the mother's body; hence there is little danger of infection from other young in a confined space. When built, primate nests are abandoned as soon as they become fouled with wastes. This evolutionary adaptation in primates has eliminated the problem of nest contagion among infants. Yet this adaptation raises the problem of the primate infant freely soiling the mother with urine and fecal matter. Female gorillas pay regular and very specific attention to grooming and cleaning of the area about the anus of their infants after defecation and are themselves groomed by another gorilla after being soiled by an infant. It is necessary for human adults to undertake quite explicit and repeated steps over a period of several years to make an infant surrender their free-soiling physiological autonomy and eventually accept cultural controls concerning defecation and urination.

In doing so the infant has learned to recognize the meaning of accumulating bowel and bladder pressures and to understand that, despite these body pressure signals, it cannot evacuate when needed physiologically but rather when specific adults require such release in particular places and at specific times. Thus the physiologically based human species-characteristic behavior form of free soiling is gradually transformed in a series of *transactional, or doubly contingent,* culturally structured events into a cultural process. It is in this way that organic bridgeheads to socialization are begun.

In this context it is useful to know that in this text cultural transmission is viewed as a *doubly contingent,* or *transactional* process. The question of the "point of time" at which this process begins, and terminates, is of theoretical importance. The assumption used in the text is that the cultural transmission process begins, and ends, when significant personal *transactions* start, and cease, between parents or their surrogates (e.g., nurses, "baby-tenders," teachers, and so on) and children in terms of learning cultural information.[5] It should be recognized that the cultural transmission process is also shaped and directed in significant respects by social and culture factors determining parental courtship, mate selection, and sexual activity, as well as maternal diet and health during conception and pregnancy. This theoretical position does not say that an individual ceases to learn vital information in later life. However these factors usually do not involve significant interactions of a *doubly contingent,* or *transactional,* type between individuals and their parents or parent-surrogates.

Repression of Smell   Systematic studies of the human infant's sense of smell have concluded that there is little discrimination of odor and that infant responses to odors are highly variable. While these experiments often have been confounded by imposition on the infant of the investigator's own culturally structured concepts concerning smells, basic research does support the general conclusion that the human infant appears to have a repressed, or limited, sense of smell.

Smell usually depends upon close physical proximity and the moisture content of the air. Odors from the object giving off a smell are very quickly diluted beyond any possibility of olfactory perception. High-flying birds of prey such as eagles have had to depend upon their sense of vision in hunting over large land areas. Carrion-feeding birds such as the condors and vultures, which should have an acutely developed sense of smell to find their food sources, instead have also had to depend on keen vision

---

[5]For a review and discussion of parental and surrogate cultural transmission, see Weisner and Gallimore, 1977.

because of the extreme dilution of odors with distance and moisture content of the air. Hawks and owls, hunting much closer to the land surface, have also been forced to rely on vision as well as a smell sense to locate food.

The human repression of smell is not an ancestral animal trait. Reptiles have a highly developed sense of smell, more so than either their bird or mammal descendants. It is likely that long-term adaptation to life in the air and high trees led eventually to recession and repression of the sense of smell among both birds and primates. As a consequence of this evolutionary heritage, *Homo sapiens sapiens* infants are born with a species-characteristic form of an organic repression of smell.

Emphasis of Sight The development of stereoscopic color vision as the consequence of the first primate locomotor adaptation of grasping and the second primate adaptation of special sensory organization has meant that for at least the past 55 to 60 million years primates have possessed the ability to see clearly the world in which they live. A dependence by an animal upon the sense of smell as a primary means of dealing with its environment restricts it to very limited amounts of space. Environmental contact through smell depends on natural energy units consisting of chemical molecules arranged in a particular pattern to comprise a substance. A molecule is the minimal energy unit of any chemical compound and is governed in its actions and relations with other molecules by certain invariable physical laws. For example, a chemical molecule cannot move at the speed of light. The speed of diffusion of any odor is limited by the physical properties of the molecules in a particular combination.

The primate and human vision sense is based, however, on a very different natural energy unit. Sight depends on quantum units of light which move at the absolute velocity of all physical forms in the universe. The eye of *Homo sapiens sapiens* has been demonstrated to respond to only one quantum unit of light. Since a quantum unit of energy is basic in the universe, this means the eye of *Homo sapiens sapiens* is nearly perfectly adapted to its physical world. At night a human is capable of detecting the light of one candle over very long distances, measured in miles.

The human infant quickly exhibits a high level of visual acuity, sensitivity, and coordination, although born with an incompletely developed optic nerve and with ciliary muscles not mature enough to permit complete accommodation (adjustment of the thickness of the lens) to bring light to full focus on the retinal structures. In the first few days of life an infant becomes quite sensitive to changes in intensity of visual stimuli. By the fifteenth to twentieth day after birth, most human infants discriminate quickly among colors and can follow objects. A few hours after birth most infants show rudimentary coordination and convergence of the eyes and easily fix an object and probably perceive depth of a field. At eight weeks most human infants have such visual responses well organized in their visual explorations of their environment. These visual responses of the infant are among the earliest complex behavior patterns to become organized and functional in an infant's adaptations to the cultural and social environments.

Well before the time a baby has gained motor control over its trunk and limbs, it is skilled and able to visually explore and to command its world of visual reality. Long before the human infant can actually physically manipulate reality, it is "sizing it up" visually and is well prepared to apprehend, and thus comprehend, meaningful visual messages carried across long distances in an instant by the medium of quantum units of light. Emphasis of sight may thus be said to serve as an organic bridgehead in the process of cultural transmission.

Emphasis of Hearing   The sense of hearing in primates is not as efficient as in many mammals that depend on sound comprehension for survival. For instance, bats and dogs seem to possess a much greater and more refined ability to discriminate and to locate sounds well beyond the hearing range of any primate. Because of the placement of their ears, most primates have only a limited sound-sensing ability, or an idea of the direction of sounds. This is so because sound waves strike primate ears in an off-center manner, usually reaching one ear before the other. The sense of hearing is not particularly efficient in humans since the distance of a sound-producing source cannot be accurately discriminated unless the sense of sight is used to make distance judgments on the basis of learned comparisons of volume and other clues, especially cultural ones.

This general sensory mode was retained, however, through millions of years of primate evolution in the high forests at perhaps the same level of functioning as in the ground-dwelling preprimates and apparently was not affected by the demands of tree life, as was the sense of smell.

While acuity of hearing seems to have bestowed no particularly naturally selective advantages on the evolving primates, it was not a disadvantage to life in the high forests. By the time of the evolving *hominoids* of the Miocene period, the ancestral primate hearing sense seems to have been intact and still functioning. Later when the evolution of *Homo* had proceeded to the point where the products of reflection and learning could be transmitted to succeeding generations through the use of articulate communication in the form of language, a sense of hearing came to play a vital part in evolving human biology.

Newborn human infants have a low level of hearing acuity in the first few days after birth, more as a result of mucus in the middle ear than lack of maturation of the auditory structures. The infant soon responds quickly and strongly, however, to different intensities and durations of sounds.

Human newborns do not seem to respond well to pitch differences. Pitch discrimination appears to develop to a generally high level after the first few months of life. Newborn human infants are generally well prepared biologically to hear and discriminate among the sounds of the world into which they are born. Hearing thus serves as an organic bridgehead in cultural transmission.[6]

Absolute Nutritional Dependence   Human infants are completely dependent upon others for their care and feeding. In Chapter 5 we will see how this fact has come to be the basis for the myth of *feral* (wild animal-like) children. The feral child myth recognizes more than a common-sense observation that human infants die unless nurtured by others. It also clearly notes the evolutionary organic roots of all mammalian and primate societies. In the course of the evolution of these kinds of animals, there has been a broad trend toward *meta-organisms*, or societies, where many individual animals comprise increasingly larger units for mutual satisfaction of their basic needs and individual survival, so that an animal, apart from a social grouping, is often unable to survive.

The basic mammal evolutionary adaptation is a nutritional one, as is illustrated today by the surviving primitive egg-laying mammals. The platypus and echidna (spiny anteater) suckle young born through laying eggs. Another major adaptation of the mammals was that of the marsupial. Marsupial young are born alive in an extremely immature state and must live for an extended time in a pouch on the mother's belly. This provides warmth and some measure of protection for the quasi-fetal young, while they nurse on nipples contained within the pouch. A further major evolutionary adaptation of the mammals was the endoparasitic placenta; the fetus remains in the mother's body until mature for birth, while taking nutriments directly from the bloodstream, rather than from a nipple on the outside of the body, as when the fetus is ectoparasitic.

The special evolutionary adaptation of combining the primitive mammalian adaptation of suckling the newborn by means of external teats and of the placental mammal adaptation of endoparasitic development, which provides for some safety in the bony shelter of the pelvic basin, is the foundation for the absolute nutritional dependence of the primate infant. In the course of primate evolutionary changes, newborn infants tended to become smaller, more helpless, and very much more physically immature. Today among the different types of primates, nutritional dependency

---

[6]For discussions of research concerning human infant vision, hearing, speech, and space perceptions, see Cohen and Salapatek, 1975a, 1975b.

TABLE 2–1   The Trend Toward Nutritional Dependency in the Primate Order

Primate form	Pregnancy period	Period of absolute nutritional dependency on mother or mother-surrogate	Suckling period	Social independence	Primate form
Humans	266 days	One year or more	1–2 years	6–8 years	Humans
Apes	Chimpanzee, 235 days Gibbon, 290 days	3–6 months	2–3 months	12–18 months	Apes
Monkeys	Rhesus, 166 days Marmoset, 150 days	1–3 weeks	2–4 weeks	2–4 months	Monkeys
Lemurs	111 to 145 days	1–3 days	2 days to 2 weeks	2–3 weeks	Lemurs

needs become increasingly greater from lemur to man, with the suckling period increasing from several days to a few weeks to one or two years.

Thus a human infant is born with a nutritional dependency upon its parents that is long-lasting and important for its subsequent development. This species-characteristic behavior is important in cultural transmission, for it is in the time, and the conditions, of prolonged nutritional dependency that a number of events occur (see Chapter 5) that are necessary for development of an essential "humanity." However this species-characteristc form alone is not responsible for humanizing an infant. This statement also applies to each one of the species-characteristic forms described in this chapter; no one species-characteristic behavior form can be said to be solely responsible for humanization of an infant.

Infantilization   The term *infantilization* refers to a broad tendency in the evolution of primates that had as its consequence the fact that, in adult form, *Homo sapiens sapiens* is a "fetalized ape." Modern adult apes such as the gorilla have a number of "rugged" body characteristics, including heavy brow ridges and massive forward jutting jaws. These physical characteristics are not present in a newborn gorilla. It is clear from the fossil evidence now available that the adult forms of early progenitors of *Homo sapiens sapiens* were also possessed of similar rugged body characteristics such as heavy brow ridges and projecting heavy jaws. When the evolutionary evidences for *Homo* are considered together, it is clear that the more *gracile*, or finely developed in structure, humans have become, the more they have come as adults to resemble an infant ape. As human hands became more useful in grasping, throwing, tearing, and lifting, and as the human brain became more vital in behavior than use of heavy jaws and tooth structure in defense and food getting, evolving humans reversed the early general trend in primate evolution of moving from gracile (light) to rugged (heavy) physical characters. Thus *Homo sapiens sapiens* adults have the smooth round heads characteristic of an ape infant and do not possess the *supraorbital* (brow) ridges or *prognathous* (jutting) jaws so typical of contemporary apes. *Homo sapiens sapiens* also has skull sutures, or lines between bones, that close late in body growth and relative body hairlessness, both fetal ape characteristics.

The evolutionary adaptive advantages of infantilization for *Homo sapiens sapiens* are significant for understanding the cultural transmission process. The smallness of the human face is related directly to the size of the brain case. *Homo sapiens sapiens* adults have a more massive brain than any other contemporary primate adult. The adult gibbon has an average brain case capacity of 97 cc.; the chimpanzee, 400 cc.; the orangutan, 416 cc.; and the gorilla, 519 cc. In contrast, contemporary human adults have an average brain case capacity of 1450 cc. These differences in brain size are related to the fact that human infants persist for a long period after their birth in a fetal stage of active brain growth, which is typical of fetal monkeys and apes. In the rhesus monkey and the gibbon, the most active period of brain growth is before the time of birth, when about 70 percent of the adult brain size is reached. After birth gibbon and monkey brains grow at the same rate as the rest of their bodies. The gorilla and chimpanzee have a brief period of rapid brain growth just after birth, so that 70 percent of adult brain size is reached in the first year of life. A *Homo sapiens sapiens* infant has only 22 percent of its adult-sized brain at birth. Despite a rapid increase in brain size in the first and second years of life, 70 percent of the human adult-sized brain is not gained until the first quarter of the third year, and 80 percent of the adult-sized human brain is not reached until near the close of the fourth year of life. *Homo sapiens sapiens* infants continue for three years following birth in a growth activity that is typically fetal in monkeys and some apes. Thus human babies have a delayed brain growth during the very long period of their nutritional dependency on adults.

Bloom's (1964) analysis of studies of human learning and physical development provides some indications of the importance of infantilization of the brain in humans with respect to demonstrated adult intelligence. Bloom has concluded that, in terms of intelligence measured at age 17 by any one of several standardized tests, at least 20 percent is developed by age 1, 50 percent by age 4, 80 percent by age 8, and 92 percent by age 13.

While there is obvious difficulty in developing and then administering "intelligence" tests to adult monkeys and apes, the general pattern of maturation of intelligence in these animals appears to follow the pattern of body growth common to these forms. Thus the "wild" rhesus monkey, which has an intrauterine period of 166 days, an infant period of 1.5 years, a juvenile period of 6.5 years, and an adult period of about 20 years, seems to develop at least 80 percent of its mature intelligence in its early years. A "wild" chimpanzee, which is intrauterine for 235 days, infantile for 3 years, juvenile for 8 years, and adult for approximately 30 years, also appears to develop at least 80 percent of its mature intelligence in its early years. So it seems likely that among contemporary monkeys and apes "intelligence" develops rapidly and early and that these primates probably are functioning at nearly the full level of an adult "intelligence" capacity by at least the beginning of their juvenile growth period.

The vital fact in understanding human infantilization is that there is a general "biological slowing" of infant growth so that the human brain and learned behavior develop together during the long period of nutritional dependency on parents. It is important not to draw the conclusion from this discussion that intelligence in *Homo sapiens sapiens* is related only to a larger brain size. It is reasonably clear now that normal human cranial capacity ranges from a lower limit of about 900 cc. to an upward limit of 2000 cc., with an average of 1450 cc. Anatole France, a Nobel Laureate and celebrated novelist, had a brain size of slightly over 900 cc. Idiots may have brain sizes of 1600 to 1800 cc. Thus it can be said that, within a broad range, neither human cranial capacity nor brain size is related to intelligence or functional capacity.

It can also be said that infantilization of the human newborn is a vital organic bridgehead to cultural transmission since this neotenous evolutionary feature (*neoteny*—"remaining ever young") means mature humans do not act generally with reference only to their species-charactistic behavior forms because these forms have been supplemented in *Homo sapiens sapiens* by cultural behavior forms learned in a socialization process.

In the long-term physical dependence on others of the human species, an infant comes to acquire through cultural learning those ways most other animals have fixed in their genetic structure. Animal adaptations in evolution ordinarily become gene traits, but the basic human evolutionary adaptation to the natural world is culture, which must be learned by a child using biological features of a special kind and which are comprised, in part, of species-characteristic forms.

It should be noted that infantilization and absolute nutritional dependency are both features of the general biological principle of *neoteny*. The features have been discussed separately here since they are special aspects of the biological heritage of a newborn human which serve, uniquely in each instance, as organic bridgeheads in cultural transmission. It would also be theoretically possible to discuss absolute nutritional dependency as a feature of infantilization. The delayed growth of the brain and a corresponding delay in the development of general intelligence, however, clearly seem to be different orders of phenomena and so warrant separate discussion from the fact of the human infant's nutritional dependency on its parents.

It has been said that play among humans, particularly in the form of games, is a neotenous feature.[7] Games can thus be seen as reflecting the continuation in adult humans of an immature behavior characteristic which usually ceases among other animals during the juvenile growth period. Recent comparative, or transcultural, studies of human games appear, however, to indicate organized forms of human play are associated with particular types of cultural transmission and personality traits and so serve to promote certain cultural ideas, concepts, or life styles. For instance, games of chance tend to occur in cultures where individual demonstrations of responsibility are highly rewarded. Games of strategy tend to occur in cultures where an emphasis is placed on unquestioning obedience. Games of skill tend to occur in cultures where displays of individual achievement are frequently and directly rewarded. In addition, cultures which have the most "severe" cultural transmission practices, such as early weaning, toilet training, independence training, or repeated verbal and physical punishments, tend to have much more complex forms of games than do cultures with much less "severe" cultural transmission practices. In those cultures where new games are introduced on a regular basis, cultural transmission practices tend to be much more "severe" in their form.[8] If these transcultural studies of human games are meaningful, it would be expected that individuals demonstrating a high degree of personal responsibility, obedience, and achievement would be found in cultures where the form of games is more complex and the cultural transmission practices tend to be much more "severe." It is possible to conclude from these data that in the long period of human cultural evolution—that is, over the past two to three million years—humans have discovered ways to direct, or to shape, a neotenous feature of their biology in such a manner as to utilize a species-characteristic form to achieve particular goals in cultural transmission. This conclusion would be based, however, on circular logic and a form of "illegitimate" teleological reasoning (see Chapter 4). In other words, to explain how games played by humans contribute to the successful operation of the cultural transmission process or the development of particular types of

[7]C.F. Bruner, Jolly, & Sylva, 1976. See also Rayner, 1976; G. Bateson, 1972; J. Lieberman, 1977. It should be noted that Bateson views play as a ritual aspect of human communication.

[8]See Roberts & Sutton-Smith, 1962, 1966; Sutton-Smith & Roberts, 1970; Bruner, *et al.*, 1976. See also Schwartzman, 1976.

personality traits is to reason in a logical style that notes games produce a particular kind of cultural transmission process; therefore, a particular kind of cultural transmission process is necessary for and leads to certain kinds of games.

This kind of logic and reasoning is also found in statements which claim that both human "curiosity" and "flexibility " of responses are species-characteristic neotenous entities. No credible scientific evidence presently supports such claims. Some humans learn to be more, or less, curious or flexible in their behavior, depending upon the cultural system in which they are enculturated. Human curiosity and flexibility do not appear, however to be nonexceptionable, or universal, in the human population, and in common with human game playing, apparently are not physically-chemically based, as species-characteristic behavior forms. Thus explaining individual curiosity, flexibility, or game playing as a feature of neoteny in *Homo sapiens sapiens* requires both circular logic and illegitimate teleological reasoning and results in statements that at best seem inappropriate.

In conclusion of this brief discussion of the species-characteristic traits of newborn humans, it should be noted again that it is very difficult at this point in cultural transmission research to say with any certainty whether one species-characteristic behavior is more important than others. While infantilization is vital as an organic *bridgehead* to cultural transmission because it provides for the very long time involved in the process of learning culture, it is not possible to say that this form is the most crucial of all human species-characteristic behavior forms.

Summary of Human Species-Characteristic Behavior Forms

In the preceding pages a brief account has been given of seven species-characteristic forms: (1) *random movement,* (2) *free soiling,* (3) *organic repression of smell,* (4) *organic emphasis of sight,* (5) *organic emphasis of hearing,* (6) *absolute nutritional dependence,* and (7) *infantilization.* A suggestion was also made, and brief illustrations offered, that there are at least ten other possible human species-characteristic forms that have had little systematic study in relation to their role in the process of cultural transmission. The point of this discussion of species-characteristic behavior forms has been to provide an awareness that there are physiologically and chemically based forms of activity typical of humans that apparently are not generally subject to modification, except through very long-term and repeated exposure to learning and situational experiences. The seven species-characteristic behavior forms briefly described here have been listed in the order in which they appear subject to whatever modification is possible; random movement appears the most modifiable through long-term learning and situational experiences, while the species-characteristic form of infantilization seems least modifiable through any type of life experience. It is important, however, to remember that all seven species-characteristic forms appear to be affected very little by learning when compared with other classes *(reflexes, drives, capacities)* of biological structures possessed by newborn humans. These other three classes, which are increasingly more modifiable through experience, are illustrated and discussed in some detail below.

It is useful to note that scholars in a variety of disciplines continue to debate as though there is little contemporary understanding of the details of human biology as the products of a complex evolution spanning at least 70 million years among the primates.

A differentiation in clear and concise terms between human species-characteristic forms, reflexes, drives, and capacities allows us to advance beyond sterile arguments that pit "nature" (e.g., human biology) against "nurture" (e.g., cultural and social learning)—that is, *"heredity vs. environment,"* toward a conceptual understanding that rejects such a limited theoretical position for one that accepts data of human evolution and the products of such evolution as one side of a cybernetic equation, $[C \leftrightarrow B]$ in which events in human biology (B) are dependent on events in a human culture system (C),while events in a human culture system are, in turn, dependent on those in human biology. Repeated arguments in the "nature vs. nurture" style pose "nature" as more important in human life, as in a work by E. O. Wilson (1978), or pose "nurture" as more important than "nature," as in Sahlins' penetrating and insightful critique of sociobiology (Sahlins, 1976). Such arguments miss the essential point of the *cybernetic,* or interactive, basis of human biology and culture.[9]

REFLEXES

Taxes The second major class of biological equipment possessed by the newborn human infant that serves as an organic bridgehead in cultural transmission is termed *reflexes.* All organisms are born with "stimulus-

---

[9]It is important to note here that some biologists, particularly those specializing in human genetics (cf. Dawkins, 1976; Cavalli-Sforza & Feldman, 1981), have taken the position that "nature" (e.g., human biology) takes precedence, or first priority, over "nurture" (e.g., culture) to the point of defining cultural transmission as essentially a biological process. Thus, Dawkins (1976, 206) defines as a new "replicator," a unit he terms a *meme* and uses the concept of a *meme pool* to discuss *memes* as, "living structures, not just metaphorically, but technically." Some other biologists and biologically trained anthropologists reject this proposition and seek to work with the idea of a "coevolution" between human biology and culture (cf. Alexander, 1979; Dunham, 1979). However even this approach tends to adopt the "nature" side of the *nature-nurture* debate.

bound" behavior forms—that is, because of a particular genetic heritage, members of a species will behave in stereotyped ways in response to particular stimuli in their environment. The simplest forms of adaptation by an animal to its environment are designated *taxes*. An example of a *taxis* would be an instance in which an organism orients itself in such a way that it can maintain equal stimulation of two bilaterally symmetrical sensory receptors or an instance in which an organism alternates right and left movements to equalize stimulation at successive intervals through time. Another illustration would be the instance of a response of an organism with two "eye" receptors to the stimulus of bright light. If the light source is moved laterally, the organism will change its orientation because one "eye" is receiving more light than the other. If one "eye" is blocked or removed and the organism is subjected to such a stimulus, it will move in a circle as it seeks to equalize the light stimulus. Such an effort to orient to a specific stimulus in the environment, continuously made and specifically guided by an external stimulus, is called a *taxis*.

In many instances a taxis is part of a whole complex of taxes. It is very difficult to separate the specific adaptive mechanisms involved at this level of an organism's behavior. For example, fish usually are oriented in water with the ventral (belly) surface downward, an orientation that depends on both gravitational and light taxes. If light comes into a tank of fish from the side rather than from the surface of the water, certain species of fish will orient themselves in a heads-up or heads-down angle to the surface. If the effects of gravity are removed when the labyrinth of the inner ear is destroyed by surgery, some species of fish will orient themselves ventral side up if the light comes up from below them. So precise analysis of taxes becomes difficult when there are factors that naturally interfere wih a basic orientation of an animal to stimuli in its environment. Too, not all taxes occur in uncomplicated forms. Even the simplest organisms, such as protozoa, show individual variability in their behavior and are not completely stereotyped in their acts. This is because all organisms are responsive to several features of their environment, including their own internal states, and so are usually making several different responses to varying stimuli at the same time.

Taxes appear to be almost nonexistent in humans. The higher in the phylogenetic, or evolutionary, scale, the more modes of behavioral adaptation are found in organisms, resulting in less stereotyped behavior in orientations to stimuli. Protozoa, simple metazoa, worms, insects, fish, amphibians, reptiles, birds, and "lower" mammals (such as the platypus and echidna) show a decreasing amount of taxes in the sequence in which they are listed here. "Higher" mammals, including all primates and especially humans, exhibit little taxes behavior. Figure 2–1 illustrates this fact in a schematic diagram.

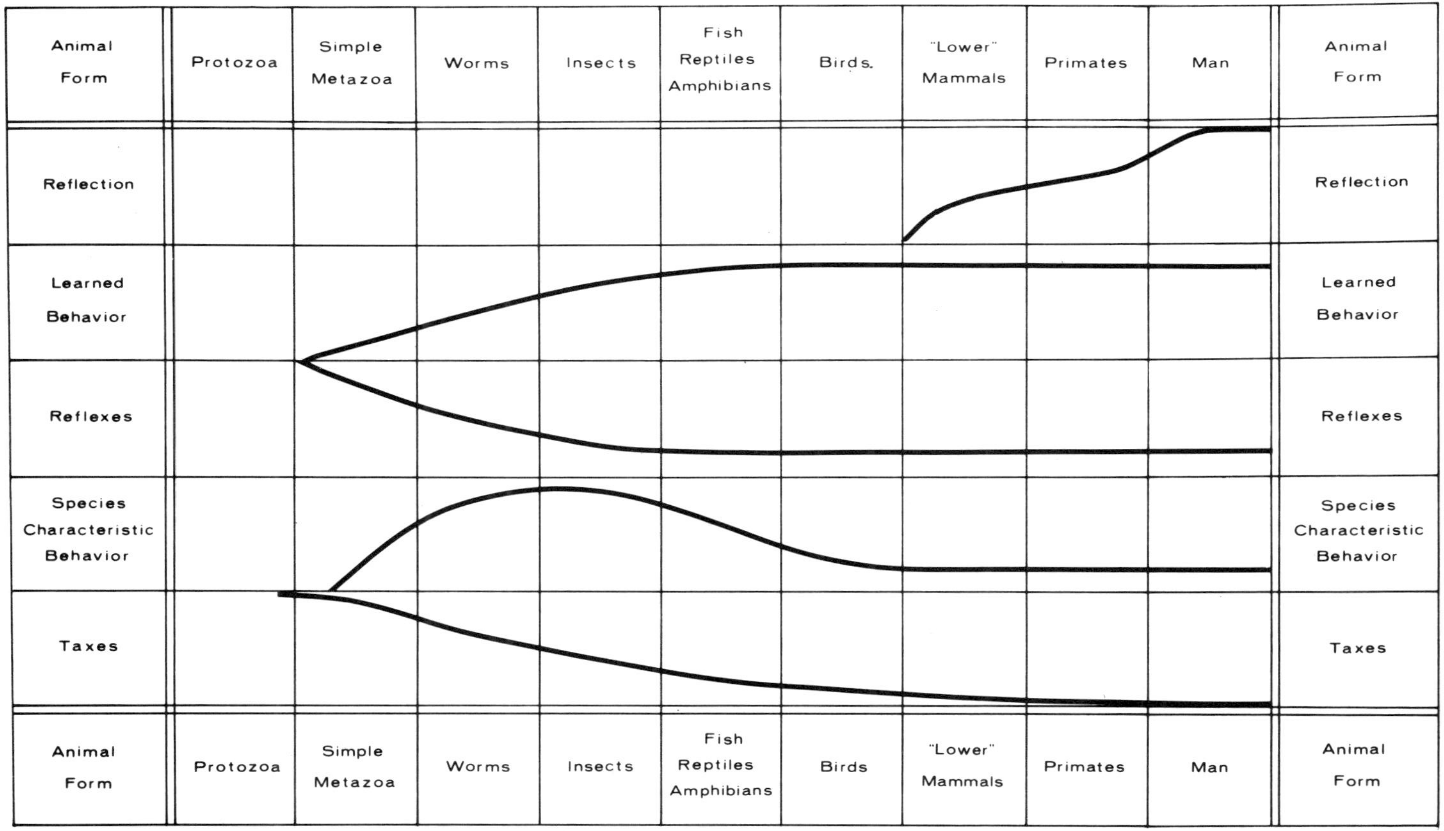

FIGURE 2–1 Schematic diagram of phylogenetic scale relationships in adaptive activity. (Adapted from Dethier, V.G., and E. Stellar. 1970, *Animal Behavior: Its Evolutionary and Neurological Basis.* Englewood Cliffs, N.J.: Prentice-Hall, Inc.)

The Nature of Reflexes

Reflexes are similar to taxes for they are relatively fixed or stereotyped responses to stimuli derived from genetically based nervous system structures and their functionings. In many animals it is very difficult to make a distinction between taxes and reflexes. The general distinction used by students of animal behavior is that taxes usually involve an orientation of the whole body of an animal to a stimulus. In contrast, while reflexes may involve all of an animal's body in response to a stimulus, usually they involve only part of an animal's body, such as constriction of the pupil in response to bright light or a flexing of a limb to a pain stimulus. Reflexes appear also to have greater variability and modifiability than do taxes, especially among higher vertebrate animals, particularly primates.

There are two general classes of reflexes: (1) *tonic* reflexes are slow, long-lasting responses to stimuli involved in such body processes as maintaining equilibrium, posture, and muscular tone, and (2) *phasic* reflexes are rapid, short-term responses to stimuli such as the one seen in the flexing of a limb under a painful stimulus. Reflexes are integrated at different levels and in complex ways in the nervous systems of the "higher" animals.

While it is theoretically possible to make an analysis of some of these complex reflex processes in terms of more simple reflex processes, it is now clear that, in the course of evolutionary change, particularly in the primate order, reflexes have tended to become subject to the modifying and mediating influence of higher neural mechanisms such as the brain cortex. Reflexes in humans can be altered in their stereotyped forms through learning of culture.

Kinds of Human Reflexes　A human infant is born possessing a wide range of reflexes: (1) *superficial* reflexes (such as mucous membrane or skin reflexes), (2) *deep* reflexes (such as biceps, knee), and (3) *visceral* reflexes (such as heartbeat, salivary glands, radial muscles of the iris). A partial listing of these human reflexes is provided in Table 2–2. Most human reflexes are based in or are directly mediated through the spinal cord. The spinal cord integrates reflex behavior occurring in the trunk and limbs and conducts nervous impulses concerning reflex activity to and from the brain. The basic spinal neural mechanism for integrating reflexes is termed the *reflex arc.*

The spinal cord is connected through special nerve systems branching off from it with the automatic nervous system, which innervates the viscera, blood vessels, and other smooth muscles of the body. The autonomic system is divided into two major parts: (1) a sympathetic nervous system branch, lying along the middle region of the spinal cord and sending out a diffuse

TABLE 2–2 Some Human Reflexes

I Superficial reflexes
   A. Mucous membrane reflexes
      1. Corneal (eye blink)
      2. Nasal (sneeze)
      3. Pharyngeal (gag)
      4. Uvular
      5. Palatal
   B. Skin reflexes
      1. Interscapular
      2. Upper abdominal
      3. Lower abdominal
      4. Cremasteric
      5. Gluteal
      6. Plantar
      7. Anal
II Deep reflexes
   A. Maxillary
   B. Biceps
   C. Triceps
   D. Periosteroradial
   E. Periosteoulna
   F. Wrist
   G. Patellar
   H. Achilles tendon
III Visceral reflexes
   A. Pupillary reflexes
      1. Pupillary
      2. Consensual
      3. Accommodation
      4. Ciliospinal
   B. Oculocardiac reflex
   C. Carotid sinus reflex
   D. Bulbocavernosus reflex
   E. Bladder and rectal reflexes
   F. Mass (Riddech) reflex
   G. Salivary
   H. Smooth muscle of bronchi
   I. Glands of respiratory passage
   J. Smooth muscles in walls of alimentary tract
   K. Glands of alimentary tract
   L. Liver
   M. Sphincters of alimentary tract
   N. Uterine muscle
   O. Pilomotor muscles
   P. Smooth muscle of skin blood vessels
   Q. Smooth muscle of blood vessels of abdominal viscera
   R. Smooth muscle of blood vessels of salivary gland and external genitalia
   S. Sweat glands

network of nerve fibers to the organs it innervates, and (2) the parasympathetic nervous system branch which arises from the most posterior regions of the spinal cord and brain and goes directly to the specific organs it innervates. In general, the sympathetic branch of the autonomic nervous system functions in reflexes that expend body energy (increased blood pressure, heartbeat rate, pupil dilation). The parasympathetic branch of the autonomic nervous system is generally reparative in its functions, for it is related to sleep, digestion, and so on.

In adult humans, if the influence of the brain on spinal reflex arcs is undamaged, the complex nature of reflexes increases greatly. This is because there is a nervous conduction to and from the brain by means of bundles of nerve fibers which are located on the peripheral parts of the spinal cord. In the course of vertebrate evolution the basic structure of the spinal cord has undergone very little change. As the forebrain area enlarged in primate evolution, however, the ascending nerve bundles on the peripheral areas of the spinal cord extended into the forward area of the brain itself (thalamus), while the nerve bundles descending from the brain came to originate in the highest portion of the brain (cortex). These nerve tracts became more compact, while also becoming more separate, thus permitting greater refinement and segregation of reflex arc functions. These evolutionary changes mean that in humans most reflex behavior is integrated and sorted out at several different levels of the central nervous system, including the brain. A reflex may be directly modified, or inhibited, by the higher brain centers on the basis of sensory data reaching it from other body parts. Thus learned behavior or a complex of learned attitudes resulting in an emotional or cognitive interpretation of the reflex experience can delay, modify, or block a reflex action.

Reflexes Can Be Modified   Reflex responses mediated through and interpreted by the brain, as is the case with nearly all human reflexes, become very complex neurosensory phenomena that considerably expand and enhance the behavioral potentials of a human being. Most importantly, however, these properties of human biological structure and function mean that a newborn human has the potential to learn to greatly modify reflexes, which does not appear possible in other animals. A human infant will live on a reflex arc basis; its heart will beat, it will breathe, and it will digest its food and eliminate wastes on a fairly automatic basis, without effort on its part. But a human infant, providing there is no central nervous system damage, has an opportunity to learn to culturally modify at least some reflexes in a quite significant manner. The fact is, of course, that many cultures do not systematically attempt to modify, repress, or inhibit most reflexes through enculturation. Persons in many cultures, including American culture, may even deny that such reflex changes are possible. There is now, however, substantial evidence that *Homo sapiens sapiens* reflexes are capable of modification through learning. Chapter 4 discusses this point in some detail.

DRIVES

A third major class of biological equipment possessed by a newborn human infant that can serve as an organic bridgehead in cultural transmission is known variously by the terms *drive, need, impulse, tension, urge, or appetite.* In the broadest sense all these terms refer to a complex of biological states of an organism and the stimuli leading or motivating it to a given behavior. Although there are some conceptual differences between these several designations, the term *drive* will be used here for the sake of brevity in discussion. Drives usually are seen by psychologists as representing a dynamic force behind the motivations to action of a human being. Drives have been used as explanations for and as answers to such questions as, "To what is apparent spontaneity of human behavior due?" and "Why in the absence of learning and fatigue does a human response to a constant stimulus change from time to time?"

A Theoretical Model

Scholars in biology and psychology have developed a general theoretical model, which has several major variations, to answer such questions. This model notes that all changes in an organism's activity not clearly attributable to *species-characteristic behavior* or to *reflexes* result from some kinds of changes in the quantity and distribution of physical, chemical, or electrical energy. This energy is created within the organism and is then "discharged," "released," "blocked," "deflected," or "stored." It is this energy that is said to motivate the organism to specific action. Despite more than a century of intensive research and discussion on the matter, however, it still is not clear whether such "energy" really exists and whether there is any scientific rationale for *drive* (*urge, need,* and so on), explanations of human behavior being based upon physiological processes that have yet to be clearly demonstrated. Many recent studies of human motivation continue to assume that some kind of body energy must underlie spontaneous human behavior (behavior not tied to or elicited by any visible stimulus). It is most often assumed that such "energy" arises from a complex physical-chemical interplay among reflexes and between reflexes and other genetically transmitted body features, such as species-characteristic behavior forms. Yet a serious question remains of whether motives to human action are ultimately reducible to a finite sequence and specific types of organic structure (such as a central nervous system) discharging some kind of "energy" that makes a human being "want" to act in certain spontaneous ways. Whether or not motivation theorists formulate new conceptual models that dispense with concepts of inner energy states leading humans to goal-directed actions to reduce physical tensions caused by energy accumulation, it seems clear that a newborn human possesses biological features directly involved in the process of cultural transmission and clearly different conceptually from *species-characteristic behavior* and *reflexes*.

Inner States and Later States

In newborn humans the biological features said to be related to drives appear to be primarily related to preservation of the individual through metabolic maintenance. This requires the acquisition of oxygen, water, carbohydrates, amino acids, and other essential metabolic elements used by the human body. It also requires maintenance of a constant ionic composition of the blood, a relatively constant body temperature level, the elimination of wastes and toxic body byproducts, and so on. Human metabolic maintenance also requires concentrated periods of sleep, rest, and wakefulness alternated in specific sequences to allow recovery from activities. These requirements are especially crucial for a newborn human and have been considered by many human behavior theorists as the bases of all other *drives, needs, urges,* and *tensions* that are developed or acquired later in human life (for example, the need for intimacy or for prestige).[10]

While basic research in the area of developmental psychology is attempting to identify the neurological and physical-chemical correlates of human infant and child behavior and continues to be wide-ranging and searching, the amount of description and analysis of the precise ways that drives originate and function in the newborn human is still limited. The most extensive descriptions of the ways drives arise and function in the newborn human are still to be found in psychoanalytic and psychiatric literature.

A View of Infant Inner Life

Until recently psychologists and psychoanalytic scholars have tended to portray human infants in a similar manner as far as drives are concerned: The newborn human infant was pictured by classic psychoanalysis and orthodox psychology as an undifferentiated passive recipient of stimulation calling into play its various drives. Bettelheim (1967) has pointed out that he believes this view of human infancy arose from a myth created by these scholars concerning the infant's "golden age," when it was assumed to not exist psychologically and to respond only through its various drives. Ac-

---

[10]Hinde (1960, 1974) provides a good review of variations of the "classic" energy models in his study of human motivation.

cording to Bettelheim we imposed our wishful adult views onto the inner life of the infant, to make it passive and receptive, sheltered from all the stresses of later human life. Spitz (1946) pictured the human infant's condition as *anaclitic*—that is, characterized by such extreme dependence that all "psychological" functioning in the newborn is qualified or suppressed by the presence and operation of drives, particularly the hunger drive.

A Change of View

Recently, there has been a withdrawal from this position as extreme. A newborn human is now viewed by many psychoanalytic, psychiatric, and psychological scholars as an active, competent being in constant reciprocal interaction with its environment. Current psychological studies of human development make it clear that there is adequate empirical evidence to support such a general theoretical shift. This shift still leaves the reader interested in the cultural transmission process with a choice between one of several energy models as the basis of drives and with little accurate understanding of how drives are used to transform a human organism into a human being in the course of a cultural transmission process.

The Rubber Band Analogy

The general energy model for the explanation of drives leaves something to be explained, particularly in the classic psychoanalytical view, which says the hunger drive is supposed to become operative about 18 to 36 hours after birth, when the blood sugar level of the infant drops markedly. The hunger drive then takes precedence over and is more vital than other body processes by creating a tension that can be reduced only by specific acts of the mother or a mother-surrogate, such as a "wet nurse." A rubber band analogy often is implied in such tension reduction explanations of infant behavior. When a new rubber band is stretched to near its breaking point, the molecules within the structure are rearranged because of heat and pressure. If the tension on the rubber band is released and the structure is allowed to return to its normal shape, a slight change in the original structure occurs resulting from the permanent changes in molecular arrangement created in the initial stretching process. Each time the rubber band is stretched again, a further molecular rearrangement occurs until the structure begins to assume a new shape.

Thus, some scholars have said that when the internal tension created by lowering of the glycogen level, which leads the infant to many kinds of random behavior such as sucking and head turning, is finally reduced by a feeding act by the mother or mother-surrogate, there is a basic change in the hunger drive because of the specific ways in which the tension was reduced by the mother or her substitute. These scholars also say that each reduction of this tension leads to added modification of the hunger drive, until finally the drive is "socialized" and the human infant begins to assume individual management of the drive.

Contrary Evidence

Recent experimental studies of satiation and hunger drive reduction in human and other mammal infants (rats, cats, puppies, monkeys) tend to indicate that the rubber band analogy, which presumes the hunger drive to be shaped by adult acts lowering the infant's glycogen level, is too simple. Studies of newborn human infants indicate that babies sucked as much when satiated and experimentally aroused as when they were deprived of food but equally aroused experimentally. It can thus be concluded that the descriptions of the hunger drive behavior in newborn humans are confounded by a lack of specific knowledge concerning the ways a baby is aroused or stimulated by other factors internal and external to its being. It may be that a revision in thinking will have to occur concerning the function of drives in cultural transmission, similar to the effort that took place in the instance of the concept of instinct and its replacement by the concept of species-characteristic behavior. This does not mean that the concept of *drive* is not a useful way to begin thought about this class of biological equipment in newborn humans. It does mean that at present it is exceedingly difficult to say that a specific drive, dealt with in a particular way by adults in an enculturation process, invariably leads to specific behavior form in a human infant.[11]

CAPACITIES

Possible and Actual Capacity

A fourth major class of biological equipment possessed by the newborn human infant, which can serve as an organic bridgehead in cultural transmission, has been termed variously as *capacity* and *potential*. The term *ability* is sometimes also used to denote a *capacity*. In the broadest sense *capacity* refers to the fact that the human infant is born possessed of gene patterns that can come into play at particular stages of growth and development only when elicited through specific combinations of biological, social and cultural circumstances. Each human infant possesses the *possibility* of body growth and maturation.

---

[11]The problem of causality has greatly concerned scholars studying the consequences of the socialization process for more than three decades. For instance, see Orlansky, 1949; Lindesmith & Strauss, 1950; Chess, Thomas & Birch, 1959; Kagan & Klein, 1973; Shweder, 1979. It may be that the problem of determining cause-effect relation between socialization events involving *drives* and later adult behavior is one of a *conceptual focus* rather than a lack of causation.

Whether infants actually grow and act, as well as the ways infants grow and act, depends upon the fact of their survival and the ways they are cared for and learn as they do mature. A child's strength, speed afoot, balance, body flexibility, coordination, dexterity, learning, and so on, depend first on the presence of specific patterns of genes and secondly on whether these *capacities* are brought into play through their being developed and expressed in particular cultural, social, and biological circumstances.

An Example of a Distinction   An example of the distinction being made here between the *possible* as opposed to the *actual capacities* of human individuals is that of peoples living on the islands offshore from Asia (Japan, Taiwan, Philippines, Borneo, Celebes, Java, Sumatra) who have traditionally had a subsistence diet comprised largely of white polished rice. Whatever their other physical characteristics (skin color, hair color, and form), these people are short, ranging in stature on the average from 5 feet, 1 inch to 5 feet, 5 inches. Explanations for this average short stature have ranged from a lack of minerals in the soils to the fact that these peoples all belong to the Mongoloid race, or clinal population. However, none of the explanations is sufficient to understand the average short stature among island Asian peoples. Soils vary considerably in their mineral content from Japan to Java. Members of the Mongoloid clinal population living on the Asian mainland vary greatly with respect to their stature.

One factor that the people of island Asia share is their diet of white polished rice. In World War II Europeans and Americans who were forced for long periods as prisoners of war to subsist entirely on white polished rice developed the diseases of pellagra, black tongue, hyperkeratosis, staggers, and edema. These diseases are generally not found among the peoples of island Asia eating a diet mainly of white polished rice. Experimental animals raised on a white polished rice diet are much smaller than other animals of the same genetic strain raised on diets normal for such animals. A white polished rice diet introduces a basic amino acid deficiency; there is enough protein in such rice to sustain life but not enough to encourage or allow full growth. The peoples living on the Asian islands have become genetically adapted to the white polished rice amino acid deficiency and so now do not usually suffer the diseases that afflict other humans who eat such a diet. This genetic adaptation by island Asian people has resulted, however, in an average short stature.

The taller tropical island peoples of the Pacific who live to the east of island Asia are believed to be the descendants of the peoples who ate white polished rice. They are taller because they have developed a diet rich in animal proteins and most vitamins, including such foods as fish, pig, yams, taro, and coconuts.

The people of island Asia have the *capacity* for larger size, both in stature and weight, but have not actually realized this capacity because of their basic subsistence diet of white polished rice. Marked changes in social and cultural patterns following World War II have altered this traditional diet as a part of life in this geographic area and will likely result in significant changes in the average stature of some island Asian (Japan, Taiwan, Philippines) peoples. This average stature change has proceeded most rapidly in post–World War II Japan among the children born since 1950.

Statements concerning human capacities thus have little scientific meaning unless they also include an exact specification of the biological, cultural, and social contexts in which a capacity is manifested. Studies of twins, discussed in Chapter 5, are vital to understanding human capacities because they allow some specifications of the ways biological, social, and cultural factors can affect the *actual capacities* as opposed to *possible capacities* of human individuals.

Research on Capacities

The scientific literature on human capacities is fragmented and unclear. Research on the nature of human capacities has been concentrated in three areas: (1) *motor functions* (strength, speed, coordination), (2) *cognitive functions* (concepts of mass, weight, number, logical thought), and (3) *learning.* Data of human capacity have generally been derived in these three areas by the methods of factor analysis and psychological tests.

A newborn human appears to be equipped with a very wide range of possible development in each of the three capacity areas that have been studied. As infants mature, and depending upon the circumstances in which they mature, their capacities become more amenable to direct observation and testing. After about age four children seem to exhibit in very broad outline their adult motor, cognitive, and learning capacities.

The Capacity for Learning

The learning capacity has been the most-investigated human capacity. Psychologists now generally agree that social and cultural experiences play a central role in human learning. Studies of the human capacity for learning indicate that a human infant is born possessed of genes that fix very broad limits for the possible development of this capacity but that humans are not genetically equipped in any way that ensures that such potential will be realized automatically.[12]

How and *what* infants and children learn at particular times in their maturation becomes crucial to understanding the development of their learning capacity. Benjamin Bloom (1964) and others have also argued that the human learning capacity is also dependent upon the *quality* of an individual's past learning experiences and is not a result of any innate human

---

[12]For instance, Cattell & Dreger, 1977.

impetus to learning. Thus the character of learning experiences—their soundness, distinction, and excellence, as defined in social and cultural terms—is said to promote and to stimulate the operation of the human capacity for learning in individuals.[13]

Studies of human capacities usually have been confined to Western European cultures. Some studies, using what are said to be "culture-fair" (or "culture-free") methods, have been made of psychomotor, cognitive, and learning capacities in a few non-Western cultures or on small groups of individuals from non-Western cultures. In this respect the observations of Sarason and Gladwin (1958, 142) still hold; no accurate tests currently exist to transculturally measure human capacities. It is reasonable to say that, while capacities are part of the biological equipment of the newborn human, little is known concerning the expression and range of human capacities.

UNDERSTANDING THE LINKS
BETWEEN HUMAN BIOLOGY
AND CULTURE

It is important to reaffirm the point that research efforts seeking to define specific links between human biology and culture must be undertaken in the context of contemporary knowledge concerning human evolution and behavior. It should also be understood that research concerning the links between human biology and culture is limited, and rightly so, by ethical, moral, and legal codes which prohibit most laboratory and surgical experiments on human infants and children.

There can be no question that it is fundamentally wrong to use human infants and children in any ways liable to cause them harm, simply to prove a scientific point. The search for knowledge of specific links between human biology and culture developed in a cultural transmission process is thus required to draw upon data and conclusions of experimental studies of the relationships between biology and behavior in a wide variety of animals, including various kinds of nonhuman primates. The results of most such experimentation, however, are of limited use in the study of the cultural transmission process. The results of recent, and excellent, experimental studies using laboratory animals would seem helpful to the study of human cultural transmission. For example, the studies by Butler, Suskind, and Schanberg (1978) concluded that an increase in the enzyme *ornithine de-carboxylase* (ODC), said to be vital to the rapid growth and differentiation

---

[13]The studies of six cultures by John and Beatrice Whiting and their associates (Whiting & Whiting, 1975) provide richly detailed accounts of the quality of learning in different contexts. See the discussion in Chapter 3 of the Whiting "six cultures" project.

of preweanling rat pup brain and heart tissue, is caused by the nurturing behavior of rat mothers. Butler et al. report that isolating preweanling rat pups from their mothers for as little as one hour leads to 50 percent reduction in brain and heart tissue ODC and that ODC activity is rapidly restored to a high level in rat pup brain and heart tissue after a pup is returned to its mother or a surrogate rat mother.

In their experimental studies Butler et al. tested the hypothesis that significant ODC decrease in the brain and heart tissue of isolated preweanling rat pups is a function of some factor in rat nutrition by surgically tying the nipples of lactating rat mothers, who could not nurse pups but could exhibit all other kinds of normal rat nurturing behavior. Rat pups placed with ligated but otherwise nurturant rat mothers showed a significant increase in brain ODC activity, while pups placed with anesthetized but unligated and lactating rat females showed a 55 percent decline in ODC brain activity. To ensure that adrenal hormones had not increased because of physiological stress among rat pups from a lack of mothering and had inhibited ODC activity in brain and heart tissue, Butler et al. surgically removed the adrenal glands from rat pups used in their experiments. Maternally deprived preweanling rat pups again showed significant decreases in ODC activity in brain and heart tissues. Butler et al. have concluded from their experimental work that ODC activity is not regulated by rat nutrition or adrenal glands, but is directly dependent upon the nurturant behavior of rat mothers.

Since there are ethical, moral, and legal prohibitions on surgically removing the adrenal glands of human infants or ligating the nipples of lactating human mothers for experimental purposes, it would seem appropriate to apply conclusions from the Butler et al. study to try to understand a specific link between infant human biology and culture by directly applying the conclusions of such laboratory research to humans (e.g., that a high level of ODC activity in human infant brain and heart tissues is caused by human maternal nurturant behavior).[14]

---

[14]In another illustration of this point, the innovative experimental surgical intervention techniques developed by Ronald Myers and his associates and Edward Taub and his colleagues for research involving nonhuman primate fetuses have demonstrated that many primate motor "programs," or typical behavior forms, are part of primate genetic endowment—that is, no sensory feedback or spinal reflex loops actually are necessary for learning the repertoire of typical (gait, posture, gesture) movements in nonhuman primates. For a discussion of this research, which involves removing primate fetuses from the uterus, performing surgery on the fetus, then replacing the fetus in the uterus for a full-term, "normal" birth, see Kolata, 1978. This experimental research is said by neurobiologists to provide new views on the complex interrelationships between the nonhuman primate central nervous system, the environment, and learned behavior.

A Problem of Application

There is a fundamental scientific problem in use of the Butler et al. experimental work or data and conclusions from many experimental and surgical studies on nonhuman animals in efforts to understand the ways that links between human biology and culture are developed in a cultural transmission process. The problem can be described in this way: Human infants are born possessed of a wide variety of species-characteristic behavior forms, reflexes, drives, and capacities whose nature makes it logically inappropriate to use data and conclusions from many of the experimental studies conducted on nonhuman animals. For example, if conclusions from the Butler et al. study were applied literally to human infants, it would lead to an error. It is clear that whatever the specific links may be between the nurturing behavior of human mothers and enzyme, or hormone, activities in the brain and heart tissue of human infants, these links *do not increase* the levels of ODC and lead to rapid growth and differentiation of human infant brain and heart tissue. Human infants are characterized at birth by the neotenous features of infantilization and absolute nutritional dependency that produce delayed body growth, including brain and heart tissue growth, during the first years of life. As noted earlier a human infant has only 22 percent of its adult-sized brain at birth and has acquired only 80 percent of the adult brain size by the close of the fourth year of life.[15] So the nurturant behavior of human mothers does not lead to rapid growth and differentiation of infant brain and heart tissue. Rather, human nurturing behavior is linked to a *slowing of the growth rate* of human infant brain, heart, and other vital tissues, possibly through stimulating in infants high levels of a yet unknown or specified enzyme or hormone whose action is quite different from the effects of *ornithine decarboxylase* in rat pups.

It should be noted that a large number of studies of severe deprivation of ordinary human nurturant behavior tends to indicate that such isolation contributes to a wide variety of maladaptive behavior forms in human infants and young children, including infantile autism (see Chapter 5), a marked lessening of "mental abilities," a significant lack of personal adjustment and personality development in infants and children, severe anxiety, and a clinical syndrome in newborn infants that includes extreme apathy, eventual refusal of all social contacts, and the onset of a number of physiological imbalances and diseases related to isolation from consistent nurturing behavior by mothers.

---

[15]This is in contrast to the structure of the nonhuman primate central nervous system, which is essentially complete at birth.

It can be suggested that all of these consequences of severe isolation in human infants may be dependent upon the absence in maternally deprived infants and young children of a certain level of an enzyme, or enzymes, or possibly hormones, which act to retard growth and differentiation of human infant body tissues, particularly in the brain and other structures of the central nervous system. In fact, human infants and young children who are severely maternally deprived may experience a marked "speeding up" of brain and central nervous system tissue growth and differentiation due to the reduction or absence of a crucial enzyme, enzymes, or hormones which act to inhibit such growth during the first years of life. In turn, severe maternal deprivation leads to a number of kinds of maladaptive human infant and child behavior forms.

Monkey Mothering and Peer Groups

Some other kinds of human isolation and deprivation may also contribute in a significant way to the lack of an enzyme or hormones required to suppress rapid growth or tissue differentiation in human infants and children. It is possible that the absence of regular peer group contacts for a human infant and child may also directly contribute to a failure to suppress human infant and child growth enzymes or hormones and may lead directly to a wide variety of personal maladaptations. A large body of experimental and laboratory work involving social isolation in nonhuman primates, particularly macaque and rhesus monkeys, was conducted over a thirty-year period by Harry Harlow (1959, 1966, 1969) and his associates. These studies indicate that the long-term consequences of isolation for these types of monkeys include compulsive rocking and swaying, repeated thumb and finger sucking, skin pinching and tearing when startled, high levels of aggression, and an inability to copulate as adults. All of these infant and young monkey behavior forms are considered by Harlow and others to be socially maladaptive. In considering application of Harlow's studies to understanding the socialization process, it would be helpful to know that in these nonhuman primates the brain and other nervous system structures are largely mature and complete at birth. Thus, Harlow and his associates could not have been dealing experimentally with the postnatal growth and differentiation of central nervous system tissues vital to monkey social behavior and learning. Rather, Harlow was studying a wide variety of complex sensory feedback mechanisms necessary for infant and young macaque and rhesus monkeys to be able to "fine-tune" their social behavior. This conclusion is supported by neurosurgical experiments performed on primate fetuses by Patricia Goldman and her associates (Kolata, 1978) at the National Institute of Mental Health. Goldman and her colleagues have conducted research on the social behavior consequences of the removal or severe injury to the *prefrontal cortex* of the monkey brain. Surgical removal of the prefrontal cortex in juvenile or adult monkeys results in poor performance in tasks requiring social learning. Monkeys who experience surgical removal of the prefrontal cortex at 50 days of age perform normally on tests of social behavior until they are about one year old, when their learning performances begin to diminish sharply. However, these monkeys continue to learn social behavior forms at a higher level than do monkeys whose prefrontal cortex was surgically removed when they were juveniles or adults. Goldman and her associates have reported that monkeys whose prefrontal cortices were removed surgically about two-thirds of the way through their fetal development appear to be able to completely overcome the effects of such a severe brain injury and to perform within the normal range of behavior of monkeys that have not had such experimental surgery. During study of the brain of a two-and-one-half-year-old monkey whose prefrontal cortex had been removed earlier through fetal neurosurgery, Goldman and her associates discovered that the form of the brain in this surgically impaired monkey was very different from the brain of normal monkeys and even from the brains of monkeys whose prefrontal cortices were removed after their birth.

The brain of the fetally impaired monkey had "anomalous" folds and indentations both close to and far away from the site of the surgical injury. Neurons from the thalamus, a brain structure through which complex sensory impulses pass to reach the cerebral cortex, or top layer of cells on the brain, which usually project to the prefrontal cortex, appeared to have been "rerouted" during growth to other parts of the brain rather than to have degenerated, as in the instance of monkeys which had the prefrontal cortex removed after their birth.[16] Goldman has speculated that the morphological changes in the brain of fetally impaired monkeys allowed these monkeys to compensate for the loss of their prefrontal cortex and to learn social behavior in a normal manner for that animal. Goldman cautions, however, that further research is needed to support this conclusion.[17] The importance of the surgical and behavioral research on monkey fetuses removed from and then replaced in the uterus is that it clearly indicates

---

[16]It has been known for some time that human patients with diseased or impaired cerebellums and an eye disorder in which the eyes move involuntarily cannot be taught to correct the eye disorder. However, recent studies by David A. Robinson, professor of ophthalmology and biomedical engineering at Johns Hopkins University, indicate that both patients and experimental animals with an undamaged cerebellum can, in fact, learn to overcome even severe "eye jump" problems, apparently through a type of "rewiring" activity carried out in the cerebellum in a form that Robinson notes may be an example of *"self-repair"* by the brain of an otherwise healthy adult.

[17]For a general discussion of the work of Goldman and her associates, see Kolata, 1978.

the vital role that complex sensory, or experience, "inputs" may have in the development of normal adult monkey social behavior.

If the research by Harlow and his associates concerning infant and young monkey isolation from ordinary maternal and peer group social contact is combined with the neurosurgical studies of Goldman and her colleagues, it is possible to conclude that normal social behavior in adult monkeys depends upon earlier, and adequate, maternal and peer group social contacts which produces the stimulation of complex sensory "inputs" in an infant, which in turn leads to a differentiation of brain and central nervous system sensory structures required for learning social behavior forms.

Although there are exciting possibilities in research which joins Harlow's observational and Goldman's fetal surgical procedures in experimental research on nonhuman primates, an important question remains concerning the application and use of such knowledge and conclusions in study of the cultural transmission process. It is not and should not be possible to remove the prefrontal cortices of human fetuses during their gestation in order to demonstrate the vital role of social behavior by mothers or peers in stimulating the post-birth growth and differentation of infant neural sensory structures required for learning "normal" adult patterns of social and cultural behavior. So we shall be required to either use, or disregard, these kinds of data.

A Matter of Evidence and Choice

It is worth repeating that uncritical use of nonhuman experimental data and conclusions in the study of the socialization process can result in inappropriate statements concerning the links between human biology and culture. This problem is readily apparent in the review by Barchas (1976) of a field of sociological study that has come to be termed *physiological sociology*. Here some sociologists use nonhuman experimental data and conclusions to interpret human social behavior and to form general conclusions concerning the nature of human society. At present these interpretations and conclusions appear to have minimal value since they have been reached uncritically—that is, without regard to the problems in use of nonhuman experimental data in human studies. This does not mean, of course, that use of all nonhuman experimental data or conclusions must be avoided. To the contrary, there are research data and conclusions based on particular types of field, laboratory, or experimental research using nonhuman animals that appear appropriate for use in study of the socialization process. Some of these conclusions and data are cited in Chapters 1 and 4. It is appropriate to note here that all scientific research has intrinsic merit. A decision that data and conclusions from a particular experimental or laboratory study using nonhuman animals is not useful in seeking to determine the nature of links between human biology and culture forged in a socialization process is not a comment on the inherent value of such research.

CONCLUSIONS

There is a basic paradox in the fact that, although human culture can easily be demonstrated to persist beyond the life span of any one person, without human individuals there seems to be no identifiable place, or *locus,* in nature for this phenomenon. Pareto (1935), in a theory of "culturology," and Kroeber (1952), in a theory of the "superorganic," sought to ignore this paradox through considering the concepts of culture and society as being generally unrelated to the acts or concerns of individuals.

It now is clear that the fundamental locus of culture in the natural world is the cultural behavior of the individual. If this is so, then the key scientific questions become, "How does an individual human being acquire cultural behavior forms?" and "If cultural behavior forms are not transmitted genetically, then how does an individual acquire them?"

These are among some of the principal questions in the study of the nature of the socialization process. Evidence is examined in Chapter 5 that clearly indicates that human cultural behavior forms are acquired in a socialization process and do not automatically appear in the human individual, as would be expected if these forms were genetically transmitted as species-characteristic behavior forms.

This chapter has been concerned with assisting you to gain an understanding that specific features of human biology serve as the points of transition between the human individual and culture. The answer to the question, "If cultural behavior forms are not transmitted genetically, then how does an individual acquire them?" must begin with a specification of those aspects of human biology, such as *species-characteristic behavior, reflexes, drives,* and *capacities,* that are amenable to modification through experience in a socialization process and therefore can serve as the organic bridgeheads, or key links, between human biology and culture.

Any discussion of the cultural transmission process must thus proceed from the basis of specific knowledge concerning the nature and functioning of the several types of organic bridgeheads to socialization. Despite our present limited knowledge of these links between culture and human biology, it is likely that advances in specific understanding of the ways they are interrelated will come through basic research on the manner in which these organic bridgeheads are modified, accentuated, or limited in a socialization process.

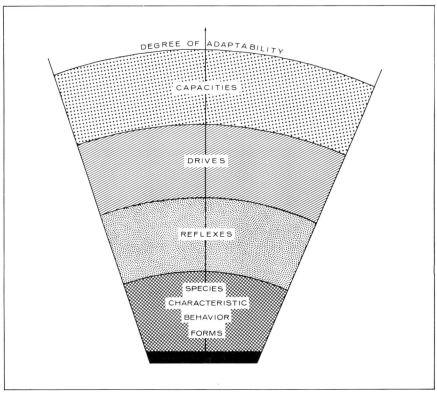

FIGURE 2–2 Relationship between increasing levels of behavior organization and the degree of adaptability in species-characteristic behavior forms, reflexes, drives and capacities.

SUMMARY

A human infant is born possessing at least four interrelated classes of biological features that serve as organic bridgeheads in socialization: (1) *species-characteristic behavior*, (2) *reflexes*, (3) *drives*, and (4) *capacities*. The preceding pages have briefly described these organic bridgeheads and have noted some of the conceptual problems involved in discussions of these phenomena. It should be remembered that each of these classes is interrelated with the others in very complex ways, most of which are not yet understood or even fully identified, and that each one is a human evolutionary product. The point of this chapter has been that culture, the natural ecology of humans, begins to affect the activities of the human organism through the specific biological features possessed by a human infant. It is important to recall the fact that each of these aspects of human biology is, in varying degrees, amenable to modification through cultural and social learning experiences.

REFERENCES CITED AND SUGGESTED READINGS

AINSWORTH, M.D.S. 1967. *Infancy in Uganda: Infant Care and the Growth of Love.* Baltimore, Md.: John Hopkins University Press.

ALEXANDER, R.D. 1979. *Darwinism and Human Affairs.* Seattle: University of Washington Press.

BARCHAS, P. 1976. "Physiological Sociology: Interface of Sociological and Biological Processes." In A. Inkeles, J. Coleman, & N. Smelser (eds.), *Annual Review of Sociology,* Vol. 2. Palo Alto, Calif.: Annual Reviews, Inc., pp. 299–334.

BATESON, G. 1969. Metalogue: "What is an Instinct?" In T.A. Sebeok (ed.), *Approaches to Animal Communication.* The Hague: Mouton, pp. 11–30.

———. 1972. "A Theory of Play and Fantasy." In G. Bateson, *Steps to an Ecology of Mind.* New York: Ballentine, pp. 177–193.

BATESON, P.P.G., & R.A. HINDE. 1976. *Growing Points in Ethology.* Cambridge, England: Cambridge University Press.

BETTELHEIM, B. 1967. *The Empty Fortress.* New York: Free Press.

BINDRA, D. 1959. *Motivation: A Systematic Reinterpretation.* New York: Ronald.

BLOOM, B. 1964. *Stability and Change in Human Characteristics.* New York: John Wiley.

BLURTON-JONES,N. 1972. *Ethological Studies of Child Behavior.* London: Cambridge University Press

BRAIN, J.L. 1977. "Sex, Incest and Death: Initiation Rites Reconsidered." *Current Anthropology,* 18, 191–208.

BRONFENBRENNER, U. 1977. "Toward an Experimental Ecology of Human Development." *American Psychologist,* 32, 513–531.

BRUNER, J., A. JOLLY & K. SYLVA. 1976. *Play—Its Role in Development and Evolution.* New York: Basic Books.

BULLOWA, M., J.H. FIDELHOLTZ, & A.R. KESSLER. 1975. "Infant Vocalization: Communication Before Speech." In T.R. Williams (ed.), *Socialization and Communication in Primary Groups.* The Hague: Mouton, pp. 253–281.

BURTON, R. 1973. "Folk Theory and the Incest Taboo." *Ethos,* 1, 504–516.

BUTLER, S.R., M.R. SUSKIND, & S.M. SCHANBERG. 1978. "Maternal Behavior as a Regulator of Polyamine Biosynthesis in Brain and Heart of the Developing Rat Pup." *Science,* 199, 445–447.

CATTELL, R., & R. DREGER (eds.). 1977. *Handbook of Modern Personality Theory.* New York: Halstead.

CAVALLI-SFORZA, L.L., & M.W. FELDMAN. 1981. *Cultural Transmission and Evolution: A Quantitative Approach.* Princeton, N.J.: Princeton University Press.

CHESS. S., A. THOMAS, & H. BIRCH. 1959. "Characteristics of the Individual Child's Behavioral Responses to Their Environment." *American Journal of Orthopsychiatry,* 29, 791–802.

COHEN, L.B., & P. SALAPATEK (eds.). 1975a. *Infant Perception: From Sensation to Cognition—Basic Visual Processes,* Vol. 1. New York: Academic Press.

———. 1975b. *Infant Perception: From Sensation to Cognition—Perception of Space, Speech and Sound,* Vol. 2. New York: Academic Press.

COHEN, Y.A. 1964. *The Transition from Childhood to Adolescence.* Chicago: Aldine.

CONDON, W.S., & L.W. SANDER. 1974. "Neonate Movement Synchronized with Adult Speech: Interactional Participation and Language Acquisition." *Science,* 813, 99–101.

DAWKINS, R. 1976. *The Selfish Gene.* New York: Oxford University Press.

DETHIER, V.G., & E. STELLAR. 1970. *Animal Behavior.* (3rd ed.) Englewood Cliffs, N.J.: Prentice-Hall.

DeVos, G. 1975.   "Affective Dissonance and Primary Socialization; Implications for a Theory of Incest Avoidance." *Ethos*, 3, 165–182.

Dobzhnsky, T. 1973.   *Genetic Diversity and Human Equality.* New York: Basic Books.

Dunham, W.H. 1979.   "Toward a Coevolutionary Theory of Human Biology and Culture." In N. Chagnon & W. Irons (eds.), *Evolutionary Biology and Human Social Behavior: An Anthropological Perspective.* Belmont, Calif.: Buxbury Press, pp. 35–59.

Eibl-Eibesfeldt, I. 1975a.   *Ethology: The Biology of Behavior.* New York: Holt, Rineart & Winston.

———. 1975b.   "Aggression in the !Ko-Bushman." In T.R. Williams (ed.), *Psychological Anthropology.* The Hague: Mouton, pp. 317–331.

Etkin, W. 1967.   *Social Behavior from Fish to Man.* Chicago: University of Chicago Press.

Fox, R. (ed.). 1975.   *Biosocial Anthropology.* London: Malaby Press.

Frank, L.K. 1938.   "Cultural Control and Physiological Autonomy." *American Journal of Orthopsychiatry*, 8, 622–626.

Freud, S. 1940.   *An Outline of Psychoanalysis.* London: Hogarth.

Frings, H., & M. Frings. 1977.   *Animal Communication.* Norman: University of Oklahoma Press.

Gellhorn, E. 1967.   *Principles of Autonomic-Somatic Integration.* Minneapolis: University of Minnesota Press.

Gottlieb, G. (ed.). 1976.   *Neural and Behavioral Specificity: Studies on the Development of Behavior and the Nervous System.* New York: Academic Press.

Gould, S.J. 1977.   *Ontogeny and Phylogeny.* Cambridge, Mass.: Harvard University Press.

Harlow, H.F., & M.K. Harlow. 1966.   "Learning to Love." *American Scientist*, 54, 244–272.

———. 1969.   "Effects of Various Mother-Infant Relationships on Rhesus Monkey Behaviors." in B.M. Foss (ed.), *Determinants of Infant Behavior*, Vol. 4. London: Methuen, pp. 15–36.

Harlow, H.F., & R.R. Zimermann. 1959.   "Affectional Responses in the Infant Monkey." *Science*, 130, 421–432.

Harrison, G., J. Weiner, J. Tanner, & N. Barnicot. 1977.   *Human Biology: An Introduction to Human Evolution, Variation, Growth and Ecology.* New York: Oxford University Press.

Hersher, L., J.B. Richmond, & A.U. Moore. 1963.   "Modifiability of the Critical Period for the Development of Maternal Behavior in Sheep and Goats." *Behavior*, 20, 311–320.

Hinde, R.A. 1955.   "The Modifiability of Instinctive Behaviour." *Advancement of Science*, 12, 19–24.

———. 1960.   "Energy Models of Motivation." *Models and Analogues in Biology*, No. XIV, 199–213.

———. 1974.   *Biological Bases of Human Social Behavior.* New York: McGraw-Hill.

Hinde, R.A., & N. Tinbergen. 1958. "The Comparative Study of Species-Specific Behavior." In A. Roe & G.G. Simpson (eds.), *Behavior and Evolution.* New Haven, Conn.: Yale University Press, pp. 251–268.

Howells, W. 1973.   *Evolution of the Genus Homo.* Reading, Mass.: Addison-Wesley.

Hunt, J. McV. 1960.   "Experience and the Development of Motivation: Some Reinterpretations." *Child Development*, 31, 489–504.

Kagan, J., & R.E. Klein. 1973.   "Cross-Cultural Perspectives on Early Development." *American Psychologist*, 28, 947–961.

KARELITZ, S., & V.R. FISCHELLI. 1962. "The Cry Thresholds of Normal Infants and Those with Brain Damage." *Journal of Pediatrics*, 61, 679–685.

KAUFMAN, I.C. 1975. "Learning What Comes Naturally: The Role of Life Experience in the Establishment of Species Typical Behavior." *Ethos*, 3, 129–142.

KENDON, A. 1972. "Some Relationships Between Body Motion and Speech, An Analysis of an Example." In A. Seigman & B. Pope (eds.), *Studies in Dyadic Communication*. New York: Pergamon Press, pp. 177–210.

KLOPFER, P.H., & J.R. HAILMAN. 1974. *An Introduction to Animal Behavior: Ethology's First Century*. 2nd ed. Englewood Cliffs, N.J.: Prentice-Hall.

KOLATA, G.B. 1978. "Primate Neurobiology: Neurosurgery with Fetuses." *Science*, 199, 960–961.

KROEBER, A.L. 1952. "The Superorganic." In A.L. Kroeber (ed.), *The Nature of Culture*. Chicago: University of Chicago Press, pp. 22–51.

KROGMAN, W.M. 1972. *Child Growth*. Ann Arbor: University of Michigan Press.

LABARRE, W. 1954. *The Human Animal*. Chicago: University of Chicago Press.

LEVI-STRAUSS, C. 1958. *Anthropologie Structurale*. Paris: Libraire Plon. (*Structural Anthropology*. New York: Basic Books, Vol. 1, 1963; Vol. 2, 1976.)

———. 1962. *La Pensee Sauvage. (The Savage Mind.)* Paris: Librairie Plon. Chicago: University of Chicago Press, 1966.

LIEBERMAN, J.N. 1977. *Playfulness: Its Relationship to Imagination and Creativity*. New York: Academic Press.

LIEBERMAN, P. 1967. *Intonation, Perception and Language*. Cambridge, Mass.: M.I.T. Press.

———. 1975. *On the Origins of Languages: An Introduction to the Evolution of Human Language*. New York: Macmillan.

LIEBERMAN, P., E.S. CRELIN, & D. KLATT. 1972. "Phonetic Ability and Related Anatomy of the Newborn and Adult Human, Neanderthal Man and the Chimpanzee." *American Anthropologist*, 72, 287–307.

LIND, J. (ed.). 1965. *Newborn Infant Cry*. Uppsala, Sweden: Almquist & Wiskells.

LINDESMITH, A.R., & A.L. STRAUSS. 1950. "A Critique of Culture—Personality Writings." *American Sociological Review*, 15, 587–600.

LORENZ, K. 1965. *Evolution and the Modification of Behavior*. Chicago: University of Chicago Press.

MCBRIDE, G. 1968. "On the Evolution of Language." *Social Science Information*, 7, 81–85.

———. 1975. "Interactions and the Control of Behavior." In T.R. Williams (ed.), *Socializaiton and Communication in Primary Groups*. The Hague: Mouton, pp. 329–337.

MCEWEN, B. 1976. "Interactions Between Hormones and Nerve Tissue." *Scientific American*, 235, 48–58.

MEAD, M. 1942. "Anthropological Data on the Problem of Instinct." *Psychosomatic Medicine*, Vol. 4. Baltimore, Md.: Williams & Wilkins, pp. 396–397.

———. 1976. "Towards a Human Science." *Science*, 191, 903–909.

MEAD, M., & F.C. MACGREGOR. 1951. *Growth and Culture*. New York: Putnam's.

MENZEL, E.W., Jr. (ed.). 1972. *Precultural Primate Behavior*. Basel: S. Karger.

OMARK, R., M. OMARK, & M. EDELMAN. 1975. "Formation of Dominance Hierarchies in Young Children." In T.R. Williams (ed.), *Psychological Anthropology*. The Hague: Mouton, pp. 289–315.

ORLANSKY, H. 1949. "Infant Care and Personality." *Psychological Bulletin*, 46, 1–48.

PARETO, V. 1935. *General Treatise on Sociology (The Mind and Society)*. New York: Harcourt Brace Jovanovich.

RAPAPORT, D. 1958. "The Theory of Ego Automony: A Generalization." *Bulletin of the Menninger Clinic*, 22, 13–35.

RAYNER, C. (ed.). 1976. *The Rand McNally Atlas of the Body and Mind*. Skokie, Ill. Rand McNally.

ROBERTS, J., & B. SUTTON-SMITH. 1962. "Child Training and Game Involvement." *Ethnology*, 1, 166–185.

———. 1966. "Cross-Cultural Correlates of Games of Chance." *Behavior Science Notes*, 3, 131–144.

RÓHEIM, G. 1943. *The Origin and Function of Culture*. Garden City, N.Y.: Doubleday, Anchor Books (republished in 1973).

SAHLINS, M. 1976. *The Use and Abuse of Biology: An Anthropological Critique of Sociobiology*. Ann Arbor: University of Michigan Press.

SARASON, S.B., & T. GLADWIN. 1958. "Psychological and Cultural Problems in Mental Subnormality: A Review of Research." *Genetic Psychology Monographs*, 57, 3–290.

SCHILLER, C. (ed.). 1957. *Instinctive Behavior*. New York: International Universities Press.

SCHWARTZMAN, H.B. 1976. "The Anthropological Study of Play." In B. Siegel, A.R. Beals, & S.T. Tyler (eds.), *Annual Review of Anthropology*, Vol. 5, 289–328. Palo Alto, Calif.: Annual Reviews, Inc.

SCOTT, J.P. 1972. *Animal Behavior*. Chicago: University of Chicago Press (2nd rev. ed.).

SHWEDER, R.A. 1979. "Rethinking Culture and Personality Theory, Parts I, II." *Ethos*, 7, 255–278.

SPITZ, R. 1946. "Anaclitic Depression." *Psychoanalytic Study of the Child*, 2, 313–342.

STEVENSON, H.W., E.H. HESS, & H.L. RHEINGOLD. 1967. *Early Behavior: Comparative and Developmental Approaches*. New York: John Wiley.

SUTTON-SMITH, B., & J. ROBERTS. 1970. "The Cross-Cultural and Psychological Study of Games." In Gunther Luschen (ed.), *The Cross-Cultural Analysis of Games*. Champaign, Ill.: Stipes, pp. 100–108.

THORPE, W.H. 1956. *Learning and Instinct in Animals*. Cambridge, Mass.: Harvard University Press.

TIGER, L., & R. FOX. 1971. *The Imperial Animal*. New York: Dell Pub. Co., Inc.

TINBERGEN, N. 1951. *The Study of Instinct*. Oxford: Oxford University Press.

VON CRANACH, M., & I. VINE (eds.). 1973. *Social Communication and Movement: Studies of Interaction and Expression in Man and Chimpanzee*. New York: Academic Press.

VONFRISCH, K. 1953. *The Dancing Bees*. London: Methuen.

WASHBURN, S., & R. MOORE. 1974. *Ape into Man: A Study of Human Evolution*. Boston: Little, Brown.

WASHBURN, S.L., & H. YAHRAES. 1969. "The Origins of Aggressive Behavior." In *Mental Health Program Reports*, No. 3. Washington, D.C.: National Institute of Mental Health.

WEISNER, T., & R. GALLIMORE. 1977. "My Brother's Keeper: Child and Sibling Caretaking." *Current Anthropology*, 18, 169–190.

WHITING, B., & J.W.M. WHITING. 1975. *Children of Six Cultures*. Cambridge, Mass.: Harvard University Press.

WILSON, E.O. 1978. *On Human Nature*. Cambridge, Mass.: Harvard University Press.

WOHLWILL, J.F. 1973. *The Study of Behavioral Development*. New York: Academic Press.

CHAPTER THREE
MODELS OF LEARNING
AND SOCIALIZATION

This chapter provides a brief review of two major theoretical models of learning widely used in socialization studies: (1) *Thorndike-Hull behaviorism* and (2) *Freudian personal character processes*.[1] These often-used models of learning are then contrasted with case study data of the process of enculturation among the Papago, a native North American society. The chapter concludes with some brief comments concerning possible use of some other and more recent models of learning in the study of cultural transmission and current transcultural studies of the contexts of learning.

THORNDIKE-HULL BEHAVIORISM

The most elaborate and precisely formalized model of learning used in the study of cultural transmission is found in the efforts of Hull to integrate the "conditioned response" learning formulations of Pavlov with the concept of "learning through reinforcement" from the studies of

[1]Learning has been defined (Hilgard, 1956, 3) as the process by which an activity originates or is changed through reacting to an encountered situation, provided that the characteristics of the change in activity cannot be explained on the basis of inherited response tendencies, maturation, or temporary states (fatigue, drugs) of the organism.

Thorndike. This model of learning consists of a set of generalizations derived largely from observation of behavior of nonhuman organisms (pigeons, rats, cats, monkeys) subjected to experimental conditions.[2] This model is usually termed *behavioristic*, since it is based on data obtained from measurements of the visible behavior of organisms and is not generally concerned with certain sense events, such as thinking, feeling, and desiring, occurring within an organism.

Behaviorists postulate that all action by any organism, including humans, is an effort to satisfy physiological needs. A corollary of this postulate proposes that physiological needs are the source of all other needs of an organism, including any social or cultural needs. In whatever form it is used, behaviorism holds the concept of learning to be of central importance in understanding the activity of an organism. Learning is conceived by behaviorists as a process in which drives are met, or supplemented, by adaptive action, which enables an organism to act relevantly to its physiological requirements.[3]

Thorndike and Learning Concepts

Fundamental for an understanding of the behavioristic learning model are two concepts first formulated prior to World War I from experimental studies by E. L. Thorndike and later revised and elaborated by Clark Hull. These are the concepts of (1) *trial and error* and (2) *reward and punishment*. Thorndike noted in his observations of the behavior of cats, chickens, and monkeys that, in the course of numerous encounters with its environment, an organism tends to show increasing modification of behavior and an increase in skill of movement as a consequence of an apparent elimination of "wrong moves" and a consolidation of "correct moves." Thorndike concluded from his experimental studies that the general trend of behavior in all animals is to more efficient satisfaction of innate needs. Later experimental evidence indicated that rewards (such as food or water) or punishments (such as electric shock or other noxious stimulation) administered to an organism had a specific effect on behavior

---

[2]There are a number of learning theories, generally classed as: (1) *stimulus-response reinforcement* theories, as in the work of Pavlov (1927, 1928), Thorndike (1911, 1932, 1933, 1935), or Hull (1942, 1943, 1950, 1951, 1952); (2) *stimulus-response contiguity* theories, as set forth by Guthrie (1935, 1952); (3) *dual theories of learning*, as represented by the works of Skinner (1938, 1953) and Mowrer (1950); (4) *cognitive, "sign,"* or *holistic* learning theory, as represented in the works of Tolman (1932, 1951), Stern (1938), Allport (1937), Angyal (1941), and Leeper (1951); (5) *gestalt* theory, as in the works of Wertheimer (1923, 1925), Koffka (1924), and Kohler (1925); (6) *field learning* theory, as found in the works of Lewin (1935, 1936); and (7) *functional learning* theory, as represented in the works of Woodworth (1918, 1929). The discussion in this chapter is concerned with details of the *stimulus-response reinforcement* model of learning since it has greatly influenced research in studies of socialization.

[3]Asch (1952, 12–13) has given a concise review of behavioristic premises.

directly preceding the administration of rewards or punishments. On the basis of that evidence Thorndike formulated the *principle of reinforcement*, or as it is currently designated, the *law of effect*. This principle asserts that the response of an organism to a stimulus is automatically strengthened if it is followed by a reward. Conversely, the response of an organism to a stimulus is automatically extinguished if followed by punishment. To Thorndike the administration of rewards and punishments to an organism, as it went about seeking to reduce its physiological needs, was a satisfactory means of explaining the behavior of all organisms, including humans.

Hull and Learning Concepts

Thorndike's concepts of learning were subjected to a number of revisions and extensions from 1925 to 1945. The most widely used revision is Hull's formulation of the postulates of stimulus-response reinforcement learning. Hull's theory of learning evolved from his efforts to synthesize Thorndike's conception of the law of effect and Pavlov's postulates of conditioned learning. Pavlov and Thorndike both had formulated their initial conceptions of learning by the early 1900s. Although these theories were similar in several ways, they differed profoundly in one respect. Pavlov's "conditioned reflexes" were preparatory movements (salivation) by an organism directed at particular goals (eating). Such movements were not believed by Pavlov to be *instrumental* in attaining a goal. In contrast, Thorndike's law of effect attempted to explain goal-directed or *instrumental* behavior. Thorndike's experimental subjects had to undertake movements to escape from confinement in order to attain food. Thorndike assumed that rewarded movements (escape for attainment of food) became a lasting part of the sensorimotor systems of an animal because of physiological satisfactions achieved as a consequence of movements to a goal.

Hull formulated a theory of learning that combined Thorndike's principle of instrumental learning with Pavlov's neurophysiologically based concept of conditioned learning. To accomplish this, Hull assumed that in all organisms, including humans, there exists an innate sensorimotor network. This network is designed so that any stimulus (such as food) that would begin agitation in the sense organs would be transmitted automatically as an electrical-chemical impulse via the nervous system to the muscles, thus bringing about motor activity leading to direct movement of an animal toward the source of stimulus. When a second stimulus occurred with the first—for example, a ringing bell and food—the second stimulus could, if presented often enough, set off motor patterns derived from lasting and remaining traces of the first stimulus, although the first stimulus was absent. Hull further assumed that, once an organism regularly responded to the second stimulus, the reintroduction of the first stimulus could be said to act as a reinforcement of the conditioned (or second) stimulus. Thus Hull's model of learning rests on conditions established by research of Thorndike and Pavlov attempting to explain the manner by which organisms acquired habitual ways of behavior.

To provide a complete explanation of instrumental uses of acquired habits in the behavior of organisms, however, Hull turned to the concept of *need*, which he later elaborated to the more inclusive concept of *drive*. Hull identified conditions of need as identical with the basic somatic processes of hunger, thirst, sleep, and so on. He noted that unsatisfied needs in an organism set up internal stimulations that had to be removed through motor activity. Thus a state of need was viewed by Hull as a condition of somatic tension, or disequilibrium, that ultimately had to be reduced through motor activity for survival of the organism. In his experimental research Hull attempted to demonstrate that the specific effect of internal tension caused by somatic need was to motivate, or "drive," the organism to random trial-and-error efforts. When the organism behaved in such a way as to reduce or eliminate a need driving it to action, the relationship between the stimulus situation (somatic needs) and the response actions (trial-and-error behavior) was supposed by Hull to be automatically strengthened and subsequently retained as a basic pattern of behavior. Hull further held that in later situations of a similar nature an organism would respond to its somatic needs in a form consistent with initial reductions of the drive to behavior, particularly if on subsequent occasions the need was reduced in a more useful manner. Hull believed that through the duplication of sequences of primary reinforcement an organism would learn to reduce its drives by behaving in habitual ways.

Thus, according to Hull, learning is the association and reinforcement of any number of stimulus-response connections stemming from the reduction of basic body needs. Hull's revision of Thorndike's ideas, through the joining of Pavlov's concept of the conditioned reflex with the construct of drive reduction, led to a model of learning based on the assumption that the sources of energy for learning in all organisms are found in and derived from somatic or body needs. Under the laws of this model, primary body tensions are designated as having the capacity to impel an organism to behavior. All modification of behavior, or learning, is derived from and is a function of innate needs.

The Concept of Secondary Drives

In the course of formulating a stimulus-response reinforcement learning model, Hull gave attention to the question of *secondary drives*—that is, drives that develop as a consequence of positive reinforcement of stimuli arising from the environment of the organism. In earlier formulations of his postulates of learning, Hull utilized the concept of *drive* to refer to either external or internal sources of stimulation of basic body processes.

In later statements of theory Hull offered more precise comments concerning drives derived from stimuli external to the organism. At the same time he considered the possibilities of reinforcement for such "secondary" drives. The revised concept of secondary drives may be illustrated by the example of "fear" as a secondary drive. The primary somatic drive is an avoidance response to pain, which produces the basic drive stimulus. Neutral stimuli associated with the drive to avoid pain give rise to fear responses, similar in form to the responses of the organism to pain. The consequences of the associated, or learned, responses subsequently produce a drive stimulus that serves as a *secondary drive*. Thus an otherwise neutral stimulus may become a secondary drive for an organism, if such stimuli are associated with a lessening of a primary drive response.

The Concept of Acquired Drives

The general postulates of the Thorndike-Hull learning model have been used as a basis for several theoretical efforts to systematically analyze human social and cultural behavior. Perhaps the most influential generalization of the Thorndike-Hull learning model to studies of human behavior is found in the work of Miller and Dollard (1941). Proceeding generally from Hull's synthesis of the learning formulations of Thorndike and Pavlov and specifically from Hull's concept of secondary drives, Miller and Dollard advanced the concept of *acquired drives* as an explanation for human motivations to instrumental behavior that develop as a direct consequence of positive reinforcements of stimuli derived from their social and cultural environments.

In seeking to apply Hull's concept of secondary drive to human behavior, Miller and Dollard began by modifying his earlier drive-reduction assumption to a form that has been termed *drive-stimulus reduction learning*. According to this theory, drives arising as a consequence of behavior through which an organism seeks to reduce the effects of stimulation are held to be identical to basic, or innate, drives that lead to attempts to escape injurious stimuli. Thus the theoretical basis for learning was expanded by Miller and Dollard to incorporate all sources of stimulation from human social and cultural environments. Miller and Dollard proceeded to propose a hierarchy of human drives, commencing with Hull's primary, or innate, drives, then proceeding to a series of "learnable drives" such as fear, gregariousness, social conformity, prestige seeking, desire for money, and imitativeness, and then subsequently to higher mental processes. Choosing human imitation for their detailed study of acquired drives, Miller and Dollard note that imitative behavior is essential to survival of a human society through production of group action and in maintaining social conformity and discipline.

Influence of Thorndike-Hull Learning Concepts

The principles of learning that form the Thorndike-Hull behaviorism model and the Miller-Dollard extension of this theory have now been widely diffused to all areas of scholarship concerned with studies of human behavior. The impact of these conceptions of learning on the social sciences has been profound. Between 1940 and 1960 the basic formulations of the Thorndike-Hull model of learning and its extensions in the works of Miller and Dollard were widely accepted by many anthropologists and sociologists because these ideas offered support for studies of human culture and society and provided a basis for denial of the doctrine of instinct.

FREUDIAN PERSONAL CHARACTER PROCESSES

A number of attempts have been made to extract a theory of learning from the writings of Sigmund Freud.[4] This has not been an easy task, for the human problems Freud dealt with were not those that most concerned behavioristic learning theorists. However the consensus of scholars attempting to find a general learning theory in Freud's work appears to be that, while the propositions of classic psychoanalysis are complex and so diffusely stated that it is difficult to subject them to empirical test, learning concepts and a form of learning theory exist in the totality of Freud's works. Perhaps the most formidable difficulty in dealing with Freudian learning concepts lies in the changes by Freud in his statements of theory over half a century.

Despite these problems in analysis of Freudian learning theory, there are several major parallels between Freudian theory and learning formulations by behavioristic theorists. There are three psychoanalytic principles similar to Thorndike-Hull behavioristic learning concepts: (1) *the pleasure principle*, (2) *the reality principle*, and (3) *the principle of repetition-compulsion*.

Freud's statements concerning humans' search for pleasurable experiences and avoidance of painful stimuli correspond to the Thorndike-Hull formulations of the law of effect. The common ground between these ideas is the assumption of genetically transmitted human need states leading

---

[4]For detailed discussion of Freud's views and their uses in studies of human behavior, see Hall (1954), Hall and Lindzey (1957), and Munroe (1955). No attempt is made here to deal with the writings of those scholars called by Hall and Lindzey (1957, 143) "major revisionists" of psychoanalytic theory. Freud's statements concerning learning are far more elaborate than those offered by others seeking to modify his ideas.

to somatic disequilibrium, consequently requiring the lowering of such tensions for the survival of the organism.[5]

As formulated by Freud, the *reality principle* holds that, rather than seeking immediate pleasure, humans will try to identify and eliminate through a series of random moves those stimuli that potentially bring pain. This concept is similar to the trial-and-error learning formulations of the Thorndike-Hull behavioristic learning theory. The Freudian conception of *repetition-compulsion* also corresponds to Thorndike-Hull behavioristic learning formulations concerning acts that do not "extinguish" under repeated negative reinforcement, that is, acts once learned that are usually resistant to extinction by adverse stimuli.

In addition to these parallels, other topics in Freud's writings concerning learning have been explored by learning theorists. These include Freud's concerns with the origin, development, and operation of individual personality. In specific Freudian studies of anxiety, aggression, repression, forgetting, and recall, the interests of learning theorists centered on those aspects of personality clearly within behavioristic conceptions of innate need or drive states.

Learning theorists have generally ignored, however, those aspects of Freud's work pertaining to personality development and functioning that cannot be directly related to behavioristic assumptions or experimentally based conceptions of the nature and operation of basic drives. For the most part Thorndike-Hull behavioristic learning theory is concerned primarily with present behavior forms whose nature could be circumscribed precisely in a limited time under experimental conditions. The present-time orientation of Thorndike-Hull behavioristic learning research resulted in inattention by learning theorists to broad areas of Freudian ideas. Freud's writings provide substantial evidence of his concern with historical continuities in individual personality and contain two learning concepts that appear central to his general theory of human behavior. These concepts are *identification* and *introjection*.

In an early work Freud (1910) refers to his theory of personality as a dynamic conception which reduces mental life to the interplay of reciprocally urging and checking forces. Terming these forces *cathexes,* Freud used this concept in subsequent writings as denoting the investment of a charge of psychic energy in objects external to the organism (*object cathexes*) or in the self (*ego cathexes*). Freud held that the human organism possessed at birth a primitive psychological structure operated by a limited amount of psychic energy generated from inherited body needs and seen in individual behavior as instincts seeking gratification.

---

[5]For Freud, instincts seeking gratifications lead to states of body tension that must be lowered. In the Thorndike-Hull model, drives arising from innate states lead to consummatory responses by the organism.

Freud supposed that for an infant all psychic energy is dissipated in random, gross motor activity. Later as the human individual matured, social and cultural environmental circumstances caused the primitive psychological structure to undergo a series of specific modifications through transformation of the basic psychic energy into purely psychological processes such as perception, memory, ideas, and feeling. Thus as the human organism, with specific inherited body need states, comes into more direct and continuous contact with objects and events in its surroundings and begins to be aware of itself it begins to transform body need energy into psychological energy and eventually becomes able to deal with objects or events by *cathecting*—that is, perceiving and retaining their qualities in the form of memories, ideas, and feelings. As the human individual becomes more mature and experiences added contacts with various parts of its environment, greater amounts of body energy flow into and make up complex and intimately interrelated *perceptual, mnemonic,* and *ideation* systems, which form the basic personality structure.

Cathexes, Identification, and Incorporation

Freud's earliest and best-known statements concerning the origin, development, and functioning of personality noted that permanent traits of character were perpetuations of inherited basic body needs. Later as he modified his theory of personality, Freud set forth the notion that individual personal character is developed equally from inherited body needs and cathexes as the mechanisms through which specific social and cultural forms and their symbols are *incorporated* into the organism. He believed that through incorporation specific *identifications* are made with parental and other authority figures and their symbols.

Freud conceived *identification* as the general transformation of a cathexis for the perception (or memory) of an object or event into a cathexis for a perception of the self. *Incorporation* similarly represents a general change in cathexis from a psychological content with an outer referent to a psychological content with a self, or inner, referent. Thus through cathexes the world of the objective and external becomes transformed into properties of the individual self.

Id, Ego, and Superego

Freud published several accounts of the structuring of individual personal character through the transformation of body need energy into psychological processes and the operation of these processes through the mechanisms of identification and incorporation. His final formulations of personality theory identified the primary divisions, or portions, of personal character by the designations of *id, ego,* and *superego.* For Freud the mechanisms of identification and incorporation were of particular importance in the inception, development, and operation of the superego. Freud believed the superego was the last and most vital of the provinces of personality to be formed. Although identification and incorporation were also said to be operative in the origin of the id and ego, Freud believed these processes to be the basic means by which the superego is developed and maintained through the life span of an individual.

Freud postulated that the superego originates in early childhood through substitution of identifications with parents for earlier, conflicting feelings of hate and love created by parental denials of satisfaction of the child's basic body needs. Thus the superego is formed from both early and subsequent cathexes of parents and parental behavior. Such cathexes, once incorporated into the existing character structure and forming the superego, become the prototypes for the child's subsequent social relationships with other persons, especially those in positions of authority and those representing the moral and ethical codes of a society. Freud noted that the formation and operation of the superego by means of cathexes and their transformations particularly are related to the special qualities of parents and their surrogates as punishing and rewarding agents. These *introjected* parental qualities serve, said Freud, as the basis for the two major divisions of the functioning superego, the conscience and the ego-ideal. Punishing qualities of parents and their surrogates become cathected into that aspect of superego Freud terms the *conscience*, while rewarding qualities are cathected into that aspect of the superego called the *ego-ideal*. Freud held the ego-ideal to be the personality mechanism that sets standards of personal ethical conduct, as these standards were directly incorporated from the parents and their surrogates. Conscience was viewed by Freud as a personality mechanism acting in the role of a censor or judge, setting specific punishments for the self for violation of ego-ideal standards.

Freud felt that most rewarding and punishing identifications that were incorporated into the self, in the formation and subsequent operation of the superego, were primarily in the form of direct parental commands, threats, accusations, or specific exhortations and encouragements. He noted, however, that the severity, or strength, of superego is determined not by the severity of parental treatment of the child but by the strength of the cathexes for parents and parent-surrogates that are subsequently transformed into cathexes for the child's self. Thus the innate reservoir of body energy for cathectic processes is seen by Freud as being of more fundamental importance than is actual parental behavior in the socialization process. Freud felt that parents generally follow their own superego dictates in rearing children. Thus the child's superego is not, according to Freud's ideas, a direct consequence of parental behavior but rather is a precipitate, first of the child's cathectic energies, and then of the parental superego structure. According to Freud the superego of each member of a human generation represents the accumulated influences of the social and cultural behavior of past generations on the present social behavior of the individual as these influences are mediated by the biologically inherited energies available for the processes of cathecting social and cultural objects or events.

In summary, Freud held that a child learns the social and cultural traditions of his or her group by cathectic processes of identification with parents and their surrogates and the incorporation of such identifications into the character structure and particularly the superego. As agents of a social and cultural tradition, parents and their surrogates use specific rewards and punishments to lead children to accept the demands of a culture. As a consequence of such rewards and punishments and through the processes of identification and incorporation, the superego portion of character takes on the role of external authority, forcing conformity of the self to group traditions.

Influence of Freudian Learning Concepts

Freudian concepts of character formation and operation have had a great influence on research in the social sciences. For instance, Kluckhohn (1944; 590) in reviewing that influence has noted that American anthropology has seemed to find only in Freud's ideas the basis for a workable cultural psychology. Hallowell disagreed with Kluckhohn's opinions of the fundamental importance of Freud's propositions in anthropological research, particularly as it has been concerned with learning. In reviewing the uses of learning models and concepts used in anthropologoy, Hallowell (1954; 214–215) concluded that Thorndike-Hull behavioristic theory has furnished the major model for research. Recent publications and particularly the literature of socialization and enculturation studies, however, tend to show that the Freudian model of learning continues to be used as widely as the Thorndike-Hull behavioristic model of learning.

MODELS OF LEARNING AND UNDERSTANDING PAPAGO ENCULTURATION

Attempts to employ either the Thorndike-Hull or Freudian learning models have been largely unsuccessful in fully and adequately describing the ways children are encultured in different societies. One reason for this is that children seem to "learn" culture in a variety of ways not accounted for in either the Thorndike-Hull behavioristic or Freudian personal character models of learning. The following brief case study of the main features of enculturation among the Papago, a native North American society, is intended to emphasize the ways human symbolic and reflective capacities enter into and are an integral part of the socialization process. Referring to the discussion of learning concepts will assist you as you read.

THE PAPAGO WAY OF LIFE

The Papago now number about 16,000 persons. About 10,500 Papago live on three federal reservations in the vicinity of Tucson, Arizona. Most Papago occupy a 2.75-million-acre reservation located in traditional Papago lands west of Tucson. The area is in a physiographic zone known as the Sonoran Desert, which is characterized by less than five inches annual rainfall and daily temperatures that for seven months of the year may rise over 100°F.

Most Papago living on reservations work in cattle ranching and farming. Some 3,000 Arizona Papago work away from the reservations as laborers and technicians for large agricultural mining or industrial firms in the Phoenix and Tucson areas. Before the Europeans arrived, Papago lived by hunting desert animals, gathering desert plants, and growing agricultural products such as beans and corn on farms irrigated by floodwaters coursing through the desert after heavy seasonal rains.

The Papago have a continuous cultural heritage which reaches back at least 10,000 years. During that time the Papago, who are very adaptable in unusual situations, have met the challenges of a hostile environment and contacts with alien cultures. Although they are a hospitable people, they tend to avoid contacts with strangers. This tendency, combined with ob-

Papago family (circa 1893). (Courtesy American Museum of Natural History.)

stacles presented by the harsh desert environment, was the reason that, prior to 1880, the Papago had only sporadic contacts with the Europeans who settled in their land. In fact, the Papago remained generally unaffected by European culture for nearly 200 years after the first Spanish missions were built to the south of their desert homeland.

Focal Values in Papago Enculturation

Five related *focal values* appear to impart characteristic uniqueness to Papago enculturation:[6] (1) *children who cannot talk cannot understand;* (2) *children who cannot understand cannot be expected to exhibit appropriate social behavior;* (3) *children will learn appropriate social behavior when ready and capable of doing so;* (4) *adult social behavior is the sole standard of conduct;* and (5) *children are desirable because they increase the status of parents as adults.* These five focal values are seen regularly in Papago life and are significant in understanding Papago enculturation because of their direct relationship to choices of actual or potential action on the part of adults in elicitation of desired social behavior in the maturing child.

Obtaining Focal Values

These five focal values have been abstracted from two reciprocally related sets of behavioral data. The first data set consists of statements by Papago adults concerning the worthwhileness of personal conduct and of cultural goals. Such statements of value, secured by means of interviews and use of various tests, reveal many desirable and potential cultural goals, principles of Papago conceptualization, and ideal order among possible behavior forms. However the statements do not put Papago informants to

Papago tribal council chairman Enos Francisco (left) and son. (T. R. Williams, 1953.)

[6]DuBois (1955) uses the concept of *focal value* as a means of denoting a *second-level abstraction* of value from observed social behavior. At the *first,* or *specific value,* level of abstraction are found statements or judgments of worthwhileness of behavior. *Second-level* or *focal value,* abstractions are statements synthesizing a series of first-level values. In turn, *third-level,* or *basic postulate,* statements reflect abstractions from a series of focal value statements organized around third-level judgments of worthwhileness of behavior.

the test of actual behavior, where they become responsible for making specific choices between *ideal* and *actual* cultural values.

The second set of data from which these five Papago focal values have been abstracted may be termed *behavior kinds*—that is, records of well-identified Papago adults behaving repeatedly in ways that can be counted and classified. Behavior kind data are comprised of an observer's descriptive accounts of people interacting socially in regular ways and of the objects they make and use in shaping their environment. Such behavioral kind data are assumed to reflect culturally standardized preferences, or judgments, concerning worthwhileness of particular behavior forms, as mediated through individual perceptions of social goals, ends, and so on. The five focal values listed here have been abstracted through the process of systematically relating the first set of data or ideas expressed by Papago adults about worthwhileness of behavior to the second set of data, or behavior kinds.

An added dimension of Papago value, which is not usually immediately available, can be gained in following disparities noted to exist between the first and second sets of data. Thus following observations of behavior, some Papago statements of worthwhileness were found to be justifications of the informant's actual course of actions, which ran counter to prevailing judgments of worthwhileness made by most members of Papago society. This dimension of value provides data concerning behavior kinds not judged appropriate by the community, yet of sufficient merit to be known, used, and transmitted by some adults seeking publicly to gain approval for their behavior or to discredit the conduct of others when their own social actions appear to be beyond limits of worthwhile Papago conduct.

The focal values presented here are useful in two ways in considering the question of how Papago children learn desired forms of behavior. First, the focal values comprise the essence of a Papago learning theory, with special reference to Papago ideas concerning the ways that desired forms of behavior are best transmitted to children. Second, study of Papago focal values allows concepts derived from the Thorndike-Hull behavioristic and Freudian models of learning, such as *reward* and *punishment*, to be used in an examination of both data of Papago enculturation and the formal learning concepts and models.

Papago Enculturation

The first two focal values appear to be guides in most enculturation activities by Papago adults from a child's birth through the fifth to seventh year. The third focal value is applied by adults generally in enculturation activities between the fifth to seventh through the twelfth to fourteenth year. After the fourteenth year a Papago is expected to conform to adult standards of social behavior.

Children are desired and welcomed in Papago society as important additions to the maintenance and functioning of the culture. However this welcome seems to be without consideration by adults of any intrinsic worth of a child as a person. No general merit appears to be attached to childhood behavior independent of its specific approximation to adult behavior. The pronounced worth given to Papago adult behavior appears to imbue all Papago judgments concerning learning by children with a tone that has been mistaken by observers for "permissiveness." On initial observation Papago adults appear to have exaggerated respect for their children. It is misleading, however, to describe Papago enculturation behavior as permissive, since such a classification is based on a category of experience peculiar to European and American life. The idea of permissiveness assumes the intrinsic merit of a child as a basis for parental indulgence of behavior. Imposition on Papago behavior of this European and American cultural *theme* (see Chapter 8), with its Western assumption concerning the basic nature of humans, can lead to misinterpretation of the nature of Papago enculturation. Papago adults view enculturation with reference to five focal values whose sum is to give to parents and other adults a specific concern that a child eventually becomes an adult whose behavior conforms to adult standards. The specific course of a child's progress to adulthood generally is of little significance to most Papago adults, since they assume that children will in time behave as adults do.

In the initial period of a child's life, from birth through five to seven years, adults give little specific attention to the beginnings of child behavior that approximate adult behavior. Younger children are simply not expected to behave in ways that are adult. Thus Papago adults make no public observance of events in the initial period of a child's life. There are no ceremonies for physical maturation, such as first steps, the initial haircut, loss of teeth, and so on. Similarly little concern is exhibited by adults at the presence or absence of any type of first actions or social achievements by

Papago boys, second grade, Sells, Arizona School. (T.R. Williams, 1953).

a child. This lack of concern is reflected also in the general absence of specific age-grading terms for children in the first five to seven years of life or in special ritual actions by Papago adults that specifically align children with their kin and the supernatural. Papago believe that a ceremony of formal social acceptance is unnecessary, since a child unable to talk and understand does not comprehend the complex reciprocal rights and duties of Papago kinship. Alignment of a child with the supernatural is viewed by the Papago as unnecessary; children are said to derive their protection from supernatural forces directly from their relationships with parents and ritual specialists and only incidentally from the fact of participation in any special rituals. Children are present at most adult gatherings, including those of considerable religious or political significance, but unless child is in grave danger of physical harm, few efforts are made by adults to prevent behavior by children that disrupts or interferes with adult proceedings.

The first two focal values also operate directly in enculturation of particular physiological systems (hunger, thirst, sexual, bowel, bladder) in the first five to seven years of a child's life. However Papago children are cared for with little general reference to adult management of these physiological systems. Infants and young children usually are fed on demand. Unless a mother is pregnant, weaning is of incidental concern. No adult foods or ways of eating are forbidden to children. Bowel and bladder processes tend to be treated with few general adult concerns for signs of physiological autonomy. Little significance is attached to matters of personal cleanliness or grooming by children. Sexual behavior in young children is generally ignored. No attempts are made to lead young children to be independent of adults or peers in any behavior.

This general Papago enculturation process continues in the period from the fifth to seventh through the twelfth to fourteenth years. However among themselves, adults begin in this time to use the third focal value in

Papago girls, second grade, Sells, Arizona School. (T.R. Williams, 1953.)

commenting on behavior by a child not approximating adult standards. Few comments are made directly to children regarding failure or success in uses of adult behavior forms. By their eighth to ninth year, most Papago children begin to exhibit knowledge and some use of acceptable adult Papago behavior. In this age period children assume some regular household duties. Although sporadic efforts toward such an assumption are made by children as young as three or four years old, by the tenth year both boys and girls are making some contributions toward family economic activities. Such duties are not usually assigned; most children take up chores without seeking adult direction. No ritual observances are offered by adults in recognition of an older child's assumption of some adult tasks or to signal use of adult behavior forms in systems of control and appropriate releases of sex, aggression, dependence, cleanliness, modesty, and so on.

The age period of 14 to 16 years and on through the end of the teens is marked by a gradual display of increasingly more responsible adult behavior. Papago adults say, "When a child does an adult's work, he is an adult." Public recognition of increasing responsibility by children is minimal, however, with open note of attempts at more complex adult tasks being avoided by adults. A primary adult privilege—social seniority—is accorded to older children as they assume a proportionately larger share of responsible adult tasks and successfully approximate adult behavior standards in their activities. The privileges of seniority enable an older child, when addressed by adults, to speak as an adult on matters judged to be of concern to adults. While seniority is related directly to age in later life and particularly after the birth of a first child to a young married couple, among adolescents and young adults it is more related to a greater assumption of adult responsibility and exhibition of expected forms of behavior.

Learning in Papago Enculturation

In application of the Thorndike-Hull and Freudian models to human learning, the concept of reward has come to denote two broad categories of behavior by adults with reference to children: (1) *material rewards* and (2) *verbal rewards.* Material reward has been given the meaning of a tangible remuneration as an incentive for repetition of approved forms of behavior by a child. Verbal reward generally denotes use of speech forms by adults to elicit desired behavior or to approve and encourage repetition of approved behavior. Following the concepts of the Thorndike-Hull model, Miller and Dollard (1941) noted that sometimes there is an *intrinsic reward* factor for a child in particular social situations. Unlimited freedom of social action at particular times may thus be viewed as a rewarding event. In extending the concepts of the Freudian model of learning, Ruesch and Kees (1956) suggested that *action language*—movements used by adults to convey concepts, specific words, numbers, or objects—to children can also serve as statements of reward. Thus a child can ascertain approval of his or her behavior by adults through the nonverbal, or paralinguistic, messages of approval conveyed in culturally standardized adult body postures, gaits, gestures, or movements.

The concept of punishment has also come to be extrapolated from the Thorndike-Hull and Freudian learning models to include several categories of behavior: (1) *physical punishment,* (2) *verbal punishment,* (3) *intrinsic situational punishment,* and (4) *action language punishment.* Physical punishment includes both blows and physical isolation. Verbal punishment includes all uses of speech intended by adults to convey disapproval of the child's behavior. Verbal punishment may include direct disapproval of behavior; threats of physical punishment; direct denial of nurture or affiliation; threats, suggestions, or implications of denial of material recompense or special social privileges; threats of social isolation; ridicule or shame; actions meant to produce fear; and verbal frustration—that is, confusing issues by volume of words or use of meanings unknown to the child. Punishment through intrinsic situational factors is involved when children are confronted regularly with aspects of social situations that denote disapproval of some behavior forms; such confrontations imply chastisement simply for being a child. Thus for a child, fulfillment of particular social roles may involve a form of punishment for being a child. As a theoretical category, action language punishment has come to include all of the threatening, menacing, abusive, and ominous gestures, body postures, or demeanors by the adults of society with reference to child behavior.

Papago Rewards and Punishments   An analysis of Papago enculturation through use of theoretical concepts of reward and punishment from the

Teenage Papago girls, Gu Achi, Arizona. (T.R. Williams, 1956.)

Thorndike-Hull and Freudian learning models provides the following data. Papago adults rarely give children tangible remunerations as incentives for repetition of desired behavior. Use of speech forms to elicit approved behavior is infrequent among the Papago. Praise is generally absent in the Papago enculturation process. Permission to behave is seldom given as approval for exhibition of action. Parents and parent-surrogates almost never strike or physically threaten children. Striking, slapping, pushing, or touching a child violates an adult pattern of supernational sanction for control of social behavior. Adults say that a mysterious illness and eventual death will befall any individual who touches another Papago in anger. Physical activities are seldom restricted for children as a disapproval for behavior. It is uncommon for Papago children to be isolated for behavior. In the instance of one major restriction of action imposed on children, the limitations are those also imposed for adults. Certain locations are known sources of physical danger at particular seasons. Thus in the summer season of heavy rains and flash floods, children and adults avoid the many drywash stream beds crisscrossing Papago country. Locations likely to contain harmful animals are known and avoided by both adults and children.

Verbal disapproval of behavior is uncommon among the Papago. Direct adult prohibitions or orders to children for social action are not often heard. Threats of physical violence, by blow or isolation, are uncommon. Disapproval of a child through denial by adults of their nurture or affection is rare. Direct revocation of social privilege or suggestion of denial of approval is uncommon. Threats of social isolation are rare. There is a paucity of disapproval of children by means of verbal frustration. Ridicule is used very sparsely and then only in the sporadic instance of nonapproved

Teenage Papago boys, Santa Rosa School, Gu Achi, Arizona. (T. R. Williams, 1956.)

behavior by a child over 14 years old which is noticed by the general community. When an older child interrupts the conversation of adults or directly questions adult behavior or meanings, he or she may be rebuked by means of a teasing commentary, generally addressed to onlookers, which draws an analogy between the behavior of a coyote and the child: "It is known that coyotes run about sticking long noses into the business of other people."

Techniques of producing in children a consciousness of personal shortcoming, impropriety of behavior, or personal disgrace are seldom used by the Papago. Reproaches for child behavior that shame or lead to a sense of personal denigration are scarce. Disapproval through use of fearful personalized supernaturals is sporadic and generally confined to recounting adult fears in myth, legend, and folk stories. The fears expressed by adults are usually apprehensions common to most adult Papago and center upon particular events, objects, and animals. The sense of terror that may sometimes be imparted through stories regularly told to groups of children by adults is diffused to the entire gathering, rather than focused on the real or anticipated misdeeds of one child. Children are rarely purposely terrified or deliberately alarmed for a particular behavior.

Other Concepts for Understanding Learning

In contrast, less frequently used theoretical categories of learning appear to provide for a more detailed understanding of learning in Papago enculturation. The method of imparting states of emotion or meaning by culturally standardized action language is used by Papago adults to convey their covert notice of child behavior. Thus although adults take no direct note of the behavior of young children, they do appear to exhibit action language preferences for the behavior of older children and adolescents. Among themselves, adults are often amused at failures of younger children to succeed in tasks deemed a necessary part of Papago life. A clumsy use of eating utensils, awkward handling of work tools, or inappropriate performance of work tasks may evoke humor that for the most part appears unnoticed by the younger child. However by their ninth to eleventh year, most children have clearly noticed the action language forms of approval for completion of a difficult task or for making repeated attempts to undertake work beyond their physical capacities or knowledge. The primary action language form seems to be a series of body postures used by adults to convey pride in the older child's efforts at approximation of adult standards of behavior. These postures are illustrated in the ways in which older children and adolescents will exaggerate action language postures of approval by adults for completion of difficult tasks. Boys initially mastering the difficult technique of staying on a bucking horse sometimes verbalize action language reward by fathers and other male kin by saying, "I ride like a man," while simultaneously striking poses similar to those used by adult onlookers to impart approval through action language.

Papago action language forms of disapproval appear much more subtle than those used in expressing approval for exhibition of desired behavior. Action language disapproval is expressed by body postures that convey some note of particular behavior forms used by older children and adolescents. Adults may move, stand, or sit in any one of a series of Papago culturally conventional positions of inattention while observing or listening to older children. Such adult body positions generally denote adult personal detachment and imply to older children and adolescents a nonapproval of their actions.

Some circumstances of social action that denote approval or disapproval of child behavior are also used by Papago adults as enculturating techniques. Most societies publicly laud appropriate social behavior exhibited by persons holding key social positions. The forms of commendation vary from the award of a medal for bravery to general public approval as a "good person." This process may also be self-administered—that is, persons holding or anticipating key social assignments commend themselves through performing in a manner they know to be expected and approved by the community. For Papago children approvals for expected behavior appear mostly self-administered. In behaving as if they occupied adult status, Papago children gain acceptance for their right to be assigned to the adult social positions.

Many situations of social action involving Papago adults and children possess intrinsic commendation factors through the implied desirability of adult status. Other intrinsic situational approvals are occasionally derived from adult social positions being ascribed to children because of reputations of their kin or the nature of economic, political, or religious behavior powers wielded by a child's parents or relatives. The most persistent Papago intrinsic situational rewards are found, however, in the nearly unlimited freedom of social action permitted to children of all ages. Such freedom of action appears to permit a long-term rehearsal of approved adult behavior with a minimum of adult interference in a child's attempts at adult behavior forms. When not actually attempting adult tasks, younger children spend much of their time playing at adult ways appropriate for adults of their sex. Approval of exhibition of behavior approximating that of adults appears self-administered when children play alone, as is common among four-to-six-year-olds. In play groups that are common among 7- to 12-year-olds, children assume a variety of adult roles, thereby creating situations of social action that in part duplicate intrinsic situational commendations for exhibition of desired adult behavior forms.

Many circumstances of Papago social behavior in which children regularly participate appear to imply disapproval of any behavior other than adult behavior. Papago adults make a variety of judgments of worthwhileness regarding forms of social deference. Among the Papago such deference is given to all seniors in age, usually regardless of the senior's sex, social or economic rank, or degree of kinship. A well-behaved younger person generally is humble, unobtrusive, and reserved in speech and action with a senior person. These same personal characteristics usually mark the social relationships of younger persons with those only a few years their senior. The pattern of deference permits a senior person to expect constant attention to their wishes in most situations. This pattern is rarely questioned by juniors. In addition, the powers and privileges of seniority are based on a belief which holds that a senior must consider fairly the interests and desires of their juniors. Seniors rarely impose hardships on juniors. Public ridicule and gossip are directed at the adult who abuses the powers and privileges of seniority. However in application of the pattern of deference to children, particularly younger children, adults follow the several focal values imparting structure to Papago enculturation. As a consequence, the reciprocal obligations of a senior to a junior become greatly diluted, or are entirely absent, in social situations involving adults and younger children.

CONCLUSIONS FROM A CASE STUDY

Comparing these data of Papago enculturation with conceptions of learning contained in the Thorndike-Hull and Freudian models leads to the conclusion that these models yield little information in answering the question of *how* Papago children learn expected behavior. Conversely, using concepts of learning much less frequently employed in studies of human learning of culture appears more productive in analyzing how Papago children learn to behave in ways acceptable to Papago adults.

Both the Thorndike-Hull and Freudian models of learning place primary emphasis on, and proceed from, premises that assume the fundamental role of drives in all human learning and action. Concepts formulated following these models therefore tend to stress the necessity of reducing human learning to physiological bases and properties. It is also important to note that attempts to extend principles of these models to human learning soon have proceeded to a very different level of analysis, through acknowledging the existence of a basic human capacity for learning through symbolic and reflective processes. The discussions and research of Mowrer, G. W. Allport, Murray, Sears, Verplanck, and many others in extending the ideas of the Thorndike-Hull learning model to human learning are quite similar to the discussions of Sullivan, Fromm, Horney, Kardiner, and Erickson, among others, in seeking to apply Freudian concepts to human learning. Generally these scholars have acknowledged human reflective and symbolic processes to be as fundamental in human learning as the need or drive processes accentuated by Thorndike, Hull, and Freud.

Drive, Reflective, and Symbolic
Processes in Socialization

The distinction between drives, or needs, and reflective and symbolic processes is one that has not been given a satisfactory definition in contemporary studies of cultural transmission. Reflectivity is the distinctively human capacity to regularly go beyond observed properties of particular objects or events to draw, on the basis of past or present experiences, added inferences about unobserved properties of such objects or events.[7] This capacity involves an attention to symbolic reproductions of past experiences that allows consideration of alternative possibilities of immediate and future behavior to enter into a consideration of present conduct. The *Homo sapiens sapiens* reflective capacity is dependent for effective operation on acquisition of human language. Unlike drives that are elicited through physical and chemical changes within the body, the human reflective capacity does not seem to become operative, except at a minimal level, unless the individual has the opportunity to acquire the language employed by members of a culture.

Human reflection does not appear to be related to any human capacities other than language; therefore it does not appear to be stimulated through particular uses of capacities developed independently of reflection. Studies of experimental isolation of adults, so-called brain washing, and deculturation (see Chapter 5) demonstrate that the human capacity for reflection is not characterized by a tendency to return to a low level of operation once it is initiated. While sensory disturbances may be created by extreme physical isolation, extreme social isolation in itself may not impair or alter the adult capacity to reflect. The level of reflective capacity is dependent on the cultural forms of behavior available to an individual in an enculturation process as he or she matures. The capacity for reflection tends to be characterized by a concern with future and nonsensory events rather than immediate and sensory-based behavior. While drives must be reduced in brief periods, the capacity for reflection may operate at sustained levels over long periods with apparently little effect on the nature of the survival of the human organism. The human capacity for reflection appears *polyphasic*—that is, capable of several operations at one time.

The defining of essential differences among human drives, reflectivity, and symboling will continue as basic research is conducted on the nature of each and as studies proceed on mutual influences between drives and the reflective and symboling capacities. Research conducted by Miller and others, as cited in the next chapter, gives substantive evidence that human reflection may possibly alter human physiological processes in lasting ways. Such "operant conditioning" research may lead to increased un-

---

[7]Devereux (1975) notes that the human capacity to anticipate possible problem situations is a vital part of the socialization process.

derstanding of the nature of drives, reflection, and symboling in human learning of culture.

Phylogenetic Reductionism

Confusion between drives and the capacities for reflection and symboling has resulted in a regular and widespread use of an assumption about learning in the socialization process. The assumption may be termed *phylogenetic reductionism*. Hull (1945, 56) set forth explicitly the nature of the phylogenetic reductionistic assumption when he noted that all behavior of the individuals of a given species and that of all species of mammals, including humans, occurs according to the same set of *primary* (biological) laws. In a review of learning theory, Hilgard (1956, 461) has commented on Hull's assumption by noting that, while such a position is more often implied than asserted, it is strange that the opposite point of view is not more often made explicit, that is, through evolution, capacities at the human level have emerged for retaining, reorganizing, and foreseeing experiences that are not approached by other animals, including other primates. Simpson (1950) has observed that, while it is important to realize that humans are animals, it is even more important to realize that the essence of human nature lies precisely in those characteristics not shared with any other animal. Peters (1958) notes that such a conclusion seems rather obvious. However with some exceptions, such as brief discussions by Gregory Bateson (1942), Cora DuBois (1944, 1949), and some others (see Bandura, 1969), very little attention has been given to the consequences of learning theories used in attempts to differentiate between the different levels and kinds of learning involved in socialization.

PROBLEMS OF APPLYING
LEARNING THEORIES

As noted, data offered here with regard to Papago enculturation suggests a conclusion that the Thorndike-Hull and Freudian models of learning do not provide adequate theory for understanding how Papago children learn culture. These data of Papago enculturation also suggest the difficulties for observers of actually applying the specific concepts of the Thorndike-Hull and Freudian learning models in field research settings in other, non-Western cultures. Papago adults do not appear to be concerned with enculturating their children. It is very difficult for an individual from another culture to discern what would fit the Thorndike-Hull or Freudian definitions of "learning" by Papago children. Yet Papago children obviously do learn their culture. One reason for this problem is that the Thorndike-

Hull and Freudian conceptions of human learning stress the somatic basis, or the drive level, of learning, while the Papago enculturation process is primarily concerned with the regular use of reflective and symbolic capacities of children in learning culture. It becomes apparent from the case study of Papago enculturation that too little attention has been given in the formulation of the Thorndike-Hull and Freudian models to the role of symbolic and reflective capacities in learning culture. More than a quarter of a century ago Honigmann (1954, 430–431) noted that the Thorndike-Hull learning theory, with its emphasis on reward and punishment, helps us to understand the way some patterns of cultural behavior become established but is not adequate to explain all patterning of personal character. Honigmann also said that attention must be devoted not only to *what* is transmitted in the learning process but also to *how* that transmission takes place. Hallowell (1953, 610) made a similar observation when he pointed out that the learning process has been conceptualized too simply in the past since we now know that to say that the individual acquires culture through learning in a socialization process is only a confession of ignorance as to what this process actually involves. Both Honigmann (1967) and Clausen (1968) have also emphasized that a valid general learning theory is essential for study of socialization.

SOME OTHER LEARNING MODELS

At least two other general models of learning appear to provide for a more adequate understanding of the richness and great complexity of how infants and children learn in the socialization process. The models, developed by Albert Bandura and Jean Piaget, provide some ways of accounting for regular use by infants and children of reflective and symbolic capacities in learning culture.

Bandura and Cognitive Social Learning Theory

Proceeding from a belief that the theoretical conceptions of the Thorndike-Hull learning model were too narrow to be applied to human learning, Albert Bandura and his associates have developed a learning model that emphasizes the ways infants and children learn through observing the behavior of other persons that appears to be rewarded.[8] This

---

[8]Bandura's learning model is described in Bandura, 1969, 1973, 1977; Bandura & McDonald, 1963; Bandura & Walters, 1963, and Bandura, Ross, & Ross, 1963.

is not a matter of a child simply imitating other persons to obtain nurturance from them, as proposed by Miller and Dollard (1941) in their extension of the Thorndike-Hull learning model, or imitating in an effort to secure parental influence, power, and strength, as suggested by Kagan (1958) and J. W. M. Whiting (1960). Rather by watching others behave, human infants and children form concepts through use of their capacities for reflection and symboling. Such concepts are then used to guide acceptable personal behavior. Bandura notes that children can also form concepts of acceptable behavior from radio, television, books, and newspapers.

Bandura also points out that as children observe their own behavior and reflect upon the degree to which it is acceptable to adults, they form concepts which are retained as symbolic patterns. Thus Bandura's cognitive social learning model makes human knowledge, thought, and understanding the keys to explanation of human learning. In Bandura's theory the Thorndike-Hull and Freudian conception of stimuli external to human individuals controlling all of their behavior, or initiating body responses which give rise to behavior, has been replaced by a belief that all stimuli are signals used by humans to help them choose a course of action. Hence in the cognitive social learning theory model, it is the individual's conception of a stimulus, not the stimulus itself, which shapes and guides human behavior.

This learning model provides ample time for human infants and children to examine and try out actions that they see to be within the range of their personal ability and to avoid actions that are judged to be harmful or beyond their capability. Since in this learning model human infants and children reflect upon and make judgments about what has happened or is happening to them, they cannot be made to behave or be manipulated by acts of reinforcement directed or imposed by adults.

Papago Enculturation and Cognitive Social Learning Theory

The model of human learning developed by Albert Bandura and his associates can be used to explain why Papago adults do not appear to be overly concerned with enculturating their infants and children; adults have chosen to permit infants and children to regularly use their reflective and symbolic capacities in learning culture. In shifting the theoretical focus for understanding learning in the cultural transmission process, Bandura and others have moved away from the Thorndike-Hull and Freudian theories that primarily emphasized biological drives as the key aspect of all human learning and action. A key theoretical problem remains, however, in applying the cognitive social learning model to completely understand how Papago infants and children learn their variety of culture. The problem is that cognitive social learning theory does not specify either the nature

Papago house constructed in traditional style, Gu Achi, Arizona. (T. R. Williams, 1953.)

or the ways of operation of the human capacities that are the central elements in the theory. Thus in following this theory we still do not really know quite how reflection and symboling, as physiologically based processes "interior" to or "inside the heads" of Papago infants and children, are specifically related to their behavior as individuals. In other words, although the cognitive social learning theory model informs us about the reasons that we have not been able to adequately understand the Papago enculturation process in terms of the Thorndike-Hull and Freudian learning models, we are left to consider the problem that the cognitive social learning model also tells us very little about the ways human capacities actually work in the process of learning culture. However there is another model for human learning, developed by Jean Piaget, which may be applied to consideration of this problem.

An Organismic Model for Learning

Piaget's model for human learning, in common with Bandura's, is centered upon cognition, or "knowing," by infants and children. However Piaget's conception of cognition is that it is an innate biological system which serves to provide and maintain a balance between the human organism and its environment. Piaget emphasizes that the biological system for cognition functions the same way and has the essential features of all human biological systems, such as respiration or digestion. Thus Piaget sees human cognition working in the same way as any other human biological system in that it takes in and uses whatever elements it needs to operate.[9]

[9]It should be noted that Heinz Werner (1948, 1957) also developed an organismic model of human learning which proceeds from the same basic assumptions.

assimilation — when child learn new exp, will relate to
the world in term of its existing schemata
accomodation — form new schemata eg · imitation

101   *Models of Learning and Socialization*

Piaget notes that the human system for cognition depends for its growth on other human biological systems, particularly those used for sensing and motor activity. The other biological systems make it possible for a human individual to come in contact with the environment, take in their experiences, and then, through the biological system for cognition, to know and understand the world. Piaget shares with cognitive social learning theorists a view that human individuals actively use their environment to construct their personal view of the world.

Piaget's model stresses the continuity of learning through the human life span and is termed by Piaget as a *genetic epistemology* approach to human learning—that is, a model for understanding the development of learning about knowing by humans as they grow. In this model of learning, all knowledge comes through the actions of an individual experiencing the environment; an infant experiences the objects and events going on about it and so comes to know about these events and objects. Piaget stressed that knowledge does not come from the objects or events a child experiences, or from "inside" the individual, but from the interactions that build up firm links of knowledge between objects and events and the individual. It is in this way that maturing children interact with the environment through experience and develop their human biological system for cognition.

The essence of the organismic model of learning developed by Piaget lies in the construction by infants and children of various *schemes* for knowing and understanding. Thus infants come to know through experience that both a rubber ball and a grapefruit are round and can be rolled, but that when thrown, the ball will bounce, whereas grapefruit will not bounce. It is from this type of knowing that infants and children build up various *schemes* for *coordinated behavior*—that is, a child learns that, while both round rubber balls and grapefruit can be rolled and thrown, these two actions are exclusive.

In Piaget's model for human learning, cognition is built through the operations which are termed *assimilation* and *accommodation*. Infants and children incorporate, or *assimilate*, new ways of knowing through use of previously acquired schemes for knowing. *Accommodation* occurs when an infant or child revises their schemes to fit new knowledge that has been assimilated through experience and does not blend with an existing scheme. Piaget notes that there must be a balance, or equilibrium, between old learning schemes and new learning schemes if an individual is to progress in knowing. Piaget notes that there is a genetically transmitted impetus for each human individual to seek *equilibration*, or a required balance between growing and knowing. Piaget says that transitions from one stage of a child's growth and knowledge depend on a balance being disturbed by assimilation of new knowledge so that cognitive development proceeds to another one of the stages characteristic of human intellectual life and learning.

The earliest or first stage of cognitive development, termed by Piaget as the *sensorimotor*, begins at birth and lasts through the second year of life.

A second stage of cognitive development, which Piaget calls the *representational stage*, lasts from three years to eleven or twelve years of age and is characterized by two periods: (1) the *preoperational* and (2) the *concrete-operational.* The third stage of cognitive development, which begins at eleven or twelve years of age and lasts through adult life, is termed by Piaget as the *formal operational* stage.

These stages may be briefly described in this way: Most of the first two years of life is spent by an infant building a framework of concepts about events and objects that are directly experienced. This framework establishes the basic cognitive skills of the individual and sharpens the ability to remember, to use symbols, and to imagine. In the third through seventh years of life, in the *preoperational* period of the *representational* stage of cognitive development, children begin to remember their experiences in essentially symbolic terms; imagining and symbolizing increasingly replace direct exploration of objects and events. This activity heightens the child's abilities to reason and form concepts. In the eighth to eleventh or twelfth years of life, in the *concrete-operational* period of the *representational* stage of cognitive development, children begin to comprehend a new type of knowing which involves *reversible transformation*—that is, using words and metaphors for understanding.[10] It is in this period of cognitive development that children finally become proficient in use of logical operations to represent reality. Finally, in the *formal operational* (or *propositional*) stage of cognitive development, which begins after eleven or twelve years of age and lasts throughout life, children develop formal logical reasoning that is composed of a large number of "if . . . then" statements—that is, "*if* I turn this switch, *then* the ignition will start the car."

Papago Enculturation and Organismic Learning Theory

When applied to the question of how Papago children learn their culture, it is apparent that the cognitive model developed by Piaget provides some theoretical conceptions that solve the major problem raised in using the cognitive social learning model to understanding Papago enculturation. Piaget's theory helps us understand what may be taking place "inside the heads" of maturing Papago individuals—that is, the ways human capacities

---

[10]Piaget noted that young children have great difficulty in knowing that transformations of perceptual features usually do not alter other properties of a substance. Thus an unhappy child at four years of age may be satisfied by a parent pouring out a soft drink into a tall, narrow glass from a short, squat container to convince the child that the amount being given has more than doubled. A nine-year-old child has usually learned to realize that if the soft drink is poured back into the short, squat container from the tall, narrow glass it will show that the drink in the tall glass has not doubled at all. Reversible transformation allows a child to prove to him/herself mentally that the amount of the soft drink remains the same in both glasses.

Desert scene near Gu Achi, Arizona. (T. R. Williams, 1953.)

are used in the course of enculturation. Using an organismic model of learning, we can see how Papago infants and children actively reach out, size up, and then seize on forms and patterns of Papago culture. We can also see, through use of Piaget's concepts of *assimilation* and *accommodation* and his definitions of particular stages of cognitive development, how it is possible for a Papago child to progress, essentially alone, from a dependent infant to a socially and culturally competent adult without much direct adult guidance. For example, using Piaget's model, we now know why most Papago children between 9 and 11 years of age clearly note the action language forms used by adults to convey approval or disapproval of behavior; in this *concrete-operational* period of the *representational* state of cognitive development, as defined by Piaget, all human children begin to regularly use metaphors, their own and those of others, for understanding and knowing. Thus Papago children, in common with all human children, are cognitively prepared to reach out and learn for themselves expected ways of behavior. At this age children do not need to learn from direct reward or punishment being administered to them by parents or other adults. The organismic learning model developed by Piaget can thus be used to significantly extend our understanding of the Papago enculturation process.

It should be noted, however, that the Piaget model for cognitive learning also leaves us with a theoretical problem in completely understanding the cultural transmission process. Although this model assists us greatly in understanding the ways human capacities operate in cultural transmission, we are left with the vital question of the nature of the human biological

Papago family, Gu Achi, Arizona. (T. R. Williams, 1954.)

system, as postulated by Piaget, which is said to be the base from which, and through which, human learning develops and operates. In viewing cognitive learning as a biological system, Piaget poses a question of importance in a final understanding of the cultural transmission process. That question is one of finding a way to describe the postulated innate human biological system upon which all learning is said to rest. This problem cannot be addressed in a limited space as part of a work concerned with the process of socialization. It is helpful to be aware, however, that the question exists and does not have a satisfactory answer in current learning theory.

DESCRIBING LEARNING
ENVIRONMENTS

The careful specification of the nature of the learning environments experienced by human infants and children in a wide variety of cultural and ecological settings is a vital part of comprehensive learning theory for use in describing and analyzing how infants and children learn culture. The most detailed accounts of human learning environments for infants and children are found in the reports of six cultures studied by Beatrice and John W. M. Whiting (1975) and their associates, as well as in studies conducted recently by other students of the Whitings.

Using essentially the Miller and Dollard (1941) extension of the Thorndike-Hull learning model and proceeding from a detailed field guide first developed in 1954 and later revised (J. Whiting, 1966), the Whitings studied enculturation in six cultures in widely separated locations (Kenya, India, Mexico, U.S., Philippines, Okinawa) with very different linguistic, ethnic, and ecological backgrounds. Their study was founded upon precise descriptions of behavior events using techniques of naturalistic observation developed by Barker and Wright (1954) and others (cf. Barker & Wright, 1951; Sears, 1953). The plan of the six cultures research was to have each field research team write a general ethnography of the culture being studied, as well as a detailed description of child-rearing and child life at each cultural level. The general ethnographies were published first in one volume (B. Whiting, 1963) and later as separate books (LeVine & LeVine, 1966; Minturn & Hitchcock, 1966; Romney & Romney, 1966; Fischer & Fisher, 1966; Nydegger & Nydegger, 1966; Maretzki & Maretzki, 1966). In addition, the plan of six cultures project called for use of standardized interviews of the mothers of all children selected to be observed (Minturn & Lambert, 1964) and to have each field team collect a large number of similar observations of the behavior of children in everyday settings. The analysis of these behavior observations is reported in a work by Beatrice and John W. M. Whiting (1975). An earlier work (Whiting & Child, 1953) suggested that there are at least nine transculturally valid categories of enculturation behavior: nurturance, succorance, sociability, achievement, dominance, submission, aggression, responsibility, and self-reliance. Using that study as a basis, the observers in six cultures selected "sample" children and recorded a series of behavior events involving those children in particular settings (house or yard; adjacent pasture or garden; school or school play yard; other public places). The observers noted the persons present and the kinds of interactions taking place between children and other individuals. Initial tabulation by the Whitings of observational data in the six cultures studied indicated that approximately 20,000 behavioral acts had been described for 134 children, with an average of 150 acts for each child in a variety of cultural settings (Whiting & Whiting, 1975, 56). These data provide the most complete account of the learning environments experienced by human infants and children now available and tell us more, in greater detail, about the precise settings children occupy, the behavior of their caretakers and teachers, the work tasks assigned by adults to children, and the workload of mothers caring for children than is to be found anywhere in the scientific literature.

The results of the Whiting et al. techniques for describing the learning environments of infants and children are particularly amenable to use of modern statistical analysis. A number of students of the Whitings have employed these observational and statistical analytic procedures in other cultures to add significantly to our knowledge of human learning environments. For example, Gerald Erchak (1975), in a careful study of the "non-social behavior" of young Liberian Kpelle children, and Susan Seymour (1975), in a sound study of enculturation in a setting of rapid social and economic change in an Indian city, both provide data of human learning environments using modifications of the observational and analytic procedures first used in the six cultures project.[11]

It should also be noted that significant descriptions of human learning environments, using different research procedures, have been provided for Liberian Kpelle culture by Michael Cole, John Gay, and their associates (1971) and for four East African cultures (Hehe, Kamba, Pokot, Sebei) by Robert Edgerton and his associates (1965). Although not comparable to data on human learning environments provided by the Whitings and their students, the information provided by Cole, Gay, Edgerton, and their associates is a valuable addition to our understanding of the way in which human learning is shaped and directed by cultural, social, and ecological contexts.

DATA OF LEARNING ENVIRONMENTS AND LEARNING MODELS

It seems clear that valid data of human learning environments are a requisite for finally understanding how infants and children learn culture. It would seem that this is so without regard to the particular learning model used to describe and analyze socialization. It appears to be particularly appropriate to combine data of human learning environments with use of a cognitive social learning model or an organismic learning model, in which knowing by infants and children is held to be the key to their learning. It seems reasonable to suppose that the environment in which cognition develops must play a vital role in human learning. It should be noted that it is only in the study of socialization by the Whitings that we presently have an effective combination of a fully developed learning model (Thorndike-Hull) and detailed descriptions of different contexts of learning. Such combinations are not yet available in the instance of cognitive social learning or organismic learning models. This is unfortunate since it appears that these learning models, or some combination of them, given the theoretical problems noted previously, have great promise for developing a general

---

[11]Draper (1974) reports on other studies of human learning environments using the Whiting techniques of study.

theory of human learning for use in understanding the socialization process.[12]

CONCLUSIONS

The study of human learning is complex and involves a number of very difficult unresolved conceptual issues. As noted, a valid general human learning theory is essential for study of the socialization process. Current models for understanding human learning provide some elements for use in understanding cultural transmission, but no one of the available learning models, standing alone, appears likely to be developed into a valid general learning theory. This is particularly so because these models, and their major variations, tend to ignore to some greater or lesser degree the environments in which human learning occurs. For the present, it seems useful to combine the cognitive social learning model set forth by Bandura with the precise techniques for describing human learning environments evolved by the Whitings in attempting to find ways to understand the richness and complexity of the socialization process.

SUMMARY

This chapter began with brief reviews of some details of two major models of learning widely used in socialization studies. Following this discussion, case study data of the process of enculturation among the Papago, a North American Indian society, were presented to note the roles of reflective and symbolic learning in the socialization process. Then two other

[12]A review of recent works concerned with human learning in a socialization process indicates little movement toward a goal of dealing with this problem. See, for instance, P.H. Liederman, S.R. Tulkin, & A. Rosenfeld (eds.), 1977, *Culture and Infancy: Variations in the Human Experience,* New York Academic Press: H.R. Schaffer & P.E. Emerson, 1976 (1964); *The Development of Social Attachments in Infancy,* Lafayette, Ind.: Monographs of the Society for Research in Child Development, Vol. 29, No. 3 (Kraus Reprint, Millwood, N.J., 1976); C.E. Snow & C.A. Ferguson (eds.), 1977, *Talking to Children: Language Input and Acquisition,* New York: Cambridge University Press; M. Lewis & L.A. Rosenblum (eds.), 1974, *The Effect of the Infant on Its Caregiver,* New York: John Wiley; J.H. Stevens, Jr., & M. Mathews (eds.), 1978; *Mother/Child, Father/Child Relationships,* Washington, D.C.: National Association for the Education of Young Children; M.D.S. Ainsworth, 1978, *Patterns of Attachment: A Psychological Study of the Strange Situation,* Hillsdale, N.J.: Lawrence Erlbaum Associates; H.R. Schaffer, 1971, *The Growth of Sociability.* Harmondsworth: Penguin; H.R. Schaffer, 1977. *Mothering.* Cambridge, England: Cambridge University Press; H.R. Schaffer (ed.), 1975. *Studies in Mother-Infant Interaction.* Ross Priory: University of Strathclyde-New York: Academic Press; G. Clezy, 1979. *Modification of the Mother-Child Interchange in Language, Speech and Hearing.* Baltimore, Md.: University Park Press.

models of learning, which focus on cognition, were examined. The chapter concluded with comments concerning ways human reflective and symbolic capacities are involved in learning culture and with some suggestions for future research on the socialization process.

REFERENCES CITED AND SUGGESTED READINGS

ALLPORT, G.W. 1937. *Personality: A Psychological Interpretation.* New York: Holt, Rinehart & Winston.

ANGYAL, A. 1941. *Foundations for a Science of Personality.* New York: The Commonwealth Fund.

ASCH, S.E. 1952. *Social Psychology.* Englewood Cliffs, N.J.: Prentice-Hall.

BANDURA, A. 1969. "Social Learning Theory of Identificatory Process." In D.A. Goslin (ed.), *Handbook of Socialization Theory and Research.* Skokie, Ill.: Rand McNally. pp. 213–262.

————. 1973. *Aggression: A Social Learning Analysis.* Englewood Cliffs, N.J.: Prentice-Hall.

————. 1977. *Social Learning Theory.* Englewood Cliffs, N.J.: Prentice-Hall.

BANDURA, A, & F.J. McDONALD. 1963. "Influence of Social Reinforcement and the Behavior of Models in Shaping Children's Moral Judgements." *Journal of Abnormal and Social Psychology,* 67, 274–281.

BANDURA, A., D. ROSS. 1963. "Imitation of Film-Mediated Aggressive Models." *Journal of Abnormal and Social Psychology,* 66, 3–11.

BANDURA, A., & R.H. WALTERS. 1963. *Social Learning and Personality.* New York: Holt, Rinehart & Winston.

BARKER, R.G., & H.F. WRIGHT. 1954. *Midwest and Its Children.* Evanston, Ill.: Row, Peterson.

BARKER, R.G., & H.F. WRIGHT. 1951. *One Boy's Day: A Specimen Record of Behavior.* New York: Harper & Row, Pub.

BATESON, G. 1942. "Social Planning and the Concept of Deutero-Learning." In L. Bryson & L.K. Finkelstein (eds.), *Science, Philosophy and Religion,* Conference on Science, Philosophy and Religion, New York. Garden City, N.Y.: Country Life Press, pp. 81–97.

BLOOM, B. 1977. *Human Characteristics and School Learning.* New York: McGraw-Hill.

CASTETTER, E.F., & R. UNDERHILL. 1936. "The Ethnobiology of the Papago Indians." *University of New Mexico Bulletin,* Ethnobiological Studies in the American Southwest, No. 2, Biological Series, Vol. IV, No. 3. Albuquerque: University of New Mexico Press.

COLE, M. *et al.* 1971. *The Cultural Context of Learning and Thinking.* New York: Basic Books.

DEVEREUX, G. 1975. "Time: History versus Chronicle; Socialization as Cultural Preexperience." *Ethos,* 3, 281–292.

DRAPER, P. 1974. "Comparative Studies of Socialization." *Annual Review of Anthropology,* 3, 263–277.

DUBOIS, C. 1944. *The People of Alor.* Minneapolis: The University of Minnesota Press.

————. 1949. "Attitudes toward Food and Hunger in Alor." In D.G. Haring (ed.), *Personal Character and Cultural Milieu.* Syracuse: Syracuse University Press, pp. 196–204.

————. 1955. "The Dominant Value Profile of American Culture." *American Anthropologists*, 57, 1232–1239.

EDGERTON, R. 1965. "Cultural Versus Ecological Factors in the Expression of Values, Attitudes and Personality Characteristics." *American Anthropologist*, 67, 442–447.

ERCHAK, G.M. 1975. "The Non-social Behavior of Young Liberian Kpelle Children and Its Social Context." In T.R. Williams (ed.), *Socialization and Communication in Primary Groups*. The Hague: Mouton, pp. 27–39.

FISCHER, J., & A. FISCHER, 1966. *The New Englanders of Orchard Town, U.S.A.* Vol. 5, Six Cultures Series. New York: John Wiley.

FREUD, S, 1905. "Three Contributions to the Theory of Sex." In *The Basic Writings of Sigmund Freud.* pp. 553–629. New York: Random House, 1938.

————. 1908. "Character and Anal Erotism." In *Collected Papers*, Vol. II, pp. 45–50. London: Hogarth Press, 1924.

————. 1910. "Psychogenic Visual Disturbance according to Psycho-Analytical Conceptions." In *Collected Papers*, Vol. II, pp. 105–112. London: Hogarth Press, 1924.

————. 1911. "Formulations Regarding the Two Principles in Mental Functioning." In *Collected Papers*, Vol. IV, pp. 12–21. London: Hogarth Press, 1925.

————.1912. "Types of Neurotic Nosogenesis." In *Collected Papers*, Vol. II, pp. 113–121. London: Hogarth Press, 1924.

————. 1913. "Totem and Taboo." In *The Basic Writings of Sigmund Freud*, pp. 807–930. New York: Random House, 1938.

————. 1914. "On Narcissism: An Introduction." In *Collected Papers*, Vol. IV, pp. 30–59. London: Hogarth Press, 1925.

————. 1920a. *A General Introduction to Psychoanalysis.* New York: Boni & Liveright.

————.1920b. *Beyond the Pleasure Principle* (translation). New York: Liveright.

————. 1921. *Group Psychology and the Analysis of the Ego* (translation). New York: Liveright, 1922.

————. 1923a: *The Ego and the Id* (translation). London: Hogarth Press, 1927.

————. 1923b. "The Libido Theory." In *Collected Papers*, Vol. V, pp. 255–268. London: Hogarth Press, 1924.

————. 1925. "Negation." In *Collected Papers*, Vol. V, pp. 181–185. London: Hogarth Press, 1950.

————. 1926. *The Problem of Anxiety* (translation). New York: W.W. Norton & Co., Inc. 1936.

————. 1930. *Civilization and Its Discontents.* London: Hogarth Press.

————. 1933. *New Introductory Lectures on Psychoanalysis.* New York: W.W. Norton & Co., Inc.

————. 1938. *The Basic Writings of Sigmund Freud* (translation). New York: Modern Library.

————. 1939. *Moses and Monotheism.* New York: Knopf.

————. 1940. *An Outline of Psychoanalysis.* New York: W.W. Norton & Co., Inc.

GUTHRIE, E.R. 1935. *The Psychology of Learning.* New York: Harper & Row, Pub.

————. 1952. *The Psychology of Learning.* (revised). New York: Harper & Row, Pub.

HALL, C.S. 1954. *A Primer of Freudian Psychology.* Cleveland, Ohio: William Collins Publishers, Inc.

HALL, C.S. & G. LINDZEY. 1957. "Freud's Psychoanalytic Theory of Personality." In C.S. Hall & G. Lindzey (eds.), *Theories of Personality.* New York: John Wiley, pp. 32–55.

HALLOWELL, A.I. 1953. "Culture; Personality and Society," In A.L. Kroeber (ed.), *Anthropology Today.* Chicago: University of Chicago Press, pp. 597–620.

————. 1954. "Psychology and Anthropology." In J. Gillin (ed.), *For a Science of Social Man.* New York: Macmillan, pp. 160–226.

HILGARD. E.R. 1956.   *Theories of Learning* (2nd ed.) New York: Appleton-Century-Crofts.

HILGARD, E.R., L.S. KUBIE, & E. PUMPIAN-MINDLIN. 1952.   *Psycholanalysis as Science.* Stanford, Calif.: Stanford University Press.

HONIGMANN, J.J. 1954.   *Culture and Personality.* New York: Harper & Row.

————. 1967.   *Personality and Culture.* New York: Harper & Row.

HULL, C.L. 1942.   "Conditioning: Outline of a Systematic Theory of Learning." *The Psychology of Learning, Chapter 2, National Society for the Study of Education 41st Yearbook,* Part II, pp. 61–95.

————. 1943.   *Principles of Behavior.* New York: Appleton-Century-Crofts.

————. 1945.   "The Place of Innate Individual and Species Differences in a Natural-Science Theory of Behavior." *Psychological Review,* 52, 55–60.

————. 1950.   "Behavior Postulates and Corollaries—1949." *Psychological Review,* 57, 173–180.

————. 1951.   *Essentials of Behavior.* New Haven, Conn.: Yale University Press.

————. 1952.   *A Behavior System: An Introduction to Behavior Theory Concerning the Individual Organism.* New Haven, Conn.: Yale University Press.

JOSEPH, A., R.B. SPICER, & J. CHESKY. 1949.   *The Desert People.* Chicago: University of Chicago Press.

KAGAN, J. 1958.   "The Concept of Identification." *Psychological Review,* 65, 296–305.

KARDINER, A. 1939.   *The Individual and His Society.* New York: Columbia University Press.

————. 1945.   *Psychological Frontiers of Society.* New York: Columbia University Press.

KIMBALL, S., & J. BURNETT. 1973.   *Learning and Culture.* Seattle: University of Washington Press.

KLUCKHOHN, C. 1944.   "The Influence of Psychiatry on Anthropology in America during the Past 100 Years." In J.K. Hall, G. Zilboorg, & H.A. Bunker (eds.), *One Hundred Years of American Psychiatry.* New York: Columbia University Press, pp. 589–617.

KOFFKA, K. 1924.   *The Growth of the Mind* (translated by R.M. Ogden). London: Kegan Paul, Trench, Trubner & Co., Ltd.

KOHLER, W. 1925.   *The Mentality of Apes* (translated by E. Winter). New York: Harcourt Brace Jovanovich.

LEEPER, R.W. 1951.   "Cognitive Processes." In S.S. Stevens (ed.), *Handbook of Experimental Psychology.* New York: John Wiley, pp. 730–757.

LeVINE, R. 1963.   "Behaviorism in Psychological Anthropology." In J.M. Wepman & R.W. Heine (eds.), *Concepts of Personality.* Chicago: Aldine, pp. 361–384.

LeVINE, R.A., & B.B. LeVINE. 1966.   *Nyansongo: A Gusii Community in Kenya,* Vol. 2, Six Cultures Series. New York: John Wiley.

LEWIN, K. 1935.   *A Dynamic Theory of Personality* (translated by D.K. Adams & K.E. Zener). New York: McGraw-Hill.

————. 1936.   *Principles of Topological Psychology* (translated by F. Heider). New York: McGraw-Hall.

MARETZKI, T.W., & H. MARETZKI. 1966.   *Taira: An Okinawan Village,* Vol. 7, Six Cultures Series. New York: John Wiley.

MILLER, N.E., & J. DOLLARD. 1941.   *Social Learning and Imitation.* New Haven, Conn.: Yale University Press.

MINTURN, L., & J.T. HITCHCOCK. 1966.   *The Rājpūts of Khalapur, India,* Vol. 3, Six Cultures Series. New York: John Wiley.

MINTURN, L., & W. LAMBERT. 1964.   *Mothers of Six Cultures: Antecedents of Child Rearing.* New York: John Wiley.

MOWRER, O.H. 1950.   *Learning Theory and Personality Dynamics.* New York: Ronald Press.

MUNROE, R.L. 1955.   *Schools of Psychoanalytic Thought.* New York: Dryden.

NYDEGGER, W.F., & C. NYDEGGER, 1966.   *An Ilocos Barrio in the Philippines,* Vol. 6, Six Cultures Series. New York: John Wiley.

PAVLOV, I.P. 1927.   *Conditioned Reflexes.* London: Oxford University Press.

———. 1928.   *Lectures on Conditioned Reflexes* (translated by W.H. Gantt). New York: International.

PETERS, R.S. 1958.   *The Concept of Motivation.* London: Routledge & Kegan Paul.

PIAGET, J. 1926.   *The Language of the Child.* (translated by M. Warden). New York: Harcourt Brace Jovanovich.

———. 1928.   *Judgement and Reasoning in the Child* (translated by M. Warden). New York: Harcourt Brace Jovanovich.

———. 1932.   *The Moral Judgement of the Child* (translated by M. Gabain). Boston: Routledge & Kegan Paul.

———. 1951.   *Play, Dreams and Imitation in Childhood* (translated by C. Gattegno & F. Hodgson), New York: W.W. Norton & Co., Inc.

———. 1952a.   *The Child's Conception of Number* (translated by C. Gattegno & F. Hodgson). Boston: Routledge & Kegan Paul.

———. 1952b.   *The Origins of Intelligence in Children* (translated by M. Cook). New York: International Universities Press.

———. 1954.   *The Construction of Reality in the Child* (translated by M. Cook). New York: Basic Books.

———. 1976.   *The Grasp of Consciousness: Action and Conception in the Young Child.* Cambridge, Mass.: Harvard University Press.

PIAGET, J., & B. INHELDER. 1969.   *The Psychology of the Child.* Boston: Routledge & Kegan Paul.

ROMNEY, K., & R. ROMNEY. 1966.   *The Mixtecans of Juxtlahuaca, Mexico,* Vol. 4, Six Cultures Series. New York: John Wiley.

RUESCH, J. & W. KEES. 1956.   *Nonverbal Communication: Notes on the Visual Perception of Human Relations.* Berkely: University of California Press.

SIMPSON, G.G. 1950.   *The Meaning of Evolution.* New Haven, Conn.: Yale University Press.

SKINNER, B.F. 1938.   *The Behavior of Organisms: An Experimental Analysis.* New York: Prentice-Hall, 1966.

———. 1953.   *Science and Human Behavior.* New York: Macmillan.

SPICER, E.H. 1941.   "The Papago Indians." *The Kiva, Arizona Archaeological and Historical Society,* 6, 21–24. Tucson: Arizona State Museum.

STERN, W. 1938.   *General Psychology from the Personalistic Standpoint.* New York: Macmillan.

THORNDIKE, E.L. 1911.   *Animal Intelligence.* New York: Macmillan.

———. 1932.   *The Fundamentals of Learning.* New York: Columbia University Teachers College

———. 1935.   *The Psychology of Wants, Interests and Attitudes.* New York: Appleton-Century-Crofts.

THORNDIKE, E.L. 1933   "An Experimental Study of Rewards." *Teachers College Contributions to Education,* No. 580.

TOLMAN, E.C. 1932.   *Purposive Behavior in Animals and Men.* New York: Appleton-Century Crofts.

———. 1951.   *Collected Papers in Psychology.* Berkeley: University of California Press.

UNDERHILL, R., 1934.   "Notes on Easter Devils at Kawori'k on the Papago Reservation." *American Anthropologist,* 36, 515–516.

———. 1936.   "The Autobiography of a Papago Woman, Chona" (Memoirs). *American Anthropological Association* 46, 3.

———. 1938a.   "A Papago Calendar Record." *Anthropological Bulletin Series,* Vol. 2, No. 5. Albuquerque: University of New Mexico Press.

———. 1938b.   *Singing for Power: The Song Magic of the Papago Indians of Southern Arizona.* Berkeley: University of California Press.

———. 1939.   "Social Organization of the Papago Indians." *Columbia University Contributions of Anthropology,* Vol. 30. New York: Columbia University Press.

———. 1940.   "The Papago Indians of Arizona and Their Relatives the Pima." *Sherman Pamphlets,* No. 3. Lawrence, Kansas: Publication of the Branch of Education, Bureau of Indian Affair, Department of the Interior.

———. 1946.   *Papago Indian Religion.* New York: Columbia University Press.

VERPLANCK, W.S. 1955.   "Since Learned Behavior Is Innate and Vice Versa, What Now?" *Psychological Review,* 62, 139–144.

WERNER, H. 1948.   *Comparative Psychology of Mental Development* (translated by E. Garside). New York: International Universities Press.

———. 1957.   "The Concept of Development from a Comparative Point of View." In D.B. Harris (ed.). *The Concept of Development: An Issue in the Study of Human Behavior.* Minneapolis: University of Minnesota Press. pp. 125–148.

WERTHEIMER, M. 1923.   "Untersuchungen zur Lehre von der Gestalt, II" (translated and condensed as "Laws of Organization in Perceptual Forms.") In W.D. Ellis (ed.), *A Source Book of Gestalt Psychology.* New York: Harcourt Brace Jovanovich,

———. 1925.   "Uber Schlussprozesse im Produktiven Denken" (translated and condensed as "The Syllogism and Productive Thinking.") In W.D. Ellis (ed.), *A Source Book of Gestalt Psychology.* New York: Harcourt Brace Jovanovich, 1938.

WHITING, B. 1963.   *Six Cultures: Studies of Child Rearing.* New York: John Wiley.

WHITING, B.B., & J.W.M. WHITING. 1975.   *Children of Six Cultures: A Psycho-Cultural Analysis.* Cambridge, Masss.: Harvard University Press.

WHITING, J.W.M. 1941.   *Becoming a Kwoma.* New Haven, Conn.: Yale University Press.

———. 1960.   "Resource Meditation and Learning by Identification." In I. Iscoe & H.W. Stevenson (eds.), *Personality Development in Children.* Austin: University of Texas Press, pp. 112–126.

WHITING, J.W.M. & I.L. CHILD. 1953.   *Child Training and Personality.* New Haven: Yale University Press.

WHITING, J.W.M. 1966.   *Field Guide for a Study of Socialization,* Vol. 1, Six Cultures Series. New York: John Wiley.

WILLIAMS, T.R. 1958.   "The Structure of the Socialization Process in Papago Indian Society." *Social Forces* 36, 251–256.

WOODWORTH, R.S. 1918.   *Dynamic Psychology.* New York: Columbia University Press.

———. 1929.   *Psychology* (rev. ed.). New York: Holt, Rinehart & Winston.

CHAPTER FOUR
OPERANT CONDITIONING
AND SOCIALIZATION

This chapter begins by discussing ethnographic reports of some of the ways culture and human biology appear to become interrelated in the socialization process. Then a brief account is given of the concept of *operant conditioning* and the ways this special learning reseach procedure has been used experimentally to study various kinds of interrelationships between behavior and body functions. The chapter concludes with a discussion of some implications for the study of socialization to be drawn from ethnographic data and experimental studies of operant conditioning.

ETHNOGRAPHIC REPORTS OF
VOLUNTARY CONTROL OF
REFLEXES

The practitioners of the Indian religious discipline of yoga regularly engage in a series of body exercises requiring voluntary control of some reflexes. These reflexes are believed by most Europeans and Americans to be beyond any kind of voluntary control. For example, in the exercise of diaphragm raising, a yoga practitioner stands nearly erect, knees a little bent, with the upper torso leaning slightly forward, and tries to force all the air from the lungs, then pulls the rib cage up sharply in a simulated inhalation, causing an extremely deep depression of the abdomen, which results in a sharp raising of the entire diaphragm muscle.

In the yoga practice of voluntary vomiting, an individual drinks a half dozen or so full containers of water, bends sharply forward, places hands on knees, and exhales deeply. Then the abdominal muscles are sharply contracted upward and backward and quickly relaxed. These sharp upward contractions and downward relaxations are repeated at a rate of six to ten each minute, until the contents of the stomach are vomited.

Another method of stomach cleansing used in yoga exercises is to swallow a thick piece of heavy cloth, about two to four inches wide and some ten feet in length. After all the cloth is in the stomach, except the end clasped firmly between the teeth, the practitioner engages in the two techniques of diaphragm raising and the sharp abdominal contraction-relaxation, with special attention to voluntary use of the *rectus abdominis* muscles. First the diaphragm is sharply raised. Then the part of the abdomen above the pubic arch is voluntarily pulled downward and forward to expose beneath the surface of the skin the long, flat *rectus abdominis* muscles, extending vertically on either side of the abdomen. These two muscles are manipulated by the yogi through rapid contraction and relaxation, first on the right side, and so on, in a rolling, rhythmic sequence. After about 20 or 30 minutes of such rolling manipulation of the *rectus abdominis* muscles, the diaphragm is relaxed and the cloth is pulled from the stomach.

Physiological studies of the autonomic functions in yoga practitioners have shown a lower rate of respiration, an increase in skin resistance, and no consistent changes in heart rate or blood pressure during their exercises. Electroencephalograms have shown marked change during yoga exercises and meditation on yoga practices.[1]

Voluntary Control of Pain Reflexes

Voluntary control of pain reflexes is widely known and practiced in human cultures. Among the accounts of voluntary control of pain reflexes are the acts of young male Cheyenne Indians during a religious ritual, the Sun Dance (Jorgensen, 1972). Cheyenne boys were taught by adults to believe that self-torture was a special way to achieve the psychological state necessary for access to the supernatural visions sent by the creator to those mastering displays of pain. One principal technique of self-torture prac-

[1]See Wenger, Bagchi, & Anand, 1961; Anand, China, & Singh, 1961; Wenger & Bagchi, 1961.

Cheyenne Sun Dance initiates (circa 1890). (Courtesy American Museum of Natural History.)

Sun Dance ritual (circa 1892), Piegon Reservation, Alberta, Canada. (Courtesy American Museum of Natural History.)

ticed by the Cheyenne during the Sun Dance was to drive small wooden skewers under the skin of the upper back or chest and then to attach the skewers to leather thongs. The skewers were inserted by a Cheyenne *shaman*, a specialist in ritual actions. The young man would be tied up to the top of a high pole to hang for long periods suspended by the thongs attached to the skewers inserted under his skin.

Another example of voluntary control of pain reflexes is to be found in behavior during the initiation rituals for membership in the *Onayanakia* order of the Zuni Indian "Great Fire Fraternity." Stevenson (1904, 495) notes that participants in the Onayanakia initiations regularly walked and stomped in the glowing coals of large fires, then scooped up great handfuls of hot coals to literally bathe themselves in red-hot embers. Stevenson also describes participants placing burning coals in their mouths, holding hot embers in their hands, and engaging in a prolonged rubbing of live coals on the backs of each other and the initiates, all without seeming to show pain responses of any type.[2]

Still another illustration of voluntary control of pain reflexes is to be found in reports of ritual firewalking from the central Pacific islands such as Raiatea and Fiji and from the western Pacific islands such as New Britain. In the act of firewalking, individuals make their way across a surface of irregularly shaped rocks that have been heated to an incandescent glow by burning hardwood logs placed beneath the rock surface. The fire pit usually is eight to ten yards square, but often is smaller. Before the act begins, the surface of the hot rocks is swept clear of burning embers and hot wood cinders. A ritual specialist then conducts a series of prayers, songs, and dances with the onlookers participating. Then the persons participating in the walk move slowly and deliberately across the glowing bed of rock to the opposite side of the fire pit.[3]

Preparation of fire pit, Fiji (1970) (Courtesy Hiram Walker Inc.)

[2]For a contemporary report of Zuni fire handling, see Tedlock, 1973.

[3]For a detailed eyewitness account of personal participation in firewalking by an American surgeon, see Feigen, 1969. Freeman (1976) has described a firewalking ritual in *Kapileswar* Village in the state of Orissa, India, and also notes the drastic consequences of a failure in belief and ritual among these firewalkers (Freeman, 1980).

The ritual acts of firewalking, fire initiation, and pole swinging are closely associated with patterns of religious belief in the cultures where they have occurred. The participants in these rituals are enculturated to believe that an inability to feel pain or to display hurt in special situations that ordinarily would cause great pain and harm places humans in a closer relationship to the powerful supernatural forces controlling their destiny.

Observations of yoga exercises and acts of pain reflex suppression make it clear that these activities are learned and within the physical capability of most adult humans. The fact that most Americans or Europeans do not voluntarily control these reflexes does not mean Indian yoga practitioners, Cheyenne, Zuni, Polynesians, and Melanesians have special human biological features. It means only that it is possible for humans to learn to exercise firm, voluntary control over many reflexes. The fact that one culture does not choose to learn voluntary control of reflexes should not be taken to mean that cultural use of some, or even all, reflexes is beyond possibility for humans.

ETHNOGRAPHIC REPORTS OF VOLUNTARY CONTROL OF DRIVES

The concept of *drive* was described in Chapter 2 as referring to a complex of biological states of an organism and the stimuli motivating it to a given behavior. It was also noted that most scholars studying drives have assumed that some type of body energy lies "behind" spontaneous behavior in organisms. The principal sources of body energy underlying basic drives are said to be derived from activities of an organism directed toward acquisition of metabolic ingredients essential for survival and action. Some essential drives in humans are directed toward (1) acquisition of oxygen, (2) acquisition of water, (3) acquisition of carbohydrates, (4) acquisition of amino acids, (5) acquisition of vitamins and minerals, (6) maintenance of a constant ionic composition of blood, (7) elimination of body wastes, and (8) concentrated periods of sleep and rest.

Some substances required by humans for metabolism may be stored in the body for future use, but a daily average intake of metabolic requirements, discharge of wastes, and sleep are still essential to maintain body functioning and physiological balance. A prolonged deficiency in acquiring foodstuffs, in discharge of wastes, in sleep, and so on, leads to progressive loss of body weight and muscle strength, emaciation, and a general inability to carry on usual activities.

A study of the ethnographic reports of the varied ways the world's people seek to meet their common human metabolic requirements leads to two conclusions: (1) human metabolic requirements can be met in very diverse ways, and (2) where some of the metabolic requirements of a human population cannot be supplied for a period of time, special patterns of cultural behavior will be used to compensate for metabolic needs in the form of a voluntary decrease in or restriction of individual action.[4]

Diverse Ways of Meeting Human Metabolic Requirements

The different ways humans meet their metabolic requirements can be illustrated by some examples from the ethnographic literature concerning the ways hunger and thirst are treated by some of the world's peoples.

The Vedda of Ceylon regularly ate at least five different kinds of quite rotten wood, often garnished with honey, bark, leaves, or varieties of fruits. Among some South American *Guiana* tribes, when their cassava root bread is scarce, greenheart tree seeds are prepared with rotten wood in a bread substitute. There are reports of humans eating small pebbles after a meal. The peasant peoples of Styria, in southeast Austria, are reported to have taken from two to five grains of arsenious acid each day with their food as a "seasoning" to avoid disease.

The practice of eating clay is reported to have taken place among peoples of the Amazon River basin. Schoolboys in Morocco have been reported to regularly eat potter's earth to promote learning in school. Clay eating is a feature of the behavior of pregnant women in some northern Borneo cultures. Children and adults in rural Mississippi are reported to have eaten clay and certain soils to alleviate hunger.

Humans learn to tolerate and prefer putrefied materials to meet the hunger drive. The Dusun of northern Borneo place meat from a variety of animals, including house rats, in sealed bamboo tubes, allow the meats to spoil to liquefaction in the heat of the sun, and then consume it with rice. A sauce used on rice dishes by Vietnamese people is prepared from putrefied materials.

Humans have obtained their metabolic requirements from nearly every possible source of food, including other humans. The Indians of South America eat monkeys, sometimes with hair still on the body, frogs, iguanas, grubs, bees, the larvae of any insect, and head lice. The Shoshone Indians of Utah were reported to have eaten over one hundred kinds of seeds, roots, and nuts. The Dusun of northern Borneo eat snakes, gibbons, anteaters, mice, rats, and a great many different kinds of insects. While *food cannibalism* is based on a great variety of cultural meanings and is a limited practice with unclear origins, it was known among some tribal groups in South America, Melanesia, Africa, and in Meso-America. Human flesh was occasionally sold in aboriginal markets in New Britain. Among tribal peoples in parts of Africa, in a countryside plentiful with wild game,

---

[4]The second conclusion was formulated initially by Gillin (1944).

human flesh was sometimes a part of the diet. It should be noted that food cannibalism among contemporary humans is an uncommon and rarely used means of satisfying the hunger drive.[5]

Because of the limitations of a harsh environment or because of specific cultural choices, some human groups have subsisted on diets restricted almost entirely to animal products. The Eskimo live primarily by consuming meat and fish, rarely eating vegetable products. In contrast, the Bemba of Africa live almost entirely on one type of grain and some vegetables and rarely eat meat.

The kinds of liquids taken by humans in meeting their metabolic requirements vary greatly. Humans slake their thirst with water and animal products, both milk and blood, and with a broad range of vegetable products such as fruit juices, juices from plant stalks and leaves, and cocoa, coffee, and tea. Fermented animal and vegetable products are also used regularly to reduce thirst.

Cultural Patterns and Voluntary
Control of Metabolic Requirements

In humans the hunger drive occurs periodically; however the periodicity of this drive is highly patterned by cultural learning. All cultures practice taking food at least once in 24 hours, with standard intervals of four to five hours between the first and second meals and five to six hours between the second and third meals. In pre–World War II Europe, four meals each 24 hours was a standard procedure in the German and English cultures, while five and six meals were eaten in parts of Scandinavia. Among the Bemba of East Africa it was usual to eat a single meal at varying times each day. The Dusun of northern Borneo eat two meals each day, early each morning and at dusk.

A concentration on a single meal, or two meals, or six meals in 24 hours requires that infants and children be enculturated in ways that will lead them to voluntarily "feel hungry" at the appropriate times. In cultures that eat many meals each day, the enculturation process must focus on children having the hunger drive specifically elicited at regular intervals. In general, in the cultures that eat a single meal each day, such as the Bemba, children are enculturated to a voluntary control of the hunger drive by being permitted light snacks throughout the day. Only as Bemba

---

[5]Harner (1977,1978) has proposed that Aztec cannibalism was the consequence of a thousand years of population growth in the central valley of Mexico and the increase in intense pressures upon domestic plant crops and animals. Since Meso-Americans raised only semidomesticated ducks, turkeys, and hairless dogs, the Aztec peoples, growing more numerous each year, turned to eating the flesh of captives taken in war. Harner notes the Aztec religion and government practices, unlike those of any goverment or religion ever known, turned increasingly to favoring food cannibalism as a source of protein. Harner's views have been questioned by Ortiz de Montellano (1978) and supported by Harris (1980, 420–422). See also Harner, 1980.

children approach adolescence or in time of food shortages are they required to give up the snacks and to concentrate on eating only one daily meal.

Because of regular periods of short food supplies, many cultures have developed patterns of fasting for most adult members, which make a virtue of the necessity of long periods of hunger. As a specific cultural pattern for voluntarily delaying or displacing the hunger drive, fasting rarely lasts longer than three days. In some cultures, such as the Papago Indians of Arizona, the usual adult pattern of fasting at times of short supplies of food was also practiced in a purification ritual for warriors returning after battle. If a Papago warrior had taken an enemy life in battle, he usually fasted for a period of 16 full days, drinking only water in which a handful of corn had been allowed to soak.

Humans have used many substances that in moderate amounts diminish sensibility, relieve pain, and produce lassitude, stupor, or sleep as an aid in voluntarily delaying the meeting of their metabolic requirements. For example, Indian porters of the South American Andean Mountains have been accustomed to chewing coca leaves instead of eating when walking over the mountains with heavy burdens. The cocaine in the coca leaves tends to inhibit hunger and fatigue.[6]

Some peoples afflicted with chronic, long-term food shortages have used cultural patterns to voluntarily reduce their regular total daily caloric intake well below the levels necessary for human survival. For example, the Bemba of Africa live in an area with barren soils, and uncertain seasonal rainfall where the animals and people are subject to regular attacks of severe diseases. The Bemba grow "finger" millet and have no cattle because of the presence of the tsetse fly. Millet is grown on an 8 to 13 acre field cleared of low trees and shrubs by a hand axe and prepared with a simple hoe. A Bemba meal consists of millet porridge "eased" down by a vegetable relish and, on very rare occasions, meat and fish. In the Bemba language the word *nbwali* stands for the millet porridge. This word occurs repeatedly in proverbs, folk tales, puns, jokes, folk songs, and riddles and is a one-word surrogate for many ordinary daily affairs. In this respect, *nbwali* is somewhat comparable to the word *bread* in English, as in the expressions, "Give us this day our daily bread," "Earning our bread and butter," and so on. A Bemba will say, "How can a man refuse to help his mother's brother who has given him *nbwali* all these years?"

In Bemba ritual and ceremony, *nbwali* stands for *life* and *health*. In this way the term plays an important part in tribal political actions, in female initiation, marriage ceremonies, in kinship relations, and is not spoken by

---

[6]For a review of the ways humans use plant products to allay hunger and fatigue and to induce trance behavior, see Schultes, 1969.

those who feel possessed by evil spirits. Thus the Bemba concentration on a single food runs as a theme throughout their culture.

Bemba rarely produce enough of a millet crop to last the entire year. The last three months of the year are termed by Bemba as the "hunger months." When millet becomes scarce the whole community life slows in pace and is affected. Adults reduce their meals, and millet beer is no longer brewed. Children eat only one small meal late each day and are allowed none of the frequent snacks they have been given in the other months of the year. Most Bemba experience times of severe hunger when they must go two or three days without eating. Then the people stay in their huts, where they take large amounts of water and inhale snuff to reduce their hunger.

Systematic samples of individual Bemba diets show that the number of calories eaten each day averaged 1706 per adult male, compared to an average of approximately 3000 calories for adult male Americans and Europeans. The average adult Bemba male daily caloric intake in one typical year was from a low of no calories through 286 calories to a high of 3164 calories. The Bemba live consistently at a subsistence intake of calories well below that felt to be adequate for human health, normal activity, and attainment of an ordinary life span.[7]

When a Bemba village or family obtains an unexpected supply of meat, it is an occasion for suspension of the ordinary rules and courtesies of eating; everyone gorges until all the meat has been eaten. At such times Bemba life is described as characterized by intense excitement, with adults and children singing and dancing in spontaneous ways not seen in ordinary Bemba activities, because the oppressing fear of constant hunger has been temporarily lifted from them.

Thus facing a chronic shortage of food, the Bemba have developed a set of culturally patterned behaviors, beliefs, and values that serve to focus their attention on voluntary control of hunger.

CULTURAL STRUCTURING OF SOME OTHER HUMAN BIOLOGICAL FEATURES

In addition to reflexes and drives, there are some other aspects of human biology that appear to be subjected to cultural shaping, particularly in the forms of individual voluntary control, release, and use. For example, the consistency of human feces appears to vary widely among cultures, even

---

[7]Tolley (1948) has concluded that the average daily caloric intake over a year or longer cannot fall below 2000 calories if a population is to survive.

in instances where diets are similar. Mead (1956, 610) reports that the degree of constipation or looseness of the bowels is subject to specific cultural structuring among Iatmul of New Guinea and among the Manus of the Admiralty Islands. The Iatmul spend a great deal of time teaching their children not to step in human or animal feces but otherwise follow relaxed enculturation practices with regard to sexual activity or training schedules of feeding, weaning, independence, or aggression. Mead notes that the Iatmul have loose and frequent stools. The Manus people, living as the Iatmul do on sago, fish, and yams, spend a great deal of time training children to be sexually prudish and are rigid in their enculturation schedules for feeding, weaning, independence, and aggression. Mead notes that Manus adults have hard, formed stools and defecate once a day at approximately the same time.

Mead concludes from these data and studies of American and European adults that the degree of constipation or looseness of feces is subject to cultural standardization in an enculturation process—that is, it is possible for a general somatic alteration to be taught to every person born into a culture, as in the case of the Iatmul or Manus, where the process, once begun, may be irreversible for the individuals involved.

Circumstances that produce individual nausea and vomiting are also highly structured culturally. In some cultures vomiting is a feared behavior, and the ordinary reaction of extreme disgust is defecation. Mead reports that the Arapesh of New Guinea pattern eating in such a way that throughout the enculturation process strong ties are stressed between the eaters and what remains after they have eaten, while the social relations between parents and children, husband and wife, elders and youth are conceived specifically in terms of which person is responsible for feeding the other person. Thus vomiting is considered as a violation of proper social relations between individuals. In this cultural setting the Arapesh view defecation as the "proper" and "acceptable" reaction to extremely upsetting or nauseous situations.

A heavy flow of saliva is not always associated with food, as it is in American and European cultures. Fijian men report that they experience a very heavy flow of saliva at the sight of a beautiful woman.[8]

Cannon (1936, 1942) has noted that individuals can become convinced that they are a victim of witchcraft to the point where they experience such severe disturbances of body functioning that they die. Many irregularities in circulatory and respiratory functions are said to be the results of cultural beliefs concerning magic. Thus the idea of "magical fright," which is known

---

[8]See Quain, 1948, 332.

widely in Middle American cultures, is said to cause severe irregularities in pulse functions.[9]

Other vascular responses are also culturally patterned. For instance, blushing, a peripheral vascular response, tends to be essentially a facial response among most Europeans and Americans. There are ethnographic reports that, when extremely discomforted socially or caught up in a situation that is culturally defined as "embarrassing," many of the world's peoples do not blush on the face. Rather, the peripheral vascular system response to such social and personal situations is exhibited on other body parts, such as the surface of the chest, the upper arms, or the thighs.

Fatigue is another aspect of human biology that is highly culturally structured. Human definitions of and responses to fatigue are quite culturally variable.[10]

The way individuals gesture, walk, stand, sit, and move in specific social situations also varies greatly among cultures. Mead (Mead & MacGregor, 1951) has observed the enculturation of motor patterns among Balinese children. She finds that, compared to American children, Balinese children are taught to emphasize the outward rotation and extension of the little finger sides of their hands rather than the inward rotation and closure of the thumb and forefinger sides of the hands, as is typical in American enculturation of children. Balinese children are also enculturated to have a type of "meandering" body posture, in which some limbs or parts are relaxed and flexible while other parts are flexed or tense. Balinese children are also taught to move smoothly from a posture of complete relaxation to one of great tension. In contrast, American children are enculturated to sit or stand with all body parts in the same degree of tension-relaxation and to move from one extreme (relaxation) to the other (tension) through well-defined body sequences.[11]

It has also been noted that certain aspects of human reproductive physiology are culturally structured, particularly where cultures have developed patterns of ceremonial continence, celibacy, and activities that increase or decrease male and female fertility.[12]

---

[9]Johnson and Herron (1973) note that in the U.S. there are more than 400,000 sudden deaths each year from heart attacks suffered by persons in the prime of life and known to be in good health, with no history of heart disease. One hypothesis used by a number of investigators to explain such deaths is that "psychological variables" contribute to creation of heart rhythms that can be suddenly fatal. A technical account and references to current research on sudden cardiac death can be found in Braunwald, 1980, 800–802, 1924–1925. See also Garfield, 1979; Scherlis, 1976; Friedman, 1977; Gillin, 1948, 1951.

[10]For some examples of cultural patterning of fatigue, see Mead, 1946, 676; Benedict, 1946, 180–181, 230, 257, 268.

[11]See Mead & MacGregor, 1951.

[12]See Ford & Beach, 1951; Coon, 1950.

Cultural concepts of numbers, time, and sequence are also imposed on particular features of human biology. Mead notes the frequent relationship between the sacred or magical number of a culture and the day on which a baby's umbilical cord falls off. In Bali, where the mother is in a special state of ritual isolation for three days, the cord tends to fall off in three days. Among the Iatmul of New Guinea, where five is the magical number, the cord tends to fall off in five days.

There is also a cultural structuring of biology in different societies with regard to the time involved in the healing of wounds. In the hot, tropical climate of New Guinea and Indonesia, the problem in wound healing is to close the wound. Mead (1956) points out that among the Iatmul wounds close slowly, even with medical attention.

The Iatmul manifest very little concern with most wounds. However Mead notes that, in Bali, where there is a great fear of any injury to the surface perfection of the body, wounds heal very rapidly. Balinese insist on keeping the smallest cuts open for several days with continuous applications of wet dressings to avoid the tendency of a wound to heal and then to fester under the scab. Balinese wounds apparently tend to heal more rapidly even when dressings are not used. In the United States most wounds, even those surgically induced, are supposed to take from 7 to 14 days to heal. In fact, wounds do tend to heal within this period.

A THEORY FOR
UNDERSTANDING THE
SOCIALIZATION PROCESS

The discussion so far in this chapter has proposed that there are specific relationships between various features of human biology, such as reflexes and drives, and particular cultural features. The theory of socialization upon which these suggestions have been based has not been discussed. A brief statement of this theory should help clarify some of the questions that have been raised.

What has been said to this point is derived from the following theoretical paradigm:

1. The preoccupations of adults in a society, which are cultural preoccupations, result in children becoming similarly preoccupied, through time, as a function of their various responses to adult pressures to conform, their own physiological processes, and use of their reflective, symbolic, and cognitive capacities.
2. In turn, the derived preoccupations of children help to shape adult attitudes and values concerning their own preoccupations.
3. Therefore the form of the socialization process in any particular culture represents a historically developed working arrangement between a local

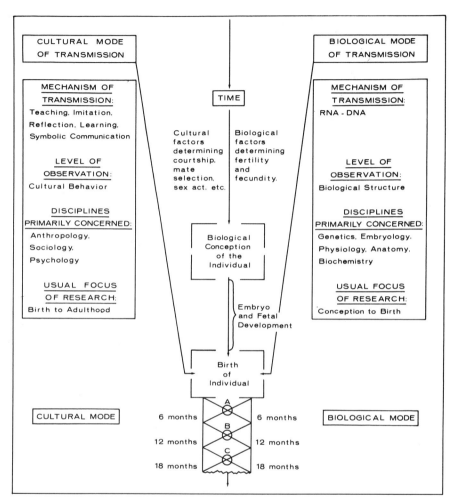

CULTURAL MODE OF TRANSMISSION		BIOLOGICAL MODE OF TRANSMISSION
MECHANISM OF TRANSMISSION: Teaching, Imitation, Reflection, Learning, Symbolic Communication	TIME	MECHANISM OF TRANSMISSION: RNA - DNA
	Cultural factors determining courtship, mate selection, sex act. etc.	Biological factors determining fertility and fecundity.	
LEVEL OF OBSERVATION: Cultural Behavior		LEVEL OF OBSERVATION: Biological Structure
DISCIPLINES PRIMARILY CONCERNED: Anthropology, Sociology, Psychology	Biological Conception of the Individual	DISCIPLINES PRIMARILY CONCERNED: Genetics, Embryology, Physiology, Anatomy, Biochemistry
USUAL FOCUS OF RESEARCH: Birth to Adulthood	Embryo and Fetal Development	USUAL FOCUS OF RESEARCH: Conception to Birth
	Birth of Individual	
CULTURAL MODE	6 months ⊗ A ⊗ B ⊗ C 6 months	BIOLOGICAL MODE
	12 months 12 months	
	18 months 18 months	

FIGURE 4–1 Biological and cultural modes of transmission in the socialization process. (After Davis, K. 1949. *Human Society*. New York: The Macmillan Co.)

cultural tradition, which provides for the preoccupations of adults, and the concerns and behavior of maturing infants and children.[13]

Some brief specific examples of this *doubly contingent,* or *transactional,* theoretical socialization paradigm might be helpful. In the Arapesh culture of the Admiralty Islands of the Southwest Pacific, parental preoccupation with the intake of food eventually results in a child's preoccupation with food intake, which is a function of the Arapesh child's response to parental pressures and their own physiological functions. As an Arapesh child dem-

[13]This summary of theory proceeds from one first presented by Mead (1956, 610).

onstrates a derivative preoccupation with intake of food, they in turn shape their parent's cultural preoccupation with the intake of food. The further and later training given to an Arapesh child in bowel and bladder sphincter control depends on the prior training given them in regard to eating, on the child's responses to that previous training, and on the parent's responses to those responses by the child. Arapesh children's sphincter training is also dependent upon cultural behavior forms that are standard for stages of life not yet reached by a child. A parent's training of Arapesh child with regard to sphincter control reflects not only the prior training for food intake but also the Arapesh cultural belief that dying old people must attempt to control their body functions and still drag themselves to the edge of the village to defecate. Thus Arapesh children have their biology culturally shaped and directed through responses to them by their parents and through their parents' responses to their responses. The Arapesh parents also apply consistently to the children, by evaluating the children's responses to their concerns, cultural definitions appropriate for behavior at stages of life not yet reached by a child. This theoretical paradigm is illustrated in its major outlines in Figure 4–2.

Adult preoccupations become the preoccupations of children; Tambunan Dusun (Sensuron) female ritual specialists entering into trance state on behalf of child at right. (T.R. Williams, 1959.)

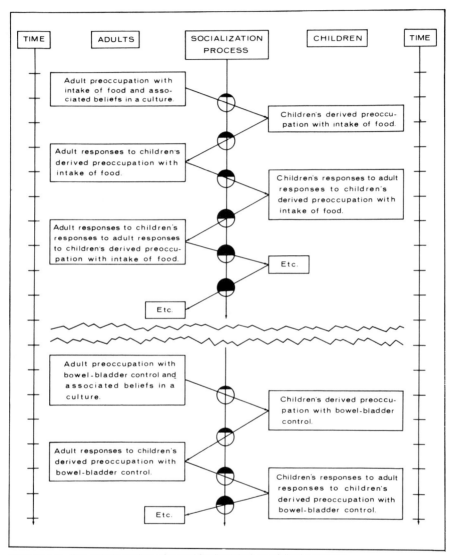

FIGURE 4–2 Theoretical paradigm of mutual feedback in the socialization process.

In this theoretical model for the socialization process, culture is viewed not as a set of external events, or stimuli, to which the individual is subjected without protection or recourse but as one of two primary facts in the development of the individual (the other primary fact is human biology). Culture thus results in a child having, as an adult, a biological structure, a kind of biological functioning and a set of behavioral attributes very different from individuals who have been enculturated in another cultural tradition.

In this theory, immersion in a culture through regular social contacts with other individuals who have been immersed in a similar way develops in the growing human organism a large number of specific biological and behavioral tendencies and abilities that become increasingly more irreversible.

For example, Samoans are enculturated from their birth to sit on the floor. As adults, Samoans sit cross-legged for hours without fatigue. At the same time Samoans learn to sit on the floor, they also learn a whole group of cultural behavior forms and values directly related to this sitting position. A Samoan must learn that it is rude to talk while standing up. They must learn that, before they use either or both hands in accepting a cup, they must pay attention to the relative distances at which their fellows on their right and left are seated. They must learn that their back is considered outside the formal circle of social intercourse as they sit on the floor, so they can wipe food from their hands on their back, or on the back of their head, or on the house-post on which they lean but that they must never wipe food on their front to avoid giving grave social offense. A Samoan must learn that the person who stands up when another person is seated is one of higher social rank. They must learn that they must bow low if they pass before a seated person of equal or higher rank. All of these complex behavioral patterns are in turn directly related to a whole system of social status-role behavior. If we ask an adult Samoan to sit on a chair at a social occasion, we ask much more of him than merely to sit in a different position. In revising their basic posture orientation, from floor to chair, a Samoan is disturbing the whole of their usual personal perceptions in social relations. They become truly disoriented, for they are asked to "feel" and to perceive in ways that a previous lifetime of experience has not prepared them for. And a Samoan's disorientation in this situation will be quite different from that experienced by members of another culture to whom sitting has quite different cultural significance.[14]

Although adult Samoans may learn to deal with Americans or Europeans, they will react essentially in terms of being Samoan—that is, by "feeling" about and "perceiving" social situations with the integrated sum of both their biology and their cultural beliefs and values. Adult Samoans may learn to adapt to a new culture, but they will do so by confronting the new culture situation in terms of this "Samoan-ness," which has been de-

[14]This example is written in the "ethnographic present" to provide understanding of relationships between culture and biology in the process of socialization. Samoans use chairs today without any sense of disorientation, unless they have been enculturated following traditional Samoan ways.

veloped in them from a complex, lifelong interplay between their individual biology and their Samoan culture. As adults they will not, and in fact cannot, fully discard their "Samoan-ness" when confronting a new culture. They will attack the problems involved in culture contact by use of their essential "Samoan-ness." Because of this, adult Samoans regularly facing a situation of contact with another culture will display very many regularities and uniformities in their responses to the new culture.

The Appearance of Abilities

When phrases such as *voluntary control, voluntary meeting, voluntarily,* and so on were used earlier in this chapter, they were not meant in the everyday sense of conscious, willful, or deliberate. Rather, these terms were used in the conceptual sense that it is through the complex and reciprocal interplay of human biology and culture over the long time of socialization that an individual comes as an adult to be possessed of an *ability* that has been developed uniquely out of the socialization process. This *ability* (and not a *capacity*) might be defined as the way adult individuals in any culture can, through time, generate out of the complexly interrelated biological and cultural materials available to them, specific ways of altering, shaping, or directing the internal and physiological, as well as the external and social, events directly affecting them.

Figure 4–3 illustrates the way in which culture and human biology mutually and reciprocally interact through time in a socialization process to produce the *ability* of adults to voluntarily deal with basic aspects of their biology, such as reflexes and drives. The open circle (A) at the point of intersection of the arrows from *culture to biology* and *biology to culture* represents the place at which a specific human ability, present at birth *neither* in human genetic materials nor in culture, can appear in the human process of socialization. After about six months of life (B), the open circle has some shading, representing the beginnings of a particular ability as the consequence of the reciprocal interplay between culture and human biology in the socialization process. If a culture emphasizes a particular ability, the circles at each successive intersect between culture and biology will become more shaded (C to F).

This conceptual way of considering a human ability developing from the mutual and reciprocal feedback between biology and culture in a socialization process underlies the discussion in the earlier part of this chapter. It is important to remember that this chapter has focused on only one of the several abilities humans can develop in a socialization process—that is, an ability to voluntarily control specific features of their biology. Humans have the *potential* for developing many different kinds of abilities through the socialization process. For example, in addition to the *ability* for voluntary

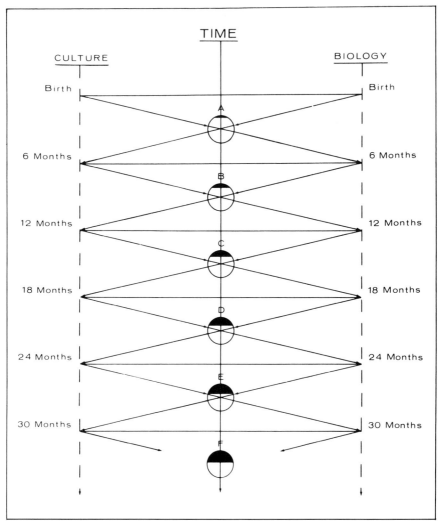

FIGURE 4–3 The emergence of human abilities through the interplay of culture and biology in the socialization process.

control of features of their biology, *Homo sapiens sapiens* can develop abilities to be highly creative intellectually and artistically, to become culturally innovative, to be penetrating and efficiently perceptive in social relations, to be highly independent of the other persons in a society, to be and remain nonaggressive, and so on.

Whether individuals in a society possess any of these particular abilities appears to depend upon whether the conditions of reciprocal interplay between culture and human biology are maintained throughout a particular enculturation process. Whether certain abilities are developed also depends on the priorities set within a culture for the stimulation of and provision for some abilities as compared to others. For example, it seems that in American culture we have chosen to give a relatively low priority to development of an ability to voluntarily control most features of biology in favor of an emphasis on abilities that are ranked more highly, such as intellectual creativity in technological and managerial behavior. In this theoretical sense many Americans are enculturated in such a manner as to ensure the development of some kinds of abilities rather than some others. But then, so are yoga practitioners, Cheyenne Sun Dancers, and Polynesian firewalkers.

In considering how a people come to have voluntary control over some features of their biology, it is vital to recall that *voluntary* should not connote yoga novices standing with their eyes tightly closed while trying very hard to make their exercises in diaphragm raising successful; rather, we should recall that yoga novices are Indians who have been raised to adulthood in a specific Hindu cultural context in which year upon year of mutual, reciprocal feedback between culture and human biology constantly prepares a man to become a yogi if he so chooses by developing consistently over a long time a set of circumstances that favor appearance of the *ability* to voluntarily control certain features of human biology. Thus wherever voluntary control of features of human biology occurs, it does so because the enculturation process in a society provides for the conditions for a human ability to do so.[15]

The theoretical distinction between a human capacity (see Chapter 2) and a human ability essentially lies in the fact that a *capacity* appears to be a genetically transmitted "organic bridgehead" already possessed by humans at birth, whereas *abililties* appear to be developed out of the mutual feedback process between culture and biology through the long period of socialization. Human capacities seem related to human abilities in very complex ways, which at present are understood only vaguely. It appears that, if the basic human capacities for reflection and for symboling are impaired, deficient, or incapable of being expressed because of disease or accident, then there will be no real emergence from the socialization process of an ability for voluntary control over features of biology. However if the capacities for reflection and symboling are not impaired in any way and if the socialization process as expressed in the enculturation practices of a particular society provides for the emergence of the ability for voluntary control of features of biology, then humans in that situation will be able,

---

[15]Byers (1972) discusses the transition from "biological rhythm to cultural pattern," while Condon and Sander (1974) describe the ways one-to-two-day-old human infants move in unison with the speech patterns of a caretaking adult. For discussions of acquisition of human skills (abilities), see Bilodeau, (1966), and Barber, 1974.

through use of their reflective and symboling capacities, to learn such voluntary controls of biology as may be specified in a culture.

This theoretical point is very important in understanding the discussion in this chapter because it is quite apparent now that there may be a wide range of possible human abilities, when used in conjunction with human capacities, which can lead to new dimensions of human experience, including significant voluntary control of human biological features.

EXPERIMENTS IN OPERANT CONDITIONING

In the past three decades experimental psychologists have developed a method of learning research that has been termed *operant conditioning*. The basic studies of operant conditioning were undertaken by Skinner.[16] In considering the Thorndike-Hull learning model, Skinner noted that the law of effect, which specifies that the response of an organism to a stimulus is automatically strengthened if it is followed by a *reward* and automatically extinguished if followed by a *punishment*, involves a simple time relationship between a response and a consequence. Skinner used the term *operant* to describe the time relationship between response and consequence.

Skinner Boxes

In his efforts to study the time relationship factor in learning, Skinner developed a soundproof box containing a lever that could be pressed by the animal used in the experiment. Lever pressing by the subject, whether accidental or purposeful, delivered a reward in the form of food. If the subject, such as a rat or a pigeon, is placed in the Skinner box, it will not seek out the lever initially and depress it. However when the subject accidentally depresses the lever, it will receive a reward, usually food. Each time the subject presses the lever, it receives a reward. As the subject repeatedly depresses the lever without the interference or influence of the experimenter, it receives further rewards and is said to condition itself "operantly."

Measures of Behavior

The typical measure of behavior made in Skinner box is the *rate* of lever pressing, that is, the number of times in a given period the subject depressed the lever to receive a reward. Automatic response-recording

---

[16]See Skinner, 1938; see also Skinner 1948, 1953, 1957, 1969, 1972; Skinner & Ferster, 1957; Skinner & Holland, 1961; Evans, 1968.

devices have been attached to the experimental box so that a continuous graph recording of the number and rate of lever depressions can be made, even in the absence of the experimenter. The recording device moves a pen across paper at a constant speed. Each time the experimental subject depresses the lever, the recording pen moves higher on the paper; if no responses are made by the subject, the pen traces a horizontal line. As the subject makes increasingly more responses more quickly, the pen line will ascend on the paper in a way that shows the experimenter, by the steepness of the ascending line, not only how many times the lever was depressed but also how rapidly the lever was depressed.

Schedules of Reinforcement

In training animals in this type of experimental device, Skinner and other psychologists have used different *schedules of reinforcement*—that is, they have varied the number of times an animal was rewarded for pressing the box lever. A schedule of reinforcement asks the question, "What happens if, rather than rewarding the subject every time it pressed the lever, it is reinforced (rewarded) for only some of its responses?"

Experimental psychologists use four main types of schedules of reinforcement to seek answers to this question: (1) fixed ratio schedules, (2) variable ratio schedules, (3) fixed interval schedules, and (4) variable interval schedules. A fixed ratio schedule of reinforcement involves a response (lever pressing) being reinforced (rewarded) after a fixed number of unrewarded responses counted from the last rewarded response. A variable ratio schedule of reinforcement is similar to the fixed ratio schedule, except that reinforcements are scheduled randomly and arbitrarily. A fixed interval schedule of reinforcement involves the reward of the first response which occurs after a specific length of time, measured from the last rewarded response. Variable interval schedules of reinforcement are similar to the fixed interval schedules except that reinforcements are scheduled for random and arbitrary intervals of time.

Partial Reinforcement Effect

In varying the ways experimental animals were rewarded for lever pressing, Skinner and other psychologists discovered that animals rewarded only part of the time appear to build up a greater operant strength—that is, are more resistant to loss of the rewarded behavior (lever pressing)— than were the animals rewarded each time they pressed the lever. This learning result has been called the *partial reinforcement effect* (PRE). Skinner made no attempt to explain why partial reinforcement schedules affect experimental subjects so they appear more resistant to loss of the rewarded behavior than animals continually rewarded. He simply reported these data and left interpretations of the PRE phenomenon to others. Skinner's concern in his research has been in using what he considers the only two reliable and basic measures of behavior: (1) the rate of responding and (2) the number of responses made by a subject after all rewards available to it have been stopped.

However many other experimental psychologists have tried to explain PRE learning. One reason for a wide interest in this particular fact of operant learning is that outside the psychological laboratory, in the human world, most rewards seem to be provided by adults to maturing infants and children in an intermittent manner, very much like the variable interval schedules of reinforcement used in operant experimental studies. Adult responses to children are seldom precisely consistent in form each time they occur and may not always involve the same "reward." The PRE formulation seems to be an adequate explanation for humans learning culture. This is, of course, a conception of human learning that views children acquiring culture because adults do something to them. However the discussion of Papago enculturation in Chapter 3 shows that in some cultures rewards and punishments for behavior are administered by children to themselves more often than by adults. Thus the socialization process is vastly more complex than can be explained by PRE. A large number of human operant learning studies have been conducted in the past 30 years, many of which have focused on infants and young children as experimental subjects. A large number of studies of human operant learning have also been conducted to discover whether human physiological functioning can be permanently influenced or altered.

Human Operant Conditioning

Studies of operant learning by infants and children are of two kinds: (1) activities involving bar pressing, knob pulling, window pressing, and box opening; (2) activities involving behavior patterns such as thumb sucking, verbalizing and vocalizing, stuttering, and smiling.[17] Operant research involving the first type of activities typically uses Skinner box devices. In laboratory studies with infants, Rheingold, Stanley, and Cooley (1962) employed an experimental "crib" similar to the one illustrated in Figure 4–4, I. Many operant learning research projects using preschool and school-age children have used operant devices similar to the one developed by Bijou (1957) (Figure 4–4, II) or the one developed by Gewirtz and Baer (1958) (Figure 4–4, III).

---

[17]For reviews of such research, see Bijou & Baer, 1966; Honig, 1966; Catania, 1968; Reynolds, 1975; Leitenberg, 1976.

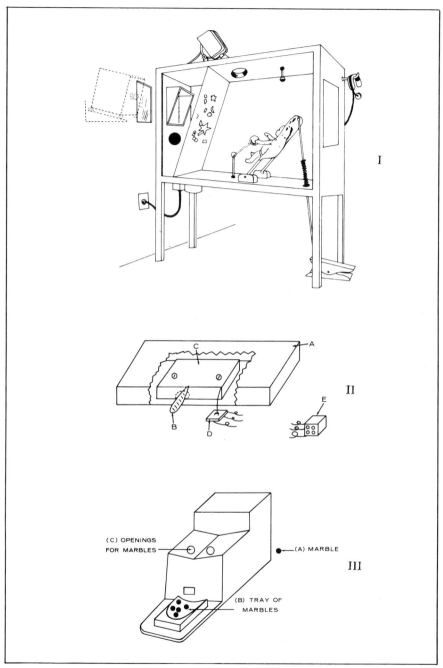

FIGURE 4–4 I, Experimental crib used in operant studies of infants. II, Operant conditioning device used in studies of preschool children. *A.* Cover box; *B,* handle of lever; *C,* modified sponge mop assembly; *D,* switch for recording electrical contact; *E,* recording device. III, Operant conditioning device used in studies of school-age children.

In operant learning studies using experimental cribs, infant subjects are seated in a special chair, so that they are partially reclining. They face a screen on which brightly colored, moving images are projected for an instant, if they reach out with either hand and merely touch a ball mounted on an upright lever and placed within their reach. The ball lever may be made into the antenna of an oscillator circuit serving as a sensitive relay to automatically show the number of operant responses of the infant over a given period.

In studies using lever-pressing-type devices, preschool and school-age children have been given the opportunity to use a lever as they choose to do so, with rewards such as a movie or music being presented to the child as long as they keep the lever either depressed or lifted, depending on the act to be rewarded in experimental situations. In a somewhat more complex type of study of operant conditioning, preschool and school-age children sit before a device with two holes in its top surface and an opening at the base of the front. When the child takes marbles from the tray under the opening in the base and drops them through the two openings in the top of the device, they drop a series of internal switches that record the response and control the dispensing of the reward (food, music, pictures, and so on).

In studies of operant conditioning of thumb-sucking behavior, rewards presented to preschool and school-age children are withdrawn when they suck their thumbs. Children are exposed to long sessions of sound movie cartoons. At the times they suck their thumbs, the movies are shut off. When the children take their thumbs from their mouths, the movies continue. The rate and time response of the children in this situation are "judged" by observers screened behind one-way glass. When a child sucks a thumb, the judges each depress a recording device and hold it as long as thumb sucking continues. This procedure of operant conditioning, which punishes thumb sucking and rewards thumb removal, is said to have yielded increasingly greater depression of thumb-sucking rates and times after three experimental sessions spaced a few days apart.[18]

The verbal and vocal behavior responses of infants have been studied using modifications of the operant conditioning techniques just described. These studies involved observing and recording the discrete sounds of infants, ignoring their coughs, whistles, squeaks, and noisy breathing snorts. Little note was taken during the studies of the phonetic characteristics of infant sounds. In one early study of this type, the observation time used was a set of three 3-minute periods, three times a day for two days. This served as a baseline for the study. During the first two days of the research, the experimenter stood motionless over the crib of the infant being observed, while an associate stood away from the crib, out of the infant's sight, recording vocalizations by the baby. In the next two days of the study,

[18]See Baer, 1962a.

vocalizations were rewarded by a smile from the observer who was standing over the crib, by use of the sounds *tsk, tsk, tsk,* and by a light touch administered to the baby's abdomen. In the final two days of the study, the same procedures used in the first two days were repeated. This particular study reported that during the two days the observer rewarded vocalizations the rate of the baby's vocalizations nearly doubled that recorded in the study baseline rate. Furthermore the study reported the rate of vocalization by the infants studied dropped back during the last two-day period almost to the baseline rate. This particular operant conditioning experiment was repeated with some minor changes in procedures, and the results reported were similar to those of the first study.[19]

More complex studies of operant conditioning of vocalization and verbal behavior have been undertaken with older children. These studies have sought in various ways to "shape" or "control" the use of children's speech through operant procedures—that is, rewarding successively closer approximations to the desired speech response until the subjects learned to verbalize the precise way desired by the experimenters.[20]

It has been concluded from studies of stuttering in children that it is possible to "weaken," or lessen, hesitant speech patterns by means of operant learning procedures. In one well-known study children wearing earphones in an isolated setting were presented a 6000-cycle tone at an intensity of 105 decibels.[21] To provide for an ongoing operant level of speech during the experiment, children read aloud from materials considered by the experimenters to be easy and interesting for their particular age levels. If a child exhibited any hesitation, stoppage, repetition, or prolongation in speech as they read, the experimenters judged it to be stuttering behavior. Children were operantly conditioned through schedules of *avoidance* and *escape.* In *avoidance* conditioning the 105-decibel tone was continuously present and five-second termination was dependent upon a child's stuttering. In *escape* conditioning a one-second blast of the 105-decibel tone was presented through the child's earphones following each stuttering response. The results of this research showed that the presentation of the tone as a consequence of stuttering weakened the stuttering speech pattern and that halting the tone when the child stuttered strengthened or led to an increase in stuttering speech.

Efforts have been made to operantly condition smiling behavior in infants. In one well-known study four-month-old infants were observed over eight separate, five-minute intervals, during which the experimenter stood motionless over a baby's crib, holding her expressionless face about

---

[19]See Rheingold, Gewirtz, & Ross, 1959.
[20]See Lovaas, 1961; Baer, 1962b.
[21]See Flanagan, Goldiamond, & Azrin, 1958.

15 inches from the infant's face.[22] The rate of each infant's smiling was noted during these eight session. Then in operant conditioning sessions that consisted of from ten to twelve 5-minute sessions the experimenter rewarded smiling by the infant by smiling in return and also by cuddling the baby. The rate of smiling was counted during these periods. During a later set of observations comprising fifteen 15-minute periods, the experimenter, using the same research procedure as in the first set of observations (standing over the crib with an expressionless face), counted the number of smiling responses by the infant subjects. The study concluded that the rate of smiling during the *conditioning period* (when the experimenter smiled back and cuddled the infant) was considerably higher than the rate during the *operant period* (the first time the experimenter stood motionless over the infant and counted smiling responses). The rate of smiling in the *extinction period* (the second time the experimenter stood motionless over the infant and counted smiling responses) was lower than during either the operant (the first) or the conditioning (the second) period.

Respondent Conditioning Studies

The term *respondent* was used by Skinner during the time he was defining the concept of operant conditioning. A *respondent* is an unlearned reaction to a specific stimulus, or an unconditioned response to an unconditioned stimulus. The contraction of the pupil of the eye in bright light and the galvanic skin reaction to electric shock are examples of respondents. Pavlov's learning experiments (see Chapter 3) were concerned with respondent conditioning. In contrast, *operants* are said by Skinner to be responses on the part of an organism that occur because of, but are not elicited by, known stimuli. Hence *respondents* and *operants* are the conceptual opposites of one another.

Pavlov reported as early as 1879 that changes in heart and blood system functioning were related to his conditioning of dogs. He noted that as dogs were trained to salivate at the presentation of stimuli such as tones and lights rather than at the taste or sight of food the *conditioning* process also produced clear physiological changes in the dogs. Pavlov did not concern himself with this question in later studies; however Pavlov's observations led other persons to investigate the physiological changes accompanying *respondent conditioning*. In the past half century many studies have been conducted on this subject which have produced a large body of knowledge and contributed substantially to understanding the process of learning.

[22]See Brackbill,1958.

Physiological Changes and Operant Conditioning

After 1950 interest in psychology grew in studying any physiological changes that accompany the operant conditioning process. This interest stemmed in part from the growth of new experimental devices which made possible a more carefully controlled situation for observing and measuring such physiological changes. Because the ideas involved were incomplete and respondent research had a long tradition, operant conditioning studies of physiological changes at first tended to concentrate on short-lived respiratory and cardiovascular responses to operant experimentation with laboratory animals. Then operant conditioning studies began to focus on longer lasting physiological changes in experimental animals involving the endocrine system, the gastrointestinal system, and infectious disease processes. Recent studies of operant conditioning of physiological states have concentrated on seeking durable physiological changes in the cardiovascular system and in brain functions in laboratory animals.[23]

Research on operant conditioning of physiological states in laboratory animals has produced various results. For example, when rats were confined on a small perch and had to move their heads to lift a panel to avoid a bright light being flashed directly into their eyes, their respiration rate increased greatly during the conditioning periods and decreased to normal during the extinction periods.[24] When cats were subjected to intermittent punishment by blasts of air and electric shock during feeding and had to press levers or lift lids to avoid the punishments, they exhibited elevations in blood pressure and a decline in a blood plasma substance termed *pepsinogen* during the conditioning periods.[25]

In another set of experiments rats had electrodes implanted in different areas of their brains so that when they pressed a lever they administered a low-voltage discharge to a part of the brain. This research showed that the self-administered electrical stimulations during a conditioning period produced significant changes in rat heart rates when the electrodes were placed in particular parts of the brain such as the hypothalamic region. The research also found that when electrodes were implanted in another part of the rat brain (septal area) the heart rate was significantly decreased during the conditioning period.[26]

[23]Brady (1966) has provided a review and discussion of much of this research until 1965. See also Honig, 1966; Catania, 1968; Reynolds, 1975; Leitenberg, 1976. For reviews of this literature from 1965 through 1975, see also Mastofsky, 1975. See also the issues of *Biofeedback and Self-Regulation*, Vol. 1 (1976) to Vol. 5 (1980).

[24]See Eldridge, 1954.

[25]See Shapiro & Horn. 1955.

[26]See Malmo, 1961; Perez-Cruet, Tolliver, Dunn, Marvin, & Brady, 1963.

Similar research demonstrated that there are changes in animal brain wave patterns in operant learning situations. For example, monkeys were prepared for research by surgical implantation of electrodes deep into their brains. During experimental periods they were restrained in special chairs; the electrodes were attached to special brain wave recording instruments. Then the monkeys were subjected to several different operant conditioning procedures, including lever pressing to obtain sugar pellets or to avoid a mild electric shock punishment. Through the course of the conditioning periods, marked changes were noted in brain wave activity patterns of the monkeys. In the extinction periods of research, these changes were no longer noted.[27]

More durable physiological changes, as the consequences of operant conditioning, have been reported from a large number of recent experimental studies. In one well-known study, rats were operantly trained to lick fluid from the end of a tube in order to avoid electric shocks to their feet. Each lick postponed the shock for 15 seconds. Rats could avoid all shocks by licking the tube each 15 seconds. These animals were subjected to this procedure in alternating one-hour periods (one of conditioning, one of rest), 24 hours a day for 20 days. In this time the subjects consumed twice their normal intake of fluids and almost doubled their body weights. These rats did not lose weight or body fluids in the period of extinction.[28]

A broad range of hormonal changes have also been reported in operant conditioning of rhesus monkeys. Marked and permanent alterations in thyroid, gonadal, and adrenal hormones were produced by a continuous stress administered to the monkeys over a 72-hour period by means of a special conditioning technique. Some of the hormonal processes that changed did not return to their normal values until nearly three weeks after the extinction period of research.

Miller and Operant Conditioning of Physiological Processes

In a series of experiments over the past 15 years, Neal Miller and his associates at Rockefeller University have further refined procedures and a theory for research on operant conditioning of basic physiological states.[29] Miller is interested in demonstrating that the learning that occurs in "classic" or respondent conditioning and the learning that occurs in operant conditioning are not two different kinds of learning, but rather are manifestations of the same phenomenon expressed under different conditions.

---

[27]See Hearst, Beer, Sheatz, & Galambos, 1960.

[28]See Williams & Teitelbaum, 1956.

[29]See Miller, 1969, 1973, 1975. See also Stoyva, 1976. Miller and Dworkin (1975) have described some of the problems with the research described here.

Miller's experiments are discussed in the following paragraphs as examples of operant conditioning leading to durable changes in physiology. The discussion does not comment on Miller's proposal that there is one kind of learning with different facets; that theoretical topic is beyond the scope of an introductory work on socialization.

In one research project Miller and an associate spent one 45-minute operant conditioning session each day for 40 days experimenting on the salivation of dogs. Dogs in one group were rewarded with water when they showed a burst of salivation so they would be operantly conditioned to increase their salivation. Dogs in a second group were rewarded whenever there was a long time interval between their spontaneous bursts of salivation so they would be operantly conditioned to decrease salivation.

Miller noted that the group of dogs rewarded for increases in salivation seemed to be more aroused and active during the experiment. Concerned that all his experiment had accomplished was to change the level of skeletal and muscle activity of the dogs, which in turn affected their salivation and therefore ruled out evidence of operant conditioning, Miller tried a second experiment. In this experiment he began by paralyzing dogs with curare to make certain that skeletal movements did not affect the salivation process. This experiment was abandoned when it was found that the use of curare drug resulted in continuous and large amounts of salivation in all the experimental dogs used and caused such a thick saliva that instruments were fouled beyond any possibility of recording.

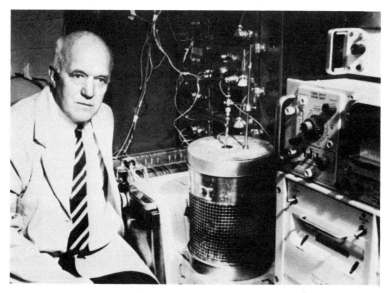

Professor Neal E. Miller with equipment for rewarding free-moving rat for changes in heart rate. (From laboratory of Neal E. Miller, Rockefeller University, 1971.)

Miller and his associates then turned to a study of operant conditioning of the heartbeat rate in rats that had been paralyzed with curare. Two groups of experimental rats were rewarded with direct electrical stimulation of certain areas of their brains as they showed changes, either an increase or decrease, in their heartbeat rates in an operant conditioning situation. The rats rewarded in this fashion showed both increases and decreases in their heart rates, but the amount of change in heart rate was still so small that Miller developed another, similar experiment in heart rate change to see if he could "shape" the operant changes. In the shaping process he immediately rewarded the first, very small change in paralyzed rat heart rates that occurred in the desired direction, either an increased rate or a decreased rate, then required progressively larger changes in heart rate for further rewards. In this experiment Miller and his associates quickly produced significant operant conditioning changes.

Miller then turned to the questions of whether these operantly conditioned rats could bring their responses under voluntary control and whether these operantly conditioned responses in the form of increased and decreased heart rates would be "remembered." These two questions were of interest to Miller because they involved two of the more important characteristics of operant learning; discrimination learning and memory had been believed to be not typical of respondent, or "classic," conditioned learning.

Miller experimented with rats in a procedure similar to the one used in his previous research to see whether they could learn to give a significant response in heart rate changes when a flashing light and a tone were associated with the reward. His experiment demonstrated that the rats did learn to clearly discriminate between rewards accompanied by a light and tone rewards not accompanied by these stimuli.

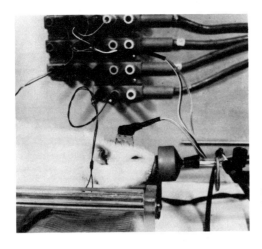

Rat paralyzed by curare, artificially respirated by a face mask, and rewarded by direct electrical stimulation of the brain for learning changes in heart rate. (From laboratory Neal E. Miller, Rockefeller University, 1971.)

Miller and his associates then took rats that had been put through one operant conditioning session and returned them to their cages for three months. Then these rats were curarized again and returned to the operant conditioning situation. Miller notes that these rats showed a good, reliable memory of their initial and brief training.

Miller also sought to demonstrate that the paralyzed rats could be operantly conditioned to avoid, or to "escape" from, a mild shock delivered shortly after a shock signal had been given to the rat. During the first ten seconds after the shock signal, the paralyzed rat could turn off the mild shock by making the "correct" (increased or decreased) change in its heart rate by a required amount. If the rats did not make a correct response in the ten-second period after the shock signal, they were given a continuous shock of electrical current until they made the correct response, which then turned off both the shock and the shock signal. Each of the rats in this experiment showed considerable operant learning when escape and avoidance were used as rewards in the conditioning process.

Next Miller turned to experiments in operant conditioning of the heart rate of rats in a non-curarized, or "normal," state. In his first experiments he had sought to rule out through the use of curare the possibility that his subjects were somehow learning the performance of skeletal and muscle responses that were indirectly causing the changes in heart rates being recorded. As he repeated his basic experiments, he found that rats not paralyzed by curare showed the same basic changes in heart rates under operant conditioning but did not show any skeletal or muscle changes that could be related to such heart rate changes. In fact, Miller found that, while greater changes in heart rate were being learned by the rats, there were increasingly smaller amounts of respiratory and muscle activities.

Miller then turned to testing the precise nature of the types of physiological changes possible in operant conditioning. First, using curarized rats he demonstrated that operant conditioning of intestinal contractions is possible in these mammals. In another experiment he determined that the rate of urine formation by the kidney could be changed in curarized rats rewarded by direct electrical stimulation of the brain. In a further experiment Miller and his associates demonstrated that the stomach walls of curarized rats can be operantly conditioned to contract and expand and that vasomotor responses affecting the amount of blood in the stomach mucosa, or wall, were amenable to operant conditioning, Miller then turned to research on peripheral vasomotor responses in operant conditioning. He found that curarized rats rewarded by electrical stimulation of the brain could be operantly conditioned to show quite specific and significant changes in the amount of blood in the vessels of their extremities (tails, ears). Miller also demonstrated that changes in systolic blood pressure of curarized rats could be operantly conditioned.

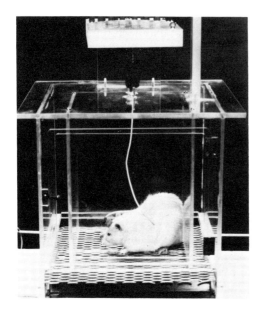

Apparatus for rewarding free-moving rat for changes in heart rate. (From laboratory of Neal E. Miller, Rockefeller University, 1971.)

Encouraged by their success in operant conditioning of so many different and specific visceral functions, Miller and his associates turned to experiments on the operant conditioning of brain wave changes. First, cats were equipped with electrodes attached to their brain surfaces. The electrodes picked up the cumulative effects of electrical activity over a considerable area of the brain and a permanent record, called an electroencephalogram, was made during the research. When the cats were aroused and active, the electroencephalogram showed fast, low-voltage electrical activity. When the cats were quiet, drowsy, or sleeping, the electroencephalogram showed slow, high-voltage activity. The cats were rewarded in the operant conditioning process with direct electrical stimulation of a specific area of the brain (medial forebrain bundle). This stimulation for reward produced a slight average lowering of voltage recorded on the electroencephalogram record. One group of cats was rewarded for showing an increased rate of slow, high-voltage brain electrical activity, and another group was rewarded for showing an increased rate of fast, low-voltage activity. Both groups appeared to become operantly conditioned to changes of rates of brain wave activity. Since the cats were able to move about during the research, it was not clear whether the changes in the rates of brain waves were in some way related to their freedom of movement. In order to rule out the consequences of muscle tension and movement on brain wave changes, curarized cats were subjected by Miller to operant conditioning and were found to exhibit a rate of brain wave changes similar to that found in the freely moving cats.

In another experiment Miller and his associates sought to determine whether animals could be operantly conditioned to maintain their total physiological balance, or homeostasis. Rats were injected with a hormone (ADH) that was antidiuretic—that is, which prevented loss of body fluids—if they chose one arm of a T-shaped maze. If they chose the other arm of the T-maze, they were injected with an isotonic saline solution. The ADH hormone permitted water to be reabsorbed in the kidney so that a smaller volume of more concentrated urine was formed. Thus for normal rats loaded in advance of the experiment with water, the ADH injection interfered seriously with excess water excretion required for homeostasis, while the isotonic saline solution allowed the excess water to be excreted. The rats in the experiment learned to select the side of the T-maze that assured them of an injection of saline so that their glandular response could restore their physiological balance. Miller concluded from this, and from two similar control experiments, that rats could learn in an operant manner to make specific glandular and visceral responses that would restore a physiological balance.

Many scholars have sought to duplicate and extend Miller's results in operant conditioning of specific features of physiology through research on human subjects. For example, in an experiment conducted at the Harvard Medical School, Shapiro, Tursky, Gershon, and Stern (1969) developed automatic instruments that yielded a continuous measure of a human subject's systolic blood pressure on each successive heartbeat.[30] This device was then used in operant conditioning of systolic blood pressure in 20 normal male subjects between 21 and 27 years of age. The subjects were given 25 trials, with each trial being 25 seconds long. The beginning of each trial was indicated by a blue light. Ten subjects were rewarded for increasing their systolic pressure, while ten subjects were rewarded for decreasing their systolic pressure. The reward used was a brief flash of red light and a short tone of moderate intensity. The results of this study tend to confirm the fact that a specific feature of human physiology, such as systolic blood pressure, can be operantly conditioned. Similar operant conditioned research was undertaken by, among many others, Engle of the National Institute of Child Health and Human Development in Bethesda, Md., on human heart rate and rhythms; by Kamiya of the Langley Porter Institute in San Francisco on brain waves; and by Lang of the University of Wisconsin, Madison, on human heart rates.

[30]For Miller's comments concerning replication and use of his research, see Miller & Dworkin, 1975; Miller, 1975. The literature reporting operant conditioning experiments on human physiology is often termed biofeedback and self-control research. For references to a wide range of this research see Jonas, 1973; Miller, 1973, 1974; Schwartz, 1975. See also Vol. 1 (1976) to Vol. 5 (1980) of *Biofeedback and Self-Regulation*. See also Barber, 1971; Stoyva, 1972, 1979; Shapiro, 1973; Miller 1974; DiCara, 1975; Barber, 1976; Kamiya, 1977.

In another series of experiments concerned with the physiological effects of "transcendental meditation," a Hindu form of concentrating the reflective process on body functions, Wallace (1970) of the University of California at Los Angeles noted the oxygen consumption, heart rate, skin resistance, and the electroencephalogram measurements of subjects before, during, and after their state of meditation. He reports that there were "significant changes" in all of these physiological measures during the time of meditation for each of 15 subjects. During meditation oxygen consumption and heart rates decreased markedly, skin resistance increased, and the electroencephalogram showed specific changes in some brain wave frequencies. Wallace believes all these changes were the consequence of the meditation process.

It should be pointed out that Miller and others have warned that, in addition to the question of whether the effects of operant conditioning really are durable in humans, there is a question in human operant studies of whether the changes recorded as learning represent operant learning of physiological responses or are the unconscious learning of those muscular and skeletal responses that are known to produce physiological changes. Miller feels that the experimenters working with operant conditioning of human physiological functions are developing the scientific controls and procedures to be able eventually to answer these questions. He believes that the cumulative results of this research now tend to demonstrate that the human autonomic nervous system can be brought for the most part under voluntary control through operant conditioning techniques. Orne and Paskewitz (1974) believe that some caution should be exercised in accepting uncritically all conclusions from operant learning research. In their experimental work on aversion situational effects on brain waves, Orne and Paskewitz determined that the anticipation of an electric shock by an individual did not depress *alpha* brain wave activity in a feedback, or operant, setting even though the electric shock was associated with experimental subjects all reporting anxiety and showing increased heart rates and skin conductance responses. The result was contrary to the conclusions of previous studies dating as far back as 1929, in which it was noted repeatedly that the apprehension and worry of experimental subjects always resulted in the depression of the *alpha* brain wave. It had been assumed by Orne and Paskewitz that as their subjects were trained operantly to increase the level of their alpha brain waves they would be learning to regulate the level and degree of their anxiety. In fact, the opposite effect occurred as the result of their study. After a review of many studies, Schwartz (1975) also cautions that biofeedback studies, particularly research concerned with the patterning and self-regulation of human physiological processes, must be used with caution. However Jonas (1973) does not share the views expressed by Schwartz, Orne and Paskewitz, and others and proposes that a science of visceral learning has been developed.

Conclusions: Operant Conditioning Studies

The concept of operant conditioning and the research evidence that has been derived in the study of this kind of event provides a vital departure from models of learning in which various "external" influences automatically produced behavioral responses by an organism. Now there is a systematic way to consider that humans can learn through directing, regulating, and shaping their own responses to many different types of stimuli, whether or not these arise within the body or in the environment. Research on operant conditioning has greatly clarified the specific relations between behavior and biology.

The application of operant research procedures to human behavior is severely limited by ethical and moral considerations, which are quite proper and should continue. It is unlikely that any investigator will try to curarize a human infant or adult to fully control skeletal and muscle influences on operant conditioning of specific physiological processes. Thus whether operant research procedures lead to long-lasting changes in humans and really are the consequence of operant learning remains an open question. It is possible that research on human volunteers afflicted with diseases of a potentially fatal or severely limiting nature can provide some additional evidence concerning the application of operant conditioning techniques to humans. Patients suffering from fatally high blood pressure or severe spastic colitis, asthma, cardiac arrhythmias (irregular heartbeat), insomnia, or epilepsy may be greatly helped through attempts at therapeutic alleviation of their conditions by use of operant conditioning methods. In turn, such therapeutic alleviation and change may possibly provide research data for answers to the questions of the durability and specific nature of operant learning in humans.

CONCLUSIONS

The first part of this chapter noted that there are ethnographic reports suggesting a variety of specific relationships between culture and human biology. Until recently, ethnographic accounts as diverse and esoteric as yoga exercises, Cheyenne pole swinging, Zuni fire initiations, Polynesian firewalking, the food practices of South American Indians, Bornean, and African peoples, varying conditions of constipation, diarrhea, and nausea among New Guinea peoples, magical fright in Meso-America, blushing and fatigue patterns, different ways of walking, standing, and sitting, different culturally styled gestures, and the different ways that number, sequence, and time concepts seem to be related to human biology in different cultures seemed to have little place in understanding cultural transmission.

The development of socialization theory and emergence of operant conditioning methods in psychology, however, have brought these customs to the forefront of research seeking to understand the specific ways human culture and biology became interrelated in a process of socialization.

Anthropologists have long been able to cite the different ways humans blush in different circumstances. However these facts meant little until the development of precise experimental procedures in the operant conditioning of peripheral vascular responses—that is, until it was demonstrated by Miller and his associates that one kind of mammal could learn to voluntarily control and adjust the flow of blood to the surfaces of its extremities, with more or less blood flowing to the tip of a tail or to the right rather than the left ear. Human customs in meeting starvation conditions, in defecation, wound healing, and so on, were only of passing interest until the demonstration in operant conditioning research of the specific ways some mammals can direct and control contractions of the intestine and stomach, as well as the amount of blood flow to the stomach wall.

Now using these different kinds of data, it is possible to begin thinking more clearly about the mutual, reciprocal feedback process between culture and human biology. Studies of operant conditioning not only indicate how particular processes might be controlled by humans on their own volition but also may indicate how long-term immersion in a culture develops a great number of human abilities that in time become firmer and more irreversible.

Operant conditioning research may also make a contribution to a more precise understanding of socialization by providing a broader theoretical base for study of that process. In the preceding chapter an effort was made to show that too little attention had been given in formulations of the major models of learning to the ways human capacities, particularly reflection and symboling, were directly involved in the process of socialization. The case study data from Papago enculturation was presented to provide an illustration of some of the ways an enculturation process can become focused on capacities such as reflection and symboling. An attempt was made to demonstrate that Papago adults rarely depended primarily upon their "doing something"—that is, overtly rewarding or punishing— to children as they mature. Rather, Papago adults have placed the general burden of the enculturation process on their children, who must interpret, define, and choose for themselves behavior that might be rewarded or punished by adults if the adults did in fact actively administer such rewards and punishments.

In the sense of the traditional learning models, Papago enculturation seems so transparent in its texture as to be nonexistent. If you set out to describe Papago enculturation using the Thorndike-Hull behavioristic model, for example, you could find very little actual "classic conditioning" of children by adults. However the concept and results of operant conditioning research clearly show that Papago children contribute greatly to enculturating themselves in the context of Papago culture. In fact, operant conditioning research suggests the following theoretical statement concerning Papago enculturation:

> Papago children become enculturated by regularly selecting for themselves the features of their behavior which, if they were adults, they would reward. Then after engaging in such behavior, Papago children administer rewards to themselves for behaving in a manner which, if they were Papago adults and if adults provided rewards, they would reward to show their approval. Papago children become enculturated through regularly selecting for themselves features of their behavior which, if they were adults, they would punish. Then after such behavior, Papago children may administer punishments to themselves for behavior in a way which, if they were Papago adults and if adults provided punishments, they would punish to show their disapproval. In the course of administering to themselves the rewards and punishments Papago adults know but generally avoid using, Papago children can be said to be operantly conditioning themselves to their culture.

The key features of such self-administered rewards and punishments in Papago enculturation would seem to be the genetically transmitted human capacities for reflection and symboling. Papago children, in common with children in other cultures, are born with capacities to go beyond the observed properties of a specific object or social event, to draw conclusions on the basis of their past experiences concerning unobserved properties of objects or events, and also to symbolically reproduce these conclusions and project them into the future so they can consider alternative possibilities of immediate and future behavior before they act. In this way Papago children can come to administer to themselves rewards and punishments for their behavior that are consistent with cultural standards and values they are not actively taught but must be observed and about which they must draw proper conclusions.

It is clear that these genetically transmitted capacities and their specific uses in this type of learning of culture are not confined to Papago children. These capacities have been noted in use in enculturation in most other cultures. For example, in observing the ways Alorese children learn adult views that food is valuable, important, and in uncertain supply, DuBois (1941) used the concepts of *absorptive learning* and *psychic osmosis* to note that these Indonesian children learn for themselves proper attitudes toward food from observing, reflecting upon, and symbolically reproducing for themselves the cultural values of adults about food and hunger. Gardner (1966) has described a similar enculturation process among the Paliyans of South India. Paliyan children appear to be subjected to only a minimum of adult direction as they learn their culture. In fact, the form of Paliyan enculturation closely resembles Papago enculturation in making children essentially responsible for learning their culture. An examination of the records of enculturation processes described by trained observers (see Appendix) leads to the hypothesis *that considerably more of human culture is transmitted to children through an operant conditioning self-enculturation use of the capacities for reflection and symboling than through use of overt parental rewards and punishments for behavior of children.* The Papago style of allowing children to almost enculturate themselves is an unusual one among the world's cultures. However this is also true of the style of enculturation proposed under the formulations of the Thorndike-Hull and other behavioristic models of learning. In fact, there is no example to be cited of such a culture.

The enculturation process in contemporary American society appears to be a combination of some quite specific forms of rewards and punishments for certain kinds of behavior, especially sexual, anal, aggression, and dependence learning, with a substantial amount of reliance on children enculturating themselves in broad areas of the culture such as technology, political values, and social organization. Americans tend to assign to their children the responsibility for learning by themselves many substantive features of American culture. American adults are then surprised when they discover that self-enculturation may result in serious misunderstanding of and rapid changes in culture.[31] When the adults of a culture allow children to reward or to punish themselves for behaving in ways which, if they were adults, they would reward or punish, they risk having children seriously misperceive the style, flavor, intents, and latent meanings of a culture. In some cultures, such as the Kaoka speakers of Guadalcanal, adults use comments at specific points in children's enculturation to ensure that they do not misperceive values of behavior held important in adult life.[32]

TELEOLOGICAL REASONING IN STUDIES OF SOCIALIZATION

It is important not to conclude from the discussion and examples in this chapter that humans are born with an *innate* striving, or impetus, to move through the socialization process toward the specific goal of acquiring and using culture. Human infants are born into an ongoing cultural system.

---

[31]Mead suggests that the American enculturation process now also involves children informing their parents about vital elements of American culture and thereby reversing the traditional form of the enculturation process (Mead, 1970).

[32]See Hogbin, 1965, 33–34.

They are equipped with biological features that they can use in a long-term process of learning culture. But whether human infants learn culture depends upon a large number of complex, nonbiological factors over which an infant has no effective control. In order to learn culture, infants must be born with certain biological features unimpaired, must live and grow, and must be in a situation of regular communicative contact with adults (see Chapter 5). Human infants will not learn culture simply because they are born possessing some biological features such as reflexes, drives, and capacities that can be used to learn culture; there is no demonstrable "grand design," or larger plan, for socialization. The kind of reasoning which explains events in terms of their contribution to goals or ends of a larger plan is termed *teleological.* In a limited sense the concept of socialization is *teleological* because it looks forward to the goal of humans acquiring culture. The concept is teleological in another limited sense since it also looks back to the beginnings of the process of transmitting acquiring culture.

The whole idea of teleological explanation has a basic logical problem inherent in it. On the one hand, teleological explanation involves a demonstration that it is a fundamental part of what is explained to have specific goals which themselves contribute to the success of a larger whole or design. Thus the physiological working of the human kidney would be explained teleologically by saying that the regular removal of tissue wastes contributes to homeostasis and therefore to the continuation of the life of the organism. What is being explained (the workings of the kidneys) is teleologically accounted for when it is said to have specific consequences for a larger complex (homeostasis) and system (life).

On the other hand, teleological explanations can easily be reversed— that is, the thing to be explained (the workings of the kidney) is understood because it has the consequences it has for a larger system (life). In this kind of a reversed teleological explanation, the end brought about (the workings of the kidneys) is viewed as "designed" by "something" or "someone" as part of a plan to ensure the success of the larger system.

An understanding of these two kinds of teleological explanation, termed by Spencer in 1879 as *legitimate* and *illegitimate,* might be found in two examples.[33] First we ask the question, "How do we explain the form of marriage among the Dusun of Borneo?" Then we apply the two types of teleological explanations to seek our answer. The first kind of teleological explanation, which Spencer calls *legitimate,* would note that the form of marriage among the Dusun is to be explained by observing that it produces the integration and cohesion of large and unrelated social groups. This form of explanation looks forward to a goal or purpose for the form of Dusun marriage. The second kind of teleological explanation, which Spen-

[33]See Spencer, 1879. For a contemporary discussion of teleology, see Woodfield, 1976.

cer terms *illegitimate*, would ask an opposite question about the form of Dusun marriage—that is, "Why does marriage among the Dusun take this particular form?" This question presupposes that Dusun marriage is part of an original and larger design, or plan, for human marriage and looks back to that plan to understand the form that Dusun marriage has taken.

This chapter and text seek to discuss at a beginning level several aspects of the socialization process. The discussion is not primarily concerned with explaining the consequences of the socialization process for individual learning and behavior. There has been no attempt to account teleologically for the socialization process by saying that it has specific consequences for a larger complex (the learning of individual behavior) or system (culture or society). It was suggested in the first chapter that the process of socialization arose in the course of the long-term, reciprocal, mutual feedback [C ↔ B] between human biology and behavior. The socialization process is to be accounted for as an emergent evolutionary fact of both the human body and natural ecology of humans—that is, culture— and is best explained in these terms. There is no scientific evidence that the socialization process is the consequence of and exists because of some grand design or plan. The socialization process apparently arose as a natural, chance occurrence in the long time of human physical evolution and adaptation to culture as the natural ecology of humans. The socialization process clearly did not arise solely from human biology, or only from culture, and is not to be explained finally in terms of its intended or actual consequences for either human biology or culture.

CIRCULAR REASONING IN STUDIES OF SOCIALIZATION

It should be noted that there has been no attempt in this chapter, or this book, to explain some of the ways the mutual, reciprocal feedback process between human biology and culture functions through use of circular reasoning or logic. An example of circular reasoning would be to say, "B causes C to behave in ways 1, 2, and 3; therefore C causes B to behave in ways 1, 2, and 3." This chapter has attempted to set forth some data and to explain a few of the ways that human biology and culture may become interrelated through a socialization process. It may appear on casual reading that what has been said is circular in form. The intention here has been only to give some brief indications that the biological and cultural modes of transmission in the socialization process become complexly interrelated through time through a *doubly contingent* feedback from one mode into the other. It has also been suggested that, in the course of this long-term feedback process, abilities are developed that are not present in the biology or behavior of a newborn child. The biological precursors—that is, signs or indications—of such abilities are part of the genetic heritage of all humans. The development of abilities depends upon the specific conditions and history of the local culture into which a human child is born and especially upon the conditions, through a long period of time, in which the mutual interplay between biology and culture takes place. There is no intention to say that B (biology) causes C (culture) to develop in ways X,Y, and Z and that therefore C (culture) causes B (biology) to develop in ways X, Y, and Z. There is also no intention to claim that human abilities arising in the course of the socialization process cause biology to influence culture, which in turn causes culture to influence biology.

SUMMARY

This chapter has been concerned with discussing some of the ways culture and human biology become interrelated in the socialization process. It began with some ethnographic examples of the various ways humans culturally structure reflexes, drives, and some other features of their biology. That portion of the chapter concluded with a brief summary of the socialization theory used in the chapter and text. The second part of the chapter was concerned with a brief account of the concept of learning through operant conditioning and of the ways this research method has been used to alter various types of physiological processes and behavior in laboratory animals and in human subjects. It was noted that data and conclusions of operant conditioning research provided some innovative ways to understand ethnographic accounts of humans learning in a socialization process to control reflexes, drives, and other features of human biology. The chapter ended with a discussion of some of the ways conclusions from operant conditioning studies, when joined with the kinds of ethnographic data discussed in the first part of the chapter, may provide for a broader theoretical base for the concept of socialization.

REFERENCES CITED AND SUGGESTED READINGS

ANAND, B., G. CHINA, & B. SINGH. 1961. "Some Aspects of Electroencephalographic Studies in Yogis." *Electroencephalography and Clinical Neurophysiology,* 13, 452–456
BAER, D. 1962a. "Laboratory Control of Thumbsucking by Withdrawal and Representation of Positive Reinforcement." *Journal of Experimental Analysis of Behavior,* 5, 525-528.
————. 1926b. "A Technique of Social Reinforcement for the Study of Child Behavior: Behavior Avoiding Reinforcement Withdrawal." *Child Development,* 33, 847–858
BARBER, T. 1974 "Implications for Human Capabilities and Potentialities." In L.V. Dicara, *et al.* (eds.), *Biofeedback and Self-Control, 1974.* Chicago: Aldine, pp. 53–71.

BARBER, T. (ed.) 1971. *Biofeedback and Self-Control, 1970.* Chicago: Aldine.

BARBER, T. (ed.). 1976. *Biofeedback and Self-Control, 1975–1976.* Chicago: Aldine.

BENEDICT, R. 1946. *The Chrysanthemum and the Sword.* Boston: Houghton-Mifflin.

BIJOU, S. 1957. "Methodology for an Experimental Analysis of Child Behavior." *Psychological Reports,* 3, 243–250.

BIJOU, S., & D. BAER. 1966. "Operant Methods in Child Behavior and Development." In W. K. Honig (ed.), *Operant Behavior; Areas of Research and Application.* New York: Prentice-Hall, pp. 718–789.

BILODEAU, E.A. (ed.). 1966. *Acquisition of Skill.* New York: Academic Press.

BRACKBILL, Y. 1958. "Extinction of the Smiling Response in Infants as a Function of Reinforcement Schedule." *Child Development,* 29, 115–124.

BRADY, J. 1966. "Operant Methodology and the Experimental Production of Altered Physiological States." In W. Honig (ed.), *Operant Behavior: Areas of Research and Application.* New York: Prentice-Hall, pp. 609–633.

BRAUNWALD, E. (ed.). 1980. *Heart Diseases: A Textbook of Cardiovascular Medicine.* Philadelphia: Saunders.

BYERS, P. 1972. "From Biological Rhythm to Cultural Pattern." Unpublished doctoral dissertation, Columbia University, New York.

CANNON, W.B. 1936. *Bodily Changes in Pain, Hunger, Fear and Rage.* New York: Appleton-Century-Crofts.

———. 1942. "Voodoo Death." *American Anthropologist,* 44, 169–181.

CATANIA, A.C. (ed.). 1968. *Contemporary Research in Operant Behavior.* Glenview, Ill.: Scott, Foresman.

CONDON, W.S., & L.W. SANDER. 1974. "Neonate Movement Is Synchronized with Adult Speech; Interactional Participation and Language Acquisition." *Science,* 183, 99–101.

COON, C. 1950. "Human Races in Relation to Environment and Culture with Special Reference to the Influence of Culture on Genetic Changes in Human Population." *Cold Spring Harbor Symposia on Quantitative Biology,* 15, 247–258.

DICARA, L.V. (ed.). 1975. *Biofeedback and Self-Control, 1974.* Chicago: Aldine.

DUBOIS, C. 1941. "Attitudes Toward Food and Hunger in Alor." In L. Spier, A. Hallowell, & S. Newman (eds.), *Language, Culture and Personality: Essays in Memory of Edward Sapir.* Menasha, Wis.: Sapir Memorial Fund, pp. 272–281.

ELDRIDGE, L. 1954. "Respiration Rate Change and Its Relation to Avoidance Behavior." Unpublished doctoral dissertation, Columbia University, New York.

EVANS, R.I. 1968. *B. F. Skinner: The Man and His Ideas.* New York: Dutton.

FEIGEN, G. 1969. "Bucky Fuller and the Firewalk." *Saturday Review,* July 12, 1969, pp. 22–23.

FLANAGAN, B., I. GOLDIAMOND, & N. AZRIN. 1958. "Operant Stuttering: The Control of Stuttering Behavior through Response-Contingent Consequence." *Journal of Experimental Analysis of Behavior,* 11, 173–177.

FORD, C., & F. BEACH. 1951. *Patterns of Sexual Behavior.* New York: Harper & Row, Pub.

FREEMAN, J.W. 1976. *Scarcity and Opportunity in an Indian Village.* Menlo Park, Calif.: Cummings Publishing Co.

———. 1980. "Trial by Fire." In J.P. Spradley & D.W. McCurdy (eds.), *Conformity and Conflict.* Boston: Little, Brown, pp. 333–342 (first printed in *Natural History Magazine,* January, 1974).

FRIEDMAN, M. 1977. "Some Pathophysiologic Phenomena Observed in Subjects Exhibiting Type A Behavior." In D.T. Mason (ed.), *Advances in Heart Disease.* New York: Grune & Stratton, pp. 73–83.

GARDNER, P. 1966. "Symmetric Respect and Memorate Knowledge: The Structure and Ecology of Individualistic Culture." *Southwestern Journal of Anthropology,* 22, 389–415.

GARFIELD, C.A. (ed.). 1979. *Stress and Survival.* St. Louis, Mo.: C. V. Mosby.
GEWIRTZ, J., & D. BAER. 1958. "Deprivation and Satiation of Social Reinforcers as Drive Conditioners." *Journal of Abnormal and Social Psychology*, 57, 165–172.
GILLIN, J. 1944. "Custom and Range of Human Response." *Character and Personality*, 13, 101–134.
———. 1948. "Magical Fright." *Psychiatry*, 11, 387–400.
———. 1951. *The Culture of Security in San Carlos.* New Orleans, La.: Middle American Research Institute.
HARNER, M.J. 1977. "The Ecological Basis for Aztec Sacrifice." *American Ethnologist*, 4, 117–135.
———. 1978. "Reply to Oritz de Montellano." Paper presented to The New York Academy of Sciences, November 17, 1978.
———. 1980. "The Enigma of Aztec Sacrifice." In J.P. Spradley & D.W. McCurdy (eds.), *Conformity and Conflict.* Boston: Little, Brown, pp. 208–215 (first printed in *Natural History Magazine*, April, 1977).
HARRIS, M. 1980. *Culture, People and Nature.* New York: Harper & Row, Pub., (3rd. ed.).
HEARST, E., B. BEER, G. SHEATZ, & R. GALAMBOS. 1970. "Some Electrophysiological Correlates of Conditioning in the Monkey." *EEG and Clinical Neurophysiology Journal*, 12, 137–152.
HOGBIN, I. 1965. *A Guadalcanal Society: The Koaka Speakers.* New York: Holt, Rinehart & Winston.
HONIG, W.K. (ed.). 1966. *Operant Behavior: Areas of Research and Application.* New York: Prentice-Hall.
JOHNSON, D., & C.R. HERRON. 1973. "Head, Heart: Deadly Pair." *New York Times*, December 2, 1973, p. E-7.
JONAS, J. 1973. *Visceral Learning: Toward a Science of Self-Control.* New York: Viking.
JORGENSEN, J.G. 1972. *The Sun Dance Religion.* Chicago: University of Chicago Press.
KAMIYA, J. 1971. *Biofeedback and Self-Control: An Aldine Reader on the Regulation of Bodily Processes and Consciousness.* Chicago: Aldine.
KAMIYA, J. 1977. *Biofeedback and Self-Control, 1976–1977.* Chicago: Aldine.
KLUCKHOHN, C. 1954. "Culture and Behavior." In G. Lindzey (ed.), *Handbook of Social Psychology*, Vol. II. Cambridge, Mass.: Addison-Wesley, pp. 921-976.
LANGNESS, L.L. 1975. "Margaret Mead and the Study of Socialization." *Ethos*, 3, 97–112.
LEITENBERG, H. (ed.). 1976. *Handbook of Behavior Modification and Behavior Theory.* Englewood Cliffs, N.J.: Prentice-Hall.
LOVAAS, O. 1961. "Interaction Between Verbal and Nonverbal Behavior." *Child Development*, 32, 329–336.
MALMO, R. 1961. "Slowing of Heart Rate After Septal Self-Stimulation in Rats." *Science*, 133, 1128–1130.
MASTOFSKY, D. (ed.). 1975. *Behavior Control and Modification of Physiological Activity.* Englewood Cliffs, N.J.: Prentice-Hall.
MEAD, M. 1946. "Research on Primitive Children." In L. Carmichael (ed.), *Manual of Child Psychology.* New York: John Wiley, pp. 667–706.
———. 1956. "The Concept of Culture and the Psychosomatic Approach." In D. G. Haring (ed.), *Personal Character and the Cultural Milieu.* Syracuse, N.Y.: Syracuse University Press, pp. 594–622.
———. 1970. *Culture and Commitment: A Study of the Generation Gap.* New York: Natural History Press & Doubleday.
MEAD, M., & F. MACGREGOR. 1951. *Growth and Culture.* New York: Putnam's.
MILLER, N.E. 1969. "Learning of Visceral and Glandular Responses." *Science*, 163, 434–445.

————. 1973. "Introduction: Current Issues and Key Problems." In N.E. Miller, *et al.* (eds.), *Biofeedback and Self-Control, 1973. An Aldine Annual on Bodily Processes and Consciousness.* Chicago: Aldine.

————. 1975. "Biofeedback: Evaluation of a New Technique." In L.V. DiCara, *et al.* (eds), *Biofeedback and Self-Control, 1974.* Chicago: Aldine, pp. 51–52.

MILLER, N.E. (ed.). 1974. *Biofeedback and Self-Control, 1973.* Chicago: Aldine.

MILLER, N.E., & B. DWORKIN. 1975. "Visceral Learning: Recent Difficulties with Curarized Rats and Significant Problems for Research." In L.V. DiCara, *et al.* (eds.), *Biofeedback and Self-Control, 1974.* Chicago: Aldine, pp. 83–103.

NEEDHAM, A.E. 1964. "Biological Considerations of Wound Healing." In W. Montagna & R.E. Billingham (eds.), *Advances in Biology of Skin,* Vol. 5. Oxford: Pergamon, pp. 1–29.

ORNE, M.T., & D.A. PASKEWITZ. 1974. "Aversive Situational Effects on Alpha Feedback Training." *Science,* 186, 458–460.

ORTIZ DE MONTELLANO, B.R. 1978. "Aztec Cannibalism: An Ecological Necessity?" *Science,* 200, 611–617.

PEREZ-CRUET, J., G. TOLLIVER, G. DUNN, S. MARVIN, & J. BRADY. 1963. "Concurrent Measurement of Heart Rate and Instrumental Avoidance Behavior in the Rhesus Monkey." *Journal of Experimental Analysis of Behavior,* 6, 61–64.

QUAIN, B. 1948. *Fijian Village.* Chicago: University of Chicago Press.

REYNOLDS, G. 1975. *A Primer of Operant Conditioning.* Glenview, Ill.: Scott, Foresman (rev. ed.).

RHEINGOLD, H., J. GEWIRTZ, & H. ROSS. 1959. "Social and Conditioning of Vocalizations in the Infant." *Journal of Comparative and Physiological Psychology,* 52, 68–73.

RHEINGOLD, H., W. STANLEY, & J. COOLEY. 1962. "A Crib for the Study of Exploratory Behavior in Infants." *Science,* 136, 1054–1055.

SCHERLIS, S. 1977. "Report of the Committee on Stress, Strain and Heart Disease." *Circulation,* 55, 2–11.

SCHULTES, R. 1969. "Hallucinogens of Plant Origin." *Science,* 163, 245–254.

SCHWARTZ, G.E. 1975. "Biofeedback, Self-Regulation and the Patterning of Physiological Processes." *American Scientist,* 63, 314–324.

SHAPIRO, A., & P. HORN. 1955. "Blood Pressure, Plasma Pepsinogen and Behavior in Cats and Subjected to Experimental Production of Anxiety." *Journal of Nervous and Mental Disease,* 122, 222–231.

SHAPIRO, D., B. TURSKY, E. GERSHON, & M. STERN. 1969. "Effects of Feedback and Reinforcement on the Control of Human Systolic Blood Pressure." *Science,* 163, 588–590.

SHAPIRO, D. (ed.). 1973. *Biofeedback and Self-Control, 1972.* Chicago: Aldine.

SKINNER, B. 1938. *The Behavior of Organisms.* Englewood Cliffs, N.J.: Prentice-Hall, 1966.

————. 1948. *Walden Two.* New York: Macmillan.

————. 1953. *Science and Human Behavior.* New York: MacMillan.

————. 1957. *Verbal Behavior.* Englewood Cliffs, N.J.: Prentice-Hall.

————. 1969. *Contingencies of Reinforcement; A Theoretical Analysis.* Englewood Cliffs, N.J.: Prentice-Hall.

————. 1972. *Beyond Freedom and Dignity.* New York: Knopf.

SKINNER, B.F., & C.B. FERSTER. 1957. *Schedules of Reinforcement.* New York: Appleton-Century-Crofts.

SKINNER, B.F., & J.G. HOLLAND. 1961. *The Analysis of Behavior.* New York: McGraw-Hill.

SPENCER, H. 1879. *The Data of Ethics.* New York: A. L. Burt.

STEVENSON, M.C. 1904. *The Zuni Indians.* Washington, D.C.: 23rd Annual Report of the Bureau of American Ethnology.

STOYVA. J. 1976. "Self-Regulation: A Context for Biofeedback." *Biofeedback and Self-Regulation,* 1, 1–6.

STOYVA, J. (ed.). 1972. *Biofeedback and Self-Control, 1971.* Chicago: Aldine.

STOYVA, J. (ed.). 1979. *Biofeedback and Self-Control, 1978–1979.* Chicago: Aldine.

TEDLOCK, D. 1973. "In Search of the Miraculous at Zuni." Paper presented to *IX International Congress of Anthropological and Ethnological Sciences,* Chicago, No. 1356, August 18–September 9, 1973.

TOLLEY, H. 1948. "Populations and Food Supply." *Chronica Botanica,* 11, 217–224.

WALLACE, R. 1970. "Physiological Effects of Transcendental Meditation." *Science,* 167, 1751–1754.

WENGER, M., & B. BAGCHI. 1961. "Studies of Autonomic Functions in Practitioners of Yoga in India." *Behavioral Science,* 6, 312–323.

WENGER, M., B. BAGCHI, & B. ANAND. 1961. "Experiments in India on 'Voluntary Control' of the Heart and Pulse." *Circulation,* 24, 1319–1325.

WILLIAMS, D., & P. TEITELBAUM. 1956. "Control of Drinking Behavior by Means of an Operant Conditioning Technique." *Science,* 124, 1294–1296.

WOODFIELD, A. 1976. *Teleology.* Cambridge, England: Cambridge University Press.

ZBOROWSKI, M. 1952. "Cultural Components in Responses to Pain." *Journal of Social Issues,* 8, 16–30.

CHAPTER FIVE
SOCIALIZATION
RESEARCH STRATEGIES
Studies of
Isolated Children, Twins,
and the Critical
Period Hypothesis

This chapter begins with a discussion of two types of evidence now available that aid in illustrating the ways human biology and culture become inter-related in the socialization process. The first comes from studies of children isolated for long periods from the enculturation process in their society. The second is derived from studies of twins who share the same, or nearly the same, genetic heritage and who are enculturated separately in the same society. The first type of evidence illustrates that, if an infant has its basic drives met even at the most minimal levels, it will mature biologically, although fitfully, and perhaps well below its potential growth pattern. However there will be no accompanying development of cultural and social behavior forms, for these must be acquired by an infant in the context of regular communicative contact with other persons. The study of twins, the second type of evidence, helps us see more clearly that, while individuals sharing a common genetic heritage can be very much alike biologically, they may also behave quite differently, depending on the enculturation processes they are exposed to as they grow up. The chapter concludes with a discussion of an influential hypothesis often unstated or implied in so-cialization research.

ISOLATED CHILDREN

Types of Studies

A significant amount of evidence demonstrating the fundamental ways in which species-characteristic behavior forms, reflexes, drives, and capacities may serve as organic bridgeheads in socialization is found in studies of isolated infants and children. This literature is extensive and fragmented into loosely related topics. Sociologists have tended to study socially and culturally isolated infants and children. Psychologists have generally studied twins separated from one another at or near birth and raised in different social and cultural environments. Some psychologists concerned with clear definitions and evidence in support of a "critical incidents" or "critical periods" hypothesis have worked with experimentally isolated laboratory animals to study the long-term effects of the deprivation of maternal care and social contact. Physicians and psychiatrists have usually studied severely emotionally disturbed, or autistic, children and children isolated socially and culturally because of immobilizing biological limitations such as blindness or brain damage at birth.

To make such accounts easier to understand, this widely scattered literature on social and cultural isolation has been categorized under general headings. It is important to know that this discussion is concerned with the vital question, "What happens to an infant or child raised in conditions of extreme physical or social isolation, with a minimum of cultural and social learning?" Studies of isolated infants and children demonstrate in a unique manner the role of the socialization process in the development and expression of what ordinarily is taken to be human "nature" and human "personality." The studies of isolated infants and children tend to strongly support the statement that most of the behavior we feel to be "normal" in *Homo sapiens sapiens* does not in fact occur outside of a process of socialization.

Feral Children: An Apocryphal Tale

Studies of isolated human infants and children labor under a heavy burden of folk tales concerning children who are supposed to have been raised by animals. All of us are familiar with the tale of Romulus and Remus, legendary founders of Rome, who were said in the ancient Roman folk tales to have been suckled and cared for by a wolf mother. Many of us have read, or have had read to us, stories such as Kipling's *Mowgli*, the boy supposedly raised from infancy by wolves and friend of Bagheera, the black panther. An American television series has depicted a young boy being raised with tigers.

Unfortunately these folk myths have also become established in the literature concerned with studies of isolated infants and children. Stories such as those of the "Hessian Wolf Boy," Amala and Kamala, the so-called "Wolf Girls of Midnapore," Parasram, the "Wolf Boy of Agra," and Victor, "the Wild Boy of Aveyron," have tended to provide support, more often from the fact of the great length of time the tale has been in print (Victor was found near Aveyron, France, in 1799) than from any credible scientific proof, for the folk-culture myths that human infants and children can be raised by animals.[1]

The Basis of Myth

Bettelheim (1967) has examined this literature and has concluded that such tales arise from the fearful delusions in parents created by the presence of severely emotionally disturbed, or austistic, children in human society. Bettelheim also believes that the feral infant and child myths reflect a human desire to want to believe that a benign nature looks after lost or abandoned children. When isolated autistic children have come to public attention, it appears, says Bettelheim, that we are unwilling to admit that such individuals could have a human past. We need desperately to believe, Bettelheim points out, that only the most incredible accidental circumstances could reduce a child to such a "subhuman" state.

Bettelheim concludes that some reports of feral children (Amala and Kamala; Parasram) appear to him to be instances of <u>autistic children—that is, children who have been abandoned emotionally by parents and so pushed beyond their capacity to cope with reality</u>. Bettelheim also notes that some cases of reputed feral children could be instances of "feeble-mindedness" caused by a limited genetic capacity for learning or by brain damage at birth, which make possible the animallike behavior typically recounted in stories of feral individuals. Reported feral behavior includes profound withdrawal from contacts with other people, desire for sameness, mutism, an inability to laugh, and very disorderly personal appearance, including matted hair and dirty skin. The descriptions by Kanner (1943, 1944, 1949) and Bettelheim (1959, 1967) of the behavior and appearance of autistic children lends support to the conviction of Bettelheim that most accounts of feral infants and children have been descriptions of recently abandoned autistic individuals.

It could be concluded from the examination of organic bridgeheads to socialization that human infants deserted by adults before they can care

---

[1]See Itard, 1932; Silberstein & Irwin, 1962; Rauber, 1888; Singh & Zingg, 1942; Gesell, 1940; Ogburn, 1959. It should be noted that, while Victor was not reported to have been raised by animals, it is implied that he had some type of nonhuman help in staying alive. See Lane, 1976.

for themselves will die. There is no credible evidence to demonstrate that any adult animal, including all of the adult primates, could adequately care for a human infant, especially in terms of meeting demands of species-characteristic behavior, reflexes, and drives, to enable an infant or child simply to survive the time of their utter dependency.

Autistic Children

Prior to about 1940 infants and children with severe emotional and behavioral impairments were believed to be brain damaged or to be "feeble-minded." After this date some physicians, clinical psychologists, and psychiatrists began to recognize that some infants and children with severe disturbances in behavior showed little or no neurophysiological deficiencies. Some persons began to recognize that such children, with apparently "normal" physical equipment for their ages, were typified by quite similar ways of acting. A central feature of these actions was an extreme disturbance of contacts with other persons to the point where an infant or child seemed totally unaware of their environment. Bettelheim's case history descriptions (1967) of "Laurie," "Marcia," "Joey," "Ken," and "Mitchell" vividly portray the very different and seemingly inexplicable behavior of the infant and child afflicted with autism.

The Roots of Autism Bettelheim and Kanner have hypothesized that autism is a *functional disturbance* and has its roots in a child being born into a cultural and social environment in which it is deserted emotionally and cared for in ways that emotionally traumatize it to the point where it can be said that a parent, or in some instances both parents, actually do not wish the child to live. Thus, for Bettelheim, Kanner, and others, autism stems from a realization by an infant or child that nothing can be done about a world that sometimes offers some unwanted satisfactions and that is very frustrating in even those few satisfactions allowed. Because of repeated frustrations and because they cannot obliterate themselves as parents expect them to do, autistic infants and children in time begin to withdraw from all contacts with others and become incapable of engaging in behavior dealing with other human beings.

A contrary hypothesis for the origin of autism may be formulated from a study conducted in London at the Institute of Psychiatry that suggests that genetic and prenatal influences are the likely cause of autistic behavior. In this study 11 pairs of identical and 10 pairs of fraternal twins were examined for symptoms of autism. In four pairs of the identical twins, both twins clearly were found to be autistic. In contrast, there were no such autistic pairs among the ten pairs of fraternal twins. The obstetric records of all pairs of twins were examined to determine whether brain injury at, or shortly following, birth was responsible for the autism afflicting the four pairs of identical twins; there was no evidence of birth injuries to any identical or fraternal twin. These data suggest that the basis for infantile and child autism is not solely *functional*, or acquired, as proposed by Bettelheim, Kanner, and others.

Marcia   Whatever the causes of autism, close observation of the victims of infantile and childhood autism for very long periods has dramatically demonstrated the role that socialization plays in the process of taking on, through learning, most of those attributes we ordinarily associate with being human. Autistic children are so "unhuman" in their actions that state institutions have refused them care. Marcia (Bettelheim, 1967), at three years of age, had stopped looking at the world and at people by regularly stuffing her fingers in her eyes. Sometimes she sat for hours, tapping her chin with her fingers while staring fixedly and without sign of comprehension at movement about her. At the age of 10 Marcia sat for hours in a yogalike position, either motionless or excitedly rocking up and down. She would say "no," but never "yes," and would echo only a few words in a whisper. Marcia had to be dressed; the act of dressing required infinite patience in waiting for her to finally whisper her private language utterance of "fas . . . EN," her plea to be helped. Marcia was obsessed that people meant to devour her and had confused the phrase "we eat her" with the word *weather* and so was compulsively concerned with a watch on the daily movement of weather. Bettelheim also says that she often refused food to keep herself from being devoured, as she had to devour the food.

Joey   Joey functioned as a machine, a mechanical boy, run by imaginary machines created by him and beyond his control. His body movements were those of a complex machine. Bettelheim (1967) notes that it often took a conscious act of will to make himself perceive Joey as a child. When Joey was "at rest," he remained as motionless as a machine. Joey carried a series of tubes, small motors, and so on with him, which he believed served as sources of power for his machine body. When he started up from his motionless machine existence, he would come "alive" in a machine fashion, with noises of a berserk nature. Wherever Joey went, he laid down an imaginary wire to an imaginary power source and insulated himself with a wire to a piece of furniture. He could eat, sleep, play, defecate, read, or move only with his power "plugged in" because it ran his body. Bettelheim (1967) says that Joey's pantomime was so skilled and his concentration so contagious that those who watched him seemed to suspend their own existence and become observers of another reality.

Thus studies of autistic children demonstrate the ways in which a lack of socialization or incomplete socialization may produce disorganization of behavior in an otherwise physically capable and healthy child.

Cases of Extreme Social and Cultural Isolation

Feurbach's account in 1832 of the isolation of a boy named Kaspar Hauser posed quite precisely, for the first time, the question of, "What happens to the person who is raised in extreme social and cultural isolation?"[2] This instance of isolation now appears to be one of a lost or abandoned older autistic child who somehow managed to survive. When found, Kaspar was bereft of many responses and actions usually associated with a boy of his age. Since the accuracy of the reports by Feurbach is in general question, it was not until reports by Davis of the case of Anna and by Mason and Davis of the case of Isabelle that reliable descriptions of extreme instances of social and cultural isolation became available.

Anna   Anna was an illegimate child whose grandfather so disapproved of her mother's behavior that he forced the baby to be confined in an upstairs room where the infant was provided only the physical care needed to keep her alive. Anna was infrequently moved from one position to another, and her clothing and bedding were rarely changed. Apparently she had no friendly instruction and minimal social contact. Anna was found and taken out of the room when she was six years old. She could not walk or talk and showed no behavior that could be called "intelligent." She was emaciated and badly nourished, apathetic, expressionless, and apparently indifferent to everything about her. She made no movements on her own behalf to feed, dress, or care for herself. Davis (1949) has noted in describing Anna's case that her condition shows how little her purely biological resources alone could contribute to making her a complete person.

At the age of 10½ years Anna died from hemorrhagic jaundice. However she had made considerable progress in learning social and cultural behavior in the four years after she was discovered. She had learned to follow verbal directions, could identify a few colors, build with play blocks, and respond to "attractive" and "unattractive" pictures. She cuddled and played with a doll. She had learned to talk in phrases. She could repeat words clearly and tried regularly to carry on a conversation. She learned to wash her hands before and after eating and to care for her teeth by brushing. She tried to help in the care of other children in the county home setting where she was being cared for by untrained persons. She learned to walk well and to run without falling. While she was easily excitable, Anna was reported to have a pleasant disposition. In all, at the time of her death, Anna's social behavior was estimated to be that of a child of two and one-half to three years of age. A complete interpretation of Anna's development was made impossible by her death. It is probable that Anna was somewhat

[2]For a discussion of Feurbach's account of Kaspar Hauser, see Wagler, 1928.

"mentally deficient" from the outset. It is quite clear, however, that Anna made extraordinary progress in her social and culture learning in a very short period. This case illustrates the point that communicative contact is one of the elements making up the essence of the socialization process.

Isabelle Another well-documented case of extreme social and cultural isolation is that of Isabelle, who was found at six years of age in circumstances very much like those in which Anna was discovered (Davis, 1949). Isabelle was an illegitimate child and was kept in seclusion because of her illegitimacy. Her mother was a deaf mute. Isabelle and her mother spent most of their time together in a darkened room. She communicated with her mother by means of gestures and did not develop her speech beyond a few croaking sounds. She was suffering badly from rickets because of her diet and lack of sunlight. When found, her actions seemed to show "fear" and "hostility." At first, after taking her from her isolation, observers were unsure whether Isabelle could hear. It was concluded that her behavioral development was approximately that of a 19-month-old child. The first medical specialists to work with Isabelle pronounced her to be "feeble-minded," but the trained persons in charge of her care began a carefully designed program to teach her to speak and act. At first Isabelle showed little response, but over the next months she began to exhibit more skills in her use of language and in her behavior. Then she went rapidly through each of the "stages" of social and cultural learning said to be typical of children in American society. In less than three months after speaking her first words she was putting sentences together. Ten months later she could identify words and sentences printed on cards and pages. She could write legibly, add to ten, and retell a story in the general sequence in which it had been told. In another seven months she had an estimated vocabulary of between 1400 and 2000 words and was capable of asking and answering complex questions.

So beginning at age six with an apparent level of social and cultural learning of between one and two years, Isabelle reached a social and cultural level typical of an American six-year-old in a two-year period. Another way to state this would be to say that in two years Isabelle learned the social and cultural skills ordinarily believed to take six years for American children to learn. Isabelle eventually entered a public school, where she took part in school activities without special provisions for her. By the time she was 14 years old she was in the sixth grade, where her teachers rated her as a competent and well-adjusted student. Isabelle is reported to have completed high school with better-than-average grades, to have married, and to have her own "normal" family.

The Crib Sisters Kagan and Klein (1973, 958–959) have provided additional evidence of the effects of severe social and cultural isolation in human infants and children. Two sisters, a year apart in age, were restricted to a crib in a room with no toys and minimal social contact by their mother who believed she was unable to care for them. The two infants were taken from their crib to another room only to be fed and bathed. According to an older sister of the two girls, the infants spent about 23 hours each day alone in their barren crib. When local law enforcement authorities learned of this treatment, the girls, who were 2½ and 3½ years old, were removed from their crib and taken to a hospital. On examination they were found to be malnourished, severely retarded in height and weight, and judged to be seriously retarded psychologically. After a month in the hospital the sisters were placed as foster children with a middle-class family with several young children. The sisters remained in their foster home for more than 12 years. The sisters were tested by Jerome Kagan, a leading scholar in child development, five times between 4 and 9 years of age, and were reinterviewed and tested at 14½ and 15½ years of age.

Kagan states that the younger sister has performed "consistently better" on all tests than the older sister over a ten-year period. He also notes that the IQ scores of the younger sister have increased steadily, from a Stanford-Binet score of 74 at 4½ years, following two years in her foster home, to a Wechsler Full Scale IQ score of 88 at age 14. The older sister's IQ scores also increased but not as dramatically as her younger sister's scores. Kagan notes that the scores of the sisters on a battery of child development tests were consistently "competent" for their ages. He also points out that their interpersonal behavior was "in no way different" from that of the average rural Ohio adolescents that the sisters lived among. Kagan and Klein (1973, 959) conclude that, while there is some question about the competence of the older sister, the younger sister now performs at an average score level on a wide range of tests of development of cognitive functioning despite 2½ years of severe isolation.

Comparisons and Contrasts

Isabelle's case is different from Anna's in several important respects. Although both girls were judged to have a very low "intellectual" level to begin with and both reached a considerably higher level of social and cultural skills than when first brought from their situations of isolation, Isabelle telescoped into two years the same kinds of learning Anna took four and one-half years to acquire or did not acquire at all prior to her death. This suggests that Isabelle had a greater learning capacity to begin with and that Anna probably was somewhat deficient in such a capacity. However it should be recalled that Isabelle had prolonged and very expert training, while Anna did not. Davis (1949) says that if Anna had started her speech patterns earlier, after being brought from her isolation, she might have progressed more than she did.

What is important is that there would appear from these instances of extreme isolation to be a process of accelerated recovery in which the isolated child goes through what have been said to be the usual stages of socialization at a more rapid pace than is the instance in "normal" development of cultural learning. At present no one knows the age at which a person can be removed from extreme social and cultural isolation and still fully acquire culture. Davis estimates it could be as old as 15 years or as young as 10 years.[3] Whatever the case may be, it is quite obvious that the human propensity for acquiring culture is very durable and quite "tough" in the adverse circumstances of extreme isolation.

Degrees of Isolation: Biological, Social, Cultural

The cases of Anna and Isabelle illustrate the extreme in cultural isolation. However there are a number of other, less extreme forms of isolation that are also important in understanding socialization. Generally these are of two types: (1) *immobilizing isolation* and (2) *nonimmobilizing isolation*. Immobilizing isolation is generally the result of infants and children being biologically incapable of participating in the socialization process. These children include all those born with deficient capacities for learning and cognition, those born with brain damage, deafness, muteness, or blindness, or those suffering from diseases that seriously harm the central nervous system.

Being Immobilized

There are many degrees of immobilizing isolation, ranging from the child with cerebral palsy to children afflicted by rheumatic fever. In most instances such children regularly miss participating in some significant aspects of the socialization process. Thus a mentally deficient or brain-damaged child cannot hope to compete for high-status positions that are earned through success in athletic competitions and in schools, colleges, and universities. Children not severely immobilized sometimes can learn successfully to participate in the ongoing life of society through substitution of one or another of their psychomotor, cognitive, or learning capacities that remain unimpaired by illness. Many reliable accounts have been written about individuals who have been born with severe limb handicaps and have subsequently learned to drive an automobile, type, use a pencil, and so on.

---

[3]Curtiss, Fromkin, Rigler, Krashen, and Krashen (1975) report on the language development of Genie, a girl removed by police in 1970 from her home at age 13 years, 9 months, and placed first in a hospital for almost a year, and then as a member of a foster family. In 1974 at nearly 18 years of age and after nearly four years of training, Genie was using language, although incompletely and at a low level, despite nearly 14 years of isolation and abuse. See also Curtiss, 1977.

Persons born with severely immobilizing defects can also learn to overcome them if other capacities remain unimpaired and are of high potential. The account of Helen Keller's recovery from her nearly total cultural isolation because of her blindness and deafness is a dramatic example of the ways other capacities, in this instance the use of the sense of touch, can sometimes break down the barriers of immobilizing isolation. The cases of autistic children who have recovered also indicate that even the most severe isolation, which is nearly fully immobilizing, can sometimes be overcome with patient and long-term efforts to engage children in caring about themselves and others.

Not Being Immobilized

Nonimmobilizing isolation from the socialization process is of three types: (1) *social*, (2) *locational*, and (3) *cultural*. These kinds of isolation are characterized by the fact that infants are born with unimpaired or undamaged species-characteristic behavior forms, reflexes, drives, and capacities, but because of some particular feature of their local culture, they are unable to participate fully in the enculturation process.

Social Isolation

The best-known examples of social isolation are those in which individuals are said to have culturally ascribed "defects" of race, class, caste, clique, clan, club, or religion, so that children find it very difficult to gain access to full participation in the enculturation process of their society.

Social isolation can range from factors almost inconsequential because they can be overcome, as in the instances of children who attend sessions for private language or religious instruction after completion of their public school day, to those of major consequence, as in the instances of children unable to obtain only minimal public schooling because of their race, economic or social class, or religion.

In a large and heterogenous society, such as the modern American society, many diverse factors of social isolation are in operation. Each person has been isolated to some degree from some aspects of all possible cultural learning. The factors of social isolation with the greatest effect on American infants and children, such as race, social and economic class, and religion, may bar them from lifelong and effective participation in their society by causing them to be regularly isolated from the practical knowledge, details, and basic ideas widely shared in their society.[4]

---

[4]Montagu (1972) has suggested that a whole range of "behavioral deficits" are found in children who have experienced brain damage through being isolated in impoverished social environments where they are seriously malnourished. See also Joffe, 1969; Stott, 1966; Montagu, 1962.

There are also some factors of social isolation that derive from biological bases but are not immobilizing. Generally such factors are physical disfigurements that limit certain kinds of social action and learning. These factors, which vary greatly from culture to culture, include facial and body warts, moles, scars, large birthmarks, harelips, gross overweight and underweight, dwarfism, giantism, and grotesque misshapenness ("hunchback"), missing or deformed limbs, and so on. Individuals afflicted with such disfigurements often find themselves blocked off from learning and participating in many activities in their culture. Thus it is rare to see an American corporation executive, public official, or professor with such nonimmobilizing but biologically based defects.

Locational Isolation

Factors of locational isolation are found to some degree in all large societies. Individuals are born and often live in only one region of the geographic territories occupied by their society. If a society is large and spreads across large land areas, regional isolation may play an important part in the enculturation process of a society. This is especially so where there is a limited technology, which does not include high-speed transportation, television, and radio, all of which tend to break down barriers of locational isolation. In most of the larger societies of the world, some significant differences in the enculturation process occur because of locational isolation. Thus Kagan and Klein (1973) have noted that infants and children living in subsistence farming communities in Guatemala are isolated in significant ways from Guatemalan culture.[5]

This is also true in the United States. Accents, folk culture content (in some regions a "sack" is a "poke," while in others it is a "bag"), and even styles of posture, gesture, and gait are recognizable and are often used as bases for permitting social access to facilities and ideas.[6]

Locational isolation also includes housing and neighborhood features. Growing up in a particular section of a city or county may result in a whole range of isolating factors coming into play, including an individual's access to recreation, housing, education, medical care, transportation, and communication. The street address of children is vital to their enculturation for when they go to a neighborhood school they may be limited by social

---

[5]Kagan and Klein also note that infants in Guatemalan subsistence farming communities receive little attention from adults in the first year of life and, as they mature, appear to an observer from another culture to be "mentally retarded,"—that is, are listless and show little interest in events taking place about them. However Kagan and Klein say that by 11 years of age these Guatemalan children have become as active and alert as a "middle-class" American child of the same age. Kagan and Klein conclude from their study that "environmental factors" may slow down or speed up the emergence of intellectual competency but that the capacities for symbolism, memory, and inference will emerge strongly in children growing up in normal, or "natural," environments.

[6]Americans "carry," "tote," or "heist" their food; some "carry groceries in a bag," others "tote vittles in a poke," while others "heist food in a sack."

definitions that impose upon them a special pattern of access to their society's broad range of cultural behavior.

Isolated from a Culture

Cultural isolation includes all those factors related to an individual being unable to gain access to the widely shared patterns of learned behavior transmitted in a society from one generation to the next. These factors include linguistic, customary behavior, and value judgment forms of action and belief. Some individuals in American society are unable to participate in many patterns of American culture because they do not speak English or speak and comprehend the language badly. Of the more than one million native Americans living in the territory of the United States, nearly one quarter do not speak English as a "first" language. Many speak so little English as to be incapable of carrying on a simple conversation. There are millions of foreign-born residents of the United States, a large number of whom speak very little English. Typically the children of these persons, both native American and immigrant, are handicapped in their access to the dominant patterns of American culture. Language is a formidable isolation factor, especially when coupled with other factors of locational and social isolation.

Many individuals have been isolated from widely shared cultural patterns in their societies because of their having learned particular beliefs or ways of action that are especially provincial or parochial in form and meaning. In the United States, for example, success in certain occupations such as banking, medicine, dentistry, law, and military service as an officer is often limited or enhanced by whether a person has a particular set of values. Thus it is difficult to reach and to retain an executive position with a laborer's values. The attitudes and judgments expected by boards of directors in large corporations are not usually learned by children of laborers. In some instances the American system of free public education has made it possible for the child of a laborer to learn to express and even to comprehend the values of other occupational groups, providing, of course, other significant factors of isolation were not operating in the individual's life career. The factor of cultural isolation in socialization can affect large segments of a society organized by castes or classes based on specialized education and occupations.

Individuals in Extreme Situational Isolation; Reversing the Socialization Process

There are other instances of isolation that are extreme in nature and that may be as inescapable as the various factors of immobilizing and non-immobilizing isolation. For adults, and even children, these situations can lead to a reversal of the socialization process. The first evidence of this came from experimental studies of human isolation through the use of drugs or mechanical devices that obstruct or muffle senses. However these experimental situations are not as totally overwhelming as are situations in which there remains no hope of escape and relief.

Nazi Death Camps and Reversal of Enculturation

Bruno Bettelheim worked with autistic children in Germany from 1932 until 1934. Then he was imprisoned in a Nazi concentration camp until 1938. In these years, as a trained observer of human behavior, he sought to defend himself psychologically from the constant danger and inescapability of the camp by trying to study clinically the reactions of his fellow prisoners. Bettelheim (1943) witnessed in many of his fellows a continuous *deculturation process*, or a constant wearing away of those learned attributes of self and many forms of cultural behavior that had characterized the German prisoners before their arrest. Bettelheim's observations are mostly confirmed by Cohen's (1953) study of concentration camp behavior.[7] In the camps the first response of many prisoners to their danger was to pay the minutest attention to every sign of harm, to each guard, to the prisoner foreman, to each noise in the distance, and to each abrupt or large-scale movement. Finally after long-term stress caused by such concerns, prisoners either "converted" themselves from their Judaic religion to a synthetic faith and action or moved on to a form of psychological adaptation that involved paying less attention to mortal danger and more to self-preservation actions such as trying to find "safe" or less difficult job assignments, making friends to share a confidence with, and finding a better place to sleep.

Converts to Death   The Nazi prisoners who responded to the constant danger by professing a synthetic religion became increasingly more focused on extreme dangers in the camp to the exclusion of every other matter, so that all actions by everyone, prisoners as well as guards, became destructive in design and intent. Bettelheim (1967, 77) notes that for these prisoners nothing existed except the unrelieved prospect of death. Psychologically these prisoners responded to external dangers with ego defenses that caused continuing debilitation of their acquired selves to the point of an autisticlike withdrawal from all contacts with life and reality.

Converts to Life   In contrast, the Nazi prisoners who moved on from initial perception of a mortal danger to concerns with self-preservation adapted psychologically by hopeful thinking and daydreaming and by plotting revenge and making elaborate plans to this particular end. There apparently was considerably less debilitation of self resources for such pris-

---

[7]See also Vaughan, 1949; Leighton, 1963; Wilkins, 1967; Biderman, 1967; Cohen & Taylor, 1973; DesPres, 1976. See also Kellerman, 1977.

oners. Through these insignificant actions, in terms of "normal" situations, many of these prisoners survived psychologically and were not subject to deculturation. Bettelheim is of the opinion that these persons saved their lives and selves in an extreme situation by taking a hand in their own fate, through forcing their attention toward something besides the never-ending threat of death.

Prisoners of War and Reversal of Enculturation

An extensive study of Americans captured and imprisoned by the North Koreans and Chinese in the Korean War confirms Bettelheim's conclusions about extreme situational isolation possibly producing a reversal of the socialization process. Although this study set out to identify ". . . those attributes, those traits or skills which are required by soldiers to aid them in resisting the enemy if captured" (U.S. Senate, 1956, 79), it also produced quite valuable knowledge regarding the ways the socialization process may be reversed. In the study a total of 3323 repatriated American prisoners were separated into two groups: (1) those who actively resisted the enemy while prisoners and (2) those who "participated" (or "collaborated") in enemy activities while prisoners. Based on the interviews conducted by armed services personnel, about 500 individuals of the second group were recommended for court-martial, dishonorable discharge, or other forms of less than honorable separation from the U.S. armed forces. A civilian psychologist working under contract to the U.S. Army later made a study of these individuals and of a sample of other noncollaborating soldier prisoners of similar rank, race, length of service, length of captivity, and places of imprisonment. Using the personnel dossiers of all the prisoner soldiers in the study, the psychologist obtained more than 300 items of "personal information" and developed 27 "rating scales" to judge the reported prison camp actions of the prisoners in terms of their civilian and military backgrounds.

A Study of Collaboration This study showed that 70 percent of all the Americans held as prisoners during the Korean War, whether court-martial proceedings had been used or not after release, had made at least one contribution to the enemy's propaganda effort.[8] The main effort with the

---

[8]In the period between 1972 and 1974, four Japanese soldiers from World War II finally emerged from their long-term, self-imposed isolation. Pvt. Shoichi Yokoi hid in the jungles of Guam for 27 years and was discovered by two hunters in January 1972. Pfc. Kinshichi Kozuka and Lt. Hiro Onoda hid on Lubang Island in the Philippines until surprised by a Philippine government patrol in October 1972; Kozuka was killed and Onoda was wounded as they tried to flee from the patrol. Lee Kuang Huei, an army draftee from then Japanese-occupied "Formosa" (Taiwan) lived for 29 years on the Indonesian island of Morotai, afraid he would be executed if he surrendered. Lee, whose Japanese name was Teuro Nakamura, finally turned himself in to Indonesian police authorities in December 1974. The Japanese government estimates that some 3750 unaccounted-for World War II soldiers may still be hiding in remote areas of the Pacific carrying out orders to not surrender to the enemy.

prisoners by the Korean and Chinese captors was to have the soldiers "accept communism as a social and economic system above and beyond their prior beliefs and concepts" (U.S. Senate, 1956, 89). The most common method used in seeking this change in values among the American prisoners was a simple classroom-type lecture approach rather than widespread brutality and torture, use of drugs or sex, and so forth. Some lectures were conducted for their captors by American prisoners. As a consequence of these lectures, 39 percent of all prisoners signed enemy propaganda petitions, 22 percent made propaganda recordings, 11 percent wrote propaganda articles, 5 percent wrote petitions, 5 percent circulated petitions among their fellows, and 16 percent had full-time propaganda jobs (U.S. Senate, 1956, 88). At least 10 percent of the prisoners of all ranks were regular informers for their captors.

Brainwashing and brainwashing   The vital point of this study is that the techniques usually associated by the public with the "brainwashing" process—individuals isolated from all normal associations and their usual environment, deprived of food, water, and sleep, subjected to gross physical brutality, and kept in solitary confinement except when undergoing long periods of brutal indoctrination and interrogation—generally were not used on most of the American prisoners who participated in the enemy war effort.[9]

Even more important for studies of human response to extreme isolation and consequent possible reversal of the socialization process was the fact that a research psychologist, after careful study using standard psychological methods, could find little difference between those who resisted all efforts at value change and those who participated in their captors' efforts. The psychologist noted that there were no significant differences between these two groups with respect to age, education, civilian occupation, marital status, or the region of the country from which they came or in which they were born. There was a slight difference in the two groups in terms of their general intelligence levels. The servicemen who were the

[9]The specific methods (Schein, 1956) used by Korean and Chinese captors in "brainwashing" included: (1) enforcement of trivial demands to develop compliance to commands; (2) repeated suggestions concerning the futility of resistance; (3) use of unpredictable favors or kindness; (4) use of threats to cultivate anxiety, dread, or despair; (5) personal degradation through denial of body care and hygiene; (6) control of perceptions by alternating access to light and darkness in order to fix prisoner attention on their situation of captivity and danger; (7) isolation to focus prisoner concern on survival; and (8) debilitation by starvation, exposure to heat and cold, and failure to treat illness. It should be noted that prisoners who were subjected to such brutalizing forms of treatment were left listless, were extremely depressed, were subject to bursts of anger, had nightmares, and had difficulty in personal relationships. Many prisoners having strong convictions, pride in self, and loyalty to their service and country also died under such treatment. DesPres (1976) provides a description of such methods and their effects on Nazi and Russian death camp prisoners. See also Winokor, 1955; Lifton, 1956.

most active collaborators were somewhat less intelligent, as measured by tests administered at the time of enlistment or induction.

Other factors   The factor of cooperation with, or resistance to, their captors by Americans thus appeared to have been based on some other aspect of their experience. The psychologist directing the study concluded that whether prisoners collaborated with their captors depended largely on their response to the captors' promises of immediate material rewards, such as more blankets, a warmer hut, or new clothes, rather than on the purely ideological inducements offered by the Chinese and Korean guards and interrogators. Offers of special treatment and privileges in the severe living conditions of the Korean prisoner-of-war camps, especially during the harsh winters, seems to have been the key to the prisoners' behavior. It appears that the offers of material rewards for cooperation with captors were real and were usually fulfilled for those Americans willing to pay the price of cooperation.

Thus 70 percent of the American prisoners in the Korean War were induced by their captors to abandon some basic American values to maintain other values. Studies of American values indicate that the American conception of "material well-being," which was used as a lure to collaboration by Korean and Chinese captors, is a very old, widely shared, and deeply felt American value.

Analysis of American values suggests that the focal value (see Chapter 8) of material well-being is vital in American culture since it appears directly linked to a basic American premise—that of believing humans are the masters of the universe. Americans hold this premise in most life situations. The value of material well-being notes that a high standard of living is an inherent and natural "right" to be demanded by all Americans and that success in attaining material goods (a new car, house, suit) carries a moral sanction; it is believed not only to be "right" to seek out comfort but also to be a moral virtue of a high order. Americans have relatively little tolerance for pain, brutality, or threat of death since these all interrupt access to success in gaining material well-being. Americans are usually repelled by contact with poverty and misery and try to seek an immediate release from such situations. It appears that the captors of the American soldiers were well aware of the intensity and long history of the focal value of material well-being in American life and used it deliberately to their advantage in seeking collaboration from prisoners.

Values in deculturation   When the experience of American prisoners of the North Koreans and Chinese is compared with the experience of the Nazi concentration camp and Russian death camp prisoners, a clear indication emerges that not only can humans in extreme situations suffer from a deculturation process but also that this process consists at least partly of a personal striving to adjust new and peculiar circumstances to be congruent with values ordinarily learned in a process of socialization.[10]

Extreme Isolation—Conclusions

Studies of individuals in situations of extreme isolation tend to support the general conclusions noted in earlier chapters concerning the complex ways the biological and the cultural transmission processes become interrelated in the life career of individuals undergoing a process of socialization. The cases of autistic children, Anna, and Isabelle show the vital place of communicative contact in socialization. Studies of extreme situational isolation demonstrate that it is possible to reverse the socialization process or at least to bring about a refocusing of acquired basic values in such a way that one focal value, or even a basic premise of a culture, comes to take precedence over all other values or premises in the fight to live and to escape from extreme isolation.

It should also be noted that there now is substantive evidence from eyewitness testimony, autobiographies, and personal diaries that using illegal, forced imprisonment in a penal institution, a "mental hospital," or as a hostage as a governmental strategy of personal and political harassment and constraint can also create an extreme situation of isolation and may lead to reversal of the socialization process. Some nations of the modern world employ the authority of the modern practice of psychiatry (Szasz, 1970) to use mental hospitals as political prisons for ideological dissenters. Persons illegally held in such situations for long periods suffer from the same effects as the prisoners in Nazi, Russian, Korean, Chinese, and Vietnamese camps, especially if they are held captive among genuinely ill individuals. There are strong indications that the process of growing old and dying may also involve a reversal of the socialization process. In studies by Anderson (1969) and Marshall (1975), some aged Americans appeared to be systematically deculturated as preparation for their status as aged persons and as individuals facing death.

These data all seem to indicate that the socialization process could be effectively studied from observing and analyzing the effects of extreme situations. Most studies of socialization concentrate now on developmental, or ontogenetic, factors. It may be as useful to learn about the ways extreme situations may break apart the links forged between biology and culture in a socialization process.

---

[10]The experiences of American prisoners held for a long period during the Vietnam War also confirm this conclusion.

TWIN STUDIES

Additional scientific evidence demonstrating the ways in which human biology and culture become related in a socialization process is found in the literature of twin studies.

Identical and Fraternal Twins

There are two types of twins: *monozygotic* ("one egg" or "identical") and *dizygotic* ("two egg" or "fraternal") twins. Monozygotic twins are derived from the same fertilized ovum because of an accident of development in the course of initial cell division after conception; monozygotic twins have identical genetic materials. Dizygotic twins are derived from an almost simultaneous impregnation by sperm of two ova; dizygotic twins do not have identical genetic materials since the sperm and the ova that joined in the two instances of fertilization have different assortments of genetic materials.

Monozygotic twins are always of the same sex and have the same features of skin, hair, and eye pigmentation and blood group type. Monozygotic twins are also alike in many other physical-chemical factor compositions, including those of their saliva and urine, and they manifest similar patterns of brain electrical activity. It usually is possible to determine from such physical similarities whether twins are monozygotic or dizygotic. The chemical (saliva, urine) similarities of monozygotic twins may remain even in the cases of such twins being separated shortly after birth and raised in very different home environments.

Twin Studies and Their Limits

It seems that careful study of twins, especially monozygotic twins, would provide detailed information concerning the ways different environments, both between cultures and within the same culture, will affect the same gene materials as children mature. It would appear that studies of monozygotic twins separated at birth and then raised in very different circumstances could provide clear answers to the special questions concerning the ways the biological and cultural modes of transmission in socialization become interrelated and function together. Unfortunately this has not been the case, for a significant amount of twin research over the past half-century has demonstrated that even monozygotic twins show consistent individual differences, although they were raised in the same family setting.

Twins T and C Gesell and Thompson (1929) studied monozygotic twins "T" and "C" for a period of 14 years after their birth. The method of "co-twin control" was employed in this study; twin T would be given early special training in such actions as block building, manual coordination, and so on, while twin C was left untrained. At first twin T excelled in such skills, but twin C was just as skilled when she reached the same level of physical development. This long-term study demonstrated that there were a number of persistent differences between T and C. T was quicker, while C was more careful. T used straight lines and angles while drawing, while C consistently drew curved lines. T gave quicker attention, but C was more alert. T learned a bit more quickly, but C was more adept in a social situation. It can be concluded from this study that even monozygotic twins reared together will show basic differences in their learning and behavior.

Mabel and Mary   Newman's (1937) description of "Mabel" and "Mary" makes the conclusion easy to accept that monozygotic twins reared in quite different settings are very different because of their different home environments, unless these data are contrasted with the work of Gesell and Thompson. Monozygotic twins Mabel and Mary were separated shortly after their birth. Mabel lived in a country home and grew up working at strenuous farm chores. She completed the eighth grade in a rural school. Mary grew up in a city of medium size. She completed high school in city schools. She became a music teacher after her graduation. Mabel and Mary both lived in fairly well-to-do homes. At 29 years of age Mabel and Mary were studied and found to be at least 17 points different on the Stanford-Binet intelligence test. Mary was judged to be high-average and Mabel was judged to be low-average in intelligence. Mabel was phlegmatic and slow in her social responses. Mary was very excitable. Mabel was very "masculine" in appearance and had a "masculine walk" and a large, 138-pound, hard-muscled frame. Mary was quite "feminine," with a 110-pound, soft-muscled body. Mabel and Mary seemed quite unlike the identical twins they were, in nearly every aspect, except for a general "family" resemblance. Thus this case would seem to demonstrate the striking way in which different cultural environments produce very different individuals even though they share the same gene stuff. Based on works such as the Gesell and Thompson study, this conclusion is not as valid as it appears, however. This is because use of conclusions from twin studies has been confounded by research comparing monozygotic and dizygotic twins reared in different and similar environments ignoring three crucial points: (1) that twins separated by adoption are not often randomly placed in their new homes, (2) that the home environments of separated monozygotic twins sometimes could be more alike than the environments of separated dizygotic twins, and (3) the size of the sample, or number of twins compared in studies, has usually been limited.

Cattell (1960) has argued that the style of twin research, similar to the one used in the study of Mabel and Mary, should be modified to another type of methodological approach, which he terms *multiple abstract variance analysis*. This method, which is essentially statistical in form and content, involves study of variations in four factors: (1) differences in the environments between families with twins, (2) differences of heredity between families with twins, (3) differences of environments for individuals within the same family, and especially for twins, and (4) differences of heredity between siblings in the same family, including twins. Cattell claims this approach avoids the artificial and limited nature of the twin study method by seeking to determine the relative importance and specific relations between the biological and cultural modes of transmission in socialization.

Recent Efforts in Twin Studies

Efforts have been made recently by psychologists to account for such research problems and questions concerning methods used in twin studies to investigate the interrelations between biology and culture in socialization. Newman and his associates (1966) have published an account of their conclusions from many types of twin studies, particularly monozygotic twins raised apart. Loehlin and Nichols (1976) have reported their conclusions based on studies of 850 sets of twins. Scheinfeld (1973) has offered comments concerning the nature of the relationships of human heredity and the socialization process derived from twin studies. A long-term study by Thomas Bouchard, a psychologist, and his colleagues at the University of Minnesota currently involves the most comprehensive study undertaken of monozygotic twins raised apart.[11]

The Bouchard research team has 17 specialists, including 6 psychologists, 2 psychiatrists, and 9 medical specialists of various types. Each one of the 15 pairs of monozygotic twins reared apart studied so far have been given several dozen written tests, which ask approximately 15,000 questions ranging from family and childhood environments to fears, values, aesthetic and musical tastes, and reading habits. Each pair of twins studied by the Bouchard team has undergone three comprehensive psychological tests and several ability, vocabulary, and intelligence tests. In addition, each pair of twins has been asked for a detailed medical history and have been examined physically through use of electrocardiograms, chest X-rays, heart and lung tests, allergic responses, and brain wave responses to various stimuli. Bouchard notes that a study of these test results, conducted over a six-day period while the twin pairs were at the University of Minnesota,

[11]See Holden, 1980.

will occupy at least five or six years. One very tentative conclusion to be drawn from this work is that the degree of coincidental behavior among monozygotic twins reared apart is much greater than had been demonstrated in other twin studies. This is particularly true in the area of emotional problems—for instance, mild depression and phobias of various kinds. A second tentative conclusion to be drawn from this ongoing study is that scores on standard intelligence tests taken by most of the Minnesota twins do not differ anymore than those scores on two tests taken by the same individual at different times. Where there are significant differences in intelligence scores by the Minnesota twins reared apart, there are also considerable differences in education.

Twin Studies and Socialization

Vandenberg (1966) has reviewed the contributions of the twin research method to the study of socialization and concludes that, while the twin study method has contributed greatly to understanding the broad outlines of the nature of the interactions of the biological and cultural modes of transmission in socialization, the method has distinct limitations for future research. However twin studies continue to be a basic source of data for learning about the ways human biology and culture are interrelated and function together to produce a socialized human being.

THE CRITICAL PERIODS HYPOTHESIS

Origin and Nature of the Hypothesis

Beginning in the middle 1920s several individuals observed phenomena which suggested the idea that there are vitally important points, periods, or stages in the behavioral development of organisms when the organism was most receptive to specific stimulation from its environment. The studies of von Senden (1960) on the behavior of congenitally blind persons after corrective eye surgery led him to the conclusion that visual space and shape perception in humans depends on specific experiences that must occur early in life for normal vision to be present. At the same time, Piaget (1926, 1932) was conducting his pioneering studies of language and reasoning development in infants and young children. Piaget also concluded that there is a time of quite limited duration when infants or children must be exposed to certain learning experiences if specific actions are to become a regular part of their adult behavior. Somewhat later Lorenz (1952) reached a similar conclusion from his observations of animal behavior. He noted that there are antecedent, or earlier, experiences that must occur very early in the life of an animal if it is later to perform successfully in more complex ways.

Spitz (1946) also reached the same conclusion after observing the behavior of orphaned and abandoned infants and children raised by hospital staff members. He suggested that human infants have a special stage of increased efficiency for learning specific cultural responses, before which such responses cannot be acquired and after which the chances of learning them are markedly reduced. During this time Gesell (1954) also formulated a theoretical model of child development in which the interplay and reciprocal influence of two opposite and supposedly biologically inherited tendencies to behavioral integration and differentiation were said to occur at critical times of limited duration.[12]

A Critical Periods Statement

In essence, these scholars all were formulating a hypothesis that can be briefly summarized as follows:

> There are critical periods, or stages, in the development of all animals, including humans, during which the individual is more receptive to learning from particular kinds of experiences. These periods are of very limited duration. If an experience is to become a regular part of an individual's later behavior, it has to be acquired during the critical period when the individual is most ready to learn from that kind of experience. Earlier or later exposure to such experience will produce little or no effect on the individual's later actions.

Research Efforts

This hypothesis produced great interest among those conducting socialization research since it promised, once particular behavior forms were identified and their critical periods specified, an understanding of the acquisition of culture and of personality development and possible solutions to a whole range of difficult social problems such as delinquency, alcoholism, divorce, and so on.

After World War II a variety of efforts were made to provide experimental evidence to support the critical periods hypothesis. Research efforts centered upon studies of (1) sensory processes, (2) imprinting, and (3) the social and sexual behavior of experimental animals. The results of these studies have often been generalized to humans and then used in research on the socialization process, either as hypotheses for research or

---

[12]Gesell's theoretical model provides for a number of critical periods during maturation, with some occurring in late childhood and adolescence.

as unstated assumptions concerning the nature of humans and the phenomenon of socialization.

Critical Periods in Sensory Processes

A number of studies of sensory deprivation (Hess, 1961) have been made to test the critical periods hypothesis. In one test of the effects of early vision deprivation on later ability to perceive movements, four groups of cats were exposed to four different sets of conditions: (1) a normal laboratory environment, (2) one hour each day of diffuse light, (3) a normal laboratory environment, but with the cat's movements restricted by a special harness, and (4) one hour each day of free-moving light. The cats in the second and fourth groups were raised from birth to eight weeks of age in total darkness and were then placed in one of the conditions noted above. After the experimental period all the cats were tested for their abilities to choose visually between a rotating and a stationary X, placed on two doors that had to be pushed to obtain a food reward. The cats of the second and third groups could not discriminate between the rotating and stationary X's, whereas the cats of the first and fourth (or control) groups did so without apparent difficulty.

In a second study using the same conditions of experimentation, cats were subjected to three tasks of visual discrimination learning: (1) discrimination of light and dark, (2) discrimination of horizontal and vertical stripes, and (3) discrimination of a black dot, a stationary dot, and a bouncing dot. No differences were found among the four groups of cats in discrimination of light and dark, and only slight differences were found between the control (first and fourth) and other (second and third) groups with regard to discrimination between horizontal and vertical stripes. However there was a marked difference between the cats of the first and fourth groups and those of the second and third groups with respect to discrimination of movement. The control (first and fourth) groups learned the discrimination of movement after 450 and before 900 trials, whereas the other groups (second and third) still had not learned to discriminate movement after 2000 trials.

These studies, and others similar to them, seem to indicate that at least in some animals there are specific times, of limited duration, in which certain sensory experiences must occur if the animal is to behave "normally" as an adult. However it has also become obvious from these studies that there are significant differences in critical periods of sensory learning in different kinds of animals. The fact that cats apparently must be subjected to movement discrimination experiences in the first five months of life does not seem applicable to members of other animal groups such as fish, birds, and amphibians and cannot even be generally extended as a principle to other kinds of mammals such as rats or monkeys.

Imprinting

A century ago, in the course of observing the behavior of young animals, Spalding (1873) noted that infant birds, ducklings, goslings, and chicks seemed to follow their parents as soon as they were hatched. He also noted that these young animals would as easily follow many other kinds of substitute parents; chicks would follow an adult duck or human as well as a hen. Spalding also pointed out that after a young bird had followed a substitute parent for a time it usually would not then follow its own parent.

Spalding's observations provided the basis for an intensive effort to understand the nature of *imprinting*, as the tendency to follow parents or substitute parents has been termed recently. Thorpe (1963) has summarized the results of research since Spalding's time concerning the imprinting process in this manner: (1) imprinting is a process of social attachment that seems to be confined to a specific period of limited duration and often to a particular set of environmental circumstances; (2) once a following attachment is formed by an animal, it tends to be extremely strong and often irreversible; (3) imprinting is often completed prior to the development of other behavior patterns with which imprinted behavior finally will be linked; and (4) the imprinting process is characteristic of an entire species, rather than being an individual activity.

Hess (1961) has further refined these observations through noting that (1) an animal can become attached to a "parent object" even though it may not be the biological parent or a member of the same species, (2) an animal may become attached to physical objects as easily as to other animals, and (3) even after long separation from the "imprinted object," an imprinted animal will continue to demonstrate "following" behavior toward that object.

The critical period for imprinting in some animals is very early and brief. For example, chicks have been shown to have a maximum receptivity to imprinting 16 hours after hatching and usually cannot be imprinted after 32 hours or later following hatching. In many other animals, however, the period during which imprinting occurs is delayed significantly if the animal is deprived of visual experiences after birth. The "following" response is also "lost" at a much earlier age in socially reared chicks and ducks than in isolated chicks and ducks. Isolated chicks have shown a very wide variation in their initial responses to an imprinting object, ranging from flight, fear, and apathy to aggression.

Imprinting in Humans Many studies have been undertaken of the possibilities of an imprinting process in humans. These studies have been inconclusive regarding existence of any type of human imprinting process. It seems that critical periods for imprinting experience become less fixed and much more complex as the phylogenetic scale is ascended.

(history) evolution of animal

In addition, attempts to experimentally demonstrate critical periods in human infants have confounded biological and cultural factors, such as one study of the smiling response in infants stimulated at feeding by the presentation of smiling human adult portraits. It was concluded from this study that the human smiling response is a function of the age at which a smiling adult face (or portrait) is first presented to the infant, thus indicating existence of a critical period for imprinting human smiling.[13] Transcultural studies of emotional responses provide evidence, however, that casts doubt on the validity of generalizations concerning the existence in humans of a critical period for a smiling response. Despite arguments by some ethologists to the contrary, humans do not seem to have a natural and universal "language" of emotion, including forms of smiling, greeting, grief, and so on. The meanings attached to such behavior forms are highly culturally structured.[14]

Critical Periods in Development of Social and Sexual Behavior

It was noted in Chapter 1 that humans and other primates share many structural characteristics. This is especially so in the instance of the primates of the *Hominoidea* group, which includes chimpanzees, gorillas, orangutans, gibbons, and modern humans. Humans and the chimpanzee are particularly alike in upper body anatomy, blood serum proteins, chromosome number and form, and dentition. They also share a great many behavioral characteristics, including the ability to use tools. Humans share considerably fewer structural and behavioral features with lemurs, loris, tarsiers, marmosets, macaques, and baboons. Among all the primates the fewest features of structure and behavior are shared between humans and lemurs.

However because of the availability and size of monkeys, particularly those of the genus *Macaca*, species *mulatta* (the rhesus monkey), experimental studies seeking to understand critical periods in human social and sexual behavior have often been based on this particular kind of primate. Since monkeys share fewer characteristics of structure and behavior with humans than is the case for some other primates (e.g., members of *Hominoidea*), there are fundamental questions concerning the conclusions drawn from such studies. Comparative experimental studies may not reveal as much as has been expected or hoped because the basic logical fault in using monkeys in studies of human critical periods learning is that more than 30 million years of separate evolutionary development is involved in monkey and human social and sexual behavior.

---

[13]Eimas and Miller (1980) have presented some experimental evidence in support of their proposal that human infants must come to know the acoustic cues for speech in a relatively brief period of time.

[14]See La Barre, 1947.

Isolated and Motherless Monkeys   Many studies have been made of monkeys reared in laboratories and subjected to various kinds of experimental tests. For example, Mason (1961) raised six monkeys in conditions of "social restriction" and then compared them at 2½ years of age with a group of six monkeys born and raised in a wild, or free-ranging, environment. Mason found the restricted monkeys to be more aggressive socially and to seldom engage in grooming behavior, a regular feature of free-ranging monkey behavior. The socially restricted monkeys were said to possess sexual responses that were "inefficient," "unintegrated," and "disorganized" in comparison to the "normal" sexual responses of the free-ranging group. Socially restricted male monkeys seemed unable to mate when given a choice of females. The free-ranging animals made mating choices quickly. In situations in which a choice was possible between engaging in social or isolated activities, the socially restricted monkeys seemed indifferent to each other and to prefer isolation.

In other observations of groups of socially restricted and free-ranging monkeys, Mason noted that when exposed to unfamiliar environments socially restricted monkeys exhibited crouching, self-clasping, and rocking behavior, while free-ranging monkeys explored widely as well as played normally in the same situation. It was concluded from these studies that the first year of life in monkeys is a "true critical period" for development of their basic social and sexual responses.

To demonstrate the validity of this hypothesis, Masson studied 12 one-year-old "normal" laboratory monkeys, placing 6 of them in a setting of individual isolation and housing the other six together in pairs. Later the paired monkeys demonstrated less self-clasping, thumb sucking, and grasping behavior and cooperated more easily in learning tasks demanding social action. When the two groups were placed together at 2½ years of age, the isolated monkeys remained more apart from social play than any of the paired monkeys but otherwise behaved as would be expected. Mason concluded that these data also provided evidence that the first year of life is a crucial period in a monkey's experience.

In other studies of critical periods in social and sexual development, Harlow (1959a) placed infant monkeys (1) with wire surrogate mothers that were "hard," "cold," and "unresponsive" and (2) with terry cloth and foam rubber surrogate mothers that were "soft," "warm," and "unresponsive." When these two groups of young monkeys were later exposed to stressful stimuli in the form of a colorful and noisy toy drummer, the wire-reared monkeys were fearful, disorganized, and withdrawn, while the foam-rubber-reared monkeys were generally organized, composed, and even curious.

Harlow (1958) also investigated the hypothesis that learning is better before love than after love, using monkeys reared by both wire and terry cloth surrogate mothers in a variety of novel experiments. Monkeys raised with the cloth mother surrogates did not appear to suffer any impairment of their ability to perform a variety of tasks or harm to their normal growth, in comparison to mother-reared monkeys. Both wire and the cloth surrogate-reared monkeys were less responsive than mother-reared monkeys in some sexual and social behavior forms; surrogate-reared monkeys played less, were less curious, and were more frequently engaged in self-clasping, rocking behavior. Suomi and Harlow (1972) have also demonstrated that the bizarre and stereotyped behavior by isolated monkeys can be changed by placing them with monkeys three months younger for a 26-week period.

On the basis of these and many other experiments with surrogate-reared monkeys, Harlow has concluded that monkeys raised apart from their mothers found it very difficult as adults to develop and engage in usual monkey social and sexual companionship with their "normal" mother-reared counterparts. Harlow also concluded that the development of affection between a mother and an infant monkey was a necessary antecedent, or condition, for a later normal development of affection between young monkeys; surrogate-reared monkeys seemed unable to relate affectionally to other monkeys. Harlow believes that critical periods exist in monkey social and sexual development with a number of crucial antecedent experiences necessary before later normal social and sexual behavior can develop.

Conclusions from Critical Periods Experiments

Studies of sensory development and imprinting have clearly demonstrated the existence of some critical periods for learning in cats, fishes, ducks, chickens, rats, and mice. There are antecedent experiences that must occur early in the maturation of these animals if they are to perform more complex behaviors later. However it is apparent that there are significant differences between these species and other kinds of animals with regard to existence and functioning of critical periods in behavior. The studies of sensory functions and imprinting and the studies of monkey and human infants suggest that, if they exist, critical periods become much less fixed and much more diffuse as significant natural boundaries, such as phyla, class, order, family, and so on, are passed, particularly where differences between animals become less of degree and more of kind. Studies to date of the application of the critical periods hypothesis to humans have produced no scientifically acceptable evidence that such critical periods exist which are specifically antecedent to consequent adult human behavior forms. This does not mean that earlier learning in humans is not the basis of later learning; it simply means that the critical periods hypothesis has not yet been demonstrated in humans.[15]

The Psychoanalytic Critical Periods Hypothesis

It would be inappropriate in a discussion of the critical periods hypothesis not to briefly consider similar ideas developed in psychoanalytic studies with regard to the existence of critical periods in human development and the relations between these periods and their consequences for later behavior.

During the 1920s and 1930s a body of psychoanalytic theory was developed that predicted that infants and children would modify their behavior because of rewards and punishments received from adults in five "primary" learning areas: (1) oral, (2) anal, (3) sexual, (4) dependency, and (5) aggression. Oral learning clues are said to be received by children especially in the ways they are fed and weaned. Anal clues are said to come to children especially in the ways they are made to control their anal sphincters. Sexual clues are said to come from activities by adults that especially draw children's attention to their genitals. Dependency clues are said to come to children from stimulations by adults for children to be dependent on them. Aggression clues are said to come from stimulation by adults for children to act in aggressive ways. The basic hypotheses used in such studies are

1. Early permissiveness or indulgence by adults in any one of the five primary learning areas will accentuate and heighten the capacity of that area to evoke satisfaction in later life.
2. Early restrictions or frustration in any one of the five primary learning areas will accentuate, heighten, or evoke conflict, guilt, shame, incapacity, and frustration in later life.

Thus psychoanalytic theory has predicted that there are specific critical periods (feeding, weaning, toilet training, and so on) which take place in human development and which are then directly related to particular adult forms of behavior. It must be noted that recent psychoanalytic theory has not predicted that a single event was a cause of a later specific adult

---

[15]Although Kessen *et al.* (1970, 297) first state that, while nearly all research on human infancy has led to the conclusion that early learning does not seem to be related to later behavior, they later (1970, 309) also say that this conclusion is ". . . so much against good sense and common observation" that they plan to ignore it. Kagan and Klein (1973) point out that there is at least adequate evidence to be certain that each child carries an "inherent" (or species-characteristic) schematic blueprint for learning that is very little affected by experiences in early infancy.

behavior. Rather, it has been felt by many psychoanalytic theorists that a series of similar, or related, events focused in a period of time on and about one of the primary learning areas (oral, anal, sexual, and so on) could lead directly to particular kinds of later adult behavior.

Consequences and Critiques

This particular theory and hypotheses derived from it have stimulated much research in the fields of anthropology, psychology, sociology, education, and social work. However in the late 1940s and during the 1950s strong critiques were published concerning the psychoanalytic variation of the critical periods hypothesis (Orlansky, 1949; Lindesmith & Strauss, 1950; Sewell, 1952). Recently Shweder (1979) has offered a similar statement. All of these critiques note that no firm research evidence has been offered demonstrating that in fact such critical periods in infancy were invariably related to any particular later human behavior. The authors of these critiques, particularly Shweder (1979), seem to imply that in general the early specific experiences of human infants are not related to later patterns of behavior. Although there is doubt concerning this particular psychoanalytic variation of the critical periods hypotheses, research and vigorous discussion of this theory has drawn attention to the socialization process and has stimulated a greater concern for improving observational methods and the design of research seeking to demonstrae specific cause-and-effect sequences in human behavior.

Isolated and Autistic Children and the Concept of Critical Periods

The critical periods hypothesis involves a major theoretical problem as a useful statement for understanding socialization when considered in the context of reports of isolated children. The credible accounts of Anna and Isabelle and the "crib sisters" indicate that there are no really critical periods in development of most of those skills and acts that traditionally have been said to be requisites for being human.

Anna, Isabelle, and the "crib sisters" were prevented from having the kinds of experiences at the times other children in American culture do that serve as the basis for later acquisition of more complex cultural ways. The careful descriptions of these children make it clear that, when found, they were without most of those cultural and social behavior forms that would ordinarily be present in American children of the same age. Yet Anna and the "crib sisters," with only routine custodial care by persons untrained for teaching "retarded" or "slow-learning" children, acquired and began to regularly display attributes and skills that have been thought to be difficult or impossible to display unless specific earlier, or antecedent, experiences were present and undergone by a child. The evidence of Isabelle's transition in two years from an estimated cultural and social level of less than a two-year-old American child to that of six-year-old American child, while under the care of professionally trained and quite sympathetic persons, raises this question even more dramatically concerning the application of a critical periods hypothesis to humans. If there are critical periods of limited duration in human acquisition of culture during which certain experiences must occur if they are to be a regular part of an individual's later cultural behavior, then these experiences must either be many years in length or so very diffuse in nature, such as regular physical contact with at least one other human, even though that person is socially and culturally deficient, that the general assumptions of the critical periods hypothesis are not applicable in their original form to humans and the socialization process. The evidence of Isabelle's having a routine later schooling, marrying, and raising her own "normal" family also indicates that, if critical periods do exist in socialization, much later exposure to the "usual" experience of human society and culture not only can produce marked and quite dramatic effects on the course of acquisition of culture but also can erase, or completely overlay, many of the emotional traumas and stresses of extreme early isolation. It may be that both quality and intensity of learning and behavior allowed by parent-surrogates and care-takers is vital in the process of recovery by isolated and autistic children.

The case histories (Bettelheim, 1967) of children who have "recovered" from their long-term states of autism with skilled and special care and have then gone to lead socially and culturally ordinary adult lives also make it apparent that the critical periods hypothesis, as it has been formulated, probably is only broadly applicable to the socialization process.[16] Formerly autistic children have been reported as adults to have earned doctoral degrees, to be teaching college courses in several academic disciplines, to be working in demanding business occupations, and to have married and regularly assumed the normal routines of raising their own children. If such reports are valid—and there are no reasons to believe they are not—then it is likely that socialization does not operate primarily through specific events occurring in finite periods early in a child's life.

Some Future Directions of Research

It is quite possible, of course, that other procedures of research, especially in the developing areas of human psychobiology, brain chemistry, and operant conditioning (see Chapter 4), may provide dramatic new evi-

---

[16]These recoveries also raise fundamental questions concerning the genetic basis for autism suggested by the research on autistic twin pairs.

dence of some specific interrelations between biology and culture that must occur at precise times in physical maturation for a child to begin acquiring culture. The various experiments on animals with strychninelike chemicals and with some antibiotics have tended to demonstrate, at least in rats, mice, and goldfish, that there may be natural chemical substances which enhance or prevent certain kinds of learning. Strychninelike compounds have been used experimentally to "raise" the levels of learning in "less intelligent" animals to the performance levels of so-called "bright" animals of the same species. When these limited data are considered in the context of the evidence cited so far in this discussion, including those of autistic and isolated children, it is clear that acquisition of culture involves extremely complex interrelationships between biology and culture that obviously have to be "time-bound"—that is, have to take place in some identifiable span of time. Continued research possibly will begin to provide some indications of specifically when and how socialization is related to events in the maturation of infants and children.

CONCLUSIONS

Data from studies of isolated and autistic children and studies of twins demonstrate the fact that, without regular communicative contact with parents and other agents of socialization, the process of cultural transmission is modified or altered in significant ways. These studies provide acceptable evidence that without a socialization process there is little that can be recognized as a *human being* in the everyday sense of the term.

Newborn humans take on the ideas, habits, thoughts, emotions, and preoccupations of the generations that have preceded them in their cultures. These ways, many of which are quite specific to a local society, are not transmitted to children through their genes. Infants must learn to walk, sit, talk, love, hate, fear, hope, and so on by participating in a process of enculturation. If infants and children are denied access to or cannot fully participate in the enculturation process and fail to learn the ways necessary to behave as a human being, through communicative contacts, instruction, imitation, and reflection, they will be severely limited in their ability to make full use of possibly unique combinations of their gene material.

Data of the consequences of extreme situational isolation, while far from complete, tend to show that the socialization process is capable of being reversed, even after a long period of time. The fact that the socialization process is so plastic in its form is important for understanding the nature of that process.

Although limited by certain research problems, twin studies show promise as a general method for seeing some of the ways biology and culture may become interrelated in the socialization process. These studies highlight the complex nature of these relationships and make it clear that neither "nature" (biology) nor "nurture" (culture) is more important as an aspect of socialization. On the contrary, twin studies assist us in seeing the fallacy of the nature vs. nurture (or heredity vs. environment) arguments of the past.

misleading argument

SUMMARY

This chapter has discussed studies of isolated and autistic children and twins in an effort to provide some understanding of the way in which human biology and culture may become related in the socialization process. The chapter also included an account of the ways in which socialization might be "reversed" or significantly altered in situations of extreme isolation.

This discussion has also been concerned with an examination of a key hypothesis that has often been unstated or is implied in socialization research. The origins and the general nature of the critical periods hypothesis were briefly examined. Comments on some of the methodological and theoretical problems of applying conclusions from this research to humans were noted before a brief discussion of a major variation of the critical periods hypothesis used by psychoanalytic scholars in their studies of socialization. Comments were also made on the application to humans of the psychoanalytic critical events version of the critical periods hypothesis. The chapter concluded with a series of observations regarding the meaning of the critical periods hypothesis when contrasted to data derived from studies of isolated and autistic children.

REFERENCES CITED AND SUGGESTED READING

ANDERSON, B.C. 1969. "The Process of Deculturation: Its Dynamics among the Aged." Paper read before the 1969 annual meeting, American Anthropological Association, New Orleans, La. November, 1969.

BETTELHEIM, B. 1943. "Individual and Mass Behavior in Extreme Situations." *Journal of Abnormal and Social Psychology*, 38, 417–452.

———. 1959. "Feral Children and Autistic Children." *American Journal of Sociology*, 64, 455–467.

———. 1960. *The Informed Heart: Autonomy in a Mass Age.* New York: Free Press.

———. 1967. *The Empty Fortress.* New York: Free Press.

BIDERMAN, A. 1967. "Life and Death in Extreme Captivity Situations." In M. Appley & R. Trumbull (eds.), *Psychological Stress.* New York: Appleton-Century Crofts, pp. 242–277.

CATTELL, R.B. 1960. "The Multiple Abstract Variance Analysis Equations and Solutions for Nature-Nurture Research on Continuous Variables." *Psychological Review*, 67, 353–372.

CLARIDGE, G., S. CANTER, & W. HOME. 1973. *Personality Differences and Biological Variations: A Study of Twins*. Elmsford, N.Y.: Pergamon Press.

COHEN, S., & L. TAYLOR, 1973. *Psychological Survival: The Experience of Long-Term Imprisonment*. New York: Pantheon.

CURTISS, S. 1977. *Genie*. New York: Academic Press.

CURTISS, S., V. FROMKIN, D. RIGLER, M. KRASHEN, & S. KRASHEN. 1975. "An Update of the Linguistic Development of Genie." In D.P. Dato (ed.), *Developmental Psycholinguistics: Theory and Applications*. Washington, D.C.: Georgetown University Press.

DAVIS, K. 1940. "Extreme Social Isolation of a Child." *American Journal of Sociology*, 45, 554–565.

———. 1947. "Final Note on a Case of Extreme Isolation." *American Journal of Sociology*, 52, 432–437.

———. 1949. *Human Society*. New York: Macmillan.

DENNIS, W. 1938. "Infant Development Under Conditions of Restricted Practice and Minimal Social Stimulation: A Preliminary Report." *Journal of Genetic Psychology*, 53, 149–158.

———. 1960. "Causes of Retardation Among Institutionalized Children." *Journal of Genetic Psychology*, 96, 47–59.

DESPRES, T. 1976. *The Survivor: An Anatomy of Life in Death Camps*. New York: Oxford University Press.

EIMAS, P.D. & J.L. MILLER. 1980. "Contextual Effects in Infant Speech Perception." *Science*, 209, 1140–1141.

ERIKSON, E.H. 1939. "Observations of Sioux Education." *Journal of Psychology*, 7, 101–156.

———. 1943. "Observations on the Yurok: Childhood and World Image." *University of California Publications in American Archaeology and Ethnology*, Vol. 35, No. 10.

———. 1950. *Childhood and Society*. New York: W. W. Norton & Co., Inc.

———. 1956. "Growth and Crises of the Healthy Personality." In C. Kluckhohn & H.A. Murray (eds.), *Personality in Nature, Society and Culture*. New York: Knopf, pp. 185–225.

FROMM, E. 1943. "Sex and Character." *Psychiatry*, 6, 21–31.

———. 1949. "Psychoanalytic Characterology and Its Application to the Understand of Culture." In S.S. Sargent & M.W. Smith (eds.), *Culture and Personality*. New York: Viking Fund.

GESELL, A. 1940. *Wolf Child and Human Child*. London: Methuen.

———. 1954. "The Ontogenesis of Infant Behavior." In L. Carmichael (ed.), *Manual of Child Psychology*, (2nd ed.). New York: John Wiley, pp. 335–373.

GESELL, A., & THOMPSON, H. 1929. "Learning and Growth in Identical Infant Twins: An Experimental Study by the Method of Co-Twin Control." *Genetic Psychology Monograph*, 6, 1–124.

GOFFMAN, E. 1961. *Asylums: Essays on the Social Situation of Mental Patients and Other Inmates*. Garden City, N.Y.: Doubleday.

GOLDMAN-EISLER, F. 1956. "Breast Feeding and Character Formation." In C. Kluckhohn – H.A. Murray (eds.), *Personality in Nature, Society and Culture*. New York: Knopf, pp. 146–184.

GRAY, P.H. 1958. "Theory and Evidence of Imprinting in Human Infants." *Journal of Psychology*, 46, 155–166.

GUITON, P. 1958. "The Effect of Isolation on the Following Response of Brown Leghorn Chicks." *Proceedings of the Royal Physiological Society, Edinburgh*, 27, 9–14.

HARLOW, H. 1958. "The Nature of Love." *American Psychologist*, 13, 673–685.

———. 1959a. "Affectional Response in the Infant Monkey." *Science*, 130, 421–432.

———. 1959b. "Basic Social Capacity of Primates." In J.N. Spuhler (ed.), *The Evolution of Man's Capacity for Culture*. Detroit, Mich.: Wayne State University Press.

———. 1961. "Social and Sexual Behavior." In *Critical Periods of Development: Report on a Conference*, Social Science Research Council, Items 15, 16–17.

HARLOW, H., & M.K. HARLOW. 1962. "Social Deprivation in Monkeys." *Scientific American*, 207, 136–146.

———. 1965a. "An Analysis of Love." *Listener*, 73, 255–257.

———. 1965b. "Romulus and Rhesus." *Listener*, 73, 215–217.

HARLOW, H., M.K. HARLOW, & S.J. SUOMI. 1971. "From Thought to Therapy: Lessons from a Primate Laboratory." *American Scientist*, 59, 538–549.

HARLOW, H., F. SCHILTZ, & M.K. HARLOW. 1969. "The Effects of Social Isolation on the Learning Performance of Rhesus Monkeys." In C.R. Carpenter (ed.), *Proceedings of the Second International Congress of Primatology*, Vol. I. New York: Karger.

HESS, E.H. 1957. "Effects of Meprobamate on Imprinting on Water Fowl." *Annals*, New York Academy of Science, 67, 724–733.

———. 1959. "Two Conditions Limiting Critical Age for Imprinting." *Journal of Comparative and Physiological Psychology*, 52, 515–518.

———. 1961. "Imprinting." In *Critical Periods of Development: Report on a Conference*, Social Science Research Council, Items 15, 14–15.

HOLDEN, C. 1980. "Twins Reunited." *Science 80*, 1, 55–59.

HRDLICKA, A. 1931. *Children Who Run on All Fours*. New York: McGraw-Hill.

HUSEN, T. 1960. "Abilities of Twins." *Scandinavian Journal of Psychology*, 1, 125–135.

ITARD, J.M.G. 1932 *The Wild Boy of Aveyron*. Englewood Cliffs, N.J.: Prentice-Hall, 1962.

JOFFE, J.M. 1969. *Prenatal Determinants of Behavior*. Elmsford, N.Y.: Pergamon Press.

JOHNSON, R.C. 1963. "Similarity in I.Q. of Separated Identical Twins as Related to Length of Time Spent in Same Environment." *Child Development*, 34, 745–749.

JUEL-NIELSEN, H., & B. HARVALD. 1958. "The Electroencephalogram in Uniovular Twins Brought Up Apart." *Acta Genetica*, 8, 57–64.

KAGAN, J. 1964. "American Longitudinal Research on Psychological Development." *Child Development*, 35, 1–32.

———. 1973. "Growing Up Normal. *Science News*, 103, 8.

KAGAN, J., & R.E. KLEIN. 1973. "Cross-Cultural Perspectives on Early Development." *American Psychologist*, 28, 947–961.

KANNER, L. 1943. "Autistic Disturbances of Affective Contact." *Nervous Child*, 2, 217–250.

———. 1944. "Early Infantile Autism." *Journal of Pediatrics*, 25, 211–217.

————. 1949. "Problems of Nosology and Psychodynamics of Early Infantile Autism." *American Journal of Orthopsychiatry*, 19, 416–426.

KELLER, H. 1911. *The Story of My Life*. New York: Grosset & Dunlap.

KELLERMAN, J. 1977. "Psychological Effects of Isolation in Protected Environments." *American Journal of Psychology*, 134, 563–565.

KESSEN, W., *et al.* 1970. "Human Infancy: A Bibliography and Guide." In P.H. Mussen (ed.), *Carmichael's Manual of Child Psychology*. (3rd. ed.) New York: John Wiley.

KOCH, H.L. 1966. *Twins and Twin Relations*. Chicago: University of Chicago Press.

LABARRE, W. 1947. "The Cultural Basis of Emotions and Gestures." *Journal of Personality*, 16, 49–68.

LANE, H. 1976. *The Wild Boy of Aveyron*. Cambridge, Mass.: Harvard University Press.

LEIGHTON, D., J. HARDING, D. MACKLIN, A. MACMILLAN, & A. LEIGHTON. 1963. *The Character of Danger*. New York: Basic Books.

LIFTON, R.J. 1956. "Thought Reform of Western Civilians in Chinese Communist Prisons." *Psychiatry*, 19, 173–195.

LILLY, J.C. 1956. "Effects of Physical Restraint and Reduction of Ordinary Levels of Physical Stimuli on Intact Healthy Persons." New York: Group for the Advancement of Psychiatry, *Symposium Number Two*, pp. 13–20.

LINDESMITH, A.R., & A.L. STRAUSS. 1950. "A Critique of Culture-Personality Writings." *American Sociolgical Review*, 15, 587–600.

LORENZ, K. 1952. *King Solomon's Ring: New Light on Animal Ways*. New York: Harper & Row, Pub.

————. 1965. *Evolution and Modification of Behavior*. Chicago: University of Chicago Press.

LOEHLIN, J.C., & R.C. NICHOLS. 1976. *Heredity, Environment and Personality: A Study of 850 Sets of Twins*. Austin: University of Texas Press.

MANDELBAUM, D. 1941. "Wolf-Child Histories from India." *Journal of Social Psychology*, 17, 24–44.

MARSHALL, V.W. 1975. "Socialization for Impending Death in a Retirement Village," *American Journal of Sociology*, 80, 1122–1143.

MASON, N.K. 1942. "Learning to Speak after Six and One-half Years of Silence." *Journal of Speech Disorders*, 7, 295–304.

MASON, W.A. 1961. "Social and Sexual Behavior." In *Critical Periods of Development: Report on a Conference*, Social Science Research Council, Items 15, 15–17.

MELZACK, R. 1964. "Early Experience: A Neuropsychological Approach to Heredity-Environment Interaction." In G. Newton (ed.), *Early Experience and Behavior*. Springfield, Ill.: Chas. C Thomas.

MOLTZ, H. 1960. "Imprinting: Empirical Basis and Theoretical Significance." *Psychological Bulletin*, 57, 291–314.

————. 1963. "Imprinting: An Epigenetic Approach." *Psychological Review*, 70, 123–138.

MOLTZ, H., & L.H. STETTNER. 1961. "Some Parameters of Imprinting Effectiveness." *Journal of Comparative Psychology*, 54, 279–283.

MONTAGU, M.F.A. 1962. *Prenatal Influences*. Springfield, Ill.: Chas. C Thomas.

————. 1972. "Sociogenic Brain Damage." *American Anthropologist*, 74, 1045–1061.

NEWMAN, H.H. 1937. *Twins: A Study of Heredity and Environment*. Chicago: University of Chicago Press.

————. 1940. *Multiple Human Births*. New York: Doubleday.

————. 1966. *Twins: A Study of Heredity and Environment* (rev. ed.) Chicago: University of Chicago Press.

New York Times. 1977. "New Research in Autism." April 24, 1977, p. 6E

OGBURN, W.F. 1959. "The Wolf Boy of Agra." *American Journal of Sociology*, 64, 449–454.

ORLANSKY, H. 1949. "Infant Care and Personality." *Psychological Bulletin*, 46, 1–48.

PIAGET, J. 1926. *The Language and Thought of the Child.* London: Kegan Paul, Trench, Trubner.

———. 1932. *The Moral Judgment of the Child.* London: Kegan Paul, Trench, Trubner.

RAUBER, A. 1888. *Homo Sapiens Ferus, oder die Zustande der Verwilderten.* Leipzeg: J. Brehse.

RIESEN, A.H. 1961. "Sensory Processes." In *Critical Periods of the Development: Report on a Conference,* Social Science Research Council, Items 15, 13–14.

RUTTER, M. 1972. *Maternal Deprivation Reassessed.* London: Penguin.

SALK, L. 1962. "Mothers' Heartbeat as an Imprinting Stimulus." *Transactions of the New York Academy of Sciences*, 24, 753–763.

SCHEIN, E.H. 1956. "The Chinese Indoctrination Program for Prisoners of War: A Study of Attempted Brainwashing." *Psychiatry*, 19, 149–172.

———. 1957. "Methods of Forceful Indoctrination: Observations and Interviews." New York: Group for the Advancement of Psychiatry. *Symposium Number Four*, pp. 253–284.

SCHEINFELD, A. 1973. *Twins and Supertwins.* Baltimore, Md.: Penguin.

SCOTT, J.P. 1962. "Critical Periods in Behavioral Development." *Science*, 138, 949–958.

———. 1963. "The Process of Primary Socialization on Canine and Human Infants." *Monograph of the Society for Research in Child Development*, 28, 1–47.

SEWELL, W.H. 1952. "Infant Training and the Personality of the Child." *American Journal of Sociology*, 58, 150–159.

SHATTUCK, R. 1980. *The Forbidden Experiment.* New York: Academic Press.

SHIELDS, J. 1962. *Monozygotic Twins.* London: Oxford University Press.

SHWEDER, R.A. 1979. "Rethinking Culture and Personality Theory I, II." *Ethos*, 7, 255–278; 279–311.

SILBERSTEIN, R.M., & H. IRWIN. 1962. "Jean-Marc-Gaspart Itard and the Savage of Aveyron: An Unsolved Problem in Child Psychiatry." *Journal of the American Academy of Child Psychiatry.* 1, 314–322.

SINGH, J.A.L., & R.M. ZINGG. 1942. *Wolf Children and Feral Man.* New York: Harper & Row, Pub.

SPALDING, D.A. 1873. "Instinct, with Original Observations on Young Animals." *British Journal of Animal Behavior*, 2, 2–11.

SPITZ, R. 1946. "Anaclitic Depression." *Psychoanalytic Study of the Child*, 2, 313–342.

STOTT, D.H. 1966. *Studies of Troublesome Children.* New York: Humanities Press.

SUOMI, S.J., & H. HARLOW. 1972. "Social Rehabilitation of Isolate Reared Monkeys." *Developmental Psychology*, 6, 487–496.

SZASZ, T. 1970. *Ideology and Insanity: Essays on the Psychiatric Dehumanization of Man.* Garden City, N.Y.: Doubleday.

THORPE, W. 1963. *Learning and Instinct in Animals.* London: Methuen.

UNITED STATES SENATE. 1956. *Communist Interrogation, Indoctrination and Exploitation of American Military and Civilian Prisoners.* Hearings before the Permanent Subcommittee on Investigations of the Committee of Government Operations, U.S. Senate, June 19, 20, 26, 27, 1956. Washington, D.C.: U.S. Government Printing Office.

VANDENBERG, S.G. 1966. "Contributions of Twin Research to Psychology." *Psychological Bulletin*, 63, 327–352.

VAUGHAN, E.H. 1949.   *Community under Stress: An Internment Camp Culture.* Princeton, N.J.: Princeton University Press.

VON SENDEN, M. 1960.   *Space and Sight: The Perception of Space and Shape in the Congenitally Blind before and after Operation* (translated by Peter Heath). New York: Free Press.

WAGLER, L. 1928.   *Die Bilanz einer hundertjaehrigen Hauserforschung.* Nuremberg.

WEIDMANN, U. 1956.   "Some Experiments of the Following and the Flocking Reactions of Mallard Ducklings." *British Journal of Animal Behavior,* 4, 78–79.

WILKINS, W. 1967.   "Group Behavior in Long-Term Isolation." In M. Appley & R. Turnbull (eds.), *Psychological Stress.* New York: Appleton-Century-Crofts, pp. 278–296.

WINOKUR, G. 1955.   "Brainwashing—A Social Phenomena of Our Time." *Human Organization,* 13, 16–18.

YARROW, L.J. 1961.   "Maternal Deprivation: Toward an Empirical and Conceptual Re-Evaluation." *Psychological Bulletin,* 58, 459–490.

CHAPTER SIX
KINSHIP, KIN GROUPS, AND SOCIALIZATION

This chapter examines various ways in which the socialization process is related to some major forms of human behavior. The discussion begins with some brief comments on ways of thinking systematically about culture. The discussion continues with ethnographic examples of the relationship between kinship, kin groups, and socialization. The chapter concludes with some observations concerning the study of kinship, kin groups, and socialization.

SUBSYSTEMS AND PATTERNS OF CULTURE

Human culture can be thought of as a system containing at least four *subsystems*: (1) social relations, (2) language, (3) technology, and (4) ideology.[1] A large number of whole categories of culture, or *patterns*, make up each subsystem of culture. Table 6–1 lists many of the patterns that can be grouped under the headings of different cultural subsystems.[2]

[1]It is important to note that some anthropologists would include fewer, or more, subsystems of culture and perhaps would use different labels for the subsystems.

[2]For an example of a listing of the major patterns of culture used by anthropologists in their studies, see Murdock, 1969.

TABLE 6–1 Subsystems and Patterns of Culture

SOCIAL RELATIONS PATTERNS	23. Adulthood	12. Machines
	24. Old age	13. Tools
1. Kinship	LANGUAGE PATTERNS	14. Property
2. Kin groups	1. Speech	15. Exchange
3. Community	2. Vocabulary	16. Marketing
4. Territory	3. Grammar	17. Finance
5. State	4. Phonology	18. Labor
6. Government	5. Semantics	19. Transportation
7. Law	6. Style	IDEOLOGY PATTERNS
8. Justice	7. Signs	1. Arts
9. Daily routine	TECHNOLOGY PATTERNS	2. Religious belief
10. Recreation		3. Ecclesiastical belief
11. Entertainment		4. Numbers
12. Status-role	1. Food quest	5. Measures
13. Class	2. Animal husbandry	6. Ideas about nature
14. War	3. Agriculture	7. Ideas about humans
15. Health	4. Food processing	8. Ideas about society
16. Sickness	5. Clothing	9. Ideas about culture
17. Death	6. Adornment	
18. Sex	7. Shelter	
19. Reproduction	8. Processing of materials	
20. Infancy	9. Construction	
21. Childhood	10. Equipment	
22. Adolescence	11. Energy	

There may be more, or less, patterns in a particular cultural subsystem than noted here. Some patterns could be included in other subsystems, depending on the nature of the cultural theory used. The concept of *pattern* is a generalization by an observer about what people regularly do or, should do.

A conceptual model of culture using these ideas might be represented as in Fig. 6–2. The four subsystems of culture are shown, with circles linked to one another by lines, representing the major patterns making up each subsystem. The lines are meant to indicate a long-lasting relationship of interdependence between each of the patterns in a subsystem. The lines are also drawn to show long-lasting relationships of interdependence, or functional relations, between patterns in one subsystem and patterns in the other cultural subsystems. This is intended to convey the idea that culture is a complex, integrated whole, or system, of many interrelated parts, each one dependent on the other.

The patterns described in this chapter, and the chapters to follow, have been chosen for discussion because they have been more clearly described and analyzed in their relations to socialization than have other cultural patterns. A full theoretical understanding of socialization may require careful study of the ways all patterns, in each subsystem of culture, are related to that process. This appears to be a basic requirement of a system of ideas, and statements concerning these ideas, that propose to

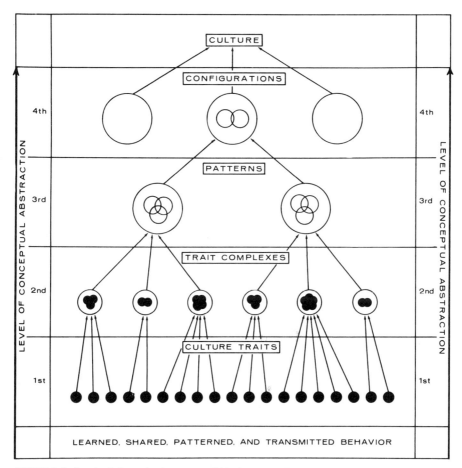

FIGURE 6–1 Levels of abstraction in conceptualizing the nature of culture.

explain and account for the observed and confirmed data of cultural transmission. We now understand, as we did not at the turn of the twentieth century (cf. Chamberlain, 1896, 1901; Kidd, 1906), that knowing about the social setting in which culture is transmitted is as vital as knowing the details of what is being learned by children as they mature.

ETHNOGRAPHIC EXAMPLES—
ARUNTA AND ASHANTI

Knowledge concerning kinship and kin groups is important for understanding socialization. As infants and children learn various social behavior forms, they develop patterns of personal action that become part of their lifelong model for relations with others in a wide variety of social situations.

FIGURE 6–2 Relations of interdependence of patterns in subsystems of culture. Note: The number of patterns in each subsystem of culture does not correspond to the number of patterns listed in Figure 6–1; this diagram is intended only as an ideal conceptual model.

While this is not the only model for behavior that children learn, it does seem vital to their access to other aspects of culture. The following pages briefly summarize data concerning the ways kinship, kin groups, and socialization are interrelated in two cultures: the Arunta of central Australia and the Ashanti of West Africa. These data are summarized to emphasize the point, first made in the works of Fortes (1938), Kluckhohn (1939), and later by Parsons, Bales, and Olds (1955), that socialization also is, as Wills (1979, 877) has observed, a "context sensitive" and "communicative" process. In other words, the various settings in which learning, maturing infants and children and communicating adults interact in the family, local group, school, or society must be viewed as being at least as important in the process of socialization as specific features of human biology or any of the discrete practices of child training used by adults to transmit culture.[3]

Arunta Kinship, Kin Groups, and Enculturation

Europeans began to settle the Australian continent in 1788. It has been estimated that at that time there were perhaps 300,000 Australian natives, divided into some 500 tribal groups widely scattered over all of the Australian continent. At the beginning of the nineteenth century the native population of the central desert of Australia, an area of some 200,000 square miles, was estimated at 18,000 persons, organized into approximately 25 to 50 different tribes. The largest central Australian desert tribe is known as the Arunta (also known as the Aranda).[4]

In 1896 the Arunta numbered about 2000 persons. Arunta technology was quite limited. Crude tools and weapons made of stone and wood were used in hunting, in the gathering and preparing of food, in protection, and

Temporary Australian native camp, northwestern South Australia (circa 1920) (Courtesy American Museum of Natural History.)

[3]Wills (1979, 883) also points out that both cultural and linguistic study is increasingly focused now on the "universal bedrock" of how culture is learned and communicated, rather than on what is being communicated and learned. See also McCormack & Wurm, 1976; Williams, 1975; Richards, 1974, 1977; Sander, 1977; Bernstein, 1968; Blount, 1972; Lewis & Rosenblum, 1977; Goodman, 1971; Goody, 1973; Pilner, Krames, & Alloway, 1973; McGrew, 1975; Stross, 1972; Whiting & Whiting, 1976.

[4]For some readings on Arunta culture and society, see the discussions and references in Basedow, 1925; Berndt & Berndt, 1964; Davidson, 1926; Elkin, 1933, 1954; Elkin & Berndt, 1950; Mathews, 1907, 1908; Pink, 1936; Radcliffe-Brown, 1930; Róheim, 1925 & 1933; Spencer, 1928; Spencer & Gillen, 1927, 1938; Service, 1963, 3–26; Murdock, 1934, 20–47.

in war. The Arunta did not use the bow and arrow, an important tool among many of the world's isolated and nomadic peoples. The Arunta made no pottery or baskets, used no cooking utensils, and wore no clothing. Each Arunta *nuclear* (mother, father, biological offspring) family was almost a self-contained economic unit. A typical permanent Arunta encampment usually consisted of a father, a mother, and their children. This social unit lived in shelters of interlaced sticks made into low-domed structures thatched with grasses. Nuclear families moved regularly as they hunted through the local dry desert territory for kangaroo, wallaby, emu, and smaller birds and animals. Family members also gathered seeds, roots, edible fungi, bird and reptile eggs, the pupae of moths, caterpillars, beetles, flies, ants, and rodents. In their temporary hunting camps nuclear families built a low stick-and-grass wall to shelter themselves from the sun and wind.

Kin Groups   Arunta nuclear families feel themselves to be a part of a larger unit of related nuclear families. Anthropologists have named these loose collections of nuclear families *local groups*. Arunta local groups are *exogamous* and *virilocal*.[5] The local group of a male would contain his father, his father's father, his brothers, and eventually, his sons, his sons' sons, and all the brothers and unmarried sisters of these men. A male's married sisters and their children lived in the local groups of their husbands. His local group would also contain wives brought into the local group from other local groups.

The Arunta practice a system of marriage exchange in which a male marries his mother's mother's brother's daughter's daughter, or a "second cross-cousin," while his sisters marry the brothers of his wife. Thus a man's wife comes from a local group that contains his mother's mother's brother's patrilineal relatives, a local group different from the one in which his father had chosen a wife. In this way the Arunta use kinship to bind together four to eight local groups. Such kin ties were vital to the stability of Arunta social life since they had no formal political or governmental organization to regulate daily life.

Among the Arunta the term *wife* refers to all females of the kin category ("second cross-cousins") from which males would select a wife. A man's grandparents address him and he addresses them by use of the same kin term. The children of a man's brothers are called by one term, while the children of a man's sisters are called by a different kin term. A man's father's brother is addressed by the same term as father, while mother's

---

[5]*Exogamy* is a rule of marriage that requires an individual to take a wife or husband from outside of the local, or kin, groups to which they belong. A *virilocal* family kin group is a type of extended family kin group in which the bride is required to reside with the groom, either in or close by the household of the groom's parents. This kin group is also called a *patrilocal* family kin group.

brother is addressed by a special kin term. A man's mother and mother's sisters are addressed by the same term, while father's sisters are addressed through use of a separate kin term. Arunta also distinguish between parallel cousins (mother's sister's and father's brother's children) and cross-cousins (father's sister's and mother's brother's children). A man also addresses the children of his brother and sister in a parallel and cross fashion, that is— the children of sisters and brothers are addressed through use of the same term used for a man's daughters or son.

The Enculturation Process of the Arunta   Arunta infants spend most of their time with their mother. She carries the baby as she goes about her search for food and as she walks from one camp to another. When she kneels, digging for roots or grubs, the infant lies in a curved wooden food-carrying dish. Sometimes babies are carried in a net bag slung from their mother's forehead over and down her back. As they grow older, babies sit astride their mother's shoulders, clutching her hair. Arunta infants learn very early that the women their mother calls "sister" will also care for them, even nurse them. They also learn that father's mother or mother's mother may concentrate her affection on them and serve as a mother as well. Male babies learn, too, that there are many men besides their biological father whom they will call "father." Male infants learn that these men will address a boy as "son" and will act toward them in the same way as their father does when he cares, protects, or disciplines them. In some Australian native local groups, a male child learns that certain men older than his own father

Arunta older woman and daughter (date unknown).
(Courtesy American Museum of Natural History.)

will sometime assume a formal responsibility greater than his biological father for his enculturation. Among the Arunta, a baby's father's father and father's father's brothers have a large share of formal responsibility for enculturation. In some special instances mother's mother's brothers also will take on duties of enculturation as well as the biological father.

Arunta children learn the content of kinship terms as they interact daily with specific people. They are informed repeatedly by adults who individuals are and how they should act toward them. A boy may be told by an adult, "This person is your sister; you call her (kin term), and you must look after her. When you get older you must give her some of the meat you catch and she will give you vegetable foods. You are not to say her name, but when she gets married, her husband will give you gifts. If her husband treats her badly, you must take her part." On another occasion he may be told about a little girl walking by him, "She is your mother-in-law. You must not look at her face to face, or speak to her, but later when she is married you will sent her gifts of meat. If she bears a daughter, she may give her to you for a wife."

Arunta children often rehearse kin behavior in play situations. For instance, children play at being husbands and wives making separate windbreaks and fires and pretending to cook food. Sometimes they also play at adultery, with a boy running away with the "wife" of another boy. Adults generally indulge this play, which often mixes up actual kin categories. However when children who really will address each other as mother-in-law and son-in-law try to play such games together, they are quickly separated by adults with sharp rebukes.

Thus children must learn early that some persons in particular kinship categories have to be dealt with in ways that are very restrained and circumspect, that other individuals must be completely avoided, and that, while some others cannot be spoken to, some individuals can be the subjects of broad, joking speech. Children must also learn that there are persons with whom they can interact socially in complete freedom and that there are others with whom all social interaction must be marked by a very high degree of mutual cooperative actions in both ordinary and ritual events.

For instance, a male must learn to avoid his mother-in-law, to never speak her name, and to avoid speaking to her except through intermediaries or by use of a special language, if no one is available to relay his immediate concerns. A female must learn to turn away quickly and face the opposite direction when she sees or is told her son-in-law is approaching her. She must learn the special restrictions on the way she handles meat given to her by her son-in-law. However she also comes to know that if she is in trouble she can expect aid from her son-in-law, particularly if anyone abuses or threatens her in his hearing. A son-in-law is expected to be implacable in seeking revenge from those inflicting injury or death on his mother-in-law.

Arunta male (date unknown). (Courtesy American Museum of Natural History.)

Boys must also learn that a similar, although not as severely restrictive, avoidance relationship is expected between the persons addressed as father-in-law, wife's brother, sister's husband, and wife's mother's brother. Girls must also learn such general avoidance patterns for the persons they address as husband's brother, sister's husband, and husband's mother's sister.

Arunta children soon learn to know which categories of kin they can be open with in their speech and action. For instance, a man's father's sister, who is addressed as "father" in some Australian native societies, regularly is available to a boy for advice and counsel as he grows up. A boy comes to know that he is expected to be emotionally close to and frank with his sisters and that he is their champion, protector, and if need arises, disciplinarian. If a brother overhears a sister being scolded by her husband, he may take up his spears and threaten her and all of her sisters, actual and classificatory (classificatory kin terms are those that classify certain relatives under one term), including the sister actually involved. Brothers learn that they are responsible for the general good behavior of anyone they call "sister." Sisters must learn to avoid engaging in sexual acts in sight of their brothers. Brothers are supposed to speak in whispers when near sisters, and both avoid speaking each other's personal name.

Arunta children learn that persons who share the same names comprise a special kin status category and must behave toward and with each other with regard to their special bond. Such persons are expected to be close friends and to aid each other in economic and personal affairs. They also learn the special kin status terms and role behavior forms for individuals who undergo initiation rituals together (see Chapter 7), who have been born at the same time, or for all those persons who have shared with them some extraordinary event, such as a victory in a fight. In all, an Arunta child must learn more than ten categories of such kinship terms and associated ways of behavior.

Arunta children also learn a very complex series of special hand signs, which indicate all the different kinship terms and roles they must know for ordinary and special social behavior. These signs are unitary—that is, each one stands for a separate and distinct kinship term and its associated ideal role forms. These signs are part of a much larger hand sign vocabulary used by Arunta to communicate complex information across a distance. Arunta children regularly practice these signs and try them on each other as they play.

Kin Groups of the Arunta

Patrilineal Descent   Arunta kin groups include *unilineal descent* groups, *clans,* and *moieties.*[6] Arunta children must learn the ways these groups are formed and influence their daily life if they are to function successfully as adults. The Arunta unilineal descent group is based on patrilineal descent.[7] Children are affiliated with the named group to which their father belongs and, in the case of boys, are formally initiated into it at puberty in a series of complex ceremonies. Children learn that their father's patrilineal kin group holds and controls use of land in its own name. They learn that, with permission, other friendly patrilineal groups can enter the land claimed by their father's descent group and can hunt or gather foods within its limits. They also learn that other patrilineal descent groups must always avoid the special locations where sacred objects are stored. These sites are the *totem centers*—that is, the resting places of the spirits of the human ancestors of the patrilineal descent group to which their father belongs. Children are told that when a woman who has married a man in their descent group becomes pregnant it is because she was impregnated by a totem spirit of her husband's patrilineal descent group. Thus Arunta children learn to know their father as a "social" father but not as their progenitor, since they learn they have been created by the totem spirits of the descent group. Arunta children come to understand that they are forever

[6]In a unilineal descent group, an individual is said to be related to one line of male, or female, relatives. A clan is a type of unilineal descent group which is based on a working compromise that some relatives by marriage, or *affines*, are to be included, whereas some relatives by birth, or *consanguineal* relatives, are to be excluded. Clans may trace their descent from the same known, or even mythical, ancestor. A moiety is a unilineal kinship group; usually societies with moieties have only two such groups, so that an individual is a member of one moiety or the other. based on residence + choice

[7]Patrilineal descent occurs when kinship ties are traced only through relatives in the father's line of kinship.

Arunta spearman (date unknown). (Courtesy American Museum of Natural History.)

Arunta hunter (date unknown). (Courtesy American Museum of Natural History.)

bound to the land of their father's descent group because they are totem spirit children. If Arunta children think of "home," it is always in terms of the special totem spirit locations of their father's patrilineal descent group and not with reference to the location of their nuclear family's permanent camp. Thus the Arunta term *home* has essential religious and magical meaning because it refers to the resting places of a patrilineal descent group's ancestor spirits.

Arunta boys receive two names. One name is sacred and secret, associated with the totem spirits who have fathered him, and known only to the old man who made the personal totem symbol, or *churinga*, that is used at a boy's initiation into his father's patrilineal descent group. A secret name is never made known to women and uninitiated children and is used only on important ritual occasions celebrated by the men of the descent group. Boys and girls also receive a personal name, which may not refer in any way to the patrilineal descent group to which they belong. Arunta also use nicknames and special age, sex, and achievement terms in speaking to other persons.

Arunta girls must learn that, although they are members of their father's descent group because they are also totem children, they must move out of the totem lands at their marriage to join the patrilineal descent group of their husbands. Girls come to know, however, that their primary spiritual and emotional ties are expected to always remain with the descent group of their father. Thus while they have to leave their totem lands, they do not give up their spiritual heritage by their absence.

Arunta children must also learn that all power in the lands of their descent group is held by the oldest men of their father's patrilineal descent group. They come to know that the most important of these older males is the *inkata*, or totem leader, who conducts all the sacred rituals of the

Arunta woman and daughter (date unknown). (Courtesy American Museum of Natural History.)

descent group. They learn that the *inkata* can magically communicate with the totem symbols, whether these are represented in the forms of animals or plants. They also come to know that an *inkata* is responsible for the care of the personal *churinga* of each person born into the descent group. Arunta children learn that their *churinga* is stored in one of the sacred totem places and is taken out and used in important rituals such as the *mbanbiuma*, or totem increase ritual, which is held each year at the time when the animal or plant totem representative of a father's descent group produces fruit or seed or bears its young. Uninitiated boys, girls, and women are barred from the secret ritual activities in which the *inkata* magically seeks to increase the numbers of totem plants or animals. The *inkata* symbolically eats a portion of a totem animal or plant and then finally passes the totem animal or plant to all the initiated boys and men of the descent group so they may also make a symbolic communion with the totem spirit. Children take part in the public portion of the *mbanbiuma* ceremony, when everyone belonging to their father's patrilineal descent group feasts on the totem animal or plant. In this way women, girls, uninitiated boys, and special guests from other patrilineal descent groups can also share in the magical protection of the totem spirits of a descent group.

Clans   Among the Arunta, clans are formed by alliances among those patrilineal kin groups which claim their common descent from mythical ancestors or totem spirits. Arunta clans are patrilineal and exogamous— that is, children automatically belong to their father's clan and must marry persons not members of the same clan. Thus the Arunta clan does not consist of individuals able to trace their actual kinship across the boundaries of the several patrilineal descent groups making up this consanguineal kin group. Rather, individuals are members because they belong to particular patrilineal descent groups who have linked themselves together since they claim a totem or ancestor in common.

The patrilineal descent groups that comprise Arunta clans usually live in the same area or adjacent areas. Arunta believe all forms of life share certain attributes and feel that these derive from a mythical past, or *alchera* ("dream time"), when the self-created hero ancestor, *numbakulla*, made all the various totems and natural geographic features and deposited them about the Arunta territory, after imbuing them with spirits from his own body. Thus Arunta clans are based on more than a recognition of inclusion of persons who share a common area, or totem; their heritage has derived from *numbakulla's* mythical spirit many vital attributes that are palpable, observable, and sacred since these qualities all come from the *alchera* time. This special relationship is symbolized for members in the displays of special, sacred clan decorative art patterns and particular clan myths, songs, and stories. Arunta linguistic terms, as well as special dialects, are also used

Ngatatjara rock painting, Puntutjarpa rock shelter, northern Warburton Range, Western Australia (date unknown). (Courtesy American Museum of Natural History.)

Australian native child and female (date unknown). (Courtesy American Museum of Natural History.)

by clan members to show their special qualities of relationship. This is particularly so in use of "secret" clan names and the dialect used only in special secret rituals.

Since the clans are exogamous, every Arunta child's parents must belong to different clan groups. Hence within the nuclear family two special and different clan dialects are known and used by mothers and fathers. As an Arunta boy grows up, he first learns the clan dialect of his mother, despite the fact that he is to be a member of his father's clan. Then as he grows older, he comes to learn and use the dialect of his father's clan. The clan dialects used in a local area are similar enough for a general mutual understanding between members of different clans, yet different enough to ensure the distinctive nature of each clan. Thus Arunta children must forge a personal as well as a social identification in the context of learning two distinctive dialects. However this is not an unusual situation in Arunta daily social life, which continually places individuals in situations of having to seek a delicate balance between social sameness and differences and social unity and separation in nearly every facet of the kinship and kin group activity.

Arunta children learn that there is one nonalterable entity in their life, that of their totem spirit. Arunta children learn that their spirit returns after their death to the totem center to await reentry into another human body. Thus the many tugs and pulls created by having to cope with and balance clan dialects and other opposing features of kinship and kin group life are counterbalanced by the specific knowledge for a child that, whatever occurs, they are part of all that has or will exist spiritually and magically in Arunta life.

Arunta clans meet on certain occasions to narrate the complete myths of the dream time, or *alchera*. Members of one clan cannot own or cannot formally know a complete myth from the *alchera* times. Even though Arunta children, with parents from different clans, learn and can often repeat all the parts of myths not "officially owned" by their father's clan, elders of the clans must meet formally in order to bring together the parts of ritual stories necessary to increase their totems. Arunta children and most women are barred from all totemic rituals to protect them from the very powerful forces basic to human existence that are believed to be present at the ceremonies. Clans are summoned to ritual meetings through use of special message sticks, feathered strings, or miniature copies of sacred objects. Arunta children play at making and sending clan message forms.

Clans maintain an effective internal discipline of members through the threat and practice of sorcery and magic. Every clan has a sorcerer skilled in the magical arts of defending clan members against harm by other clan sorcerers and believed capable of turning harmful magic against outsiders. All clan sorcerers are also suspected of being capable of using harmful magic for personal reasons or from sheer whimsy. Thus few clan members willingly seek to offend the sorcerer and usually follow his wishes.

Arunta discipline for children involves few severe restrictions, beyond those associated with totem centers and activities, rare physical punishment, and a considerable amount of direct, continuing verbal instruction by specific adults in the primary family and patrilineal descent group. After puberty, when both boys and girls have undergone a series of formal initiation rituals, there is a shift in authority and instruction in enculturation from the primary family and patrilineal descent group to the clan. Then the clan sorcerer becomes a visible and threatening figure of severe discipline for unusual behavior. In addition, after a child's puberty rituals all adult members of the clan ideally are entitled to intervene in the initiated child's behavior when they view it as inappropriate. Before initiation clan members rarely interfere with the rights of adults in the nuclear family and patrilineal descent group to instruct, discipline, or reward a child. After initiation it becomes the responsibility of all adult clan members to ensure proper conduct.

Moieties   Arunta regularly distinguish all persons by their membership in one or the other of the two large groups made up of the relatives of their father and mother. This is so even if a person is actually not a relative but a member of a clan linked to their father's or mother's clan. These two inclusive groups comprise the Arunta *moiety* system. Arunta moieties are named social units and have totems, special linguistic uses, rituals, and taboos generally similar to those of clans. The moieties are exogamous—that is, a person must marry into the opposite moiety. Among the Arunta, moieties are also patrilineal. Thus Arunta children automatically become members of their father's moiety. Arunta moieties divide persons on a *horizontal scale*—that is, without regard to their age, sex, or knowledge, and with reference only to whether individuals are members of the group of father's or mother's relatives.

Arunta also separate persons socially on the basis of a *vertical scale*—that is, with reference to adjacent generations. Thus an individual's generation is differentiated from father's generation and son's generation but not from father's father's or son's son's generation. These two organizing principles of horizontal (or moiety) separation and of vertical (or adjacent) generation separation have been combined by the Arunta in the southern part of the central Australian desert into a social system that has been technically termed a *four-class system*. This means that an Arunta child must learn that there are four distinct kin groupings, in addition to their primary family, patrilineal descent group, and clan, that are important in daily life. These four groups of persons, consisting of the two moieties and the two generational groups, are important to a child because they define the locations of possible marriage partners and set the very important rules of etiquette for respect and avoidance between persons in adjacent generations. As noted earlier an Arunta man ordinarily selects a wife from the group of his mother's mother's brother's daughter's daughters. In the Arunta four-class system, only one of the four classes includes marriageable persons such as mother's mother's brother's daughter's daughters. That same class also includes some women, such as first cross-cousins, who cannot marry a man. However Arunta in the northern part of the central Australian desert have created eight, rather than four, named classes of kin by regularly separating first cross-cousins from second cross-cousins.[8] Thus the eight classes of the northern Arunta are derived from the two moieties and two adjacent generations and by distinguishing between first and second cross-cousins in each of the two moieties. This very complex cognitive map of different social groups must be learned by an Arunta child, for without it the kinship terms and ways of behaving associated with them would be confusing. Children learn to depend first and regularly upon kin terms used in their nuclear family and descent groups and only later come to use the terms that need to be employed in dealing with clan, moiety, and all marriage-class relatives.

Ashanti Kinship, Kin Groups, and Enculturation

When Europeans came to the west coast of Africa in the late sixteenth century, they found many small native chiefdoms, each with its own capital town and political organization. By the late seventeenth century the economic and military pressures of the Europeans had caused a series of wars, during which some of the independent native kingdoms had allied themselves into states. One of these states was formed in the geographic area that later became the British colony of the Gold Coast, now the independent nation of Ghana. The African people who allied to form this powerful state through the eighteenth and nineteenth centuries belonged to tribes called *Ashanti*.[9] The native Ashanti state lasted until conquered by British forces in two bitter wars fought in 1873–1874 and 1900–1901.

Originally the Ashanti may have been sedentary farmers on the grasslands of the western Sudan. Under constant pressure from raids by nomadic Moslem peoples, however, small Ashanti groups began to migrate westward, finally settling in the tropical forests near the West African coast. The Ashanti forest villages were very small and isolated from one another until the arrival of the Europeans. The total Ashanti population is now estimated to be more than one million persons.

The Ashanti forest lands are very fertile, hot, and somewhat mountainous. Heavy rains fall from April to November and are followed by a very dry season. The Ashanti have been afflicted with a wide variety of serious tropical diseases, including malaria, typhoid, typhus, cholera, leprosy, elephantiasis, sleeping sickness, intestinal parasites, and skin diseases.

Ashanti technology includes hand-modeled pottery and wood carvings, made by specialists. Iron is worked with a bellows and charcoal fire

---

[8]A *cross-cousin* is a father's sister's or mother's brother's child.

[9]For readings on Ashanti culture and society, see discussions and references in Busia, 1951, 1955; Fortes, 1949, 1950; Hoebel, 1954; Matson, 1953; Rattray, 1923, 1927, 1929; Service, 1963, 366–386.

by experts adept at making axe and hoe blades, hammer heads, nails, knife blades, and spear points, as well as finely detailed chains, containers, bells, and a variety of ornaments. Before their contact with Europeans, Ashanti made bark cloth for clothing. In the late seventeenth century Ashanti men learned to make small looms and to weave cotton fabrics with complex designs. Intricate designs are stamped onto cloth worn as clothing.

Ashanti live in scattered villages and small towns in houses of wooden sticks and daubed-on mud wall construction, with roofs of grass or leaf thatching. Houses of wealthier Ashanti are usually arranged in compounds, that is, connecting buildings facing inward onto a central courtyard. Less affluent Ashanti live in small rectangular dwellings. Most Ashanti houses have a wide veranda along the length of one side of the structure. Houses of both the poor and the rich often have painted and carved designs on the exterior walls and roof support posts.

Except for the craft specialists, Ashanti gain their living by farming crops of manioc, yams and plaintains, millet, beans, peanuts, and onions and by raising fruit and oil palm trees. Oil palm products are used in a wide variety of cooking and domestic activities and are made by Ashanti into liquor. Because of the fertile land and climate, some vegetable crops are harvested twice a year. Fields are prepared by burning off the weed or forest cover and then are cultivated with an iron hoe blade. Fields are located outside villages and towns, so that Ashanti often must travel some distance to their farms.

Ashanti Kinship Groups   Most Ashanti live in dwelling groups, or *fie*. A *fie* ideally consists of persons connected by matrilineal descent and incorporated by ties of affinity.[10] By Ashanti law and custom the *fie* is the place where a person's matrilineage is located. If possible, women return to their childhood *fie* to bear their children. Children become citizens in an Ashanti chiefdom because they are born in their mother's mother's *fie*. However the dwelling group is not necessarily a place where fathers, mothers, and their children live together. In a stable Ashanti community about half the people live in matrilineal *fie* under female heads, and only about one-third of all married women live with their husbands, with the remainder living with matrilineal kin. In the evenings in an Ashanti village, many children are to be seen carrying prepared foods from the houses in which they reside with their mothers to the houses where their fathers are residing. Ashanti children may sleep in their mother's *fie* but often will eat their meals in their father's. It is considered contemptible for a man to live in his wife's house and normal for him to live in the house of his mother or one of his sisters.

---

[10]Matrilineal descent occurs when kinship ties are traced only through relatives in the mother's line of kinship. *Affinity* refers to ties through marriage.

The Ashanti dwelling group does not have a common food supply and does not share incomes for mutual support of members. Aid given within the *fie* occurs because members are matrilineal kin and not because they reside in it. A dwelling group usually contains three or more generations, consisting of a mother, her children, and her mother. Both men or women can be the head of a *fie*, depending on whether they are senior in age or generation to other members of the group. *Fie* heads usually own the house in which the group lives.

Although the *fie* centers upon one woman and her children and the children of her daughters, men living in it actually become heads of such groups about twice as often as women. Such a position for a man means simply that, because of the menstrual taboo on women, he must publicly represent the *fie* in the place of the senior female member of the group. Every Ashanti aspires to have his or her mother settled in her own *fie*, since concepts of personal dignity are closely related to one's mother being head of such a group or to residing in one's mother's *fie*. Ideally a man is supposed to set up his own dwelling group at marriage and to have his wife and children live with him, but the economic problems involved in building a house usually are too great for most young Ashanti men. So they continue to live on after marriage in the *fie* of their mother or sister, while their wife and young children stay in the *fie* of the wife. In addition, the ties of matrilineal kinship for both the young husband and wife are as strong as those imposed initially by marriage and parenthood. Although the cultural ideal is for the young Ashanti man to set up a *fie* and to have his wife and children with him, the traditions of the matrilineage exert strong tugs to another way of behaving.

There is no more basic social tie for the Ashanti than the one between a mother and her children. This tie is considered the ultimate element of all Ashanti social life. Children rarely question their mother's position of privilege, deference, or rank in the *fie*. When the senior female of a *fie* dies, her children may separate and establish independent dwelling groups of their own. More often than not, however, the *fie* is maintained by the sisters, daughters, or granddaughters of the deceased women, while her sons try to move out to set up their own.

A woman must try to reconcile her duties to her husband with her strong attachment to her mother and mother's mother, to her sisters, and to her mother's mother's sisters. A man has to reconcile his duties to his wife with his strong attachment to his mother and mother's mother, to mother's sisters, and to his own sisters. Ashanti men and women also have to try to balance out their relations to their own children and the children of their own sisters and brothers.

An Ashanti man is the legal guardian of his sister's children's rights, for they are his legal heirs. If a man's sister dies, his wife cannot expect him to exclude his sister's children from the *fie*. Ashanti say that men use cross-cousin marriage—that is, men marry their father's sister's daughters and mother's brother's daughters—as a way to unite their love of their own children with their loyalty to and responsibility for their sister's children. However less than ten percent of Ashanti women actually marry their cross-cousins. Ashanti seek to balance the social stresses that occur in the matching of ties of maternal kinship and parenthood by saying that a father is responsible for the care, support, and guidance of his children until they are adolescents, when they become the primary responsibility of their mother's brother. A man and his wife's brothers will try not to share the same *fie* to avoid the conflicts of loyalty that will arise in enculturation. Ashanti children must learn to handle the stresses generated by their form of social organization.

Ashanti kinship terminology is of the *Crow* type—that is, father's sister's son is called by the term used for father, while father's sister's daughter is called by the term used for father's sister. Mother's brother's son is called "son" and mother's brother's daughter is called "daughter," while all parallel cousins are called by the terms used for siblings.[11] Ashanti address all women of their mother's generation as "mother." All the men of their mother's generation are called "mother's brother," while all men and women of their mother's mother's generation and all the children in their grandchildren's generation are called by the same term. Ashanti women address all members of their children's generation as "child," while men address all members of their children's generation as "sister's child." Any male member of an individual's father's lineage may also be addressed as "father," while any female member of father's lineage may be called *"female father."*[12]

The regular care of Ashanti infants is the general responsibility of their mother. This is often formally shared with their mother's mother so that daily farming and other economic tasks may be carried out. This

[11]Comparisons of the pattern of kinship indicate there are six kinds of kin systems. The principle of classification used in defining the six systems depends upon the way people address their cousins. In the *Eskimo* system all cousins are equated with each other and are differentiated from an individual's (or *Ego's*) brothers or sisters. In the *Iroquois* system terms for brother and sister are extended to parallel cousins (*Ego's* mother's sisters and father's brother's children), and there are separate terms for cross-cousins (*Ego's* father's sisters and mother's brother's children). In the *Hawaiian* system terms for brothers and sisters are used to address all cousins. In the *Omaha* system, *Ego* calls father's sister's son by the term used for a nephew, while the father's sister's daughter is called by the term used for niece. The mother's brother's son is called by the term for mother's brother and the mother's brother's daughter is called by the term used for mother. All parallel cousins are called by the terms used for brothers and sisters. In the *Sudanese* system each cousin is called by a distinct term that is different from the ones used for brothers and sisters. The *Crow* system is described above. There is a possibility of classifying Ashanti cousin terminology as *descriptive* rather than as *Crow*. A *descriptive* kin system uses terms for cousins that are derived from other "elementary" kin terms (*Fa, Mo, Br, Si*). See Murdock, 1967, 66.

[12]A *lineage* is a unilineal consanguineal kinship group descended from a named and known ancestor who lived only five or six generations before *Ego*.

practice may cause some problems between a young mother and her own mother, since it is not uncommon for the mother's mother to argue strongly that she has the final say in raising an infant because a baby belongs more to the matrilineage (or *abusua*) than to its parents. This argument is usually overcome by a baby's mother when she notes that a moral and spiritual bond exists between a mother and her child that is much stronger than the one between mother's mother and her grandchildren. Ashanti mothers traditionally make all personal efforts to ensure their children's welfare. Ashanti mothers are symbols for protection and support of their children. Children grow up expecting to fully obey and to defer to their mother. Ashanti believe disrespect to one's mother is a grave religious offense since mothers represent all female ancestors. Ashanti children learn very early that an offended mother will not punish or publicly ridicule her children. They also learn to fear the dangers of the special form of witchcraft (*bayi*) that only a mother can loose upon children regularly unmindful of her wishes and commands. Children learn that mother's sisters are to be treated and responded to as their own mother would be, for Ashanti consider it disgraceful conduct to differentiate between their mother and her sisters in any public way. Ashanti children expect that their unruly behavior will be dealt with by their mother's brother as their mother's disciplinary representative. Although children may show temper toward their mother's brother, they also learn very quickly that he speaks for and with the authority of his sister.

The relationships between an Ashanti father and his children are marked by the fact that he is recognized as the sole contributor of two basic aspects of each child's personality, called *sunsum* and *kra*. A child's *sunsum* dies with him or her, but his or her *kra* returns to the Ashanti creator god. A father is believed to directly transmit his own personality to each of his children. When a father's *sunsum* is alienated through magic or witchcraft, Ashanti believe a child's personality will be affected, too. Thus it is not uncommon for fathers to want to be ritually treated along with their ailing children. The bond between an Ashanti father and his son is particularly close and affectionate because it is felt they share the same personality more fully than do father and daughter. Until a child's puberty, fathers are held formally responsible for the behavior of their children, especially their sons. Because they share the same *sunsum*, fathers are legally liable in Ashanti law for the behavior of their sons. Mothers are held accountable for the immoral acts of their daughters because of the "blood" (or matrilineage) ties between them. Although a girl inherits her personality from her father, she is directly accountable to her mother, who in turn is legally liable for their daughter's actions.

Initially and for a time immediately after a child's birth, the relations between Ashanti fathers and children are based solely on that fact of biological paternity. However when a man finally chooses a personal name for each of his children, he passes on, in addition to his *sunsum* and *kra*, a pride in the traditions of his own ancestors. The right of naming provides an Ashanti father with further opportunity to bind his children to his own consanguineal kin group.

Despite their personal liability for their sons' acts, Ashanti fathers have no legal authority over children. A father cannot require his children to live in his *fie*, nor can he claim their custody if he divorces his wife. It is believed a duty of fathers to feed, clothe, and train their children, whether they reside in their mother's *fie* or not. Ashanti fathers are supposed to help all their children get started in their adult lives by providing economic aid, advice, and directions.

Ashanti fathers are said to be exacting in requiring their children's obedience, deference, and respect. Fathers do not hesitate to physically punish children when they misbehave. The Ashanti say that the ties of love and respect for a father's contributions to their *sunsum* and *kra* make children willing to submit to a more severe discipline than they would receive from their mother or members of their mother's kin group. Children cannot inherit their father's property; however a father can make small bequests to children during his lifetime. Ashanti believe that to insult or deprecate a father is a grave wrong against his ancestors, as well as the creator, which will bring them continuing bad luck. Ashanti believe that no father can love his sister's children as much as his own children. In organized warfare an Ashanti father prefers his sons to accompany him into battle, rather than to have his sister's son by his side.

Ashanti children learn, however, that their mother's oldest living brother within the matrilineal kin group, traced from their mother's mother's mother, is the male of the parent generation with sole legal authority over them. A mother's brother will not discipline a child unless he is requested to do so by his sister. A mother's brother can and does command obedience to his wishes. Ashanti mother's brothers have had the power to pawn their sister's son to secure a loan for his own use; a young boy could be put to work for other persons, as security against default on a loan to his mother's brother. A mother's brother can demand financial help from his sister's son, as he can also generously provide for his sister's son's welfare. It is expected that a sister's son will repay the help provided by his mother's brother by treating his own sister's sons generously as they grow up or by assisting other matrilineal kin in need. The prime aspect of this relationship is the fact that the sister's son is the legal heir of his mother's brother. The importance of this is seen in the fact that a man's own children will address his sister's son as "father" to show respect to him as their potential legal guardian should their mother's brother die. A man can address his mother's brother's wife as "wife" because he will inherit her as a wife if his mother's brother should die. However no other social relationship of Ashanti children is as ambivalent as the one with their mother's brother. The ideal is that mother's brother and sister's son are like father and son. The reality, which involves the problems of inheritance and of the legal authority of the mother's brother, is that such relations are very stressful for children, despite the fact that the mother's brother and the sister's children often live in the same dwelling group.

Ashanti Enculturation   Ashanti children learn to pay great respect and deference to the parents of both their father and mother, since grandparents ideally embody the essence of Ashanti ways. Because of her position as the link between children and their matrilineage, the mother's mother has great influence on the enculturation of an Ashanti child. She takes pride in her grandchildren's conformity to Ashanti ideal ways, cares for them regularly during infancy, and provides them with lavish displays of affection. Grandparents rarely punish their grandchildren for minor disobedience. They will ask a child's mother or father to administer discipline to children for serious misbehavior, since grandparents, and especially the mother's mother, are supposed to maintain harmony in the dwelling group. Children learn from all their grandparents the traditional Ashanti knowledge and folklore, such as proverbs, tales, myths, and songs. Grandparents regularly recount to children the histories and fortunes of their particular kin group and ancestors. If Ashanti children have living great-grandparents, they regard them with near-religious awe because these old persons form a human link to the long-dead ancestors. Children learn that the kin term for grandparent (*nana*) is used by an Ashanti as the title of greatest respect when addressing or referring to their chief or king and that chiefs, priests, and political leaders use the reciprocal term (*nana*) in addressing their followers. Thus the relationship between grandparents and grandchildren are the formal models of behavior throughout the Ashanti political, religious, and legal institutions.

Ashanti children also learn to be respectful to their father's sisters as a symbol of their father. A father's sister may scold her brother's children for their misbehavior since she represents to children all of the claims, privileges, and authority of their father's matrilineage. Since under the ideal Ashanti practice of cross-cousin marriage, their father's sister is a potential mother-in-law and is formally charged under Ashanti law with looking after the ways her brother treats the property her children will inherit, children do not often seek out their father's sister for help or affection. The father's sister may act for her brother at the time of the ritual naming of his children.

Ashanti children must also learn to regularly defer to and be respectful of older brothers and sisters. Older siblings are able to physically and verbally punish a younger brother or sister for misbehavior and are responsible to their parents for assistance to a younger sibling in trouble or in need of help. These privileges and responsibilities are especially given to the firstborn, who is said by Ashanti to be the "head" of the children's group. Parents continually stress the need for sibling unity and presenting a common front against misfortune or personal attack. The only real informality permitted in Ashanti social relations occurs between siblings. Brothers and sisters may joke and tease and be somewhat immodest in dress in the presence of one another. These forms of behavior are considered unthinkable with other persons. Children learn that brothers and sisters trust and confide in each other on all vital matters and that as adults they will continue to do so, to the exclusion of their own husband or wife. Siblings will entrust highly personal confidences to each other that they would not share with their parents, wives, or children. Ashanti children are taught that siblings are supposed to unite in the face of opposition from spouses or children.

Ashanti children learn to understand messages sent and repeated by adults across long distances by use of "talking drums." Cedar wood and elephant ear membrane drums are used in sets to imitate, through drum beats, the tones of Ashanti words. The Ashanti language, like many African languages, is tonal—that is, a large amount of meaning for most words is demonstrated in the sounding of the word. Drums are used by Ashanti to closely reproduce the tones of words and punctuation in *set holophrases*— that is, very complex ideas are expressed in stylized beats that are so well known that all who hear the "language" can quickly and precisely understand the messages sent on the drums. Children learn early to read these messages, which usually summon political leaders to meetings, give public notice of the death of important persons, and discuss vital events such as impending war, widespread disease, and so on. Some special drums are used only to broadcast traditional proverbs that stress loyalty, duty, hard work, and other ideal personal virtues. Drummers, with the minstrels who sing traditional songs at rituals and on special occasions, transmit a substantial amount of culture to children as they mature in Ashanti society.

Ashanti Kin Groups The Ashanti believe children are physically a composite of the "blood" (*mogya*) of their mother and the "spirit" (*ntoro*) of their father. The link between each Ashanti generation is believed to be provided by the mother's blood. Every child is a member by birth in his or her mother's "blood group," or *abusua*. Every child is also a member of his or her father's "spirit group," or *ntoro*.

The Ashanti *abusua* is a matrilineal kin group consisting of all the persons of both sexes who trace their descent through the female line to a named, real, common female ancestor who lived some 10 to 12 generations before their mother's generation. The *abusua* group is much more important in a child's social life than the *ntoro*, or patrilineal, kin group because it is the social unit where the most important Ashanti economic, political, and religious activities occur. Matrilineal descent determines the right to own and use land, inheritance of most other property, political succession, social rank, many statuses, and formal titles. However every Ashanti matrilineage has a male head, chosen from among the males of the kin group. The head (*abusua panin*) is formally responsible for the welfare of all lineage members and is expected to settle disputes between them. He is also supposed to lead in organizing its rituals, ceremonies, and economic and political activities. He oversees the marriages, divorces, and remarriages of lineage women, makes offerings to the female ancestors, cares for ancestor shrines, deals with the lineage gods, and holds in trust the sacred symbols of the lineage. The male Ashanti matrilineage head also represents the entire lineage at the councils of the heads of all the matri-lineages in a village, town, or district.

One of the important functions of a man acting as a lineage head is to be a combined symbolic mother's brother and father to all its children. If Ashanti children wish special, formal permission to engage in out-of-ordinary ways, they seek out their mother's brother and the head of the segment of their lineage (or *yafunu*) in their dwelling group (if this is a man other than their mother's brother) and then go to the matrilineage head to request the permission they need. As children proceed from the generally constrained and formalized contact with their mother's brother and the *yafunu* head to the head of their lineage, they experience a marked change of attitude. Matrilineage heads look upon children in the kin group as their own children and so are much less formal and more openly affectionate, evenhanded, and considerate of a child's feelings than a mother's brother and the *yafunu* head need to be with children asking special favors or aid.

A lineage head chooses a senior woman of the kin group to assist him in watching over women's morals, to supervise girls' initiation ceremonies, to make peace in lineage quarrels, to be the genealogical expert for the group, and to serve as a symbolic mother for the entire lineage. In this role she is the living symbol of the fact that lineage members all share "one blood," or *mogya*.

Ashanti matrilineages have a *segmentary* structure. The segments, called "children of one womb," or *yafunu*, generally consist of the descendants of a common female ancestor not more than four or five generations antecedent to the persons making up a segment. Most often a *yafunu* consists of matrilineal kin whose female parents and grandparents grew up in a single dwelling group, or *fie*, as a group of siblings. The kinship terms of reference and address that are used in the *yafunu* are those applied to all members of the maximal matrilineage. The members of a *yafunu* may all be part of one *fie* or may live in adjacent *fie*. The number of segments in one Ashanti matrilineage varies from generation to generation because the *yafunu* tend to disappear as the founding female ancestors die.

An old, established Ashanti village is divided into a number of "wards" (*brono*), each one of which is occupied by the male and female members of one matrilineage. Neighborhoods within the *brono* consist of groupings of the several segments, or *yafunu*, of the maximal matrilineage. The numbers of matrilineages in a village vary, but usually at least half the population belongs to two or three lineages, while the remainder are members of "stump lineages"—that is, matrilineal kin groups brought into the community by migrants, refugees displaced by wars, or occupational specialists such as weavers, smiths, and woodcarvers.

A maximal lineage is regarded by Ashanti as a local branch of one of the seven or eight widespread matrilineal clans, or *mmusuaban*. The lineages of one clan are regarded as the matrilineal descendants of a single, remote female ancestor for whom a mythological birth and magical life is claimed and in whose name special rituals are observed and certain shrines and religious symbols are maintained. Ashanti usually do not know the names of their clan ancestors but may still behave toward each other in daily affairs as if they were members of the same matrilineage. The matrilineal clans have a vital function in Ashanti social life because they are the social units that ensure that every Ashanti individual belongs to a kin group that is named and known both in location and in Ashanti history. In the recent past clans may have had special totem animals and special totem rituals.

Children's membership by birth in their father's patrilineal kin group, or *ntoro*, involves them with persons said to share the same *sunsum*, or personality. Ashanti view an individual's personality as the "child" of his or her father's *ntoro* kin group. The number of Ashanti *ntoro* varies from area to area. Ashanti say there are from 7 to 12 such patrilineal kin groups. Each *ntoro*, and hence each member of such a group, is believed by Ashanti to be under the protection of a particular god, or *abosom*. The god of a *ntoro* is said to share the *sunsum* and *kra* (personality and life force) of the creator god (or *Onyankopon*), as Ashanti children share the *sunsum* and *kra* of their father. Thus Ashanti children learn early that their *sunsum* and *kra*, derived from their father, is a heritage from the *abosom* of their father's patrilineal kin group, given to it by the god of all Ashanti.

Each *ntoro* has a special name, which indicates the dominant personality type to be expected from its members. Some names of Ashanti *ntoro* are, in translation, "the tough," "the human," "the liberal," "the fanatic," "the audacious," and "the fastidious." Thus children are born with their personality not only fully shaped and inherited from their father but also firmly fixed for their lifetime by the character stereotypes ascribed to all members of a *ntoro*. Each *ntoro* group also uses special surnames, so its members can be distinguished easily by their characteristic name.

Each patrilineal kin group has some special taboos to observe. Thus the *ntoro* called *Bosommuru* ("the distinguished") cannot eat or harm an ox, python, or dog. These animals are totems, said to have given special services to the *ntoro* god or founding ancestors. Each *ntoro* has a "sacred day" on which it ritually purifies its members. The *ntoro* gods are associated specially with rivers, lakes, and the sea. A sacred day ceremony usually involves "washing the spirit" of the *ntoro* in a purification ritual to cleanse the *sunsum* and *kra* of all the members of this kin group. Ashanti children are present at these special ritual activities. At these times they learn the sacred lore of the *ntoro*, such as the special form of greeting used between members of the group to enable them to fully identify one another. Ashanti children's principal contacts with most members of their father's *ntoro* are at the times of the sacred-day ceremonies.

Ashanti children must also learn to comprehend the ways their society is formally stratified into large groups of persons. In addition to kinship terms and kin groupings, Ashanti order their social life through identifying certain ideal and expected behavior forms with occupational and ritual specialties (smith, weaver, woodcarver, priests), ranks (kings, chiefs, nobles, commoners, slaves), income (wealthy, poor, destitute), mobility (geographic changes of residence because of politics, war, famine, disease), and education (apprentice to an occupational or ritual specialist). Ashanti children must learn about these categories of persons and the social ways associated with them because everyday conversation and life are permeated by reference and action with respect to whether particular individuals have such socially meaningful characteristics. Ashanti society is open—that is, it is possible for the children and grandchildren of slaves or of unredeemed pawns (children of a man placed in forced labor by his mother's brother as security on a loan) to attain positions of social and economic power and great political influence. An Ashanti chief swears a sacred oath on taking office which includes a formal declaration that he will never reproach subjects for being the descendants of slaves or pawns, thus ensuring lower-ranked and poor children the opportunity to regain or to gain new social positions of greater prestige and influence.

Comparison and Contrast—Arunta and Ashanti Enculturation

Case study data from Arunta and Ashanti cultures have been presented to illustrate the point that there are great variations in the patterns of kinship and kin groups, so that children growing up in some societies learn specific ideas about these patterns of culture markedly different from those learned by children in other societies. Some principal differences in patterns of Arunta and Ashanti kinship and kin groups are summarized in Table 6–2.

TABLE 6–2 Some Contrasts between Arunta and Ashanti Patterns of Kinship and Kin Groups

	ARUNTA KINSHIP AND KIN GROUPS*	ASHANTI KINSHIP AND KIN GROUPS*
Family organization	Independent polygynous families with sororal polygyny permitted; co-wives live in the same quarters	Small, extended polygynous families with sororal polygyny permitted but not frequent; co-wives live in separate quarters
Social group focus	Local groups (exogamous, patrilocal)	Dwelling groups (exogamous, avunculocal with virilocal and duolocal alternatives)
Cousin terms	Iroquois cousin terminology	Crow cousin terminology (possibly descriptive type)
Cousin marriage	Nonlateral cousin marriage; preferred with *MoMoBrDaDa* or *FaMoBrSoDa*	Duolateral cousin marriage; matrilateral cross-cousin marriage preferred
Property exchange at marriage	Dowry or transfer of property from bride's kinsmen to kinsmen of the groom	Bride-price or transfer of property from groom's kinsmen to kinsmen of the bride
Community organization	Clan communities; each community consists of a single exogamous clan	Agamous communities; community has no localized clan or marked tendency to exogamy or endogamy
Kin groups	Patrilineages are a major consanguineal kin group	Matrilineages are a major consanguineal kin group; segmentary matrilineages have social functions
Kin groups	Clans; exogamous kin groups formed of patrilineal descent groups whose membership live in one community	Clans; exogamous kin groups whose core membership lives in more than one community
Kin groups	Moieties formed of two maximal patrilineages	Patrilineages are present and perform special ritual and social functions
Settlement pattern	Fully migratory bands	Compact and relatively permanent settlements in villages or towns
Social stratification	No stratification by occupation, income, education, social classes, or social mobility	Social stratification by occupation, rank, income, and education; recognized social classes with mobility possible in and between classes
Status-role terms	Family, in-law, generational, lineage, clan, and moiety status terms	Family, in-law, generational, lineage, clan, and nonfamily (chief, lord, commoner) status terms

*See also Murdock, 1967, 13, 27, 66–69, 94–97, and Service, 1963, 747–762.

However it is also important to note that, despite such marked differences, the enculturation process in Arunta and Ashanti cultures has some fundamental similarities. Both cultures utilize their patterns of kinship to provide for a very large number of parent-surrogates, or alternates, so that culture is transmitted to and acquired by children effectively and well. In both cultures there is wide opportunity for infants and children to learn from and observe many people acting in the ways that must be known for successful adult behavior. This broad diffusion of the responsibility for the cultural transmission process through use of the patterns of kinship and kin groups means that in both Arunta and Ashanti cultures widely shared concepts, ideas, and ways of acting are elaborated on and regularly emphasized by many individuals other than a child's biological parents.

In both Arunta and Ashanti cultures the competing demands on children by different kin groups are balanced in the enculturation process through use of concepts such as totem and life spirits and supernatural forces. In these cultures competing kin groups subject infants and children to contrary pressures for social sameness and difference and for social unity and separation. These competing kin group demands can be quite intense, for example, when an Ashanti boy must choose to obey the commands of his father or his mother's brother or when an Arunta girl must be loyal to her father's descent group as well as to the local group in which she resides with her husband.

Such competing and highly personal demands are met in both Arunta and Ashanti cultures through appeals to nonhuman beings, spirits, and forces. For instance, Arunta seek a balance in such competing kin group demands through myths of the *alchera*, or dream times, when there were no clan or moiety divisions in Arunta society and all Arunta were believed to have belonged to one small local group. Arunta also use the concept of total spirit descent from one powerful creator god to balance competing kin group demands. Thus Arunta children learn that, although they are regularly subjected to conflicting demands by kin groups with different concerns, such pressures are only incidental to the basic fact of all Arunta being part of one group. As in the case of Arunta children, Ashanti children also learn to meet the demands upon them by different kin groups through reference to a common, mythical past, totem spirits, and a common descent. In both Arunta and Ashanti cultures children learn to understand that such pressures are immediate and situational and what really matters is the fact of being "Arunta" or "Ashanti" and living as a member of the society.

Finally both the Arunta and Ashanti enculturation processes essentially depend upon the various special social roles played by the parents of mother and father in the transmission of the ideal history and beliefs of these cultures. It is primarily from grandparents and the brothers and sisters of grandparents that Arunta and Ashanti children learn the ways these cultures came into being, the ways they have met past challenges and tests in the human and natural worlds, and the reasons used to justify special social forms or acts. In both cultures grandparents also provide children with their basic understanding of the ways the many parts of culture are supposed to be interrelated. This aspect of the cultural transmission process in Arunta and Ashanti cultures provides for children's basic understanding of the *ethos* and *eidos*, or the overall cultural form and style of Arunta and Ashanti life. In other words, it is from grandparents that Arunta and Ashanti children have their enculturation in those dominant ways of thought and behavior which constitute the "flavor" and the "coherence" of Arunta and Ashanti cultures.

Comparisons with Other Cultures   These three features of enculturation—that is, use of the pattern of kinship to provide a large number of parent-surrogates in cultural transmission; balancing of competing kin group demands through use of concepts of common descent, totem, life spirits, and forces; grandparents providing the principal portrayal of cultural history and cultural *ethos* and *eidos*—which are common to Arunta and Ashanti cultures, are also to be found in the process of cultural transmission in many other societies.

For example, the Appendix of this text provides a bibliography of enculturation in 128 societies. A careful review of data of enculturation in these societies indicates that the three features of enculturation noted in common between Arunta and Ashanti cultures also appear to be present in 99 (or approximately 77 percent) of 128 cultures. Table 6–3 notes the names of the cultures in which these three features of enculturation seem to be present. In 29 of the 128 societies, one or more of these three features of enculturation are missing, or ethnographic data are so unclear that it is very difficult to be certain concerning the presence or absence of such features of cultural transmission.

There are six societies (American, English, French, German, Israeli, Russian) of the 128 cultures in the Appendix in which all three features of enculturation seem absent. These societies also have contrasting kinship and kin group forms. All of these six societies are industrialized and urbanized. Each one of the 99 societies listed in Table 6–3 with the three features of enculturation present have in common the fact that they have possessed a nonindustrial economy and were organized in nonurban forms of social living.

These data suggest that the three features of enculturation found in 99 cultures of a 128-culture sample may illustrate the point that as industrialization and urbanization occur and belief and values associated with industrialization and urbanization are introduced into and spread through a culture: (1) the number of parent-surrogates is progressively reduced; (2) kin group demands are increasingly replaced by demands made on individuals by technological institutions ("the firm," "the company," "the guild," "the craft," "the union") with the consequence that traditional social balancing mechanisms (conceptions of totem, life spirits, and forces) are no longer effective; and (3) grandparents become unable to serve as guides

TABLE 6–3 128-Culture Sample for Three Features of Enculturation*

NEW WORLD CULTURES (39)		PACIFIC CULTURES (31)		OLD WORLD CULTURES (58)	
North America (26)	Central and South America (13)	Australia, Indonesia, Borneo, New Guinea, Pacific Islands (31)	Eurasia (15)	Europe and Circum-Mediterranean (11)	Africa (Sub-Saharan) (32)
3 features present (24)	3 features present (9)	3 features present (28)	3 features present (10)	3 features present (4)	3 features present (25)
Apache	Camayura	Alor	Ainu	Arab	Ashanti
Arapaho	Jivaro	Arapesh	Andamanese	Lapp	Azande
Cheyenne	Kaingang	Arunta	Baiga	Riffians	Baganda
Comanche	Sherente	Bali	Chenchu	R'wala	Basuto
Eskimo	Siriono	Chamorro	Deoli		Bemba
Flathead	Tenetehara	Dobuans	Lakher		Bena
Hopi	Wapisiana	Dusun	Lepcha	One or more features absent or data unclear (6)	Bushmen
Hupa	Witoto	Fijians	Palaung		Chagga
Kaska	Yagua	Ifaulk	Yakut	English	Chewa
Klamath		Ifugao	Yukaghir	French	Dahomean
Kutenai	One or more features absent or data unclear (4)	Ilocos		German	Gusii
Kwakiutl		Kwoma	One or more features absent or data unclear (6)	Israeli	Kikuyu
Navaho	Abipon	Lesu		Russian	Lamba
Omaha	Ona	Malaitans	Balahi	Zadruga	Masai
Paiute	San Pedro	Malekula	Chinese		Ngoni
Papago	Warrau	Manus	Japanese		Nuer
Sanpoil		Maori	Koryak		Nyakyusa
Slave		Marquesans	Okinawan		Pygmies
Taos		Murngin	Rājpūts		Swazi
Teton		Ontong-			Tallensi
Dakota		Pukapukans			Tanala
Wichita		Samoans			Tiv
Winnebago		Tikopia			Tswana
Zuni		Trobriands			Yoruba
		Trukese			Zulu
One or more features absent or data unclear (3)		Ulithians			
		Wogeo			One or more features absent or data unclear (7)
American		Yungar			
Mexican					Bapedi
Puerto Rican		One or more features absent or data unclear (3)			Kongo
					Pondo
		Javanese			Thonga
		Kiwai			Tonga
		Nauru			Turkana
					Venda

*The time of the "ethnographic present" is about 1948–1950. Inclusion of Japanese and Chinese data is on the basis of reports of traditional, nonindustrial life. References for cultures listed here may be found in the Appendix. It should be noted that many of these cultures have alternative names (e.g., the Bemba also are termed the Awemba, Babemba, or Wabemba). See Textor (1967), Appendix One, for an alphabetic listing of culture names and their alternatives. See also Murdock et al., 1958.

for children to the *ethos* and *eidos* of a culture. In fact, descriptions of the enculturation process in contemporary industrialized and urbanized cultures (see Appendix) make it apparent that there are very few parent-surrogates in enculturation, that competing kin group concerns actually are minimal or entirely absent, and that schools and other social, political, and economic institutions have largely taken over the special roles of grandparents in transmitting culture history and cultural *ethos* and *eidos* conceptions. Bronfenbrenner's (1970) studies of American and Russian childhood and enculturation show that two of the world's most industrialized and urbanized societies have turned significantly away from use of the three features of enculturation that appear in many of the world's cultures.[13] This change may also be found in many of the world's industrialized and urbanized cultures, particularly those recently undergoing rapid change toward urban, industrial life.

Socialization and Urban Life

A specific relationship between socialization and industrial, urban life has been proposed by Wallace (1970, 147–148), who notes in commenting on McClelland's (1961) hypothesis concerning "achievement motivation" in socialization that there is a "substantial correlation" between strong maternal encouragement of a child's independence strivings and a high achievement motivation in adult life and economic enterprise, particularly in industrial societies. Wallace points out that studies by LeVine (1966) among the Ibo in Nigeria and DeVos (1968) in Japan report data which support his hypothesis.[14] In a number of other studies of the relationship between patterns of kinship and kin groups and socialization in China, India, Japan, and the United States, Hsu (1963, 1965, 1971) also suggests that there are some specific relationships between socialization and industrial, urban life that are focused through cultural conceptions of social life, particularly kinship and kin groups, and learned by infants and children as they mature in these cultures.

Using a very different theoretical and methodological approach, Konner (1976) has reviewed research on humans and other primates concerning interactions of infants and juveniles with their peers and nonpeers and concludes that human peer groups are fabrications of highly developed industrial societies and do not seem to be natural features of the human groups important in the psychological and social development of infants.

---

[13]Ariès (1962) provides a clear indication that the three features of enculturation were present in Western Europe prior to the industrial revolution.

[14]It should be noted that, while DeVos (1968) points out that achievement motivation is closely tied to Japanese enculturation, it does not always lead to economic or industrial success, as apparently it does among Ibo traders, as reported by LeVine. See also Caudill & Schooler, 1973; B. Whiting, 1969.

Konner supports this conclusion through use of data on modern primates, early human hunter-gatherer cultures, the culture and behavior of the present-day !Kung San peoples of Southwest Africa and studies of children conducted in Boston and London.

It is clear that the patterns of kinship and kin groups in a culture are directly related to the enculturation process found in the culture. However it is not yet as clear whether the enculturation process is related, and in what specific ways it is related, to many other patterns in other subsystems of culture. This is because conclusions, such as those offered previously concerning the three features of enculturation and urban, industrial life, the relationship between enculturation for achievement and industrial and economic success, or the relationship between an industrial economy and the formation of human peer groups, must now be qualified by both theoretical and methodological exceptions.

The Problem of Bias in Comparative Studies

In comparing transcultural data of enculturation, it is necessary to take care that the cultures chosen for comparison have been independent of one another, with no history of borrowing of culture or use of the same language.[15] Scientific logic suggests great care in making any statements which imply or state that all the patterns of a culture are equally involved in determining the state, or condition, of either the whole culture or any of its subsystems. Simply to assert that two or more patterns of a culture, such as kinship and exchange, or marketing, are interdependent begs the question of whether they actually are linked. Such an assertion also ignores the important theoretical problem of whether all cultural patterns are equally independent—that is, whether each one has an equal capability of survival when separated from the other patterns in a cultural system.

The statements made here concerning the presence or absence of three features of enculturation in 128 cultures are drawn from a comparative sample in which some cultures do have historical and linguistic relationships. This fact biases the conclusions noted earlier. It would similarly bias any conclusions about socialization where there were demonstrable relationships of cultural diffusion and language between the cultures in-

---

[15]This has been termed *Galton's Problem* by Naroll (1961, 1964, 1968) and others (Naroll & D'Andrade, 1963; Driver & Chaney, 1968) and is derived from Galton's (1889) comment on a paper by Tylor (1889) in which Galton pointed out the serious problem that arises in comparing cultural forms when cultures share a common history or language, as for example, Polynesian cultures such as the Maori of New Zealand and Hawaiians of the Hawaiian Islands or the Athabascan-language-speaking Dogrib of Northwest Canada and the Apache of New Mexico and Arizona.

cluded in a sample.[16] The statements concerning the three features of enculturation do not include any consideration of whether each feature is equivalent or differentially weighted. This may also bias the conclusions offered here and in any other transcultural study of the interrelations between a pattern of culture and the process of socialization.

Whether the statement advanced here concerning the effects on the socialization process of the transition from nonindustrial, nonurban life to industrial, urban living is of worth and will be borne out by further study of the ethnographic literature and in field studies, the point of the illustration is that the process of socialization is not only related to patterns of kinship and kin groups but should also be considered as interdependent with other patterns in other cultural subsystems.

CONTEXTUAL AND HOLOCULTURAL STUDIES OF SOCIALIZATION

Two quite different methodological approaches are used in contemporary comparative studies of the socialization process. The two approaches may be termed as *contextual* and *holocultural*.

The Contextual Method

One of the fundamental theoretical insights of modern anthropology has been that culture is a complexly interrelated whole. Cultural anthropologists have learned that when studying a culture such as the Dusun of Borneo, they should be aware that the ways Dusun mothers hold their babies and the form of disposal of a baby's umbilical cord may be linked to the form of Dusun songs or the style of designs woven by Dusun into baskets and carved or painted on Dusun houses and grave structures. An anthropologist expects that all of these cultural forms, which occur as part of different subsystems of Dusun culture, when viewed in their special relation of interdependence through the history of Dusun culture, can offer profound insights in the analysis of the patterns of culture widely shared in Dusun society. In other words, cultural anthropologists have learned that no cultural pattern or form, whether in Dusun, Arunta, or Ashanti culture, stands alone and unrelated to the other aspects of culture.

A cultural anthropologist does not learn the importance of a *contextual* method of cultural analysis by reading descriptions of culture, although reading ethnographic accounts is a very important part of preparation for

---

[16]*Diffusion* refers to the geographic spread of customs and social institutions among different cultures due to intercultural borrowing.

field research. Rather, he or she learns about the ways patterns of culture are interrelated by being totally immersed in different cultures for a long period.

Cultural anthropologists live in other cultures where they become intensely aware of new social environments as they make consistent efforts to interact regularly with their neighbors on terms they comprehend and in their language. In the process of totally experiencing another and very different culture, an anthropologist comes to understand and be able to illustrate that cultures are wholes, made of complexly interdependent parts, each of which can be finally understood only in its relations to other parts of a culture.

The sensitivity to the *contextual* (or *holistic*) nature of culture gained by cultural anthropologists through long-term field studies produces a unique theoretical outlook. This outlook deeply affects modern anthropological writings and is the background against which much of cultural analysis is conducted and judged by contemporary cultural anthropologists.[17]

The contextual method for comparative study of socialization is based on inferences drawn concerning this process after repeated readings of a large number of entire ethnographic sources. After reading, and rereading, of entire ethnographic sources for 128 cultures (see Appendix), this statement was formulated:

> As industrialization and urbanization occur, the numbers of parent-surrogates are progressively reduced, kin group demands are increasingly replaced by demands made on children by technological institutions, and grandparents are no longer able to serve as guides for children to the ethos and eidos of a culture.

It is important to understand that this statement was not first developed as a formal hypothesis and then validated by use of data abstracted from ethnographic studies in a sample of 128 selected cultures. Rather, this statement is a *reasoned inference* based on a method of repeated readings of a large number of ethnographic sources.

The method of drawing a socialization inference after repeated reading of a large number of entire ethnographic sources was first described and used successfully by Cohen (1964) in a comparative study of the events involved in the transition from childhood to adolescence.

The contextual method is also a time-honored procedure of ethnographic research, in which a field worker makes detailed notes, later ana-

---

[17]For a critique of use of the contextual, or holistic, method in the social sciences, see Phillips, 1976. Phillips concludes that a holistic method can be error-prone and misleading unless carefully used by highly trained persons. For a different view, see Spindler, 1967.

lyzes these notes through repeated readings, and then draws reasoned inferences from them.[18] It is worth repeating that sensitivity in the use of the contextual method, whether in field study or in comparative social-ization research, is best gained by repeated, long-term immersion in other cultures as a participant-observer.[19]

It should be noted that among others, Textor (1967, 9) has described this conventional cultural and social anthropological method as being an activity based on the ". . . hope that one's creative intellect would succeed in generating hypotheses or perceiving patterns," and as being "impres-sionistic cross-cultural thinking" that seeks to substitute creative insight and originality of thought for methodological rigor, quantification, and sus-tained attention to the solution of difficult research problems.

However Naroll (1973, 312) takes a different view of the use of the contextual method when he concludes that ". . . the original insights, orig-inal discoveries, great illuminations about social and cultural affairs usually come from minds meditating long about particular cases deeply studied— rarely from statistical studies of necessarily much simplified data." One widely acknowledged example of the application of the contextual method is to be found in a study by Mead (1938–1949) concerning the relationships between patterns of kinship and kin groups and the enculturation process in Arapesh culture.

The Holocultural Method in Study of Socialization

The term *holocultural* refers to a method of study that involves com-parative analysis of cultural data taken from a worldwide sample of societies. This method was first used by Edward Tylor in an 1889 study of the interrelationships between kinship and marriage patterns in culture; in this sense, the holocultural method is as time-honored through use as is the contextual method. Tylor searched the written ethnographic records avail-able to him for "adhesions" between the practice of married males being forbidden to speak to their wife's mother (mother-in-law avoidance) and the practice of a married man going to live with his wife's family (matrilocal residence). Tylor's study of the records of culture available to him led him to the conclusion that when mother-in-law avoidance was practiced in a culture, matrilocal residence was also common. Thus in modern terms Tylor noted a strong, positive *correlation* between mother-in-law avoidance and matrilocal residence.

Since Tylor's adhesions, or correlational, method depended upon the

---

[18]In the development of socialization research this method was used with notable success by Mead (1928, 1935, 1949), Kluckhohn (1947, 1954), and others, including J.W.M. Whiting, 1941, and DuBois, 1944.

[19]For one discussion of participant-observation in field study, see T.R. Williams, 1967.

availability of a large number of descriptions of different cultures, for a long period its use was limited to scholars with very good personal libraries, access to major university and museum libraries, or personal notes copied through many years of study.

However between 1937 and 1943 a file of basic ethnographic descriptions of many different types of cultural and social forms was begun by George Murdock and his associates at the Institute for Human Relations at Yale University.[20] The file, now known as the Human Relations Area File, is based on abstracting descriptions of specific cultural and social forms from ethnographic accounts and then storing them according to an index covering the major categories of culture and society. This index, or outline of cultural materials, "now covers 79 major headings with 631 subdivisions" (Murdock, 1971). In 1943 the Yale file contained data abstracted from 150 cultures. By 1957 because of various demands for use, particularly in holocultural research, the file included data from 565 cultures. In 1967 the cross-cultural file had expanded to 862 cultures (Murdock, 1967). By 1980 the Human Relations Area File contained data from 1167 cultures (Barry & Schlegel, 1980) of the over 4000 cultures that Murdock et al. (1958, v.) have estimated are known to history and ethnography.[21] Murdock and White (1969) have selected a "standard cross-cultural sample" of 186 cultures which is widely used in holocultural research. Duplicate sets of the cross-cultural file are now maintained at more than 20 centers in the United States and abroad, with microfilm sets of the files for a limited number (usually 50) of cultures also available in many libraries around the world.

J.W.M. Whiting (1954, 1968), Ford (1967), and Bock (1969, 356–363) have described the ways the Human Relations Area Files may be used to formulate and then test, using modern statistical procedures, any one of a number of holocultural hypotheses concerning relationships between various patterns of culture. Thus Horton (1943) used the files and the holocultural method to determine possible relationships between use of alcohol and certain cultural features, while Ford (1945) conducted a study of the correlations between certain cultural features and human reproduction. In 1949 Murdock published a landmark holocultural study of the statistically demonstrated correlations among kinship terms, descent rules, marriage rules, and residence rules in 165 cultures. O'Leary (1969, 1971, 1973) and Naroll (1970, 1973) list more than 350 holocultural studies. Naroll, Michik, and Naroll (1976) and Levinson (1977b) have made available a summary and discussion of 1350 theoretical propositions tested or developed by means of worldwide cross-cultural studies—that is, through

---

[20]For an account of the development of this cross-cultural file, see Murdock et al., 1969. See also Ford, 1970.

[21]Naroll (1973, 315) also estimates that there were between 4000 and 5000 cultures in the world in the nineteenth century.

use of the holocultural method.[22] Udy (1973) and Vermeulen and deRuijter (1975) have discussed the underlying assumptions and procedures of such holocultural studies.

The holocultural, or statistical, procedure has been employed frequently in socialization research to systematically seek to reduce the complexity of human cultural and social phenomena and to try to demonstrate relations of interdependence between socialization and various patterns of culture. Today the model for most such research is an innovative and original study by Whiting and Child (1953). This study proceeded in a series of five steps. First the authors abstracted specific data of infant care and of some later patterns of adult behavior from the ethnographic literature of 75 nonliterate, nonindustrial, and nonurban societies. Then the authors constructed a set of ratings for the severity of care of infants in these 75 societies with respect to enculturation of feeding, excretory, aggression, dependency, and sexual behavior. They also constructed a set of ratings, noting the presence or absence of particular adult patterns of behavior in each of the samples studied. The modern statistical procedure known as the *correlational method* was then used by Whiting and Child to determine if there were any links of interdependence between specific patterns in infancy and later patterns of adult behavior. Finally on the basis of these statistical procedures, Whiting and Child formed some general conclusions concerning the ways some specific patterns in human child care appeared causally related to later adult patterns of behavior.[23]

Whiting and Child's holocultural method and correlational procedures have been used by many others for more than 25 years to try to show relations of interdependence between specific patterns in infant and child care and adult patterns of behavior and personality in some 20 areas of culture and society, ranging from art styles, games, and sex taboos to mother-infant sleeping arrangements.[24] Table 6–4 lists 65 conclusions (Williams, 1978) reached through use of the holocultural method in the study of socialization. Many of these research conclusions are restated and expressed in a different form in Levinson (1977b) and discussed in Naroll et al. (1976).

[22]It should be noted that the *reasoned inference* drawn through use of the contextual method of socialization research concerning the relationship of socialization and urban, industrial life, first published in the 1972 edition of this text, was included in their study by Naroll et al. (1976) and Levinson (1977b) as a "hypothesis" and noted as not being supported as a holocultural proposition, despite the fact that the inference was reached by the contextual method.

[23]For the conclusions reached by Whiting and Child, see their 1953 text.

[24]Socialization practices have been tested for their interdependence with various cultural and social features, including (1) adult achievement motivation, (2) adolescent peer group influence, (3) artistic activity, (4) criminal behavior, (5) climate, (6) cross-sex identity, (7) dreams, (8) games, (9) infantile stimulation and adult male stature, (10) female initiation rites, (11) male initiation rites, (12) menarcheal age and infant stress, (13) mother-child households, (14) narcissism, (15) Oedipus complex, (16) pregnancy, (17) premarital sex relations, (18)

TABLE 6–4 Some Conclusions Reached Through Use of the Holocultural Method in Study of Socialization

1. Harsh parental treatment during infancy leads to cultural beliefs that the spirit world is harsh and aggressive (Spiro & D'Andrade, 1958; Lambert, Triandis, & Wolf, 1959; Whiting, 1959a).
2. Societies in which mothers have few economic responsibilities and are little involved in the ceremonial life of the community tend to be more indulgent with their infants than in societies where mothers have such responsibilities (Murdock & Whiting, 1951; Whiting, 1961; Minturn & Lambert, 1964).
3. The degree of infant indulgence in a society is proportional to the number of adults living in a household (Whiting, 1961).
4. Exclusive mother-infant sleeping arrangements produce a strong identification of a child with the mother (Whiting, Kluckhohn, & Anthony, 1958).
5. Stressful infantile stimulation of males produces more rapid growth and greater adult skeletal length (Landauer & Whiting, 1964; Gunders & Whiting, 1968; Whiting & Landauer, 1968).
6. Stress during infancy leads to a wide range of adult song styles and polyphonia; lack of stress in infancy leads to adult monotonic singing (Ayres, 1968).
7. Adequate physical growth and psychological development during the earliest months of infancy profoundly influence all subsequent growth and psychological development (Harrington & Whiting, 1972).
8. Societies with early weaning, early independence training, and early training in modesty tend to explain illness as the responsibility of the patient (Whiting & Child, 1953).
9. Early socialization of infants and children produces a stronger identification with parents and a greater degree of guilt over contravening parental values (Whiting & Child, 1953; Whiting, 1960).
10. Household structure is a significant determinant of the age of socialization; nuclear households are earliest for weaning and independence training, while mother-child households are the latest in weaning and independence training of infants; extended and polygynous households fall between the extremes of nuclear and mother-child households in age of socialization (Whiting, 1959a).
11. The age of weaning in monogamous societies is related to a feeling of patient responsibility for illness (Whiting, 1959a).
12. Societies which engage in severe childhood socialization practices tend to produce more complex forms of decorative art (Barry, 1957).
13. Societies which engage in severe childhood socialization practices have more complex game forms (Sutton-Smith & Roberts, 1970). *severe self disciplining*
14. Societies which engage in severe childhood socialization practices tend to have ascetic *& life* mourning customs (Friendly, 1956).
15. As new types of games are added to a culture, there is an increased severity in childhood socialization practices (Sutton-Smith & Roberts, 1970).
16. The degree of pressure exerted upon a child by adults during the status change from infancy to childhood ("transition anxiety") is directly related to household structure; societies with nuclear family households are significantly more severe in the degree of pressure exerted than are societies with extended family households (Whiting et al., 1966b).
    → in independent household - band like soc

sexual division of labor, (19) sexual differences in behavior, and (20) subsistence economy. For some statements of some specific conclusions from these areas of study, see Table 6–4. For citations to these studies in the period from 1953–1976, see Whiting (1961), Barry, Bacon, & Child (1967), LeVine (1970), Harrington & Whiting (1972), O'Leary (1969, 1971, 1973), Textor (1967), Naroll (1973), Naroll et al. (1976), Levinson (1977b), and Barry & Schlegel (1980). See also Draper (1974), Tindall (1976), Williams (1978). Table 6–4 includes specific citations following each conclusion. The sources cited in Table 6-4 may be found in the various references listed above.

TABLE 6-4 *(continued)*

17. Children develop an anxious preoccupation with the type of behavior system severely punished by adults ("negative fixation") (Whiting & Child, 1953).

18. Severity of weaning ("oral anxiety") is strongly related to adult "oral explanations" for illness (e.g., sickness is caused by ingestion of magically poisoned food or by spells cast verbally) (Whiting & Child, 1953).

19. Severity of weaning ("oral anxiety") is associated with the importance in a society of beliefs in romantic love as a basis for marriage (Rosenblatt, 1966).

20. The severity of aggression training is directly related to explanations in a society for adult illness involving aggression, including hostility or disobedience to spirits, poison injected into a patient, and use of magical weapons by a *shaman* (Whiting & Child, 1953).

21. The severity of independence training is directly related to dependence explanations for adult illness or to a belief that illness is caused by "soul stealing" or "spirit possession" (Whiting & Child, 1953).

22. Societies with severe toilet training practices tend to have therapeutic practices involving washing or cleansing, the adherence to cleanliness taboos, or the retention of feces (Whiting & Child, 1953).

23. Societies with severe sexual training practices tend to have adult beliefs that abstention from sexual intercourse by a patient would have a benefical therapeutic affect (Whiting & Child, 1953).

24. Societies with severe sexual training practices have elaborate menstrual taboos (Stephens, 1962).

25. Societies with severe sexual training practices have prolonged taboos on sexual intercourse during pregnancy (Ayres, 1954).

26. Societies with severe childhood socialization practices produce adults with diminished "ego strength" or an inability to be assertive in life situations (Allen, 1967).

27. Societies with sororal polygyny are significantly less severe in weaning practices than are societies with nonsororal polygyny (Murdock & Whiting, 1951).

28. Societies with severe sexual training practices are characterized by polygyny (Murdock & Whiting, 1951).

29. Societies with severe aggression training practices are characterized by extended family households (Whiting, 1959b).

30. Children will be severely punished for aggressive behavior in societies where many people must share cramped living quarters (Minturn & Lambert, 1964).

31. In societies where sorcery is an important explanation for adult illness, infants and children will be severely socialized with respect to both aggression and sexual behavior (Whiting & Child, 1953).

32. Love magic is present in societies which are most severe in their sexual socialization practices (Shirley & Romney, 1962).

33. Societies with severe socialization of aggression during childhood are likely to use folk tales in which the "hero" directs aggression toward enemies or strangers and not toward friends (Wright, 1954; Whiting & Child, 1953).

34. Societies with severe socialization of aggression are very likely to have beliefs that spirits cause illness and that illness-causing spirits are more likely to be animal than human (Whiting & Child, 1953).

35. Small societies with no formal system of social control will possess polygynous households and severe sexual socialization practices or extended family households and severe aggression socialization practices (B. Whiting, 1950; LeVine, 1960).

36. Girls are socialized to be nurturant, obedient, and responsible, and boys are socialized to achieve and be self-reliant in societies where large animals are hunted, or where grain rather than root crops are grown, or where large or milking animals are kept, or where fishing is not important, or where the settlement pattern is nomadic rather than sedentary and where polygyny is high (Barry, Bacon, & Child, 1957).

TABLE 6-4 *(continued)*

37. Societies which emphasize sexual distinctions in patterns of residence, in kin groups, in kinship terminology, in authority succession, in eating arrangements, and in required attendance at childbirth usually do not have institutionalized transvestism (Munroe, J. Whiting, & Hally, 1969).
38. Societies which exert strong pressures on boys for self-reliance and independence conceive supernatural beings as aggressive (Lambert, Triandis, & Wolf, 1959).
39. Societies that severely punish older children for disobedience, irresponsibility, lack of self-reliance, and lack of achievement have a high frequency of theft (Bacon, Child, & Barry, 1963).
40. Societies with low infant indulgence and severe weaning practices will have a high frequency of theft (Bacon, Child, & Barry, 1963).
41. Societies with low indulgence of children and high achievement demands will have a high consuuumption of alcohol by adults (Barry, 1965).
42. Games of chance occur in societies where responsibility is highly rewarded in child training (Roberts & Sutton-Smith, 1962, 1966).
43. Games of strategy occur in societies where emphasis is placed on obedience in child training (Roberts & Sutton-Smith, 1962, 1966).
44. Games of skill occur in societies in which reward for achievement in childhood is frequent (Roberts & Sutton-Smith, 1962, 1966).
45. Societies with a high accumulation of food place strong pressures on infants and children to be responsible and obedient and deemphasize achievement in both boys and girls, independence in boys, and self-reliance in girls (Barry, Child, & Bacon, 1959).
46. A close relationship between a mother and an infant son as a consequence of (1) their sleeping together with the father excluded for at least a year, or (2) the mother being prohibited from having sexual intercourse for at least a year after an infant's birth, or (3) both of these events occurring together will result in measurable consequences which are manifested in cultural adjustments at the time of a boy's adolescence. These adjustments will involve either an initiation ceremony involving at least one, and possibly several, of the factors of (1) tests of endurance, (2) painful hazing by adult males of the society, (3) seclusion from women, and (4) genital operations, or a boy may be required to change his residence in order to separate him from his mother and sisters, and this may also involve receiving instructions from members of a "men's house" or a mother's brother. If both the factors specified in mother-infant sleeping arrangements are present in the socialization practices of a culture, the consequences for a boy at adolescence are more severe and the initiation rites much more elaborate (Whiting, Kluckhohn, & Anthony, 1958).
47. Absence of a father during a boy's infancy will lead to primary cross-sex (feminine) sexual identity in boys (Burton and Whiting, 1961).
48. Societies with male initiation rites at adolescence intend them to overcome primary cross-sex (feminine) identity and to substitute a primary male identity and behavior forms (Burton & Whiting, 1961).
49. The aim of the socialization process in all human societies is to produce adults whose "attributed statuses" (those assigned to *Ego* by others), "subjective statuses" (those *Ego* thinks he fills in a society), and, "optative statuses (those which *Ego* wishes to occupy in a society) are fully congruent (Burton & Whiting, 1961).
50. Both male solidarity and male initiation rites at adolescence are a consequence of conflict in sexual identity engendered in infancy (Young, 1962; Whiting, 1962).
51. Circumcision rites occur in societies which clearly differentiate boys from girls throughout infancy and childhood (Harrington, 1968).
52. Aggression among males as "protest masculinity" is found more often in societies where fathers have a low salience (presence) during infancy but high status later in a child's life (B. Whiting, 1965).

TABLE 6-4 *(continued)*

53. Polygynous societies, in which fathers often sleep and eat apart from an infant, are more likely to value glory in war (Whiting, 1969).

54. Exclusive mother-son sleeping arrangements in infancy are associated with concepts of glory in war (Whiting, 1969).

55. The probability of a boy becoming delinquent will be the highest where the separation of a mother and father occur during early infancy of a boy and the mother later remarries (Whiting, Kluckhohn, & Anthony, 1958).

56. Cross-sex identity may be openly expressed in societies if both the primary and secondary identifications of a boy are feminine and often will be demonstrated in the practice of the *couvade* (Munroe, Munroe, & Whiting, 1965).*

57. The *couvade* is a significant index of the wish by a male to act out the feminine role in a society (Burton & Whiting, 1961).

58. Societies which regularly practice the separation of fathers from infant males, particularly during very early infancy, will have adult males characterized by some feminine patterns of behavior and individual expressions of cognitive cross-sex identity (D'Andrade, 1962; Carlsmith, 1963; Sutton-Smith & Rosenberg, 1968; Harrington, 1979).

59. Female initiation rites occur most often in societies where a girl, as an adult, will not be forced to leave her parent's household (Brown, 1963).

60. Female initiation rites that focus on subjecting a girl to enduring painful activities are found in societies where infant and childhood sexual identity are in conflict (Brown, 1963).

61. Female initiation rites are found in those societies in which women are important in subsistence activities (Brown, 1963).

62. Societies with chronic scarcity of food tend to produce individuals characterized by a high degree of personal independence and self-reliance (Barry, 1967).

63. Circumcision rites in adolescence are associated with a hot, rainy, tropical climate (e.g., a hot, rainy, tropical climate is associated with protein deficiency in infancy and the presence of kwashiorkor; low protein availability and the risk of kwashiorkor are correlated with an extended postpartum sex taboo to allow a mother time to nurse an infant through a critical stage when kwashiorkor might develop and before becoming pregnant again. The postpartum sex taboo is significantly correlated with the social institution of polygyny, providing alternative sexual partners for males. In turn polygyny is associated with mother-child households, child training by women, and resultant cross-sex identity. In societies where patrilocality is also practiced, there will be male initiation rites to resolve male sex identity problems) (Whiting, 1964; Whiting et al., 1966).

64. Children raised in cultures whose visual environments consist of flat horizons and round houses are less susceptible to optical illusions that depend on assumptions of right angles for their effects but are much more susceptible to optical illusions that relate to the perception of the length of a vertical line relative to a horizontal line (Segall, Campbell, & Herskovits, 1966).

65. Designs made or drawn by men and women depend on the differences in usual role requirements for men and woman in a society and will be reflected in the usual child-training practices for boys and girls in a society (Harrington & Whiting, 1972).

---

*The term *couvade* is used by cultural anthropologists to describe the form of behavior when a husband undergoes a ritual confinement and engages in ritual acts for a period of longer than one day which symbolically indicates that he is associated with the birth of an infant to his wife. This practice is found among a limited number of cultures (e.g. *Siriono, Shoshone,* in four widely separated geographic regions.

Textor (1967) has used a computer in an effort to statistically demonstrate some relationships between specific practices of socialization and various patterns of culture. Using data from a sample of 400 cultures and the holocultural method, Textor abstracted a large number of *dichotomous,* or contrasting, features of culture (for example, cultures in which wife lending or wife exchange is present; cultures in which wife lending or wife exchange is unimportant or absent), which were then put through a computer in a series of four "runs" to contrast each dichotomous feature against all other such features. This technique produced almost 20,000 different correlations, which were then printed out by the computer in the form of 480 tables showing statistical measures of the *strength* ("phi coefficient"), *significance* ("chi square" and "Fisher Exact Test"), and the *probability* ("P value") of the correlations between particular dichotomous features.

Approximately 116 of the 480 tables in Textor's study seem concerned specifically with relationships of interdependence between features of socialization and other aspects of culture. Each one of the 116 tables indicates the specific number of cultures in the sample of 400 for which Textor found ethnographic data concerning particular features of socialization either unclear or unreported. In the 116 tables the number of societies for which socialization data are unclear or unreported average approximately 336 (or 84 percent) of the 400-culture sample.

Textor notes that he believes that this research procedure employs a contextual, rather than an "atomistic," approach to seeking relations of functional interdependence between features of culture and adult behavior. Textor's belief that the holocultural method, particularly as used in comparative, statistically based studies, is essentially the same as the contextual method also appears to be shared by Naroll (1973, 316). Naroll notes that, while the most common criticism of the holocultural method once was that it extracted particular cultural traits from the whole cultural context in which they were "embedded," anthropologists have now come to realize that holocultural studies are, by nature, "explicit tests" of cultural contexts. However it appears that many cultural anthropologists do not share the belief that the contextual and holocultural methods are essentially the same procedure of socialization research.[25]

It is important to note that the holocultural method continues to be widely employed in the study of socialization to investigate a variety of problems and concerns and to generate many new conclusions.[26] For ex-

---

[25]Among others, see Köbben (1952, 1967, 1970), Schapera (1953), Barnes (1971), and Spindler (1967).

[26]Williams (1978) has noted that there is almost no sustained attention to a socialization research conclusion once it is formed by use of either research procedure. See also Vermeulen & deRuijter, 1975; Udy, 1973.

ample, in a holocultural study of the interrelations between the socialization process and kinship and kin group patterns, Munroe and Munroe (1980), using a worldwide sample of 84 societies, tested the hypothesis that the higher the number of families occupying a single dwelling, the higher the degree of permissive behavior by mothers living in that dwelling in dealing with the enculturation of their infants and children. Munroe and Munroe concluded that their hypothesis was statistically validated in their use of the holocultural method and speculated that multifamily living serves to reduce "socialization pressure" (or nonpermissive child-rearing) in a variety of ways.[27]

Barry and his associates, employing the holocultural method, statistical techniques, and a worldwide sample of 186 cultures, have presented a set of socialization codes for infancy (Barry & Paxson, 1971) and childhood (Barry, Josephson, Lauer, & Marshall, 1976, 1977) which are said to indicate the degree to which various cultural transmission traits, such as "toughness" (or fortitude, aggression, competitiveness) or "maturity" (or, self-reliance, achievement), are inculcated during these life periods. The quantitative measures used in this research are said by Barry et al. to provide new information about the most important attributes of socialization. As an example, Barry et al. (1977, 219) conclude from their holocultural research that "regardless of the sex and age of the child, the caretaker tends to be female and the parental residence tends to be slightly female. Authority and disciplinarian are predominantly male; this tendency is stronger for authority and for non-parent than for parent." This holocultural socialization study also indicates that the most frequent technique for exhorting the child is by example, that corporal punishment is the most frequently used method of discipline, and that the use of ceremonies as a rewarding technique increases in late childhood and is more frequent for boys than girls. In all, Barry and his associates have stated more than 20 additional holoculturally derived conclusions (see Table 6–4) concerning the socialization process.[28] Barry and his associates (Schlegel & Barry, 1979) have also used the holocultural method and a worldwide sample of 186 cultures to derive another half-dozen conclusions concerning socialization

[27]These ways include dilution of specific parent child interactions and demands on children by the presence of other adults, curbing a child's parent-directed emotional outbursts through the presence of other adults and allowing a parent a choice between other adults or a child for social interactions. See also Munroe & Munroe, 1971. See also number 30, Table 6–4.

[28]This work follows earlier holocultural study by Whiting and Child (1953) and Barry et al. (1967) reporting various "codes" on socialization practices, the holocultural work by Barry et al. (1959) reporting that the traits necessary for adult subsistence activities are inculcated in childhood, and by Barry & Paxson (1971) noting that various aspects of personality are shaped by socialization experiences in infancy.

and initiation rituals. In addition, Cone (1979, 291) has used the same holocultural procedure to determine the validity of the hypothesis that "the differences in adult personality commonly described for pastoralists as compared to agriculturalists are a result of differences in the context of adult life rather than child-rearing practices." Cone (1979, 294) concludes that her holocultural analysis suggests that the substantial differences reported in the ethnographic literature between the personalities of pastoralists and agriculturalists do not appear to be the result of distinctly different socialization practices but are more likely to be a response to the circumstances of adult life.[29]

Problems of Statistical Analysis

The holocultural method and statistical techniques for analyzing data continues to be a widely used approach in socialization study. It should be noted, however, that basic theoretical questions remain regarding use of the holocultural method and modern statistical techniques to deal with data of the socialization process.

For example, any type of statistical treatment of cultural data inevitably violates the assumed integrity of an integrated cultural whole through the practice of abstracting specific aspects of culture and then treating them as being capable of being analyzed alone, without reference to any other aspects of culture. Statistical analysis of cultural data usually gives little attention to the different levels of conceptual abstraction involved and often treats data of culture traits as comparable to data of cultural patterns and configurations. Statistical analysis of cultural data also usually tends to hold constant the important theoretical variables of common or dissimilar cultural forms, or meanings. Statistical treatment of cultural data also involves the error of holding cultural phenomena to be strictly equivalent and capable of manipulation as if they truly represented dynamically equivalent natural entities.[30]

The nineteenth-century physical science theories from which modern statistical procedures have been derived are based on the assumption that nature is dynamically equivalent in all of its parts—that is, each part or

[29]The general ethnographic literature on pastoralists that indicates that they are independent, aggressive, proud, and directly express emotions has been supported by the East African research of Edgerton (1971) and Goldschmidt (1971) and the Andean work of Bolton, (1976). In contrast, the work of Barry et al. (1959) and Whiting and Whiting (1971) indicates pastoralists have personalities quite different from the image found in the ethnographic studies by Edgerton, Goldschmidt, Bolton, and their associates.

[30]For further discussion of these points, see Kluckhohn, 1954, 958–960; Bateson, 1947, 651; and Williams, 1959.

aspect of any natural phenomenon corresponds conceptually to all other parts or aspects of the same phenomenon wherever it is found, such as the study of carbon atoms in physical chemistry. Under the doctrine of the dynamic uniformity or equivalence of nature, a chemist would assume that all carbon atoms are exactly the same, whether in the laboratory or the far reaches of the universe. This nineteenth-century assumption is reflected clearly in the *laws of thermodynamics.*

Statistical studies of cultural phenomena began in the mid-nineteenth century by treating all aspects of human behavior as dynamically equivalent. However by the second decade of this century, it had become apparent that this assumption was not applicable to study of culture. The development of a major part of cultural theory since early in the present century has been markedly away from the conception of dynamic equivalence. The efforts to use statistical procedures in analysis of interrelationships in the socialization process or other cultural phenomena tend to ignore these aspects of cultural theory.

This does not mean that all statistical treatment of cultural data is in basic error or should be avoided. Indeed there are very many problems in the study of culture that involve measurable incidence and intensity— that is, where counting, weighing, and scaling are useful and very important techniques. For instance, Fortes has clearly demonstrated how certain aspects of the Ashanti pattern of kinship (for example, marital residence patterns) become evident only through use of a statistical description. The study of the data of archaeology or cultural data from a time long past often fruitfully employs statistical methods. Physical anthropological studies also employ modern statistical procedures to great advantage. However Fortes, in common with Kluckhohn and others, notes that a singular dependence upon purely statistical procedures, with their inherent lack of accounting for contextual nature of cultural phenomena, are not likely to contribute to the main, unresolved problems in the study of culture.[31]

The dependence on statistical techniques in research seeking to demonstrate relations of interdependence between the socialization process and various patterns of culture, such as kinship and kin groups, has led to a situation in which the total context, internal dynamics, qualities, and regular articulation of cultural parts are being bypassed for the sake of an apparent, but theoretically misleading, ease in formulating, "testing," and "confirming" holocultural hypotheses of interdependence in socialization. Recently some limited uses have been made of matrix algebra and topological mathematics, the mathematics of nonlinear partial differential and integro-differential equations, and of Markov process analysis in new efforts to develop a mathematics that can account for the known nature of cultural

---

[31]See Fortes, 1949, 59; Kluckhohn, 1954, 959.

data and accommodate a general theory of culture widely used in modern anthropology.

Uses of these mathematical techniques so far have been largely unsuccessful, however, for the same reasons that statistical analysis has failed or has been largely unsuccessful in efforts to demonstrate relations of interdependence between the socialization process and various patterns of culture. Until a mathematics is developed and available for study of cultural phenomena that accounts fully for contextual integrity, dynamic interrelatedness, and so on, it may be preferable in socialization research to use a contextual abstraction process to produce general descriptive statements, rather than giving an appearance of scientific certainty and accuracy through use of statistical devices such as "P values," "phi coefficients," "chi square," the "Mann Whitney U test," and "Fisher Exact Tests."[32] Norbert Wiener (1950, 26), a widely respected mathematician, has pointed out that scientists do not have the right to give the impression of a mathematical analysis of complex and difficult-to-understand situations and events unless they use a language they can fully understand and correctly apply. Short of this, Wiener noted, a purely descriptive account of the gross, or whole, appearance of a phenomenon is more scientific.

Political Socialization

Before 1960 political scientists and legal specialists gave little formal attention to the question of the *political indoctrination* or the *political socialization* of children (Jaros, 1973, 8). However since the mid-1960s there has been a rapid development of new courses, books, articles, and doctoral dissertations concerned with how children learn to behave politically.[33] Fromm (1941) explored this question using a psychoanalytic learning model and concluded that the way parental power is exercised plays a dominant role in shaping a child's later, adult patterns of political action. Using a similar learning model Erikson (1950) interpreted the ways power was structured within the American family as the basis for training in personal compromise that is related to the pattern of politics in the United States. The views of political learning expressed by Fromm and Erikson, somewhat modified, are also expressed in the work by Adorno (1950) on the devel-

[32]See, for instance, Cone (1979, 291) who notes, "Given the standard image of pastoralists, it is not surprising to find these societies ranked low on the dimension of compliance vs. assertion (p < .03 "Mann Whitney U Test").

[33]See, for instance, Langton, 1969; Jaros, 1973; Dennis, 1973; Wilson, 1974a, 1974; Beck, 1974; Bennett, 1975; Easton & Hess, 1975; Guzman, 1976; Hirsch, 1971; Niemi, 1974; Renshon, 1977; Schwartz & Schwartz, 1975; Stacey, 1978. See also Arnstein, 1971; Yinger, 1971; Christiansen, 1972; J.B. Williams, 1972; Cohen, 1973; Badar, 1974; Schulman, 1975; Brewer, 1976; Jones, 1976; Woefel, 1976; Bookman, 1977; McAuliffe, 1977; Trotter, 1980; Tapp, 1971.

opment and expression of the authoritarian personality. It still is not clear, however, how the pattern of politics in a culture is transmitted by adults to infants and children. As Jaros (1973, 137) and others have noted, the processes of political socialization are presently viewed by political scientists and lawyers as "extremely complex." Recent study of political socialization has rejected the earlier assumption that children are educated to politics in any simple and direct way. While research in this field concerning "transnational," or comparative, study of political socialization (cf. Wilson, 1974) has concluded that the socialization process affects, as Jaros (1973, 137) notes, the basic features of whole political systems, there still is uncertainty about why this is so and how it occurs.

CONCLUSIONS

It is clear that there are significant links, or interrelationships, between the socialization process and the cultural patterns of kinship and kin groups. Yet until recently the nature of these links has remained uncertain. Now, however, ethnographic reports based on modern conceptions of field research are providing specific insights into the ways the patterns of kinship and kin groups are related to socialization. For example, Gonzales (1979) has published an account of the ways that drawings by Garifuna (Black Carib) children are quite consistent with the details of the patterns of kinship and kin groups in Garifuna society, while Walter (1979) gives an intriguing description of the ways the kin relations between mother's brother and sister's son in East Fiji provide a means for Fijian children to learn that personal control in the domestic, or family, group provides legal access to the resources which sustain the group. Goody (1973) has described the ways kinship and kin group patterns are complexly woven through the enculturation process among the Gonja of northern Ghana, while Sorenson (1971) provides an account of the ways learning of kinship and kin group patterns are involved in cultural change among the Fore of the highlands of New Guinea. Boram (1980) describes the ways infants and children among the Oksapmin, an isolated horticultural society living in the Victor Emmanuel Range of Central New Guinea, learn to employ kinship and kin group patterns of behavior in a wide range of Oksapmin daily affairs, ranging from gardening to religious ritual.

When details contained in ethnographic accounts of the relationships between patterns of kinship and kin groups and enculturation are added to conclusions derived from holocultural and statistically based studies, there is a point to be made that clearly transcends any questions concerning research methodology. The point, which has also emerged sharply from the case study data on Arunta and Ashanti enculturation, kinship, and kin groups, is that a full understanding of the socialization process requires specific knowledge of the ways that infants and children in regular communicative contact with adults in a culture learn the conceptions, which are often exceedingly complex, of kinship and kin groups that will become effective guides to all of their social relations with other persons throughout their adult lives.

This conclusion is supported by Murdock (1971), who believes, based on his holocultural study of data from nearly 1200 societies concerning patterns of kin behavior between relatives of the opposite sex, that the remarkable uniformity of such behavior in different world regions and among cultures with quite diverse economies and languages can only be explained through use of "basic psychological principles of learning and personality development" and the structural organization of the "nuclear family" which are ". . . the same for all mankind."[34] In other words, Murdock, widely acknowledged as the scholar most responsible for development of the holocultural research method, concludes that a cultural feature of kin behavior which has puzzled anthropologists since Tylor's (1889) era has a better theoretical explanation in the facts of the universal human nuclear family and fundamental principles of human learning. This general conclusion can be used to set the stage for future research concerning the relationships between patterns of kinship and kin groups and the socialization process.

SUMMARY

This chapter has been concerned with a discussion of some of the possible interrelationships between socialization and the patterns of kinship and kin groups. The chapter began with a brief summary of some ways of thinking about culture and the topics of kinship and kin groups. Then case study data from ethnographic accounts of Arunta and Ashanti societies were presented to illustrate some of the differences and similarities in the ideas and ways of behaving that children may learn concerning the patterns of kinship and kin groups. The chapter concluded with a comment on two principal methods of research used in socialization study and present challenges in the study of the relationships between patterns of kinship, kin groups, and the socialization process.

---

[34]Murdock's conclusion (1971, 440) rejects the two dominant theoretical explanations used in contemporary anthropology—that is, the "historical" and the "functional/structural" explanations. A historical explanation for the remarkable similarity of these holoculturally derived data would refer the similarities to geographic centers of innovation and areas of diffusion. A functional-structural theoretical explanation would note that the similarity of data is the consequence of independent, parallel adjustments of behavior to fit similar structural features, such as types of kin groups, rules of descent, or postmarital residence.

REFERENCES CITED AND SUGGESTED READINGS

ADORNO, T.W. 1950. *The Authoritarian Personality.* New York: Harper & Row, Pub.

ARIÈS, P. 1962. *Centuries of Childhood: A Social History of Family Life.* New York: Knopf.

ARNSTEIN, F.T. 1971. *Political Mobilization and Political Socialization at the University of Michigan.* Unpublished Ph.D. dissertation. University of Michigan, Ann Arbor, Michigan.

AYRES, B. 1973. "Effects of Infant Carrying Practices on Rhythm in Music." *Ethos,* 1, 387–404.

BACON, M., H. BARRY, III, & I. CHILD. 1965. "A Cross Cultural Study of Drinking: II. Relations to Other Features of Culture." *Quarterly Journal of Studies on Alcohol,* Supplement 3, 29–48.

BACON, M., I. CHILD, & H. BARRY, III. 1963. "A Cross Cultural Study of Correlates of Crime." *Journal of Abnormal and Social Psychology,* 66, 291–300.

BADAR, G.A. 1974. *Ideology and Political Socialization of Egyptian Youth.* Unpublished doctoral dissertation, George Washington University, Washington, D.C.

BARNES, J. 1971. *Three Styles in the Study of Kinship.* Berkeley: University of California Press.

BARRY, H., III. 1957. "Relationships Between Child Training and the Pictorial Arts." *Journal of Abnormal and Social Psychology,* 54, 380–383.

BARRY, H., III, M.K. BACON, & I.L. CHILD. 1967. "Definitions, Ratings and Bibliographic Sources for Child Training Practices of 110 Cultures." In C.S. Ford (ed.), *Cross-Cultural Approaches.* New Haven, Conn.: HRAF Press, pp. 293–331.

BARRY, H., III, I.L. CHILD, & M.R. BACON. 1959. "Relation of Child Training to Subsistence Economy." *American Anthropologist,* 61, 51–63.

BARRY, H., III, L. JOSEPHSON, E. LAUER, & C. MARSHALL. 1976. "Traits Inculcated in Childhood: Cross-Cultural Codes 5." *Ethnology,* 15, 83–114.

———. 1977. "Agents and Techniques for Child Training: Cross-Cultural Codes 6." *Ethnology,* 16, 191–230.

BARRY, H., III, & L.M. PAXSON. 1971. "Infancy and Early Childhood: Cross-Cultural Codes." *Ethnology,* 10, 466–508.

BARRY, H., III, & J.M. ROBERTS. 1972. "Infant Socialization and Games of Chance." *Ethnology,* 11, 296–308.

BARRY, H., III, & A. SCHLEGEL (eds.). 1980. *Cross-Cultural Samples and Codes.* Pittsburgh, Pa.: University of Pittsburgh Press.

BASEDOW, H. 1925. *The Australian Aboriginal.* Adelaide: Preece.

BATES, E. 1976. *Language and Context: The Acquisition of Pragmatics.* New York: Academic Press.

BATESON, G. 1947. "Sex and Culture." *Annals of the New York Academy of Science,* 47, 647–660.

———. 1972. *Steps to an Ecology of Mind.* New York: Ballantine.

BECK, P.A. 1975. *Setups: Political Socialization across the Generations.* Washington, D.C.: American Political Science Association.

BENNETT, W.L. 1975. *The Political Mind and the Political Environment.* Lexington, Mass.: Lexington Books.

BERNDT, R., & C. BERNDT. 1964. *The World of the First Australians.* Chicago: University of Chicago Press.

BERNSTEIN, B. 1968. *Language, Primary Socialization and Education.* London: Routledge.

BLOUNT, B.G. 1972. "Aspects of Luo Socialization." *Language in Society,* 1, 235–248.

BOCK, P. 1969. *Modern Cultural Anthropology.* New York: Knopf.

BOLTON, C. 1976. "Pastoralism and Personality: An Andean Replication." *Ethos,* 4, 463–482.

BOLTON, R. 1978. "Child-Holding Patterns." *Current Anthropology,* 19, 134–135.

BOOKMAN, A.E. 1977. *The Process of Political Socialization among Women and Immigrant Workers.* Unpublished doctoral dissertation, Harvard University, Cambridge, Mass.

BORAM, C. 1980. *Oksapmin Children.* New Haven, Conn.: HRAFlex Books.

BREWER, R.M. 1976. *Black Adolescent Politicization: A Study in Political Socialization.* Unpublished doctoral dissertation, Indiana University, Bloomington, Ind.

BRIM, J.A., & D.H. SPAIN. 1974. *Research Design in Anthropology: Paradigms and Pragmatics in the Testing of Hypotheses.* New York: Holt, Rinehart & Winston.

BRONFENBRENNER, U. 1970. *Two Worlds of Childhood: U.S. and U.S.S.R.* New York: Basic Books.

BROWN, J. 1963. "A Cross-Cultural Study of Female Initiation Rites." *American Anthropologist,* 65, 837–853.

BUSIA, K. 1951. *The Position of the Chief in the Modern Political System of Ashanti.* London: Oxford University Press.

———. 1955. "The Ashanti." In C.D. Forde (ed.), *African Worlds.* London: Oxford University Press, pp. 190–209.

CAUDILL, W. 1973. "The Influence of Social Structure and Culture on Human Behavior in Modern Japan." *Ethos,* 1(3), 343–382.

CAUDILL, W.A., & C. SCHOOLER. 1973,. "Child Behavior and Child Rearing in Japan and the United States: An Interim Report." *Journal of Nervous and Mental Disease,* 157, 323–338.

CHAMBERLAIN, A.F.C. 1896. *The Child and Childhood in Folk-Thought.* New York: Macmillan.

———. 1901. *The Child: A Study in the Evolution of Man.* London: Scribner.

CHRISTIANSEN, N.E. 1972. *Family Socialization as Related to Adoption of Culturally Radical Values by Youth.* Unpublished doctoral dissertation, University of Minnesota, Minneapolis.

COHEN, R.S. 1973. *Analysis of Familial Effects on the Political Socialization of Black and White Youth.* Unpublished doctoral dissertation, University of Illinois, Urbana-Champaign.

COHEN, Y. 1961. *Social Structure and Personality: A Casebook.* New York: Holt, Rinehart & Winston.

———. 1964. *The Transition from Childhood to Adolescence.* Chicago: Aldine.

———. 1968. "Macroethnology: Large Scale Comparative Studies." In J.A. Clifton (ed.), *Introduction to Cultural Anthropology: Essays in the Scope and Methods of the Science of Man.* Boston: Houghton-Mifflin, pp. 402–448.

CONE, C.A. 1979. "Personality and Persistence: Is the Child the Parent of the Person?" *Ethnology,* 18, 291–301.

DAVIDSON, D. 1926. "The Basis of Social Organization in Australia." *American Anthropologist,* 28, 529–548.

DENNIS, J. 1973a. *Socialization to Politics: A Reader.* New York: John Wiley.

DENNIS, J. 1973b. *Political Socialization Research: A Bibliography.* Beverly Hills, Calif.: Sage Publications.

DEVOS, G. 1968. "Achievement and Innovation in Culture and Personality." In E. Norbeck, D. Price-Williams, & W.M. McCord (eds.), *The Study of Personality: An Interdisciplinary Appraisal.* New York: Holt, Rinehart & Winston, pp. 348–370.

———. 1973. *Socialization for Achievement: Essays on the Cultural Psychology of the Japanese.* Berkeley: University of California Press.

DRAPER, P. 1974. "Comparative Studies of Socialization." In B. Siegel, A. Beals,

& S. Tyler (eds.), *Annual Review of Anthropology,* 3, 263–277. Palo Alto, Calif.: Annual Reviews, Inc.

DRIVER, H., & R. CHANEY. 1968. "A Sixth Solution to the Galton Problem." *American Anthropological Association Bulletin,* 1, 35–36.

DUBOIS, C. 1944. *The People of Alor.* Minneapolis: University of Minnesota Press.

EASTON, D., & R. HESS. 1975. *Eight City Study of Child Political Socialization, 1961–1962.* Ann Arbor, Mich.: Inter-University Consortium for Political and Social Research.

EDGERTON, R. 1971. *The Individual in Cultural Adaptation: A Study of Four East African Tribes.* Berkeley: University of California Press.

ELKIN, A. 1933. "Studies in Australian Totemism." *Monographs,* No. Two (*Oceania* 3, Nos. Three and Four; 4, Nos. One and Two).

———. 1954. *The Australian Aborigines: How to Understand Them* (2nd ed.). Sydney: Angus and Robertson.

ELKIN, A.R., & C. BERNDT. 1950. *Art in Arnhem Land.* Chicago: University of Chicago Press.

ERIKSON, E.H. 1950. *Childhood and Society.* New York: W.W. Norton & Co., Inc.

FARBER, B. 1975. "Bilateral Kinship: Centripedal and Centrifugal Types of Organization." *Journal of Marriage and Family,* 37, 871–888.

FERGUSON, C., & C. SNOW. 1977. *Talking to Children: Language Input and Acquisition.* London: Cambridge University Press.

FORD, C. 1945. "On Comparative Study of Human Reproduction." *Yale University Publications in Anthropology,* 32, 1–111.

———. 1967. *Cross-Cultural Approaches.* New Haven, Conn.: HRAF Press.

———. 1970. "Human Relations Area Files: 1949–1969; A Twenty-Year Report." *Behavior Science Notes,* 5, 1–61.

FORTES, M. 1938. *Social and Psychological Aspects of Education in Taleland.* London: International African Institute.

———. 1949. "Time and Social Structure: An Ashanti Case Study." In M. Fortes (ed.), *Social Structure.* London: Oxford University Press, pp. 54–84.

———. 1950. "Kinship and Marriage Among the Ashanti." In A.R. Radcliffe-Brown & D. Forde (eds.), *African Systems of Kinship and Marriage.* London: Oxford University Press, pp. 252–284.

FROMM, E. 1941. *Escape from Freedom.* New York: Farrar & Rinehart.

GALTON F. 1889. Comment on a paper by Edward B. Tylor: "On a Method of Investigating the Development of Institutions; Applied to the Laws of Marriage and Descent." *Journal of the Royal Anthropological Institute,* 18, 245–272.

GOLDSCHMIDT, W. 1971. "Introduction: The Theory of Cultural Adaptation." In R. Edgerton, *The Individual in Cultural Adaptation: A Study of Four East African Tribes.* Berkeley: University of California Press.

GONZALEZ, N.L. 1979. "Sex Preference in Human Figure Drawings by Garifuna (Black Carib) Children." *Ethnology,* 18, 355–364.

GOODMAN, M.E. 1971. *The Culture of Childhood.* New York: Teachers College Press.

GOODY, E. 1973. *Contexts of Kinship: An Essay in Family Sociology of the Gonja of Northern Ghana.* New York: Cambridge University Press.

GUNDERS, S.M., & J. WHITING. 1968. "Mother-Infant Separation and Physical Growth." *Ethnology,* 7, 196–206.

GUZMAN, R.C. 1976. *The Political Socialization of the Mexican American People.* New York: Arno Press.

HARRINGTON, C., & J. WHITING. 1972. "Socialization Process and Personality." In F.L.K. Hsu (ed.), *Psychological Anthropology.* Cambridge, Mass.: Schenkman, pp. 469–507.

HILL, R., & R. KÖNIG. 1970. *Families in East and West: Socialization Process and Kinship Ties*. The Hague: Mouton.

HIRSCH, H. 1971. *Poverty and Politicization: Political Socialization in an American Subculture*. New York: Free Press.

HOEBEL, E. 1954. "The Ashanti: Constitutional Monarchy and the Triumph of Public Law." In E.A. Hoebel (ed.), *The Law of Primitive Man*. Cambridge, Mass.: Harvard University Press, pp. 211–254.

HOLY, L. 1976. "Kin Groups: Structural Analysis and the Study of Behavior." In B. Siegel, A. Beals, & S. Tyler (eds.), *Annual Review of Anthropology*, 5, 107–131. Palo Alto, Calif.: Annual Reviews, Inc.

HOMANS, G. 1950. *The Human Group*. New York: Harcourt Brace Jovanovich.

———. 1961. *Social Behavior: Its Elementary Forms*. New York: Harcourt Brace Jovanovich.

HORTON, D. 1943. "The Functions of Alcohol in Primitive Societies: A Cross-Cultural Study." *Quarterly Journal of Studies on Alcohol*, 4, 199–320.

HSU, F.L.K. 1963. *Caste, Clan and Club*. New York: Van Nostrand.

———. 1965. "The Effect of Dominant Kin Relationships on Kin and Non-Kin Behavior: A Hypothesis." *American Anthropologist*, 67, 638–661.

———. 1971. "Psychological Homeostasis and Jen: New Concepts for Advancing Psychological Anthropology." *American Anthropologist*, 73, 23–44.

HYMAN, H. 1969. *Political Socialization: A Study in the Psychology of Political Behavior*. New York: Free Press.

INKELES, A. 1969. "Social Structure and Socialization." In D.A. Goslin (ed.), *Handbook of Socialization Theory and Research*. Skokie, Ill.: Rand McNally, pp. 615–632.

———. 1975. "Becoming Modern: Individual Change in Six Developing Countries." *Ethos*, 3, 323–342.

JAROS, D. 1973. *Socialization to Politics*. New York: Holt, Rinehart & Winston.

JONES, M.A. 1976. *Black Consciousness and Political Socialization*. Unpublished doctoral dissertation. University of Illinois, Urbana-Champaign.

KELLY, R.C. 1977. *Etoro Social Structure*. Ann Arbor: University of Michigan Press.

KIDD, D. 1906. *Savage Childhood: A Study of Kafir Children*. London: A. and C. Black.

KILBRIDE, P.L., & J.E. KILBRIDE. 1974. "Sociocultural Factors and the Early Manifestation of Sociability Behavior Among Baganda Infants." *Ethos*, 2, 296–314.

KLUCKHOHN, C. 1936. "Some Aspects of Contemporary Theory in Cultural Anthropology." Unpublished doctoral dissertation, Harvard University, Cambridge.

———. 1939. "Theoretical Bases for an Empirical Method of Studying the Acquisition of Culture by Individuals." *Man*, 39, 98–103.

———. 1941. "Patterning as Exemplified in Navaho Culture." In L. Spier, A.I. Hallowell, & S. Newman (eds.), *Language, Culture and Personality: Essays in Memory of Edward Sapir*. Menasha, Wisc.: Sapir Memorial Publication Fund, pp. 109–130.

———. 1947. "Some Aspects of Navaho Infancy and Early Childhood." *Psychoanalysis and the Social Sciences*, 1, 37–86.

———. 1949. *Mirror for Man*. New York: Whittlesey House.

———. 1951. "Values and Value Orientations in the Theory of Action." In T. Parsons & E. Shils (eds.), *Toward a General Theory of Action*. Cambridge, Mass.: Harvard University Press, pp. 388–433.

———. 1954. "Culture and Behavior." In G. Lindzey (ed.), *Handbook of Social Psychology*. Reading, Mass.: Addison-Wesley, pp. 921–976.

KÖBBEN, A. 1952. "New Ways of Presenting an Old Idea: The Statistical Method in Social Anthropology." *Journal of the Royal Anthropological Institute,* 82, 129–146.

———. 1967. "Why Exceptions? The Logic of Cross-Cultural Comparisons." *Current Anthropology,* 8, 3–34.

———. 1970. "Comparativists and Noncomparativists." In R. Naroll & R. Cohen (eds.), *Handbook of Method in Cultural Anthropology.* Garden City, N.Y.: Natural History Press, pp. 581–596.

KONNER, M.J. 1976. "Relations among Infants and Juveniles in Comparative Perspective." *Social Science Information,* 15, 371–402.

KUHN, T. 1966. *The Structure of Scientific Revolutions.* Chicago: University of Chicago Press.

LACHMAN, R. 1976. "Effects of Industrialization and Socialization on 'Core' and 'Periphery' Values in Personal Modernity." Unpublished doctoral dissertation, University of Pennsylvania, Philadelphia.

LAMBERT, W.W., & R. WEISBROD (eds.). 1971. *Comparative Perspectives on Social Psychology.* Boston: Little, Brown.

LANDAUER, T.K., & J. WHITING. 1964. "Infantile Stimulation and Adult Stature of Human Males." *American Anthropologist,* 66, 1007–1028.

LANGTON, K.P. 1969. *Political Socialization.* New York: Oxford University Press.

LEVINE, R. 1966. *Dreams and Deeds: Achievement Motivation in Nigeria.* Chicago: University of Chicago Press.

———. 1970. "Cross-Cultural Study in Child Psychology." In P.H. Mussen (ed.), *Carmichael's Manual of Child Psychology,* Vol. 2. New York: John Wiley, pp. 559–612.

LEVINSON, D. 1977a. "What Have We Learned from Cross-Cultural Surveys?" *American Behavioral Scientist,* 20, 757–792.

———. 1977b. *A Guide to Social Theory: Worldwide Cross-Cultural Tests,* Vols. I–V. New Haven, Conn.: Human Relations Area Files.

LEWIS, M., & L.A. ROSENBLUM (eds.). 1977. *Conversation and the Development of Language.* New York: John Wiley.

LEWIS, O. 1956. "Comparisons in Cultural Anthropology." In W.L. Thomas (ed.), *Current Anthropology Today.* Chicago: University of Chicago Press, pp. 259–292.

MATHEWS, R. 1907. "Notes on the Aranda Tribe." *Journal and Proceedings of the Royal Society of New South Wales,* 41.

———. 1908. "Marriage and Descent in the Aranda Tribe, Central Australia." *American Anthropologist,* 10, 88–102.

MATSON, J.N. 1953. "Testate Succession in Ashanti." *Africa,* 23, 224–232.

MCAULIFFE, J.P. 1977. *Political Socialization Within Two Yugoslav Subcultures.* Unpublished doctoral dissertation, University of Wisconsin, Madison.

MCCLELLAND, D. 1961. *The Achieving Society.* New York: Free Press.

MCCORMACK, W.C., & S.A. WURM (eds.). 1976. *Language and Man: Anthropological Issues.* The Hague: Mouton. World Anthropology Series, Sol Tax, General Editor.

MCGREW, W.C. 1975. *An Ethological Study of Children's Behavior.* New York: Academic Press.

MEAD, MARGARET. 1928. *Coming of Age in Samoa.* New York: Morrow.

———. 1934. *Kinship in the Admiralty Islands.* New York: Anthropological Papers, American Museum of Natural History, Vol. 34, Pt. 2.

———. 1935. *Sex and Temperament in Three Primitive Societies.* New York: Morrow.

———. (ed.). 1937. *Cooperation and Competition Among Primitive Peoples.* New York: McGraw-Hill.

———. 1938–1949. "The Mountain Arapesh," I–V. *Anthropological Papers of the American Museum of Natural History*, 36, 145–349; 37, 317–451; 40, 163–419; 31, 289–390.

———. 1947a. "On the Implications for Anthropology of the Gesell-Ig Approach to Maturation." *American Anthropologist*, 49, 59–77.

———. 1947b. "The Concept of Culture and the Psychosomatic Approach." *Psychiatry*, 10, 57–76.

———. 1949. *Male and Female*. New York: Morrow.

———. 1976. "Towards a Human Science." *Science*, 191, 903–909.

MULFORD, C.L., G.E. KLONGLAN, & R.D. WARREN. 1972. "Socialization, Communication, and Role Performance." *Sociological Quarterly*, 13, 74–80.

MUNROE, R.H., & R.L. MUNROE. 1971. "Household Density and Infant Care in an East African Society." *The Journal of Social Psychology*, 83, 3–13.

———. 1980. "Household Structure and Socialization Practices." *The Journal of Social Psychology*, 111, 293–294.

MURDOCK, G.P. 1934. *Our Primitive Contemporaries*. New York: Macmillan.

———. 1949. *Social Structure*. New York: Macmillan.

———. 1967. *Ethnographic Atlas*. Pittsburgh, Pa.: University of Pittsburgh Press.

———. 1971. "Cross-Sex Patterns of Kin Behavior." *Ethnology*, 10, 359–368.

———. 1981. *Atlas of World Cultures*. Pittsburgh, Pa.: University of Pittsburgh Press.

MURDOCK, G.P., & D.R. WHITE. 1969. "Standard Cross-Cultural Sample." *Ethnology*, 8, 329–369.

MURDOCK, G.P. 1958. *Outline of World Cultures*. New Haven, Conn.: HRAF Press.

———. 1969. *Outline of Cultural Materials* (3rd rev. ed.). New Haven, Conn.: HRAF Press.

NAROLL, R. 1961. "Two Solutions to Galton's Problem." *Philosophy of Science*, 28, 15–39.

———. 1964. "On Ethnic Unit Classification." *Current Anthropology*, 5, 283–291.

———. 1968. "Some Thoughts on Comparative Method in Anthropology." In H. Blalock, & A. Blalock (eds.), *Methodology in Social Research*. New York: McGraw-Hill, pp. 236–277.

———. 1970. "What Have We Learned from Cross-Cultural Surveys?" *American Anthropologist*, 72, 1227–1288.

———. 1973. "Holocultural Theory Testing." In R. Naroll & F. Naroll (eds.), *Main Currents in Cultural Anthropology*. New York: Appleton-Century-Crofts, pp. 309–353.

NAROLL, R., & R. D'ANDRADE. 1963. "Two Further Solutions to Galton's Problem." *American Anthropologist*, 65, 1053–1067.

NAROLL, R., G.L. MICHIK, & F. NAROLL. 1976. *Worldwide Theory Testing*. New Haven, Conn.: Human Relations Area Files Press.

NIEMI, R.G. 1974. *The Politics of Future Citizens: New Dimensions in the Political Socialization of Children*. San Francisco: Jossey-Bass.

NIEMI, R.G., & B.I. SOBIESZEK. 1977. "Political Socialization." *Annual Review of Sociology*, 3, 209–233.

O'LEARY, T. 1969. "A Preliminary Bibliography of Cross-Cultural Studies." *Behavior Science Notes*, 4, 95–115.

———. 1971. "Bibliography of Cross-Cultural Studies: Supplement I." *Behavior Science Notes*, 6, 191–203.

———. 1973. "Bibliography of Cross-Cultural Studies: Supplement II." *Behavior Science Notes*, 8, 123–134.

OLSEN, N.J. 1974. "Family Structure and Socialization Patterns in Taiwan." *Amer-*

ican Journal of Sociology, 79, 1395–1417.

PARSONS, T., R. BALES, & J. OLDS. 1955. *Family, Socialization and Interaction Process.* Glencoe, Ill.: Free Press.

PERRINJAQUET, R. 1979. "Habitat as a Universe of Child Socialization in Industrial Societies." *International Social Science Journal*, 31, 457.

PHILLIPS, D.C. 1976. *Holistic Thought in the Social Sciences.* Stanford, Calif.: Stanford University Press.

PILNER, P., L. KRAMES, & T. ALLOWAY (eds.). 1973. *Communication and Affect: Language and Thought.* New York: Academic Press.

PINK, O. 1936. "The Landowners in the Northern Divisions of the Aranda Tribe." *Oceania*, 6, 275–305.

PLATTNER, S., & L. MINTURN. 1975. "A Comparative and Longitudinal Study of the Behavior of Communally Raised Children." *Ethos*, 3, 469–480.

PLOG, S.C., & R.B. EDGERTON (eds.). 1969. *Changing Perspectives in Mental Illness.* New York: Holt, Rinehart & Winston.

POPPER, K. 1959. *The Logic of Scientific Discovery.* New York: Basic Books.

RADCLIFFE-BROWN, A. 1930. "The Social Organization of Australian Tribes." *Oceania*, 1, 34–63.

RATTRAY, R. 1923. *Ashanti.* Oxford: Clarendon Press.

———. 1927. *Religion and Art in Ashanti.* London: Oxford University Press.

———. 1929. *Ashanti Law and Constitution.* London: Oxford University Press.

RENSHON, S.A. (ed.). 1977. *Handbook of Political Socialization: Theory and Research.* New York: Free Press.

RICHARDS, M.P.M. 1974. "First Steps in Becoming Social." In M. Richards (ed.), *The Integration of a Child into a Social World.* New York: Cambridge University Press, pp. 83–97.

———. 1977. "Interaction and the Concept of Development: The Biological and Social Revisited." In M. Lewis & L.A. Rosenblum (eds.), *Conversation and the Development of Language.* New York: John Wiley, pp. 187–206.

ROBERTS, J., M. ARTH, & R. BUSH. 1959. "Games in Culture." *American Anthropologist*, 61, 597–605.

ROBERTS, J., & B. SUTTON-SMITH. 1962. "Child Training and Game Involvement." *Ethnology*, 1, 166–185.

———. 1966. "Cross-Cultural Correlates of Games of Chance." *Behavior Science Notes*, 1, 131–144.

ROBERTS, J., B. SUTTON-SMITH, & A. KENDON. 1963. "Strategy in Games and Folk Tales." *Journal of Social Psychology*, 61, 185–199.

RÓHEIM, G. 1925. *Australian Totemism.* London: G. Allen and Unwin.

———. 1933. "Women and Their Life in Central Australia." *Journal of the Royal Anthropological Institute*, 63, 241–250.

SANDER, L.W. 1977. "The Regulation of Exchange in the Infant-Caretaker System and Some Aspects of the Context-Content Relationship." In M. Lewis & L.A. Rosenblum (eds.), *Conversation and the Development of Language.* New York: John Wiley, pp. 133–135.

SCHAPERA, I. 1953. "Some Comments on Comparative Method in Social Anthropology." *American Anthropologist*, 55, 353–361.

SCHLEGEL, A., & H. BARRY, III. 1979. "Adolescent Initiation Ceremonies: A Cross-Cultural Code." *Ethnology*, 18, 199–210.

SCHULMAN, D.C. 1975. *Political Socialization in Voluntary Organizations: A Test of the Influence of Involvement on Political Participation.* Unpublished doctoral dissertation, State University of New York at Buffalo.

SCHWARTZ, D.C., & S.K. SCHWARTZ (eds.). 1975. *New Directions in Political Socialization.* New York: Free Press.

SCHWARTZ, T. (ed.). 1976. *Socialization as Cultural Communication: Development of a Theme in the Work of Margaret Mead.* Berkeley: University of California Press.

SCHWEDER, R.A. 1973. "The Between and Within of Cross-Cultural Research." *Ethos,* 1, 531–545.

SERVICE, E. 1963. *Profiles in Ethnology.* New York: Harper & Row, Pub.

SORENSEN, E.R. 1971. *The Evolving Fore: A Study of Socialization and Cultural Change in the New Guinea Highlands.* Unpublished doctoral dissertation, Stanford University.

SPENCER, B. 1928. *Wanderings in Wild Australia.* London: Macmillan.

SPENCER, B., & F. GILLEN. 1927. *The Arunta: A Study of a Stone Age People* (2 vols.). London: Macmillan.

———. 1938. *The Native Tribes of Central Australia* (2 vols.). London: Macmillan.

SPINDLER, G. 1967. "Foreword." In R.B. Textor (ed.), *A Cross-Cultural Summary.* New Haven, Conn.: HRAF Press, pp. vii–ix.

SPIRO, M., & R. D'ANDRADE. 1958. "A Cross-Cultural Study of Some Supernatural Beliefs." *American Anthropologist,* 60, 456–466.

STACEY, B. 1978. *Political Socialization in Western Society: An Analysis from a Life-Span Perspective.* New York: St. Martin's Press.

STEPHENS, W. 1962. *The Oedipus Complex: Cross-Cultural Evidence.* New York: Free Press.

STREHLOW, T.G.H. 1947. *Aranda Traditions.* Melbourne: Melbourne University Press.

STROSS, B. 1972. "Verbal Processes in Tzeltal Speech Socialization." *Anthropological Linguistics,* 14, 1–13.

SUTTON-SMITH, B., & J.M. ROBERTS. 1963. "Game Involvement in Adults." *Journal of Social Psychology,* 60, 15–30.

———. 1964. "Rubrics of Competitive Behavior." *Journal of Genetic Psychology,* 105, 13–37.

———. 1967. "Studies in an Elementary Game of Strategy." *Genetic Psychology Monographs,* 75, 3–42.

TAPP, J.L. (ed.). 1971. "Socialization, the Law and Society." *Journal of Social Issues,* 27, 1–229.

TEXTOR, R. 1967. *A Cross-Cultural Summary.* New Haven, Conn.: HRAF Press.

TINDALL, B.A. 1976. "Theory in the Study of Cultural Transmission." In B. Siegel, A. Beals, & S. Tyler (eds.), *Annual Review of Anthropology,* 5, 195–208. Palo Alto, Calif.: Annual Reviews, Inc.

TRIANDIS, L., & W. LAMBERT. 1961. "Sources of Frustration and Targets of Aggression: A Cross-Cultural Study." *Journal of Abnormal and Social Psychology,* 62, 640–648.

TROTTER, C.R. 1980. *Teachers as Agents of Political Socialization.* Unpublished doctoral dissertation, University of Toronto, Toronto.

TYLOR, E. 1889. "On a Method of Investigating the Development of Institutions: Applied to the Laws of Marriage and Descent." *Journal of the Royal Anthropological Institute,* 18, 245–269.

UDY, S.H., JR. 1973. "Cross-Cultural Analysis: Methods and Scope." In B. Siegel, A. Beals, & S. Tyler (eds.), *Annual Review of Anthropology,* 2, 253–270. Palo Alto, Calif.: Annual Reviews, Inc.

VERMEULEN, C.J., & A. DERUIJTER. 1975. "Dominant Epistemological Presumptions in the Use of the Cross-Cultural Survey Method." *Current Anthropology,* 16, 29–52.

WALLACE, A.F.C. 1970. *Culture and Personality.* New York: Random House.

WALTER, M.A. 1979. "The Mother's Brother and the Sister's Son in East Fiji: A Descent Perspective." *Ethnology,* 18, 365–397.

WELCH, M.R. 1978a. "Socialization Anxiety and Patterns of Economic Subsistence." *Journal of Social Psychology*, 105, 33–36.

———. 1978b. "Linking Subsistence Economy and Socialization Practices." *Journal of Social Psychology*, 105, 315–316.

———. 1978c. "Childhood Socialization Differences in African and Non-African Societies." *Journal of Social Psychology*, 106, 11–15.

WENTWORTH, W.M. 1978. "Context and Understanding: An Inquiry into Socialization Theory." Unpublished doctoral dissertation, University of Virginia, Charlottesville.

WHITING, B. 1969. *The Effect of Urbanization on the Behavior of Children.* Cambridge, Mass.: Graduate School of Education, Harvard University.

WHITING, B.B., & J.W.M. WHITING. 1971. "Task Assignment and Personality: A Consideration of the Effect of Herding on Boys." In W.W. Lambert & R. Weisbrod (eds.), *Comparative Perspectives on Social Psychology.* Boston: Little, Brown, pp. 33–45.

———. 1976. "Aloofness and Intimacy of Husbands and Wives." In T. Schwartz (ed.), *Socialization as Cultural Communication: Development of a Theme in the Work of Margaret Mead.* Berkeley: University of California Press, pp. 91–115.

WHITING, J.W.M. 1941. *Becoming A Kwoma: Teaching and Learning in a New Guinea Tribe.* New Haven, Conn.: Yale University Press.

———. 1954. "The Cross-Cultural Method." In G. Lindzey (ed.), *Handbook of Social Psychology.* Reading, Mass.: Addison-Wesley, pp. 523–531.

———. 1961. "Socialization Process and Personality." In F.L.K. Hsu (ed.), *Psychological Anthropology.* Homewood, Ill.: Dorsey, pp. 355–399.

———. 1968. "Method and Problems in Cross-Cultural Research." In G. Lindzey & E. Aronson (eds.), *Handbook of Social Psychology.* Reading, Mass.: Addison-Wesley.

WHITING, J.W.M., & I.L. CHILD. 1953. *Child Training and Personality.* New Haven, Conn.: Yale University Press.

WHITING, J.W.M., R. KLUCKHOHN, & A. ANTHONY. 1958. "The Function of Male Initiation Ceremonies at Puberty." In E. Maccoby, T. Newcombe, & E. Hartley (eds.), *Readings in Social Psychology.* New York: Holt, Rinehart & Winston, pp. 359–370.

WIENER, N. 1950. "Some Maxims for Biologists and Psychologists." *Dialectica*, 4, 22–27.

WILBERT, J. (ed.). 1976. *Enculturation in Latin America: An Anthology.* Latin American Studies 37. Los Angeles: University of California at Los Angeles, Latin American Center Publication.

WILLIAMS, J.B. 1972. *Family Power Structure and Political Socialization: A Synthesis and Comparison of Two Models.* Unpublished doctoral dissertation. Vanderbilt University, Nashville, Tenn.

WILLIAMS, T.R. 1958. "The Structure of the Socialization Process in Papago Indian Society." *Social Forces*, 36, 251–256.

———. 1959. "A Critique of Some Assumptions of Social Survey Research." *The Public Opinion Quarterly*, 23, 55–62.

———. 1967. *Field Methods in the Study of Culture.* New York: Holt, Rinehart & Winston.

———. 1969. *A Borneo Childhood: Enculturation in Dusun Society.* New York: Holt, Rinehart & Winston.

———. 1972a. "The Socialization Process: A Theoretical Perspective." In F. Poirier (ed.), *Primate Socialization.* New York: Random House, pp. 207–260.

———. 1972b. *Introduction to Socialization: Human Culture Transmitted.* St. Louis, Mo.: C.V. Mosby.

———. 1975a. "On the Origin of the Socialization Process." In T.R. Williams (ed.), *Socialization and Communication in Primary Groups*. The Hague: Mouton, pp. 233–249.

———. (ed.). 1975b. *Socialization and Communication in Primary Groups*. The Hague: Mouton.

——— (ed.). 1975c. *Psychological Anthropology*. The Hague: Mouton.

———. 1978. "Socialization Research: Planning for the Future." In D.B. Shimkin, S. Tax, & J.W. Morrison (eds.), *Anthropology for the Future*. Champaign-Urbana: University of Illinois Department of Anthropology, pp. 142–161.

———. 1979. "Comment on a Theory of Cultural Transmission by F. Gearing. et al." In F. Gearing & L. Sangree (eds.), *Toward a Cultural Theory of Education and Schooling*. The Hague: Mouton, pp. 151–166.

WILLS, D.D. 1977. *Culture's Cradle: Social Structural and Interactional Aspects of Senegalese Socialization*. Unpublished doctoral dissertation, University of Texas, Austin.

———. 1979. "Learning and Communicating." *American Anthropologist*, 81, 874–888.

WILSON, R.W. 1974a. *The Moral State: A Study of the Political Socialization of Chinese and American Children*. New York: Free Press.

———. 1974b. *Learning to Be Chinese: The Political Socialization of Children in Taiwan*. Cambridge, Mass.: M.I.T. Press.

WINCH, R.F., & D.T. CAMPBELL. 1969. "Proof? No. Evidence? Yes. The Significance of Tests of Significance." *American Sociologist*, 4, 140–143.

WOEFEL, J.C. 1976. *Significant Others and the Political Socialization Process*. Unpublished doctoral dissertation, University of Michigan, Ann Arbor.

WRIGHT, J.D. 1975. "Political Socialization Research—Primacy Principle." *Social Forces*, 54, 243–255.

YINGER, R.E. 1971. *Socialization, Settings and Political Attitudes: A Study of Veterans and Non-Veteran Students*. Unpublished doctoral dissertation, Florida State University, Tallahassee.

CHAPTER SEVEN
STATUS-ROLE, CLASS, AND SOCIALIZATION

This chapter is concerned with the ways the cultural patterns of status-role and class are related to the socialization process. The discussion begins with an examination of the concept of status-role and an account of transitions in status-role that may be required of children as they mature in a culture. The second part of the chapter briefly examines the concept of social class and notes some studies of relations between class and the socialization process. The chapter concludes with comments concerning the part played by these patterns in the socialization process.

STATUS-ROLE AND SOCIALIZATION

Each human culture possesses patterns that are concerned with details of work to be undertaken for survival of the society, clear definitions of the ways jobs or tasks are to be performed, and the usual practices of recruitment of individuals to such tasks. Malinowski (1944) noted that these patterns, which he termed a *cultural charter*, are sometimes explicitly stated in a culture's rituals, informal law, myths, folk tales, songs, jokes, riddles, proverbs, puns, and ideology. However some features of a cultural charter must be determined from statements about behavior made by persons recruited to perform specific tasks. Some features of a cultural charter can be determined only through direct observation of the behavior of individuals performing specific tasks.

Conceptions of Status-Role

In an influential work Linton (1936) defined *status* as a "polar position" in a pattern of reciprocal social behavior. He also noted that a polar position consisted of a collection of social rights and duties. Linton termed the precise ways rights and duties are put into effect as "roles." Linton illustrated these definitions by pointing out that persons occupying similar polar social positions would tend to behave in similar ways.

For example, at times of ritual feasting and celebration among the Dusun of northern Borneo, it is usual for men to sit scattered about the interior central area of a house. On the other hand, women walk about or stand as they serve food and drink or prepare food. Later when gong music begins or singing commences, women enter the main feasting area and walk freely among the men during dancing and song harmony. It is not until near the end of a feast, however, that women are supposed to be seated among the men.

Dusun culture also prescribes that, on meeting, younger men address older and unrelated women as "aunt," while older women must reciprocate through addressing younger, nonrelated males as "nephew." Similarly younger women are supposed to address unrelated older males as "uncle," while older men must respond to such greetings by using the term "niece."

In addition to these social statuses and their associated roles, which are based on criteria of sex and age, Dusun must learn and use at least 11 + 2 other status-role classifications. Figure 7–1 notes the 13 different status-role classes that could be involved in the instance of the social situation when a middle-aged Dusun male meets a young Dusun woman walking along a village path. Based on their estimate of the situation, each individual would have to choose appropriate ways of behaving toward the other person. In most instances, except for sex and age, the many statuses held by each adult in the Dusun cultural system can be freely entered, filled, and left. However the roles associated with each Dusun status can be performed only in a face-to-face situation, after decisions by an individual based on an estimate of the polar social positions potentially occupied by another person. A young Dusun woman meeting her mother's older brother on a village path should have full knowledge of all of the polar positions that could be occupied by the older man in the Dusun social system (see Fig. 7–1). Hence she could quickly choose to show the appropriate role behavior toward the older man, without the risk of major personal offense. In the Dusun cultural charter, *age, sex,* and *kinship* status-roles tend to dominate personal relationships. Thus on meeting an older man, a younger Dusun

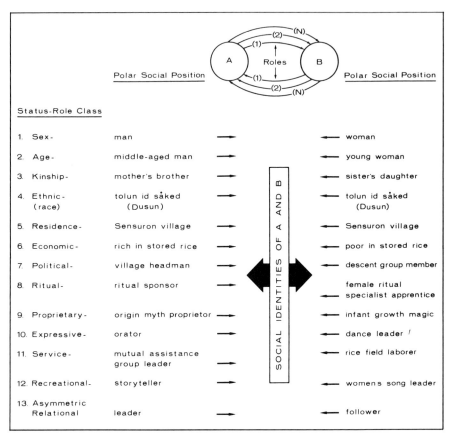

FIGURE 7–1 Some Dusun status-role definitions. (After Linton's conceptions of role-status, 1936; see also Goodenough, 1965.)

woman would not ordinarily behave in roles usual for her service status as a "rice field laborer," or in role ways reflecting her *expressive, proprietary, recreational,* or other statuses. However at certain times, such as during a special ritual observance to protect the entire community from epidemic disease, a face-to-face meeting between a young Dusun woman and her mother's older brother might be dominated by her ritual status as a *female ritual specialist* capable of conducting the special magical acts involved in the village ceremony. An older Dusun man with the primary responsibility for organizing and economically sponsoring a ritual would probably behave toward a younger woman in a deferential manner, since as a ritual specialist the younger woman has a supernatural "power"—that is, she is believed to be in contact with the most fearful and omnipotent forces and beings of the universe.

The 13 status-role classes listed in Fig. 7–1, which follow Linton's concepts of status-role, appear to be universal in human culture—that is,

TABLE 7–1   Some Service Status Differentiations in the Northern Borneo Tambunan Dusun Village of Sensuron—1959, 1960

Bamboo wall maker	Fence maker	Midwife	Rubber gardener
Bark cloth maker	Gong trader	Money lender	Salt trader
Basket weaver	House builder	Musical instrument	Smith
Blow pipe maker	Hunter	maker	Spear maker
Blow pipe dart and	Irrigation ditch builder	Palm thatch maker	Tray maker
case maker	Jar trader	Plow and yoke maker	Tobacco gardener
Bridge builder	Kerabau (water	Pottery maker	Tobacco shredder
Butcher	buffalo) breeder	Rattan knot specialist	Weaver
Dam builder	Knife maker	Rattan rope maker	Wet rice farmer
Dry rice farmer	Male ritual specialist	Rice mill maker	Wood carver
Female ritual	Male ritual specialist	Rice and palm wine	
specialist	apprentice	maker	
Female ritual	Mat maker	Ritual symbol maker	
specialist			
apprentice			

to occur in the charters of all human societies. There may also be other status-role classes. Substantial variations occur between societies in the total numbers of subclasses in particular status-roles.

For instance, in 1959 and in 1960 the Dusun cultural charter in the interior mountain village of Sensuron specified a total of approximately 43 subclasses within one (the service status) of the 13 classes of status-role.

Table 7–1 notes these Dusun service status differentiations. In contrast, in July 1980 more than 400 different service status differentiations were listed in the Yellow Pages of the telephone book for the city of Columbus, Ohio. Some examples are listed in Table 7–2. Thus in terms of service status differentiations, the village of Sensuron, with a 1960 population of 947 persons, contrasts markedly with the city of Columbus, Ohio, with a 1970 population of 539,677 persons. Such status differentiation contrasts between an isolated Dusun community and an American city also seems to extend to other differentiations in the statuses used in these two cultures, with the exception of the status of kinship. In the instance of kinship Sensuron Dusun status differentiations are much more numerous than those used in the American city of Columbus, Ohio.[1]

At present no complete accounts exist for all the status differentiations in any cultural charter or of the many roles attached to each of the statuses within the major status groups. It may be possible that, while there are approximately 13 status groups in the human cultural charter and a great many differentiations within each status class, the numbers of human roles can encompass all of the discrete ways humans behave in social situations.

[1]For some contrasts between Sensuron Dusun and American kinship status-role differentiations, see Williams, 1962, and Schneider, 1968.

TABLE 7–2 Some Examples of Service Status Differentiations in the Columbus, Ohio, Telephone Book—July, 1980 (A through C listings only)

Abstracters	Benefit plan consultants	Caterers
Accordion players	Beverage analysts	Cattle breeders
Accountants	Bicycle dealers	Cement contractors
Acoustical consultants	Biographers	Ceramic engineers
Actuaries	Blacksmiths	Certified public accountants
Advertising counselors	Boarding school consultants	Cesspool builders
Aerial crop dusters	Boat brokers	Chair dealers
Air ambulance services	Boiler dealers	Chaplains
Aircraft brokers	Bonding companies	Chauffeur services
Ambulance drivers	Bonesetters	Chemists
Animal dealers	Book dealers	Chemical engineers
Antique dealers	Booking agents	Child guidance counselors
Apothecaries	Bottle manufacturers	Chimney builders
Appraisers	Bowling instructors	Chiropodists
Arborists	Boxing and crating services	Chop suey manufacturers
Architects	Brake lining manufacturers	Church decorators
Asphalt paving contractors	Brass foundries	Cigar dealers
Attorneys	Brassiere manufacturers	Circular printers
Auctioneers	Brewers	Citizenship instructors
Auditors	Bricklayers	Claim adjusters
Automobile dealers	Bridge builders	Clipping services
Baby sitters	Building wreckers	Coal analysts
Bacteriologists	Butchers	Collection agencies
Bail bondsmen	Cabinet makers	Copy preparation services
Bakers	Cafeteria consultants	Correspondence schools
Bands	Caisson contractors	Cosmetic therapists
Bankers	Campaign managers	Coupon redemption centers
Barbecue builders	Candy brokers	Court reporters
Barbers	Carpenters	Crematory services
Baseball ticket agents	Carpet dyers	Criminologists
Baton twirling instructors	Carshakers	Custom house brokers
Bell manufacturers	Cartoonists	

Thus the great number of roles associated with statuses presently is a significant barrier to broad generalizations concerning the nature of status-role behavior.

Ascribed and Achieved Status-Role

One useful generalization has evolved from the many efforts to describe and analyze the numbers of statuses and their associated roles. This is the idea of grouping many different types of status-roles according to whether a cultural charter *ascribes* them—that is, automatically assigns them to individuals—or whether status-roles must be *achieved*—that is, learned through performance or demonstration. Linton (1936) first suggested the usefulness of such general classifications of status-role forms. Linton's suggestions have been developed and discussed over the past three decades by sociologists and anthropologists. Table 7–3 notes the ways Banton, Na-

TABLE 7–3 A Classification of Ascribed and Achieved Status-Role*

	ASCRIBED STATUS-ROLE				ACHIEVED STATUS-ROLE				
	SEX	AGE	RACE	KINSHIP	PROPRIETARY	EXPRESSIVE	SERVICE	SYMMETRICAL	ASYMMETRICAL
	Status-role based on sexual characters	Status-role based on chronological maturity	Status-role based on racial features	Status-role based on kin relations	Status-role based on special learning, knowledge, or skill	Status-role based on demonstration of special beliefs, creativity, or communicative abilities	Status-role based on occupational activities	Status-role based on social relationships of equality	Status-role based on social relationships of inequality
	—	Baby	—	—	—	—	Teacher	—	—
	Male	Boy	Dusun	Son	—	—	Accountant	Partner	Leader, follower, Chairman, member
	Female	Woman	American	Mother	Potter	Artist	Biologist	Colleague	
		11 years old	Eskimo	Mother's brother	Carver	Orator			
					Shaman	Dancer			

*Banton, M. 1965 *Roles*, London: Tavistock, p. 31; Nadel, S.F. 1957. *The Theory of Social Structure*. Glencoe, Ill.: Free Press; Southall, A. 1959. "An Operational Theory of Role," *Human Relations* 12:17–34.

del, and Southall, among others, have suggested that Linton's conception of ascribed and achieved status-roles may be modified in terms of recent studies.

Status-Relationships and Social Identities

In considering some of the problems of analysis of status-role, Goodenough (1965) has proposed a redefinition of the concept. He points out that, although Linton initially recognized polar social positions to consist of a cluster of social rights and duties and ideas concerning the ways these are put into effect in social situations, Linton then made the conceptual error of discussing status as referring only to kinds of persons, such as "teacher," "woman," and so on. Goodenough notes that most writers since Linton have followed this error without question, treating a social category, such as "brother" or "chief," together with all of its associated rights and duties, as one indivisible conceptual unit called a *status*.[2] For Goodenough the "formal properties" of status involve only social rights, duties, privileges, powers, liabilities, and immunities and the ordered ways these are distributed in a culture. Goodenough believes it would be much more useful to refer to social categories, or kinds of persons, as *social identities*, while reserving the term *status* for specific combinations of social rights, duties, and so on. Thus Goodenough would describe and analyze ascribed and achieved *social identities*, and others, following Linton, would study ascribed and achieved *statuses*.

While adopting Linton's definitions of status-role as he considered some new ways to analyze basic social interactions, Goffman (1961) also noted that there was analytic efficiency to be gained in identifying the rights and duties usually associated with particular "social positions." Goodenough and Goffman agree that, in any social relationship, one individual's social *rights* over another are those things that one person, A, can demand of another, B, whereas social *duties* are those things that B owes to A.

Goodenough also notes that social rights and duties between A and B serve to set the formal boundaries for interpersonal behavior. Thus as hostess for a dinner party, an American woman may personally request that her guests wear "informal" clothing. It is her *social right* to make such a request. In turn, it is the *social duty* of guests to dress informally. However, a hostess has no *social right* to dictate the color, style, or design of informal dress. It remains the privilege of a guest to make such choices, providing they fully observe their duty toward a hostess exercising her social right in issuing an invitation to her home. Goodenough terms such a reciprocal right-duty pair as a *status relationship*. He also notes that status relationships

[2]See for instance, Merton, 1957, 368–370.

can often be found widely repeated in a culture.[3] Thus when entering new social situations, individuals must know the ways status relationships may be applied.

A Trukese status relationship   Children growing up on Truk, a Pacific island, must learn all of the ways status relationships carry over into different social situations. For instance, the duties associated with one Trukese social right—that of claiming "social rank"—involve at least six discrete activities.

1. To regularly use the special honorific greeting *fääjiro* when encountering a person of higher social rank.
2. To avoid being physically elevated over a person of higher social rank and therefore to engage in crouching or crawling if a higher-ranked person is seated.
3. To avoid face-to-face social interactions with persons of higher social rank unless specifically requested by them to do so.
4. To honor all requests made by persons of higher social ranks.
5. To not speak harshly to or scold persons of higher social rank.
6. To avoid striking persons of higher social rank.

Table 7–4 notes Goodenough's summary of the ways these social duties for Trukese individuals are carried from one situation to another when there are persons present who can claim the right of higher social rank.[4] This particular Trukese status relationship (the *right* of claiming social rank; the *duty* of not setting oneself above a person with higher rank) is somewhat difficult for Americans and Europeans to conceive since status relationships in these cultures involving the right of claiming social rank and the duty of social deference are based on different social and cultural premises.

Status-Role Number and Complexity

In considering the ways status relationships, or status-roles, are learned in the socialization process, it is important to recall that no culture provides children with analytic diagrams, such as Table 7–4, to study as they mature. For instance, Trukese children, in common with children in all human societies, master great complexity of social behavior (Table 7–4 includes 246 social duty actions) for each one of the status relationships or status-role classes used in their local societies.

[3]Goffman (1961) uses the concept of *role set* in essentially the same way Goodenough (1965) has defined a *status relationship.* See also Merton, 1957, and Gross, Mason, McEachern, 1958.

[4]The Trukese pattern of social rank is manifest in the taboo of "setting oneself above another." For ease of discussion, this has been glossed, or interpreted, here as "claiming social rank." For further details see Goodenough, 1951, 111–119.

TABLE 7–4 Status Duty of Not Setting Oneself Above Another in Trukese Society*

SOCIAL RELATIONSHIP IN WHICH STATUS DUTY IS OWED	MUST SAY *Fääjiro*	MUST CRAWL	MUST AVOID	MUST OBEY	MUST NOT SCOLD	MUST NOT FIGHT
1. Non-kinsman to chief	Yes	Yes	Yes	Yes	Yes	Yes
Non-kinsman to *jitag*	Yes	Yes	Yes	Yes	Yes	Yes
2. Man to female neji	No	Yes	Yes	Yes	Yes	Yes
Man to Wi's *mwääni*	No	Yes	Yes	Yes	Yes	Yes
Woman to So of *mwääni*	No	Yes	No(?)	Yes	Yes	Yes
Woman to *mwääni*	No	Yes	Yes	Yes	Yes	Yes
Woman to So of Hu's older *pwiij*	No	Yes	Yes	Yes	Yes	Yes
Woman to Wi of *mwääni*	No	Yes	Yes	Yes	Yes	Yes
3. Man to older *pwiij*	No	No	Yes	Yes	Yes	Yes
Woman to older *pwiij*	No	No	Yes	Yes	Yes	Yes
4. Man to male *neji*	No	No	No	Yes	Yes	Yes
Man to Wi of older *pwiij*	No	No	No	Yes	Yes	Yes
Woman to Da of *mwääni*	No	No	No	Yes	Yes	Yes
Woman to Da of Hu's *pwiij*	No	No	No	Yes	Yes	Yes
Woman to So of Hu's younger *pwiij*	No	No	No	Yes	Yes	Yes
Woman to Da of Hu's *feefinej*	No	No	No	Yes	Yes	Yes
Woman to So of Hu's *feefinej*	No	No	No	Yes	Yes	Yes
Woman to Hu of older *pwiij*	No	No	No	Yes	Yes	Yes
Woman to Da's Hu	No	No	No	Yes	Yes	Yes
Woman to So's Wi	No	No	No	Yes	Yes	Yes

TABLE 7-4 *(continued)*

SOCIAL RELATIONSHIP IN WHICH STATUS DUTY IS OWED	MUST SAY *Fääjiro*	MUST CRAWL	MUST AVOID	MUST OBEY	MUST NOT SCOLD	MUST NOT FIGHT
5. Man to younger						
pwiij	No	No	No	No	Yes	Yes
Man to Wi's						
older pwiij	No	No	No	No	Yes	Yes
Woman to						
younger pwiij	No	No	No	No	Yes	Yes
Woman to So of						
pwiij	No	No	No	No	Yes	Yes
Woman to Hu's						
older pwiij	No	No	No	No	Yes	Yes
6. Man to Wi of						
younger pwiij	No	No	No	No	No	Yes
Woman to own						
So	No	No	No	No	No	Yes
Woman to Hu's						
younger pwiij	No	No	No	No	No	Yes
7. Man to semej	No	No	No	No	No	No
Man to jinej	No	No	No	No	No	No
Man to feefinej	No	No	No	No	No	No
Man to Hu of						
feefinej	No	No	No	No	No	No
Man to Wi	No	No	No	No	No	No
Man to Wi's						
younger pwiij	No	No	No	No	No	No
Woman to semej	No	No	No	No	No	No
Woman to jinej	No	No	No	No	No	No
Woman to own						
Da	No	No	No	No	No	No
Woman to Da of						
pwiij	No	No	No	No	No	No
Woman to Hu	No	No	No	No	No	No
Woman to Hu of						
younger pwiij	No	No	No	No	No	No
Woman to Hu's						
feefinej	No	No	No	No	No	No

Translations of Trukese linguistic terms (from Goodenough, 1951, 94, 186–187).

jinej, "my mother"—that is Mo, MoMo, MoSi, FaSi.

jitag, specialist in law, war, diplomacy, and rhetoric.

feefinej, "my sister."

mwääni, "my brother."

neji, "my child"—that is, So, Da, SiCh, BrCh.

pwiij, "my siblings of the same sex,"—that is, Br, Si.

semej, "my father,"—that is, Fa, FaFa, FaBr, MoBr.

*Goodenough, 1951, 113; 1965, 13.

In another theoretical context Wallace (1961, 157) has proposed that there is evidence in all human societies of a tendency toward individual effort in reducing all social experience to some meaningful kind of order, as Goodenough suggests for status relationships, but at the same time also working toward greatly increasing the complexity within any classification of order that may be created. Thus while there may be 5, 7, 9, or 13 status-role relationship scales in any culture, it would be expected that there would be great complexity of behavior associated with each individual scale, without regard to the number of scales used. In fact, human status-role (or status relationships) are characterized by enormous complexity and at the same time by systematic ordering of such complexity. This is reflected in the example of the one Trukese status relationship noted in Table 7–4; Trukese children must learn not only the right of claiming social rank in many different social situations, but they must also learn the complex ways this right has been expanded by different definitions of social duty in each social situation. Figure 7–2 illustrates the idea of role expansion of a status scale, following Goodenough's example of a Trukese status relationship.

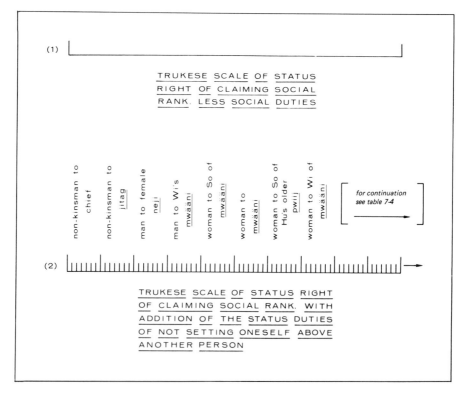

FIGURE 7–2 Expansion of complexity in a status relationship scale in Trukese society. (Goodenough, 1951, 1965.)

Summary

In summary, there are at least two ways of thinking about the number and complexity of status-roles. First, following the concepts of status-role advanced by Linton and refined recently by others, there are at least 13 major status classes, each one possessing numerous internal differentiations and with a nearly infinite number of associated roles. These major classes seem to have order, when classified into "ascribed" or "achieved" status-roles. On the other hand, following the concepts formulated by Good-enough, the number of status relationships in a cultural charter will be limited to only seven (plus or minus two). Wallace's estimate of the tendency of humans to strive toward increasing the internal complexity of categories used to make order of their experience, when added to Goodenough's theoretical estimate, would seem to explain why so few status relationships can accommodate the very great complexity of human social relations.

All of these ideas are vital in considering the ways in which infants and children learn the details of the human cultural charter. Without a theory for making specific estimates of the numbers and types of tasks to be performed, the different ways these tasks will be carried out, and so on, which are specified in all cultural charters, it becomes a nearly impossible task to comprehend how infants and children can ever begin to grasp clearly, and in so brief a time, all of the many details and vast complexity apparently required in every society for successful social performances.

Added Dimensions of Status-Role

A major problem in considering estimates of the number and complexity of status-roles or status relationships to be learned by children in the process of socialization is that there are a wide variety of other cultural features which are also involved in such behavior. For instance, human social interaction usually involves personal demeanor, including whole body orientations, movements, gestures, and physical distance or proximity of the persons involved. Thus the demeanor of the hostess toward a guest at the time of the issuance of a dinner party invitation can carry specification of what is intended by her use of the term *informal*. If an invitation is offered by a hostess to a male guest while she engages in sexually suggestive movements, it could indicate to a male guest a definition for informality quite different from the one to be noted by a hostess seated half a room distant while she issues her invitation for an "informal" dinner.

The use of features of costume to provide specific clues regarding status-role or status relationships is also common to all human societies. The forms of such features vary widely between societies, however, ranging from the full-dress uniform of a United States Navy admiral to the wooden ear and lower lip plugs worn by adult Botocudo Indian women of the Amazon River Basin. For an admiral or a Botocudo woman, incumbency in a particular status-role or status relationship may be symbolized through clues of costume, so that others of a society will know immediately, in a new situation, with whom they must be socially concerned. The responses of persons in a social situation are often to the clues manifested in features of costume which show status-role behavior potentials—that is, which indicate the possession of personal, political, or other kinds of power. Features of costume may also show the nature of status-role attachment or the degree of involvement of a person in a particular status-role. The ear and lip plugs worn by Botocudo women, who ordinarily go about their affairs unclothed, symbolizes all of their feminine modesty, for without such plugs women are reported to feel "undressed" and hence as embarrassed as an American hostess might be if she appeared at her informal dinner party without wearing any clothing.

The styling of hair to indicate different sex, age, and service status-roles is also quite widespread in human society. Such styles have also been used to denote specific clan or other kin group memberships, notably in some North American Indian and some African societies. In addition, cosmetic paints used as body and facial decorations, jewelry, tattoos, and regular practice of body deformations and mutilations, including foot and head binding, scarification, circumcision, subincision, and tooth filing, are used in human societies as indicators of status-roles. These clues to status-role may be combined with other clues of costume, hair styles, and demeanors.

Thus it is usually necessary for children to learn multiple cultural clues for many different status-roles or status relationships, which can vary from time to time and in different social situations in complex combinations. In addition, children in most human societies must learn a very intricate and widely used status-role terminology. For instance, in the Trukese social relationship in Table 7–4, children must learn details of when and how to use the honorific greeting *fääjiro*. American children must learn to say "sir" and "ma'am" at appropriate times and places and to avoid public rudeness in use of status-role terms noting less than ideal status-role conditions of age, sex, service, and so on ("funny old man, " "old bag," and so on). Among the Swazi, a native people of Southeast Africa, status-role terminology is highly developed for distinguishing among commoners, nobles, and royalty. Swazi children are confronted very early in life with learning a quite complex vocabulary for successful social interaction.[5] Severe personal and economic penalties are imposed in Swazi society and many other societies for failure to regularly use precise status-role terminology. Such penalties

[5]See Kuper, 1947, 1952, 1963; Drucker, 1939.

range from the possibility of long-term imprisonment for an American Marine private showing open disrespect for his superior officers by use of foul language, to the complete social ostracism, and possible execution, that would have been imposed on a Hawaiian "commoner" violating the personal taboos (*tapu*) of a king or queen through use of inappropriate status-role terminology.

Children in all human societies must also learn and correctly use a system of status-role *worth*. American Supreme Court justices, physicians, nuclear physicists, scientists, and government scientists have been ranked as the most influential and important of more than 100 well-known jobs specified in the American cultural charter. Table 7–5 lists the worth rankings given by Americans for some well-known status-roles. Nonliterate cultures also rank status-roles in a similar manner. For instance, 165 northern Borneo Dusun adults (82 men, 83 women) living in Sensuron in 1959 and 1960 verbally ranked the service statuses listed in Table 7–1 according to

TABLE 7–5   Status-Role Prestige of Occupations in the United States, 1925–1963*

25 HIGHEST-RANKED OCCUPATIONS	25 LOWEST-RANKED OCCUPATIONS
Supreme Court justices	Garage mechanics
Physicians	Truck drivers
Nuclear physicists	Fishermen (who own boats)
Scientists	Clerks in stores
Government scientists	Milk route men
State governors	Streetcar motormen
Federal government cabinet officers	Lumberjacks
College professors	Restaurant cooks
Representatives (in Congress)	Singers (nightclub)
Chemists	Filling station attendants
Lawyers	Dock workers
Diplomats in foreign service	Railroad section hands
Dentists	Night watchmen
Architects	Coal miners
County judges	Restaurant waiters
Psychologists	Taxi drivers
Ministers	Farm hands
Corporate board members	Janitors
Mayors of large cities	Bartenders
Priests	Clothes pressers in a laundry
State government department heads	Soda fountain clerks
Civil engineers	Sharecroppers
Airline pilots	Garbage collectors
Bankers	Street sweepers
Biologists	Shoeshiner

*Hodge, R. W., P. M. Siegel, & P. Rossi, "Occupational Prestige in the United States." 1964. *The American Journal of Sociology,* 70, 286–301.

TABLE 7–6 Prestige Rankings of 43 Service Statuses in the Northern Borneo Tambunan Dusun Village of Sensuron, 1959–1960

Male ritual specialist	Smith	Butcher	Bridge builder
Female ritual specialist	Spear maker	Ritual symbol maker	Rice and palm wine maker
Hunter	Knife maker	Female ritual specialist apprentice	Rubber gardener
Midwife	Bark cloth maker	Male ritual specialist apprentice	Tobacco gardener
Dry rice farmer	Weaver		Gong trader
Wet rice farmer	Bamboo wall maker	Pottery maker	Jar trader
Irrigation ditch builder	Basket weaver	Musical instrument maker	Salt trader
Dam builder	Mat maker	Rattan rope maker	Kerabau (water buffalo) breeder
Blow pipe maker	Tray maker	Rattan knot specialist	Tobacco shredder
Blow pipe dart and case maker	Rice mill maker		Fence maker
House builder	Wood carver		Money lender
	Plow and yoke maker		
	Palm thatch maker		

the "honor" and "personal power" accorded to persons who held such status-roles. The results of this verbal survey are noted in Table 7–6.[6]

In many cultures it is necessary for children to learn the subtle indications that distinguish such signs of *worth* from status-roles *esteem* signs. For instance, most adult Americans know that the two shoulder bars of a Marine captain, when compared to the two sleeve stripes of a Marine corporal, are signs of the worth placed upon the services of the two men to the Marine Corps. Many Americans also know that, if the corporal wears a pale blue ribbon with five white stars over his left blouse pocket and the captain has no such ribbon, the corporal is entitled to greater personal esteem, despite his lesser "worth," or rank, for he is a holder of the Congressional Medal of Honor, the highest symbol of wartime valor awarded by his country.

While learning the ways demeanor, costume, hair styles, cosmetics, jewelry, tattooing, body mutilations, status-role terminology, and worth and esteem signs may be features of status-role or status relationship behavior in a society, children must also be able to regularly distinguish between the *performance* of a role and a regular *performer* of a role. To use Goffman's (1961) example, children must know that, in an American funeral home, the three status-roles of the funeral director, the bereaved, and the deceased must be performed regularly but that only the funeral director will be a continuing, or regular, performer in that status-role or status relationship. Children in every society must come to know or to be able to judge from

[6]The methodology used in measurement of service status worth in a Dusun community follows Warner's (1960) ideas, as amended by Kornhauser (1953) and by Pfautz and Duncan (1950) and as developed in other forms in the work of Hollingshead (1949) and Kaufman (1944). For a discussion of the problems and methods in measurement of status-role worth, see Svalastoga (1965).

evidences available to them in a specific social situation which persons will likely never again or only rarely again engage in particular status-roles. A child's level of awareness of and success in learning the difference between performance of a status-role and a regular performer of a status-role may lend shape to their subsequent social interactions.

Children must also learn details of the commitment of persons to certain of the status-roles they are assigned or fill regularly in a society.[7] For example, Dusun children must come to know and understand the clues that alert Dusun adults to the fact that the old man who often sits and makes or repairs children's toys, tells children stories, or shows them the rudiments of carving a knife handle, weaving a rattan rope, or "old ways" to play a popular game, is also the leading male ritual specialist of the village and area. Dusun children must learn to perceive, from the clues given off in the old man's dress, hair style, tattoos, and particularly his demeanor, that he holds and exercises substantial authority over his fellows which is derived from a ritual specialist's ready access to the supernatural world. Dusun children younger than six years old have usually not learned to perceive the fact that, while the old man may hold other important status-roles in Dusun society, he has fully committed himself to the male ritual specialist status-role as a central fact of his personal existence.[8] Similarly in each culture children must learn, either from direct instruction by adults or peers or from their own observations, the significant clues of status-role commitment. Failure to learn such clues or to exercise social judgments based on them can lead to repeated unsuccessful social performances.

At some point in the process of socialization, children must also learn to understand the social functions of status-role—that is, to know and generally understand the part played by "proper" (or "eufunctional") status-role behavior in the continuing maintenance of the cultural patterns comprising the cultural charter. Children must also learn the ways "improper" (or "dysfunctional") status-role behavior can contribute to the dissolution or destruction of patterns in a cultural charter. Status-role behavior must also generally be viewed by children in terms of its *manifest* and *latent* functions. Where the effects of "proper" status-role acts are openly acknowledged and acclaimed, such social behavior has a manifest function; in situations where the effect of eufunctional status-role behavior is not foreseen but tends to contribute to maintenance of a local cultural charter, such behavior has a latent function.[9] At present there is little descriptive

[7]See Becker, 1960, and Goffman, 1961, for a discussion of the concept of status-role commitment.

[8]For a brief description of Dusun conceptions of the supernatural and the activities of male ritual specialists, see Williams, 1965.

[9]See Merton, 1957, for discussions of the social functions of status-role.

data or analytic understanding of the exact ways most individuals come to generally perceive the necessity of eufunctional status-role acts.

Clubs, Age-Sets, and Cultural Transmission

Some cultures have chosen to make status-role behavior related to age and sex the basis of special social groupings. Such groups have been designated by the terms *club, fraternity, association, sodality,* and *age-grade* or *age-set*. Recruitment to a kin group is based on birth. In contrast, the principle of recruitment to a club is based almost entirely on the attribute of sex, whereas recruitment to an age-set is based principally on chronological age.[10]

An understanding of clubs and age-sets is important for analysis of the socializaton process because cultures with such social groups tend to use them regularly for the transmission of locally significant cultural forms.

Clubs are usually restricted to males.[11] Women's clubs, which are common in American culture, are so uncommon in other cultures that Schurtz, in a 1902 study, concluded that women must be fundamentally unsociable. A modern theoretical interpretation of the predominance of male clubs in human social life would note that the tasks assigned to women in cultural charters usually leave little time for formation of and activities connected with voluntary, nonkinship groups.

In some human societies cultural charters assign males the general responsibility for knowledge of action toward supernatural beings and forces.[12] In some societies men are also given the primary responsibility for defense from external attack and for maintenance of internal order. Societies that assign men exclusively to these tasks also seem to provide them with substantial freedom from routine tasks. Thus men in such cultures actually spend only a small proportion of their time working, since the conduct of war or religious ritual does not occupy great amounts of time in everyday life in a majority of human cultures.[13]

When clubs occur in a culture they usually take one of two forms. A club may be wholly inclusive—that is, be composed of all of the men or all the women is a society—without regard to other status-roles. Clubs may

---

[10]For a comparative discussion of clubs, see Webster, 1908, and Hsu, 1963.

[11]Bohannan (1963, 154) says that "social groupings based on sex are rare" and notes that the criterion of marital state usually also applies in accepting members to such groups.

[12]For a discussion, see Simmons, 1945; Hickman, 1962; Brown, 1963; and Textor, 1967.

[13]Textor (1967, 160–161) reports from a 400-culture sample that only 41 cultures appear extremely bellicose and regularly seek warfare, while another 46 cultures exhibit only "moderate" or "negligible" bellicosity toward other societies. Data of the amount of bellicosity in the remaining 313 cultures of the sample could not be ascertained from the ethnographic literature.

also be highly exclusive, with only a select number of men or women.[14] Whether clubs are inclusive or exclusive, they are focused almost exclusively upon either sacred activities—that is, concerned with the supernatural or sacred activities—or are concerned with nonmystical and nonmagical events. Clubs focused upon sacred activities almost always conduct their affairs in secrecy, with nonmembers facing severe punishment or even death if they are caught observing ceremonies or sacred objects. Clubs focused upon secular activities usually make a point of public displays of their special concerns. On occasion in some cultures the clubs that ordinarily are secretive present public activities, while secular clubs sometimes hold secret meetings.

Among Central Australian native cultures, such as the Arunta, all married men form an inclusive, sacred club. Similar inclusive, sacred clubs are found widely in West Africa, particularly among cultures now in the nations of Nigeria, Liberia, Sierra Leone, and the Republic of the Congo. In these areas, particularly in Sierra Leone and Liberia, women have also formed inclusive, sacred clubs that rival men's clubs in social prestige and political power. The Temne, Limba, and Mende of Sierra Leone and the Kpelle of Liberia have required both boys and girls, on completion of their puberty rituals (see following), to become members of sacred, inclusive clubs for males or females.[15] In these cultures a substantial amount of particular kinds of cultural information, especially information concerning magic, ritual, and the supernatural, is made available to children only through the inclusive, sacred clubs.

Inclusive, secular clubs were formed by many of the American Plains Indians, particularly the Cheyenne, Crow, Kiowa, and Wind River Shoshone societies. These clubs were open to all males, without regard to their age or marital status, as long as they expressed concern with fighting their best in time of war.[16]

Males in Northwest Coast American Indian societies, such as the Kwakiutl, and among the Pueblo Indians of the American Southwest, including the Hopi and Zuni, formed exclusive sacred clubs concerned essentially with magic, sacred ritual, and the supernatural.[17]

Among the Hopi and Zuni, children are led by adults to believe there are named supernatural beings, termed *katcina* (or *kachina*), who control rainfall and crop fertility and appear as masked ceremonial figures at cer-

[14]Clubs have also been classified as "voluntary" and "involuntary" in type (Hsu, 1963, 207).

[15]For discussions of Kpelle inclusive, secret clubs, see Gibbs, 1962, 1965; Welmers, 1949.

[16]For discussions of Cheyenne inclusive, secular clubs, see Grinnell, 1915, 1923; Hoebel, 1960.

[17]For a discussion of Kwakiutl exclusive, secret clubs, see Boas, 1895. For the Hopi, see Titiev, 1944.

Model, Hopi black ogre *katcina* (1969). (Courtesy Museum of Nothern Arizona.)

Model, Hopi butterfly katcina (1969). (Courtesy Museum of Northern Arizona.)

Hopi *katcina* dance (date unknown). (Courtesy Museum of Northern Arizona, Neil Judd Collection.)

Hopi village (circa 1900). (Courtesy Museum of Northern Arizona.)

tain times of the year. The *katcina* figures are adult males who are members of a *kiva*, or exclusive sacred club, generally concerned with maintaining the well-being of their community through magical and religious ceremonies. Boys between eight and ten years old are subjected by masked and elaborately costumed *katcina* figures to a public initiation ritual. Boys are sponsored by ceremonial "fathers" and are prepared for their ordeal by tales recounting the powers and deeds of the feared supernatural and reminded that *katcina* beings have carried rude and ignorant children off to the "other world." The boys to be initiated into the *kiva* are then taken to the entrance of the *kiva* structure and publicly beaten by *katcina* figures. Four days after their public whippings, boys are taken into the *kiva* structure with their ceremonial fathers, where the unmasked *katcina* figures dance and sing a ceremonial welcome to the new *kiva* members. Here the initiates learn that they have been severely beaten and thoroughly frightened by their own fathers and brothers.

Exclusive secular clubs are found widely distributed in the Melanesian culture region. For instance, the Suai of Bougainville Island, in the Solomon Islands, have male clubs concerned primarily with providing members with regular public feasts, at which great amounts of scarce foods are consumed.[18]

Clubs may also be *corporate groups*—that is, social groups that legally acquire and hold property in the form of land, ritual gear, and scarce economic goods transmitted from generation to generation in the name of the club. As corporate entities depending on a local legal system, clubs may have a social position that entitles them to special protection, favored treatment, and privileges not accorded to other, nonkin groups.

All cultures use designations for social categories made up of persons at the same stage, or time, of their life cycles. There is great variation between cultures in designations used for life cycle stages. The term *age-grade* refers to the categories of people recognized by cultures as being at the same point ("baby," "old man," "adolescent") in their lives. Such collectivities of persons have no real social identity or corporate functions.

However some cultures have formed *age-sets,* or social groups based on the principle of recruitment of persons of the same age, without regard to their kinship relations. The crucial distinction between an age-grade and an age-set is that age-sets are corporate social groups in which the major criterion of membership is chronological age. The use of age as a basis for status-role behavior is found in all cultures, but the forming of corporate, nonkin, exclusive social groups based solely on age is a practice found in less than five percent of all cultures. In one survey of cultural features (Murdock, 1957), only 23 of 547 cultures were noted as possessing age-sets.[19] Approximately three-quarters of the 23 cultures possessing age-sets are located in Africa, with the remainder in other world culture regions. In Africa, where only 15 percent of all cultures have age-sets, such groups are most common among East African cultures, such as the Nandi and Kikuyu. Despite the low incidence of age-sets among all human cultures, such corporate, nonkin groups play a vital role in enculturation in societies in which they occur.

---

[18]For a description of Suai exclusive, secular clubs, see Oliver, 1955.
[19]See Murdock, 1957, 1967; Coult & Habenstein, 1965.

Kikuyu boys, Kenya (date unknown). (Courtesy American Museum of Natural History.)

Kikuyu girls, Kenya (date unknown). (Courtesy American Museum of Natural History.)

For instance, among the Nandi of Kenya, males are grouped into a number of age-sets.[20] The first age-set is comprised of all boys under 12 years old. Boys advance to the second age-set after an initiation ritual. Such rituals are held once every seven or eight years. Newly initiated boys become "junior warriors" and for four years are subordinate to a third, or "senior warrior," age-set. At the end of four or more years, on the "retirement" of their seniors, the junior age-set advances to become the senior warrior age-set. Retiring age-set warriors are permitted to marry and begin a routine of daily life and work, generally free of the demands of warfare and keeping internal order in their society.

[20]For a description of Nandi age-sets, see Hollis, 1909. For a comparison of some other East African age-sets, see Prins, 1953.

After their marriages Nandi males progress steadily through a series of additional age-sets, each with greater prestige, political and economic powers, and corporate functions; as members of an "old man" age-set, Nandi males can finally hold ultimate social authority.

Among the Zulu of South Africa, age-sets are formed and function in ways similar to those of the Nandi, except that the organization of age-sets is very closely controlled by the Zulu king.[21] After their initiation all the members of a junior warrior age-set from a local community report to the king's community, where with junior warrior age-sets from other communities they are organized into a special fighting unit, numbering several thousand men.

Zulu "armies" are formed of many such fighting age-sets. A Zulu age-set remains on duty as a fighting unit for approximately ten years. Then all of the men of an age-set are released by the king to return to their local communities and are permitted to marry, have families, and assume the age-status of Zulu "elder," a term referring to all Zulu males from about 25 to 65 years of age. At 65 the men of the "elder" age-set become Zulu "ancestors"—that is, are formally retired from active participation in the daily affairs of their communities.

Thus Nandi and Zulu age-sets function as the basic units of military organization, aid in maintenance of internal order, and serve as units for large-scale labor. In addition, despite their somewhat different definitions of age for membership, age-sets in these societies become the basis of formal local government. In both societies age-sets also function as a *law group*—that is, as a means to protect the personal rights of members. A personal dispute in Nandi and Zulu society between members of different age-sets or with a kinsman becomes a dispute involving whole age-sets. In addition to these functions, Nandi and Zulu age-sets are also charged with responsibility for conduct of certain special rituals concerned with warfare and safety. Thus for Nandi and Zulu boys direct access to most knowledge concerning defense, law, government, and political actions is confined to understanding gained as members of age-set groups.

Among the Nyakyusa of Tanzania, the organization of age-sets is considerably less concerned with warfare and internal peace-keeping activities.[22] At about six years of age, boys join an age-set ranging in age up to 11 or 12 years. Until they become 12 years old, boys of an age-set spend most of each day together, tending herds of their fathers' cattle. At age 12 boys join another age-set, which lives together in a separate "boys' village." Boys return to parental households only for their meals. The remainder of their time is spent working in their fathers' gardens and in various social activities centered upon the "boy's village." Life in an age-set village is highly organized and centers upon individuals learning to work closely with

[21]For a description of and references to Zulu age-sets, see Service, 1963.
[22]For a description of Nyakyusa age-sets, see Wilson, 1951.

others. When the members of an Nyakyusa age-set village are between 20 and 25 years old, they begin to marry and bring wives to the village, where permanent households are established. At the time a man marries, his father deeds him garden land. A married man no longer works for his father as a garden laborer and regularly takes meals in his new household.

When all or most members of an age-set village have married and within about ten years from the time of the last marriage, the fathers of sons living in the age-set village hand over to the age-set all governmental powers and the final responsibility for internal village affairs. A few years later the young sons of the members of the age-set village begin to set up their own community near the village of their fathers. Thus in Nyakyusa society the age-set takes on social functions often associated with kin groups in other cultures. In addition, for older boys it supplants the nuclear family in daily social life and becomes the central focus of the social organization, which is the dominant feature of adult life.

The Ngoni of Malawi separate all boys at the appearance of their "second teeth"—that is, six or seven years old—and place them in an age-set dormitory located within their community.[23] Boys live and eat in the dormitory until they marry or become seriously ill. Ngoni age-set dormitories function as residential "schools" for regular, formal instruction in war, economic, and ritual activities. Boys are instructed by their seniors in the age-set dormitory in the proper ways of social and personal deference and are taught that age and physical strength are the principal criteria of public decision making and authority in Ngoni society.

The transition to life in an age-set is generally an abrupt one, whether among the Nandi, Zulu, Nyakyusa, or Ngoni. In each society young boys are well fed and cared for and are described by trained observers as being socially confident to the point of being "impudent" (Read, 1968, 49). In the first months after joining the age-set, boys in each of the age-set cultures described here have to adjust quickly to being regularly hungry, since only their age-set seniors eat well and fully, to being punished regularly for talking out of turn, and to a nearly complete lack of adult protection and concern for their physical and emotional well-being. Ngoni men view age-set dormitory life as a primary way to ensure that boys learn traditional Ngoni culture without the "soft" and "unmanly" influence of women. Similarly Nandi, Zulu and Nyakyusa males justify age-set life as the best preparation for boys to learn and participate in adult life.

In a comparative study of the forms and functions of age-sets, Eisenstadt (1965, 54) advances the hypothesis that such groups occur in societies in which the regular allocation and distribution of status-roles is not based on membership in kinship groups. At first glance such a hypothesis appears to be useful. It seems logical, in Western European and American terms, that when status-roles are not available in and through kinship groups a

[23]For a discussion of Ngoni age-sets, see Read, 1956, 1960, 1968.

significant social alternative, such as age-sets, would be developed by a society. However this logic does not tend to hold when a study is made of the available comparative data of status-role. Most societies allocate and distribute status-roles outside of kinship groups without forming or using age-sets. Hence Eisenstadt's hypothesis is not sustained, perhaps because his work has not attended to the broader theoretical question of the ways *informal social groups* can also be involved in the allocation, distribution, and learning of status-roles in a society. Some examples of informal social groups in human societies would be children's play groups, neighborhoods, work teams, feasting societies, craft groups, "gangs," and "blood brother-hoods." Informal social groups are usually formed only for brief periods, for attainment of certain limited social aims.[24] Such groups usually function with the cultural values and norms of behavior widely employed in the culture in which the informal group exists. Individuals voluntarily become part of such informal social groups because they share the special interests or preferences manifested by the group. When children become part of informal social groups, they have a special and unofficial opportunity for learning important features of their local culture as these are employed by older members of the group in fulfillment and attainment of their special interests. Hence informal social groups can occupy an important place in an enculturation process, since they make it possible for children to have repeated access to cultural content generally used by adults and without the special hazards of discipline, censure, and authority for misbehavior or failures to learn often imposed on children by kinship and other formal social groups, such as churches and schools.

In not considering the ways that informal social groups can be involved in the allocation, distribution, and learning of status-roles in a society, Eisenstadt apparently missed the point that age-sets have other social counterparts that can provide individuals access to and knowledge concerning status-roles important to society.

Ritual Transitions in Status-Role

Between the ages of 11 and 15 years, children experience fundamental biological changes involving sexual maturation. The gradual changes, which are summed up by the term *puberty*, are taken in most cultures to mark a point between the status-roles of childhood and adulthood. However the biological changes that occur in puberty may be socially recognized by a culture in varying degrees and forms. In some cultures, such as those

---

[24]In contrast, formal social groups exist over long periods of time and have four distinctive features: (1) a set of clearly stated group aims, (2) specific controls for behavior of members, (3) high valuation on "proper" intergroup relationships, and (4) expectation of inclusive personal knowledge by each member concerning all other members.

Satina, a Dusun girl, age 15 years, from
Sensuron village, Tambunan district,
Sabah, Malaysia (T.R. Williams, 1960).

on the central Pacific islands of the Samoa group, there are few formal
social or ritual recognitions of sexual maturity. The Samoan transition from
the status-roles of childhood to those of adulthood is marked by a gradual
development of new activities and concerns and has no periods of induced
social crises or personal stress.[25] A similar lack of concern for special social

[25]See Mead, 1928.

or ritual recognitions of puberty is also found in many other Pacific island cultures, as well as in many native North American Indian cultures.[26]

However cultures in other world areas, including some American Indian cultures such as the Hopi and Zuni, ritually observe puberty for one or both sexes. These observances do not always occur at the onset or even during the actual time of puberty, since cultural definitions of when children take on the status-roles of adults may not at all coincide with the specific biological changes occurring in puberty.

The ritual acts used by cultures to symbolize the transition from childhood to adulthood status-roles vary in the degree of their complexity, public drama, and the amount and duration of personal pain imposed upon children subjected to these ceremonial and symbolic events. It is not uncommon for such ritual acts to involve a form of the symbolic "death" of infancy and childhood status-roles as a quite socially limited and culturally unproductive state and of the symbolic "rebirth" of children in the status-roles of adults, able to enter fully into the affairs and engage in concerns of adult society. To illustrate some of the ways status-role transitions may be formally defined in a culture, a brief description will be given of the ritual acts used by the Arunta of Central Australia to mark the onset of adulthood.[27]

Arunta initiation rituals   Arunta boys usually undergo the first of a complex series of initiation rituals between 10 and 12 years of age. On occasion, when a boy has been regularly rude and disrespectful to the older men of his local group, he may be made to wait until he is between 14 and 16 years old before undergoing the first of the ritual acts marking a transition to adult status-roles.

The appearance of a boy's pubic or facial hair and other physical signs of sexual development are used by the Arunta as criteria for eligibility for initiation. Most Arunta boys have only vague general ideas concerning the rituals they face, since most of these events are conducted in secret and are rarely discussed by adults. As the time for initiation approaches, a boy may begin to boast to his friends that the "old men" will never catch him and that he is not afraid of whatever they will do to him. However most boys are reported to look forward to the initiation rituals as an opportunity to gain adult freedoms and privileges.

[26]While many Pacific island cultures practice *superincision* (a limited form of circumcision) on boys sometimes between infancy and marriage, this act does not appear to be associated with puberty or to be a ritual indication of the transition from childhood to adulthood. For a discussion of the ritual treatment of boys in a Pacific island culture, see Gifford, 1929.

[27]For some other descriptions of ritual observances of status-role transitions from childhood to adulthood, see Radcliffe-Brown, 1922; Gibbs, 1965, 197–240; Dozier, 1966, 57–65, 1970, 140–142, 155–162; Richards, 1956.

Arunta initiation rituals follow very traditional forms, which vary only slightly from one generation to the next. The rules and practices governing these rituals are said by Arunta to have been handed down from mythical ancestors.

Among the Arunta the entire series of initiation rituals follows the broad pattern of events that occur at the death of an aged and respected person. Thus as a boy is led from the camp by the old men, women will wail for him as they do at death, while "bullroarers" (a flat board rapidly whirled at the end of a string) sound in the distance, to represent the voices of spirits waiting to "swallow" the novice and then vomit him up again to be reborn, as is believed to happen at the death of an individual.

Arunta boys tend to be passive subjects in the course of initiation rituals. They are also more nearly "pupils" and "learners" during their initiation than at any other time during their lives. The training and learning at the time of Arunta initiation centers upon boys learning the broad outline of secret knowledge of adult males, particularly ideas concerned with myth, magic, and special rituals for increase of sacred totems. Some details of secret knowledge are also transmitted over many years following completion of the initiation rituals.

The Arunta ritual transition in male status-roles involves four major events, occurring over a period of several years. First a novice is taken away from his home camp by a group of old men, as women wail and the bullroarers sound. When the old men first enter a camp, a boy is told by a parent that a mythical python has come to swallow his foreskin, and he is encouraged to take refuge with his mother, while his wailing adult female relatives take up spears, form a protective ring about the boy and his mother, and threaten the old men. As the men approach the boy, the women flee in mock terror and then finally prostrate themselves, wailing as they do at the time of death.

The boy is led by the old men to a location used regularly to hide sacred totems. Here fully initiated men draw blood from their arm veins, then paint the novice with blood, and ritually drink some of it. It is believed the "blood rite" gives an Arunta boy longevity, courage, and new strength. The ritual is also said to symbolically represent and therefore show the presence of mythical clan ancestors. Then in rapid succession a boy may have his nasal septum pierced, a middle upper front tooth knocked out, and be painted with a solution of red ochre. Arunta sometimes perform the septum-piercing operation before the first initiation ritual to save the great pain which comes with the tooth-knocking blow following the piercing operation. The septum hole is said to be made to enhance a boy's looks. The practice of tooth evulsion is said to create a permanent look on the boy's face which resembles certain dark rain clouds and so to magically

Australian native totemic ritual dance (date unknown), Cundeelee, Western Australia, Ngatajara. (Courtesy American Museum of Natural History.)

enhance his influence and control over the rainfall so vital in the desert life of the Arunta.

Patterns depicting clan totems are drawn in the red ochre smeared over the novice's body. The ochre is said to symbolically represent clan blood and strength. At the conclusion of these ritual acts, a novice is given some general instructions in secret lore and knowledge, then sent with other novices to live in seclusion. During the 9 to 12 months of seclusion, novices must engage in certain ritual acts and avoid social contacts with their parents and female relatives.

The second stage of Arunta initiation rituals begins when novices are led back from seclusion by the old men to their home camp for a "tossing rite" and "presentation of gifts." The tossing rite involves male adults throwing the novice high in the air four times and then throwing burning coals and sticks over the heads of the women dancing about the boy. Arunta believe that these acts symbolize the growing of a novice to the vigor and strength of manhood. Arunta also believe these acts express symbolically the conventional antagonism between the two generations (old and young) involved in the ritual.

Older men begin the second part of the initiation ritual by drawing blood from their arm veins and using it to secure down feathers on their bodies, which are placed in ways to denote sacred totem patterns. Then novices are seated and covered to keep them from seeing the totemic acts conducted by the old men. However novices are kept informed on the meanings of the songs they hear during the totemic rites. After this act the covering is removed, and the novice is permitted to see some of the ritual dancing by the old men and some of the major totemic emblems of their clan.

Australian native ritual bloodletting (date unknown), Laverton, Australia. (Courtesy American Museum of Natural History.)

Australian native men form a "human table" for use in circumcision ritual (date unknown), Warburton Range, Australia. (Courtesy American Museum of Natural History.)

Then just before a ritual circumcision is performed, all the other men make a path for the novice while holding smoking tree boughs and singing sacred songs. Several younger adult men kneel at the end of the path and form a "human table" on which the novice is circumcised. After his foreskin has been cut, the novice is led back to his seclusion camp, while the main Arunta camp picks up and moves some distance away, as is the custom at the death of an adult. Before the novice is led off to a second period of seclusion, he is ceremonially presented two bullroarers and is allowed to sound them for the first time. A novice remains in seclusion until his penis heals. During this time old men may again cut their arm veins and cover a novice's head and chest with their blood to symbolize the boy's entrance into adult life.

When the circumcision scar is fully formed, a novice is permitted to return to his home camp, where he is ceremonially welcomed as an adult by his parents and close relatives. Immediately after his return home a novice is taken by close male relatives on a journey of the water holes and totemic locations in the countryside claimed by his local group and clan.

Before the third stage of ritual transition from childhood to adulthood, a boy is given from 12 to 24 months of regular, secret instruction in the magic, myths, and symbols of his local group and clan. These instructions are given in intensive sessions by old men especially knowledgeable in Arunta lore and belief, providing examples of dances, showing objects, recounting folk tales, and singing songs.

At the close of this period of instruction, a novice leaves his home camp, to the wailing sounds of women and low rumble of the distant bullroarers. Once again the novice lives in seclusion, until completion of all of the third-stage rituals. The third portion of the initiation process begins after a lengthy period of dancing by old men. Then a novice is again led to a table formed by kneeling younger men, laid on his back, and subjected to subincision, a surgical operation in which the urethra is slit open along most of the length of the penis. The novice is then placed face up on the ground, while the men cut open their own subincision scars and dance across the prostrate boy, dripping blood on him to symbolize his rebirth as an adult male. Arunta are said to believe that the penis represents the mythical python, while the incisure cut represents the uterus of the mythical "Fertility Mother." Thus the subincised penis of a novice symbolically represents in the same body part the male and female sex organs. Arunta are also said to believe that the blood from a subincisure cut symbolizes both the blood of afterbirth and of menstruation; covering the prostrate initiate with reopened subincision wounds of initiated men symbolizes his "birth" into adult life.[28]

On completion of the subincision ritual, a novice returns to his home camp. For the next 12 months he is given further special instructions in myth, magic, and ritual. During this time there may be other brief ritual acts, including a repetition of the "blood rite" used in the first stage of the initiation process, ritual feasting to properly introduce the novice to ancestor spirits, and a ritual during which the most sacred totem objects (*djilbilba* boards) are revealed and explained to the novice. It is common for a novice

[28]For some discussions and reviews of other meanings of the subincision ritual, see Cawte, Djagamara, Barrett, 1966; Singer & DeSole, 1967; Cawte, 1968. For a psychoanalytic interpretation of the subincision ritual, see Bettelheim, 1954.

to reopen his subincisure wound during these rituals and to join in the dancing by the initiated men.

The fourth and final stage in the ritual transition from childhood to adulthood for Arunta boys involves a ritual of cicatrization, or scarring, of their bodies. The novice lies face down while older men make 3 to 12 broad cuts across his back. This ritual may be repeated a second and third time, with cicatrices being made on the novice's upper arms and thighs and across his lower abdomen. Healed and well-formed scars are signs that a novice has completed all four stages of initiation. Arunta boys are usually permitted to marry after the healing of the scars from the cicatrization ritual; however there are other ceremonies at which he is permitted to be only an onlooker. A novice is also prohibited from attending other ritual acts until fully knowledgeable about sacred lore.

Arunta boys may also be subjected to a variety of other initiation ritual practices. It is not uncommon for a novice to have fingernails pulled off and to have his head severely cut or bitten bloody during the first and second stages of the ritual transition.

Arunta girls also undergo a series of formal ritual acts marking the transition from childhood to adulthood status-roles. This initiation process is less formal and dramatic and is not as prolonged as the one for boys. Girls receive no direct instruction in sacred knowledge, and the entire community generally does not become involved in the rituals marking the initiation of a girl.

At the first signs of puberty, particularly the appearance of either pubic hair or at the time of first menstruation, a girl leaves to spend a week in seclusion at a shelter built some distance away from her home camp. During her seclusion a girl usually observes several taboos on food, listens to the stories and tales of an older woman who visits with her, and receives instructions concerning sexual and marriage behavior.

At the end of the period of seclusion, a girl bathes and is then ritually decorated by older women with body paint, shells, and ornaments and led back to her home camp with songs, shouts, and cries describing her new status-role as a woman. If a girl has not been given in marriage before the ritual seclusion period, arrangements are made immediately after her return home to secure her marriage. If she has been given in marriage before her seclusion, this social fact is formally confirmed by handing her over to her husband and his kin. This handing-over act can involve ritual sexual intercourse between the girl and a group of her husband's male kin. If arrangements for marriage have been made but not formally confirmed by public announcements, a girl may be "captured" by her future husband and several of the men he calls "brother" while she is out gathering food. Then these men may have sexual intercourse with the girl to confirm her adult status-role.

On her return after a week of seclusion, a girl who has not been given in marriage, either formally or informally, may undergo a further series of ritual acts of initiation while waiting for marriage arrangements. Then shortly after return from her seclusion, a girl is led back into the bush by a small group of older women and men. After a series of brief rituals she will be subjected to a ceremonial cutting of either her vulva, perineum, or hymen. After this act is completed, a girl is decorated with red ochre, white clay, and string and shell necklaces. Before returning to the main camp she may have her nasal septum ritually pierced and be subjected to a ceremony of cicatrization to mark her new status-role as a woman.[29]

Although other rituals take place in a woman's life, particularly at the time of childbirth, the rituals which occur at puberty emphasize a state of sexual maturity and ability to bear children and are seen by the Arunta to mark the formal transition from dependent daughter and child to generally independent wife and woman.

Studies of Initiation Rituals

Wherever ritual acts, particularly those involving formal public drama and severe personal pain, are found associated with the social recognition of puberty, a general cultural theme (see Chapter 8) seems involved—a recognition of the transition from childhood to adulthood. However since many cultures do not formally recognize this transition, a substantial question remains of why there would be such a wide range of ritual practices involved in the way a common human biological fact is viewed by different cultures.

Cohen (1964) has considered this question by studying the social functions and meanings of the various forms of ritual acts that occur during the transition from child to adult. Using a research sample of 65 societies, Cohen first classed each society in his sample as (1) concerned with enculturation of children for *social interdependence*—that is, where individuals are prepared emotionally and personally to be "anchored" in kin groups such as lineages and clans—and (2) concerned with enculturation of children for *social independence*—that is, where individuals are prepared to be "anchored" in the nuclear family. Cohen's contextual analysis of ethnographic data for the 65 societies led him to conclude that 28 societies enculturated children for social interdependence (or life anchored in kin groups), whereas 37 societies enculturated their children for social independence (or life anchored in the nuclear family).[30] Cohen's contextual analysis of

---

[29]It should be noted that initiation rituals for girls may vary between local groups of Arunta in the time sequence involved and rituals used. There is great variation in such rituals among Australian aboriginal societies.

[30]Cohen's research sample includes 54 of the cultures listed in the Appendix.

ethnographic data also revealed that formal initiation rituals marking a status-role transition between childhood and adulthood were used by 18 (or approximately 65 percent) of the 28 societies that enculturate children for social interdependence. In contrast, Cohen found that 36 of the 37 societies that encultrate children for social independence do not use rituals to mark the status-role transition from childhood to adulthood.

On the basis of Cohen's analysis it could be concluded that the wide scope of human concern over status-role transitions at puberty, ranging from an almost total lack of interest among Samoans to the elaborate ritual dramas and personal pain of the Arunta, may depend on the form of the patterns in a culture's social relations subsystem. In other words, Cohen's data suggest that whether a culture socially marks a transition in status-roles from child to adult depends on the position (nuclear family or kin group) children will ordinarily occupy during their adult social life.

In another comparative study of ritual transitions in 75 societies, Brown has suggested from her analysis of ethnographic descriptions of female initiation rituals that formal and ritual observances of a status-role transition occur when a young girl continues to reside at least half the time in her mother's household after her marriage—that is, when a society practices *uxorilocal* or *bilocal* residence after marriage.[31]

Brown also suggests that when a society depends heavily on the work of girls and young women to make a notable contribution to subsistence activities formal initiation rituals will be held to mark the transition from the status-roles of girl to woman.

In addition, Brown proposes that those few (10 of 75) societies that subject a girl to great pain during status-role transition rituals do so because of a basic need to overcome severe conflicts of sexual identity fostered in female infants and young girls by their acute awareness that the scarce social and material resources on which they depend and therefore greatly desire are usually controlled by adult males.

In another study of ritual transitions in status-roles, Young (1962) has made a comparative analysis of the social functions of male initiation rituals which seems to broaden the conclusions offered by Cohen and Brown. Young notes that male initiation rituals appear to be caused by the presence in a society of an exclusively male club or organization. This male club, in turn, is caused by a type of "middle level" economic system neither producing great surpluses of goods nor functioning close to a survival level, which Young believes to be finally caused in its turn by the physical envi-

---

[31]See Brown, 1963. *Uxorilocal* (or *matrilocal*) residence after marriage refers to the practice whereby a newly married couple lives in the household, or domicile, of the wife's family. *Bilocal* residence refers to the practice whereby a newly married couple may choose to live near the parents of either spouse. For a discussion of the problems in use of such classifications, see Bohannan, 1963, 86–99.

ronment of a culture. Hence for Young the presence (or absence) of male initiation rituals, such as those found among the Arunta, depends on a cause-effect sequence which he postulates as (1) *physical environment type* → (2) *"middle level" of economic production* → (3) *presence of exclusive male organizations* → (4) *use of male initiation rituals at puberty.*

Thus Brown and Young have extended Cohen's conclusions concerning the social functions of initiation rituals to include other cultural practices such as (1) certain marital residence patterns, (2) particular subsistence activities and types, (3) levels of economic organization and activity, (4) the presence of exclusive male organizations, (5) the presence of certain climatic types, and (6) degree of conflict in sexual identity common to a society. Brown's and Young's explanations seem to imply, as does Cohen's, that the reason some cultures do not formally observe a transition from childhood to adulthood is because of a distinct lack of concern with specific cultural patterns, such as marital residence practices, subsistence practices, and sex identity conflicts.

Whiting (1964), in his work on the causal effects of climate on ritual circumcision in the status-role transition from child to adult, has provided some indications that there may be further and alternative ways not only of viewing this particular transition but also of more broadly defining and considering the origins and causal effects of all such ritual transitions.

Whiting and his associates have noted statistically the effects of several factors on the status-role transitions from child to adult. Their argument, complexly structured, involves a number of major assumptions concerning the ways certain patterns and climate are interrelated and the ways specific cultural practices are interrelated, including (1) the practice of a mother and infant sleeping together for a long period during infancy while the father sleeps separately, (2) the practice of a postpartum taboo on sexual intercourse between parents for a year or more after a child's birth, and (3) virilocal residence after marriage.[32]

Whiting (1964) has pointed out that there is a significantly biased geographical distribution of societies in which boys are circumcised during ritual observances of the status-role transition from child to adult; such a ritual practice commonly occurs in the tropical climate zones of Africa and a few Pacific islands, while it is absent entirely in tropical South America, as well as in North America, and statistically is insignificant as a practice among Eurasian cultures. Whiting believes that the three cultural practices just noted (exclusive mother-child sleeping arrangements, prolonged postpartum sex taboo, virilocal residence) occur together as a basic cultural solution to certain environmental problems essentially found in hot, wet, humid, tropical areas.

---

[32]*Virilocal* (or *patrilocal*) residence refers to the practice whereby a newly married couple lives in the household, or domicile, of the husband's family.

In a tightly reasoned presentation based on statistical analysis of the distribution of these three culture traits, Whiting demonstrates the direct association between circumcision and tropical climate. His findings reveal that exclusive mother-child sleeping arrangements seem strongly influenced by the average winter temperatures experienced by a culture; that a prolonged postpartum sex taboo is strongly influenced by protein deficiency in a nursing mother's diet, which in turn is a function of a rainy, tropical climate; and that virilocal residence is directly associated with the practice of polygyny (see Chapter 6), which in turn is directly associated with a prolonged postpartum sex taboo.

Whiting's fundamental theoretical contribution in this work is his basic concern for deriving a new method for understanding the difficult problem of causality in studies of the socialization process.[33] He notes correctly that the correlation method used in socialization studies cannot indicate the *direction* of causation. Whiting also points out that, in research on the socialization process, the direction of causation of phenomena must rest for now on estimates of the "relative plausibility" (Whiting, 1964, 524) of the observer's assumptions made about causal direction. In the study described here Whiting did not assume that temperature and climate are the *effect* of customs, such as mother-child sleeping arrangements, a prolonged postpartum sex taboo, or the practice of virilocal residence at marriage. Any association, notes Whiting, between a climatic variable and a culture trait can only be plausibly interpreted either as an *effect* of climate on the culture trait or as an effect of climate upon some other culture trait, or pattern, which in turn has a direct effect upon the trait in question. Thus Whiting notes that it is not reasonable to assume that exclusive mother-child sleeping arrangements cause a tropical climate or that a postpartum sex taboo causes a rainy climate. Whiting's basic theoretical contribution in this work, which is an important one in socialization research, is his proposal of a systematic way to think about causation in studies of the socialization process in which some variables, such as ecological factors, determine the cultural patterns associated with them. Whiting's approach considerably broadens the suggestions for the causes of ritual observances of the transition from childhood to adulthood offered by Cohen, Brown, Young, and others and points the way to development of a genuine mathematical, rather than a statistical, approach to scientific studies of causation in the process of socialization.

CLASS AND SOCIALIZATION

Individuals behaving with respect to the same polar social positions—that is, status-roles—often develop awareness of their common interests, par-

---

[33]Whiting first formally expressed this concern in a work on the social functions of male initiation rituals. See Whiting, Kluckhohn, & Anthony, 1958. See also Whiting, 1973.

ticularly in contrast to the interests of other individuals. When a large number of persons in a society act upon awareness of their common status-role positions, they may constitute a social class.

The personal interests and awareness that arise from holding similar polar social positions in one society may be quite different in other societies. In many societies such interests center upon the acquisition and use of scarce resources, such as food, tools, land, and "money." However classes have also been formed on the basis of shared religious belief and action or on the conditions of personal freedom—that is, differentiations between "master" and "slaves." Classes have been based on exhibitions of courage in warfare, courtesy, and "handsomeness" of personal appearance.[34] Classes also may "cross-cut" kin groups in a society, as was the case among the Aztec of Mexico, in which the "honorary lords" were recruited from all Aztec clans.

Life Chances and Class

There are strong indications, regardless of how social class is measured or defined, that opportunities to stay alive, to be born alive, and to grow to adulthood are related to relative social class position; there seems little question now that, at least in American and Western European societies, the infant death rate markedly decreases with increasing family income and therefore with differential class position. Both the frequency and duration of disabling and crippling infant and child illnesses are also demonstrably related, in the United States, to family income and therefore to social class position of the parents. The general state of American infant and child physical well-being—that is, the state of nourishment and therefore the potential for growth and development—are also directly affected by the social class of parents.

For a contemporary American child the opportunity to learn the culture, particularly in formal educational settings such as schools and colleges, is directly affected by occupations of parents and hence by the social class of parents. There is a clear relationship in the United States between amount of adult schooling, occupational achievement, and annual income. This relationship, which generally results in those persons with the least schooling being employed in the least desirable and lowest prestige manual labor and farm occupations and receiving the lowest annual incomes, means that children of such parents have less opportunity for formal education, especially beyond the primary school grades. In American society the highest annual incomes and lifetime earning expectations generally appear to be restricted to persons completing four or more years of

---

[34]See Richardson, 1940, and Mishkin, 1940, for a description of the kinds of common interests used by the Kiowa, a North American Indian society, to define social classes.

college education. The relationship between parental education, occupation, and income also seems to significantly affect the development of a wide range of infants' and children's abilities and potentials (see Chapters 2 and 4), particularly those apparently vital in further learning of complex social and cultural information. In other words, whether American children develop some individual potentials and abilities to learn appears directly related to their relative social positions, which are generally dependent in turn upon the social class position of parents. As noted earlier, class position also contributes directly to the kinds and degrees of social and cultural isolation experienced by children. When a social class position has produced long-term social or cultural isolation, persisting over several familial generations, consistently different forms of social and cultural behavior can arise. Such behavior differences can be in cultural ideology, forms of kinship and kin groups, or judgments of the worth of some kinds of social behavior, such as sexual and "criminal" activities, as well as in "taste" for dress, personal adornment, and displays of personal power and prestige. Statistics of arrests in the United States for deviant sexual and criminal behavior clearly indicate that persons with the least education and annual income have a significantly greater chance of arrest and conviction than "middle-class" citizens. The research evidence of the relationships between social class and "life chances" was noted in the early 1900s by scholars concerned with studies of American and European societies. Comments concerning differential life chances in particular social classes led to increasing attention being paid to research seeking to relate social class and the process of socialization. In most such research the focus of concern has been on the consequences for the individual of having matured in nuclear family and kin group settings in specific social classes. It has been assumed in much of this research that, since nuclear families and kin groups will have the economic resources, knowledge, and power typical of other families and kin groups in the same class, children will occupy essentially the same social class positions as their parents. It has also been assumed in such research that the enculturation of children by adult members of a nuclear family and kin group involves the transmission of particular cultural and social knowledge, as well as styles of personal behavior usual for the social classes of adults.

Research on Social Class and Socialization

Steere (1964) has noted that in the United States concern about relationships between social class and the socialization process extended over a period of more than 100 years before any systematic attempts were made by scholars to define and study such phenomena. A 1929 publication by Lynd and Lynd concerning life in an American community contained five chapters on enculturation in the "family" and schools, with particular reference to the ways social class affected a child's life chances. This research may be said to be the first modern attempt to give specific attention to reporting and analyzing empirical data for specific evidence of relationships between social class and cultural transmission. This work was followed by more detailed empirical studies of social class and the socialization process made by Anderson (1936), Davis and Dollard (1940), Warner and Lunt (1941), Davis, Gardner, and Gardner (1941), Davis and Havighurst (1946), Havighurst and Taba (1949), Havighurst and Neugarten (1955), and others.

A key research method in empirical studies of relations between class and socialization from 1929 through the late 1950s was to contrast the specific enculturation practices of different classes within one community. Thus in a study based on a sample of 100 white and black, lower- and middle-class mothers in Chicago, Davis and Havighurst (1946, 1947) and Ericson (1946) noted that middle-class American families, whether white or black, were inflexible in following a rigid schedule of infant and child feeding, weaning, toilet training, and discipline, whereas lower-class white and black families were flexible in regard to such enculturation practices. These data of class differences in enculturation were interpreted, in the context of psychological theories prevailing in the 1940s, as tending to produce children with markedly different personalities. Middle-class children raised under inflexible schedules of enculturation were said to become very demanding, self-assertive, and rigid adults, particularly with respect to control of their sexual and aggressive impulses. In contrast, lower-class children enculturated under a more flexible schedule of training than were middle-class children were believed to become adults with a more spontaneous ability to cope successfully with their aggressive and sexual impulses.

A 1946 analysis by Green of the kinds and levels of children's anxiety resulting from a concern with securing love through successful performances according to parental expectations concluded that middle-class children, when compared to lower-class children, were made more neurotic by middle-class enculturation practices. Green assumed that his conclusion was valid because it seemed clear from the earlier empirical research concerning relations between social class and the socialization process, and particularly enculturation practices in American society, that middle-class parents focused on maintaining very tight controls for sexual and aggressive impulses in order to aid their child in gaining a more successful status-role achievement and greater mobility between social classes. Green also assumed that lower-class children were free from most impulse control training because of a lack of any adult concern with success in status-role achievement. Hence Green concluded that lower-class children were much less anxious and neurotic because they were not made to conform to parental concerns about tightly controlled sexual and aggressive impulse controls. The conclusions drawn by Green were strongly supported by data of American social class and enculturation reported by Davis and Havighurst and by Ericson. Thus by extension of this argument, a relationship between class and the socialization process seemed clearly defined.

However a study by Sewell (1952), based on interviews with the mothers of 165 rural Wisconsin children, concerned relationships between reported early childhood enculturation practices and observations of later behavior by mothers and teachers concluded that it was entirely unwarranted to make any inferential move from supposedly class-determined enculturation practices to later childhood behavior and personality characteristics. In 1954 Maccoby, Gibbs, and their coworkers presented the results of a study of 198 "upper-middle" and 174 "upper-lower" class mothers living in the Boston metropolitan area; the study was especially concerned with the relationship between social class position and enculturation practices. This work found that parents in the "upper-middle" class were more "permissive and less severe" than were parents of the "upper-lower" class. These data, which were a reversal of data offered by Davis and Havighurst and by Ericson in their Chicago study of social class and the socialization process, were interpreted by Maccoby et al. as possibly reflecting either (1) basic changes through time in the child-rearing practices of the American "lower" and "middle" classes or (2) different definitions of social class in the Chicago and Boston studies.

In a response to the study by Maccoby et al., Havighurst and Davis (1955) offered a reanalysis of their earlier data, based on a subsample they believed to be more comparable to the ages of mothers interviewed in the Boston study of social class and socialization. On the basis of their second analysis, Davis and Havighurst concluded that there were in fact "substantial and large" disagreements between the Chicago and Boston studies, which they attributed either to basic errors in research procedure and method in the different studies or to fundamental changes in child-rearing practices in the United States.

Noting the marked differences in the Chicago and Boston studies, Sewell and Haller (1956) designed a research project to test whether there really could be any relationship between the social class of a family and a child's "personality adjustments," or behavior. On the basis of a study of 1462 children in grades four through eight in what was termed a "culturally homogeneous" small Wisconsin town with a wide range of status-roles and distinct social classes, Sewell and Haller concluded that in fact there was a statistically "positive and significant" association between their measures of differential social status, or class, and a child's personality adjustment. This study indicated, as Davis and Havighurst had concluded, that the contrasts and differences between the Chicago and Boston studies of social class and personality were the result either of methods used or of profound changes in class orientations with respect to enculturation.

In a final report on the Boston study, Sears, Maccoby, and Levin (1957) noted that the evidence of their research clearly pointed to the fact that middle-class American mothers were generally more permissive and less punitive toward their children than were working-class mothers. The research conducted by Barker and Wright (1954) and by Miller and Swanson (1958) concerning social class and personality also appeared to lend substantial support to the conclusions of Sears et al.

In 1957 Littman, Moore, and Pierce-Jones published the results of research on social classes and socialization conducted in Eugene, Oregon. Using a sample of 206 pairs of white parents, each with identifiable social class differences and whose children were of preschool or school ages, these authors conducted detailed interviews on specific enculturation practices. On the basis of their statistical analyses of interview responses and measures of the parents' social class differences, they concluded there are in fact no profound differences in enculturation practices because of the social classes of parents. Littman et al.

This contradiction of both the Chicago and Boston studies concerning a relationship between social class and personality was followed by a study by Sewell and Haller (1959) that statistically demonstrated that Green's (1946) conclusions were essentially correct—that is, there is a specific relationship between a child's anxiety and neurosis and the social class of his parents. However Sewell and Haller's data of class and anxiety were exactly the opposite of those noted by Davis and Havighurst (1946), Ericson (1946), and Green, since lower-class children seemed to be more anxious than were middle-class children. Sewell and Haller explained this reversal by noting that lower-class children were acutely aware of their social class positions, in contrast to the positions of their middle-class schoolmates, which led them to "frustrations" and "anxieties" resulting from their desire to change social class but inability to control any means to cause the desired change. Sewell and Haller (1959, 519) also supported this conclusion by noting that Davis had earlier (1944) demonstrated and documented the existence of the production of high levels of personal anxiety in children because of their concerns over their inability to change social classes.

At this point, because of the conflicting theoretical views and conclusions of these and other studies, Bronfenbrenner (1958) reviewed research concerning relationships between social class and the socialization process, particularly as this relationship affected personality development.[35] Bronfenbrenner pointed out that after World War I there had been a marked

---

[35]See also White, 1957.

increase in the awareness of middle-class American parents that they were being portrayed in scientific literature, as well as in popular accounts, as rigid, demanding, and inflexible parents and as causing lasting harm to the personalities of their children. Hence the new awareness by middle-class Americans of their parental acts had rapidly altered their whole orientation from rigid and inflexible to permissive and flexible enculturation practices. Bronfenbrenner concluded that middle-class American parents were in the process of becoming similar to working-class parents in their attitudes toward enculturation. Bronfenbrenner also proposed that the essential differences between the Chicago and Boston studies of social class and personality were not the result of methods of research but reflected rapidly changing attitudes in different regions of the United States.

In a review of research concerning the relationships between social class and the socialization process, Sewell (1961) noted Bronfenbrenner's conclusions regarding the influence of changing views of American parents in studies of class and socialization. Sewell pointed out that the confusion of theory from such studies represents conclusions that were founded upon such limited and biased research samples that no reliable scientific conclusions could possibly have been reached by investigators. Sewell also noted that no single study seeking to relate class and enculturation was representative of the entire American society, or of any region of the United States, or even of any clearly definable social system. Sewell observed that statistical techniques used in some studies were not appropriate for the problem studied and that there was a lack of conceptual clarity in definitions of the terms *social class* and *personality*. Sewell concluded that, because of such weaknesses in theory and method, more definite conclusions about the relationship between social class position and children's personality must await future studies carefully designed and systematically conducted by theoretically sophisticated scholars. In his closing remarks Sewell also noted some of the research procedures, techniques, and theoretical approaches that could be used in seeking to conduct future research relating social class and the socialization process.

In the decades of the 1960s and 1970s research concerning relationships between class and the socialization process has tended to follow some of the directions suggested by Sewell. For instance, after earlier research seeking to relate social class position and parental authority, Kohn (1959a, 1959b, 1963) specified some patterns of cultural ideology, such as reliance upon self-direction as opposed to direction of activity imposed by the authority of social superiors, that seem to be involved in the lives of parents holding different status-role positions (Kohn, 1963). Kohn concluded that class differences in parent-child relationships are basically the product of differences in parental values reflecting differing conditions of social and cultural life, particularly those involving occupations.

Refining these ideas further Kohn, in conjunction with Pearlin (1966), conducted a "cross-national" study comparing parental values and parent-child relations in Turin, Italy, and in Washington, D.C. Pearlin and Kohn concluded that three aspects of parental occupation—(1) degree of supervision experienced, (2) whether an individual works principally with things, people, or ideas, and (3) the degree of self-reliance required in a job—are directly related to parental expectations for their children in both an Italian and an American city, with middle-class parents in both cities greatly valuing children's self-reliance, whereas lower-class parents valued their children's conformity to authority imposed by other persons. Pearlin and Kohn concluded their study by noting that a large part of the social class differences reported between the enculturation practices of middle-class and lower-class parents in two different societies reflect the fact that differing patterns of cultural ideology influence parental occupations, which in turn influence the ways parents expect children to behave.

In later studies Kohn, working in conjunction with Schooler (1969), refined the ideas of his earlier studies through a more precise specification of the cumulative effects of the amount of education and of occupational position on parental values and subsequently on adult expectations for children.

Despite such movements to more theoretically sophisticated and exacting definitions of the problem and use of new research procedures, it remains apparent that, even though social class differences in a society may be established clearly, it still is not certain that such differences have any specific or lasting effects upon the enculturation process of a society. In a review of a series of articles edited by Grey (1969) concerning relationships between social class and personality, Lauer (1970) noted, as Sewell (1961) had nearly a decade earlier, that there still was no conclusive evidence from research that indicates with clarity the nature of a relationship between social class and the socialization process, particularly in cultures where social mobility may be important. This conclusion by Lauer remains valid in the early 1980s.[36]

Since the end of World War II, with a few exceptions, such as the study by Pearlin and Kohn (1966) and in some work similar to that conducted in Ceylon by Straus (1957), there has been a lack of sustained attention to transcultural, holistic, and transtemporal variables in the study of possible relationships between social differentiation, whether in the form of class or age-grades, and the process of socialization. While this inattention is an understandable consequence of the primary professional concerns of scholars conducting research on this question, it does shape any conclusions to be drawn from the existing body of research literature. While data

[36]See Kerckhoff, 1972; Wandersman, 1973; Porter, 1974; Rosenbaum, 1975; Direnzo, 1977; Harris, 1979; Mortimer, 1975; Mortimer & Lawrence, 1979.

concerning the "life chances" of infants and children (neonatal death, infant mortality, and infant disease and malnutrition rates) seem indisputably related to the income, education, and occupations of parents in some urbanized and industrialized Western European societies and in American society, there is little empirical evidence of such a fact in the remainder of the world's nonliterate, nonurban, and nonindustrial cultures. Furthermore it is not at all certain at present that there is a transculturally and holistically valid relationship between class position and the socialization process. The large amount of evidence, which is now transculturally and holistically certain, that human adults behave generally following their earlier social and cultural experiences does not necessarily always mean that in every culture the social positions or occupations, education, or income of a child's family or kin groups significantly and determinately shape and direct enculturation and an individual's personality and behavior. It seems to follow logically, in a Western cultural and social milieu, that if life chances are affected by parental occupation and income, and early experience does influence later behavior, then there should be a direct relationship between such social and cultural phenomena. However reasonable this logical analysis and these assumptions seem to a Western European or American scholar, they may not be at all valid in other and quite different cultural settings.

A considerable amount of well-defined research, based upon prior work, remains to be accomplished before it can be said with confidence that social class directly and causally influences, or is directly related to, the socialization process in particular ways.

CASTE AND SOCIALIZATION

Some human societies have chosen to accentuate social differences by choosing to eliminate or severely restrict the possibility of access to or changes in achieved status-roles. This has sometimes been accomplished through linking specific occupations with the concept of descent—that is, through defining the essential tasks to be performed in a society as ascribed only through an individual's birth to parents with particular occupations. This practice may be reinforced by requiring children of parents holding specific occupations to practice group endogamy—that is, to marry only other children of parents holding the same occupations. A society which has social groups linked to specific occupations through descent and endogamy may be said to have *social castes*.

A society may have a number of social castes. When social castes become hierarchically organized and ranked for their worth, special qualities, and social attributes, a *caste system* may develop. Caste systems have been reported in societies of the Arabian Peninsula, Polynesia, North Africa, East Africa, Guatemala, Japan, and native North America.

Perhaps the best known example of a caste system society was that of India prior to 1947. Many different occupations served as the basis for a large number of individual castes, while most castes were joined in a complex system in which some castes were believed to have greater social worth and esteem than did other castes. The Indian caste system also had a complex religious basis and rationale, so that before being outlawed by the present Indian constitution, castes had come to have social rank and esteem based not only on occupation but also on religious practices, such as the type of ritual sacrifice followed by the members of a caste.

In a society with castes, individuals tend to derive their personal esteem, rank, and prestige from their caste membership. Caste members find most personal choices closely defined and restricted by the attributes of their caste. In addition to narrowing their choices in marriage and occupation, individuals growing up in a caste system may find their choices quite restricted in their style and color of dress, selection of foods, access to public places, political action, persons to be touched, education, and even the type of funeral permitted.

Individuals enculturated in a caste find the social group to which they belong provides the corporate and personal benefits of belonging to a trade union, a feasting society, a clan, a club, a health insurance company, a savings society, a political party, and a funeral association.

Descriptive accounts of the enculturation process in a society with a caste system are fragmentary and incomplete, especially with reference to attention to specific ways parents and other adults transmit cultural and social knowledge to infants and children and concerning the ways children behave as they learn the essential features of caste life.[37] It is clear, however, that children maturing in a caste have to learn a broad complex of definitions of status-roles. In fact, available ethnographic data appear to indicate that, while children growing up in a caste do have certain clearly defined limits on the ways they can act and upon the ideas to be learned, they also must learn the many ways they cannot act and the details of knowledge they are not supposed to acquire. In effect, enculturation in a caste or in a caste system tends to be quite complex due to "negative" culture which must be acquired—that is, because children must also learn well and quickly those aspects of culture they must not learn, yet still be aware of, in order to act as though they do not know such things. Hence it appears that the enculturation process is no less complex with regard to status-role learning in an Indian village than it would be in noncaste so-

[37]For some descriptions of enculturation features in castes or in caste systems, see Beals, 1962; Carstairs, 1958; Dube, 1955; Hutton, 1946; Lewis, 1958; Marriott, 1955; Mayer, 1960; Ryan, 1953; Tumin, 1952; Wiser & Wiser, 1963.

cieties in Truk, Samoa, the Central Australian desert, or the high plains of native North America.

CONCLUSIONS

Children in every society must learn the many details of cultural patterns concerned with the assignment of tasks, the definitions of jobs to be performed, and the formal and informal practices of recruitment to such tasks. In all cultures children learning a cultural charter must master complex and highly detailed conceptions of the social statuses and roles. Children must also come to know and effectively use cultural conceptions of their own and of other's social rights and duties as these are associated with various tasks to be performed and the instructions for carrying them out. Children must also learn and understand the clues to different status-roles or status relationships implied in the demeanor, costumes, hair styles, cosmetic uses, jewelry, tattoos, body mutilations, special terminology, and prestige signs of others.

Descriptive data is scarce at present for use in analyzing the ways infants and children actually learn and use status-roles, especially those associated with social class differences. It seems, however, that such learning should be a vital aspect of the socialization process. Goffman (1961, 87) has concluded that the learning of social rights and duties comprises the "basic unit" of the entire socialization process, since he believes that it is through such learning that all tasks in a society are allocated and arrangements are devised to ensure a regular performance of social rights and duties. In contrast, Goodenough (1965) adopts a more cautious view of the overall importance of status-role learning in the socialization process. Goodenough believes that a large amount, but not all, of social learning by infants and children in any society involves detailed knowledge of social duties to others and the specific situations in which such duties are owed.

However there is no substantive evidence that demonstrates that status-role learning has a central role in the socialization process or is critical to the existence and operation of that process. A useful theoretical approach to analysis of the socialization process would seem to be one that has no fundamental or primarily important requirements that some categories, features, or parts of that process must be chosen over others. It appears sufficient for now to say that if children are to become successful adults in a society they obviously must learn the details of cultural patterns concerned with definitions of tasks to be performed in a society, the ways such tasks are performed, and the ways persons are recruited to such tasks. In many societies children must also learn details of a cultural pattern concerned with social classes. However successful adult performance in a society also involves knowing and following the details of many other cultural patterns, including kinship, kin groups, food quest, religious belief, grammar, and so on.

SUMMARY

This discussion has been concerned with describing some of the possible relationships between the cultural patterns of status-role and class and the socialization process. The chapter began with a review of concepts and examples of status-role behavior and noted some of the kinds of signs, symbols, and ideas children must learn if they are to comprehend and successfully use status-roles. The discussion then turned to a brief review of special social groups, clubs, and age-sets, which are based on selected aspects of status-role, such as sex and age, and which in some societies are regularly used in transmission of locally significant forms of culture.

In the next part of the discussion an account was given of ritual actions used in some societies to mark the transition in status-roles culturally associated with the onset of puberty. A summary description was given of Arunta ritual observances marking puberty to illustrate the complex ways some societies have chosen to dramatize a transition from status-roles of childhood to those of adulthood. This portion of the discussion also included a review of studies seeking to explain the existence and importance of ritual transitions in status-roles at puberty. The discussion then turned to an examination of the life chances and personal expectations of individuals born to parents in different social classes. This was followed by a review of studies seeking to demonstrate a relationship between social class and the socialization process. The chapter concluded with a summary of the ways castes, a special form of social class characterized by the linking of social groups to specific occupations through descent and endogamy, may be related to the process of socialization.

REFERENCES CITED AND SUGGESTED READINGS

ACOCK, A.C., & V.L. BENGTSON. 1980. "Socialization and Attribution Processes—Actual versus Perceived Similarity Among Parents and Youth." *Journal of Marriage and the Family*, 42, 501–515.

ANDERSON, J.E. 1936. *The Young Child in the Home.* New York; Appleton-Century-Crofts.

BANTON, M. (ed.). 1965a. *The Relevance of Models for Social Anthropology.* New York: Holt, Rinehart & Winston.

———. 1965b. *Roles: An Introduction to the Study of Social Relations.* London: Tavistock.

BARBER, B. 1957. *Social Stratification.* New York: Harcourt Brace Jovanovich.

BARKER, R.G., & H.F. WRIGHT. 1954. *Midwest and Its Children: The Psychological Ecology of an American Town.* Evanston, Ill.: Row, Peterson.

BARNETT, M.A., J.A. HOWARD, L.M. KING, & & G.A. DINO. 1980. "Antecedents of Empathy; Retrospective Accounts of Early Socialization." *Personality and Social Psychology Bulletin,* 6, 361–365.

BATES, F.L. 1956. "Position, Role, and Status: Reformulation of Concepts," *Social Forces,* 34, 313–321.

BEALS, A.R. 1962. *Gopalpur; A South Indian Village.* New York: Holt, Rinehart & Winston.

BEARISON, D.J. 1979. "Sex-Linked Patterns of Socialization." *Sex Roles,* 5, 11–18.

BECKER, H.S. 1960. "Notes on the Concept of Commitment." *American Journal of Sociology,* 66, 32–40.

BENGSTON, V.L. 1975. "Generation and Family Effects in Value Socialization." *American Sociological Review,* 40, 32–40.

BERGEL, E.E. 1962. *Social Stratification.* New York: McGraw-Hill.

BERREMAN, G. 1968. "Caste: The Concept of Caste." In D.L. Sills (ed.), *International Encyclopedia of the Social Sciences.* New York: Macmillan and The Free Press, pp. 333–339.

BETTELHEIM, B. 1954. *Symbolic Wounds, Puberty Rites, and the Envious Male.* New York: The Free Press.

BIANCHI, L. 1975. "Family, Socialization and Social Classes." *Ressegna Italiana di Sociologia,* 16, 379–420.

BLOCK, J., A. VON DER LIPPE, & J. BLOCK. 1973. "Sex-role and Socialization Patterns: Some Personality Concomitants and Environmental Antecedents." *Journal of Consulting and Clinical Psychology,* 41, 321–341.

BOAS, F. 1895. *The Social Organization and the Secret Societies of the Kwakiutl Indians.* Washington, D.C.: U.S. National Museum, Reports.

BOHANNAN, P. 1963. *Social Anthropology.* New York: Holt, Rinehart & Winston.

BRAUNGART, R.G. 1971. "Family Status, Socialization, and Student Politics: A Multivariate Analysis." *American Journal of Sociology,* 77, 108–130.

BRONFENBRENNER, U. 1958. "Socialization and Social Class through Time and Space." In E.E. Maccoby, T.M. Newcomb, & E.L. Hartley (eds.), *Readings in Social Psychology,* (3rd. ed.). New York: Holt, Rinehart & Winston, pp. 400–425.

————. 1962. "The Role of Age, Sex, Class and Culture in Studies of Moral Development." *Religious Education,* 53, 5–17.

BROOM, L. 1959. "Social Differentiation and Stratification." In R.K. Merton, L. Broom, & L.S. Cottrell, Jr. (eds.), *Sociology Today.* New York: Basic Books, pp. 429–441.

BROWN, J.K. 1963. "A Cross-Cultural Study of Female Initiation Rites." *American Anthropologist,* 65, 837–853.

BURTON, R.V., & J.W.M. WHITING. 1961. "The Absent Father and Cross-Sex Identity." *Merrill-Palmer Quarterly of Behavior and Development,* 7, 85–95.

CARSTAIRS, G.M. 1958. *The Twice-Born: A Study of a Community of High-Caste Hindus.* Bloomington: Indiana University Press.

CAWTE, J.E. 1968. "Further Comment on the Australian Subincision Ceremony." *American Anthropologist,* 70, 961–964.

CAWTE, J.E., N. DJAGAMARA, & M. BARRETT. 1966. "The Meaning of Subincision of the Urethra to Aboriginal Australians." *British Journal of Medical Psychology,* 39, 245–253.

COHEN, Y.A. 1964. *The Transition from Childhood to Adolescence.* Chicago: Aldine.

COOK-GUMPERZ, J. 1973. *Social Control and Socialization: A Study of Class Differences in the Language of Maternal Control.* London: Routledge & Kegan Paul.

COULT, A.D., & R.W. HABENSTEIN. 1965. *Cross Tabulations of Murdock's World Ethnographic Sample.* Columbia: University of Missouri Press.

COUNT-van M.G. 1973. "The Validity of Parent-Child Socialization Measures: A Comparison of the Use of Assumed and Real Parent-Child Similarity with Criterion Variables." *Genetic Psychology Monographs,* 88, 201–277.

DAVIS, A. 1944. "Socialization and Adolescent Personality." In *Forty-Third Yearbook of the National Society for the Study of Education.* Chicago: National Society for the Study of Education, Part I.

DAVIS, A., & J. DOLLARD, 1940. *Children of Bondage.* Washington, D.C.: American Council on Education.

DAVIS, A., B.B. GARDNER, & M.R. GARDNER. 1941. *Deep South.* Chicago: University of Chicago Press.

DAVIS, A., & R.J. HAVIGHURST. 1946. "Social Class and Color Differences in Child Rearing." *American Sociological Review,* 11, 698–710.

———. 1947. *Father of the Man.* Boston: Houghton-Mifflin.

DAVIS, K., & W. MOORE. 1945. "Some Principles of Stratification." *American Sociological Review,* 10, 242–249.

DENZIN, N.K. 1975. "Play, Games and Interaction: The Contexts of Childhood Socialization." *Sociological Quarterly,* 16, 458–478.

DEUTSCH, M., I. KATZ & A.R. JENSEN (eds.). 1968. *Social Class, Race and Psychological Development.* New York: Holt, Rinehart & Winston.

DE VOS, G.A. 1975. "Affective Dissonance and Primary Socialization: Implications for a Theory of Incest Avoidance." *Ethos,* 3, 165–182.

DIRENZO, G.J. 1977. "Socialization, Personality and Social System." *Annual Review of Sociology,* 3, 261–295.

DOBRINER, W. 1963. *Class in Suburbia.* Englewood Cliffs, N.J.: Prentice-Hall.

DOLLARD, J. 1949 *Caste and Class in a Southern Town.* New York: Harper & Row, Pub.

DOZIER, E.P. 1966. *Hano: A Tewa Indian Community in Arizona.* New York: Holt, Rinehart & Winston.

———. 1970. *The Pueblo Indians of North America.* New York: Holt, Rinehart & Winston.

DRUCKER, P. 1939. "Rank, Wealth and Kinship in Northwest Coast Society." *American Anthropologist,* 41, 55–65.

DUBE, S.C. 1955. *Indian Village.* Ithaca, N.Y.: Cornell University Press.

DUNHAM, H.W. 1961. "Socialization Structures and Mental Disorders: Competing Hypotheses of Explanation." *Millbank Memorial Fund Quarterly,* 39, 259.

EISENSTADT, S.N. 1956. *From Generation to Generation.* Glencoe, Ill.: The Free Press.

ELLIS G.J., G.R. LEE, & L.R. PETERSEN. 1978. "Supervision and Conformity: Cross-Cultural Analysis of Parent's Socialization Values." *American Journal of Sociology,* 84, 386–403.

ELSAFTY, M. 1979. "Parental Attitudes Toward the Socialization of Children in the Egyptian Muslim Middle-Class Families." *International Journal of Sociology of the Family,* 9, 177–195.

ERICSON, M.C. 1946. "Child-Rearing and Social Status." *American Journal of Sociology,* 52, 190–192.

ESTEP, R.E., M.R. BURT, & H.J. MULLIGAN. 1977. "Socialization of Sexual Identity." *Journal of Marriage and the Family,* 39, 99–112.

FELDMAN, D.C. 1977. "Role of Initiation Activities in Socialization." *Human Relations,* 30, 977–990.

GIBBS, J.L. 1962. "Poro Values and Courtroom Procedures in a Kpelle Chiefdom." *Southwestern Journal of Anthropology,* 19, 9–20.

———. 1965. "The Kpelle of Liberia." In J.L. Gibbs (ed.), *Peoples of Africa.* New York: Holt, Rinehart & Winston, pp. 197–240.

GIFFORD, E.W. 1929. *Togan Society.* Honolulu: Bernice P. Bishop Museum, Bulletin No. 61.

GOFFMAN, E. 1956. "The Nature of Deference and Demeanor." *American Anthropologist,* 58, 473–502.

———. 1959. *The Presentation of Self in Everyday Life.* New York: Doubleday Anchor Books.

———. 1961. *Encounters: Two Studies in the Sociology of Interaction.* Indianapolis, Ind.: Bobbs-Merrill.

GOLDSCHMIDT, W. 1950. "Social Class in America—A Critical Review." *American Anthropologist,* 52, 483–498.

GOODENOUGH, W.H.. 1951. *Property, Kin and Community on Truk.* New Haven, Conn.: Yale University Publications in Anthropology, No. 46.

———. 1965. "Rethinking 'Status' and 'Role'; Toward a General Model of the Cultural Organization of Social Relationships." In M. Banton (ed.), *The Relevance of Models for Social Anthropology.* New York: Holt, Rinehart, Winston.

GREEN, A. 1946. "The Middle Class Male Child and Neurosis." *American Sociological Review,* 11, 31–41.

GREY, A.L. (ed.). 1969. *Class and Personality in Society.* New York: Lieber-Atherton.

GRINNELL, G.B. 1915. *The Fighting Cheyennes.* New York: Scribner's.

———. 1923. *The Cheyenne Indians: Their History and Ways of Life.* New Haven, Conn.: Yale University Press.

GROSS, N., W.S. MASON, & A.W. McEACHERN. 1958. *Explorations in Role Analysis: Studies of the School and Superintendency Role.* New York: John Wiley.

HANKS, M., & B.K. ECKLAND. 1978. "Adult Voluntary Associations and Adolescent Socialization." *Sociological Quarterly,* 19, 481–490.

HARRIS, A.E. 1979. "Recent Findings on Infant Socialization from North American Research." *International Social Science Journal,* 31, 415–423.

HAVIGHURST, R.J., & A. DAVIS. 1955. "A Comparison of the Chicago and Harvard Studies of the Social Class Differences in Child Rearing." *American Sociological Review,* 20, 438–442.

HAVIGHURST, R.J., & B.L. NEUGARTEN. 1955. *American Indian and White Children: A Socio-Psychological Investigation.* Chicago: University of Chicago Press.

HAVIGHURST, R.J., & H. TABA. 1949. *Adolescent Character and Personality.* New York: John Wiley.

HAVIGHURST, R.J. 1962. *Growing Up in River City.* New York: John Wiley.

HICKMAN, J.M. 1962. "Dimensions of a Complex Concept: A Method Exemplified." *Human Organization,* 21, 214–218.

HODGE, R.W., & D.J. TREIMAN. 1968. "Social Participation and Social Status." *American Sociological Review,* 33, 722–740.

HODGES, H.M., JR. 1964. *Social Stratification: Class in America.* Cambridge, Mass.: Schenkman.

HOEBEL, E.A. 1960. *The Cheyennes: Indians of the Great Plains.* New York: Holt, Rinehart & Winston.

HOLLINGSHEAD, A.B. 1949. *Elmtown's Youth: The Impact of Social Classes on Adolescents.* New York: John Wiley.

HOLLINGSHEAD, A.B., & F.C. RECLICH. 1958. *Social Class and Mental Illness: A Community Study.* New York: John Wiley.

HOLLIS, A.G. 1909. *The Nandi.* London: Oxford University Press.

HOMANS, G.C. 1950. *The Human Group.* New York: Harcourt Brace Jovanovich.

———. 1961. *Social Behavior: Its Elementary Forms.* New York: Harcourt Brace Jovanovich.

HSU, F.L.K. 1963. *Clan, Caste and Club.* Princeton, N.J.: Van Nostrand.

HUGHES, E.C. 1945. "Dilemmas and Contradictions of Status." *American Journal of Sociology,* 50, 353–359.

HUTTON, J.H. 1946.   *Caste in India: Its Nature, Function and Origins.* Cambridge, England: The University Press.

INKELES, A. 1960,   "Industrial Man: The Relation of Status to Experience, Perception and Value." *American Journal of Sociology,* 66, 1–31.

JACKSON, J.A. (ed.). 1968.   *Social Stratification.* London: Cambridge University Press.

JENNINGS, M.K. 1973.   "Review of A. C. Kerckhoff, *Socialization and Social Class.*" *Social Forces,* 52, 293.

KAHL, J.A. 1957.   *The American Class Structure.* New York: Holt, Rinehart & Winston.

KANDEL, D.B. 1978.   "Homophily, Selection and Socialization in Adolescent Friendships." *American Journal of Sociology,* 84, 427–436.

KAUFMAN, H.F. 1944.   *Prestige Classes in a New York Rural Community.* Ithaca, N.Y.: Cornell University Agricultural Experiment Station, Memoir 260.

KERCKHOFF, A.C. 1969.   "Early Antecedents of Role-Taking and Role-Playing Ability." *Merrill-Palmer Quarterly,* 15, 229–247.

――――. 1972.   *Socialization and Social Class.* Englewood Cliffs, N.J.: Prentice-Hall.

――――. 1976.   "Status Attainment Process: Socialization or Allocation?" *Social Forces,* 55, 368–381.

KOHN, M.L. 1959a.   "Social Class and Parental Values." *American Journal of Sociology,* 64, 337–351.

――――, 1963.   "Social Class and Parent-Child Relationships: An Interpretation." *American Journal of Sociology,* 68, 471–480.

――――, 1969.   *Class and Conformity: A Study in Values.* Homewood, Ill.: Dorsey.

KOHN, M.L., & E.E. CARROLL. 1960.   "Social Class and the Allocation of Parental Responsibilities."*Sociometry,* 23, 372–392.

KOHN, M.L., & C. SCHOOLER. 1969.   "Class, Occupation and Orientation." *American Sociological Review,* 34, 659–678.

KORNHAUSER, R.R. 1953.   "The Warner Approach to Social Stratification." In R. Bendix & S.M. Lipset (eds.), *Class, Status and Power.* Glencoe, Ill.: The Free Press.

KUPER, H. 1947.   *An African Aristocracy.* London: Oxford University Press.

――――. 1952.   *The Swazi.* London: International African Institute.

――――. 1963.   *The Swazi: A South African Kingdom.* New York: Holt, Rinehart & Winston.

LANHAM, B.B 1973.   "Review of R. Hill and R. Konig, *Families in East and West— Socialization Process and Kinship Ties.*" *American Anthropologist,* 75, 444–446.

LASSWELL, T.E. 1960.   "Orientations Toward Social Classes." *American Journal of Sociology,* 65, 585.

――――. 1965.   *Class and Stratum: An Introduction to Concepts and Research.* Boston: Houghton-Mifflin.

LAUER, R.H. 1970.   "Review of Alan L. Grey (ed.), *Class and Personality in Society.*" New York: Atherton, *American Sociological Review,* 35, 139.

LEVY, R.I. 1973.   *Tahitians: Mind and Experience in the Society Islands.* Chicago: University of Chicago Press.

LEWIS, O. 1958.   *Village Life in Northern India.* Champaign-Urbana: University of Illinois Press.

LINTON, R. 1936.   *The Study of Man.* New York: Appleton-Century-Crofts.

LITTLE, K. 1960.   "The Role of the Secret Society in Cutural Specialization." In S. Ottenberg & P. Ottenberg (eds.), *Cultures and Societies of Africa.* New York: Random House, pp. 199–213.

LITTMAN, R.A., R.C. MOORE, & J. PIERCE-JONES. 1957. "Social Class Differences in Child-Rearing: A Third Community for Comparison with Chicago and Newton." *American Sociological Review,* 22, 694–704.

LOEB, R. 1973. "Adolescent Groups." *Sociology and Social Research,* 58, 13–22.

LOOFT, W.R. 1973. "Socialization in a Life-Span Perspective: White Elephants, Worms, and Will-O'-the-Wisps." *Gerontologist,* 13, 488–497.

LUEPTOW, L.B. 1980. "Social Structure, Social Change and Parental Influence in Adolescent Sex Role Socialization, 1964–1975." *Journal of Marriage and the Family,* 42, 93–103.

LYND, R., & H. LYND. 1929. *Middletown.* New York: Harcourt Brace Jovanovich.

———. 1937. *Middletown in Transition.* New York: Harcourt Brace Jovanovich.

MACCOBY, E.E., P.K. GIBBS. 1954. "Methods of Child Rearing in Two Social Classes." In W.E. Martin & C.B. Stendler (eds.), *Reading in Child Development.* New York: Hartcourt Brace Jovanovich, pp. 380–396.

MALINOWSKI, B. 1944. *A Scientific Theory of Culture and Other Essays.* Chapel Hill: University of North Carolina Press.

———. 1945. *The Dynamics of Culture Change.* New Haven, Conn.: Yale University Press.

MARRIOTT, M. (ed.). 1955. *Village India.* Chicago: University of Chicago Press.

MAYER, A. 1960. *Caste and Kinship in Central India.* Berkeley: University of California Press.

McCONAGHY, M.J. 1977. "Typological Invalidity in Generation and Family Effects in Value Socialization; A Reply." *American Sociological Review,* 42, 369–372.

MEAD, M. 1928. *Coming of Age in Samoa.* New York: Morrow.

MERTON, R.K. 1957. *Social Theory and Social Structure.* Glencoe, Ill.: The Free Press.

METRAUX, A. 1946. "The Botocudo." In J. Steward (ed.), *Handbook of South American Indians.* Washington, D.C.: Smithsonian Institution, Bureau of American Ethnology, Vol. I. p. 534 ff.

MILLER, D.R., & G.E. SWANSON. 1958. *The Changing American Parent.* New York: John Wiley.

MILLER, G.A. 1956. "The Magical Number Seven, Plus or Minus Two: Some Limits on Our Capacity for Processing Information." *Psychological Review,* 63, 81–97.

MISHKIN, B. 1940. *Rank and Warfare among the Plains Indians.* American Ethnological Society, Monograph Three. Seattle: University of Washington Press.

MORTIMER, J.T. 1975. "Occupational Value Socialization in Business and Professional Families." *Sociology of Work and Occupations,* 2, 29–53.

MORTIMER, J.T., & J. LORENCE. 1979. "Work Experience and Occupational Value Socialization—Longitudinal Study." *American Journal of Sociology,* 84, 1361–1385.

MURDOCK, G.P. 1957. "World Ethnographic Sample." *American Anthropologist,* 59, 664–687.

———. 1981. *Atlas of World Cultures.* Pittsburgh, Pa.: University of Pittsburgh Press.

NADEL, S.F. 1957. *The Theory of Social Structure.* Glencoe, Ill.: The Free Press.

NARAIN, B. 1964. "Growing Up in India." *Family Process,* 3, 127–154.

OGBU, J.U. 1979. "Social Stratification and the Socialization of Competence." *Anthropology and Education Quarterly,* 10, 3–20.

OLEJNIK, A.B. 1980. "Socialization of Achievement; Effects of Children's Sex and Age on Achievement Evaluations by Adults." *Personality and Social Psychology Bulletin,* 6, 68–73.

OLIVER, D. 1955. *A Solomon Island Society.* Cambridge, Mass.: Harvard University Press.

OLSEN, N.J. 1974. "Family Structure and Socialization Patterns in Taiwan." *American Journal of Sociology,* 79, 13935–1417.

PARKER, S., J. SMITH, J. GINAT, & W. GINAT. 1975. "Father Absence and Cross-Sex Identity: The Puberty Rites Controversy Revisited." *American Ethnologist,* 2, 687–706.

PARSONS, T. 1953. "A Revisited Analytical Approach to the Theory of Social Stratification." In R. Bendix & S.M. Lipset (eds.), *Class Status and Power.* Glencoe, Ill.: The Free Press, pp. 92–128.

PARSONS, T., & R.F. BALES. 1965. *Family, Socialization and Interaction Process.* Glencoe, Ill.: The Free Press.

PAUL, B.D. (ed.). 1955. *Health, Culture and Community.* New York: Russell Sage Foundation.

PEARLIN, L.I., & M.L. KOHN. 1966. "Social Class, Occupation, and Parental Values: A Cross-National Study." *American Sociological Review,* 31, 466–479.

PFAUTZ, H.W., & O.D. DUCAN. 1950. "A Critical Evaluation of Warner's Work in Community Stratification." *American Sociological Review,* 15, 205–215.

PORTER, J.N. 1974. "Race, Socialization and Mobility in Educational and Early Occupational Attainment." *American Sociological Review,* 39, 303–316.

PRINS, A.H.J. 1953. *East African Age-Class Systems: An Inquiry into the Social Order of Galla, Kipsigis and Kikuyu.* Groningen and Djakarta: J. B. Wolters.

RADCLIFFE-BROWN, A.R. 1922. *The Andaman Islanders.* Cambridge, England: Cambridge University Press.

READ, M. 1956. *The Ngoni of Nyasaland.* London: Oxford University Press.

———. 1960. *Children of Their Fathers: Growing Up among the Ngoni of Nyasaland.* New Haven, Conn.: Yale University Press.

———. 1968. *Children of Their Fathers: Growing Up among the Ngoni of Malawi* (rev. ed.) New York: Holt, Rinehart & Winston.

REDEKOP, C. 1976. "Social Ecology of Communal Socialization." *International Review of Modern Sociology,* 6, 113–125.

REISS, A.J., O.D. DUNCAN, P.K. HATT, & C.C. NORTH. 1961. *Occupations and Social Status.* Glencoe, Ill.: The Free Press.

REISSMAN, L. 1959. *Class in American Society.* Glencoe, Ill.: The Free Press.

RICHARDS, A.I. 1956. *Chisungu; A Girl's Initiation Ceremony among the Bemba of Northern Rhodesia.* New York: Grove.

RICHARDS, M.P. (ed.). 1974. *The Integration of a Child into a Social World.* Cambridge, England: Cambridge University Press.

RICHARDSON, J. 1940. *Law and Status among the Kiowa Indians.* American Ethnological Society, Monograph One. University of Washington Press.

RICHER, S. 1979. "Sex-Role Socialization and Early Schooling." *Canadian Review of Sociology and Anthropology,* 16, 195–205.

ROSENBAUM, J.E. 1975. "Stratification of Socialization Processes." *American Sociological Review,* 40, 48–54.

RYAN, B. 1953. *Caste in Modern Ceylon.* New Brunswick, N.J.: Rutgers University Press.

SANFORD, M. 1974. "Socialization and Ambiquity—Child Lending in British West Indian Society." *Ethnology,* 13, 393–400.

SCHNEIDER, D.M. 1968. *American Kinship: A Cultural Account.* Englewood Cliffs, N.J.: Prentice-Hall.

SCHURTZ, H. 1902. *Altersklassen und Mannerbunde.* Berlin: G. Reimer.

SEARS, R.R., E.E. MACCOBY, & H. LEVIN. 1957. *Patterns of Child Rearing.* Evanston, Ill.: Row, Peterson.

SERVICE, E.R. 1963.   *Profiles in Ethnology.* New York: Harper & Row, Pub.
SEWELL, W.H. 1952.   "Infant Training and the Personality of the Child." *American Journal of Sociology,* 58, 150–159.
———. 1961.   "Social Class and Childhood Personality." *Sociometry,* 24, 340–356.
———.1963.   "Some Recent Developments in Socialization Theory and Research." *The Annals of the American Academy of Political and Social Science.* 349, 163–181.
SEWELL, W.H., & A.O. HALLER. 1956.   "Social Status and the Personality Adjustment of the Child." *Sociometry,* 19, 114–125.
———. 1959.   "Factors in the Relationship between Social Status and the Personality Adjustment of the Child." *American Sociological Review,* 24, 511.
SEWELL, W.H., P.H. MUSSEN, & C.W. Harris. 1955.   "Relationships among Child Training Practices." *American Sociological Review,* 20, 137–148.
SIEBER, R.T. 1978.   "Schooling, Socialization and Group Boundaries; Study of Informal Social Relations in Public Domain." *Urban Anthropology,* 7, 67–98.
SIMMONS, L.W. 1945.   *The Role of the Aged in Primitive Society.* New Haven, Conn.: Yale University Press.
SINGER, P., & D. DeSOLE. 1967.   "The Australian Subincision Ceremony Reconsidered: Vaginal Envy or Kangaroo Bifid Penis Envy." *American Anthropologist,* 69, 355–358.
SOUTHHALL, A. 1959.   "An Operational Theory of Role." *Human Relations,* 12, 17–34.
SPANIER, G.B. 1977.   "Sexual Socialization: Conceptual Review." *International Journal of Sociology of the Family,* 7, 87–106.
SPIRO, M.E. 1958.   *Children of the Kibbutz.* Cambridge Mass.: Harvard University Press.
STARR, J.M. 1974.   *Social Structure and Social Personality.* Boston: Little, Brown.
STEERE, G.H. 1964.   "Changing Values in Childhood Socialization: A Study of United States Child Rearing Literature 1865–1929." Unpublished doctoral dissertation, University of Pennsylvania.
STEIN, A.H., & M. BAILEY. 1973.   "The Socialization of Achievement Orientation in Females," *Psychological Bulletin,* 80, 345–366.
STRAUS, M.A. 1957.   "Anal and Oral Frustration in Relation to Sinhalese Personality." *Sociometry,* 20, 21–31.
SVALASTOGA, K. 1959.   *Prestige, Class and Mobility.* Copenhagen: Gyldendal.
———. 1964.   "Social Differentiation." In R.E.L. Faris (ed.), *Handbook of Modern Sociology.* Skokie, Ill.: Rand McNally, pp. 530–575.
———. 1965.   *Social Differentation.* New York: D. McKay.
TEXTOR, R.B. 1967.   *A Cross Cultural Summary.* New Haven Conn.: Human Relations Area Files
THOMAS, D.L., V. GECAS, A. WEIGERT, & E. ROONEY. 1974.   *Family Socialization and the Adolescent: Determinants of Self-Concept, Conformity, Religiosity and Counterculture Values.* Lexington, Mass.: Lexington Books.
THOMAS, D.L., & A.J. WEIGERT. 1971.   "Socialization and Adolescent Conformity to Significant Others: A Cross-National Analysis." *American Sociological Reviews,* 36, 835, 847.
TITIEV, M. 1944.   *Old Oraibi.* Cambridge, Mass.: Harvard University, Papers of the Peabody Museum 22.
TOUHEY, J.C. 1973.   "Child-Rearing Antecedents and the Emergence of Machiavellianism." *Sociometry* 26, 194–206.
TUMIN, M.M. 1952.   *Caste in a Peasant Society: A Case Study in the Dynamics of Caste.* Princeton, N.J.: Princeton University Press.
———. 1953.   "Some Principles of Stratification: A Critical Analysis." *American Sociological Review,* 18, 387–394.

————. 1967.   *Social Stratification: The Forms and Functions of Inequality.* Englewood Cliffs, N.J.: Prentice-Hall.

WALLACE, A.F.C. 1961.   "The Psychic Unity of Human Groups," In B. Kaplan (ed.). *Studying Personality Cross-Culturally.* Evanston, Ill.: Row, Peterson, pp. 128–163.

WANDERSMAN, L.P. 1973.   "Stylistic Differences in Mother-Child Interaction: A Review and Re-evaluation of the Social Class and Socialization Research." *Cornell Journal of Social Relations,* 8, 197–218.

WARNER, W.L. 1953.   *Amercian Life: Dream and Reality.* Chicago: University of Chicago Press.

————. 1960.   *Social Class in America.* New York: Harper & Row, Pub.

WARNER, W.L., 1949.   *Democracy in Jonesville.* New York: Harper & Row, Pub.

WARNER, W.L., & P.S. LUNT. 1941.   *The Social Life of a Modern Community.* New Haven, Conn.: Yale University Press.

WEBER, M. 1946.   *From Max Weber: Essays in Sociology.* New York: Oxford University Press (edited and translated by H.H. Gerth & C.W. Mills).

WEBSTER, H. 1908,   *Primitive Secret Societies.* New York: Macmillan.

WELCH, M.R., & B.M. PAGE. 1979.   "Sex Differences in Socialization Anxiety." *Journal of Social Psychology,* 19, 17–23.

WELMERS, W.E. 1949.   "Secret Medicine: Magic and Rites of the Kpelle Tribe in Liberia." *Southwestern Journal of Anthropology,* 5, 208–243.

WHITE, M.S. 1957.   "Social Class, Child Rearing Practices and Child Behavior." *American Sociological Review,* 22, 704–712.

WHITING, J.W.M. 1961.   "Socialization Process and Personality." In F.L.K. Hsu (ed.), *Psychological Anthropology.* Homewood, Ill.: Dorsey, pp. 355–380.

————. 1964.   "Effects of Climate on Certain Cultural Practices." In W. Goodenough (ed.), *Explorations in Cultural Anthropology.* New York: McGraw-Hill, pp. 511–544.

————. 1973.   "A Model for Psychocultural Research." American Anthropological Association, *Annual Report.* Washington, D.C., 1974.

WHITING, J.W.M., R. KLUCKHOHN, & A. ANTHONY. 1958.   "The Function of Male Initiation Ceremonies at Puberty." In E.E. Maccoby, T. Newcomb, & E. Hartley (eds.), *Readings in Social Psychology.* New York: Holt, Rinehart & Winston, pp. 359–370.

WILLIAMS, T.R. 1962.   "Tambunan Dusun Social Structure," *Sociologus,* 23, 141–157.

————. 1965.   *The Dusun: A North Borneo Society.* New York: Holt, Rinehart & Winston

————. 1966.   "Cultural Structuring of Tactile Experience in a Borneo Society." *American Anthropologist,* 68, 27–39.

WILSON, M. 1951.   *Good Company.* London: Oxford University Press.

WISER, W.H., & C.V. WISER. 1963.   *Behind Mud Walls.* Berkeley: University of California Press.

YOUNG, F.W. 1962.   "The Function of Male Initiation Ceremonies: A Cross-Cultural Test of an Alternative Hypothesis." *American Journal of Sociology,* 67, 379–396.

ZEYFERREL, M., W.L. TOLONE, & R.H. WALSH. 1978.   "Intergenerational Socialization of Sex Role Attitudes; Gender or Generation Gap?" *Adolescence,* 13, 95–108.

CHAPTER EIGHT
TECHNOLOGY, IDEOLOGY, AND SOCIALIZATION

This chapter is concerned with a discussion of some examples of the relations between the socialization process and patterns in the cultural subsystems of technology and ideology. It begins with an account of the ways the technology subsystem pattern of shelter may be related to the process of socialization. The discussion then turns to a consideration of the ways some patterns of the ideology subsystem, such as various cultural beliefs and values, including ideas about nature, society, and art, are possibly related to the socialization process. The chapter concludes with comments concerning the study of the interdependence between socialization and patterns in the cultural subsystems of technology and ideology.

TECHNOLOGY AND SOCIALIZATION

In Chapter 6 it was noted that culture can be conceptualized as having four major subsystems: (1) *social relations,* (2) *language,* (3) *technology,* and (4) *ideology.* Each subsystem is composed of a large and varying number of whole categories, or patterns, of culture. Table 6–1 lists 19 patterns which seem to be part of the cultural subsystem of technology. The technology subsystem includes all those patterns of culture invented and used by humans to transform their natural environment in ways that provide them with the materials needed for life in a particular physical setting. Specifically technology is that part of human culture which enables humans to produce from their physical environment those manufactured goods and devices, or artifacts, which make it possible for humans to survive by culturally adapting to local conditions. Artifacts include tools and containers, processed foods, shelters, transport, items of clothing and adornment, and all other material objects produced and used by members of a society. It is through invention and use of technology that humans have been able to inhabit all of the earth's varied climate zones.

Complexity of Technology

Contemporary human societies differ greatly in the complexity of their systems of technology. Some societies with a very limited technology have been restricted to one physical environment. However some other human societies have been able to range widely across sharply contrasting earth regions because of their inventions and more varied technology.

Because of the nature of their technology system, some societies have also been restricted to only one major use of their physical environment. The Plains Indians of North America hunted big game, principally the buffalo, but usually did not plant the rich earth of their area because they lacked the learned categories of behavior and belief, plans for action, and the artifacts needed to exploit this potential for a great food surplus. In contrast, the Iroquois Indians of the eastern woodlands of North America, with a more complex technology subsystem of culture, practiced hunting, fishing, food gathering, and horticulture to gain a living from their environment. Thus the type and complexity of technology possessed by a society depends on its past cultural history in gaining access to a physical setting. Changes in the technological type and complexity of a culture seem to be closely related to the nature of, and changes in, other patterns in the cultural subsystems of social relations, language, and ideology.

Sometimes individuals untrained in cultural analysis make the error of judging the nature of a whole culture only from its technology type and complexity. It is possible to make long lists of the different types of technology and of the complexity of artifacts used in gaining a living in many societies. On such a list some societies could be ranked as "simple" or "less complex" than other societies in their system of technology. However simple or advanced a cultural subsystem of technology may appear, it is not necessarily true that an entire culture is also "simple" or "less advanced" or is not as "complex" as other cultures.

Research on Technology

In the past century a great amount of research has been done on the nature of human technology. Much of the interest in the study of technology has stemmed from the fact that some early theories of human cultural evolution postulated that whole cultures were at various "stages" of social development, depending on the presumed state of their technological complexity. Studies of technology were also derived from the fact that artifacts remaining from human cultures are a principal source of evidence for study of early human history. Technology has been widely studied also because it is easier and often safer in an alien cultural setting to make detailed records of artifacts and ways of making a living from an environment than it is to ask questions about topics such as magic, cannibalism, marriage, and so on.

There have been many notable studies of selected aspects of the technology subsystem in one society.[1] The ready availability of a great number of detailed publications concerned with technology has led to attempts to make general statements about both the subsystem of technology and the part played by that aspect of culture in human cultural history and behavior. These discussions have ranged from an effort to theoretically relate artifacts to basic human needs, through attempts to undertake correlational analyses of features of technology and social relations, to use of the statistical technique of factor analysis to show that features of technology seem closely interrelated to aspects of the ideology subsystem of human culture.[2] Quite detailed and extensive studies have been made of the ways particular features of technology manifest themselves in human culture.[3] Considerable time and skill have been devoted to compiling detailed summaries of various features of human technology.[4]

Universal Categories of Technology

The result of intensive study of technology in specific cultures and of attempts to systematically compare these data has been a growing awareness among anthropologists that certain broad categories of technology are universal, or are found in all societies. The universal categories of technology are (1) food gathering or production (2) shelter, (3) clothing, (4)

---

[1]See Beals, 1935; Bogoras, 1904; Buck, 1930; Bunzel, 1929; Kroeber, 1901; Linton, 1923; Lowie, 1922; Osgood, 1940; Wissler, 1910.

[2]See Greenman, 1945; Hobhouse, Wheeler, & Ginsberg, 1915; Gouldner & Peterson, 1962.

[3]See Driver & Kroeber, 1932; Driver, 1956, & 1966; Driver & Massey, 1957; Ford, 1939; Freeman & Winch, 1957; Sawyer and LeVine, 1966.

[4]See Murdock, 1957, 1967.

tools and containers, and (5) transportation. As noted, these universal categories are not equally developed in all societies.

To illustrate the ways the process of socialization may be related to the patterns of technology, it is appropriate to select a pattern of this cultural subsystem which not only is universal in human society but also is a pattern of technology that all children are subject to as they mature in all societies. A pattern of the technology subsystem which meets these requirements is the one concerned with shelter. Infants and children in most societies have little direct, initial contact or concern with the technology patterns involved in food gathering or production, manufacture of tools and containers, or transportation. In many societies children are not required to wear clothing until they are four years of age or older. However children in all societies have direct and long-lasting experience with the technology subsystem pattern of shelter.

Explaining Shelter Variations

Contemporary human societies use shelters ranging from rock overhangs and caves through wind screens and tents to massive buildings. Shelters are constructed of nearly every available material. However comparisons of human shelter data show that, despite the seemingly endless diversity in type and materials used, humans actually make their shelters in a limited number of forms and with restricted kinds of materials. The ground plans of shelters in all human societies seem to be of only 6 types.

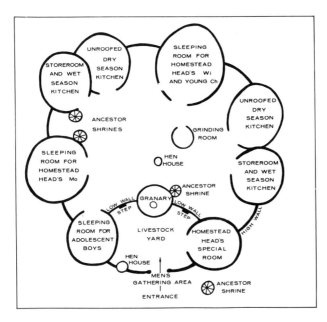

FIGURE 8–1
Diagrammatic shelter ground plan of a Tallensi (Ghana) dwelling (not to scale). (Fortes, M. 1949. *The Web of Kinship among the Tallensi*. London: Oxford University Press, p.53)

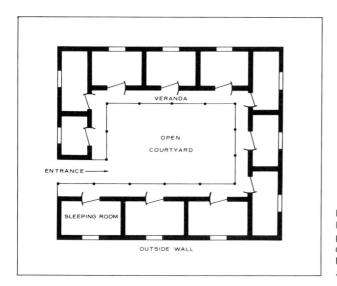

FIGURE 8–2
Diagrammatic shelter ground plan of an Ashanti (Ghana) dwelling (not to scale). (Fortes, M. 1959. "Primitive Kinship," *Scientific American*, 200, 146.)

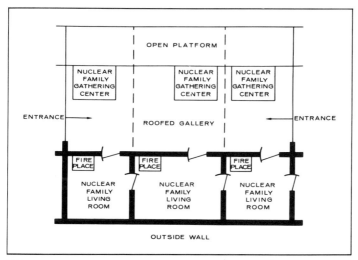

FIGURE 8–3 Diagrammatic shelter ground plan of a section of an Iban (Sarawak, East Malaysia) dwelling (not to scale). (Freeman, J.D. 1955. *Iban Agriculture*, London: Her Majesty's Stationery Office, pp. 1–5.)

The floor levels of all human shelters seem to comprise only 4 types. The construction of shelter walls involves only 11 types of material. The shape of all shelter roofs involves only 9 different types, while only 11 types of materials are regularly used for roof construction. The following outline lists these basic shelter forms, types, and materials. Figures 8–1 to 8–3 illustrate some shelter ground plan types.

Common Features of Shelter Shape, Construction, and Materials[5]

I. Ground plan of shelters
  A. Circular
  B. Elliptical or elongated with rounded ends
  C. Polygonal
  D. Quadrangular around (or partially around) an interior court
  E. Rectangular or square
  F. Semicircular
II. Floor level of shelters
  A. Elevated slightly above the ground on a raised platform of earth, stone, or wood
  B. Floor formed by or level with the ground itself.
  C. Raised substantially above the ground on piles, posts, or piers
  D. Subterranean or semisubterranean, ignoring cellars beneath the living quarters.
III. Wall materials of shelters
  A. Adobe, clay, or brick
  B. Bark
  C. Felt, cloth, or other fabric
  D. Grass, leaves, or other thatch
  E. Hides or skins
  F. Mats, latticework, or wattle
  G. Open walls
  H. Plaster, mud and dung, or wattle and daub
  I. Walls merging into roof materials
  J. Stone, stucco, concrete, or fired brick
  K. Wood, including logs, planks, poles, bamboo, or shingles
IV. Shape of roofs
  A. Beehive shaped with pointed peak
  B. Conical
  C. Dome-shaped or hemispherical
  D. Semihemispherical
  E. Flat or horizontal
  F. Gabled (with two slopes)
  G. Hipped or pyramidal (four slopes)
  H. Rounded or semicylindrical
  I. Shed (with one slope)
V. Roofing materials
  A. Bark
  B. Earth or turf
  C. Felt, cloth, or other fabric
  D. Grass, leaves, brush, or thatch
  E. Hides or skins
  F. Ice or snow
  G. Mats
  H. Plaster, clay, mud and dung, or wattle and daub
  I. Stone or slate
  J. Tile or fired brick
  K. Wood, including logs, planks, poles, bamboo, or shingles

[5]Murdock, 1967, 60–61.

There have been many attempts to explain variations in the types of human shelters and in the materials used to construct them. For the most part these explanations are "all-or-none" explanations, which select one physical, social, or cultural feature as a causative agent. A brief review of these different explanations follows, as an introduction to discussion of the possible relationships between the technology pattern of shelter and the process of socialization.

Shelter and Climate

The simplest physical determination explanation for human shelter variation is the one that says humans build shelters primarily to protect themselves from a specific climate. However the record of shelter types developed within the climate areas of the earth makes it quite clear that shelters must be built for very many reasons other than protection from climate. In fact, some groups have not built shelters even where the climate is very inhospitable. One example of such a society would be the Ona of Tierra del Fuego. The Ona lived in an almost Arctic climate, where they developed a semicircular-shaped, ground-level-floored, semihemispherical-roofed structure covered on the sides and roof with animal hides. This structure was used, however, only for special ritual purposes. Ona nuclear families regularly lived alongside such structures in a simple brush windbreak.

On the other hand, very elaborate shelters are built in climates, such as the tropical Pacific, where in terms of the effects of climate alone the human need for protection would seem to be least critical. In some societies the construction and use of shelters are the opposite of what would reasonably be expected under the climate explanation for shelter variations. The Hidatsa Indians of Missouri farmed from April through November. As they worked their summer fields of corn and beans, small, extended families lived in circular, semisubterranean, heavy-long-walled shelters with dome-shaped wooden roofs covered over with a thick layer of turf. However in the very cold period from December to March, while the Hidatsa hunted and moved their camps to follow the herds of game, they lived in "tepees" *(tipi)* or circular, ground-floored, conically shaped, hide-covered, temporary frame structures. These two types of shelters were clearly adapted to the two styles of basic subsistence practiced by the Hidatsa (farming and hunting), although under a climatic explanation for shelter types the reverse would have been expected. In fact, similar "anticlimatic" solutions for shelter are not at all uncommon in human societies.[6]

---

[6]See Rapoport, 1969; 21–24, for other examples.

Samoan house (circa 1930). (Courtesy American Museum of Natural History.)

Materials, Construction Techniques, Site Locations, and Shelter

Three other physical determination explanations for variations in human shelters say that the form of shelter in a society is determined solely by (1) the character of the materials used in building, (2) the kinds of construction techniques needed for the materials used, or (3) the site on which a shelter is constructed. No one of these explanations stands the test of comparison with the reported data of human shelters. There are many human shelters constructed of exactly the same materials but of quite different shapes. Shelters throughout the Polynesian and Melanesian Islands have been constructed through use of polished stone and shell adzes. Yet despite the use of the same adze construction technique, shelters vary greatly in their form throughout these two culture areas.

Finally there is no comparative evidence that the form of shelter in a society is determined by site location. If this particular physical determination argument were true, then shelters built on similar sites but in different societies would have the same form.

Social and Cultural Explanations

In contrast to the four physical deterministic explanations just noted, four other explanations for the forms of human shelter are based on selected social and cultural factors. In common with all of the physical deterministic explanations, each of the social and cultural explanations for variations in human shelter forms appears also to be a single causation ("all-or-none") explanation.

Need for defense   Perhaps the most typical social and cultural explanation is that humans build particular forms of shelter out of their need to defend themselves against attack. However even where the defensive needs of a society are clearly high, the specific form of a living shelter may be very different from the shelter used in time of actual war. The Masai of East Africa use a different shelter type when at war and when at peace. In Venezuela, Indian groups chronically at war, such as the Piaroa, build circular shelters, whereas the nearby Motilon build rectangular shelters. Thus the type of shelter used by a society does not seem generally related to an assumed need for defense.

Shelter and economics   Another common social and cultural explanation for human shelter form directly associates a specific economic system and a particular shelter type. However, such economic explanations do not stand the test of comparison of data of known human shelter types. The economic systems of *swidden,* or "slash-and-burn," agriculturalists living in the same area may be identical, as is the case with the Murut and Dusun societies of northern Borneo, but their house forms may vary widely. Nomadic peoples, who share a particular type of economic system based on the need for mobility to follow animals or seasonally maturing foods, vary widely in the types of shelters they use. The Mongol folding circular hut (*yurt*), the Arab folding desert tents, the collapsible tepee of the Plains Indians of North America, the hexagonal portable tent of the Tibetans,

A Tungus (Siberia) shelter (date unknown). (Courtesy American Museum of Natural History.)

and the transportable wooden houses of some American Indian societies of the Pacific Northwest are quite different forms of shelter in societies sharing an economic system based on nomadic life.

Shelter and religion A number of writers have advanced the view that human shelters basically are "religious structures" and that variations in types of structures reflect different religious systems.[7] As in the preceding instances of choosing single social and cultural factors as causative reasons for shelter types, a review of the data of human shelter and of religious beliefs in a society shows no specific correspondence. Religious factors do enter into many features of shelter construction and use, but no casual relationship has been shown to exist between the type of religious system in a society and the type of shelter it uses.

Shelter and kinship The relationship between the specific type of kinship and kin groups in a society and the typical form of its shelter has long been a subject of interest to students of culture and society. The earliest attempt to study the possible relationships between shelter form and kinship and kin groups was Morgan's 1881 account of shelter type and social organization among North American Indians. Morgan assumed in his study that the "clan" was the universal and most ancient form of human social organization and was the fundamental unit of all "primitive" society. He also assumed that, since food and household hospitality seemed to be uni-

A Toda (India) house and "dairy" (date unknown). (Courtesy American Museum of Natural History.)

[7]See Eliade, 1961.

versal among American Indians, very early human social life was probably based on a simple form of communal economic organization. From these two assumptions Morgan reasoned that the communal shelter types of the North American Iroquois, Pueblo, and Pacific Northwest Indian societies directly reflected the presence of their clans and their communal economic organization. However Morgan erred in his assumption concerning the basic and ancient nature of the clan kin grouping. Morgan did not know that food and house hospitality forms vary greatly among, and even are missing in, some American Indian societies. The social form of sharing food and living in common shelter are not generally related to the economic systems of either North American Indians or other peoples of the world.

Another attempt to directly relate types of shelter and social organization was made by Wundt, often called the "father of experimental psychology." Wundt (1928) noted that the use of a small cave by one early human nuclear family must have produced quite long-lasting social attitudes and behavior, some of which were later reflected in the building of single-family shelters. Wundt also reasoned that the occupation of a large cave by several early human nuclear families would have later produced long-lasting attitudes and behaviors that would be reflected in an extended-family-type social organization and typical multiple-family shelter types. Wundt's evolutionary psychological speculations were erroneous, since there are no evidences from comparative studies of shelter types and of social organization forms that any particular shelter form has been persistently associated with any specific type of social organization in all of the human experience.

A study by Whiting and Ayers (1968) of possible long-lasting correlations between the shape of shelter floor plans and certain social organizational features of culture has noted that in contemporary cultures some selected features of human social organization seem to be related to the

Pygmy house, Congo (1947). (Courtesy American Museum of Natural History.)

ground plan of shelters typically built in a culture. After study of a world-wide sample of 136 societies, selected in a way that ensured that no two cultures were drawn from the same culture region or linguistic unit, Whiting and Ayers concluded that the shape of a culture's basic type of shelter is directly related to (1) the form of the family and (2) whether some specific and clear distinctions are made in social relations within the family through use of different status terms and behavior. Whiting and Ayers believe the sequence of causation involved is from the social organization content of culture to the shape of the shelter floor—that is, the shape of shelter is the "dependent variable," so that as the social organizational features of culture, such as family type, change, the shape of the basic shelter also changes. This hypothesis remains to be fully tested. What is very important about Whiting and Ayers' study is their belief in use of multiple causation explanations for the form of shelter. Their research is the first to search for more than one simple reason for a shelter type.

Shelter and Cultural Structuring of Perceptions

It can be concluded from the brief survey of various single causation explanations for the variations in human shelter types that shelters are built in every culture for a very complex set of reasons. Furthermore these reasons appear to be related to and derived from the ways a people perceive the world about them and from the cultural ideologies that shape their perceptions. In other words, shelters are apparently not conceived in any human society simply as structures, but as integral and basic expressions of complexly interrelated cultural views and ideals. A more precise hypothesis states:

> Given a particular climate, materials, and the limits of a specific system of technology, what finally decides the usual form of shelter is a society are the ways a people perceive the world and their place in it.

Although this hypothesis has the appearance of another "single-cause" explanation, in fact it is a multiple-cause explanation, similar to that used by Whiting and Ayers.

It would be useful to cite some examples of the ways human perceptions are shaped by cultural experiences. A European electrical contractor working in Ghana, West Africa, noted that he was constantly confronted with the problem of his local laborers digging curved rather than straight trenches for laying conduits. The contractor would lay out a straight line between two points for his workers to follow in digging a conduit trench, but at the end of the job he invariably found the trench to have a curve in it. The laborers were recruited from the northern area of Ghana, where circular forms and styles predominate in construction and where straight lines play only a very minor role in everyday life. Thus because of their prior cultural experiences, it was as difficult for the laborers to dig a straight trench as it would be for most Americans, who have grown up in a "carpentered" or straight-lined world, to draw a perfect freehand circle.[8]

The Dusun of northern Borneo have a very complex color designation system consisting of a set of basic hues, each of which is capable of qualification through use of specific cultural modifiers, such as "hot," "old," "strong," and so on. The basic hues can also be highly refined by Dusun through use of specific event or place designations. Thus a color that has a particular hue, value, and chroma designation in the commonly used Western European and American color nomenclature system will be noted by adult Dusun to be "yellow, the color of full-grown bamboo and like the light of the sun shining through an early morning rain." In the Dusun color system the blue of a clear, tropical midday sky and the green of the underside of jungle leaves are designated by some color term. Dusun physically can "see" or differentiate between blue and green color yarns and color plates but have only one word to designate these two colors, so obviously different to Europeans and Americans. One of several possible explanations for the failure of Dusun to have separate linguistic designations and to not readily attend to the physical distinctions between blue and green is that Dusun culture has evolved in a tropical rain forest environment, where green hues and their variations dominate the environment and where Dusun live in small clearings, open only to the skies, with a heavy color border of tropical tree greens. Another explanation is that Dusun genetically lack certain kinds of macular eye pigments that make certain kinds of "blue-green" vision difficult or impossible.[9] Whatever the reason for the origins of the Dusun use of one basic color term for both blue and green hues, the fact remains that for all practical purposes, blue is green and green is blue to most Dusun adults.[10] In the same way, northern Ghanaians can "see" a straight line but live in a cultural world of curves and softened angles and so tend to respond to events in terms of this world.

Another example of the way culture shapes the basic perceptions of a people would be the fundamental inability of two young Dusun girls to see the litter in the yard about a house. When we first moved into a Dusun house in the isolated Borneo mountain village of Sensuron, my wife became concerned about the danger of accidental fire in a deep carpeting of debris under our house, which was built off the ground on hardwood piles; the

---

[8]See Herskovits, 1958, 267–268.

[9]Stiles (1946) and Wald (1949) have suggested that genetic differences in macular pigmentation may cause certain populations to have less discrimination between blue and green colors. Ray (1952, 1953) has commented at length on "blue-green confusion" in human cultures.

[10]For some other discussions of the ways color perceptions are structured by cultural experiences, see Berlin & Kay, 1969; Ray, 1952, 1953; Conklin, 1955; Monberg, 1971.

Tambunan Dusun (Sensuron) village scene (1959). (T. R. Williams.)

litter stretched in all directions to neighboring houses. One morning my wife asked the two adolescent girls working with her in our household to go under the house and to sweep the debris into a large pile and then carry it off to the nearby jungle. Several hours later she discovered the girls sitting on the lower rung of our house ladder talking heatedly with several Dusun adults concerning the task they had been assigned. The Dusun girls could see no litter in the house yard and could not understand their task, since the area looked perfectly normal to them. The argument between the girls and the Dusun adults concerned the best way of helping my wife understand that there were no broken tools or other artifacts in the yard to pick up. The Tambunan Dusun word for *litter* or *trash* is most easily translated as *waste* and refers in general only to artifacts left about a house area in a disorderly fashion. The problem of communication between the Dusun girls and my wife was not solely a linguistic one. Even after my wife's further careful explanations, the two young Dusun girls still could "see" no disorder or litter in the house area, although by this time a large crowd of our Dusun neighbors had gathered and were helping to try to figure out my wife's concerns. The event concluded when my wife decided that Dusun perceptions of order would not be changed through use of American logic, a product of another and very different cultural system. In the following days our neighbors spent a great deal of time talking about the problem of our perceptions.

Shelter and Socialization

Some anthropologists and social psychologists have made detailed studies of the ways culture and experience shape and direct the perception and cognition of a people.[11] These studies have generally concluded that the way humans see and understand themselves and the world about them is not only the consequence of genetically inherited factors and the product of their personal growth and development but also a result of the significant ways their cultural heritages prepare them to attend to or ignore selected aspects of their world. If a culture does not provide the definitions, associations, and terms for discussion and thought about particular features of the world, then individuals growing up in that culture will lack the basic ways necessary to cope in everyday affairs with some parts of their world. In other words, we usually do not see things as they really are, but as we are enculturated to see and understand them.

Research on this topic, which is very complex, has now shown that the socialization process generally involves the simultaneous development of individuals' sense of self and the objects about them and of their conceptions of time and space. This means that in discussing the ways a particular pattern in the technology subsystem of a culture, such as shelter, may be related to the socialization process, it is necessary to take specific account of the ways cultures define, discuss, and conceive objects, space, and time and the ways these are integrated by individuals in their self-concepts and are expressed in their personal actions.

Perhaps this point can be illustrated briefly by the ways a Dusun guide got himself, my 11 Dusun companions, and me lost in a mountainous, heavily forested area in the center of northern Borneo. I had selected the guide from among several persons available in the remote village we had visited for two days. I had presumed that a Dusun hunter would know his way about the area through which he hunted regularly. As it turned out, the guide had no real understanding of our direction of travel as we moved very slowly along the high, wet mountainsides. When the guide finally admitted to me that he had become completely lost from the path he had set out to follow, I asked my Dusun companions how it was possible for a local man, reportedly a skilled hunter, to become so lost in his home territory. The essence of their response was that the guide had been so busy talking and being an "important person" that he could not remember in proper sequence all of the object reference points (rocks, hill slopes, trees)

[11]See the discussions and references in Hallowell, 1951, 1955. See also Kluckhohn, 1954, 931–940. A discussion by Segall, Campbell, and Herskovits (1966) is basic to current understanding of the cultural structuring of perceptions.

which in conjunction with the passage of precisely defined spans of walking time constituted his cognitive map of the path to be followed.

Most anthropologists have had similar experiences while immersed for long periods in other cultural settings. My days with the Dusun were filled with many contrasts between the ways my Dusun neighbors and I perceived the same events and objects and organized our thoughts about them. I learned that there were profound differences separating us which could be transcended only by my learning the basic cultural postulates guiding Dusun life and by suspending as best I could my use of those postulates on which my own culture rests.

When I investigated the specific ways the technology subsystem pattern of shelter is related to the Dusun enculturation process, I found it necessary to broaden my questions and observations to include the underlying cultural postulates which guide the ways Dusun view their world. In 1959 most of the houses in Sensuron were constructed of split bamboo lashed to hardwood posts with rattan lines. The actual physical construction techniques in Dusun house-building appeared relatively simple. Ten to fifteen hardwood posts, between 20 and 30 feet in length and some 6 to 10 inches in diameter, are set upright in the ground in a pattern enclosing a rectangular area about 15 by 25 feet. Then smaller-diameter hardwood posts are tied horizontally along the outside distance between the main, upright house posts to form the edges of a floor frame. Floor frames are built about three to four feet from the ground. Next, smaller diameter posts are laid about four feet apart across the width of the house frame and tied into place with rattan lines. After this, a split, dried bamboo floor is laid out over the floor frame, trimmed at the edges of the floor, and tied down with rattan to the smaller floor-support poles. After the house floor is secured, small hardwood pole stringers are tied with rattan along the outside of the main house posts; longitudinal poles are put in place about three feet and six feet up from the floor on all sides of the house. Three-foot-wide split bamboo sections are secured vertically to these poles to form the outside house walls. After this, small hardwood poles are lashed with rattan vine from the top wall support up to the projecting tops of the main house posts, forming a peaked roof frame. A roof covering of either split bamboo half sections, or "tiles," or of sections of closely woven palm leaf *(atap)* material is then lashed across the roof frame poles to provide a watertight covering. Most Sensuron houses built in this manner are constructed in less than one day. However it usually takes months and sometimes several years, to collect and prepare all of the materials used in construction.

I found as I talked with my Sensuron neighbors that building a house is one of the most meaningful social and religious acts in a man's entire lifetime. I learned that the collection of raw materials, their preliminary preparation, and house construction involved a broad range of Dusun beliefs about human relationships to the supernatural; concepts of fortune, luck, illness, accident, and personal emotional well-being; magical practices; sacred numbers; kinship; and friendship relationships. I recorded the complex and lengthy ritual preparations that had to be used to properly select the best site for a house, to protect the builders from supernatural harm, and to ensure that occupants had lasting good fortune in their new home. I also learned that more than 40 different rattan knots and lashing techniques were used to secure house poles, frames, siding, and roof materials and that each of the rattan knots had a specific name, very complex ritual meaning, and elaborate folk tales concerning the consequences of its misuse.

I also learned from my Dusun friends that, for ritual and magical reasons, bamboo for house construction had to be cut at specific places and times of the year and that it had to be of a special diameter and length and of the "right" color. I was told of the proper ways to dry bamboo so it would be not only physically strong but "emotionally" strong as well. I soon became aware that Dusun regularly *anthropomorphized* (to attribute human properties to an object) and *reified* (to attribute human powers to an object) their houses. My Dusun friends perceived their homes as having bodies, with "arms," "legs," "muscles," "head," "belly," and so on. Dusun believe houses have to "stand" in a particular direction and not be "upside-down" on a hill slope. Dusun riddles, puns, and folk tales contain many references or allusions to house parts and appearances which are cast in human terms. I learned that Dusun perceived a house as being "young and strong," "old and weak," "fat or skinny," or "worn out."

In the course of my inquiries about the act of building a typical Dusun house, I found that an apparently simple shelter construction technique involved many of the basic postulates used by Dusun to make their world coherent. I discovered that most Dusun adults in Sensuron have a very deep and enduring emotional investment in both the shape and the details of their houses. It was very difficult for Dusun to speak easily of houses and their associated meanings, unless they turned to strong condemnations of those very few village residents with some *tolun a purak* ("European") house features, such as a tin roof or hand-sawn and nailed plank sides. Then the whole perceptual orientation of Dusun to their shelter form became readily apparent in the strong feelings of disgust, fear, and aggression displayed toward the few persons changing the traditional Dusun house style. I recorded one old Dusun woman saying, after spitting on the ground in great disgust, "You know that one (a man whose house had wooden sides and a tin roof) draws the attention of every evil spirit to this place; is it any wonder so many babies have died here this year with that man and his house in the middle of us!"

It is quite clear that many of an infant's earliest and continuing life experiences are set in the context of a particular type of shelter common to a society. These experiences appear to contribute substantially to the structuring of perceptions of the self and the environment and to the ways individuals come to view objects, space, and time. This statement does not mean, nor is it meant to imply, that the early and continuing experiences of infants and children with a particular type of shelter are critical events or are solely responsible for all of the ways they will perceive the world as adults. Such a claim would be in error, since other patterns in the cultural subsystems of technology, social relations, language, and ideology, as well as biological factors and unique life experiences, all influence and are part of the ways people perceive themselves and their world. The statement does mean, however, that if the infants and children of a society are en-culturated regularly in the context of a particular type of shelter, they probably will share as adults a perceptual set toward, preoccupation with, or "ready attention" to that special type of shelter. Furthermore it means that, as adults, such persons would be much less receptive to drastic changes in their culture's pattern of shelter since any marked change would mean altering a whole perceptual orientation toward the self and the world. As a consequence the pattern of shelter in a culture tends to remain stable over a long period of time.

Therefore if we seek to understand the interrelations of the technology pattern of shelter and the enculturation process of a particular society, we must regard both the ways adults of that society perceive shelter and the kinds of long-term life experiences and understandings infants and children gain in a particular type of shelter. We must also consider the consequences for children of having learned such perceptions from adults.

Dusun adults differ from Arunta, Ashanti, American, or other human adults not only because they have been enculturated in different cultural systems but also because those systems contain many different and uniquely interrelated patterns which contribute totally to local ways of viewing the world. In other words, it is not possible to transform a Dusun into an Arunta, or an Arunta into an Ashanti, or an Ashanti into an American simply by changing shelter types. Dusun view the world in Dusun terms and ways because they have been enculturated in the totality of Dusun culture, not simply because they have lived in a Dusun shelter.

As noted, the innovative effort by Whiting and Ayers (1968) in drawing some inferences from the shapes of shelters is one possible approach for studying the ways the human cultural pattern of shelter is related to the process of socialization. In using a carefully selected worldwide sample of ethnographic reports from 136 societies and following a statistical technique for holocultural study, Whiting and Ayers asked the specific question,

"Given the shape of the floor plan of a dwelling, what can be said, and with what degree of confidence, concerning other features of the culture?" One of their principal conclusions, which is related to the specific concerns of this discussion, was that certain "aesthetic considerations" of culture are related to the type of shelter characteristically found in a society. Using a hypothesis derived from a number of holocultural studies concerning the relations between art styles and marriage practices in a society and the development of an individual's "cognitive style" in the socialization process, Whiting and Ayers concluded from their data that it is possible to predict from a curvilinear-type floor plan that the chances are at least three to one that a society with such a shelter form practices a polygynous form of marriage.[12] Whiting and Ayers also concluded that it is possible to accurately predict that this relationship is the consequence of an "aesthetic" preference developed from a society's enculturation process, particularly when there is an intimate and exclusive relationship between mothers and infants during the first 2½ to 3 years after birth. In contrast, Whiting and Ayers believe it is possible to predict from a rectilinear-type floor that a society practices a monogamous form of marriage and that this relationship is the consequence of an "aesthetic" preference developed from a society's enculturation process in which fathers and mothers are more equally important to infants during their early years of life.

Although they seem to restrict its use only to art styles, Whiting and Ayers (1968) also appear to indicate that the phrase *aesthetic considerations* can denote the broad variety of ways humans perceive the world about them. If this is so, then this study can be taken as a partial demonstration of some transculturally meaningful relationships between shelter and socialization. It must be noted, however, that the principal point of the Whiting and Ayers study was to assist archaeologists in interpreting cultural data from their excavations of houses. In addition, the statistical methods used in their study may not account for all the contextual possibilities of data used.

The importance of such research and theory for understanding the relationships between the human pattern of shelter and the socialization process lies in the possibility of being able to specify precisely the ways shelter, or other patterns in the cultural subsystems of technology, social relations, language, and ideology produce particular effects and consequences in learning culture. At present it can be said that it is believed that such a causal relationship, for shelter, exists. However it must also be said that we do not know the precise nature and details of that relationship.

[12]For some studies suggesting causal relations between art styles, marriage forms, and socialization, see Whiting, Kluckhohn, & Anthony, 1958; Burton & Whiting, 1961; D'Andrade, 1962; Kuckenberg, 1963; Munroe, 1964; Munroe, Munroe, & Whiting, 1973.

Summary

In summary, the relationship between the socialization process and the technology subsystem pattern of shelter seems to involve much more than the ground plan, floor level, roof shape, or materials used in shelter walls and roofs. This relationship appears to involve a complex of attitudes, values, and beliefs derived from basic cultural postulates widely shared in a society that shape, direct, and guide the perceptions of individuals toward themselves and the world about them.

IDEOLOGY AND SOCIALIZATION

The ideology subsystem contains all the cultural patterns concerned with the basic style of thought, understanding, integrated assertions, and goals typical of a society. This cultural subsystem also contains all of the values, or ideals, widely shared in a society. The cultural ideas and ideals of a society sometimes are direct and actual reflections of the kinds of historical events which its members have experienced. Thus the concern of Americans with "progress" reflects an acute awareness of their culture's historic origin that required successful settlement of a continental wilderness. However the cultural ideals and ideas of a society may be fictional—that is, formed and adapted to artificial standards, after-the-fact interpretations, or partial memories of long-past historical events.

Research on Ideology

Attempts to record and compare valid statements about human cultural ideals and ideas have been a very important, although limited, part of past research and theory in anthropology and sociology. Some other scholars, notably philosophers, have also been active in the comparative study of human cultural ideals and ideas.

Attempts to study and compare human ideologies have produced a great number of terms and concepts that have been used in conjunction with a wide variety of research methods. Some examples of these different terms and concepts are given in the outline in Table 8–1.

Themes and Values in Ideology

An excellent illustration of the study of cultural ideology is to be found in Opler's discussion (1945) of *themes* in the culture of the Chiricahua Apache, a native North American society. Opler (1945;199) defines a *theme* as "a postulate or position, declared or implied, and usually controlling behavior or stimulating activity, which is tacitly approved or openly pro-

TABLE 8–1   Some Examples of Terms and Concepts Used in Studies of Cultural Ideology

I. IDEATIONAL OR COGNITIVE TERMS AND CONCEPTS	IV. ENTIRE CULTURE OR HOLISTIC ORIENTATIONS TERMS AND CONCEPTS

I. IDEATIONAL OR COGNITIVE	IV. ENTIRE CULTURE OR HOLISTIC
A. Master ideas	A. Ethos
B. Themes	B. Eidos
C. Premises	C. Total cultural pattern
D. Postulates	D. Interaction
E. Hypotheses	E. Focus
F. Common denominators	F. Plot
G. Enthymemes (unstated assumptions)	G. Style
	H. Set
II. EMOTIONAL OR AFFECTIVE TERMS AND CONCEPTS	I. Climax
	J. Social cynosure
	K. Integrating factors
A. Values	L. Sociopsychological constellations
B. Value attitudes	M. Binary oppositions
C. Interests	N. Systems of meanings
D. "Of courses"	O. Unconscious canons of choice
E. Value orientation	P. Configurations
III. ACTION OR CONATIVE TERMS AND CONCEPTS	
A. Purposes	
B. Goals	
C. Life goals	
D. Ideas	
E. Sanctions	
F. Directives	

moted in a society." Opler notes that there are many different themes in Chiricahua culture. For example, one theme notes that "men are physically, mentally, and morally superior to women." There are, says Opler, numerous "expressions" or translations of this theme in everyday Chiricahua conduct. Thus if an unborn child has "lots of life," it is said to be a boy. Chiricahua women are believed to be more unstable and excitable than men and so to do things that cause domestic or community trouble. Women are also believed to have much less willpower than men do and therefore to be easily tempted to sexual misconduct and practice of harmful magic. Chiricahua political and social leaders are men, and males always are heads of families. Women are supposed to defer to men in all social activities. Men must precede women on paths, and women must find special areas for eating away from the men. If male guests are present in a household, they must be served before any woman of the family. Women are prohibited from attending most important ceremonial and ritual activities. Menstruating women are considered a grave danger to the health of men and horses. Women are not permitted to sing dancing songs or to play at most men's games.

Another Chiricahua theme is stated by Opler as a quest for long life and an old age. Expressions of this theme are found in the fact that adults strive actively to achieve a long life through an incessant manipulation of supernatural powers and unflagging efforts in everyday life. Parents begin the quest for a long life for their children by placing their afterbirth and umbilical cord in a tree that ordinarily reaches great age, so the life and growth of the baby will parallel that of the tree. When Chiricahua children wear their first moccasins, they are led carefully through four footprints outlined with pollen, a magical symbol of long life. The annual spring haircuts of children are accompanied by prayers for their longevity. Parents seek out the blessings of very old persons, so a child will live to be at least as old as the adult. Girls must undergo a complex puberty ritual to live a long and healthy life. Very old adults command great social deference and personal respect and are expected to speak first and take the lead in social greetings.

A third Chiricahua Apache theme is termed by Opler as "validation by participation." While the wisdom of age is highly valued by the Chiricahua, it is subordinate and directly linked to personal performance. Chiricahua leaders in command during wars or in hunting parties are young men. When failing health or old age limits active participation, a leader yields readily to a younger man. Hence as long as men are fit, age is an asset. When they cannot keep pace, age does not prevent retirement. Similarly younger male ritual specialists actively and openly threaten various supernatural powers with the vigor of their magical acts. Chiricahua Apache believe that rituals for prevention and curing of disease are performed best by a vigorous and active man.

Opler has noted that Chiricahua themes are not always in perfect balance with one another and that, on occasion, one theme plays a more dominant role than others in the culture, particularly during times of great change in culture.

Another illustration of research on cultural themes is to be found in the studies by Kluckhohn (1949) of the Navaho, a native North American society. In a discussion of Navaho "ideological premises" (or themes), Kluckhohn presents an outline similar to the following:

NAVAHO THEMES

1. The Universe is orderly; all events are caused and interrelated.
   Corollary A. Knowledge is power.
   Corollary B. The basic quest is for harmony.
   Corollary C. Harmony can be restored only by orderly procedures.
   Corollary D. One price of disorder, in human terms, is illness.

2. The Universe tends to be personalized.
   Corollary A. Causation is identifiable in personalized terms.
3. The Universe is full of dangers.
4. Evil and Good are complementary, and both are ever-present.
5. Experience is conceived as a continuum differentiated only by sense data.
6. Morality is conceived in traditionalistic and situational terms rather than in terms of abstract absolutes.
7. Human relations are premised upon familistic ties.
8. Events, not actors or qualities, are primary.

Kluckhohn also presents a discussion of each of these Navaho ideological themes and corollaries in terms of their everyday expressions in Navaho life. For instance, with reference to the premise that the universe is orderly, Navaho believe no supernatural being may capriciously grant the petitions of individuals, for even the gods are bound together in specified ways that cannot be changed by gods or humans. Every feature of daily life is believed to have one or more causes, arising from the ways the event is related to other events in the cosmic scheme of things. Thus if rain does not fall at the expected season, it is because "people are too mean," or proper ritual taboos have not been followed, or someone is using witchcraft. Navaho constantly test out the order between events. Before committing themselves to a very lengthy and expensive curing ritual, Navaho will try a portion of a ritual to see if it works. If the small segment of ritual is seen to be effective, then this is taken as a sign that events are in fairly good order and that a full ritual may work. Navaho with knowledge of the ways the universe is ordered are believed to be successful and healthy because of their knowledge. Navaho strive to reduce friction in human relations in order to restore harmony and to maintain order in the universe. Navaho believe in all ritual actions, art, folklore, and songs must have a balance or a harmony in their parts and a symmetry of form. Restoration of order in life is believed to be primarily a task of putting objects and human events back into their usual and symmetrical forms.

There are also a variety of everyday expressions of another Navaho premise—that the universe is full of dangers. Navaho life is set in the context of a difficult natural environment. Winters are long and cold, summers are arid and hot, and dangerous wild animals and human enemies have been present in the Navaho lands. However Navaho accept these dangers in the terms of this first premise. Such dangers are seen to be part of the natural order of the universe. The Navaho say that it is their failure to know the exact scheme of things that causes them to see their world as a dangerous place. Navaho do not curse their destiny because they accept the fact that they can deal effectively with the lack of harmony affecting their lives only by knowing the precise order of the universe. Since they also accept their general inability to ever really know more than a small part of the order of the universe, Navaho realize that their lives will be filled with the fears that follow the constant possibilities of causing error and disharmony through some personal action. When Navaho find themselves in a situation that they define as having the potential for causing great disorder, they will tend not to act since to do so would contribute to further disorder.

A number of efforts have been made to describe the themes of different peoples, including American and European cultures. For instance, Hoebel's notable discussion (1954) of native law is organized about "basic postulates" or themes in Eskimo, Ifugao, Comanche, Kiowa, Cheyenne, Trobriand, and Ashanti cultures. Hoebel has abstracted the following 17 themes from Ashanti ethnographic data.

ASHANTI THEMES[13]

1. The gods and ancestral spirits control and direct the operation of all the forces of the universe.
2. All humans must be allowed to participate, directly or indirectly, in the formulation of laws.
3. All major contraventions of the will of the ancestors or the gods are sins.
4. The ancestors will punish the group as a whole, if the group does not punish a sinner and atone for his misdeed.
5. The ancestors will try humans in the spirit world, if they take advantage of a miscarriage of justice here.
6. Past misfortunes are repugnant to the ancestral spirits.
7. Humans are endowed with conscious will, except when drunk or misdirected by an evil spirit in certain limited situations.
8. Blood is physical in nature and is inherited through the mother, thereby creating a physical bond of continuity in matrilineal descent.
9. The spirit is inherited through the father.
10. Basic property belongs to the ancestors.
11. A headman or chief is the representative of the ancestors of the group he governs, and a stool is symbolic of the collectivity of the ancestors.
12. Men are bound to their chiefs by personal fealty as well as by kinship.
13. A man, except when he dies in battle or of natural causes, must know why he dies.
14. Cursing with a forbidden oath is killing.
15. Incest destroys the universe.
16. Menstruation is spiritually unclean.
17. The sex rights of a husband in his wife are exclusive.

DuBois (1955) has presented an outline of themes in American culture and notes that the culture is organized about four "basic premises" (or themes).

1. The universe is a mechanism.
2. Humans are masters of the universe.
3. Humans are equal.
4. Humans are perfectible.

[13]Hoebel, 1954, 252–254.

DuBois notes that systematic analysis of these premises yields the following three major "focal values":

1. A belief in material well-being which derives from the basic premise that humans are masters of the universe.
2. A belief in social conformity which derives from the basic premise that humans are equal.
3. A belief in effort and optimism which derives from the basic premise that humans are perfectible.

TABLE 8–2 Specific Values in American Life

I. Material well-being specific values
 A. A high standard of living. Americans equate economic prosperity and social progress and expect that they have a right to demand a high level of living and consumption of goods. This right is supported by health insurance, social welfare plans and operations, and political hostility toward economic and professional interest groups, organizations, and plans which threaten to limit a high standard of living.
 B. Success in material goods carries a moral sanction. Americans believe they have a right to be physically comfortable, after working hard, for virtue in daily labor carries the reward of attaining desired goods.
 C. Manual labor is dignified. Americans feel that hard work with one's hands and body is of superior worth and will "pay off" in material well-being.
 D. Military logistics shape basic strategy. Americans do not assume that, unless all is lost, personal heroism should come before providing proper supplies and equipment for fighting. Americans tend to be prepared for wars first by building bases and filling them with equipment and then starting to fight. Usually there are three times or more the number of "support" troops than "combat" troops.
 E. Pain, brutality, and death are not to be tolerated. Americans tend to be repelled by poverty, misery, cruelty, and physical suffering since these all interfere with attainment of a material well-being.
II. Conformity specific values
 A. Team work. Americans believe that no single person can master the universe, so people must work together to meet their immediate tasks to enable them to cope later with larger efforts.
 B. Self-achievement has the goal of similarity. Americans strive individually to achieve the end of being similar to others in the society.
 C. Physical barriers are unwelcome. Americans tend to believe fences, doors, walls, and other barriers separate the partners of the team in efforts to master life's problems.
 D. Hostility toward authority figures. Americans resist authority symbols because these accentuate status differences rather than conformity and team work.
III. Effort-optimism specific values
 A. Work is valuable. Americans stress work activity as so necessary that even recreation and leisure must be work to be good.
 B. Importance of education. Formal education prepares children for their work careers and activities and so is to be strongly encouraged.
 C. Vigor and impatience. Americans stress specific action now, even at the expense of planning.
 D. Emphasis on biologic youth. American cultural heroes are young, strong, good-looking, and healthy.

In turn, DuBois believes that analysis of each of these three "focal values" yields a series of "specific values" in American culture. These specific values are listed in Table 8–2. A summary of the scheme used by DuBois is presented in Figure 8–4.

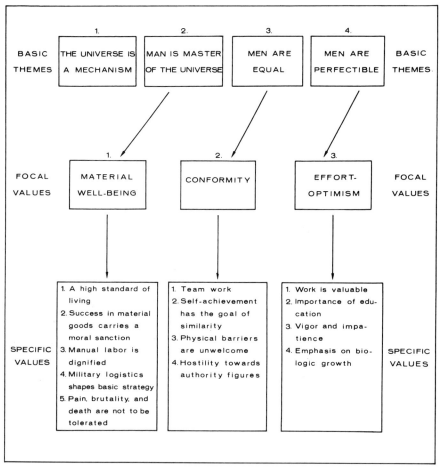

FIGURE 8–4   American themes and their associated values. (DuBois, C. 1955. "The Dominant Value Profile of American Culture." *American Anthropologist*, 57, 1232–1239.)

A major problem in the analysis of themes is that significant ideological variations in a culture have not been really accounted for in most discussions.

One effort to understand ideological, or theme, variations within and between cultures has been the research of Kluckhohn, Strodtbeck, and their associates (1961). These studies are based on the assumptions that (1) there are a limited number of common human problems for which all peoples must find some solutions and (2) in all societies there will be some differentially preferred solutions to common problems at different times. Kluckhohn et al. developed a five-section questionnaire concerned with the common problems of (1) *human nature orientation* (what is the character of innate human nature?); (2) *human-to-nature orientation* (what is the relation of humans to nature and supernature?); (3) *time orientation* (what is the temporal focus of human life?); (4) *activity orientation* (what is the usual style of a person's relationship to others?). In order to encompass the range of value variations for these assumed common human problem areas, Kluckhohn et al. defined the widest possible range of choices humans might have in each area. These choices are noted in Table 8–3.

TABLE 8–3   Value Orientations

I. Human nature orientation
   A. Evil
   B. Good and evil
   C. Good
II. Man-to-nature orientation
   A. Subjugation to nature
   B. Harmony with nature
   C. Mastery over nature
III. Time orientation
   A. Past
   B. Present
   C. Future
IV. Activity orientation
   A. Being
   B. Being-in-becoming
   C. Doing
V. Relational orientation
   A. Lineal
   B. Collateral
   C. Individualistic

Then Kluckhohn et al. presented their questionnaire to members of five differrent cultural communities located in the same general physical environment in the American Southwest. Two of the communities were native American (Navaho and Zuni), one was Spanish-American, another Mormon, and the fifth was a homestead village of American Texan and Oklahoman farmers. Before beginning actual field study the authors made specific predictions, based on the literature of each of these five communities, regarding their principal orientation on four of the five common problem areas of their questionnaire (the human nature orientation was exempted from their predictions). These specific predictions are noted in Table 8–4. This table also notes the specific results obtained by these authors through application of their value orientations research questionnaire in each of the five communities studied.

These studies of cultural ideology have established the point that there may be substantial differences between the styles of thought and understanding within different cultures.

Studies of Ideology and Socialization

Few patterns of cultural belief and value have been studied with regard to their specific relationships to the socialization process. One pattern which has had some attention is art.

Much of art is decorative. Designs or marks are made by the users or manufacturers on the artifacts and objects employed in the everyday life of a culture. Sometimes decorative art is formal—that is, it may be used to show an aesthetic preference of individuals making or using artifacts. Individual artistic expressions may also reflect a consensus of generally pleasing appearances and standards of beauty widely shared in a society.

Human art may also be symbolic in nature. Some artifacts are deliberately made and decorated with forms and designs of very special cultural meanings. Symbolic art decoration usually conveys messages about the presence of supernatural and nonhuman forces revered and feared by human beings. Thus a container with a sacred animal carved on the lid may not be just a box but represents the animal itself keeping watch over sacred objects stored within it. Objects used in religious and magical acts and rituals are usually infused with widely shared and deeply felt meanings expressed in symbolic form. The symbolic or decorative arts of a culture are not readily understood by persons unfamiliar with that tradition. For example, the "split representation" decorative and symbolic art style of the Kwakiutl, Haida, and Tsimshian peoples of the northwestern coast of North America involves the dislocation of animal, human, and spirit forms into elements that are then recombined following traditional rules and aesthetic standards that have little to do with Western European conceptions of nature. Thus it is necessary when looking at a Haida painting of a bear to imagine that the animal has been cut in two from head to tail, with a deep cleft between the eyes down to the level of the nose. The cleft head depicts two facial profiles that join at the mouth and nose. The remainder of the bear's body is similarly shown in two adjoining profiles.[14] This art form often uses the arbitrary dislocation of internal organs and other body parts, which are split off and then rejoined to the animal in some other place; a claw is made into a bird's beak, an eye becomes a leg or an arm joint, and so on.

[14]See Boas, 1927a, 1927b, 1929.

TABLE 8–4 Predicted and Observed Variations in Dominant Value Orientations in Five Southwestern American Communities*

Orientation	Spanish Americans		Texans		Mormons		Zuni		Navaho	
	Predicted	Observed	Predicted	Observed	Predicted	Observed	Predicted	Observed	Predicted	Observed
Man-to-nature	Subjugation Over With	Subjugation Over With	Over Subjugation With	Over With Subjugation	With Over Subjugation	Over With Subjugation	No prediction	With Subjugation Over	With Subjugation Over	With Subjugation Over
Time	Present Future Past	Present Future Past	Future Present Past	Future Present Past	Future Present Past	Future Present Past	No prediction	Present Past Future	Present Past Future	Present Past Future
Activity	Being Doing	Being Doing	Doing Being	Doing Being	Doing Being	Doing Being	No prediction	Doing Being	Doing Being	Doing Being
Relational	Individualistic Lineal Collateral	Individualistic Lineal Collateral	Individualistic Collateral Lineal	Individualistic Collateral Lineal	Individualistic Collateral Lineal	Individualistic Collateral Lineal	No prediction	Collateral Lineal Individualistic	Collateral Lineal Individualistic	Collateral Lineal Individualistic

*After Kluckhohn, F., and F. Strodtbeck. 1961. *Variations in Value Orientations*. Evanston, Ill.: Row, Peterson, p. 351.

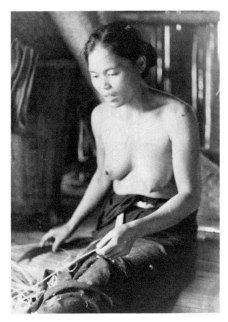

A Sensuron Dusun woman preparing rice sifting mat for harvest. (T.R. Williams, 1959)

Ethnographer's wife, Margaret Williams, preparing a meal. (T.R. Williams, 1959)

Levi-Strauss (1967) has noted that the split representation decorative and symbolic art style was also typical of the nineteenth-century Maori of New Zealand, the Neolithic cultures of China (Yangshao), Japan (Jomon), and Siberia (Amur River Basin), and among the twentieth-century Caduveo peoples of Paraguay and southern Brazil. It is also found in the prehistoric Hopewell culture of eastern North America. It is Levi-Strauss' belief that this identity of art form and style among so many cultures separated by more than 2000 years and with no known evidences of historic contact arises from the fact that all of these groups had social systems in which there were personal prestige struggles, intense rivalry between formal groups, and severe competitions for social and economic privilege as regular features of life. In other words, Levi-Strauss feels that individual artists in these different societies, widely separated in space and time, accidentally discovered, through their long-term experimentations with decorative and symbolic art, the same formal arrangement of themes of a culture organized in terms of social hierarchies and hierarchical behavior.

Unlike Levi-Strauss, other anthropologists have tended to be hesitant in making comparative studies attempting to relate art to patterns in other subsystems of human culture. However a number of studies of the possible relations between art and socialization have been published. For instance, Barry (1957) has published the results of his study of the relationships between "child training" and the "pictorial arts" in 30 nonliterate cultures. Barry began his research on the relations between art and socialization with the assumption that the personality of an individual artist is commonly expressed in their creations, so that individual differences in art styles in a culture are related directly to individual personality differences. Barry further assumed that, since the personalities of individual artists include the consequences of the influential events they have experienced while learning culture, the art styles of culture will directly reflect such events.

Next Barry proceeded to apply these two assumptions to a whole culture. He reasoned that if the assumptions were true for individuals, they would also be true for a "typical" individual in a small and relatively homogeneous population.

Using the measures of severity of socialization defined and discussed by Whiting and Child (1953) and some specific measures of art style developed by himself, Barry then conducted a statistical test for the existence of a possible correlation between (1) the severity of "socialization" in a culture and (2) typical styles of art in a culture.

Barry's research procedures began with accepting the validity of the numerical scores and rankings for each of ten measures of severity of oral, anal, sexual, dependency, and aggression socialization used by Whiting and Child (1953) in their research. Barry then sought in the ethnographic literature at least ten pictures of artworks for each of 30 native societies. He used a total of 549 pictures in all in his study. Barry then proceeded to judge each of the works of art on a seven-point scale for 18 different criteria, such as shortness of lines, presence of a border, asymmetry of design, and so on. Barry then chose to consider 11 of his 18 criteria as real measures of the complexity of the art style in a culture.

At this point Barry proceeded to employ statistical procedures to measure the possible correlations between his 11 variables of complexity of design and Whiting and Child's 10 variables of severity of "socialization" in a culture. He concluded from his statistical analysis that, for each of the

11 art variables, the cultures above the median (the point in a series chosen so that half the cases are on one side and half on the other) in complexity of art design tended also to be above average in the severity of their "socialization" of oral, anal, sexual, dependency, and aggression systems of behavior.

Barry drew the general conclusion from his data and analyses that the positive correlation between severity of socialization and complexity of design in artworks indicated a specific "connecting link" between them which he noted to be the kind of typical personality produced in a society's enculturation process. In other words, Barry believes his study of relations between art and socialization demonstrates that cultures have simple or complex art styles because the typical personality types produced in a society by severe or relaxed child training practices lead to the kind of person capable of producing either a simple or a complex art design.

In another study of the relationships between art and socialization, Fischer (1961) investigated the specific question of whether any features of culture may predispose an artist to regularly choose curvilinear (semicircular or circular) or rectilinear (rectangular) designs. Fischer began his research with the assumption that rectilinear designs represent the male body image, whereas curvilinear designs represent the female body image. He also made the assumption that humans project their society into their art.

Fischer's specific research procedures began with his accepting the validity of the judgments of art styles for 30 cultures made by Barry (1957) in his study of the relations between complexity of design and severity of socialization. Using cultural and social data taken from the summaries listed in Murdock's World Ethnographic Sample (1957), Fischer proceeded to formulate six hypotheses concerning the relationships between the art style of a culture, its typical form of social relations, and the relative prestige or security of the sexes. Fischer's (1961, 81, 84) hypotheses were as follows:

1. Design repetitive of a number of rather simple elements should characterize the egalitarian societies; design integrating a number of unlike elements should be characteristic of hierarchical societies.
2. Design with a large amount of empty or irrelevant space should characterize the egalitarian societies; design with little irrelevant (empty) space should characterize the hierarchical societies.
3. Symmetrical design (a special case of repetition) should characterize the egalitarian societies; asymmetrical design should characterize the hierarchical societies.
4. Figures without enclosures should characterize the egalitarian societies; enclosed figures should characterize the hierarchical societies.
5. Straight lines, representing the male form, as opposed to curved lines, or the female form, should be associated with societies which strongly favor male solidarity in residence.

Using Barry's criteria for design complexity, Fischer then employed statistical procedures to test these hypotheses against the ethnographic data summarized by Murdock. Fischer's statistical results tend to show a positive relationship between repetitive, open-spaced, symmetrical, and nonenclosed figure designs in the art of societies which regularly minimize individual differences in prestige and emphasized cooperation and mutual helpfulness. In contrast, Fischer's statistical data note that societies that emphasize differentiation of persons by social and economic rank and personal prestige and minimize personal cooperation will have art designs that integrate unlike elements, have little empty space, are asymmetrical, and contain enclosed figures. In addition, Fischer's statistical data concerning the relative prestige or security of the sexes (Hypothesis 5) were much less positive. To his surprise Fischer found in testing the fifth hypothesis that, while he believed from psychological studies that rectilinear, or "male," art designs would be found regularly in cultures with patrilocal or avunculocal (see Glossary) marriage residence patterns, possibly indicating that men have high prestige, quite the opposite was true. In fact, Fischer discovered a statistical association in the opposite direction—that is, curvilinear, or "female," design and a pattern of preference in a culture for patrilineal and avunculocal residence after marriage. Fischer offered an explanation for this reversal of his hypothesis by pointing out that perhaps the reason for cultures with high male prestige having a dominant "female" (curvilinear) art style was that men in patrilineal- and avunculocal-type cultures, which accorded them high prestige, were more psychologically secure and extroverted and had more time to spend looking for pleasure in the opposite sex. Hence such psychological security, says Fischer, would explain the presence in high male prestige societies of curvilinear art designs.

In reviewing Fischer's reasoning concerning the reversal of the fifth hypothesis, Whiting and Ayres (1968) point out, however, that psychological theory really suggests that psychological conflict and anxiety arising in enculturation rather than psychological security is the explanation for high male prestige in societies employing "female" art designs. This would be so, Whiting and Ayres say, simply because more sexually frustrated and anxious males would tend to be more preoccupied with the female body and thus prefer use of curvilinear, or "female," art designs. Whiting and Ayres reasoned further that, if the conflict-and-anxiety explanation for Fischer's statistical data was correct, then it could be predicted that in societies that emphasize patrilocal and avunculocal residence after marriage there would be a high degree of restrictions on children's and adolescent sex activities. Whiting and Ayres (1968, 128) report that the test of this hypothesis (societies with patrilocal and avunculocal residence have severe restrictions on premarital sex activities) in 136 societies was a statistically positive one. Whiting and Ayres conclude that patrilocal and avunculocal societies, with a preference for curvilinear art designs, tend to produce males who are more sexually inhibited because of restrictions on their sex activities in the enculturation process.

Carrying his theory of "psychological security" one step further, Fischer (1961) also reported, as part of his study, on the relationships between the form of marriage (monogamy, polygamy, and so on) in a culture and its dominant art style. He formulated two hypotheses concerning these possible relationships: (1) because of a higher degree of psychological security for men due to their sexual access to two or more women, polygamous cultures would use more curved lines in their art; and (2) because of a higher degree of psychological insecurity for men due to their sexual restriction to one woman, monogamous societies would use more straight-line designs in their art. Fischer notes that a statistical testing of these two hypotheses showed them to be valid at "a statistically significant level." However he made one important qualification of these results, with specific reference to the art designs of cultures which practice polygyny. Sororal polygyny is different, notes Fischer, from ordinary polygyny, in that the cowives are sisters and therefore because of their enculturation experiences tend more often to form a common front against the interests and wishes of an outsider, or husband. Cultures practicing sororal polygyny were found by Fischer to be "intermediate" in their art design preference, between the two extremes of curvilinear and rectilinear design. Fischer also points out that the cultures with a hierarchical social structure tend to produce a severe competition between siblings, to the point where sororal polygyny hardly would work well. This, says Fischer, is why cultures with sororal polygyny nearly all tend to have relatively simple art styles, in common with monogamous cultures. *but not nonsororal*

In reviewing these conclusions (that monogamous cultures were more likely to use a preponderance of straight lines in their art designs than were cultures practicing nonsororal polygyny), Whiting and Ayres (1968) pointed out that Fischer's use of a psychological security explanation was again contradicted by a number of recent, statistically based, holocultural studies of socialization.[15] Whiting points out that these studies, concerned generally with the specific effects of the "salience," or closeness, of the mother and father to children during the first 2½ to 3 years of life on adult cognitive styles, all note that where a culture regularly established an intimate and exclusive relationship between mothers and children the form of the family is usually polygynous. In contrast, cultures in which mothers and fathers are more equally important to children usually tend to be monogamous.

[15]See Whiting et al., 1958; Burton & Whiting, 1961; D'Andrade, 1962; Kuckenberg, 1963; Munroe, 1964; Munroe et al., 1973.

Whiting goes on to note that in cultures with a close mother-child relationship mothers are seen by children to control all the important resources and economic goods vital to children. Mothers in such cultures tend to occupy the position of highest prestige in the eyes of children. After weaning in a polygynous family, says Whiting, the preoccupation of a male child with his mother's body should continue unabated; such male children are presumed to be characterized by psychological conflict and anxiety.

In contrast, notes Whiting, in monogamous cultures children learn that both men and women equally control the resources and goods important to children. After weaning a child's preoccupation with his or her mother's body is much less intense. Such children tend to be characterized by psychological security.

Whiting and Ayres (1968) conducted their own study of the relationship between curvilinear art designs and polygyny and between rectilinear art designs and monogamy, as reported by Fischer in his study. They confirmed Fischer's positive findings in their own survey of art design and social structure (1968, 130). In contrast to Fischer and following the studies of salience in socialization, Whiting and Ayres interpret this strong association as meaning that the presence of a curvilinear art design in a polygynous culture is the result of the usual enculturation practices of such groups, in which during early childhood there is a high degree of mother-child salience. This is so, implies Whiting, because high salience in enculturation produces psychological conflict and anxiety, hence adult male concerns with curvilinear art design, whereas low salience in enculturation produces psychological security, hence a greater adult male concern with rectilinear art designs.

The general theoretical view expressed in the studies by Barry, Fischer, and Whiting is that features of enculturation give rise to some psychological characteristics that are primary determinants of artistic creativity and that these characteristics are reflected directly in the typical style of a culture's decorative and symbolic art. Barry and Whiting tend to believe that the conditions giving rise to important psychological characteristics involved in a typical art design are those found in the human socialization process. Fischer tends to look more to particular forms of human social life (hierarchical social relations, polygynous marriage preference, and so on) as being productive of those psychological characteristics that determine the typical designs of art in human culture. However Fischer also gives reference to and makes note of the socialization process in providing his explanations—for example, psychological security—for reversal of his one hypothesis and for the occurrence of particular art designs in association with specific marriage forms.

Disregarding whether the basic assumptions of these studies are correct, whether their statistical methods are accurate in transcultural analysis, or whether their logic in drawing conclusions is valid, the vital point of such innovative research is that it offers a clear demonstration that there are ways of discussing relationships between the socialization process and the ideology pattern of art.

Two other studies have been conducted of art design styles and their specific relationships to various social and cultural factors, including some features of the socialization process. Wolfe (1969) has investigated the specific question of why some cultures produce a large amount of "high-quality" art, whereas other cultures seem to produce little or no art, or art of "less quality." Wolfe used statistical procedures to test his general hypothesis that a high development of graphic and plastic art is associated with social structural features that set up barriers between males in local communities. Wolfe assumed that social barriers between males produce "emotions," which in turn would be directly reflected in the "emotions" involved in the art design and production of a culture. Wolfe then tested his hypothesis in 53 African cultures and concluded that it was generally true, at least in the case of African cultures. He notes that the statistically significant results of his research support his belief that art flourishes in those African cultures where males are divided by important social barriers, as well as where settlements are fixed and nucleated (or compact). Wolfe feels that if these African data are applicable to other world culture regions, then a transculturally valid relationship between social structure and art design may be established. Wolfe's discussion and conclusions imply that some features of the socialization process are directly involved in the art style of a culture through the "emotions" produced in particular social conditions, which are then reflected directly in the "emotions" displayed in art designs. Although he does not directly specify any enculturation practices among the 39 variables of social structure used in his study, Wolf does, in fact, include a number of features of the cultural transmission process among the variables listed.

Another study indicating some possible relationships between art and the socialization process has been reported by Dennis (1966), who notes the differences in scores on the administration of the Goodenough "Draw-A-Man" test to 6- to 12-year-old children in 40 different groups located in some 13 cultures. The test scores reported by Dennis were collected in the period between 1928 and 1962. From 1926 to about 1950 the Goodenough test was considered by many psychologists to be a "culture-free" test, which measured inherent intelligence by drawings of human figures. However by 1950 this assumption had been rejected by Goodenough. Dennis began the study reported here by noting that, while a Goodenough drawing test score obviously does not measure innate or biologically transmitted intelligence, it can be considered to show cultural and social differences in art design and drawing styles. Following this assumption Dennis proposed the hypothesis that differences in the Goodenough test scores of children in different cultures would be reflected in their representational (or decorative) art. Dennis also advanced a second hypothesis that in many cultures Goodenough test scores are "indirect" measures of modernization and cultural change toward a European and American style of technology.

Dennis also began his study with the assumptions that in non-Western cultures, with little prior contact with European and American decorative art, but with a "high level of achievement" in respect to several art forms, such as wood carving, sculpture, pottery, masks, and sand painting, children would earn high Goodenough test scores. In contrast, Dennis also assumed that in cultures with no prior contacts with European and American cultures and with a low level of artistic achievement, children would earn low Goodenough test scores. Therefore, Dennis reasoned, when children in a culture with a low level of artistic achievement begin to be exposed to a high level of artistic achievement through regular and increasing contacts with European and American decorative art, the increase in their Goodenough test scores would provide a rough index of local cultural change.

Dennis then presented test score data from the 40 groups in 13 cultures and a statistical analysis of their differences. He concluded that all of the significant differences between cultures on the Goodenough test scores seem attributable to the differences in exposure of children to representational art, either as it is native to a culture or as it has been introduced in the course of growing cultural change and modernization toward a European and American style of decorative art.

CONCLUSIONS

Studies of relationships between the socialization process and patterns in the cultural subsystems of technology and ideology presently are hampered by inattention to reporting the ethnographic details of these aspects of cultural transmission. A search of the literature of enculturation provides only fragmentary glimpses of the ways infants and children actually learn these aspects of culture.

For example, Opler (1946, 39–40) reports in a study of Jicarilla Apache Indian enculturation that when a boy is four or five years old his older brothers, father, or grandfather give him a toy bow and arrows to familiarize him with these essential adult tools. Opler notes that on occasion older men gather little boys together and teach them games that increase their skills in the use of these tools. Opler also reports that six- and seven-year-old Jicarilla boys are encouraged to get up early in the morning to run after the horses, to chase them from their night pastures to a point near the encampment where they can be caught by adult males. Boys of this age are instructed not to mistreat horses when they run after them. They are told stories of horses abandoning masters during crucial times in the hunt or in war because of mistreatment by their owners. Opler also reports that at about nine or ten years of age Jicarilla boys are taught to ride rapidly with and without a saddle. Opler notes, too, that at 12 years of age boys are made to ride past and to practice shooting arrows past each other in preparation for warfare.

These few comments on the enculturation of Jicarilla boys to skill and awareness of the two technology trait complexes of the bow and arrow and the use of the horse in war and hunting are accompanied in Opler's report by a few other brief statements concerning the ways the bow-and-arrow and horse culture trait complexes are related to some other patterns in the technology and ideology subsystems of the Jicarilla Apache culture. How- ever these brief comments do not at all provide a sense of the fullness, the great complexity of detail, and the vital importance in enculturation of these patterns of Jicarilla cultural subsystems of technology and ideology. A reading of the extensive literature on the Jicarilla and other closely related North American Plains cultures makes it clear that the enculturation process for Jicarilla boys must have been very much more complex in the learning of some cultural patterns of technology and ideology than has been reported.[16]

Such reportorial limitations, due primarily to lack of space rather than an author's interests or abilities, have not been unusual in publications concerned with cultural transmission. A need now exists, however, for studies of the enculturation process in its relation to specific patterns of the technology and ideology subsystems in order to provide the basis for meaningful transcultural generalizations concerning these aspects of cul- tural transmission.

Although only a few examples of patterns of the technology and ideology subsystems of culture have been discussed here, it is clear that the present situation in socialization research makes it difficult to offer mean- ingful general statements. It also seems quite clear that patterns of tech- nology and ideology play an important part in the socialization process. However since there is uncertainty about the specific ways technology and ideology patterns are related to cultural transmission in many different cultures, we can offer only very qualified statements. For instance, in the small sample of societies cited in Chapter 6, there appears to be a tendency for at least half of the societies, without apparent regard to other cultural and social features (such as subsistence, kinship, kin groups, class) to place on children the general burdens of properly learning technology and ide- ology patterns. In some societies, however, particularly those that are heav- ily urbanized and industrialized (such as the United States, England, France, Russia), some kinds of specific instruction in patterns of technology

[16]See the comments of Wissler, 1914; Haines, 1938a, 1938b; Hoebel, 1954, 127–176; Ewers, 1955.

and ideology do occur regularly ("vocational education," "church schools"); children are not left entirely to themselves in learning these features of their culture. Even in these urban and industrial societies, children apparently are responsible for substantial portions of their own enculturation in the patterns of technology and ideology.

This particular statement, based on a reading of the literature of enculturation in a small number of societies, is qualified by the fact that few of the studies of enculturation used in the sample fully report the specific details of learning of most patterns of technology and ideology. Hopefully this particular lack in socialization research should change rapidly as detailed field research is conducted on the enculturation of children to patterns of technology and ideology in specific societies.

SUMMARY

This chapter has been concerned with illustrating some of the ways the socialization process may be related to patterns in the technology and ideology subsystems of culture. The discussion began with an examination of possible relations between socialization and the technology pattern of shelter. Consideration was then given to the ways several ideology subsystem patterns, including ideas about nature, society, and art, might be related to socialization. The chapter concluded with brief comments concerning future studies of the interrelations between socialization and the technology and ideology subsystems of culture.

REFERENCES CITED AND SUGGESTED READINGS

ALBERT, E. 1956. "The Classification of Values: A Method and Illustration." *American Anthropologist*, 58, 221–248.

BARRY, H., III. 1957. "Relationships Between Child Training and the Pictorial Arts." *Journal of Abnormal and Social Psychology*, 54, 380–383.

BEALS, R. 1935. *Material Culture of the Pima, Papago and Western Apache*. Berkeley, Calif.: U.S. Department of the Interior, National Park Service.

BERLIN, B., & P. KAY. 1969. *Basic Color Terms: Their Universality and Evolution*. Berkeley: University of California Press.

BERNARD, H.R. (ed.). 1972. *Technology and Social Change*. New York: Macmillan.

BIDNEY, D. 1949. "The Concept of Meta-Anthropology and Its Significance for Contemporary Anthropological Science." In F.S.C. Northrop (ed.), *Ideological Differences and World Order*. New Haven, Conn.: Yale University Press, pp. 323–355.

———. 1953a. "The Concept of Value in Modern Anthropology." In A.L. Kroeber (ed.), *Anthropology Today*. Chicago: University of Chicago Press, pp. 682–699.

BOAS, F. 1911. *The Mind of Primitive Man*. New York: Macmillan.

————. 1927a. *Primitive Art.* Oslo: H. Aschehough.

————. 1927b. "Primitive Art." Oslo, Norway: Instituttet fur Sammenlingnende Kulturforskning 8, 223–224.

————. 1929. *Primitive Art.* New York: Dover (first published in 1929, republished by Dover in 1955).

————. 1930. *The Religion of the Kwakiutl Indians.* New York: Columbia University Contributions to Anthropology, No. 10.

————. 1932. *Anthropology and Modern Life.* New York: Heath.

————. 1940. *Race Language and Culture.* New York: Macmillan.

BOGORAS, W. 1904–1909. *The Chukchee, Material Culture.* New York: Memoirs of the American Museum of Natural History, No. 11.

BRANDT, R. 1954. *Hopi Ethics: A Theoretical Analysis.* Chicago: University of Chicago Press.

BUCK, P. 1930. *Samoan Material Culture.* Honolulu: Bishop Museum, Bulletin 75.

BUNZEL, R. 1929. *The Pueblo Potter.* New York: Columbia University Contributions to Anthropology, 8, 1–124.

BURTON, R., & J.W.M. WHITING. 1961. *"The Absent Father and Cross-Sex Identity." Merrill-Palmer Quarterly,* 7, 85–95.

CHISHOLM, J. 1978. "Swaddling, Cradleboards and Development of Children." *Early Human Development,* 2, 255–275.

CONKLIN, J.C. 1955. "Hanunoo Color Categories." *Southwestern Journal of Anthropology,* 11, 339–344.

D'ANDRADE, R. 1962. "Father Absence and Cross-Sex Identification." Unpublished doctoral dissertation, Harvard University.

DEFFONTAINES, P. 1948. *Geographie et Religions* (9th ed.). Paris: Librairie Gallimard.

DENNIS, W. 1966. "Goodenough Scores, Art Experience and Modernization." *Journal of Social Psychology,* 68, 211–228.

DIVALE, W.T. 1977. "Living Floor Area and Marital Residence: A Replication." *Behavior Science Research,* 12, 109–115.

DRIVER, H. 1956. "An Integration of Functional, Evolutionary and Historical Theory by Means of Correlations." *Indiana University Publications in Anthropology and Linguistics,* 12, 1–36.

————. 1966. "Geographical-Historical versus Psycho-Funcitonal Explanations of Kin Avoidances." *Current Anthropology,* 7, 131–160, 176–182.

DRIVER, H., & A. KROEBER. 1932. "Quantitative Expression of Cultural Relationships." *University of California Publications in American Archaeology and Ethnology,* 31, 211–256.

DRIVER, H., & W. MASSEY. 1957. "Comparative Studies of North Ameircan Indians." *Transactions of the American Philosophical Society* (n.s.), 47, 165–460.

DuBOIS, C. 1955. "The Dominant Value Profile of American Culture." In M. Lantis (ed.), "The U.S.A. as Anthropologists See It," *American Anthropologist,* 57, 1232–1239.

EDEL, M., & A. EDEL. 1959. *Anthropology and Ethics.* Springfield, Ill.: Chas. C Thomas.

ELIADE, M. 1961. *The Sacred and the Profane.* New York: Harper & Row, Pub.

ESSER, A.H. (ed.). 1971. *The Use of Space by Animals and Man.* New York: Plenum.

EWERS, J.C. 1955. *The Horse in Blackfoot Indian Culture.* Washington, D.C.: Smithsonian Institution Press.

FIRTH, R.W. 1936. *Art and Life in New Guinea.* London: The Studio Ltd.

FISCHER, J.L. 1961. "Art Styles as Cultural Cognitive Maps." *American Anthropologist,* 63, 79–93.

FITCH, J., & D. BRANCH. 1960. "Primitive Architecture and Climate." *Scientific American,* 203, 134–144.

FORD, C. 1939. "Society, Culture and the Human Organism." *Journal of General Psychology*, 20, 135–179.

FORGE, A. (ed.). 1967. *Primitive Art and Society.* New York: Oxford University Press.

FORTES, M. 1959. "Primitive Kinship." *Scientific American*, 200, 146–158.

FRANCK, K. 1946. "Preferences for Sex Symbols and Their Personality Correlates." *Genetic Psychology Monographs*, 33, 73–123.

FREEMAN, L., & R. WINCH. 1957. "Societal Complexity: An Empirical Test of a Typology of Societies." *American Journal of Sociology*, 62, 461–466.

GOLDENWEISER, A. 1922. *Early Civilization.* New York: Knopf.

———. 1933. *History, Psychology and Culture.* New York: Knopf.

———. 1937. *Anthropology.* New York: Crofts.

GOODY, J., B. IRVING, & N. TALANY. 1971. "Causal Inferences Concerning Inheritance and Property." *Human Relations,*24, 295–314.

GOULDNER, A., & R. PETERSON. 1962. *Notes on Technology and the Moral Order.* Indianapolis, Ind.: Bobbs-Merrill.

GREENMAN, E. 1945. "Material Culture and the Organism." *American Anthropologist*, 40, 112–117.

HAINES, F. 1938a. "Where Did the Plains Indians Get Their Horses?" *American Anthropologist*, 40, 429–437.

HALLOWELL, A.I. 1951. "Cultural Factors in the Structuralization of Perception." In J.H. Rohrer & M. Sherif (eds.), *Social Psychology at the Crossroads.* New York: Harper & Row, Pub., pp. 164–195.

———. 1954. "The Self and Its Behavioral Environment." *Explorations*, 2, 108–165.

———. 1955. *Culture and Experience.* Philadelphia: University of Pennsylvania Press. (Also republished in 1967. New York: Schocken.)

HAMMOND, P. 1966. *Yatenga: Technology in the Culture of a West African Kingdom.* New York: The Free Press.

HERSKOVITS, M. 1958. "Some Further Comments on Cultural Relativism." *American Anthropologist*, 60, 266–273.

HOBHOUSE, L., G. WHEELER, & M. GINSBERG. 1915. *The Material Culture and Social Institutions of the Simpler Peoples: An Essay in Correlation.* London: Routledge & Kegan Paul.

HOEBEL, E.A. 1954. *The Law of Primitive Man.* Cambridge, Mass.: Harvard University Press.

———. 1966. *Anthropology: The Study of Man* (3rd ed.). New York: McGraw-Hill.

KAVOLIS, V. 1968. *Artistic Expression: A Sociological Analysis.* Ithaca, N.Y.: Cornell University Press.

KEESING, R. 1981. *Cultural Anthropology.* New York: Holt, Rinehart & Winston.

KILBRIDE, J., & P. KILBRIDE. 1975. "Sitting and Smiling Behavior of Baganda Infants: The Influence of Culturally Constituted Experience." *Journal of Cross-Cultural Psychology*, 6, 88–107.

KLIMEK, S., & W. MILKE. 1935. "An Analysis of the Material Culture of the Tupi Peoples." *American Anthropologist*, 37, 71–91.

KLUCKHOHN, C. 1949. "The Philosophy of the Navaho Indians." In F.S.C. Northrop (ed.), *Ideological Differences and World Order.* New Haven, Conn.: Yale University Press, pp. 356–384.

———. 1951. "Values and Value Orientations in the Theory of Action." In T. Parsons & E. Shils (eds.), *Toward a General Theory of Action.* Cambridge, Mass.: Harvard University Press, pp. 388–433.

———. 1954. "Culture and Behavior." In G. Lindzey (ed.), *Handbook of Social Psychology.* Reading, Mass.: Addison-Wesley, pp. 921–976.

———. 1955. "Ethical Relativity: *sic et non.*" *Journal of Philosophy*, 52, 663–677.

———. 1956. "Toward a Comparison of Value-Emphases in Different Cultures."

In L.D. White (ed.), *The State of the Social Sciences.* Chicago: University of Chicago Press, pp. 116–132.

——. 1959. "The Scientific Study of Values." *Proceedings of the American Philosophical Society,* 102, 469–476.

KLUCKHOHN, C., & F. KLUCKHOHN. 1947. "American Culture: Generalized Orientations and Class Patterns." In L. Bryson (ed.), *Conflicts of Power in Modern Culture.* New York: Harper & Row, Pub., pp. 106–128.

KLUCKHOHN, C., & D. LEIGHTON. 1946. *The Navaho.* Cambridge, Mass.: Harvard University Press.

KLUCKHOHN, F., & F. STRODTBECK. 1961. *Variations in Value Orientations.* Evanston, Ill,: Row, Peterson.

KROEBER, A. 1901. "Decorative Symbolism of the Arapaho." *American Anthropologist,* 3, 308–336.

——. 1920. "Masks and Moieties as a Culture Complex." *Journal of the Royal Anthropological Institute of Great Britain and Ireland,* 50, 452–460.

——. 1941. "Salt, Dogs and Tobacco." *University of California Anthropological Records,* 6, 1–20.

KUCKENBERG, K. 1963. "Effect of Early Father Absence on Scholastic Aptitude." Unpublished doctoral dissertation, Harvard University.

LADD, J. 1957. *The Structure of a Moral Code: A Philosophical Analysis of Ethical Discourse Applied to the Ethics of the Navaho Indians.* Cambridge, Mass.: Harvard University Press.

LEIGHTON, D., & C. KLUCKHOHN. 1947. *Children of the People: The Navaho Individual and His Development.* Cambridge, Mass.: Harvard University Press.

LÉVI-STRAUSS, C. 1967. *Structural Anthropology.* Garden City, N.Y.: Anchor.

LINTON, R. 1923. *The Material Culture of the Marquesas Islands.* Honolulu: Memoirs of the B.P. Bishop Museum 8, No. 5.

——. 1952. "Universal Ethical Principles: An Anthropological View." In R.N. Anshen (ed.), *Moral Principles of Action: Man's Ethical Imperatives.* New York: Harper & Row, Pub., Chapter 32.

——. 1954. "The Problem of Universal Values." In R.F. Spencer (ed.), *Method and Perspective in Anthropology.* Minneapolis: University of Minnesota Press, pp. 145–168.

LOMAX, A., & C.M. ARENSBERG. 1977. "A Worldwide Evolutionary Classification of Cultures by Subsistence Systems." *Current Anthropology,* 18, 659–708.

LOWIE, R. 1922. "The Material Culture of the Crow Indians." *Anthropological Papers of the American Museum of Natural History,* 21, 201–270.

McELROY, W.A. 1954. "A Sex Preference for Shapes." *British Journal of Psychology,* 45, 209–216.

MEAD, M., & R. METRAUX. 1953. *The Study of Culture at a Distance.* Chicago: University of Chicago Press.

MONBERG, T. 1971. "Tikopia Color Classification." *Ethnology,* 10, 349–358.

MORGAN, L. 1881. *Houses and House Life of the American Aborigines.* Washington, D.C.: Contributions to American Ethnology. Vol. 4. (Reprinted in 1965. Chicago: University of Chicago Press.)

MUNROE, R., 1964. "Couvade Practices of the Black Caribbean: A Psychological Study." Unpublished doctoral dissertation, Harvard University.

MUNROE, R., R.H. MUNROE, & J.W.M. WHITING. 1973. "Thee Couvade: A Psychological Analysis." *Ethos,* 7, 30–74.

MURDOCK, G. 1957. "World Ethnographic Sample." *American Anthropologist,* 59, 664–687.

——. 1967. *Ethnographic Atlas.* Pittsburgh, Pa.: University of Pittsburgh Press.

NORTHROP, F. 1953. "Cultural Values." In A.L. Kroeber (ed.), *Anthropology Today.*

Chicago: University of Chicago Press, pp. 668–681.

OPLER, M.E. 1941.   *An Apache Life Way.* Chicago: University of Chicago Press.

———. 1945.   "Themes as Dynamic Forces in Culture." *American Journal of Sociology,* 51, 198–206.

———. 1946.   *Childhood and Youth in Jicarilla Apache Society.* Los Angeles: The Southwest Museum.

OSGOOD, C. 1940.   *Ingalik Material Culture.* New Haven, Conn.: Yale University Publications in Anthropology, 22.

OSWALT, W. 1972.   *Habitat and Technology.* New York: Holt, Rinehart & Winston.

PETTITT, G. 1946.   *Primitive Education in North Anerica.* Berkeley: University of California Press.

RAPOPORT, A. 1969.   *House Form and Culture.* Englewood Cliffs, N.J.: Prentice-Hall.

RAY, V. 1952.   "Techniques and Problems in the Study of Human Color Perception." *Southwestern Journal of Anthropology,* 8, 251–259.

———. 1953.   "Human Color Perception and Behavioral Response." *Transactions, New York Academy of Sciences* (Series 2), 16, 98–104.

ROBBINS, M. 1966.   "Material Culture and Cognition." *American Anthropologist,* 68, 745–748.

SAWYER, J., & R. LeVINE. 1966.   "Cultural Dimensions: A Factor Analysis of the World Ethnographic Sample." *American Anthropologist,* 68, 708–731.

SAYCE, R. 1933.   *Primitive Arts and Crafts: An Introduction to the Study of Material Culture.* Cambridge, England: Cambridge University Press.

SEGALL, M.H., D.T. CAMPBELL, & M.J. HERSKOVITS. 1966.   *The Influence of Culture on Visual Perception.* Indianapolis, Ind.: Bobbs-Merrill.

SPIER, R.F.G. 1972.   *Material Culture and Technology.* Minneapolis, Minn.: Burgess.

STEWARD, J. 1964.   *Handbook of South American Indians* (Vol. I). Washington, D.C.: U.S. Government Printing Office.

STILES W. 1946.   "Separation of the 'Blue' and 'Green' Mechanisms of Vision by Measurements of Increment Thresholds." *Proceedings of the Royal Society,* 133, 418–434.

TRIANDIS, H. 1978.   "Some Universals of Social Behavior." *Personality and Social Psychology Bulletin,* 4, 1–16.

WALD, G. 1949.   "The Photochemistry of Vision." *Documents in Opthalmology, 3, 94–137.*

WALLACE, A.F.C. 1961.   "The Psychic Unity of Human Groups." In B. Kaplan (ed.), *Studying Personality Cross-Culturally.* New York: Harper & Row, Pub., pp. 129–163.

WHITING, J., & B. AYRES. 1968.   "Inferences from the Shape of Dwellings." In K.C. Chang (ed.), *Settlement Archaeology.* Palo Alto, Calif.: National Press Books, pp. 117–133.

WHITING, J., & I. CHILD. 1953.   *Child Training and Personality.* New Haven, Conn.: Yale University Press.

WHITING, J.R., R. KLUCKHOHN, & A. ANTHONY. 1958.   "The Function of Male Initiation Ceremonies at Puberty." In E. Maccoby, T. Newcomb, & E. Hartley (eds.), *Readings in Social Psychology.* New York: Holt, Rinehart & Winston, pp. 359–370.

WHITING, J., T. LANDAUER, & T. JONES. 1968.   "Infantile Immunization and Adult Stature." *Child Development, 39,* 56–57.

WHITING, J., & B.B. WHITING. 1978.   "A Strategy for Psychocultural Research." In G.D. Spindler (ed.), *The Making of Psychological Anthropology.* Berkeley and Los Angeles: University of California Press, pp. 41–61.

WILLIAMS, T. 1969.   *A Borneo Childhood: Enculturation in Dusun Society.* New York: Holt, Rinehart & Winston.

WISSLER, C. 1910. *The Material Culture of the Blackfoot Indians.* New York: Anthropological Papers of the American Museum of Natural History, 5, Part One.

———. 1914. "The Influence of the Horse in the Development of Plains Culture." *The American Anthropologist,* 16, 1–25.

———. 1922. *The American Indian.* New York: Oxford University Press.

———. 1923. *Man and Culture.* New York: Harper & Row, Pub.

WITKIN, H.A., & J.W. BERRY. 1975. "Psychological Differentiation in Cross-Cultural Perspective." *Journal of Cross-Cultural Psychology,* 6, 4–87.

WOLFE, A. 1969. "Social 'Structural Bases of Art." *Current Anthropology,* 10, 3–44.

WUNDT, W. 1928. "Ehe und Familie in der Primitiven Gesellschaft." *Volkerpsychologie,* 7, 190–246.

ZERN, D. 1976. "Further Evidence Supporting the Relationship between Nurturer-Infant Contact and Later Differentiation of Social Environment." *Journal of Genetic Psychology,* 129, 169–170

CHAPTER NINE
LANGUAGE
AND SOCIALIZATION

This chapter is concerned with the ways language is related to the socialization process. It begins with a summary of some ideas concerning the origins and evolution of language, then turns to a brief consideration of the interrelations between language and thinking. Then data are reviewed concerning the ways humans acquire language. Finally, the possible relations between language and the socialization process are discussed in terms of the importance of language for socialization.

LANGUAGE ORIGINS AND EVOLUTION

Among contemporary primates only *Homo sapiens sapiens* is born with a genetic capacity for learning and use of language.[1] It is biologically "normal" for modern humans to learn and use language. The basic anatomical structures involved in language use by *Homo sapiens sapiens* are not essentially

---

[1] The classification of the phenomenon of language learning and use as a human *capacity*, rather than as a *species-characteristic behavior, reflex,* or *drive,* is based on a belief that the great flexibility involved in language learning and use indicates the merit of considering such a label. Whether such a classification is finally valid remains to be judged on the basis of research to be conducted on the biological bases of human behavior.

different from those possessed by other primates. All primates have lungs, teeth, lips, vocal cords, palate, nasal passages, and tongue. All primates, including *Homo sapiens sapiens,* use these structures to produce a great variety of sounds. However only contemporary humans regularly use these structures to make the sounds used in language behavior.

Fine Control

An essential difference between *Homo sapiens sapiens* and other contemporary primates in use of their similar structures for vocalizing (or "sound making") is the degree of *fine control* of pitch and resonance of sounds, made possible in modern humans because the larynx is positioned lower in the throat and is more distant from the palate area than in other primates. Among the nonhuman primates the larynx is very close to or in contact with the soft palate. The position of the modern human larynx is said to be a consequence of the human bipedal adaptation; as the *foramen magnum* (the opening for the spinal cord on the underneath of the skull) moved forward with increasingly more erect posture and locomotion and as the jaw became smaller and less rugged, the larynx of evolving *hominids* appears to have descended into the midthroat area. This created a long, uninterrupted area for sound resonation, making possible the unique low-pitched sound production that is typical of the speech of *Homo sapiens sapiens.*

Another evolutionary change which seems to have occurred among evolving *hominids,* or populations ancestral to them, and which contributes directly to a delicate control of pitch and sound resonance in vocalization in contemporary humans is the way in which the muscles of the face (see Table 9–1), and especially the *obicularis oris* which precisely closes the lips, provide for a very fine control of the front of the face area. It is likely that a fine contraction of facial muscles, and particularly the *obicularis oris* which contributed to a broad variability and range in sound production in the buccal, or mouth, cavity, would have been a naturally selective advantage

TABLE 9–1   Muscles of Facial Expression in *Homo Sapiens Sapiens*

buccinator—compresses cheek
levator labii superioris—elevates upper lip
risorius—retracts angle of mouth
mentalis—raises and protrudes lower lip, wrinkles chin
levator labii superioris alaeque nasi—dilates nose apertures
orbicularis oris—closes lips
levator anguli oris—makes facial furrows
depressor anguli oris—depresses angle of mouth
depressor labii inferioris—draws lower lip downward
zygomaticus major—draws mouth upward
zygomaticus minor—makes furrow between upper lip and nose

of some significance in animals newly developing a bipedal terrestrial social life.

For instance, modern baboons can produce many quite humanlike "grunt" sounds. Andrew (1962, 1963a, 1963b) has suggested that this is related to baboons' need for a regular transfer of social information by a more explicit and much less ambiguous means than would be possible by use of only facial expressions or body motions. It might well be that similar selective evolutionary pressures also acted upon the bipedal *hominids* as they met requirements for survival in their social groups, perhaps by making such groups into a mobile refuge on the open grasslands over which they foraged for foodstuffs; this would require vocal communication over a wide area.

These changes in the course of human evolution, which are also related to the human hearing capacity for a very close discrimination of pitch, and especially in the pitch range used in *Homo sapiens sapiens* languages, mean that, while there are no significant gross anatomical differences between contemporary humans and other primates in the structures involved in language learning and use, only modern humans have evolved a facility for repeatedly making the kinds of exact sounds that seem vital to a language system.

The ability or potential of contemporary humans to engage in imitation of sounds in their environment contributes to a greatly increased fine control over vocalization. Most primates continue to use many of the vocal sounds probably typical of their early nonprimate ancestors. Thus high short calls, or "twitter" sounds, are common among the modern primates and in many members of the *Insectivora* order. Each group of modern primates also has some significant vocalizations that are species typical, ranging from noisy expiration ("threat") sounds, a wailing and whooping call, to a rapid clicking sound. Among all the primates, however, only modern humans seem to mimic or duplicate precisely many of the calls now typically used by other members of their order of animals.

Thus fine control of vocalization in *Homo sapiens sapiens* involves a complex of biological features, including pitch production, facial muscle uses, hearing acuity, and vocal mimicry, each contributing significantly to production of the broad range of sounds used in human language. It is important not to confuse speech, or oral communication, with language. The human biological features involved in the production of speech provide a basis for language. As noted later in this chapter, language consists of a set of interelated systems that can be studied and analyzed apart from the act of oral communication.

Brain and Body Size and Language

The preceding features do not seem sufficient to account for the capacity for human language. In Chapter 1 it was noted that it seems

TABLE 9-2 Brain Size, Body Weight, and Language Learning and Use*

Primate form	Body weight (in kilograms)	Brain weight (in kilograms)	Ratio of body-brain weight	Language facility
Male, *H. sapiens* (age 2.5)	13.5	1.100	12.3	Beginning
Male, *H. sapiens* (age 13.5)	45.0	1.350	35.0	Present
Male, *H. sapiens* (age 18)	64.0	1.350	47.0	Present
Male, *H. sapiens* (age 12; dwarf)	13.5	.400	34.0	Present
Male, chimpanzee (age 3)	13.5	.400	34.0	Absent
Female, chimpanzee (adult)	47.0	.450	104.0	Absent
Male, rhesus monkey (adult)	3.5	.090	40.0	Absent

* After Lenneberg, E.H., 1964. *New Directions in the Study of Language.* Cambridge, Mass.: M.I.T. Press.

reasonable to conclude that communication of ideas by vocalization probably occurred after a significant increase in the size of the brain in the evolutionary changes occurring between the bipedal *hominids* of the Middle *Pliocene* and the *Homo* forms of the Middle *Pleistocene*.

This conclusion involves the assumption that at a certain "time threshold," or particular time period, in *hominid* evolution the unspecialized nature of a certain-sized brain, perhaps above 800 cc. made possible the invention and regular use of language. It has also been suggested that not only an absolute increase in brain size but also the increase of the *ratio* of brain weight to body size contributed significantly to the threshold appearance of human language. A comparison (see Table 9–2) of the ratio of brain size to body weight among modern primates calls this last statement into question and suggests that language learning and use is essentially a distinct capacity of humans rather than a generalized feature of the primate order that is dependent on the development of a specific size of brain and its relation to a particular size.

Lenneberg (1964, 1967) believes that language learning and use in *Homo sapiens sapiens* is a genetically based capacity that developed independently, although the brain was increasing in size. He notes further that this capacity in contemporary humans is inherited biologically and independently of a general intelligence or intellectual level. He points out that there are records of families in which the learning and use of language is lacking entirely in some members, but not in others. The appearance of this linguistic malfunction seems to follow usual human genetic patterns. There are records of persons clearly "subnormal" in intelligence but quite

TABLE 9–3 Time Required for a Given Change in the Percent Frequency of a Gene Having a Selective Advantage of 1 Percent*

DOMINANT GENE		RECESSIVE GENE	
CHANGE IN PERCENT FREQUENCY FROM	NUMBER OF GENERATIONS	CHANGE IN PERCENT FREQUENCY FROM	NUMBER OF GENERATIONS
0.01-0.1	230	0.01-0.1	900,230
0.1-1.0	231	0.1-1.0	90,231
1.0-50.0	559	1.0-3.0	6,779
50.0-97.0	3,481	3.0-50.0	3,481
97.0-99.0	6,779	50.0-99.0	559
99.0-99.9	90,231	99.0-99.9	231
99.9-99.99	900,230	99.9-99.99	230

*Boyd, W.C. 1953. *Genetics and the Races of Man.* Little, Brown, p.146.

able to speak with effectiveness, distinction, and clarity, and sometimes in several different languages. In addition, "mentally subnormal" persons, however this is demonstrated, often have brain sizes at or exceeding the *Homo sapiens sapiens* average.

Thus the origin of language learning and use may have been in the appearance of a genetic capacity that was developed independently of, but simultaneously with, other human body features, all of which contributed significantly to naturally selective advantages in life of evolving *hominid* populations. If this were the situation, the survival edge gained by language learning and using *hominids* must have been immediate and of great significance since creatures able to communicate the products of reflection and symboling directly and efficiently would have made immense gains in their survival and behavior. A genetic character that has naturally selective, or "dominant," advantage can spread very quickly throughout a species of animals (see Table 9–3). If language learning and use had its origins in a genetic change that occurred independently of, but simultaneously with, other human evolutionary changes, then the benefits that could have followed, such as a change of the coordinate use of the features of fine control of vocalizations and reflection, symboling, bipedal locomotion, and so on, were probably already in existence in more or less highly developed forms. This would mean that when the gene change for language use and learning occurred, it took place in a species that generally was biologically prepared for it and spread quickly and very successfully to and in all the succeeding groups of *hominids*.

These comments are intended to suggest that the capacity to learn and use a language is a genetic feature and not that language is itself formed or transmitted genetically. Human languages consist of basic units, termed *phonemes* and *morphemes*, of vocalization to which cultural values are arbitrarily assigned in different human cultures. Human infants are usually born possessing a capacity to mimic any of the phonemes used in any of the approximately 5000 contemporary human languages, but no human infant is born possessing knowledge of the cultural values assigned to combinations of sounds, or morphemes, specially used by their biological parents and their social groups. Infants and children must learn to duplicate precisely all of the sound combinations to which adults have traditionally given quite arbitrary cultural meanings. It eventually becomes easier for infants and children to mimic the many different combinations of sounds particularly used by the adults on whom they depend for nurture. However it may be some time before a child really learns the full use of cultural values given to special sound combinations in a society. For instance, the English word *love* can denote "desire," "courtesy," "affection," "favorite," and so on and is also used in a great many significant combinations (such as "lovelorn," "lovemaking," "lovesick," "love story"). It is many years before English-speaking children can learn most of the different cultural values assigned to even so common a combination of sounds as *love.*

HUMAN AND ANIMAL COMMUNICATION

In discussing the origins of human language it is important to note that *Homo sapiens sapiens* is not the only life form which carries on *communication* of some kind. In modern humans and among their primate contemporaries, communication involves both vocalizations and body movements. Many different kinds of animals, including bees, fish (such as the three-spined stickleback), and herring gulls, use body motions to communicate complex information among themselves concerning breeding, care of the young, social cooperation in food getting, and common defense against attacks from with or without a species. This type of communication depends on, and has different properties than are implied in, the use of the term *language.*

Linguistic scholars define human language as principally involving five systems: *grammatical, phonological, morphophonemic, semantic, and phonetic.*[2] The communicative acts of bees, three-spined sticklebacks, and most animals using essentially a kinesic form of communication do not contain

---

[2]Hockett (1958, 137–138) defines these systems as (1) *grammatical*—a stock of morphemes and the arrangements in which they occur (2) *phonological*—a stock of phonemes and the arrangements in which they occur; (3) *morphophonemic*—the code that ties together the grammatical and phonological systems; (4) *semantic*—the ways in which various morphemes and combinations of morphemes can be arranged; (5) *phonetic*—the ways in which sequences of phonemes are converted into sound waves by a speaker and are decoded from speech by a hearer.

any of these sound-based systems. No such systems have been discovered in the vocal communications of other nonhuman animals, such as wolves and whales, despite intensive and systematic research efforts by many different individuals to recognize and "decode" the vocalizations of such animals into one or all five of the systems characteristic of human language. These studies, which have also included many efforts to discover a "language" among the various species of nonhuman primates, have so far not produced evidence that can be used to say conclusively that human vocalizations, which are ordered in the five systems of human language, have any real counterparts in the vocal uses or the kinesic uses of communication by other living forms. Human language, as specialized vocalization organized into a set of five systems, is unique in the natural world.[3]

Modern Language Form

The contemporary study of thousands of "living" human languages has demonstrated that all languages spoken by humans are equally efficient, despite being learned and used in very different ecological, social, and cultural settings. The languages of groups that are not part of the industrial, urban societies of Europe and the Americas are not inferior in their structure, content, or meanings in comparison to any "modern" or "Western" languages. All contemporary human languages have a formal, recognizable grammatical structure which serves for the formulation of significant intellectual and aesthetic ideas and expressions by their speakers. No demonstrated features or characteristics set off the languages of "primitive" people from those of "civilized" peoples. On the basis of their long-term studies linguistic scholars now assume that all of the world's languages are equal in their social adequacy and complexity. There is no relationship between the fact that a group possesses a written form of language and the complexity of a language or for the possibilities of its speakers to engage in specific and complex emotional, artistic, and social expressions. In effect, there are no contemporary languages that are "natural" or "primitive" because they possess such a limited content that their speakers are severely restricted in their ability to express complex ideas, feelings, and understandings. There are no contemporary languages that are so simple in form that speakers depend more on gestures than on oral communication for exchanges of meaningful information. Where such "sign languages" exist,

---

[3]Hockett (1958, 574–585) has considered this matter carefully and has concluded that there are also seven "key properties" (*duality, productivity, arbitrariness, interchangeability, specialization, displacement,* and *cultural transmission*) characteristic of the five systems making up human language. Hockett notes that, while no system of vocal communication other than that used by humans is organized into the systems typical of human language, some few of the nonhuman vocal communication types do contain one or even several of the key properties of human language. As he points out, however, all seven key properties are always present in human language.

Children in communicative contact, Sensuron village, Tambunan district, Sabah, Malaysia. (T.R. Williams, 1959)

Infant in communicative contact with mother (standing) and mother's mother. Sensuron village, Tambunan district, Sabah, Malaysia. (T.R. Williams, 1959)

as among the Arunta, they are *paralinguistic*—that is, used to extend language rather than to supplant it.

While contemporary humans learn and use languages that differ markedly in the ways sounds are assigned arbitrary cultural meanings, contemporary languages are not themselves different in their essential features or in the ways they can be used to express complex ideas, emotions, intentions, and concerns in a particular ecological setting.

THOUGHT AND LANGUAGE

A fundamental question in studying the interrelations between language and socialization is the degree to which human thought and behavior are actually influenced by language learning and use. The basic questions of whether language learning and use affects the development of other capacities, such as cognition and learning, and whether people who speak different languages live in different realms of reality are also vital in the study of language and socialization.

Speech and Thought

Speculation concerning the ways speech and thought are related has a long history in philosophical and psychological studies. One answer to such speculations is the one given by Watson (1924), one of the founders of behaviorism in psychology. Watson asserted that human thought is silent speaking, with all thoughts having their origins as motor patterns in the larynx. Watson's statements concerning the relations between speech and thought raise obvious problems, since followed to its logical conclusion this idea means that before *homininds* developed the capacity for language learning and use and while language was developing into its contemporary form, evolving primates would be, by Watson's definition, unable to really "think" since they had no motor patterns in the larynx to enable and facilitate thought. Watson's conclusion is not reasonable today, given the body of empirical evidence demonstrating that thinking, and especially reflective thought, among evolving *hominids* must have occurred well before the development of language and its key role in cultural transmission. Watson's speculations on the link between language and thought tend to rule out all cognitive processes in all contemporary animal forms other than *Homo sapiens sapiens*. However laboratory study of learning clearly demonstrates that thought and cognition occur among a great many different kinds of contemporary animals unable to use either language or speech.

If Watson's hypothesis is followed, individuals who lose their larynx through surgery or accident should also lose their capacity to think. Experimental evidences from use of the drug curare to paralyze the larynx while testing otherwise "normal" subjects for their thinking processes have demonstrated that Watson's ideas concerning speech and thought are unacceptable.

Piaget's studies A more moderate position on the question of the relationship between speech and thought has been developed in the work of Piaget and his colleagues. Piaget assumed throughout his research that human thinking follows a particular developmental style in children, with the use of language usually coming after the attainment of a certain level of thought. Piaget and his associates have provided substantial experimental evidences, from studies of young children, of some of the intricate ways that thinking and language become interrelated. His work makes it clear that at birth, and for some time, a human language capacity and a human cognitive capacity tend to be independent entities. It seems from Piaget's studies that even though attempts are made to train younger children in special uses of language to talk about problem solving, such training is of very little use to children whose capacity for thinking has not developed to the level at which they can meaningfully consider concepts represented in the special language. Piaget's work also demonstrates that the capacities for thought and language do begin to interpenetrate one another in very young children after about 18 months to two years of age, and subsequently become so completely related that by the age of five to six years it is exceedingly difficult to sort out the primary influences of the capacity for thought or language.

Bruner's studies Systematic efforts to trace the exact ways thought and language develop and become interrelated in younger children have been made by Jerome Bruner and his coworkers at the Harvard University Center for Cognitive Studies. Bruner's research has identified three main styles of children's thinking about their experiences: (1) *enactive* (action) *representation,* (2) *ikonic* (or image) *representation,* and (3) *symbolic representation.* He notes that infants act out much of their everyday experience with their bodies and body parts, particularly their mouths and hands. Bruner believes this style of representation is the earliest way all children think about themselves and their world; in the *enactive representation* stage of cognitive development, language plays a very small part. As children mature, they develop a second thought style: simultaneous comprehension of different experiences. An example of the *ikonic representation* mode of thought would be the way an adult can "read" or think about a map that shows visually the ways hundreds or even tens of thousands of objects are generally arranged. An *ikonic* style of thought provides humans with the means to move about in a complex landscape, through the products of human life, and deal effectively with the ways these are interconnected. Young children, under the age of 3 to 3½ years, have great difficulty in simultaneous cognition, even though they have a normally developed language capacity that is being used regularly. Airlines, ship and bus lines, and other forms of public transportation which agree to carry younger children unaccompanied by their parents usually account for a child's lack of ikonic representation by attaching prominent name and destination tags to their clothing and providing adult employees as guides to help younger children overcome their inability to simultaneously relate their experiences.

Finally Bruner has demonstrated that children develop a third style of thinking about their experiences: use of written and spoken *symbols* to represent objects, activities, and their interconnections. Bruner notes that adult thought tends to be predominantly symbolic, with lesser components of ikonic and enactive thought included as needed to solve problems and deal with specific activities. He believes that the amount of adult style of thought developed through childhood depends on learning to use and understand language and its written forms. Bruner's research seems to indicate, however, that the amount of adult thought finally developed is not related to a particular language but more directly to the ways children learn and use linguistic symbols to substitute for experiences.

It is important to understand that both Piaget and Bruner share the view that the human cognition and language capacities are essentially innate programs of action which automatically unfold and develop in the course of growth and maturation. However Piaget's writings concerning the ways the cognitive and language capacities develop indicate that he views these as being much more predetermined and prefixed than does Bruner. Bruner has noted that *hominid* evolution provided a great range of possibilities for cognitive and language development. It is Bruner's belief that the unfolding of these two innately determined capacities depends primarily on the kinds of tools and objects available to infants and children as they reach particular points of physical growth. Bruner has advanced the hypothesis that the development of an infant's manual skills is vital in the later development of language and cognitive capacities because such manual skills make possible the broad strategies, or procedures, for understanding and coping with the world that must be faced by an infant and young child. Bruner feels that when a greater abundance of tools and objects is available to an infant, it will "tempt out," or draw forth, more self-initiated behavior, which when added to the presence of parents encouraging such self-initiating acts can serve as the specific precursor to the unfolding of cognition and language capacities as innate programs of action. Thus while Bruner sees the cognitive and language capacities as basic, innate human preadaptations, he also believes that only after their first appearances have been evoked by events, such as self-initiated behavior and responsive parents, will there be a significant unfolding of each capacity.

Bruner's and Piaget's ideas remain to be validated through studies in other, non-Western cultural settings. Research by J.W.M. Whiting (1971) and his associates concerning cognitive development in African infants and children tends to indicate that the development of the language capacity and of other capacities is considerably more complex than has been proposed by either Piaget or Bruner and their associates. For instance, it appears that the language capacity in different cultures interpenetrates and affects cognitive development in ways quite different from that which appears true for American or European children. Bruner's hypothesis concerning tool and object abundance, self-initiative activity, responsive parents, and unfolding of cognitive and language action, when followed to its logical conclusion, also means that children in cultures lacking those factors should show marked cognitive and language capacity differences when compared to children in cultures where the opposite is true. This logical product, from Bruner's research, is not a workable one; infants and children in cultures which do or permit few of the things Bruner seems to believe are crucial for allowing the innate programs of cognitive and linguistic action to unfold seem to have children and adults as cognitively and as linguistically capable and competent, in the terms of the local culture, as are persons in other cultures.

However there seems little question that there are two distinct capacities—cognition and language learning and use—that are involved in the socialization process; and that these capacities form in the adult an exceedingly complex reticulum, or net-like structure, that helps direct and guide human behavior.

Deaf children and thought   The research of Furth and his colleagues concerning cognitive development in congenitally deaf children also provides insight into the conclusions to be drawn from the studies of Piaget, Bruner, Whiting, and others. Deaf children, who have never heard language of any type, provide an important scientific "control group" since they are unable to engage in usual and normal language learning and formal education. Furth and others have reasoned that it may be possible to observe in deaf children whether the learning and use of language makes possible all of the levels and modes of cognitive development noted by Piaget, Bruner, and other scholars, or whether language only enriches and supports such stages as they naturally unfold in children.

Furth (1966) reports on the basis of many different kinds of research studies conducted by himself and others that deaf children appear in fact to go through the same stages and modes of cognitive development as reported for normal children by Piaget, Bruner, and others. The major difference found by Furth between deaf and nondeaf children with respect to stages and modes of cognitive development is in regard to the rate of development. Some deaf children move through the various cognitive stages and modes much more slowly than do nondeaf children. Furth attributes this to the significantly fewer opportunities usually provided to deaf children for varied experiences, rather than due to their lack of a language learning and use capacity.

Furth concludes that language learning and use has an *indirect* rather than a *causal* influence on cognitive development—that is, language learning and use is a means for speeding up and greatly enriching the development of thought since it is a vital means of efficient expressive communication about experience. However it seems that persons who are impaired or seriously lacking in their capacity for language learning and use are not usually similarly deficient in their capacity to think about their experiences. Furth's studies tend to support the suggestions of Piaget, Bruner, and others that in infancy and early childhood the cognitive and language capacities are distinct, although they become interrelated by adulthood. If this is so, then the vital problem which remains for scholars concerned with language development and the socialization process is to determine the phases in human cognitive development in which language is specifically important. A major problem for linguistic scholars is to understand the influence of cognitive development upon language learning and use—that is, to determine whether certain language processes are possible of attainment before attaining certain phases of cognitive development.

A present central concern for students of both socialization and language is to deal effectively with the problems raised by the demonstrated facts of the great lexical and grammatical diversity in different varieties of contemporary language.

Language Diversity and Human Thought

Early in the nineteenth century von Humboldt proposed the idea that individuals speaking different languages looked at and understood their social, cultural, and physical worlds in unique ways because of the grammatical structure of their language. A grammar is the arrangement of the *morphemes* (words) used in a language and their relative position in speech (Hockett, 1958, 129). The idea that the grammar form of a language determines the thoughts of its speakers persisted through the nineteenth century. It was easy for linguists and philosophers to note that a grammar was central to the structure of a language, was much more resistant to rapid change than were other aspects of language, such as its vocabulary and phonology (or typical sound style), and was a prime means of expression of such metaphysically important categories in European and American thought as "time," "space," "action," "individual," and "object." By the close of the nineteenth century, Boas and others had developed this idea as part of their efforts to define ethnology (the comparative study of culture) as a science concerned with the causal links between human thought and the form of language. Boas believed that through study of the central aspects of language, such as grammatical structure, it would be possible to discover the original forms of human cognition and to avoid all the elaborate cultural facades which have been evolved by societies to protect and preserve the original contents of their thought.

Boas (1911) was the first scholar to demonstrate clearly that what appears as a single idea in one language may be grammatically expressed in other languages by a whole series of ideas. Boas did not distinguish between the two general ways that thought categories are now known to be expressed in language—that is, through *lexical,* or word, categories and through grammatical categories. Thus to use one of Boas well-known examples, Americans employ one lexical category, *snow,* to denote that category of experience that Greenland Eskimos know by the different lexical uses: *aput* ("snow falling on the ground"), *qana* ("falling snow"), *piqsirpog* ("drifting snow"), *qimuqsuq* ("a snowdrift"), and so on.

In contrast, Boas also noted that Americans use many different lexical categories to express ideas which other peoples express in one category. Thus North American Dakota Indians express in only one lexical category *xtaka* ("to grip"), the idea of, "to kick an object" (*naxtáka*), "to bind objects into bundles" (*paxtaka*), "to bite" (*yaxtaka*), "to be near to" (*išaxtaka*), and "to pound" (*boxtaka*).

Boas also first noted concisely the ways the grammatical categories of a language may structure expressions of complex ideas. He pointed out that to use the English expression, "The man is sick," is to express the idea that "a definite single man at present sick." As Boas points out, however, a speaker of Kwakiutl, a North American, Northwest Coast native language would have to render this same expression through Kwakiutl grammar as "definite man near him invisible sick near him invisible" or as "that invisible man lies sick on his back on the floor of the absent house," depending on whether the speaker chooses to talk in terms of human visibility and nearness in the first or second person, in terms of human invisibility and nearness and in the third person, or in a definite and idiomatic sense. Boas also pointed out that in the Greenland Eskimo language this same idea ("the man is sick") would be expressed grammatically as "(single) man sick," with no expression of time or place being involved. In Ponca, a dialect of another North American Indian language (Siouan), the concept in the same English expression would have to specify whether the person was at rest or moving ("the moving single man sick"). Boas concluded from his works on the links between word and grammatical categories and thought in different languages (Boas, 1920, 1938, 1942) that human thinking was causally related to and determined by grammatical structure. From this conclusion Boas drew a corollary conclusion that if thought was determined by language structure, then all human thought was specific to the language structure which determined it.

This conclusion influenced the studies and writings of a number of persons, including Sapir, Whorf, and Lee, in trying to determine to what extent and in what ways the structure of language is related to the thought of its speakers. At various times and in different ways these scholars dealt with three general questions: (1) Are language habits specifically related to other forms of culture? (2) Do peoples with different language habits really differ profoundly in their thought habits? (3) Can linguistic habits causally determine other forms of a culture?

In general, contemporary language scholars would give each of these questions a qualified affirmative answer, without portraying the influence of language structure on human thought in the absolute terms used by Sapir, Whorf, Lee, and others. The demonstrated facts of the ways language changes, diffusion of language from one culture to another, and multi-lingualism—that is, the ways people think while regularly speaking two or more languages with very different structures—preclude acceptance of statements proposing an absolute causal relationship between language structure and thinking.

The specific qualifications of what has come to be termed the *Sapir-Whorf-Lee hypothesis*—that is, humans speaking languages with different lexical and grammatical structures hear, see, and experience the world in profoundly different ways—can be illustrated briefly through reference to some examples of the modern studies of the relations between language structure and thought.[4] These data are helpful in understanding the relationships between language and the socialization process since they illustrate that the forms of language are related to other features of culture, including its transmission.

Navaho and Papago language structure and culture   In a discussion of the ways the structure of Navaho, a native North American language, provides a broad framework for Navaho thought, concepts of reality, and under-standing, Hoijer (1951) has pointed out that speakers of Navaho must use a system of verbs that are divided into two distinct classes: the *neuter* and the *active*. Neuter verbs in Navaho are used by speakers to report general states or conditions of life and contain no meanings of tense mode or aspect but simply report a state of being, such as "being at rest," "standing," or "sitting." Some neuter Navaho verbs also report specific qualities: "to be 'blue,' 'white,' 'thin,' 'fat,' or 'tall.' " On the other hand, Navaho active verbs report specific events, movements, and actions. These are expressed mainly in regard to the aspect or mode of action and movement, rather than in a tense form. Thus the active verb *niñda:h* means "he moves to a sitting position." The Navaho speaker's emphasis here is on the incompleted action, not on the present tense expression, which is the result of translating the Navaho verb *niñda:h* into English, a language in which the present tense must be used to express the whole idea involved. If Navaho speakers wish to add a tense to the active verb form *niñda:h*, they may add the form

[4]For some discussion of the nature and validity of the Sapir-Whorf-Lee hypothesis, see Bedau (1957), Black (1959), Brown (1958), Carroll (1958), Graves (1057), Hoijer (1953), Kluckhohn & Leighton (1961), Lenneberg (1953), and Lee (1938, 1959). See also the readings on this topic in Hymes (1964).

dò (technically called an *optional enclitic*) as in *niǹdà:h-dò* ("he will be moving to a sitting position") or as in *niǹda-dò* ("he will have moved to a sitting position").

Hoijer notes that Navaho children must learn the details of five neuter and seven active verb categories in order to effectively use their language. More importantly Navaho children must understand the basic cultural distinctions which underlie all the neuter and active categories of verbs.

Hoijer points out that the conception that seems to be at the base of all five Navaho neuter verb categories is one that notes the existence of a state of events and of being, after all motion or movement has been withdrawn. In sharp contrast, Navaho active verbs report a state of being in motion, of events occurring. Thus all 12 Navaho verb categories are primarily concerned with the reporting of events, or as Hoijer terms it, *eventing,* one class having to do with "eventings in motion." However, Hoijer observes, even this basic Navaho conception of eventings seems in turn to rest on and derive from a still more fundamental Navaho conception of reality, that of the relations between concrete, specific, corporeal bodies and their movement. As an illustration of this point, Hoijer notes that in the Navaho way of speaking about an object moving, such as in the statements "he picks something up" or "he selects something," 12 different verbs are involved, all with the same prefix, *nâidi* ("the third person causes it to move upward"), but each with different enclitics, depending on the "it" being referred to in the prefix *nâidi*. Thus *nâidi-ti:h* ("the third person causes a long slender object to move upward"), *nâidi-ni:l* ("the third person causes a rigid container to move upward"), *nâidi-kà:h* ("the third person causes a fabriclike object to move upward"), and so on. This same complexity of specification of relations between bodies and their movements extends reciprocally to withdrawal of movement, such as *ʒil-siˀá* ("a round solid object lies at rest"—that is, "a mountain lies at rest") or *ʒil-ńˀá* ("solid objects lie at rest in a row,"—that is, "a range of mountains lies extending from one point to another").

Hoijer summarizes these points by noting that the Navaho language emphasizes movement and specifies precisely the nature, direction, and status of all movement in great detail. Hoijer and others, particularly Kluckhohn and Leighton (1946) and Kluckhohn (1960), have observed that patterns of Navaho culture reflect these semantic themes of Navaho language, from kinship and kin groups through patterns of ideology and technology. Navaho myths and folk tales most clearly reflect this semantic theme, since Navaho gods and folk heroes move ceaselessly from one holy place to another, trying by their motion to repair and reinstate the dynamic flux of the Navaho universe.

Another illustration of the broad relations between language categories and culture can be found in the way Papago have constructed a classification scheme for their world through the classes of the nouns used in their language. The majority of nouns used in Papago are reported by Mathiot (1962) to be of a type termed technically as *quantifiable nouns*—that is, nouns which specify the properties of *mass, aggregate,* and *individuality.* Papago regularly distinguish between features of mass and features of aggregate and individuality. For instance, the term *ʔóʔohia* ("sand") is a mass noun. However the term for "gravel," *(ʔóʔoɖ)* is an aggregate noun, as are the terms for "deer," "hair," "hailstones," or "servant." In contrast, the Papago individual noun class contains such terms as "coyote," "nose," "stone," and "wife." Both Papago aggregate and individual noun classes share the underlying characteristic of defining human experience as made up of definite bodies with specific outlines and features. In contrast, the Papago noun class for mass rests on an underlying assumption that defines experience in terms of the texture of bodies with definite outlines and features.

These two underlying assumptions, that experience has texture or definite shape and outline, are used by Papago to classify the vital features of their world into a broad two-part system of "living things," *(háʔicu dóakam)* and "growing things," *(háʔicu mo vúusañ).* The Papago class of living things includes all animated objects, such as people and animals, whereas the class of growing things refers to all inanimate objects, such as plants. An analysis by Mathiot (1962) of the Papago cultural taxonomy of experience notes that there is a stong tendency for living things to be named by use of individual nouns, whereas growing things are usually named by use of aggregate nouns. Most of the Papago taxonomy of experience consists of aggregate nouns, with only a few individual nouns. Few instances of mass nouns are found throughout the Papago taxonomic system. Thus it could be concluded that Papago tend to be concerned with definite outlines and features of their world rather than with its texture, or to state the conclusion in perceptual terms, Papago tend to see their experiences in terms of shapes and forms, rather than in terms of textures, or surface, qualities.

This structuring of the perception of reality through a particular use of noun classes, along with other linguistic features such as the number of nouns—that is, whether nouns are singular, plural, and so on—appears to contribute to the ways Papago regularly deal with their world. Most of the observers of Papago life have commented upon the style in which Papago tend to think about and behave in social situations. This style has been termed as *personal plasticity* (Joseph, Spicer, & Chesky, 1949) and *personal adaptability* (Williams, 1958). Papago individuals regularly seem to observers from other cultures to be generally "unconcerned" or "uninterested" in the formal appearances of social and cultural actions and activities, so that when confronted with real or potential personal and social conflicts or unexpected events, Papago remain placid and unruffled in their outlook, action, and demeanor. Papago life, as interpreted through the structure of the Papago language, is a continuing series of broad forms of experience. Hence as long as the forms remain intact, most Papago do not respond to immediate shifts in the specific content of such forms. In comparison with Navaho culture, which is characterized by the flux, motion, and change in forms of reality, Papago culture tends to concentrate upon a view of reality that stresses the continuity and stability of forms of experience.

LEARNING LANGUAGE

Two different types of studies have been done of the ways human infants and children learn language. The first type of study is made in a "naturalistic" manner—that is, by observers carefully noting the ways individual infants and children learn and use language in everyday contexts. A second type may be designated as "experimental," since observers tend to work with infants and children in laboratories, under carefully controlled conditions. In both types a central interest has been in description and understanding of the specific knowledge and "abilities" persons must have in order to learn and use language. Both kinds of studies have been greatly handicapped because language learning can be described only by studying actual speech behavior and responses to speech behavior. This means that early language learning and use must be inferred from events in human behavior, not all of which may correspond precisely to the "internal" events of language development in individuals.

Communicative contact through a language; Dusun man responding to greeting by ethnographer (Trus Madi, 1960). (T. R. Williams)

This research problem raises a variety of quite important questions. For example, while the cognitive capacity of young children seems to be relatively limited for the first several years of life, at the same time there is a nearly complete mastery of the structure and rules of a language in the first four to five years of life. In addition, while infants and children usually are exposed only to the selected aspects of the language spoken by their parents and those adults acting for their parents and are not given much overt language instruction, they usually master their native language equally well. The language learning process also seems to involve several stages that do not appear to be directly related to other developmental sequences in human behavior. Answers to these questions depend on research that combines the techniques of the natural and laboratory settings and solves several difficult conceptual problems, such as the one that can be termed as the "outside-inside" relations between human behavior and language learning and use—that is, ways for an observer to really know what is occurring within an infant and child as they learn language.

Cries, Babbling, and Language Learning

Some linguists and psychologists have devoted a great amount of effort to studies of the precursors, or antecedents, of language in infants and very young children. These studies have finally laid to rest a number of once-quite-fashionable notions concerning language learning. One such notion was the idea that, if left entirely alone, human infants would begin speaking a "basic" or "ancient" human language.[5] However systematic observation of both isolated and "normal" infants have produced clear evidences that children learn to speak only the language spoken by the adult members of the culture into which they are born, provided the other members of the culture expect them to do so. Thus language learning in modern humans depends on regular communicative contact with adult speakers of a language or languages. Human infants do not possess a species-characteristic tendency, so that they will begin to speak some pristine human language if they become isolated. In fact, if left entirely alone, children will not learn to speak at all, a fact well illustrated in the cases of Anna and Isabelle and other isolated children (see Chapter 5).

Another once-fashionable notion is that it is "normal" for children to learn only one language, which then becomes the precise guide for all later language use and which automatically colors or influences profoundly the later learning of all other languages. In fact, there are cultures where

---

[5]For a hypothetical reconstruction of the origin of language, see Hockett & Ascher, 1964.

children simultaneously learn two or three quite different languages.

It is quite important to understand that linguists and psychologists observing language learning currently use a fully developed conception of the nature of language. Language is not simply a set of specific calls, or distinct noises, learned by an infant in a stimulus-response fashion. Infants and children must learn a complex set of rules, or a grammar, that control the specific ways adult speakers put together minimally distinctive sounds, or *phonemes*, to make cognitively useful utterances. Thus a language is not just a large collection of special sounds that infants practice and then make automatically. A language comprises a complex set of rules that determine for the speaker the particular sequences and patterns of speech sounds to be used in particular situations. Observers of language learning now tend to concentrate their attention on the ways infants and young children acquire the rules and sound of their languages, by watching very carefully the sequences of rule acquisition and sound production and by trying to understand the ways these are interrelated with the physical growth and other behavioral maturation in the infant and child.

It was once believed that every child began learning a language by adults developing and shaping infant cries and babblings into the specific sounds of the local language. A great deal of attention was given in the 1700s, the 1800s, and early years of the 1900s to descriptions of and discussions about the ways infant cries and babblings preceded learning and use of language.[6] The general agreement among linguists and psychologists that languages—all languages—contain grammars (rules) for organizing use of distinctive sound has shown that human infants and young children do not really develop very complex rules and sounds found in all languages out of their limited crying and babbling; such rules must be learned as a language taught by adults in a culture. Isolated children (see Chapter 5) do not develop, from their crying and babbling, the distinctive phonemes and complex rules of grammar that are characteristic of language.

This does not mean that an infant's cries or first speech productions, such as babblings, may not be important for learning culture. It does mean that the learning of one subsystem of culture, language, may not be specifically and directly related to these particular features of infant life and experience.

Alternative Views

It has been suggested by Chomsky (1968) and some other linguists that every human infant is born possessing a genetic preadaptation to language learning and use, so that on the basis of a few encounters with

---

[6]For some examples of the idea that infants begin to develop their language facility from different cries and babblings, see Miller & Dollard, 1941, 81; Mowrer, 1950, 699.

samples of the language forms of the adults who nurture them, infants reinvent for themselves the rules of a grammar system and in fact almost all of the five (grammatical, phonological, morphophonemic, phonetic, and semantic) systems characterizing a language. Chomsky has indicated that this human preadaptation is of such an order that only a very few clues are needed to stimulate the competency each infant and child needs to function linguistically. Such a human predisposition seems to be portrayed by some linguists as analogous to the programs fed into a high-speed computer that allows it, on the basis of a very few bits of electronically provided and quickly scanned information, to solve an entire problem, describe a whole situation, or calculate the most probable among a wide series of consequences. These theoretical ideas have evoked wide-ranging searches for evidence to support such a hypothesis. In Bruner's studies (1975; 1978), concern is expressed with all of the ways human infants may possibly be preadapted at birth to not only acquire language but also discern for themselves the meaningful uses and logical rules of a broad scope of human activities, from technology through artistic and intellectual creativity. In fact Bruner's work tends to suggest that there may be one general species-characteristic predisposition for learning of all basic human skills, from language use, through intelligent and efficient uses of the eyes, hands, and tools, to the cognitive capacity. He proposes that this predisposition is regularly applied to reinventing the rules for forms followed in local cultures. Bruner has suggested in effect that humans are born with one basic species-characteristic behavior form, antecedent to all other such forms, that is used to test fragmentary clues from the local environment and to reorder it, then to generate automatically hypotheses that make it possible to produce a general internal comprehension of the world of experience the infant has yet to face. These highly innovative views are not yet supported by any body of strong evidence, but they do suggest that cries and babbling, along with the gestures of infants, may in some broad way be related to the learning of language and other capacities. It must be said, in conclusion, that at present such infant actions and behavior forms do not seem to be required for language learning. It must also be said that this may well be an errroneous conclusion, if acceptable evidence can be provided for a general species-characteristic preadaptation for all language and cognitive learning.

Pivot and Open Class Words

Intensive studies of the development of infant sound production by Irwin and his University of Iowa associates and by others provides substantial evidence that early sound patterns depend on and are primarily a function of individual body growth and specific changes in an infant's

Communicative contact through a language; Keningau Dusun woman teasing ethnographer (Baginda, 1963). (T.R. Williams)

anatomical and nervous systems.[7] In the first ten days of life a few phonemes are clearly articulated—for instance, *i, e, a, u, h, w,* and *k.* In the first year of life infants significantly expand their range of phoneme productions; babies of two months have an average of seven phoneme uses, at six months the average is 12 phonemes, and at 12 months the average is 18 phonemes. This still is well short of totals used in human languages; for instance, English contains 34 phonemes, while Navaho has 44 phonemes. These phoneme utterance averages are significantly influenced by the position and posture of the growing infant. The shape of the oral cavity and the soft palate are considerably affected by the on-the-back, sitting, crawling, and walking positions of the growing infant. The phonemes developed and used by infants at each age level seem to be regular in nature and not related to the languages used by the adults nurturing them; infants hearing only English also use the vowel and consonant sounds typical of German, French, and many non-Western European languages, while infants learning languages such as Dusun and Papago use phonemes typical of English.

Sometime after nine months of age infants begin to imitate directly the phonemic sound productions that emerge in their spontaneous play babblings. Psychologists now tend to agree that phonemes are not imitated from the speech of adults but are the results of self-stimulation to new

[7]See Irwin, 1947a, 1947b, 1947c, 1948a, 1948b, 1948c, 1952.

sound productions which then call the infant's attention to new types of sound production possibilities.[8]

Despite careful studies it is still difficult to determine the specific age when human infants use the first combinations of phonemes that are expressed in ways having cultural and social meaning. Recurring sequences of phonemes having cultural and social meaning are called *morphemes*. When mothers' retrospective reports from different cultures are used, it appears that the average for the first use of morphemes is about 11 months. Laboratory studies of "gifted" children indicate that some children use morphemes as early as eight months. Children in most cultures are using some morphemes by 13 to 14 months of age.

The first morphemes used by infants are employed as *total utterances*—that is, a way of communicating a whole range of complex meanings (see Table 9–4). The morpheme *mama* may come to mean to the baby and its parents, "Mama feed me," or "Mama, I am tired and wet and irritated by all the noise about me," or "Mama, please bring me the toy over there and the one here by my side that I cannot reach easily." During this period of language learning, babies do not use a grammatical system for combining morphemes into sentence utterances.

TABLE 9–4   First Morpheme Uses By One Child*

CHILD AGE	MORPHEME	CULTURAL AND SOCIAL MEANING
8 Months	Uh?	Used as an introjection and a demonstrative to distant objects, persons.
9 Months	dididi	Disapproval (loudly); comfort (softly).
10 Months	mama	Food: good taste; hungry
10 Months	nenene	Scolding
10 Months	ott!	To call an animal
10 Months	piti	Whispered "interesting"; used with a gesture.
10 Months	deh	An introjection or a demonstrative used with a gesture.

*Leopold, W.F. 1949. *Grammar and General Problems in the First Two Years, Speech Development of a Bilingual Child: A Linguist's Record* (4 Vols.). Evanston, Ill.: Northwestern University Press.

---

[8]For discussions of language development, see Bayley 1956, 1969; Bloom, 1973; Bloom, Lightbown, & Hood, 1975; Braine, 1976; Brown, 1973; Bruner, 1975, 1978; Butterfield, 1968; Clark, 1973; Clark & Clark, 1977; Eimas, Siqueland, Jusczyk, & Vigorito, 1971; Farb,1974; Ferguson & Slobin, 1973; Jakobsen, 1968; Lenneberg, 1962, 1964, 1967; Leopold, 1949; McCarthy, 1954; McNeil, 1970; Mehrabian, 1971; Menyuk, 1971; Menyuk & Bernholtz, 1969; Moskowitz, 1970; Muller, Hollien, & Murry, 1974; Nelson, 1973; Rogers, 1975; Slobin, 1972; Snow, 1977; Trevarthen, 1975.

The growth of morphemic competency in children accelerates markedly in the months and years following the onset of the first morphemic uses. Table 9–5 notes the average number of morphemes reported in one study to be those recognized and used by American middle-class Midwestern children between eight months and six years of age. At the same time children are learning increasingly greater numbers of morphemes, they are also learning to articulate them more clearly. Preschool American children are reported to pronounce approximately 32 percent of their morphemes correctly at two years of age. By three years approximately 63 percent of morphemes are correctly formed, while at six years the figure of accurate morpheme use by preschool American children rises to 89 percent. Similarly the comprehensibility of morpheme uses increases with age; 67 percent of morpheme uses by American 2-year-olds have been reported to be clearly comprehensible, with this figure rising to 89 percent for 2½-year-olds, 93 percent for 3-year-olds, and nearly 100 percent morpheme comprehensibility for 4-year-olds.[9] These data must be qualified by a notation that similar figures are generally not available from other cultures. It can be assumed that morpheme knowledge, articulation, and comprehensibility increase at the same rates for all human children, but this assumption remains to be validated in transcultural research.

In general, linguists and psychologists agree that children do not really begin to use language until they put two or more morphemes together to form primitive sentences. This typically seems to occur first at about 18 to 20 months of age. The number of two-word utterances accelerates sharply between the time of their first use by a child and about 24 to 26 months of age. The total number of different two-morpheme uses rises from between 14 and 20 uses at 18 months, to 350 to 400 at 22 months, to over 2500 at 26 months of age.

TABLE 9–5   Increase in Morpheme Use, American Children, Ages One to Six Years*

AGE IN YEARS	AVERAGE NUMBER OF SINGLE MORPHEMES USED
1	3
2	272
3	896
4	1,540
5	2,072
6	2,526

*Smith, M.E. 1926. "An Investigation of the Development of the Sentence and the Extent of Vocabulary in Young Children." *University of Iowa Studies in Child Welfare*, 3, (5).

---

[9]For some examples of well-known studies of morpheme articulation and comprehensibility, see McCarthy, 1930, 1954; Smith, 1935; Wellman, Case, Mengert, & Bradberry 1931.

Studies of the ways American and European children learn to combine morphemes into sentence utterances indicate that there are, at least for these children, specific age-related stages of development involving hierarchical and regular constructions, or combinations, of morphemes. Two-word sentences tend to include some uses of *pivot,* or "operator," morphemes. These morphemes are limited in number and are added to very slowly. Some examples of pivot words in English would be "my," "this," "see," "on," "other," "more," "there," and "all gone." A pivot morpheme such as "on" is usually the second part of a two-morpheme sentence, although it also occurs as the first morpheme. An example of a second position pivot morpheme would be in an English-speaking child's uses of "blanket on," "shoe on," "spoon on," and "hat on." Pivot morphemes can have many other morphemes, technically termed *open class* morphemes, attached to them in the first position of a two-morpheme sentence to make statements. Some examples of American children's open class morphemes in addition to those just given ("blanket," "shoe," "spoon," "hat") would be "toy," "hot," "milk," "car," "man," "woman," and "house." The open class of morphemes may contain a total of more than 200 different uses for a two-year-old American middle-class Midwestern child.

It is important to understand that young children proceed to use language at first as if there were only the pivot and open classes of morphemes, although the morphemes contained in these two classes actually belong to many different classes in adult language uses (verbs, adjectives, nouns, prepositions, and so on). However young children use them all as belonging only to the pivot or open classifications. This means that young children do not begin speaking by using or making an imitation of the language structures used by the adults who nurture them. Rather, children start language learning and use by means of a system unique to children, which is not simply an infantile imitation of adult language. Young children appear to have a grammar system quite different from the adult systems they have heard and are hearing as they begin to combine morphemes into primitive sentences. This system may be species-characteristic. This fact is important because it eliminates the confusion caused by the matter of "baby talk" in language learning.

It was assumed for a long time that infants and young children learned a greatly reduced, or simplified, version of adult grammar because they also were forming and using the same morphemes used in adult language. This assumption, in a folk or common-sense form, is widely held in many cultures. For instance, parents in cultures speaking languages as diverse as Arabic, Marathi, Comanche, Gilyak, English, and Spanish regularly speak to their children in "baby talk," to try to aid them in learning both the proper morpheme and grammatical uses of adult language.[10] Typically,

---

[10]For a discussion of "baby talk" in different languages, see Ferguson, 1964; Casagrande, 1948.

however, "baby talk" is only a very limited subsystem of the adult language, containing between 25 and 60 morphemes that cover only a very restricted range of the whole of culturally important topics, such as some kinship terms, personal names, body functions, certain qualities of life (hot, cold, wet, dirty), and morphemes for describing some animals and a few nursery games—"patty cake," "whoops-a-daisy," "peek-a-boo," and so on. "Baby-talk" morphemes are mostly open class morphemes and do not appear to provide the structure for the two-morpheme utterances of infants and young children. Thus the two-word utterance system of grammar used by infants and young children is not learned through "baby-talk" training by the adults of their culture.

Hierarchical Constructions

At about two years of age children begin to employ a few structured sentences in their play and interactions with adults and other children. This begins when a combination utterance of two open class morphemes (an "open-open" sentence) such as "woman hat" is changed by adding a pivot word such as "other" to "woman" and "hat" to make a three-unit utterance such as "other woman hat." This process is illustrated in Figure 9–1. When children reach about 2½ years of age, the use of sentences of the structured pivot-open-open (or open-open-pivot) type is an increasingly regular part of their language. At about this age children also begin to offer much more complex, multiple morpheme sentences. A number of laboratory studies indicate that by three years of age children tend to regularly use four-morpheme sentences and at four years are speaking six- to eight-morpheme sentences. At the age of five years most children are using multiple morpheme sentences, often including those with ten or more morphemes, which are increasingly structured according to the rules of grammar used by the adult speakers of the culture in which children are maturing.

From the onset of three-word-type sentences at about two years to some time close to four years of age, children tend to "overregulate" their use of morphemes as they seek to employ their unique grammar system. Thus children speaking English will typically use "strong verbs" inflected for the past tenses, in the same ways that adult speakers will inflect only "weak verbs." Some examples of this kind of inflective overregularization of morphemes in two- and three-morpheme sentences would be "goded" (for "gone"), "breaked" (for "broken"), "doed" (for "did"), "hitted (for "hit"), and "runded" (for "run"). Another example of overregularization is for English-speaking two- and three-year-olds to use plurals similar to "mouses" (for "mice"), "dogses" (for "dogs"), "foots" (for "feet"), "cateses" (for "cats"), and "manses" (for "men").

Psychological and linguistic studies of the overregularization process among two- and three-year-old European and American children tend to

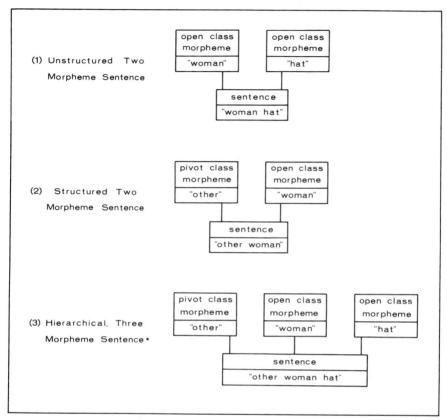

FIGURE 9–1 The transition from unstructured two-morpheme sentences to hierarchical, three-morpheme sentences. The morphemes may also be reversed in this expression, as in "woman other hat" or "hat other woman" and still be examples of a hierarchical, three-morpheme sentence.

agree that these linguistic uses represent a consistent search by young children to find and use consistent language patterns, so that they may go on, after a pattern is identified, to use it in speaking in new and more complex ways. In other words, two- to three-year-old children seem to strive in their language learning and use to seek out patterns and regularities for use in making more general statements that aid in ordering their everyday experiences.

When children reach the level of using four- and five-morpheme sentences at 3 to 3½ years of age, they begin to drop the grammar forms initially developed in speaking and to use more frequently the grammars typical of the languages spoken by the adults caring for them. This transition, from the "child grammar" to the grammar of adult languages, has been well studied only in European and American cultures. The research efforts of Piaget, Bruner, and others on cognition have provided most of the present suggestions concerning the steps in this complex transition. It is quite clear from such studies that European and American children all tend to go through the same steps in the transition from child grammar to adult grammar uses. However there is substantive disagreement currently concerning the exact specification and nature of each of these steps.

Evidence from children's behavior seems to indicate that the grammar changeover process occurs with some general kinds of steps. First, children show increasing efforts to systematize their language use and employ the overregularizations noted before. Then to break out from the limits imposed on their language use, children abandon the overregularizations for the regularities of grammatical form used by adults about them. Next, children must detect the patterns of grammar form that adults use in regular ways of speaking a language. Then children must learn to know and use well the variations from the adult grammar patterns—that is, they must comprehend and begin to use language normatively, or in a way that includes not only patterned form but also the common variations from patterns. Finally, children practice and regularly use the normative expressions of language common to and typical of the adults caring for them. These five or six steps in the transition from child grammar to adult grammar also seem to be present in other non-Western cultures. However there have been few studies of this process outside Western cultures (Harkness, 1975; Blount, 1969, 1972).

Perhaps the most important point to be made concerning this transition in language learning and use is that, although each child must face

Keningau Dusun mother in communicative contact with infant (Baginda, 1962). (T.R. Williams)

alone the almost overpowering complexities of the adult languages, most do so quite efficiently and successfully. It is clear from the literature of socialization that adults in most cultures do not provide the kind of intensive training and experience that is necessary for a child to master adult grammar forms and to make a successful transition from typical child grammar uses. These facts of language learning seem to lend weight to the conception that language learning and use is based on and proceeds from a human biological preadaptation for such behavior. However proponents of this conception of language learning and use sometimes tend to ignore some evidence that is contrary to their assumptions.

Variations in Language and Use

There are consistent indications that girls make greater progress than do boys in language learning and use, particularly in the time of first uses of language, total numbers of morphemes mastered, the time of onset of three- and four-morpheme sentences, and morpheme and phoneme comprehensibility. There also appear to be consistent variations, at least in the United States and Europe, in language learning and use specifically linked not only to the sex of the child but also to the social, economic, and ethnic settings into which children are born and are enculturated. Children whose language efforts are positively and warmly approved by the adults about them generally tend to become more highly proficient in language use and to progress quickly through the child grammar period to acquisition and regular uses of adult grammar. In contrast, children whose language efforts are deprecated or punished by adults, in any of a variety of forms, tend to lag significantly behind their "rewarded" peers, often by a matter of many months or even years; children raised in institutional settings in America and Europe generally fall well behind their age-mates enculturated in more "normal" settings. There also are research data that indicate that American and European twins and triplets may lag well behind only children in language learning and uses.

All of these data of variation in language learning and use seem to indicate that if there is a biologically transmitted preadaptation for such behavior in human infants and young children, it is very plastic, or differential, markedly influenced and easily altered by nonbiological cultural and social experiences and by biologically based sexual and health factors that affect individuals as they are enculturated. The fact of Anna and Isabelle (see Chapter 5) telescoping into a relatively brief time the language learning and uses said to ordinarily occupy children for all of the first five or six years of their lives also raises a basic question about current assumptions concerning the biological human preadaptation to language learning and use. This is not to say that the process of language learning is not fundamentally biochemical and neuroanatomical in its essence; on the contrary, it means that it may be too simplistic to try to reduce language learning and use to this level of conceptual abstraction and study. The variations of human language learning and uses are too complex and vital in human life to be explained away by a biologically deterministic, although very aesthetically appealing, assumption. It is noteworthy that even skilled and experienced scholars when faced with a very complex problem, such as the fact that infants and children learn and use adult language without much instruction, will turn to an *obscurum per obscurius* (explaining an unknown phenomenon by reference to a still more unknown phenomenon) type argument for explanation and reference.

LANGUAGE AND SOCIALIZATION

Many present accounts of the interrelations of language and socialization tend to use statements of the form, "For the sake of argument, A (language) will be considered prior to B (culture)."[11] This form of statement is logically equivalent to saying regularly that "A (language) is basic to and of underlying significance to B (culture)." These kinds of statements and the logic form they imply make brief discussions of the interrelations between language and socialization very difficult.

There no longer is a real question of whether there are such interrelations since it has been demonstrated clearly through the studies of isolated, deaf, and autistic children, of twins, and of the deculturation process that infants and children must be in regular communicative contact with other, linguistically competent adults if they are to become fully socialized. However the specific questions of *how* and *why* language affects the socialization process and vice versa remain unsettled since language cannot be reduced to or understood only by describing the cultural and social behavior of its speakers or the ways these persons have developed, arranged, and operated social, religious, economic, and other daily events. On the one hand, a language consists of whatever persons living in a culture have to know in order to vocally communicate with their fellows in a fashion that other persons will accept as corresponding to their own. On the other hand, as noted before, a language consists of a highly organized system of sounds and rules for making sounds, which can be studied, after an initial descriptive effort, quite apart from any of the behavior of individuals making the sounds and using rules of sound expression.

Today many anthropologists and anthropological linguists would accept the statement that the relation of language to culture is that of a part

---

[11]See, for instance, Bean, 1979.

Five-year-old Dusun girl in communicative contact with mother (Sensuron village, Tambunan district, Sabah, Malaysia). (T.R. Williams, 1960)

to a whole—that is, language is one subsystem of an entire culture. This means that these scholars would reject the logical form and statements that imply that language is of primary significance for all of culture. These specialists tend to see language as one of several ways of making accessible to its speakers historically created and derived concepts that individuals can employ in dealing with the events of the natural world and with each other. Language is seen as being used principally by individuals to get from the "outside" world of nature and social beings into the substance of the "inside" of a culture, by acquiring the language spoken in and typical of a culture. In this way individuals can gain some access to the "minds" and "selves" of their fellows, for language is both a way of expressing thought and feeling and of thinking and feeling about thought and emotion. Competent speakers of a language can take "into" themselves the thoughts of others in a culture and make these into their own, in the same or in some altered form. Language is not viewed as a prime mover, or first cause, in human behavior, since as one subsystem of a larger cultural whole it does not dominate all of culture. In this view of the relation of language to culture, a culture consists of many different patterns which are not "translatable" into purely linguistic forms.

In this conception of the relation between language and culture, the part played by language in the socialization process tends to be emphasized in a *facilitative* sense; thus it is *through* language infants and children come to know what others know and expect them to know. It is through language children and adults add to and change what is known and expected in a culture. It is through language that children can be reached by and respond to those persons, social agencies, and institutions (see Chapter 8) involved in the socialization process. It is also through language that children learn of the enculturation conceptual system used in their local culture; this learning enables a child to become an active participant in the process of transmitting a culture.

A contrary view of the way language is related to culture tends to be reflected in the studies of some anthropological linguists and many psychologists, linguists, and biologists. In this view language is a fully separate and easily distinguishable human behavior system that is basic for all culture and human activity. Language is generally *directive* —that is, language tends to cause and is believed responsible for human action. In one of its forms the directive argument for language proposes that adults who do not "fit" readily or are not totally "competent" in their social and cultural behavior have become so because of their failure to learn language adequately. The directive assumption concerning the relations between language and culture is involved in many of the explanations that have been offered for why and how adults come to act in similar ways when they occupy the same status positions in a social structure. In this view adults behave the same way when occupying the same status primarily because they share a language.

In the directive sense infants and children are socialized because they are born into a culture that operates from the base of a language system. Human personality, many abilities, and most individual social actions are seen as the result and consequence of having learned language. In this view individuals must also struggle against the predetermined aspects of language, only rarely transcending the tyranny of words and sounds that dominate their lives.

Another approach to the interrelations between language and socialization involves a combination of both the *facilitative* and *directive* views. While it is probably correct to note, as in the facilitative approach, that language does not dominate all human behavior and that all culture does not have linguistic components or aspects, it is equally correct, as in the directive approach, to say that many aspects of language are deeply involved and probably directly responsible for some specific kinds of human learning and action. Hallowell (1953) has demonstrated the advantages of combining the facilitative and directive approaches in his innovative and original discussions of the evolutionary growth of the interrelations of language and socialization. He has noted that today none of culture, society, or personality can really be conceived as existing apart from language, but he also notes it is still possible to analyze and subject to careful study these features (culture, society, and personality) of the human experience without assigning a high logical priority to language in its relations to culture.

Hallowell has also noted that, through language, uniquely human forms of the psychological processes of attention, perception, interest, memory, dreams, imagination, symbolic representations, ability to deal with the contrasts between the possible and the actual, the tangible and intangible, and differentiation between reality and fantasy have become operative and "alive" in humans. Thus in a theoretical approach that combines the facilitative and directive views, language is interrelated with both the formation and subsequent functioning of personality and the successes of humans in being able to comprehend and deal with culture. In this view language not only is a vehicle for socialization but also at the same time is the means by which humans become both *more* and *less* like others in a culture. Through the process of socialization and by means of language, individuals adopt those attributes of self and behavior that characterize most persons in their culture. While this is occurring, individuals also, through language, are becoming less and less psychologically like any other members of their culture, for language is not only one key to learning what others know, think, and feel, it is also a means for each individual to self-consciously reflect on and then to shape their own unique self or person-ality. Thus in this view of the role of language in socialization, new members of a culture are able simultaneously to join with and be apart from others, to be like, and yet differentiate themselves from, their fellows. Language is the means for persons to achieve "oneness" and "apartness" at the same time and is a way to handle both the social and cultural *centripedal* (pro-ceeding toward the center) and *centrifugal* (proceeding away from the cen-ter) elements of the socialization process without great harm to themselves or their society and culture. The facilitative and the directive views of language alone do not adequately explain the ways human become the kinds of adults they are when, in Kluckhohn's (1949) memorable words, they have become like all humans, some humans, no other human.

In the last few years a number of studies have combined the facilitative and directive approaches to language to provide evidences of some specific interrelations between language and the socialization process. For instance, Gumperz and his associates (Gumperz and Hymes, 1964) at the University of California at Berkeley have made a number of studies of the acquisition of language in a variety of different cultures. K. Kernan (1969) has de-scribed and analyzed the interrelations of language and the enculturation process in Samoa; Blount (1969; 1972) has described and analyzed the acquisition of language by Luo (Kenya) children; Stross (1969) has reported the details of language acquisition and enculturation among Tenjapa (Mex-ico) children; Sanches (1969) has studied the relations between encultur-ation and the acquisition of grammar by Japanese children; and C. Kernan (1969) has reported some of the interrelations between language and en-culturation in urban black American society.

These studies, and those similar to them by Howell (1967), Mathiot (1962, 1966), and others, hold promise of transcultural specification of interrelations between socialization and language. Thus Blount (1969; 1972) has identified developmental stages in the prelinguistic behavior of Luo children, which he relates to the language behavior of older child and adult caretakers, while Stross (1969) has recorded both verbal settings and Mexican children's participation in such settings in an effort to demonstrate the relative importance of direct and overheard speech on first language learning and on subsequent cultural behavior. Such studies can provide for transcultural validation of theories of language, of cognition, and of the ways language and the socialization process may be specifically interrelated.

CONCLUSIONS

In the theoretical paradigm that has been developed in this book, it is proposed that socialization is a *doubly contingent,* or transactional, process. In this theory the cultural preoccupations of adults become the infant's and child's preoccupations. Language is a medium for acquiring derived, or learned, preoccupations, as infants and children have their behavior culturally shaped by adult responses to them, by adult responses to their responses, by adult evaluations of children's responses, and by the growing ability of children to independently evaluate and judge their own responses in terms of adult expectations.

The role of language in the transactional interchange is important because it is the one human communication medium with perhaps the most lasting impact. Other communication media involved in the long-term human transactional exchanges, such as inarticulate experience (see Chapter 7) and tactile, kinesic, proxemic, and *adumbrative* (indications preceding formal communications necessary for mutual exchange of information) experiences, all have roles in the doubly contingent process of informational exchange. However language is an important way for adults to finally and fully convey their views to infants and children. It is through language that the socialization process becomes fully operative and takes on a strategic role in human life.

SUMMARY

This chapter has been concerned with a discussion of the relations between language and the process of socialization. The topic of language origin and development was examined in the first section of the chapter to provide a background of data and information for understanding some of the ways language functions in the life of contemporary humans. Then some of the relations between speech and thought and between language structure and thought were examined briefly to note the complex and pervasive nature of language. The third part of the chapter provided a brief summary of contemporary knowledge of infant and child language acquisition and use. The last section of the chapter noted some approaches to and discussed some results of studies of the interrelations between language and the socialization process.

REFERENCES CITED AND SUGGESTED READINGS

ALLEN, W.S. 1949. "Ancient Ideas on the Origin and Development of Language." *Transactions of the Philosophical Society, London,* pp. 35–60.

ALEXANDRE, P. 1972. "Review of J. H. Greenberg, *Language, Culture and Communication.*" *Language in Society,* 1, 304.

ALTMAN, S.A. (ed.). 1967. *Social Communication among Primates.* Chicago: University of Chicago Press.

ANDREW, R. 1962. "Evolution of Intelligence and Vocal Mimicking." *Science,* 137, 585–589.

———. 1963a. "Evolution of Facial Expression." *Science,* 142, 1034–1041.

———. 1963b. "The Origin and Evolution of the Calls and Facial Expressions of the Primates." *Behavior,* 20, 1–109.

BAR-ADON, A., & W. LEOPOLD (eds.). 1971. *Child Language: A Book of Readings.* Englewood Cliffs, N.J.: Prentice-Hall.

BARKER, G.C. 1945. "The Social Functions of Language." *ETC: A Review of General Semantics,* 2, 228–234.

BASSO, K.H., & H.A. SELBY (eds.). 1976. *Meaning in Anthropology* (A School of American Research Book). Albuquerque: University of New Mexico Press.

BAUMAN, R. 1974. "Review of D.M. Smith and R.W. Shuy (eds.), *Sociolinguistics in Cross-Cultural Perspective.*" *Language in Society,* 3, 103–109.

BAUMAN, R., & J. SHERZER (eds.). 1974. *Explorations in the Ethnography of Speaking.* Cambridge, England: Cambridge University Press.

BAYLEY, N. 1956. "Individual Patterns of Development." *Child Development,* 27, 45–74.

———. 1969. Manual for the Bayley Scales of Infant Development. New York: Psychological Corporation.

BEAN, S.S. 1979. "How Is the Study of Language Part of Anthropology: A Review of Language and Linguistics in Introductory Textbooks." *Language in Society,* 8, 101–109.

BECKEY, R.E. 1942. "A Study of Certain Factors Related to Retardation of Speech." *Journal of Speech Disorders,* 7, 223–249.

BEDAU, H.A. 1957. "Review of J. B. Carroll (ed.), *Language, Thought and Reality.*" *Philosophy of Science,* 24, 289–293.

BENDER, M.L., R.L. COOPER, & C.A. FERGUSON. 1972. "Language in Ethiopia: Implications of a Survey for Sociolinguistic Theory and Method." *Language in Society,* 1, 215–233.

BERNSTEIN, B. 1960. "Language and Social Class: Research Note." *British Journal of Sociology,* 11, 271–276.

———. 1961a. "Aspects of Language and Learning in the Genesis of the Social Process." *Journal of Child Psychology and Psychiatry,* 1, 313–324.

———. 1961b. "Social Class and Linguistic Development." In A.H. Halsey, J. Floud, & A. Anderson (eds.), *Education, Economy and Society.* Glencoe, Ill.: The Free Press, pp. 288–314.

———. (ed.). 1971. *Class, Codes and Control. Vol. 1—Theoretical Studies towards a Sociology of Language.* London. Routledge & Kegan Paul.

———. (ed). 1973. *Class, Codes and Control. Vol. 2—Applied Studies towards a Sociology of Language.* London: Routledge & Kegan Paul.

BIRDWHISTELL, R. 1970. *Kinesics and Context: Essays on Body Motion Communication.* Philadelphia: University of Pennsylvania Press.

BISSERET, N. 1979. *Education, Class Language, and Ideology.* London: Routledge & Kegan Paul.

BLACK, M. 1959.   "Linguistic Relativity: The Views of Benjamin Lee Whorf." *Philosophical Review*, 68, 228–238.

BLOCH, B., & G.L. TRAGER. 1942.   *Outline of Linguistic Analysis*. Baltimore, Md.: Linguistic Society of America.

BLOCH, M. 1976.   "Review of R. Bauman and J. Sherzer (eds.), *Explorations in the Ethnography of Speaking.*" *Language in Society*, 5, 229–234.

BLOOM, L. 1970.   *Language Development: Form and Function in Emerging Grammars*. Cambridge, Mass.: M.I.T. Press.

———. 1973.   *One Word at a Time: The Use of a Single Word Utterance Before Syntax*. Janua Linguarum Series Minor, 154.

BLOOM, L., P. LIGHTBOWN, & L. HOOD. 1975.   "Structure and Variation in Child Language." *Monograph of the Society for Research on Child Development*, 40, Whole No. 160.

BLOUNT, B.G. 1969.   "Acquisition of Language by Luo Children." Unpublished doctoral dissertation, University of California, Berkeley.

———. 1972.   "Aspects of Luo Socialization." *Language in Society*, 1, 235–248.

———. 1977.   "Review of S. Rogers (ed.), *Children and Language:* Readings in Early Language and Socialization." *Language in Society*, 6, 119–124.

BOAS, F. 1911.   "Introduction." In F. Boas (ed.), *Handbook of American Indian Languages*. Washington, D.C.: Bureau of American Ethnology, No. 40, 24–27, 42–43, 81.

———. 1920. "The Methods of Ethnology." *American Anthropologist, 22, 311–321.*

———. 1934.   *Geographical Names of the Kwakiutl Indians*. New York: Columbia University Contributions to Anthropology, No. 20, pp. 9–21.

———. 1938.   *General Anthropology*. New York: Heath.

———. 1942.   "Language and Culture." In *Studies in the History of Culture: The Disciplines of the Humanities*. Menasha, Wis.: Banta, pp. 178–184.

BOSSARD, J.H.S. 1945.   "Family Modes of Expression." *American Sociological Review*, 10, 226–237.

BRAINE, M. 1976.   "Children's First Word Combination." *Monographs of the Society for Research on Child Developments*. 41, Whole No. 164.

BRANDIS, W., & D. HENDERSON. 1970.   *Social Class, Language and Communication*. Beverly Hills, Calif.: Sage Publications.

BRIGHT, W.O. 1963.   "Language." In B. J. Siegel (ed.), *Biennial Review of Anthropology, 1963*. Stanford, Calif.: Stanford University Press, pp. 1–29.

———. 1966.   *Sociolinguistics*. The Hague: Mouton.

BROWN, R.W. 1958.   *Words and Things*. Glencoe, Ill.: Free Press.

———. 1973.   *A First Language: The Early Stages*. Cambridge, Mass.: Harvard University Press.

BRUNER, J.S. 1975.   "The Beginnings of Intellectual Skill." *New Behaviour*, October 9, 1975, pp. 58–61.

———. 1978.   "Acquiring the Uses of Language." The Berlyne Memorial Lecture, Toronto, 1978.

BRUNER, J.S., J.J. GOODNOW, & G.A. AUSTIN. 1956.   *A Study of Thinking*. New York: John Wiley.

BRUNER, J.S., R.R. OLVER, & P.M. GREENFIELD. 1966.   *Studies in Cognitive Growth*. New York: John Wiley.

BUTTERFIELD, E.C. 1968.   "An Extended Version of Modification of Sucking with Auditory Feedback." *Working Paper No. 43, Bureau of Child Research Laboratory, Children's Rehabilitation Unit*, University of Kansas Medical Center.

CARPENTER, E., & M. McLUHAN. 1960.   *Explorations in Communication: An Anthology*. Boston: Beacon.

CARROLL, J.B. 1953.   *The Study of Language.* Cambridge, Mass.: Harvard University Press.

———. (ed.). 1956.   *Language, Thought and Reality. Selected Writings of Benjamin Lee Whorf.* New York: John Wiley.

———. 1958.   "Some Psychological Effects of Language Structure." In P. Hoch & J. Zubin (eds.), *Psychopathology of Communication.* New York: Grune & Stratton, pp. 28–36.

———. 1964.   *Language and Thought.* Englewood Cliffs, N.J.: Prentice-Hall.

CASAGRANDE, J.B. 1948.   "Comanche Baby Language." *International Journal of American Linguistics,* 14, 11–14.

CAZDEN, C.B. 1972.   *Child Language and Education.* New York: Holt, Reinhart & Winston.

———. 1976.   "Review of T. Van der Geest, R. Gerstel, R. Appel and B. Tervoort, *The Child's Communicative Competence: Language Capacity in Three Groups of Children from Different Social Classes.*" *Language and Society,* 5, 250–254.

———. 1977.   "Review of H. Francis, *Language in Childhood: Form and Function in Language Learning.*" *Language in Society,* 6, 417–420.

CHAFE, W. (ed.). 1963.   *Aspects of Language and Culture.* Seattle: University of Washington Press.

CHAMBERLAIN, A.F. 1896.   *The Child and Childhood in Folk-Thought.* New York: Macmillan.

CHANCE, M., & C. JOLLY. 1970.   *Social Groups of Monkeys, Apes and Men.* New York: Dutton.

CHERRY, C. 1957.   *On Human Communication. A Review, a Survey, and a Criticism.* Cambridge, Mass.: M.I.T. Press.

CHOMSKY, N. 1957.   *Syntactic Structures.* The Hague: Mouton.

———. 1965.   *Aspects of the Theory of Syntax.* Cambridge, Mass.: M.I.T. Press.

———. 1968.   *Language and Mind.* New York: Harcourt Brace Jovanovich.

———. 1969.   *The Acquistion of Syntax in Children from 5 to 10.* Cambridge, Mass.: M.I.T. Press.

CHURCH, J. 1961.   *Language and the Discovery of Reality. A Developmental Psychology of Cognition.* New York: Random House.

CLARK, E.V. 1973.   "What's in a Word? On the Child's Acquisition of Semantics in His First Language." In T.E. Moore (ed.), *Cognitive Development and the Acquisition of Language.* New York: Academic Press, pp. 65–110.

CLARK, H.H., & E.V. CLARK. 1977.   *Psychology and Language.* New York: Harcourt Brace Jovanovich.

COLE, M. 1972.   "Review of R. Huxley and E. Ingram (eds.), *Language Acquisition: Models and Methods.*" *Language in Society,* 1, 290–292.

COOK-GUMPERZ, J. 1973.   *Social Control and Socialization: A Study of Class Differences in the Language of Maternal Control.* London: Routledge & Kegan Paul.

DANCE, F.E.X. 1967.   *Human Communication Theory.* New York: Holt, Rinehart & Winston.

DELAGUNA, F. (ed.). 1927.   *Speech, Its Function and Development.* New Haven, Conn.: Yale University Press. (Republished in 1963 by Indiana University Press.)

DERWING, B.L. 1973.   *Transformational Grammar as a Theory of Language Acquistion: A Study in the Empirical, Conceptual and Methodological Foundations of Contemporary Linguistic Theory.* Cambridge Studies in Linguistics, 10.

DOBZHANSKY, T. 1955.   *Evolution, Genetics and Man.* New York: John Wiley.

———. 1960.   "Individuality, Gene Recombination and Non-repeatability of Evolution." *Australian Journal of Science,* 23, 71–78.

DORE, J. 1977.   "Review of M.A.K. Halliday, *Learning How to Mean: Explorations in the Development of Language.*" *Language in Society,* 6, 114–118.

Du BRUL, E.L. 1958.   *Evolution of the Speech Apparatus.* Springfield, Ill.: Chas. C. Thomas.

DUNCAN, H.D. 1962.   *Communication and the Social Order.* New York: Buckminster.

EIMAS, P.D., E.R. SIQUELAND, P. JUSCZYK, & J. VIGORITO. 1971.   "Speech Perception in Infants." *Science,* 171, 303–306.

ELKIND, D., & J.H. FLAVELL. 1969.   *Studies in Cognitive Development.* London: Oxford.

ERICKSON, F. 1975.   "Review of J. Cook-Gumperz, *Social Control and Socialization: A Study of Class Differences in the Language of Maternal Control.*" *Language in Society,* 4, 110–113.

ERVIN-TRIPP, S.M. 1973.   *Language Acquisition and Communicative Choice: Essays by Susan M. Ervin-Tripp.* Stanford, Calif.: Stanford University Press.

———. 1974.   "Review of W.E. Lambert, *Language, Psychology and Culture.*" *Language in Society,* 3, 305–309.

ERVIN-TRIPP, S.M., & C. MITCHELL-KERNAN (eds.). 1977.   *Child Discourse.* New York: Academic Press.

FARB, P. 1974.   *Word Play: What Happens When People Talk.* New York: Knopf.

FERGUSON, C.A. 1964.   "Baby Talk in Six Languages." In J.J. Gumperz & D. Hymes (eds.), *The Ethnography of Communication.* Special Publication, *American Anthropologist,* 66, 103–114.

FERGUSON, C.A., & D.I. SLOBIN, 1973.   *Studies of Child Language Development.* New York: Holt, Rinehart & Winston.

FRANCIS, H. 1975.   *Language in Childhood: Form and Function in Language Learning.* New York: St. Martin's Press.

FURTH, H.G. 1966.   *Thinking without Language: Psychological Implications of Deafness.* New York: Free Press.

GARDNER, R.A., & B.T. GARDNER. 1969.   "Teaching Sign Language to a Chimpanzee." *Science,* 169, 664–672.

GILES, H. 1974.   "Review of S.M. Ervin-Tripp, *Language Acquisition and Communicative Choice: Essays by Susan M. Ervin-Tripp.*" *Language in Society,* 3, 145–146.

GLEASON, H.A. 1961.   *An Introduction to Descriptive Linguistics* (1st rev. ed.). New York: Holt, Rinehart & Winston.

GLEASON, J.B., & S. WEINTRAUB. 1976.   "The Acquisition of Routines in Child Language." *Language in Society,* 5, 129–136.

GRAVEN, J. 1967.   *Non-Human Thought.* Briarcliff Manor, N.Y.: Stein & Day.

GRAVES, R. 1957.   "Comment on D. Lee, Lineal and Non-Lineal Codifications of Reality; Symbolization and Value." *Explorations,* 7, 46–51, 67–73.

GREENBERG, J.H. 1963.   *Universals of Language.* Cambridge, Mass.: M.I.T. Press.

———. 1971.   *Language, Culture and Communication.* Stanford, Calif.: Stanford University Press.

GUMPERZ, J. 1958.   "Dialect Differences and Social Stratification in a North Indian Village." *American Anthropologist,* 60, 668–682.

GUMPERZ, J., & D. HYMES (eds.). 1964.   *The Ethnography of Communication.* Special Publication, *American Anthropologist,* 66, December, 1964.

HALL, E.T., & G.L. TRAGER. 1953.   *The Analysis of Culture.* Washington, D.C.: American Council of Learned Societies.

HALLIDAY, M.A.K. 1975.   *Learning How to Mean: Explorations in the Development of Language.* London: Edward Arnold.

HALLOWELL, A.I. 1950.   "Personality Structure and the Evolution of Man." *American Anthropologist,* 52, 159–173.

———. 1953.   "Culture, Personality and Society." In A.L. Kroeber (ed.), *Anthropology Today.* Chicago: University of Chicago Press, pp. 597–620.

————. 1954. "Psychology and Anthropology." In J. Gillin (ed.), *For A Science of Social Man.* New York: Macmillan, pp. 160–226.

————. 1955. *Culture and Experience.* Philadelphia: University of Pennsylvania Press.

HARKNESS, S. 1975. *Child Language Socialization in a Kipsigis Community in Kenya.* Unpublished doctoral dissertation, Harvard University.

HARPER, R.G., A.N. WIENS, & J.D. MATARAZZO. 1978. *Non-verbal Communication: The State of the Art.* New York: John Wiley.

HARRIS, Z.S. 1951. *Methods in Structural Linguistics.* Chicago: University of Chicago Press.

HEINECKE, C. 1953. *Bibliography on Personality and Social Development of the Child.* (Bound with Whiting, B.B. 1953. *Selected Ethnographic Sources on Child Training.)* New York: Social Science Research Council, Pamphlet No. 10.

HENLE, P. (ed.) 1958. *Language, Thought and Culture.* Ann Arbor: University of Michigan Press.

HILL, J.H. 1977. "Review of E. Linden, *Apes, Men and Language,* and B. Stross, *The Origin and Evolution of Language.*" *Language in Society,* 6, 274–281.

HOCKETT, C. 1958. *A Course in Modern Linguistics.* New York: Macmillan.

————. 1959. "Animal 'Languages' and Human Languages." In J.N. Spuhler (ed.), *The Evolution of Man's Capacity for Culture.* Detroit, Mich.: Wayne State University Press, pp. 32–39.

————. 1960. "The Origin of Speech." *Scientific American,* September, 1960, pp. 3–10.

HOCKETT, C., & R. ASCHER. 1964. "The Human Revolution." *Current Anthropology,* 5, 135–168.

HOIJER, M. 1951. "Cultural Implications of Some Navaho Linguistic Categories." *Language,* 27, 111–120.

————, 1953. "The Relation of Language to Culture." In A.L. Kroeber (ed.), *Anthropology Today.* Chicago: University of Chicago Press, pp. 554–573.

————. 1954. "Language in Culture." *Comparative Studies of Cultures and Civilizations, No. 3, and Memoirs of the American Anthropological Association, No. 79.* Chicago: University of Chicago Press.

HOUSTON, S.H. 1969. "A Sociolinguistic Consideration of the Black English of Children in Northern Florida." *Language,* 45, 599–607.

HOWELL, R.W. 1967. "Linguistic Choice as an Index to Social Change." Unpublished doctoral dissertation, University of California, Berkeley.

HUXLEY, R., & E. INGRAM (eds.). 1971. *Language Acquisition: Models and Methods.* New York: Academic Press.

HYMES, D. 1961a. "Linguistic Aspects of Cross-Cultural Personality Study." In B. Kaplan (ed.), *Studying Personality Cross-Culturally.* New York: Harper & Row, Pub., pp. 313–359.

————. 1961b. "Functions of Speech: An Evolutionary Approach." In F. Gruber (ed.), *Anthropology and Education.* Philadelphia: University of Pennsylvania Press, pp. 55–83.

————. 1962. "The Ethnography of Speaking." In T. Gladwin & W.C. Sturtevant (eds.), *Anthropology and Human Behavior.* Washington, D.C.: Anthropological Society of Washington, pp. 13–53.

————. (ed.). 1964. *Language in Culture and Society.* New York: Harper & Row, Pub.

————. 1974. *Foundations in Sociolinguistics: An Ethnographic Approach.* Philadelphia: University of Pennsylvania Press.

IRVINE, J.T. 1977. "Review of E. Leach, *Culture and Communication: The Logic by Which Symbols Are Connected.*" *Language in Society,* 6, 85–89.

IRWIN, O.C. 1947a. "Development of Speech During Infancy: Curve of Phonemic Frequencies." *Journal of Experimental Psychology,* 37, 187–193.

———. 1947b. "Infant Speech: Consonantal Sounds according to Place of Articulation." *Journal of Speech and Hearing Disorders,* 12, 397–401.

———. 1947c. "Infant Speech: Consonant Sounds according to Manner of Articulation." *Journal of Speech and Hearing Disorders,* 12, 402–404.

———. 1948a. "Infant Speech: Development of Vowel Sounds." *Journal of Speech and Hearing Disorders,* 13, 31–34.

———. 1948b. "Infant Speech: The Effect of Family Occupational Status and of Age on Use of Sound Types." *Journal of Speech and Hearing Disorders,* 13, 224–226.

———. 1948c. "The Effect of Family Occupational Status and Age on Sound Frequency." *Journal of Speech and Hearing Disorders.* 13, 320–323.

———. 1952. "Speech Development in the Young Child: 2. Some Factors Relating to the Speech Developmnt of the Infant and Young Child." *Journal of Speech and Hearing Disorders,* 17, 269–279.

IRWIN, O.C., & H.P. CHEN. 1946a. "Infant Speech: Vowel and Consonant Frequency." *Journal of Speech and Hearing Disorders,* 11, 123–125.

———. 1946b. "Development of Speech in Infancy: Curve of Phonemic Types." *Journal of Experimental Psychology,* 36, 431–436.

JACOBS, R.A., & P.S. ROSENBAUM. 1969. *English Transformational Grammar.* Waltham, Mass.: Blaisdell.

JAKOBOVITS, L.A., & M.S. MIRON. 1967. *Readings in the Psychology of Language.* Englewood Cliffs, N.J.: Prentice-Hall.

JAKOBSON, R. 1968. *Child Language, Aphasia and Phonological Universals.* The Hague: Mouton.

JACOBSON, R., & M. HALLE. 1966. *Fundamentals of Language.* The Hague: Mouton.

JERISON, H.J. 1955. "Brain to Body Ratios and the Evolution of Intelligence." *Science,* 121, 447–449.

JOSEPH, A., R.B. SPICER, & J. CHESKY. 1949. *The Desert People.* Chicago: University of Chicago Press.

KERNAN, C.M. 1969. "Language Behavior in a Black Urban Community." Unpublished doctoral dissertation, University of California, Berkeley.

KERNAN, K. 1969. "The Acquisition of Languages by Samoan Children." Unpublished doctoral dissertation, University of California, Berkeley.

KLUCKHOHN, C. 1949. *Mirror for Man.* New York: Whittlesey House.

———. 1960. "Navaho Categories." In S.A. Diamond (ed.), *Culture in History.* New York: Columbia University Press, pp. 65–98.

KLUCKHOHN, C., & D. LEIGHTON. 1946. *The Navaho.* Cambridge, Mass.: Harvard University Press.

———. 1961. "Notes on Some Anthropological Aspects of Communication." *American Anthropologists,* 63, 895–909.

KOHN, M.L. 1959a. "Social Class and Parental Authority." *Amercian Sociological Review,* 24, 352–366.

———. 1959b. "Social Class and Parental Values." *American Journal of Sociology,* 64, 337–351.

KROEBER, A.L. 1964. "Foreword." In D. Hymes (ed.), *Language in Culture and Society.* New York: Harper & Row, Pub., pp. xvii–xix.

LAFRANCE, M., & C. MAYO. 1978. *Moving Bodies: Nonverbal Communication in Social Relationships.* Monterey, Calif.: Brooks/Cole.

LAMBERT, W.E. 1972. *Language, Psychology and Culture.* Stanford, Calif.: Stanford University Press.

LANCASTER, J.B. 1967. "Primate Communication Systems and the Emergence of Human Language." Unpublished doctoral dissertation, University of California, Berkeley.

LEACH, E. 1976. *Culture and Communication: The Logic by Which Symbols Are Connected.* Cambridge, England: Cambridge University Press.

LEE, D.C. 1938. "Conceptual Implications of an Indian Language." *Philosophy of Science,* 5, 89–102.

———. 1959. *Freedom and Culture.* Englewood Cliffs, N.J.: Prentice-Hall.

LEHMAN, W.P. 1962. *Historical Linguistics.* New York: Holt, Rinehart & Winston.

LENNEBERG, E. 1953. "Cognition in Ethnolinguistics." *Language,* 29, 463–471.

———. 1962. "Understanding Language Without Ability to Speak: A Case Report." *Journal of Abnormal and Social Psychology,* 65, 419–425.

———. 1964. *New Directions in the Study of Language.* Cambridge, Mass.: M.I.T. Press.

———. 1967. *Biological Foundations of Language.* New York: John Wiley.

LEOPOLD, W.F. 1949. *Grammar and General Problems in the First Two Years, Speech Development of a Bilingual Child: A Linguist's Record (4 Vols.)* Evanston: Northwestern University Press.

———. 1948. "The Study of Child Language and Infant Bilingualism." *Word,* 1, 249–259.

———. 1952. *Bibliography of Child Language.* Evanston, Ill.: Northwestern University Press.

———. 1953. "Patterning in Children's Language Learning." *Language Learning,* 5, 1–14.

LINDEN, E. 1975. *Apes, Men, and Language.* New York: Saturday Review Press, Dutton.

LOTZ, J. 1950. "Speech and Language." *The Journal of the Acoustical Society of America,* 22, 712–717.

———. 1955. "On Language and Culture." *International Journal of American Linguistics,* 21, 187–189.

LOUNSBURY, F. 1960. "Language," In B.J. Siegel (ed.), *Biennial Review of Anthropology,* 1961. Stanford, Calif.: Stanford University Press, pp. 185–209.

LURIA, A.R. 1961. *The Role of Speech in the Regulation of Normal and Abnormal Behavior.* London: Pergamon.

LURIA, A.R. & F.I. YUDOVICH. 1959. *Speech and the Development of Mental Processes in the Child.* London: Staples.

LYONS, J., & R.J. WALES (eds.). 1966. *Psycholinguistic Papers.* Edinburgh: Edinburgh University Press.

MACAULAY, R.K.S. 1973. "Review of M.C. Ward, *Them Children: A Study in Language Learning." Language in Society,* 2, 310–314.

———. 1976. "Social Class and Language in Glasgow." *Language in Society,* 5, 173–188.

———. 1977. *Language, Social Class and Education: A Glasgow Study.* Edinburgh: Edinburgh University Press.

MANDELBAUM, D.C. (ed.). 1949. *Selected Writings of Edward Sapir in Language, Culture, and Personality.* Berkeley: University of California Press.

MARATSOS, M.P. 1973. "Review of W. Brandis & D. Henderson, *Social Class, Language and Communication." Language in Society,* 2, 314–319.

MATHIOT, M. 1962. "Noun Classes and Folk Taxonomy in Papago." *American Anthropologist,* 64, 340–350.

————. 1966. "An Approach to the Study of Language and Culture Relations." Unpublished doctoral dissertation, Catholic University, Washington, D.C.

McCARTHY, D. 1930. "The Language Development of the Pre-School Child." *Institute of Child Welfare Monograph Series*, No. 4. Minneapolis: University of Minnesota Press.

————. 1954. "Language Development in Children." In L. Carmichael (ed.), *Manual of Child Psychology*, (2nd. ed.). New York: John Wiley, pp. 492–630.

McLAUGHLIN, B. 1978. *Second-Language Acquisition in Childhood*. New York: Halstead Press, John Wiley.

McNEILL, D. 1970 *The Acquisition of Language: The Study of Developmental Linguistics*. New York: Harper & Row, Pub.

MEHRABIAN, A. 1971. *Silent Messages*. Belmont, Calif.: Wadsworth.

MENYUK, P. 1969. *Sentences Children Use*. Cambridge, Mass.: M.I.T. Press.

————. 1971. *The Acquisition and Development of Language*. Englewood Cliffs, N.J.: Prentice-Hall.

MENYUK, P., & N. BERNHOLTZ. 1969. "Prosodic Features and Children's Language Production." *M.I.T. Research Laboratory of Electronics Quarterly Reports*, No. 93, 216–219.

MILLER, G.A. 1951. *Language and Communication*. New York: McGraw-Hill.

————. 1954. "Psycholinguistics." In G. Lindzey (ed.), *Handbook of Social Psychology*. Cambridge, Mass.: Addison-Wesley, pp. 693–708.

MILLER, N.E. & J. DOLLARD. 1941. *Social Learning and Imitation*. New Haven, Conn.: Yale University Press.

MILLER, W.R. 1972. "Review of A. Bar-Adon & W. Leopold (eds.), *Child Language; A Book of Readings*." *Language in Society*, 285–290.

MOERK, E.L. 1977. *Pragmatic and Semantic Aspects of Early Language Development*. Baltimore, Md.: University Park Press.

MOSKOWITZ, A. 1970. "The Two-Year-Old Stage in the Acquisition of English Phonology." *Language*, 46, 426–441.

MOWRER, O.H. 1950. "On the Psychology of 'Talking Birds'—A Contribution to Language and Personality Theory." In O.H. Mowrer (ed.), *Learning Theory and Personality Dynamics*. New York: Ronald, pp. 689–707.

MULLER, E., H. HOLLIEN, & T. MURRY. 1974. "Perceptual Responses to Infant Crying: Identification of Cry Types." *Journal of Child Language*, 1, 89–95.

NELSON, K. 1973. "Structure and Strategy in Learning to Talk." *Monographs of the Society for Research in Child Development*, 38, Nos. 1 & 2.

PIAGET, J. 1929. *The Child's Conception of the World*. Atlantic Highlands, N.J.: Humanities Press.

————. 1947. *Judgement and Reasoning in the Child*. Atlantic Highlands, N.J.: Humanities Press.

————. 1954. *Construction of Reality in the Child*. New York: Basic Books.

————. 1955. *The Language and Thought of the Child*. Cleveland: Collins Publishers.

PIAGET, J., & B. INHELDER. 1948. *The Child's Conception of Space*. Atlantic Highlands, N.J.: Humanities Press.

POOLE, M.E. 1975. "Review of B. Bernstein, *Class, Codes and Control*." *Language in Society*, 4, 73–84.

ROGERS, S. (ed.). 1975. *Children and Language: Readings in Early Language and Socialization*. London: Oxford University Press.

ROMNEY, A.K., & R.G. D'ANDRADE (eds.). 1964. "Transcultural Studies in Cognition." Special Publication, *American Anthropologist*, 66, June, 1964.

RUESCH, J., & G. BATESON. 1951. *Communication: The Social Matrix of Psychiatry*. New York: W.W. Norton & Co. Inc.

SAMPSON, O.C. 1956. "A Study of Speech Development in Children 18–30 Months." *British Journal of Educational Psychology*, 26, 194–202.

SANCHES, M. 1969. "Features in the Acquisition of Japanese Grammar." Unpublished doctoral dissertation, Stanford University.

SAPIR, E. 1949. Selected Writings of Edward Sapir." In D.G. Mandelbaum (ed.), *Language, Culture, and Personality*. Berkeley and Los Angeles: University of California Press.

SCHACHTEL, E.G. 1947. "On Memory and Childhood Amnesia." *Psychiatry*, 10, 1–26.

SEBEOK, T.A. (ed.). 1968. *Animal Communication: Techniques of Study and Results of Research*. Bloomington: University of Indiana Press.

SEBEOK, T.A. & A. RAMSAY (eds.). 1969. *Approaches to Animal Communication*. Atlantic Highlands, N.J.: Humanities Press.

SLOBIN, D.I. 1972. "Children and Language: They Learn the Same Way All Around the World." *Psychology Today*, 6, 71–74.

SMITH, D.M. & R.W. SHUY (eds.). 1972. *Sociolinguistics in Cross-Cultural Perspective*. Washington, D.C.: Georgetown University Press.

SMITH, F., & G.A. MILLER. 1966. *The Genesis of Language: A Psycholinguistic Approach*. Cambridge, Mass.: M.I.T. Press.

SMITH, M.E. 1935. "A Study of Some Factors Influencing the Development of the Sentence in Preschool Children." *Journal of Genetic Psychology*, 46, 182–212.

SNOW, C.E. 1977. "The Development of Conversation between Mothers and Babies." *Journal of Child Language*, 4, 1–22.

STREHLOW, T.G.H. 1947. "On Aranda Traditions." In D. Hymes (ed.). *Language in Culture and Society*. New York: Harper & Row, Pub., 1964. (Reprinted from Strehlow, T.G.H. 1947. *Aranda Traditions*. Melbourne: Melbourne University Press, pp. xiv–xxi.)

STROSS, B.M. 1969. "Language Acquisiton by Tenjapa Tzeltal Children." Unpublished doctoral dissertation, University of California, Berkeley.

———. 1976. *The Origin and Evolution of Language*. Dubuque, Iowa: Wm. C. Brown.

TREVARTHEN, C. 1975. "Early Attempts at Speech." In R. Lewin (ed.), *Child Alive!* Garden City, N.Y.: Anchor Books, pp. 57–74.

TYLER, S.A. (ed.) 1969. *Cognitive Anthropology*. New York: Holt, Rinehart & Winston.

VAN DER GEEST, T., R. GESTEL, R. APPEL, & B. TERVOORT. 1973. *The Child's Communicative Competence: Language Capacity in Three Groups of Children from Different Social Classes*. The Hague: Mouton.

VERHAAR, J.W.M. 1975. "Review of D. Hymes, *Foundations in Sociolinguistics: An Ethnographic Approach*." *Language in Society*, 4, 352–361.

VON HUMBOLDT, W. 1836. "Über die Kawisprache." Part I. *Über die Verschiedenheit des Menschlichen Sprachbaues und Ihren Einfluss auf die Geistige Entwickelung des Menschengeschlechts*. Bonn: Dummlers Verlag.

VYGOTSKY, L.S. 1939. "Thought and Speech." *Psychiatry*, 2, 29–54.

———. 1962. *Thought and Language*. New York: M.I.T. Press and John Wiley. (Originally published in Russian in 1934.)

WALLACE, A.F.C. 1961. "The Psychic Unity of Human Groups." In B. Kaplan (ed.), *Studying Personality Cross-Culturally*. New York: Harper & Row, Pub., pp. 129–163.

———. 1962. "Culture and Cognition." *Science*, 135, 351–357.

WARD, M.C. 1971. *Them Children: A Study in Language Learning*. New York: Holt, Rinehart & Winston.

WATSON, J.B. 1924. *Behaviorism*. New York: W.W. Norton & Co., Inc.

WELLMAN, B.L., I.M. CASE, I.C. MENGERT, & D.E. BRADBURY. 1931. "Speech Sounds of Young Children." *University of Iowa Studies in Child Welfare,* 5, No. 2.

WHITING, B.B., & J.W.M. WHITING. 1971. "Task Assignment and Personality: A Consideration of the Effect of Herding on Boys." In W.W. Lambert & R. Weisbrod (eds.), *Comparative Perspectives on Social Psychology.* Boston: Little, pp. 33–45.

WHORF, B.L. 1956. *Language, Thought, and Reality.* New York: John Wiley.

WILLIAMS, H.M. 1937. "An Analytical Study of Language Achievement in Preschool Children." *University of Iowa Studies in Child Welfare,* 13, 35–46.

WILLIAMS, T.R. 1958. "The Structure of the Socialization Process in Papago Indian Society." *Social Forces,* 36, 251–256.

WITHERSPOON, G. 1971. "Navaho Categories of Objects at Rest." *American Anthropologist,* 73, 110–127.

WITUCKI, J. 1971. "A Language Pattern Co-Occurring with Violence-Permissiveness." *Behavioral Science,* 16, 531–537.

CHAPTER TEN
A SOCIALIZATION
CONCEPTUAL SCHEME

This chapter is concerned with presentation of a conceptual scheme for study of the socialization process. This discussion begins with some comments helpful in distinguishing between theory and concept in socialization research. Then a socialization conceptual scheme is provided in summary form. The chapter concludes with discussion of some ideas concerning development of a socialization conceptual scheme and a socialization theory.

THEORY AND CONCEPT IN
SOCIALIZATION RESEARCH

A *theory* is a coherent set of general statements explaining the specific ways that natural events are interrelated and interconnected.[1] In contrast, *concepts* are the product of abstract thought about the nature of the interrelations between events. Concepts may be arranged into a scheme, or plan, to assist in understanding the relationships between events or occurrences.

[1]It is helpful to understand that the term *theory* does not refer to speculation or untested ideas. It is not uncommon in the United States for theory to be confused colloquially with *hypothesis*, meaning an untried idea or opinion. It is a misunderstanding of science to believe that speaking or writing "theoretically" is to be speculative or to engage in conjecture.

An example of a conceptual scheme is the one used in chemistry and termed the *periodic table of elements*. This is a plan in which all the chemical elements, arranged according to their atomic numbers, are displayed in groups. This scheme was developed by Dimitri Mendeleev between 1869 and 1871 in an effort to understand the relationships between the 63 chemical elements then known to chemists.[2] In 1871 Mendeleev used his conceptual scheme to predict the properties of three unknown chemical elements he named *ekaboron, ekaaluminun,* and *ekasilicon.* These elements were discovered later and termed *gallium* (1875), *scandium* (1879), and *germanium* (1886).[3] Hence after a conceptual scheme has been developed, it can be used to produce new understanding. The periodic table has now been expanded to include 105 chemical elements because Mendeleev's scheme can be used to predict and then confirm the existence of new chemical elements.

Some specific rules, or procedures, are needed for stating a theory or forming a conceptual scheme. For example, as Bateson (1958, 293) noted, it is necessary to avoid confusing theory, as a series of general statements explaining the ways events are interrelated, with the thing being explained. Thus to use Bateson's example, a theoretical statement about elephants is not itself an elephant; a theoretical statement does not have tusks. A theory does not have an existence of its own, apart from the statements concerning the interconnections between events and occurrences being explained in the theory.[4] A conceptual plan for understanding the relationships between events is a uniquely human product, arising from systematic thought, and is bound by the limitations of the prior knowledge and personal dispositions of the individual(s) developing the scheme.[5]

The general approach used here in outlining a conceptual scheme for the socialization process is derived from the structural and functional the-

[2]Mendeleev's innovative plan for ordering chemical elements by their atomic numbers is based on the number of *protons,* or positive charges, in the nucleus of an atom of a particular element.

[3]*Gallium* is a rare, steel-gray, trivalent metallic element with an atomic weight of 69.72, used in high-temperature thermometers because of its high boiling point (1983 C.) and low melting point (30 C.). *Scandium* is a rare, trivalent metallic element, atomic weight 44.956, found in the mineral euxenite. *Germanium* is a scarce metallic element, normally trivalent, atomic weight 72.59, used today in making transistors.

[4]For some discussions of theory in anthropology and sociology, see Goodenough, 1969, and Homans, 1964. See also Kuhn, 1966, for an understanding of theory in the physical sciences.

[5]The French, Swedish, and German chemists experimentally confirming the existence of *gallium, scandium,* and *germanium* named the elements for their particular ethnic groups out of an intense ethnocentrism or used their own name in the formal term for the new element; Lecoq de Boisbaudran (1838–1912) used the Latin *gallus* (cock) as a translation of the French *coq* to employ his first name in designating *gallium,* the element he discovered, while Lars Nilson (1840–1899), a Swedish chemist, used the ancient name (*Scandia*) of the Scandinavian Peninsula to form the designation *scandium,* and Clements Winkler (1838–1904), the discoverer of *germanium,* employed the ancient Latin term for Germany to designate the element.

oretical tradition of modern anthropology and sociology.[6] The concept of structure is used to refer to the arrangement and interrelation of parts as they are dominated by the general character of the conceptual whole. In the following discussion the conceptual whole to be considered is the socialization process. The parts comprising that whole are the patterns of culture especially concerned with the transmission of human culture. These patterns may be said to be functionally interrelated because they result from the structure of the socialization process operating through the long period in which culture has existed as a definable and recognizable entity.

The socialization process may be conceptually viewed as consisting of a number of structurally interrelated parts. The parts of that process may be identified as (1) *personal agents,* (2) *impersonal agents,* (3) *formal social groups,* (4) *informal social groups,* (5) *a socialization conceptual system,* (6) *total human biological equipment,* and (7) *internal conditions of culture.* The functions of these specific parts of the socialization process may be identified as (A) *explicit functioning,* (B) *implicit functioning,* (C) *deutero functioning,* (D) *generative functioning,* (E) *anticipatory functioning,* (F) *developmental functioning,* and (G) *linguistic functioning.*

STRUCTURE OF THE SOCIALIZATION PROCESS

The structure of the socialization process is:

1. *Personal Agents.* In each one of the 128 cultures (see Appendix) used as the basis for development of this conceptual scheme, the process of enculturation involves transmission of culture by adults, as well as by a child's playmates and age-mates. In the initial portion of the process of socialization, a human infant is in direct contact with parents and parent-surrogates. These contacts gradually broaden to include other family members and subsequently come to include play-group members and friends.[7] Between the ages of six and ten, depending on local cultural tradition, children also begin to have direct personal contacts with adults possessing special skills, knowledge, and abilities. In cultures in which such contacts are organized systematically, transmission of particular cultural knowledge may be offered in special settings ("schools") by specially trained adults

---

[6]This tradition is discussed in Merton (1957), Levy (1952), Firth (1956), and Hallowell (1956). Portions of this discussion were first presented in Williams, 1972b.

[7]Research concerned with the consequences of the socialization process has often emphasized the importance of parental agents of cultural transmission. However there is no substantive evidence to demonstrate that only one of the different classes of personal agents of cultural transmission has more importance and is more critical to the existence and operation of the socialization process than is any other of the classes of personal agents. The structural-functional conceptual scheme proposed here has no requirements that some categories, or parts, be chosen over others as being of primary importance.

("teachers"). In cultures where such contacts are not organized, adults holding special status-role positions ("priest," "*shaman*," "craftsman," "hunter") may also serve as personal agents in the process of cultural transmission.

2. *Impersonal Agents.* Human life regularly involves contacts with many kinds of natural phenomena such as wind, sound, clouds, water, sun, plants, and animals. Although these are distributed differentially and have variable local manifestations and although contacts may vary from proximate to distant, all human groups appear to utilize them in some form or another in the transmission of culture. Humans anthropomorphize and reify some natural phenomena in songs, folk tales, proverbial sayings, riddles, and so on, which are told and sung by personal agents of socialization to infants and children. The most highly personalized of these natural phenomena become meaningful parts of the cultural transmission process. For example, the anthropomorphization and reification of the sun, moon, stars, and certain animals dominant in a local ecology—for example, "moon mother," "sun father," "wolf brother"—often take a form in which young children may come to converse directly with these natural elements as they would with a parent or a playmate. Such interactions may also occur with objects, either natural or man-made. In more technologically complex cultures, objects made by humans, such as books, radios, television sets, motion pictures, and computers, have come to occupy a similar place in the cultural transmission process.

In cultures where children are encouraged by adults to converse regularly with natural elements, the human capacity for reflexive thought, symbolizing, and language provides the opportunity for children to conduct "internal" conversations on behalf of, and in the role of, the inanimate and mute impersonal agents addressed—that is, children use their capacities for language, symbolization, and reflexivity to complete, on behalf of the impersonal agent, the "other side" of a conversation concerning their behavior or their plans for action. Thus the use of these human capacities for animating the inanimate and making personal the impersonal brings such agents fully into the cultural transmission process. In cultures possessing the kinds of technology that can actually "talk back" to children, whether in the forms of a silent exchange (for example, books) or in the forms that are verbal and often visual as well (radio, television, motion pictures), children readily acquire great amounts of cultural information.

3. *Formal Social Groups.* Each culture contains formal social groups that are involved actively in the process of cultural transmission.[8] In small societies such groups usually number from 2 to 20 persons. These groups are characterized by a face-to-face interaction between members and children. In large societies formal social groups may comprise hundreds or

[8]The features of formal social groups are noted in Footnote 24, chapter 7.

thousands of members and are characterized by face-to-face interactions occurring primarily between specially designated functionaries and representatives of the group—for example, "priest," or "president"—and maturing children.

Examples of some formal social groups, from both small and large societies, would be the family (nuclear or any of its extended forms), churches, clubs, fraternities, clans, schools, and the kibbutz. The expectations for behavior held by members of formal social groups usually correspond with expectations generally known in a culture. Thus when young members are asked to conform to formal group aims, they are in effect being subjected to a continuation of the local process of cultural transmission. Formal social groups exercise a different type of authority from that employed by personal agents in cultural transmission. If new members will not conform regularly to formal group goals and standards of behavior, they face the threat of expulsion from the group. Usually parents and parent-surrogates will not banish infants and children from their presence in any formal way. As a consequence formal social groups may take on an active role in the cultural transmission process when parents or parent-surrogates turn to the group for use of its disciplinary powers.

4. *Informal Social Groups.* Each culture contains informal social groups—that is, groups without controls for behavior of its members—with a low level of value on intergroup behavior, and organized for the inclusive knowledge of the lives of group members. Some examples of informal social groups would be play groups, neighborhood groups, work teams, feasting "societies," age groups, sex groups, economic interest groups, craft groups, "gangs," blood brotherhoods, and other such groupings organized on a nonkinship basis.

Informal social groups are organized for brief periods only for the accomplishment of limited aims. Personal relations within such groupings are marked by a "personal impersonality," with members expressing little interest in the behavior of other members outside their activities together. Such groups usually operate only within those standards of personal behavior typical of the culture in which the group exists.

Individuals become members of informal social groups because they share in the special interests of these groups. Thus when young children become part of an informal group, it is most often because they have sought it out for its special aims (to play, to learn a craft, and so on). Once part of such an informal group, however, children have a special and "unofficial" opportunity to learn the forms of a local culture, as these are used regularly by older members in the course of group action toward furtherance of their special interests. Thus informal social groups play a part in the cultural transmission process by providing repeated access to usual ideas and behavior standards transmitted in a culture.

5. *A Socialization Conceptual System.* Each culture possesses a body of culturally transmitted ideas concerning the learning capacities and potentials of infants and children and regarding the proper social positions and roles for infants and children in everyday life. Each culture also has beliefs about the nature of infant and child life, as well as a distinct set of ideas concerning the whole socialization process. Although the forms and meanings of cultural transmission concepts vary widely among cultures, all groups regularly use such concepts in the process of cultural transmission.

The existence of a socialization conceptual scheme in each local culture means adults have and know a plan for cultural transmission and use assumptions concerning it that can be referred to in the course of the long-term operation of that process. Children can also learn details of this plan as they experience it and, through a type of *autokinetic effect,* can apply it as a guide for their own cultural learning. This effect is most directly visible when children subject themselves to the norms and standards of adults, even though no punishment or censure could be applied to them for acts undertaken without adults' awareness. The existence of a socialization conceptual scheme can provide for "feedback," or regular exchange, of information between children and adults concerning the process of cultural transmission.

6. *Total Human Biological Equipment.* The phrase *total human biological equipment* refers to the fact that in the course of general biological evolution and later in the interactions between *hominid* biology and social and cultural experience, a complete biosystem that prepares the human infant to be socialized came into existence.[9]

This does not mean that since *Homo sapiens sapiens* infants are born with a biosystem that prepares them to be socialized, the socialization process is essentially biological in nature. It does mean that *Homo sapiens sapiens* infants usually are born possessing species-characteristic behavior forms, reflexes, drives, and capacities that serve together as organic bridgeheads to learning culture. However in the absence of cultural transmission, no amount of biologically transmitted readiness or active biological propensities on the part of an infant can bring the socialization process into operation. The converse is also true, for no amount of contact with the socialization process can overcome major deficiencies in the total biological system of an infant and lead to a full expression of what may be termed *humanness.*

7. *Internal Conditions of Culture.* There was a period in *hominid* evolutionary development when such populations lived more in a natural than

[9]LaBarre (1954) has provided one of the best accounts of the emergence and operations of this biosystem for socialization. Honigmann (1967, 177) has described this total system and has termed it "an active propensity for socialization," while Hallowell (1953, 612) has called it an "inherent organic potential" for socialization.

a cultural ecology. As a cultural system developed gradually over a long time, it was eventually transmitted to and acquired by *hominid* young. The cultural transmission process was probably very fitful and incomplete for hundreds of generations, as *hominids* continued to live in and under conditions of a partly natural and a partly cultural ecology. As a cultural system came into existence and slowly developed, the system began to interact more frequently with *hominid* biology. This led in turn to a powerful mutual feedback system being activated between *hominid* biology and cultural experience. Natural evolutionary selection pressures that had affected *hominid* biology became altered because of the interactions between that biology and the evolving *hominid* cultural system. This reciprocal feedback process, from *hominid* biology to culture and culture to biology, was a new phenomenon in nature, which led to rapid acceleration of events and sequences in both the *hominid* biological and cultural realms. The time intervals between significant and major biological and cultural changes began to contract sharply as the mutual feedback between *hominid* biology and culture operated to produce a vigorous interaction synthesis of both phenomena.

Perhaps more important than a "speeding up" of biological and cultural changes was the fact that the mutual feedback process between *hominid* biology and culture came to have an identifiable locus, or place, in nature in the socialization process. A conjectural model for the transition from a natural to a cultural ecology and the development of a locus for the interaction between human biology and culture in the socialization process is presented in Table 10–1.[10]

TABLE 10–1   Conjectural Model for a Transition from a Natural to a Cultural Ecology*

1. *Hominid* population(s), W, living in a natural ecology, NE, could survive more readily in a cultural ecology, CE.

2. W did not regularly produce or employ any features of a CE while living under conditions of NE.

3. A CE is produced by an interaction synthesis process between *hominid* biology, A, and *hominid* experience, B.

4. *Hominid* population(s), X, evolved from W^N with genetic frequency changes giving X the capacity to synthesize a CE from the mutual interactions between A and B.

5. X produces some features of a CE from an A and B mutual feedback process.

6. As the X population(s), produces a CE from A and B, it gains a naturally selective evolutionary advantage over population W^N and so replaces it in a habitat.

7. *Hominid* population(s), Y, evolves from X^N, with additional genetic frequency changes giving Y increased capacity to synthesize features of a CE from the mutual feedback interaction between A and B.

---

[10]This model was first published in Williams, 1972b, 233–240. See also Williams, 1975. For comment on the model, see Wills, 1979, 875–877.

TABLE 10–1 *Continued*

8. Y produces a CE from an A and B mutual feedback process.

9. As the Y population(s), produces a CE from A and B, it has a naturally selective evolutionary advantage over population X^N and so replaces it in a habitat.

10. Y transmits some of the features of CE it synthesizes from A and B to its young Y^1, who acquire some CE without their own synthesis from A and B; Y^1 also matures with and uses the capacity to synthesize CE from A and B.

11. Y^1 produces added CE features from an A and B mutual feedback process.

12. Y^1 transmits some of the CE it synthesizes from A and B to its young, Y^2. Y^1 also transmits some of the CE it has acquired from Y to Y^2. Y^2 thus possesses features of a CE that are *cumulative* in nature.

13. Y^2 produces added features of a CE from an A and B mutual feedback process.

14. Y^2 transmits some of the CE it synthesizes from A and B to its young, Y^3. Y^2 also transmits some of the CE it has acquired from Y through Y^1.

15. *Hominid* population(s), Z, evolves from Y^N, with additional genetic frequency changes giving Z increased capacity to synthesize a CE from the mutual feedback interactions between A and B. Z also possesses knowledge of features of a CE synthesized by its predecessors and culturally transmitted to it.

16. Z produces a CE (1) from an A and B mutual feedback process and (2) through integrating acquired features of a CE with the products of A $\leftrightarrow$ B synthesis. The amount and varieties of Z's CE differ significantly from that produced by any previous *hominid* populations.

17. As the Z population(s), produces CE from A and B, it has a naturally selective evolutionary advantage over population Y^N and so replaces it in a habitat.

18. Z transmits some of the CE it synthesizes from A and B to its young Z^1 who acquire some CE without synthesis from A and B; the amount of CE transmitted by Z to Z^1 and the amount of CE acquired by Z^1 are significantly increased over the amounts of CE previously transmitted and acquired by any *hominid* population. Z^1 also matures with and uses the capacity to synthesize from A and B.

19. Z^1 lives more in and under conditions of a CE than any previous *hominid* populations—that is, W^N, X^N, Y^N, and Z.

20. *Hominid* population(s), Z^N, evolve from Z^1 with additional genetic frequency changes giving Z^N increased capacity to synthesize CE from the mutual feedback interaction between A and B. Z^N produces and transmits both the CE it has synthesized and acquired from preceding generations and lives more in and under conditions of CE than has any previous *hominid* populations.

*It is important that this paradigm be understood to be only illustrative of a conjectural model for the origin and development of the socialization process. It is not meant to be used as a basis for calculations of gene frequency changes among evolving primates, for noting specific time sequences in biological or cultural evolution, nor is it to be taken as a specific explanation for the origin of particular cultural features such as social organization, language, and so on. Margaret Mead has noted (personal communication) that this conjectural model does not allow for the effects that the young may have had upon adults early in the generational process of cultural transmission.

FUNCTIONS OF THE
SOCIALIZATION PROCESS

The functions of the socialization process are:

A. *Explicit Functioning*. Each of the 128 cultures (see Appendix) in the sample used to develop a conceptual scheme for the socialization process enculturates infants and children according to specific local conceptions of the distinctive features of culture. The phrase *explicit functioning* refers to the personal involvement of adults in transmission of the features of culture they believe to be distinctive and important. For example, Bateson and Mead (1942; Mead, 1956a) report extreme concern by adult Balinese for maintaining an unimpaired body surface. This adult Balinese preoccupation is transmitted through direct comment by adults prohibiting children with open wounds or new scars from participating in religious activities. Such expressions are intentional and overt acts. This concern is part of a set of complexly interrelated cultural patterns, including wound treatment, body cleanliness, mortuary rites, and special religious rituals that the Balinese view as vital and necessary in their lives. Thus explicit functioning of the socialization process involves personal agents in a direct transmission of cultural features believed to be of significance in a culture.

B. *Implicit Functioning*. An illustration of the implicit functioning of the socialization process can also be taken from Bateson and Mead's (1942; Mead, 1956a) description of Balinese concerns for maintaining an unimpaired body surface. Balinese children learn of this adult preoccupation in at least three ways in addition to the direct and active admonitions of personal agents of socialization. These ways are (1) through the repeated expressions of concern by adults to one another concerning the time and manner of wound healing; (2) in the ways children witness and take a peripheral part in a series of mortuary rites, which are repeated over many years for each deceased individual and which involve symbolic attempts by adults to eliminate the corpse and all the objects associated with it; and (3) in the ways adults exert regular and continuing efforts to make a corpse whole and integral again through manufacture of surrogates for use in mortuary rites.

These acts by Balinese adults involve an implicit transmission to the children of the basic importance of body integrity. There is no intentional effort to relate these cultural features to children, for they are considered to be adult concerns and not educationally relevant. Thus Balinese children are also enculturated through learning about their culture in ways that do not involve explicit, overt action by adults. DuBois (1956) has termed this function of the socialization process as *absorptive*—that is, as a presentation of cultural patterns that are so consistently observed in adults that children acquire them through a "kind of psychic osmosis" (DuBois, 1956, 242).

C. *Deutero Functioning.* In the course of considering different styles of cultural transmission, Bateson (1942) and Bateson and Ruesch (1951, 215–216) noted that children may also learn culture in the acts of learning culture—that is, children may acquire culture in a *deutero*, or secondary, manner without either explicit or implicit socialization process functions being involved. Bateson (1942) illustrated the deutero function in cultural transmission by noting the ways in which some American schoolteachers and administrators provide conditions for pupils to learn specific American values, such as tolerance, equality, freedom, justice, and fairness. Students soon learn, from the contexts of such teaching, that their adult mentors believe in these values on two levels. One level is the ideal appearance of the values taught. A second level consists of the real opinions of adults involved in teaching values. When American schoolchildren learn specific values in a class setting in which no ethnically, socially, or culturally "different" children are regularly present because of their being excluded due to cultural and social patterns of inequality in income, housing, and parental educational achievements, then children have transmitted to them, in a deutero fashion, the fact that American values apply to certain kinds of Americans and not to others.[11]

D. *Generative Functioning.* Until the 1950s the socialization process was portrayed as a series of external forces imposed on infants and children as they matured in a cultural milieu. Allport (1955, 34) has noted that this view of the socialization process is essentially "mirrorlike"—that is, children are believed to simply reflect the culture known and used by the adults of their group. Allport points out that this assumption ignores the many ways infants and children actually are known to take a creative part in shaping the process of learning culture.

Among others, Maslow (1954) and Mead (1949b) have offered clear examples of the ways children take a creative part in the socialization process. In developing these ideas Goodman (1964, 1967) proposed that children can be said to generate attitudes and values out of the cultural information made available to them by adults. Bruner's studies (1956, 1966) of cognitive growth also provide empirical evidences that children can and do take an active role in the process of learning culture.

The generative function of the socialization process thus may be defined as comprising all of the ways children reflect on, think about, and

[11]The distinction between implicit and deutero functions of the socialization process resolves to cultural transmission through specific adult acts, although these are unintentional, and the contexts in which cultural learning occurs.

Tambunan Dusun mother and sons. (T.R. Williams, 1960)

sort out for themselves the content of culture available to them, in order to develop their own cognitive map of adult culture.

E. *Anticipatory Functioning.* Each of the 128 cultures in the sample provides specific preliminary clues and indications of the ways children will be expected to act as adults.[12] An example would be found in the enculturation process among the eastern highland peoples of New Guinea (Berndt, 1962, 92). Adult behavior has elements of what Americans would term "callousness" and "hostility" toward others, including infants and children. The children most admired by adults are those frequently commanding wide attention with violent temper tantrums, those bullying younger and weaker playmates, and those regularly given to excessive displays of aggressive posturing and swaggering. Children regularly carrying tales to adults are also widely admired, since this activity is viewed

---

[12]Early drafts of this conceptual scheme used the concept of *prefigurative* functioning as first defined by Margaret Mead in a discussion of the cultural determinants of sexual behavior (Mead, 1961). Mead subsequently developed a theory in which she employed the concept of *prefiguration* in conjunction with the concepts of *cofigurative* and *postfigurative* styles of cultural learning. In her comment on this scheme, Mead suggested that the concept of *anticipatory* functioning be substituted for *prefigurative* functioning. I believe it vital to maintain the integrity of the theoretical paradigm Mead has developed (Mead, 1956b, 1957, 1959, 1965, 1970) concerning the ways the learning of children reinforms adult understanding of their culture. Hence I have substituted the term *anticipatory* for *prefigurative* in developing a conceptual scheme for the socialization process.

by adults as a normal and desirable feature of adult life. Children behaving in these ways are believed to have a future as successful adults, particularly in their potential as fighters and mothers. Thus such behavior by children is analogous to specific adult acts. Although these acts by children are not adult in their form, the significant attributes of such acts anticipate approved and expected adult behavior. In acting in these ways children have an opportunity to rehearse the behavior expected of admired and respected adults.

F. *Developmental Functioning.* Following birth human growth and maturation processes are directly related to the socialization process. There is a general human biological impetus toward "completion" of the basic direction imparted to the organism through hereditary materials. Cultural transmission generally occurs in a manner calibrated with the growth and body development of infants and children–that is, as Mead (1947) notes, each major act of cultural learning occurs in a definite relationship to a child's degree of biological readiness for the act. The specific relationships between acts of cultural learning and children's biological readiness to learn create special situations in which deutero functioning of the socialization process can and often does occur. For instance, although most children learn to walk, the way they learn and the times they are permitted, or forced, to learn motor skills in reference to their actual biological capacity for walking may become a vital fact in their participation in the cultural transmission process.

Thus Balinese babies are regularly encouraged by adults to walk before crawling, so that infants suffer frequent losses of balance. This "reversal" of a human developmental process (crawl, then stand assisted, then stand unassisted, then walk alone) appears (Mead, 1947) to be related directly to the adult Balinese preoccupations with personal disorientations of any type, including those caused by use of alcohol and travel in modern vehicles. Mead suggests that the adult Balinese preoccupation with personal disorientation causes Balinese children, through a cultural structuring of developmental skills, to become concerned with an acute sensing of imbalance and motion disorientation from their being forced by adults to act in ways they cannot.

G. *Linguistic Functioning. Homo sapiens sapiens* infants are usually born with a capacity for learning and using language. Hence it is "biologically normal" for humans to learn and to use language, provided they have regular access to linguistically competent speakers of a language. Children will learn and use the language, or languages, spoken by the adult members of the culture into which they are born, provided adults expect them to do so. It is "normal" for children to undergo a series of complex transitions

Left to right, a Dusun adolescent male, mother and son, and grandmother, grandson, and granddaughter (1959, Trus Madi) (T.R. Williams)

in the process of language learning and use prior to becoming linguistically competent.

In each culture infants and children must learn to shape correctly the minimally distinctive units of sound, or phonemes, used by competent speakers of the languages being learned. Children must also learn an intricate system for joining phonemes into words, or morphemes. Children must learn a grammar that controls the specific ways adult speakers of a language join morphemes to make cognitively useful utterances. Thus language learning does not simply involve acquisition, in a stimulus-response fashion, of a large collection of sounds, made into patterns peculiar to a language. Human languages involve exceedingly complex sets of rules that determine for speakers the specific sequences and patterns of speech sounds to be employed in particular social situations. Such rules must be mastered and used by each child, essentially on their own recognizance—that is, without adult instruction, direction, or teaching.

It is through the linguistic functioning of the socialization process that infants and children come to have access to the "cognitive maps" of the adults who care for them—that is, to know what others know and expect them to know. It is through language that infants and children can reach and be reached by those individuals, social institutions, and groups involved in the socialization process. It is through language that children learn of the conceptual scheme for socialization known and used by adults caring for them. It is through language that children come to develop the uniquely human psychological forms and processes of perception, attention, interest, memory, dreams, imagination, and symbolic representations; to deal with contrasts between the actual (real) and the expected (ideal), the tangible and the intangible; and to differentiate between reality and fantasy. And it is through the linguistic functioning of the socialization process that children are able to take on the cultural preoccupation of adults, to be directly and actively instructed by personal agents of socialization, and to acquire, through the functions of the socialization process, the standard cultural meanings and meaning variations that comprise adult cultural preoccupations. It should be noted that these major aspects of the human psychological attributes (perception, imagination, and so on) are also gained in a paralinguistic manner as well as in kinesic and other nonverbal forms.

DISCUSSION: A SOCIALIZATION CONCEPTUAL SCHEME

In summary, it has been proposed that a conceptual scheme for the socialization process may be conceived as consisting of seven structural features (personal agents, impersonal agents, formal social groups, informal social groups, a socialization conceptual scheme, total human biological equipment, internal conditions of culture) and seven functional features (explicit functioning, implicit functioning, deutero functioning, generative functioning, anticipatory functioning, developmental functioning, linguistic functioning).

There are, of course, ways other than a structural-functional model to conceive the socialization process. There may be errors in the scheme outlined briefly here, arising from the number (128) of enculturation processes used in the development of the scheme, from a failure to differentiate clearly between the proposed structural or functional features, or from logical problems in use of the structural-functional model for analysis of human behavior. There may also be more structural and functional features than are presented in this conceptual scheme.[13]

It seems clear that an accurate understanding of the origin, development, and present nature of the socialization process cannot proceed without some type of conceptual scheme. In the absence of such a scheme, we shall continue to employ concepts with variable meanings and to use research methods appropriate to studies of some kinds of human phenomena, but not to the study of the socialization process.

---

[13]For instance, Gerald Erchak has suggested, in a comment on a draft of this work, that an eighth structural feature be designated as "human ecology."

It may be helpful to offer a socialization conceptual scheme mnemonic device for use in further discussions. If each one of the structural parts of the conceptual scheme presented here is diagrammatically represented as a closed square, the parts can then be combined in the form shown in Figure 10–1. It is then possible to represent each of the functions of the conceptual scheme as a boundary entity forming and maintaining the structures in Figure 10–1. In this fashion the functions of the socialization process conceptual scheme are represented as binding the several structures, one to the other, as the consequence of the operation of the socialization process through time. The incompletely formed squares on the four sides of this conceptual scheme and the missing function are meant to suggest that there may well be unrecognized structures and functions of the socialization process. Figure 10–2 offers two alternate mnemonic devices, utilizing conceptual scheme arrangements in which the structural features are noted as circles and the functional features are noted as either the points of intersections of structural features or as the several axes about which structural features are arranged.

A problem that can arise in construction and use of a conceptual scheme mnemonic device is that precision can be implied in graphic rep-

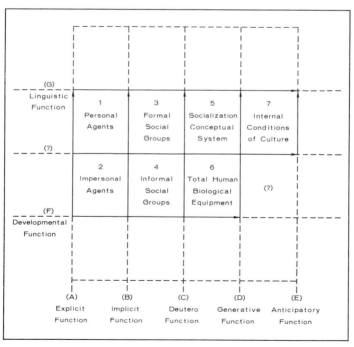

FIGURE 10–1   A mnemonic device for a socialization process conceptual scheme

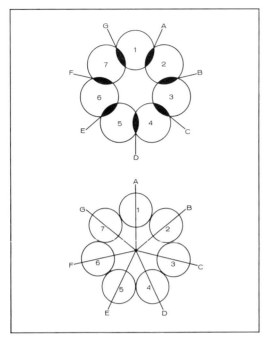

FIGURE 10-2
Two alternative socialization process conceptual scheme mnemonic devices

resentations. The structural and functional features proposed here as comprising a socialization conceptual scheme have been abstracted from descriptions of a limited number of enculturation processes. These features have not been subjected to any form of measurement—that is, they have not been "weighed," "tested for hardness," or measured for "fragility," "density," "boiling point," and so on. Even if sufficient data were available, genuine mathematical procedures for making precise measurements of socialization structural and functional features remain to be developed. When such procedures are developed, they may significantly alter any existing conceptual scheme. However, as Wiener (1950, 26) noted, until such a time it is more honest and scientifically accurate to give a descriptive account of the gross appearance of a phenomenon and to carefully avoid leaving any impression of use of analytic precision.

Finally, the development of a socialization conceptual scheme can lead to more efficient studies of enculturation processes, since such a scheme not only calls attention to many features of cultural transmission that might be overlooked but also will allow a particular enculturation process to be viewed as part of a human socialization process. Lacking a conceptual scheme base, many of the existing guides for field study (cf. Murdock, 1961; Hilger, 1960; Seligman, 1951) cannot lead observers to be alert to

Sádákàn, a Tambunan (Sensuron) Dusun man (1959). (T.R. Williams)

Bathing baby: a Dusun infant learning the preoccupations of his mother concerning relationship between dirt and illness (T.R. Williams, 1959).

important differences in and between enculturation processes that may lead to new theoretical insights.

For instance, when I began my ethnographic study of the Papago enculturation process (Williams, 1958), I had no conceptual scheme for the socialization process available for use in the field. Some years later, after developing a preliminary version of this socialization conceptual scheme, I realized during my ethnographic study of the enculturation process of the Dusun of northern Borneo (Williams, 1969) that the Papago cultural transmission process was quite different from many other such processes in a number of significant respects.[14] As noted in Chapter 3, Papago adults can rarely be seen "doing," or directly telling children anything concerning behavior or culture. One waits for long periods before anything occurs that could be said to resemble cultural transmission. Yet Papago children regularly learn their culture. In terms of the conceptual scheme developed here, the Papago enculturation process operates primarily by children generating the ways they are expected to behave as children and adults from implicit, deutero, and anticipatory types of functions.

In contrast, the Dusun enculturation process operates through a great deal of explicit instruction provided by personal agents, dependence upon use of impersonal agents of enculturation, formal and informal social groups, and a generally known and fairly explicit adult understanding of

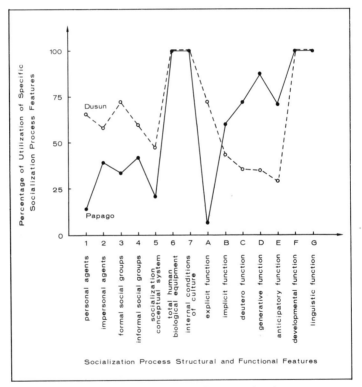

FIGURE 10–3   A comparison of Papago and Dusun enculturation processes

[14]It should be noted that, in 1959, at the beginning of my ethnographic work in Borneo, I used the six cultures field guide developed by the Whitings (J.W.M. Whiting, 1966) and recorded some data of Dusun enculturation following this theoretical approach, as well as using my own ideas concerning the socialization process. It should also be noted that although I had not been a student or associate of the Whitings, they were most generous and very professional in permitting me to use their unpublished field guide.

the local version of a socialization conceptual scheme. Dusun adults place much less dependence on implicit, deutero, and anticipatory functions than do Papago adults, choosing to rely more upon their own understandings of and abilities to transmit Dusun culture than to allow their children to generate from their enculturation experiences a conception of Dusun culture.

These general contrasts between the Papago and Dusun enculturation processes are noted schematically in Figure 10–3, which is intended to provide only a descriptive comparison of these processes and does not portray any precision of measurement of the structural and functional features involved. However using modern computer graphic techniques, it is possible to make figures, such as the one in Figure 10–3, for dozens or hundreds of enculturation processes and so to have a visual representation of the similarities and differences in human use of structural and functional features in socialization. It is vital that any impressions of precision of analysis be avoided in making such comparative analyses, since this could only delay further development of a socialization conceptual scheme.

ALTERNATE SOCIALIZATION CONCEPTUAL SCHEMES

There are four other formally stated conceptual models, paradigms, or schemes that may be used to understand the socialization process.[15] Henry (1960) has presented a paradigm for understanding education in a cross-cultural perspective, based on his long-term work in American schools and in several native cultures. Henry's paradigm is notable for its clarity of presentation. The Whitings have formulated a conceptual model for psychocultural research (Whiting & Whiting, 1975, 1978) which they have used as the basis for formulating hypotheses concerning socialization and then tested through use of the holocultural research method and in ethnographic settings. This conceptual model is elegantly concise and varies little from the original version presented in a 1953 work by J.W.M. Whiting and Child (1953, 310). LeVine (1973, 1974, 1975) has proposed a cultural evolutionary conceptual model for understanding socialization. This model is characterized by its sharp focus on questions of causation in the study of socialization and is marked by a compact presentation. Finally, Gearing and his associates (1973, 1979) have formulated a theoretical model for education and schooling which is carefully stated. Draper (1974), Spindler (1974), Cole and Scribner (1975) and Tindall (1976) have offered comments

---

[15]It is clear that a conceptual scheme for the cultural transmission process exists in the body of Mead's published work (Gordan, 1976). Elements of Mead's scheme are used in this chapter, modified by other theoretical, conceptual, and methodological views. However Mead did not present such a scheme in an integral, or formal, sense.

concerning the conceptual and theoretical work by the Whitings, LeVine, and Gearing. It should also be noted that the paradigm developed by Henry (1960) has been given little attention although it appears to offer some insights into the nature of cultural transmission in formal, or "schooling," contexts.

It may be helpful to consider briefly one of these alternative conceptual models to provide a contrast with the conceptual scheme presented in this chapter. For instance, LeVine (1973, 1974, 1975) has formulated a socialization conceptual scheme proposing that infant and child care practices—that is, the socialization process—evolved through time as adaptations to environmental features that many generations of parents perceive as frequent or especially threatening obstacles to their conscious goals for child-rearing (LeVine, 1975, 53). Thus LeVine views the socialization process as a way of eliminating a need on the part of parents and their surrogates to be repeatedly and consciously concerned with dangerous and uncertain aspects of their local world. LeVine also suggests (1975, 56) that there are three universal socialization goals held by all human parents and that the three goals constitute both "a rough developmental sequence" and "a natural hierarchy." These goals are (1) the survival and physical well-being of children, (2) development of children's behavioral capacity for "economic self-maintenance" as an adult, and (3) development of children's behavioral capacity for "maximizing other cultural values."

LeVine (1975, 57) then proposes two general hypotheses based on these three socialization goals he assumes are held by parents in all cultures:

1. In populations with high infant mortality rates, the overriding conscious concern of parents will be for the survival and well-being of children, especially in the first years of life, and enculturation practices will reflect this concern.
2. In populations with scarce or uncertain resources for subsistence, the overriding conscious concern of parents will be for children's capacity for future economic self-maintenance, and enculturation practices will reflect this concern.

Erchak (1980) has tested LeVine's two hypotheses by examining data of enculturation among the Kpelle of Liberia. Erchak (1980, 46–47) finds LeVine's two hypotheses to be "sound," at least as far as Kpelle enculturation is concerned, and suggests that they can provide a foundation for a "cultural evolutionary approach" to the transcultural study of socialization. Erchak (1980, 47) also notes that LeVine's conceptual model, which he terms a *materialist model* (or cultural materialist model) has some advantages for socialization research since it uses the evolutionary concepts of adaptation and survival, conceives humans as both biological and cultural beings, and relates individual humans to their local environments in very specific ways. Erchak (1980, 47) also notes that LeVine's conceptual scheme may seem "trivial" to some, since in essence his scheme proposes that "societies produce the kinds of people they need."

Dusun infant with mother's oldest sister; mother at right (Sensuron village, Tambunan district, Sabah, Malaysia). (T.R. Williams, 1960)

Dusun father with his daughters (Baginda village, Keningau district, Sabah, Malaysia). (T.R. Williams, 1962)

417

A brief comparison between LeVine's socialization conceptual scheme and the one offered in this chapter indicates that the two schemes share some basic features and are markedly different in many other features. Both schemes have a human evolutionary basis, relate individuals to their local environments, and view human biology and culture in an interdependent, or cybernetic, manner. However the two schemes differ greatly in the use of assumptions concerning the causal role of what Erchak (1980, 47) terms *material imperatives*—that is, subsistence activity—in human socialization. LeVine's conceptual scheme for socialization rest on the key assumption that the local ecology and the economic patterns in a culture, which are used to deal with this ecology, dictate, shape, and determine the nature of the enculturation process used in a culture. Thus LeVine has proposed a socialization conceptual scheme that is bound to human economic or subsistence types. In other words, for LeVine the socialization process consists of different variations, depending on the subsistence or economic patterns that are typically used in a society. It follows then that there is a hunter-gatherer socialization process, a pastoral nomadic socialization process, an agricultural socialization process, and so on, depending on the dominant subsistence activities used in a culture.

In contrast, the conceptual scheme presented in this chapter is not bound to a particular feature or pattern of culture. This scheme differs from the one proposed by LeVine in that it does not proceed from an assumption that any particular feature of culture takes precedence over and is more important than other cultural features. This conceptual scheme also differs from the one developed by LeVine in that it is capable of being expanded and altered through the addition of new concepts, structures, and functions. LeVine's scheme appears to have a low potential for further conceptual development and has within it the possibility of its own general conceptual limits. If there are distinct socialization processes for each major subsistence, economic, or societal type, then logically there must also be major socialization processes for each of the many variations within each subsistence or economic type. Thus hunter-gatherer peoples live in both very cold (Eskimo) and very warm (!Kung) climates, while pastoralists live in hot, dry deserts (Megarha Bedouin) and the cold tunda (Tungus); the variations in hunter-gatherer subsistence or economic patterns may be greater between such groups than between hunter-gatherers and other types of societies.

It also seems that causally linking the socialization process to a type of subsistence or economic pattern, as LeVine has in his conceptual scheme, may be a difficult avenue on which to proceed. Studies as diverse as those by Lomax and Arensberg (1977), Freeman and Winch (1957), and Murdock (1971), among others, indicate the major problems encountered in seeking to causally link a cultural pattern or process to a type of subsistence or local ecology. This problem is well exemplified in the contrasts between the works by Barry, Bacon and Child, and the Whitings and the works by Edgerton, Goldschmidt, and Bolton concerning the causal links between a pastoral type of subsistence, child-bearing practices, and adult personality type.[16]

FURTHER DEVELOPMENT OF A SOCIALIZATION CONCEPTUAL SCHEME

Kuhn (1966) has observed that in the history of science, competing conceptual schemes tend to be common in the early stages of the development of a field of study and at those times when there is a major shift from one to another theoretical or conceptual model, plan, or scheme. Thus the differences between the conceptual scheme offered in this chapter and any of the alternate schemes, plans, or paradigms simply reflect the beginning effort in the study of socialization to think abstractly about the interrelations between events in that process. The contrasts and differences between the several available conceptual schemes reflect differences in emphases on particular aspects of socialization rather than uncertainty concerning current understanding of human cultural transmission. These differences also reflect a concern by various scholars with seeking to develop more or less general conceptual schemes—that is, to focus on the most inclusive statements that may be made or to put such statements in a "middle-range" fashion. Conceptual schemes of the "middle range" seek to define what is well known and to avoid generalities that may be imprecisely stated.

In the years ahead it is likely that the several conceptual schemes now available for study of the socialization process will be combined and restated for more efficient study of cultural transmission. Rather than competing with each other, the several available schemes can serve as a basis for the future study of socialization.

APPLICATIONS OF A SOCIALIZATION CONCEPTUAL SCHEME

It is reasonable to ask whether a conceptual scheme for use in understanding the nature of the socialization process has any practical applications. It is clear there is a difference between an abstract understanding of the

[16]See Footnote 29 and the references cited in Chapter 6 for these works.

nature of a process and the practical application of such knowledge. Thus a scientific understanding of the physical events in coal gasification, or transformation of carbonized vegetable matter into synthetic natural gas, has been available for nearly a century. Now with an impending worldwide shortage of natural gas, there has been renewed interest in ways to turn abundant coal supplies into gas. Using the Lurgi process, a technology developed by Germany in World War II, it is possible to transform a million tons of coal into approximately 11.2 billion cubic feet of synthetic natural gas at a cost of between four and five dollars per 1000 cubic feet of gas. Translating an abstract or scientific understanding into practical solutions to difficult problems, such as an impending worldwide energy shortage, usually involves substantial time, effort, and great expense for development of a technology that works efficiently and is economical.

It can be suggested that some practical solutions to the difficult problems that now appear related to, or may derive from, the socialization process, such as personality and learning malfunctions, "deviant" behavior, "mental" illness, and family and marital stability, might possibly become available once an abstract understanding is reached concerning the nature of the socialization process, including its origin, evolutionary development, and present features and dynamics. Readers concerned with applying an abstract understanding of cultural transmission to a solution of practical problems, particularly as parents, or in the delivery of human services in disciplines such as medicine, education, nursing, health education, social work and counseling may find the conceptual discussion in this chapter helpful in considering and thinking about some practical procedures, plans, or policies for effectively coping with problems related to the socialization process.

CONCLUSIONS

In his work *Philosophy and the Mirror of Nature*, Richard Rorty (1979) notes that truth as a "representation," or correspondence to direct experience, is not available to humans. Rorty joins a number of other philosophers, including William James, Heidegger, Wittgenstein, Dewey, N. Goodman, Sellars, Quine, and Derrida, in concluding that "truth" has to be conceived as a conventional understanding among humans concerning their daily experiences.

This general philosophical position, which has come to be termed as the *hermeneutical circle* in contemporary scientific discourse, has been described by Rorty (1979, 319) as meaning that when we seek to isolate the basic or foundational elements of a natural process or event, we will not be able to do so, except on the basis of our knowledge of the whole fabric within which the elements occur. Such an understanding of truth makes human existence essentially *historical* and *temporal*—that is, humans simultaneously create a world and their individual identity in an ongoing discourse about what is, and what can be, by referring to what has been, so far as this can be known. The consequence of a human awareness of knowing that we know only on the basis of what we already know or can reflect on as a future is to have to try to construct some kind of meta-language or meta-knowledge—that is, a language and knowledge to talk about our language and knowledge—so we can deal with those aspects of our experience that will not fit easily into existing frameworks or conventions of human thought. A socialization conceptual scheme can be viewed as an effort at meta-knowledge or meta-language to enable us to at least consider that which we know now only by our limited personal experiences and observations as we learn culture and behave in cultural ways. There should be no misunderstanding of the intent of the conceptual scheme presented in this chapter. This scheme is not an effort to present "privileged" or "foundational" truth. Rather, it is an attempt to derive a way of talking about a realm of human experience—that is, socialization—that seems one of several keys to understanding the human experience. The scheme is also designed to assist in the continuing human discourse when we are forced to consider the unchallenged truths of today in the face of those anomalies of truth, or the new, different, and unexpected, that occur frequently in human experience.

SUMMARY

This chapter has been concerned with presentation of a conceptual scheme for study of the socialization process. The discussion began with some distinctions between theory and concept in socialization research. Then the structural and functional elements of socialization were described briefly, followed by some suggestions for organizing these elements into a conceptual scheme. The chapter concluded with a presentation of four alternate socialization conceptual schemes by Henry, the Whitings, LeVine, and Gearing and some remarks on the possible practical applications and scientific use of a socialization conceptual scheme.

REFERENCES CITED AND SUGGESTED READINGS

ALLPORT, G. 1955. *Becoming*. New Haven: Yale University.
BATESON, G. 1942. "Social Planning and the Concept of Deutero-Learning." *Symposia, Conference on Science, Philosophy and Religion in Their Relation to the Democratic Way of Life*, 2, 81–97. (Reprinted in T.M. Newcomb & E.L. Hartley (eds.), *Readings in Social Psychology*. New York: Holt, Rinehart & Winston, 1947, pp. 121–128.)

————. 1958. *Naven*. Stanford, Calif.: Stanford University Press.

————. 1972. *Steps to an Ecology of Mind*. New York: Ballantine.

BATESON, G, & M. MEAD. 1942. *Balinese Character: A Photographic Analysis*. New York: Special Publication of the New York Academy of Sciences, No. 2.

BATESON, G., & J. RUESCH. 1951. *Communication: The Social Matrix of Psychiatry*. New York: W.W. Norton & Co., Inc.

BERNDT, R. 1962. *Excess and Restraint*. Chicago: University of Chicago Press.

BRONFENBRENNER, U. 1979. "Contexts of Child Rearing: Problems and Prospects." *American Psychologist*, 34, 844–850.

BRUNER, J. 1956. *A Study of Thinking*. New York: John Wiley.

————. 1966. *Studies in Cognitive Growth*. New York: John Wiley.

COLE, M., & S. SCRIBNER. 1975. "Theorizing about Socialization of Cognition." *Ethos*, 3, 249–268.

DRAPER, P. 1974. "Comparative Studies of Socialization." in B.J. Siegel, A.R. Beals, & S.A. Tyler (eds.), *Annual Review of Anthropology*, 3, 263–277. Palo Alto, Calif.: Annual Reviews, Inc.

DUBOIS, C. 1956. "Attitudes Toward Food and Hunger in Alor." In D.G. Haring (ed.), *Personal Character and the Cultural Milieu*. Syracuse, N.Y.: Syracuse University Press, pp. 241–253.

ERCHAK, G.M. 1980. "The Acquisition of Cultural Rules by Kpelle Children." *Ethos* 8, 40–48.

FIRTH, R. 1956. "Function." In W.L. Thomas (ed.), *Current Anthropology*. Chicago: University of Chicago Press, pp. 237–258.

FREEMAN, L., & R. WINCH. 1957. "Societal Complexity: An Empirical Test of a Typology of Societies." *American Journal of Sociology*, 62, 461–466.

GEARING, F. 1973. "Where We Are and Where We Might Go: Steps toward a General Theory of Cultural Transmission." *Council on Anthropology and Education Quarterly*, 4(1).

GEARING, F., & L. SANGREE. 1979. *Toward a Cultural Theory of Education and Schooling*. The Hague: Mouton.

GOODENOUGH, W.H. 1969. *Description and Comparison in Cultural Anthropology*. Chicago: Aldine (revised edition, 1980, New York: Cambridge University Press).

GOODMAN, M.E. 1964. *Race Awareness in Young Children*. New York: Crowell-Collier Books.

————. 1967. *The Individual and Culture*. Homewood, Ill.: Dorsey.

GORDAN, J. (ed.). 1976. *Margaret Mead, The Complete Bibliography 1925–1975*. The Hague: Mouton.

HALLOWELL, A.I. 1950. "Personality Structure and the Evolution of Man." *American Anthropologist*, 52, 159–173.

————. 1953. "Culture, Personality and Society." In A.L. Kroeber (ed.), *Anthropology Today*. Chicago: University of Chicago Press, pp. 597–620.

————. 1954a. "The Self and Its Behavioural Environment." *Explorations II*, (April), 106–165.

————. 1954b. "Psychology and Anthropology." In J. Gillin (ed.), *For a Science of Social Man*. New York: Macmillan, pp. 160–226.

————. 1956. "The Structural and Functional Dimensions of a Human Existence." *Quarterly Review of Biology*, 31, 88–101.

————. 1959. "Behavioral Evolution and the Emergence of the Self." In B.J. Meggars (ed.), *Evolution and Anthropology: A Centennial Appraisal*. Washington, D.C.: Anthropological Society of Washington, pp. 33–60.

————. 1960. "Self, Society and Culture in Phylogenetic Perspective." In Sol Tax (ed.), *Evolution After Darwin*: Vol. 2, *The Evolution of Man*. Chicago: University of Chicago Press, pp. 309–371.

————. 1961. "The Protocultural Foundations of Human Adaptation." In S.L. Washburn (ed.), *Social Life of Early Man*. Chicago: Aldine, pp. 236–255.

————. 1963. "Personality, Culture and Society in Behavioral Evolution." In S. Koch (ed.), *Psychology: A Study of a Science*. New York: McGraw-Hill, Vol. 6, pp. 429–509.

————. 1965. "Hominid Evolution, Cultural Adaptation and Mental Dysfunction." In A.V.S. de Reuck & R. Porter (eds.), *Transcultural Psychiatry*. Boston: Little, Brown, pp. 26–54.

————. 1967. *Culture and Experience*. New York: Schocken Books (originally published in 1955 by University of Pennsylvania Press).

HENRY, J. 1960. "A Cross-Cultural Outline of Education." *Current Anthropology*, 1, 267–305.

HILGER, I. 1960. *Field Guide to Ethnological Study of Childlife*. New Haven, Conn.: Human Relations Area File.

HOMANS, G.C. 1964. "Contemporary Theory in Sociology." In R.E.L. Faris (ed.), *Handbook of Modern Sociology*. Skokie, Ill.: Rand McNally, pp. 941–977.

HONIGMANN, J.J. 1954. *Culture and Personality*. New York: Harper & Row, Pub.

————. 1967. *Personality in Culture*. New York: Harper & Row, Pub.

KUHN, T. 1966. *The Structure of Scientific Revolutions*. Chicago: University of Chicago Press.

LA BARRE, W. 1954. *The Human Animal*. Chicago: University of Chicago Press.

LE VINE, R. 1973. *Culture, Behavior, and Personality*. Chicago: Aldine.

————. 1974. "Parental Goals: A Cross-Cultural View." *Teachers College Record*, 76(2).

————. 1975. "Parental Goals: A Cross-Cultural View." In H.J. Leichter (ed.), *The Family as Educator*. New York: Teachers College Press, pp. 52–65.

LEVY, M.J. 1952. *The Structure of Society*. Princeton, N.J.: Princeton University Press.

LOMAX, A., & C.M. ARENSBERG. 1977. "A Worldwide Evolutionary Classification of Cultures by Subsistence Systems." *Current Anthropology*, 18, 659–708.

MASLOW, A.H. 1954. *Motivation and Personality*. New York: Harper & Row, Pub.

MEAD, M. 1928. *Coming of Age in Samoa*. New York: Morrow (1961, New York: Morrow Apollo Edition).

————. 1930. *Growing Up in New Guinea*. New York: Morrow.

————. 1935. *Sex and Temperament in Three Primitive Societies*. New York: Morrow.

————. (ed.). 1937. *Cooperation and Competition Among Primitive Peoples*. New York: McGraw-Hill.

————. 1947. "On the Implications for Anthropology of the Gesell-Ilg Approach to Maturation." *American Anthropologist*, 49, 69–77.

————. 1949a. *Male and Female: A Study of the Sexes in a Changing World*. New York: Morrow.

————. 1949b. "Psychological Weaning: Childhood and Adolescence." In *Psychosexual Development in Health and Disease*. New York: Grune & Stratton, pp. 124–135.

————. 1956a. "The Concept of Culture and the Psychosomatic Approach." In D.G. Haring (ed), *Personal Character and the Cultural Milieu*. Syracuse, N.Y.: Syracuse University Press, pp. 594–662.

————. 1956b. *New Lives for Old: Cultural Transformation-Manus. 1928–1953*. New York: Morrow.

————. 1957. "Towards More Vivid Utopias." *Science*, 126, 957–961.

————. 1959. "Closing the Gap Between Scientists and Others." *Daedalus*, (Winter, 1959), 139–146.

————. 1961. "Cultural Determinants of Sexual Behavior." In W.C. Young (ed.),

Sex and Internal Secretions (3rd ed.). Baltimore, Md.: Williams & Wilkins, Vol. 2, pp. 1433–1479.

———. 1963. "Socialization and Enculturation." *Current Anthropology,* 4, 184–188.

———. 1965. "The Future as the Basis for Establishing a Shared Culture." *Daedalus* (Winter, 1965), 135–155.

———. 1970. *Culture and Commitment: A Study of the Generation Gap.* New York: Natural History Press/Doubleday.

———. 1971a. "Options Implicit in Development Styles." In E. Tobach (ed.), *The Biopsychology of Development.* New York: Academic Press, pp., 533–541.

———. 1971b. Personal Communication (Letter) to T.R. Williams, January 12, 1971.

MEAD, M., & F.C. MACGREGOR. 1951. *Growth and Culture: A Photographic Study of Balinese Childhood.* New York: Putnam's.

MEAD, M., & M. WOLFENSTEIN (eds.). 1955. *Childhood in Contemporary Cultures.* Chicago: University of Chicago Press.

MEAD, M., & N. NEWTON. 1967. "Cultural Patterning of Perinatal Behavior." In A.F. Guttmacher & S. Richardson (eds.), *Childbearing: Its Social and Psychological Aspects.* Baltimore, Md.: Williams & Wilkins, pp. 142–245.

MERTON, R.K. 1957. *Social Theory and Social Structure* (rev. ed.). New York: Free Press.

MURDOCK, G.P. 1961. *Outline of Cultural Materials.* New Haven, Conn.: Human Relations Area Files.

———. 1971. "Cross-Sex Patterns of Kin Behavior." *Ethnology,* 10, 359–368.

Newsweek. 1977. "The Only Way to Use Coal." *Newsweek,* July 4, 1977. p. 68.

RORTY, R. 1979. *Philosophy and the Mirror of Nature.* Princeton N.J.: Princeton University Press.

SELIGMAN, B.Z. (ed.). 1951. *Notes and Queries on Anthropology: Sixth Edition, Revised and Rewritten by a Committee of the Royal Anthropological Institution of Great Britain and Ireland.* London: Routledge & Kegan Paul.

SPINDLER, G.D. 1974. "From Omnibus to Linkages: Cultural Transmission Models." *Council on Anthropology and Education Quarterly,* 5, 1–6.

TINDALL, B.A. 1976. "Theory in the Study of Cultural Transmission." in B.J. Siegel, A.R. Beals, & S.A. Tyler (eds.), *Annual Review of Anthropology,* 5, 195–208. Palo Alto, Calif.: Annual Reviews, Inc.

WHITING, B. 1980. "Culture and Social Behavior: A Model for the Development of Social Behavior." *Ethos,* 8, 95–116.

WHITING, B., & J.W.M. WHITING. 1975. *Children of Six Cultures: A Psycho-Cultural Analysis.* Cambridge, Mass.: Harvard University Press.

WHITING, J.W.M., & I.L. CHILD. 1953. *Child Training and Personality.* New Haven, Conn.: Yale University Press.

WHITING, J.W.M., & B. WHITING. 1978. "A Strategy for Psychocultural Research." In G.D. Spindler (ed.). *The Making of Psychological Anthropology.* Berkeley: The University of California Press, pp. 41–61.

WHITING, J.W.M. 1966. *Field Guide for a Study of Socialization.* New York: John Wiley.

WIENER, N. 1950. *"Some Maxims for Biologists and Psychologists." Dialectica* 4:22–27.

WILLIAMS, T.R. 1958. "The Structure of the Socialization Process in Papago Indian Society." *Social Forces,* 36, 251–256. [Reprinted in J. Middleton (ed.), *From Child to Adult: Studies in Anthropology of Education.* New York: Natural History Press, 1970, pp. 163–172.]

———. 1959. "The Evolution of a Human Nature." *Philosophy of Science,* 26, 1–13.

————. 1966. "Culture Structuring of Tactile Experience in a Borneo Society." *American Anthropologist,* 68, 27–34.

————. 1969. *A Borneo Childhood: Enculturation in Dusun Society.* New York: Holt, Rinehart & Winston.

————. 1972a. *Introduction to Socialization: Human Culture Transmitted.* St. Louis, Mo.: C.V. Mosby.

————. 1972b. "The Socialization Process: A Theoretical Perspective." In F. Poirier (ed.), *Primate Socialization.* New York: Random House, pp. 207–260.

————. 1975. "On the Origin of the Socialization Process." In T.R. Williams (ed.), *Socialization and Communication in Primary Groups.* The Hague: Mouton, pp. 233–249.

WILLS, D.D. 1979. "Learning and Communicating: Deep Process." *American Anthropologist,* 81, 874–888.

EPILOGUE

After use of the first atomic bombs, some American scientists formed an association to promote peaceful uses of the knowledge they had helped to produce. Through the decade following World War II, these scientists worked for laws and treaties for control of and placing limits on the use of atomic weapons. They also contributed to a decision to place nuclear weapons production in the hands of a civilian goverment agency. Later their efforts also helped in securing an international treaty banning nuclear weapons tests in the atomosphere. These scientists were an integral part of the movement to create a United States government agency concerned with arms control and disarmament.

Such efforts were not without personal costs to those who participated in these activities. However the example of individual scientists trying to be socially responsible for the products of their research did not go unnoticed. Today we expect that scientists will think seriously about use and control of the products of their research. Much of the current widespread concern about the quality of life in a world environment increasingly polluted by products of technology is the direct result of public activities by scientists concerned about the ways their basic inventions and understandings are being used.

At first glance a fundamental comprehension of the nature of the socialization process hardly seems to be comparable to an understanding of the nuclear processes which led to awesome weapons. Yet as time passes and our understanding of cultural transmission becomes more precise, we face questions for use of such knowledge as complex as those in other areas of science.

The time is not far distant when a scientific understanding of the process of socialization will be sufficient to be used to the great benefit or harm of humankind. We already know from accounts of isolated and autistic individuals and from studies of prisoners of war and political prisoners that it is possible to significantly alter the consequences of the human socialization process. Preliminary studies of the ways culture and biology become interrelated in the socialization process have indicated that it will be possible to literally "program" humans to acquire specific behavior, values, and beliefs. We can discern now, if only faintly, the outlines of a scientific knowledge that will give human beings an understanding of themselves that can be as formidable as nuclear weapons—that is, the power to precisely shape the wills, values, thoughts, loyalties, and views of other humans without use of drugs, degradation of their bodies, or forced routines of life.

It is true that a power to decide the content, operation, and consequences of the cultural transmission process cannot lay waste to all life as can thermonuclear weapons, or upset the world's ecological balance as can massive engineering projects to redirect climate, river flow, or sea water circulation. The power derived from understanding socialization cannot kill fish in streams, mire sea birds in oil wastes, or sear human lungs with petrochemical byproducts. But such power could be used by unscrupulous individuals to their own malevolent political and personal ends. If research on the socialization process continues to grow at the rate of the past six decades, we will be faced with trying to decide how to use our knowledge.

We already face this problem in a formative state, as we are asked to accept public policy said to be based on research on cultural transmission. In the past decade there has been evidence of this fact in vigorous arguments over the validity and effects of "remedial" childhood education programs, concerning special television programs for preschool children, about the definition of an "equal" education, and whether some classes of children are really unable to learn cultural and social forms apparently easily acquired by other classes of children. American parents are asked in advertisements to read the latest books to understand ways they can prevent their babies from becoming "bedwetters" or help them to be "better adjusted," to read more rapidly, or to achieve higher marks in school or college examinations. Popular television shows feature "experts" giving advice that is implied or actually said to be based on socialization research, and sometimes is, on topics ranging from handling infant aggression to alienation from parents in adolescence. Questions regarding which experts to believe and whether to believe them, and which public policies are scientifically sound, already are pressing upon all of us.

Such questions will become even more vexing, since the trend in American society is to the forming of public policy and to the giving of advice on the basis of research on cultural transmission. In a free society there is only one way to be certain that decisions concerning the content and operation of the cultural transmission process do not become the sole property of unprincipled individuals—that is, educating all citizens to a general understanding of the origins, nature, and consequences of that human process. Those who know American history will recognize this idea as Thomas Jefferson's solution to the problems created by the few persons in his time and society who sought to control the lives, the thoughts, and the destinies of their fellows. Jefferson believed the only certain way to protect individual freedom was to ensure that all persons had access to the things others knew, so knowledge could not be misapplied for private or political reasons.

Life in a free society near the close of the twentieth century has become more complex than Jefferson could have foreseen. Specialized knowledge has grown so vast and so technically complex that few persons can master large amounts of it; very few individuals reading these words will have full comprehension of quantum mechanics, population genetics, the literary tradition of Europe since Chaucer, linear programming of computers, the theory of viscoelasticity, and so on.

Perhaps it is not necessary for us to become thoroughly informed on all the subjects that affect our daily lives. It can be argued, after all, that we rarely give thought to electromagnetic theory when we turn on a light or to advanced principles in mechanics when we drive our automobiles. However we do think occasionally about the consequences of climbing a high-voltage transmission tower or of being in a head-on auto collision at 70 miles per hour. Our problem is to judge, each for ourselves, the kinds of knowledge affecting our personal and social destinies.

I believe it is my responsibility to point out that we now face a time when we must ensure that public policies based on socialization research are kept firmly in the hands of those persons accountable by law to being fully responsible to all those affected by policy decisions. We must be concerned that when public advice is given concerning the socialization process, it is done responsibly, with individual well-being as a foremost concern.

It may be that this epilogue will be made unnecessary by our inability to come to a full understanding of the socialization process. However I do not believe that we should postpone thinking about the subject until, as in the case of the physicists, chemists, engineers, mathematicians, and others working under the pressures of national survival in wartime, we find ourselves having produced knowledge capable of changing human life forever. The choices ahead of us are not only extinction of human life through nuclear war or devastation of the environment by misuse of technology. I think the future now also includes the possiblity of the ultimate horror of a human life bereft of individual freedom, personal dignity, spontaneity, and choice. My hope is that, as we have slowly begun to recognize the terrible consequences of nuclear weapons or of pollution of our environment, we can also begin to understand the great responsibility each one of us has for our rapidly growing knowledge of the socialization process and that together we will make all of the public decisions about the use of that knowledge. I believe that to do otherwise would be to abandon the long human quest for individual liberty and free personal choice in seeking a secure and meaningful life for our children in future generations.

APPENDIX
SELECTED READINGS
ON ENCULTURATION

Summary of Names*

Abipon	Dusun	Malaitans	Siriono
Ainu	English	Malekula	Slave
Alor	Eskimo	Manus	Swazi
American	Fijians	Maori	Tallensi
Andamanese	Flathead	Marquesans	Tanala
Apache	French	Masai	Taos
Arab	German	Mexican	Tenetehara
Arapaho	Gusii	Murngin	Teton Dakota
Arapesh	Hopi	Nauru	Thonga
Arunta	Hupa	Navaho	Tikopia
Ashanti	Ifaulk	Ngoni	Tiv
Azande	Ifugao	Nuer	Tonga
Baganda	Ilocos	Nyakyusa	Trobriands
Baiga	Israeli	Okinawans	Trukese
Balahi	Japanese	Omaha	Tswana
Bali	Javanese	Ona	Turkana
Bapedi	Jivaro	Ontong-Javanese	Ulithians
Basuto	Kaingang	Paiute	Venda
Bemba	Kaska	Palaung	Wapisiana
Bena	Kikuyu	Papago	Warrau
Bushmen	Kiwai	Pondo	Wichita
Camayura	Klamath	Puerto Ricans	Winnebago
Chagga	Kongo	Pukapukans	Witoto
Chamorro	Koryak	Pygmies	Wogeo
Chenchu	Kutenai	Rājpūts	Yagua
Chewa	Kwakiutl	Riffians	Yakut
Cheyenne	Kwoma	Russian	Yoruba
Chinese	Lakher	R'wala	Yukaghir
Comanche	Lamba	Samoans	Yungar
Dahomean	Lapp	San Pedro	Zadruga
Deoli	Lepcha	Sanpoil	Zulu
Dobuans	Lesu	Sherente	Zuni

*For alternative names of cultures, see Textor, R. 1967. *A Cross Cultural Summary,* New Haven: Human Relations Area Files, Appendix One; Murdock, G. P. 1958. *Outline of World Cultures,* New Haven: Human Relations Area Files. Spellings are the most commonly used.

Culture Region Distribution of Selected Readings on Enculturation

NEW WORLD CULTURES		PACIFIC CULTURES	OLD WORLD CULTURES		
NORTH AMERICA	CENTRAL AND SOUTH AMERICA	AUSTRALIA, BORNEO, INDONESIA, NEW GUINEA, AND PACIFIC ISLANDS	EURASIA	EUROPE AND CIRCUM-MEDITERRA-NEAN	AFRICA (SUB-SAHARAN)
American	Abipon	Alor	Ainu	Arab	Ashanti
Apache	Camayura	Arapesh	Andamanese	English	Azande
Arapaho	Jivaro	Arunta	Baiga	French	Baganda
Cheyenne	Kaingang	Bali	Balahi	German	Bapedi
Comanche	Ona	Chamorro	Chenchu	Israeli	Basuto
Eskimo	San Pedro	Dobuans	Chinese	Lapp	Bemba
Flathead	(Guatemala)	Dusun	Deoli	Riffians	Bena
Hopi	Sherente	Fijians	Japanese	Russian	Bushmen
Hupa	Siriono	Ifaulk	Koryak	R'wala	Chagga
Kaska	Tenetehara	Ifugao	Lakher	Zadruga	Chewa
Klamath	Wapisiana	Ilocos	Lepcha		Dahomean
Kutenai	Warrau	Javanese	Okinawans		Gusii
Kwakiutl	Witoto	Kiwai	Palaung		Kikuyu
Mexican	Yagua	Kwoma	Rājpūts		Kongo
Navaho		Lesu	Yakut		Lamba
Omaha		Malaitans	Yukaghir		Masai
Paiute		Malekula			Ngoni
Papago		Manus			Nuer
Puerto		Maori			Nyakyusa
Ricans		Marquesans			Pondo
Sanpoil		Murngin			Pygmies
Slave		Nauru			Swazi
Taos		Ontong-			Tallensi
Teton Dakota		Javanese			Tanala
Wichita		Pukapukans			Thonga
Winnebago		Samoans			Tiv
Zuni		Tikopia			Tonga
		Trobriands			Tswana
		Trukese			Turkana
		Ulithians			Venda
		Wogeo			Yoruba
		Yungar			Zulu

Total New World cultures—39   Total Pacific cultures—31   Total Old World cultures—58

SELECTED READINGS ON ENCULTURATION[1]

Abipon*

DOBRIZHOFFER, M. 1822. *An Account of the Abipones, An Equestrian People of Paraguay* (3 vols.). London: J. Murray.

Ainu*

BATCHELOR, J. 1895. *The Ainu of Japan: The Religions, Superstitutions, and General History of the Hairy Aborigines of Japan.* New York: Revell.

———. 1901. *The Ainu and Their Folk-lore.* London: The Religious Tract Society.

———. 1927. *Ainu Life and Lore.* Tokyo: Kyobunkwan.

HOWARD, B.D. 1893. *Life with Trans-Siberian Savages.* London: Longmans, Green.

Alor*

DUBOIS, C. 1944. *The People of Alor: A Socio-Psychological Study of an East Indian Island.* Minneapolis: University of Minnesota Press.

[1]Groups noted with an asterisk comprise the study sample referred to in Chapter 7. The readings suggested here are not "complete"—that is, inclusive of all the possible and latest references. The references listed for each society will provide students with some sources on enculturation that can be used for preliminary comparisons. This is not a research bibliography. Hence comparative statements drawn from the readings will be limited. For standard ethnographic references on each society, see G.P. Murdock. 1981. *Atlas of World Cultures.* Pittsburgh: University of Pittsburgh Press.

American*

BARKER, R.G. & H.F. WRIGHT. 1954. *The Midwest and Its Children.* Evanston, Ill.: Row, Peterson.

BRONFENBRENNER, U. 1970. *Two Worlds of Childhood: U.S. and U.S.S.R.* New York: Russell Sage Foundation.

FISCHER, J.L., & A. FISCHER. 1966. *The New Englanders of Orchard Town, U.S.A.* New York: John Wiley, Vol. 5, Six Cultures Series, B. Whiting (ed.).

GORER, G. 1948. *The American People.* New York: W.W. Norton & Co., Inc.

HAVIGHURST, R., J.P. BOWMAN, G. LIDDLE, C. MATTHEWS, & G. PIERCE. 1962. *Growing Up in River City.* New York: John Wiley.

KLUCKHOHN, C., & F. KLUCKHOHN. 1947. "American Culture: Generalized Orientations and Class Patterns." In L. Bryson (ed.), *Conflicts of Power in Modern Culture.* New York: Seventh Symposium, Conference on Science, Philosophy and Religion, pp. 106–128.

LANTIS, M. (special ed.). 1955. "The U.S.A. as Anthropologists See It," *American Anthropologist,* 57, 1113–1295.

McCLELLAND, D.C. 1961. *The Achieving Society.* Princeton, N.J.: Van Nostrand.

MEAD, M. 1942. *And Keep Your Powder Dry: An Anthropologist Looks at America.* New York: Morrow.

———. 1948. "The Contemporary American Family as an Anthropologist Sees It." *American Journal of Sociology,* 53, 453–459.

RIESMAN, D. 1950. *The Lonely Crowd.* New Haven, Conn.: Yale University Press.

SEARS, R.R., E. MACCOBY, & H. LEVIN. 1957. *Patterns of Child Rearing.* Evanston, Ill.: Row, Peterson.

WARNER, W.L. & P.S. LUNT. 1941. *The Social Life of a Modern Community.* New Haven, Conn.: Yale University Press.

WEST, J. 1945. *Plainville, U.S.A.* New York: Columbia University Press. (See also Gallaher, A. 1961. *Plainville Fifteen Years Later.* New York: Columbia University Press.)

WOLFENSTEIN, M. 1957. *Disaster: A Psychological Essay.* New York: The Free Press.

Andamanese*

MAN, E.H. 1883. "On the Aboriginal Inhabitants of the Andaman Islands." *Journal of the Royal Anthropological Institute of Great Britain and Ireland,* 12, 69–175, 327–434.

RADCLIFFE-BROWN, A.R. 1922. *The Andaman Islanders.* Cambridge, England: Cambridge University Press.

Apache*[2]

GOODWIN, G. 1942. *The Social Organization of the Western Apache.* Chicago: University of Chicago Press.

OPLER, M.E. 1937. "An Outline of Chiricahua Apache Social Organization." In F. Eggan (ed.), *Social Anthropology of North American Tribes.* Chicago: University of Chicago Press.

———. 1941. *An Apache Life Way.* Chicago: University of Chicago Press.

[2]The term *Apache* refers to different societies such as the Chiricahua Apache and the Jicarilla Apache. The Chiracahua aboriginal range was in southeastern Arizona and southwestern New Mexico. The Jicarilla aboriginal range was in northern and eastern New Mexico. Both are "Eastern" Apache. The San Carlos and White Mountain Apache are "Western" Apache.

————. 1946.   *Childhood and Youth in Jicarilla Apache Society.* Los Angeles: The Southwest Museum.

Arab*

AMMAR, H. 1954.   *Growing Up in an Egyptian Village.* London: Routledge & Paul.
GRANQVIST, H. 1931.   *Marriage Conditions in a Palestinian Village* (2 vols.). Helsingfors: Akademische Buchhandlung.
————. 1947.   *Birth and Childhood among the Arabs: Studies in a Muhammadan Village in Palestine.* Helsingfors: Söderström.
————. 1950.   *Child Problems among the Arabs.* Helsingfors: Söderström.

Arapaho*

HILGER, Sister M.I. 1952.   *Arapaho Child Life and Its Cultural Background.* Bureau of American Ethnology, Smithsonian Institute, Bulletin 148, Washington, D.C.: U.S. Government Printing Office.

Arapesh*

MEAD, M. 1935.   "The Mountain Dwelling Arapesh." In *Sex and Temperament in Three Primitive Societies.* New York: Morrow.
————. 1937.   "The Arapesh of New Guinea." In *Cooperation and Competition among Primitive Peoples.* New York: McGraw-Hill.
————. 1938—1949.   *The Mountain Arapesh.* I–V Anthropological Papers of the American Museum of Natural History, 36, 145–349; 37, 317–451; 40, 163–419; 41, 289–390.
————. 1949.   *Male and Female: A Study of the Sexes in a Changing World.* New York: Morrow.

Arunta*

SPENCER, B., & F.J. GILLEN. 1899.   *Native Tribes of Central Australia.* London: Macmillan.
————. 1927.   *The Arunta* (2 vols.). London: Macmillan.

Ashanti*

RATTRAY, R.S. 1927.   *Religion and Art in Ashanti.* London: Clarendon Press.
————. 1929.   *Ashanti Law and Constitution.* London: Clarendon Press.

Azande*

EVANS-PRITCHARD, E.E. 1937.   *Witchcraft, Oracles, and Magic among the Azande.* London: Clarendon Press.

Baganda*

AINSWORTH, M.D.S. 1967.   *Infancy in Uganda.* Baltimore, Md.: Johns Hopkins Press.
FELKIN, R.W. 1886.   "Notes on the Waganda Tribe of Central Africa." *Proceedings of the Royal Society of Edinburgh.* 13, 699–770.

HATTERSLEY, C.W. 1908. *The Baganda at Home.* London: The Religious Tract Society.

ROSCOE, J. 1902. "Further Notes on the Manners and Customs of the Baganda." *Journal of the Anthropological Institute,* (n.s.), 5, 25–80.

SEMPEBWA, E.K.K. 1948. "Baganda Folk Songs: A Rough Classification." *The Uganda Journal,* 12, 16–24.

WILSON, C.T., & R.W. FELKIN. 1882. *Uganda and the Egyptian Soudan* (2 vols.). London: Low, Marsten, Searle and Rivington.

Baiga*

ELWIN, V. 1939. *The Baiga.* London: J. Murray.

Balahi*

FUCHS, S. 1950. *The Children of Hari: A Study of the Nimar Balahis in the Central Provinces of India.* Vienna: Verlag Herold.

Bali*

BATESON, G. 1949. "Bali: The Value System of a Steady State." In M. Fortes (ed.), *Social Structure: Essays Presented to A.R. Radcliffe-Brown.* London: Clarendon Press.

BATESON, G., & M. MEAD. 1942. *Balinese Character: A Photographic Analysis.* W.G. Valentine (ed.), Vol. 2. New York: Special Publication of the New York Academy of Sciences (reprinted in 1962).

BELO, J. 1935. "The Balinese Temper." *Character and Personality,* 4, 120–146.

———. 1936. "A Study of a Balinese Family." *American Anthropologist,* 38, 12–31.

———. 1960. *Trance in Bali.* New York: Columbia University Press.

———. 1970. *Traditional Balinese Culture.* New York: Columbia University Press.

COVARRUBIAS, M. 1937. "Birth to Marriage in Bali." *Asia,* 37, 414–419.

McPHEE, C. 1946. *A House in Bali.* New York: Harper & Row, Pub.

MEAD, M. 1940. "Character Formation in Two South Sea Societies." *Transaction, American Neurological Association,* 1940: 99–103.

———. 1941. "Back of Adolescence Lies Early Childhood." *Childhood Education,* 18, 58–61.

———. 1946. "Research on Primitive Children." In L. Carmichael (ed.), *Manual of Child Psychology.* New York: John Wiley, pp. 735–780.

———. 1947. "Age Patterning in Personality Development." *American Journal of Orthopsychiatry,* 17, 231–240.

———. 1949. *Male and Female: A Study of the Sexes in a Changing World.* New York: Morrow.

MEAD, M., & F.C. MacGREGOR. 1951. *Growth and Culture: A Photographic Study of Balinese Childhood.* New York: Putnam's.

Bapedi*

DUGGAN-CRONIN, A.M. 1938. "The Bapedi (Transvaal Basotho)." In A.M. Duggan-Cronin (ed.), *The Bantu Tribes of South Africa* (2 vols.). Cambridge: Deighton, Bell (see Vol. 2, Section 2).

FRANZ, G.H. 1931. "Some Customs of the Transvaal Basotho." *Bantu Studies,* 5, 241–246.

HARRIES, C.L. 1929.   *The Laws and Customs of the Bapedi.* Johannesburg: Hortors.
PITJE, G.M. 1950.   "Traditional Systems of Male Education among Pedi and Cognate Tribes." *African Studies,* 9, 53–76, 105–124, 194–201.
WINTER, J.A. 1914.   "The Mental and Moral Capabilities of the Natives, Especially of Sekukuniland, Eastern Transvaal." *South African Journal of Science,* 12, 371–383.

Basuto*

ASHTON, H. 1952.   *The Basuto.* London: Oxford University Press.
CASALIS, E. 1861.   *The Basutos.* London: J. Nisbet.
DUTTON, E.A. 1923.   *The Basuto of Basutoland.* London: Jonathan Cape.
MABILLE, H.E. 1906.   "The Basuto of Basutoland." *Journal of the African Society,* 5, 233–251, 351–376.
MARTIN, M. 1903.   *Basutoland: Its Legends and Customs.* London: Nichols.
SHEDDICK, V.G.J. 1953.   "The Southern Sotho." In C.D. Forde (ed.), *Ethnographic Survey of Africa* (Part II). London: International African Institute.

Bemba*

RICHARDS, A.I. 1939.   *Land, Labour and Diet in Northern Rhodesia.* London: Oxford University Press.
———. 1956.   *Chisungu.* New York: Grove.

Bena*

CULWICK, A.T., & G.M. CULWICK. 1935.   *Ubena of the Rivers.* London: Allen, Unwin.

Bushmen*

LEE, R., & I. DEVORE (eds.). 1976.   *Kalahari Hunter-Gatherers: Studies of the !Kung-San and their Neighbors.* Cambridge, Mass.: Harvard University Press.
THOMAS, E.M. 1959.   *The Harmless People.* New York: Knopf.
VAN DER POST, L. 1958.   *The Lost World of the Kalahari.* New York: Morrow.
———. 1961.   *The Heart of the Hunter.* New York: Morrow.

Camayura*

OBERG, K. 1953.   *Indian Tribes of Northern Mato Grosso, Brazil.* Smithsonian Institution, Institute of Social Anthropology Publication 15. Washington, D.C.: U.S. Government Printing Office.

Chagga*

DUNDAS, C. 1924.   *Kilimanjaro and Its People.* London: Witherby.
RAUM, O.F. 1940   *Chagga Childhood.* London: Oxford University Press.

Chamorro*

JOSEPH, A., & V.F. MURRAY. 1951.   *Chamorros and Carolinians of Saipan: Personality Studies.* Cambridge, Mass.: Harvard University Press.

THOMPSON, L.M. 1947. *Guam and Its People.* Princeton, N.J.: Princeton University Press.

Chenchu*

FURER-HAIMENDORF, C. VON. 1943.   *The Chenchus: Jungle Folk of the Deccan.* London: Macmillan.
———. 1943.   *Aboriginal Tribes of Hyderabad.* London: Macmillan.

Chewa*

BRUWER, J. 1949.   "The Composition of a Cewa Village (Mudzi)."   *African Studies,* 8, 191–198.
NTARA, S.Y. 1934.   *Man of Africa.* London: The Religious Tract Society.
RICHARDS, A.I. 1950.   "Some Types of Family Structure among the Central Bantu." In A.R. Radcliffe-Brown & C.D. Forde (eds.), *African Systems of Kinship and Marriage.* London: International African Institute, pp. 297–251.

Cheyenne*

EGGAN, F.R. 1937.   "The Cheyenne and Arapaho Kinship System." In F.R. Eggan (ed.), *Social Anthropology of North American Tribes.* Chicago: University of Chicago Press.
GRINNELL, G.B. 1915.   *The Fighting Cheyennes.* New York: Scribner's.
———. 1923.   *The Cheyenne Indians: Their History and Ways of Life* (2 vols.). New Haven, Conn.: Yale University Press.
HILGER, Sister M.I. 1946.   "Notes on Cheyenne Child Life." *American Anthropologist,* 48, 60–69.
HOEBEL, E.A. 1960.   *The Cheyennes: Indians of the Great Plains.* New York: Holt, Rinehart & Winston.
LLEWELLYN, K.N., & E.A. HOEBEL. 1941.   *The Cheyenne Way: Conflict and Case Law in Primitive Jurisprudence.* Norman: University of Oklahoma Press.

Chinese*

CHIANG, Y. 1946.   *A Chinese Childhood.* London: Methuen.
FENG, H. 1948.   *The Chinese Kinship System.* Cambridge, Mass.: Harvard University Press.
FITZGERALD, C.P. 1941.   *Tower of Five Glories.* London: Cresset.
FRIED, M.H. 1953.   *The Fabric of Chinese Society.* New York: Holt, Rinehart & Winston.
HSU, F.L.K. 1953.   *Americans and Chinese: Two Ways of Life. New York: Schuman.*
HU, H.C. 1948.   *The Common Descent Group in China and Its Functions.* Viking Fund Publications in Anthropology 10. New York: Viking Fund.
YANG, M. 1945.   *A Chinese Village.* New York: Columbia University Press.

Comanche*

KARDINER, A. 1945.   "Analysis of Comanche Culture." In A. Kardiner & others (eds.), *The Psychological Frontiers of Society.* New York: Columbia University Press, pp. 81–100.
LINTON, R. 1945.   "The Comanche." In A. Kardiner & others (eds.), *The Psychological Frontiers of Society.* New York: Columbia University Press, pp. 47–80.

Dahomean*

HERSKOVITS, M.J. 1938. *Dahomey: An Ancient West African Kingdom.* New York: Augustin.

Deoli*³

CARSTAIRS, G.M. 1958. *The Twice Born: A Study of a Community of High Caste Hindus.* Bloomington: Indiana University Press.

Dobuans*

FORTUNE, R.F. 1932. *Sorcerers of Dobu.* New York: Dutton.

Dusun*

RUTTER, O. 1929. *The Pagans of North Borneo.* London: Hutchinson.
STAAL, J. 1923–25. "The Dusuns of North Borneo." *Anthropos,* 18–19, 958–977; 20, 120–138, 929–951.
WILLIAMS, T.R. 1969. *A Borneo Childhood: Enculturation in Dusun Society.* New York: Holt, Rinehart & Winston.

English*

GORER, G. 1955. *Exploring English Character.* New York: Harper & Row, Pub.
SODDY, K. (ed.). 1956. *Mental Health and Infant Development* (2 vols.). New York: Basic Books.
YOUNG, M.D., & P. WILLMOTT. 1957. *Family and Kinship in East London.* London: Routledge & Paul.

Eskimo*⁴

BRIGGS, J.L. 1970. *Never in Anger; Portrait of an Eskimo Family.* Cambridge, Mass.: Harvard University Press.
BUGGE, A. 1952. "The Native Greenlander—A Blending of Old and New." *Arctic,* 5, 45–53.
CRANTZ, D. 1767. *The History of Greenland* (Vol. 1). London: Brethren's Society.
EGEDE, H. 1745. *A Description of Greenland.* London: Hitch.
HONIGMANN, I., & J. HONIGMANN. 1953. "Child Rearing Patterns among the Great Whale River Eskimo." *University of Alaska Anthropology Papers,* 2, 31–50.
JENNESS, D. 1922. *The Life of the Copper Eskimo.* Report of the Canadian Arctic Expedition, 1913–1918. Ottawa: Acland.
LANTIS, M. 1960. *Eskimo Childhood and Interpersonal Relationships.* Seattle: University of Washington Press.
MIRSKY, J. 1937. "The Eskimos of Greenland." In M. Mead (ed.), *Cooperation and Competition Among Primitive Peoples.* New York: McGraw-Hill, pp. 51–86.
NANSEN, F. 1893. *Eskimo Life.* London: Longmans, Green.

---

³*Deoli* is a pseudonym for a community of high caste Hindus in the Indian state of Rajasthan.

⁴The term "Eskimo" refers to a number of societies scattered through the Polar Arctic from North Alaska through Northern Canada to Greenland. These groups include the "North Alaska," "West Alaska," "Polar," "Caribou," and "Copper" Eskimo.

OSTERMANN, H. 1938. "Knud Rasmussen's Posthumous Notes on the Life and Doings of the East Greenlanders in Olden Times." *Meddelelser om Grønland,* 109:1–215.
THALBITER, W. 1923a. "The Ammassalik Eskimo II. Language and Folklore," *Meddelelser om Grønland,* 40:113–564.
———. 1923b. "The Ammassalik Eskimo II. Social Customs and Mutual Aid." *Meddelelser om Grønland,* 40:575–739.

Fijians*

QUAIN, B.H. 1948. *Fijian Village.* Chicago: University of Chicago Press.

Flathead*

TURNEY-HIGH, H.H. 1937. *The Flathead Indians of Montana.* Memoirs of the American Anthropological Association, No. 47. Menasha, Wis.: American Anthropological Association.

French*

METRAUX, R., & M. MEAD. 1954. *Themes in French Culture: A Preface to a Study of a French Community.* Stanford, Calif.: Stanford University Press.
SODDY, K. (ed.). 1956. *Mental Health and Infant Development* (2 vols.). New York: Basic Books.
WYLIE, L.W. 1957. *Village in the Vaucluse.* Cambridge, Mass.: Harvard University Press.

German*

BATESON, G. 1943. "Cultural and Thematic Analysis of Fictional Films." *Transactions, New York Academy of Sciences,* Series 2, 5, 72–78.
DICKS, H.V. 1950. "Personality Traits and National Socialist Ideology." *Human Relations,* 3, 111–154.
ERICKSON, E.H. 1950. *Childhood and Society.* New York: W.W. Norton & Co., Inc.
FROMM, E. 1941. *Escape from Freedom.* New York: Holt, Rinehart & Winston.
LOWIE, R. 1945. *The German People: A Social Portrait to 1914.* New York: Holt, Rinehart & Winston.
METRAUX, R. 1955. "A Portrait of the Family in German Juvenile Fiction." In M. Mead & M. Wolfenstein (eds.), *Childhood in Contemporary Cultures.* Chicago: University of Chicago Press, pp. 253–276.
RODNICK, D. 1948. *Postwar Germans: An Anthropologist's Account.* New Haven, Conn.: Yale University Press.
WARREN, R.A. 1967. *Education in Rebhausen: A German Village.* New York: Holt, Rinehart & Winston.

Gusii*

LEVINE, R.A., & B.B. LEVINE. 1966. *Nyansongo: A Gusii Community in Kenya.* New York: John Wiley, Vol. 2, Six Cultures Series, B. Whiting (ed.).
MAYER, P. 1949. *The Lineage Principle in Gusii Society.* London: International African Institute, Memoir 24.

Hopi*

DENNIS, W. 1940. *The Hopi Child.* New York: Appleton-Century-Crofts.
SIMMONS, L.W. 1942. *Sunchief: The Autobiography of a Hopi Indian.* New Haven, Conn.: Yale University Press.
STEPHEN, A.M. 1936. *Hopi Journal of Alexander M. Stephen.* New York: Columbia University Press.
PARSONS, E.C. 1921. "Hopi Mothers and Children." *Man,* 21, 98–104.
TITIEV, M. 1944. *Old Oraibi.* Cambridge, Mass.: Papers of the Peabody Museum 22.

Hupa*

GODDARD, P.E. 1903. "Life and Culture of the Hupa." *University of California Publications in American Archaeology and Ethnology,* 1, 1–88.
TAYLOR, E.S. 1947. "Hupa Birth Rites." *Proceedings,* Indiana Academy of Science, 57, 24–28.
WALLACE, W.J. 1947. "Hupa Child Training—A Study in Primitive Education." *Educational Administration and Supervision,* 33, 13–25.

Ifaulk*

BURROWS, E.G., & M.E. SPIRO. 1953. *An Atoll Culture: Ethnology of Ifaulk in the Central Carolines.* New Haven, Conn.: Human Relations Area Files.

Ifugao*

BARTON, R.F. 1930. *The Half-Way Sun: Life Among the Head-Hunters of the Philippines.* New York: Brewer and Warren.
———. 1938. *Philippine Pagans: The Autobiographies of Three Ifugaos.* London: Routledge & Kegan Paul.

Ilocos*

NYDEGGER, W.F., & C. NYDEGGER. 1963. *Tarong: An Ilocos Barrio in the Philippines.* New York: John Wiley, Vol. 6, Six Culture Series, B. Whiting (ed.).

Israeli*

BETTELHEIM, B. 1969. *The Children of the Dream.* New York: Macmillan.
RABIN, A.I. 1965. *Growing Up in the Kibbutz.* New York: Springer.
SPIRO, M.E. 1956. *Kibbutz: Venture in Utopia.* Cambridge, Mass.: Harvard University Press.
———. 1958. *Children of the Kibbutz.* Cambridge, Mass.: Harvard University Press.

Japanese*

BENEDICT, R. 1946. *The Chrysanthemum and the Sword.* Boston: Houghton-Mifflin.
DORE, R.P. 1958. *City Life in Japan: A Study of a Tokyo Ward.* Berkeley: University of California Press.
SILBERMAN, B.S. 1962. *Japanese Character and Culture: A Book of Selected Readings.* Tucson: University of Arizona Press.
SINGLETON, J. 1967. *Nichū: A Japanese School.* New York: Holt, Rinehart & Winston.

Javanese*

GEERTZ, H. 1961. *The Javanese Family: A Study of Kinship and Socialization.* New York: The Free Press.

Jivaro*

KARSTEN, R. 1935. *The Head-Hunters of Western Amazonas.* Helsingfors: Commentationes Humanum Litterarum, Societas Scientiarum Fennica 7, No. 1.

STIRLING, M.W. 1938. "Historical and Ethnographical Material on the Jivaro Indians." *Bulletin,* Bureau American Ethnology 117, Washington, D.C.: U.S. Government Printing Office.

Kaingang*

HENRY, J. 1936. "The Personality of the Kaingang Indians." *Character and Personality,* 5, 113–123.

———. 1941. *Jungle People: A Kaingang Tribe of the Highlands of Brazil.* New York: Augustin.

Kaska*

UNDERWOOD, F.W., & I. HONIGMANN. 1947. "A Comparison of Socialization and Personality in Two Simple Societies." *American Anthropologist,* 49, 557–577.

Kikuyu*

BOYES, J. 1912. *John Boyes, King of the Wa-Kikuyu.* London: Methuen.

KENYATTA, J. 1938. *Facing Mount Kenya.* London: Seeker and Warburg.

LEAKEY, L.S.B. 1937. *White African.* London: Hodder and Stoughton.

ORDE-BROWNE, G. 1925. *The Vanishing Tribes of Kenya.* London: Seeley, Service.

Kiwai*

LANDTMAN, G. 1927. *The Kiwai Papuans of British New Guinea.* London: Macmillan.

Klamath*

PEARSALL, M. 1950. *"Klamath Childhood and Education."* Anthropological Records, 9, 339–351.

SPIER, L. 1930. *Klamath Ethnography.* University of California Publications in American Archaeology and Ethnology 30. Berkeley: University of Califronia Press.

Kongo*

WEEKS, J.H. 1914. *Among the Primitive Bakongo.* London: Seeley, Service.

Koryak*

BERGMAN, S. 1927. *Through Kamchatka by Dog-sled and Skis.* London: Seeley, Service.

CZAPLIČKA, M.A. 1914. *Aboriginal Siberia.* Oxford: Clarendon Press.

Kutenai*

TURNEY-HIGH, H.H. 1941.   *Ethnography of the Kutenai.* Memoirs of the American Anthropological Association, 36. Menasha, Wis.: American Anthropological Association.

Kwakiutl*

BENEDICT, R. F. 1934.   *Patterns of Culture.* Boston: Houghton-Mifflin.
BOAS, F. 1909. "The Kwakiutl of Vancouver Island." *Memoirs,* American Museum of Natural History, 8, 307–515.
———.1921. "Ethnology of the Kwakiutl." *Publications,* U.S. Bureau of American Ethnology, 35, 43–1481. [See also Codere, H. (ed.). 1960. *Kwakiutl Ethnography.* Chicago: University of Chicago Press.]
———. 1932. "Current Beliefs of the Kwakiutl Indians." *Journal of American Folklore,* 45, 177–260.
FORD, C.S. 1941. *Smoke from Their Fires: The Life of a Kwakiutl Chief.* New Haven, Conn.: Yale University Press.
GOLDMAN, I. 1937. "The Kwakiutl Indians of Vancouver Island." In M. Mead (ed.), *Cooperation and Competition among Primitive Peoples.* New York: McGraw-Hill, pp. 180–209.
WOLCOTT, H.F. 1967.   *A Kwakiutl Village and School.* New York: Holt, Rinehart Winston.

Kwoma*

WHITING, J.W.M. 1941.   *Becoming a Kwoma.* New Haven, Conn.: Yale University Press.

Lakher*

PARRY, N.E. 1932.   *The Lakhers.* London: Macmillan.

Lamba*

DOKE, C.M. 1931.   *The Lambas of Northern Rhodesia.* London: Harrap.

Lapp*

TURI, J. 1931.   *Turi's Book of Lappland.* London: Cape.
WHITAKER, I. 1955.   *Social Relations in a Nomadic Lappish Community* (Vol. 2). Oslo: Utgitt av Norsk Folkmuseum.

Lepcha*

GORER, G. 1938.   *Himalayan Village.* London: Michael Joseph.
MORRIS, J. 1938.   *Living with Lepchas.* London: Heinemann.

Lesu*

POWDERMAKER, H. 1933.   *Life in Lesu.* New York: W.W. Norton & Co., Inc.

Malaitans

HOGBIN, H.I. 1939. *Experiments in Civilization: The Effects of European Culture on a Native Community of the Solomon Islands.* London: Routledge & Kegan Paul.

Malekula*

DEACON, A.B. 1934. *Malekula: A Vanishing People in the New Hebrides.* London: Routledge & Kegan Paul.

LEGGATT, T.W. 1893. "Malekula, New Hebrides." *Reports of the Australian Association for the Advancement of Science,* 4, 697–708.

Manus*

FORTUNE, R.F. 1935. *Manus Religion.* Philadelphia: American Philosophical Society. Mead, M. 1930. *Growing Up in New Guinea.* New York: Morrow.

———. 1932. "An Investigation of the Thought of Primitive Children, with Special Reference to Animism," *Journal of the Royal Anthropological Institute,* 62, 73–190.

———. 1949. *Male and Female: A Study of the Sexes in a Changing World.* New York: Morrow.

———. 1956. *New Lives for Old: Cultural Transformation—Manus, 1928–1953.* New York: Morrow.

Maori*

AUSUBEL, D.P. 1961. *Maori Youth.* New York: Holt, Rinehart & Winston.

BEAGLEHOLE, E., & P. BEAGLEHOLE. 1946. *Some Modern Maoris.* Wellington, N.Z.: New Zealand Council for Educational Research.

BEST, E. 1924a. *The Maori.* Polynesian Society Memoir 5 (2 vols.). Wellington, N.Z.: Polynesian Society.

———. 1924b. *The Maori as He Was: A Brief Account of Maori Life as It Was in Pre-European Days.* Wellington, N.Z.: Dominion Museum.

BUCK, P.H. 1949. *The Coming of the Maori.* Wellington, N.Z.: Whitcombe, Tombs.

KESSING, F.M. 1928. *The Changing Maori.* Maori Board of Ethnological Research Memoir 4. New Plymouth, N.Z.: Maori Board of Ethnological Research.

RITCHIE, J.E. 1963. *The Making of a Maori.* Wellington, N.Z.: Reed and Reed.

Marquesans*

HANDY, E.S.C. 1923. *The Native Culture in the Marquesas.* Bernice P. Bishop Museum Bulletin 9. Honolulu, Hawaii: Bernice P. Bishop Museum.

LINTON, R. 1939. "Marquesan Culture." In A. Kardiner (ed.), *The Individual and His Society.* New York: Columbia University Press, pp. 137–196.

Masai*

HOLLIS, A.C. 1905. *The Masai: Their Language and Folklore.* Oxford: Clarendon Press.

MacQUEEN, P. 1909. *In Wildest Africa.* Boston: L. C. Page.

Mexican*

LEWIS, O. 1951. *Life in a Mexican Village: Tepoztlan Restudied.* Urbana: University of Illinois Press.

————. 1959. *Five Families: Mexican Case Studies in the Culture of Poverty.* New York: Basic Books.

————. 1961. *The Children of Sanchez: Autobiography of a Mexican Family.* New York: Random House.

REDFIELD, R. 1930. *Tepoztlan: A Mexican Village.* Chicago: University of Chicago Press.

ROMENY, K., & R. ROMNEY. 1966. *The Mixtecans of Juxtlahuca, Mexico.* New York: John Wiley, Vol. 4, Six Cultures Series, B. Whiting (ed.).

Murngin*

WARNER, W.L. 1937. *A Black Civilization.* New York: Harper & Row, Pub.

WEBB, T.T. 1933. "Aboriginal Medical Practice in East Arnhem Land." *Oceania,* 4, 91–98.

Nauru*

STEPHEN, E. 1936. "Notes on Nauru." *Oceania,* 7:34–63.

Navaho*

KLUCKHOHN, C. 1944. *Navaho Witchcraft.* Papers of the Peabody Museum of American Archaeology and Ethnology (Vol. 22, Number Two). Cambridge, Mass.: The Peabody Museum.

————. 1947. "Some Aspects of Navaho Infancy and Early Childhood." In G. Rohéim (ed.), *Psychoanalysis and the Social Sciences.* (Vol. 1) New York: International Universities Press, pp. 37–86.

————. 1960. "A Navaho Politician." In J.B. Casagrande (ed.), *In the Company of Man.* New York: Harper & Row, Pub., pp. 439–465.

KLUCKHOHN, C. & D. LEIGHTON. 1946. *The Navaho.* Cambridge, Mass.: Harvard University Press.

KLUCKHOHN, F., & F.L. STRODTBECK. 1961. *Variations in Value Orientations.* Evanston, Ill.: Row, Peterson.

LEIGHTON, D., & C. KLUCKHOHN. 1947. *Children of the People.* Cambridge, Mass.: Harvard University Press.

REICHARD, G.A. 1928. *Social Life of the Navaho.* New York: Columbia University Contributions to Anthropology 7.

Ngoni*

READ, M. 1956. *The Ngoni of Nyasaland.* New York: Oxford University Press.

————. 1960. *Children of Their Fathers: Growing Up among the Ngoni of Nyasaland.* New Haven, Conn.: Yale University Press.

————. 1968. *Children of Their Fathers: Growing Up among the Ngoni of Malawi.* New York: Holt, Rinehart & Winston (rev.).

Nuer*

EVANS-PRITCHARD, E.E. 1936. "Daily Life of the Nuer in Dry-Season Camps." In L.H. Dudley-Buxton (ed.), *Custom Is King.* London: Hutchinson, pp. 289–299.

————. 1940. *The Nuer: A Description of the Modes of Livelihood and Political Institutions of Nilotic People.* Oxford: Clarendon Press.

————. 1950. "The Nuer Family." *Sudan Notes and Records,* 31, 21–42.

HOWELL, P.P. 1954. *A Manual of Nuer Law.* London: Oxford University Press.

JACKSON, H.C. 1923. "The Nuer of the Upper Nile Province." *Sudan Notes and Records,* 6, 59–107.

SELIGMAN, C.G., & B.Z. SELIGMAN. 1932. *Pagan Tribes of the Nilotic Sudan.* London: Routledge & Kegan Paul.

TUCKER, A.N. 1933. "Children's Games and Songs in the Southern Sudan." *Journal of the Royal Anthropological Institute,* 63, 165–187.

Nyakyusa*

WILSON, M.H. 1950. "Nyakyusa Kinship." In A.R. Radcliffe-Brown & C.D. Forde (eds.), *African Systems of Kinship and Marriage.* London: International African Institute, pp. 111–139.

————. 1951. *Good Company: A Study of Nyakyusa Age-Villages.* London: Oxford University Press.

Okinawans*

HARING, D.G. 1969. *Okinawan Customs.* Rutland, Vermont: Tuttle.

MARETZKI, T.W., & H. MARETZKI. 1966. *Taira: An Okinawan Village.* New York: John Wiley, Vol. 7, Six Culture Series, B. Whiting (ed.).

Omaha*

FLETCHER, A.C., & F. LaFLESCH. 1911. "The Omaha Tribe." *Annual Reports of the Bureau of American Ethnology,* 27,: 17–654.

FORTUNE, R.F. 1932. *Omaha Secret Societies.* New York: Columbia University Press.

LaFLESCHE, F. 1963. *The Middle Five: Indian Schoolboys of the Omaha Tribe.* Madison: University of Wisconsin Press.

Ona*

BRIDGES, E.L. 1949. *Uttermost Part of the Earth.* New York: Dutton.

LOTHROP, S.K. 1928. "The Indians of Tierra del Fuego. "*Contributions from the Museum of the American Indians,* 10, 48–105.

Ontong-Javanese*

HOGBIN, H. I. 1930. "Spirits and the Healing of the Sick in Ontong Java." *Oceania,* 1, 146–166.

————. 1931a. "Education at Ontong Java." *American Anthropologist,* 33, 601–614.

————. 1931b. "The Social Organization of Ontong Java." *Oceania,* 1, 399–425.

Paiute*

WHITING, B.B. 1950. *Paiute Sorcery.* Viking Fund Publications in Anthropology 15, New York: Viking Fund.

Palaung*

MILNE, L. 1924. *The Home of an Eastern Clan.* Oxford: Clarendon Press.

Papago*

DENSMORE, F. 1929 *Papago Music*. Bulletin of the Bureau of American Ethnology 90. Washington, D.C.: U.S. Government Printing Office.

JOSEPH, A., R.B. SPICER, J. CHESKY. 1949. *The Desert People*. Chicago: University of Chicago Press.

UNDERHILL, R.M. 1939. *Social Organization of the Papago Indians*. Columbia University Contributions to Anthropology 30. New York: Columbia University Press.

———. 1942. "Child Training in an Indian Tribe." *Marriage and Family Living*, 4, 80–81.

WILLIAMS, T.R. 1958. "The Structure of the Socialization Process in Papago Indian Society." *Social Forces*, 36, 251–25.

Pondo*

HUNTER, M. 1936. *Reaction to Conquest*. London: International African Institute.

Puerto Ricans*

LANDY, D. 1959. *Tropical Childhood: Cultural Transmission and Learning in a Rural Puerto Rican Village*. Chapel Hill: University of North Carolina Press.

Pukapukans*

BEAGLEHOLE, E., & P. BEAGLEHOLE. 1938. *Ethnology of Pukapuka*. Bernice P. Bishop Museum Bulletin 150. Honolulu, Hawaii: The Museum.

———. 1941. "Personality Development in Pukapukan Children." In L. Spier, A.I. Hallowell, & S.S. Newman (eds.), *Language, Culture and Personality*. Menasha, Wis.: Sapir Memorial Fund, pp. 282–298.

Pygmies*

TURNBULL, C. 1962. *The Lonely African*. New York: Simon & Schuster.

Rājpūts*

MINTURN, L., & J.T. HITCHOCK. 1966. *The Rājpūts of Khalapur, India*. New York: John Wiley, Vol. 3, Six Cultures Series, B. Whiting (ed.).

Riffians*

COON, C.S. 1931. *Tribes of the Rif*. Harvard African Studies (Vol. 9). Cambridge, Mass.: Peabody Museum of Harvard University.

WESTERMARCK, E.A. 1926. *Ritual and Belief in Morocco*. London: Macmillan.

Russian*

BAUER, R., A. INKELES, & C. KLUCKHOHN. 1956. *How the Soviet System Works: Cultural, Psychological and Social Themes*. Cambridge, Mass.: Harvard University Press.

GORER, G., & J. RICKMAN. 1949.   *The People of Great Russia.* London: Cresset.
MEAD, M. 1951.   *Soviet Attitudes toward Authority.* New York: McGraw-Hill.
———. 1951.   "What Makes the Soviet Character?" *Natural History,* 60, 296–303, 336.
———. 1954.   "The Swaddling Hypothesis: Its Reception." *American Anthropologist,* 56, 395–409.
MILLER, W.W. 1960.   *The Russians as People.* New York: Dutton.

R'wala*

Musil, A. 1928.   *The Manners and Customs of the R'wala Bedouins.* New York: Czech Academy of Sciences and Arts and Charles R. Crane.

Samoans*

HIROA, TE RANGI (Peter H. Buck). 1930.   *Samoan Material Culture.* Bernice P. Bishop Museum Bulletin 75. Honolulu, Hawaii: Bernice P. Bishop Museum.
MEAD, M. 1928.   *Coming of Age in Samoa.* New York: Morrow.
———. 1928.   "The Role of the Individual in Samoan Culture." *Journal of the Royal Anthropological Institute,* 58, 481–495.
———. 1928.   "A Lapse of Animism among a Primitive People." *Psyche,* 9, 72-77
———. 1930.   *Social Organization of Manua.* Bernice P. Bishop Museum Bulletin 76. Honolulu, Hawaii: Bernice P. Bishop Museum.
———. 1937 (ed.).   *Cooperation and Competition among Primitive Peoples.* New York: McGraw-Hill.
———. 1949.   *Male and Female: A Study of the Sexes in a Changing World.* New York: Morrow.
SU'APA'IA, K. 1962.   *Samoa: The Polynesian Paradise.* New York: Exposition Press.

San Pedro*

PAUL, B.D. 1950.   "Symbolic Sibling Rivalry in a Guatemalan Indian Village." *American Anthropologist,* 52, 205–218.
———. 1950.   *Life in a Guatemalan Indian Village.* Chicago: Delphian Society.
PAUL, B.D. & L. PAUL. 1952.   "The Life Cycle." In S. Tax (ed.), *Heritage of Conquest.* Glencoe, Ill.: The Free Press, pp. 174–192.

Sanpoil*

Ray, V.F. 1933.   *The Sanpoil and Nespelem.* Seattle: University of Washington Press.

Sherente*

NIMUENDAJÚ, C. 1942.   *The Serente.* Publication of the Frederick Webb Hodge Anniversary Fund 4. Los Angeles: The Southwest Museum.

Siriono*

HOLMBERG, A.R. 1950.   *Nomads of the Long Bow.* Institute of Social Anthropology, Smithsonian Institution Publication 10. Washington, D.C.: U.S. Government Printing Office.

Slave*

HONIGMANN, J.J. 1946. *Ethnography and Acculturation of the Fort Nelson Slave.* Yale University Publications in Anthropology 33. New Haven, Conn.: Yale University Press.

Swazi*

KUPER, H. 1947. *An African Aristocracy.* London: Oxford University Press.
———. 1950. "Kinship among the Swazi." In A.R. Radcliffe-Brown & C.D. Forde (eds.), *African Systems of Kinship and Marriage.* London: International African Institute, pp. 86–110.
MARWICK, B.A. 1940. *The Swazi.* Cambridge, England: Cambridge University Press.

Tallensi*

FORTES, M. 1938. *Social and Psychological Aspects of Education in Taleland.* London: Oxford University Press.
———. 1949. *The Web of Kinship among the Tallensi.* London: Oxford University Press.

Tanala*

LINTON, R. 1933. *The Tanala.* Publication of the Field Museum of Natural History, Anthropological Series 22. Chicago: Field Museum of Natural History.
———. 1939. "The Tanala of Madagascar." In A. Kardiner (ed.), *The Individual and His Society.* New York: Columbia University Press, pp. 251–290.

Taos*

PARSONS, E. 1936. *Taos Pueblo.* General Series in Anthropology 2. Menasha, Wis.: Banta.

Tenetehara*

WAGLEY, C., & E. GALVÃO. 1949. *The Tenetehara Indians of Brazil.* New York: Columbia University Press.

Teton Dakota*

ERIKSON, E. 1939. "Observations on Sioux Education." *Journal of Psychology,* 7, 101–156.
———. 1950. *Childhood and Society.* New York: W.W. Norton & Co., Inc.
MACGREGOR, G. 1946. *Warrriors Without Weapons.* Chicago: University of Chicago Press.
MEKEEL, H.S. 1936. "An Anthropologist's Observations on Indian Education." *Progressive Education,* 13, 151–159.
MIRSKY, J. 1937. "The Dakota." In M. Mead (ed.), *Cooperation and Competition among Primitive Peoples.* New York: McGraw-Hill, pp. 382–427.

Thonga*

JUNOD, H.A. 1927. *The Life of a South African Tribe*. (2 vols.). London: Macmillan.

Tikopia*

FIRTH, R.W. 1936. *We, the Tikopia*. New York: American Book.

Tiv*

AKIGA (B. Akiga Sai). 1939. *Akiga's Story: The Tiv Tribe as Seen by One of Its Members*. London: Oxford University Press (trans. Rupert East).
BOHANNAN, P. 1954. Tiv Farm and Settlement. *London: Her Majesty's Stationery Office*.
———. 1957. *Justice and Judgment among the Tiv*. London: Oxford University Press.
BOHANNAN, P., & L. BOHANNAN. 1953. *The Tiv of Central Nigeria*. London: International African Institute.

Tonga*

COLSON, E. 1958. *Marriage and the Family among the Plateau Tonga of Northern Rhodesia*. Manchester, England: Manchester University Press.

Trobriands*

LEE, D. 1940. "A Primitive System of Values." *Philosophy of Science, 7*, 355–378.
MALINOWSKI, B. 1922. *Argonauts of the Western Pacific*. London: Routledge & Kegan Paul.
———. 1926. *Crime and Custom in Savage Society*. New York: Harcourt Brace Jovanovich.
———. 1927. *Sex and Repression in Savage Society*. New York: Harcourt Brace Jovanovich.
———. 1929. *The Sexual Life of Savages in North-West Melanesia: An Ethrographic Account of Courtship, Marriage and Family Life among the Natives of the Trobriand Islands, British New Guinea* (2 vols.). New York: Liveright.
———. 1935. *Coral Gardens and Their Magic: A Study of the Method of Tilling of the Soil and Agricultural Rites in the Trobriand Islands* (2 vols.). London: Allen and Unwin.

Trukese*

FISCHER, A.M. 1950. *The Role of the Trukese Mother and Its Effect on Child Training*. Final S.I.M. Report, Pacific Science Board. Washington, D.C.: National Research Council.
GOODENOUGH, W. 1951. *Property, Kin and Community on Truk*. New Haven, Conn.: Yale University Publications in Anthropology, 46.

Tswana*

BROWN, J.T. 1926. *Among the Bantu Nomads*. Philadelphia: Lippincott.

DORNAN, S.S. 1925. *Pygmies and Bushmen of the Kalahari.* London: Seeley.
DUGGAN-CRONIN, A.M. 1928. "The Bechuana." In A.M. Duggan-Cronin (ed.), *The Bantu Tribes of South Africa* (2 vols.). Cambridge: Deighton, Bell.
LIVINGSTONE, D. 1857. *Missionary Travels and Researches in South Africa.* New York: Murray.
SCHAPERA. I. 1938. *A Handbook of Tswana Law and Custom.* London: Oxford University Press.
———. 1940. *Married Life in an African Tribe.* London: Faber and Faber.

Turkana*

GULLIVER, P.H. 1951. *Preliminary Survey of the Turkana.* Communications from the School of African Studies 26. Capetown, South Africa: University of Capetown Press.
———. 1955 *The Family Herds.* London: Routledge & Kegan Paul.
RAYNE, H. 1919. "Turkana." *Journal of the African Society,* 18, 183–189, 254–265.
WHITE, R.F. 1920. "Notes on the Turkana Tribe." *Sudan Notes and Records,* 3, 217–222.

Ulithians*

LESSA, W.A. 1950. *The Ethnography of Ulithi Atoll.* C.I.M.A. Final Report 28. Los Angeles: University of California Press. (Mimeographed.)
———. 1966. *Ulithi; A Micronesian Design for Living.* New York: Holt, Rinehart & Winston.

Venda*

GOTTSCHLING, E. 1905. "The Bawenda: A Sketch of Their History and Customs." *Journal of the Anthropological Institute,* 35, 365–386.
STAYT, H.A. 1931. *The BaVenda.* London: International Institute of African Languages and Cultures, Oxford University Press.
WESSMANN, R. 1908. *The Bawenda of the Spelonken.* London: African World.

Wapisiana*

FARABEE, W.C. 1918. *The Central Arawaks.* Anthropological Publication of the University of Pennsylvania Museum 9. Philadelphia: University of Pennsylvania Press.

Warrau*

SCHOMBURGK, R. 1922. *Travels in British Guiana,* 1840–44 (Vol.1). Georgetown, British Guiana: Daily Chronicle Office.

Wichita*

SCHMITT, K., & I.O. SCHMITT. 1952. *Wichita Kinship, Past and Present.* Norman, Okla.: University Book Exchange.

Winnebago*

OSTREICH, N. 1948. "Trends of Change in Patterns of Child Care and Training Among the Wisconsin Winnebago." *Wisconsin Archaeologist,* 29, 39–140.
RADIN, P. 1916. *"The Winnebago Tribe."* *Annual Reports,* Bureau of American Ethnology, Smithsonian Institution, 37, 33–550.

Witoto*

WHIFFEN, T. 1915. *The North-West Amazons.* New York: Duffield.

Wogeo*

HOGBIN, H.I. 1943. "A New Guinea Infancy: From Conception to Weaning in Wogeo." *Oceania,* 13, 285–309.
———. 1946. "A New Guinea Childhood: From Weaning till the Eighth Year in Wogeo." *Oceania,* 16, 275–296.
———. 1970. *The Island of Menstruating Men.* New York: Harper & Row, Pub.

Yagua*

FEJOS, P. 1943. *Ethnography of the Yagua.* Viking Fund Publication in Anthropology 1. New York: The Wenner-Gren Foundation.

Yakut*

IOKHEL'SON, V.I. 1933. "The Yakut." *Anthropological Papers of the American Museum of Natural History,* 33, 33–225.

Yoruba*

BASCOM, W. 1969. *The Yoruba of Southwestern Nigeria.* New York: Holt, Rinehart & Winston.
DELANO, I.U. 1937. *The Soul of Nigeria.* London: Werner Laurie.
WARD, E. 1936. "The Parent-Child Relationship among the Yoruba." *Primitive Man,* 9, 56–63.
———. 1937. *Marriage among the Yoruba.* Catholic University of America Anthropological Series 4. Washington, D.C.: Catholic University of America.
———. 1938. *The Yoruba Husband-Wife Code.* Catholic University of America Anthropological Series 6. Washington, D.C.: Catholic University of America.

Yukaghir*

IOKEL'SON, V.I. 1926. *The Yukaghir and the Yukaghirized Tungus.* New York: Stechert.

Yungar*

GREY, G. 1841. *Journals of Two Expeditions of Discovery in Northwest and Western Australia.* London: Boone.

NIND, S. 1832. "Description of the Natives of King George's Sound (Swan River Colony) and Adjoining Country." *Journal of the Royal Geographic Society*, 1, 21–57.

Zadruga*[5]

TOMASIC, D.A. 1948. *Personality and Culture in Eastern European Politics*. New York: G.W. Stewart.

Zulu*

BRYANT, A.T. 1949. *The Zulu People*. Pietermaritzburgh: Shuter and Shuter.

KRIGE, E.J. 1936. *The Social System of the Zulus*. London: Longmans, Green.

MAHLOBO, G.W.K., & E.J. KRIGE. 1934. "Transition from Childhood to Adulthood Amongst the Zulus." *Bantu Studies*, 8, 157–191.

SCHAPERA, I. (ed.) 1937. *The Bantu-Speaking Tribes of South Africa: An Ethnographic Survey*. London: Routledge and Kegan Paul.

Zuni*

BENEDICT, R.F. 1934. "The Pueblos of New Mexico." In *Patterns of Culture*. Boston: Houghton-Mifflin, pp. 57–129.

———. 1935. *Zuni Mythology*. Columbia University Contributions to Anthropology 21 (2 vols.). New York: Columbia University Press.

BUNZEL, R.L. 1929. *The Pueblo Potter: A Study of the Creative Imagination in Primitive Art*. New York: Columbia University Press.

———. 1933. *Zuni Texts*. Publication of the American Ethnological Society 15. New York: G.E. Stechert.

GOLDFRANK, E.S. 1945. "Socialization, Personality, and the Structure of Pueblo Society (with particular reference to Hopi and Zuni)." *American Anthropologist*, 47, 516–539.

PARSONS, E. 1917. "Notes on Zuni, Parts I. and II." *Memoirs of the American Anthropological Association*, 4, 151–327.

STEVENSON, M.C. 1901–1902. "The Zuni Indians: Their Mythology, Esoteric Fraternities and Ceremonies." *Annual Report*, Bureau of American Ethnology, 23, 13–608.

---

[5]The term *Zadruga* referrs to a peasant cooperative association in South Slav culture and not to a specific society.

GLOSSARY

ability the skilled performance of particular kinds of learned behavior, especially those involved in specific ways of shaping, altering, or directing events, both internal and external, that affect an organism (see *capacities* and *skill*)

Abosom a native language term used by the Ashanti to refer to the gods protecting patrilineal kin groups, or *ntoro*

absolute nutritional dependence the complete dependency of the *Homo sapiens sapiens* infant on others for its care and feeding

abusua a native term for the Ashanti matrilineal kin group

achieved status a status earned or learned through performance and demonstration

acquired drive instrumental behavior that develops from positive reinforcements of stimuli arising in the social and cultural environments of an organism (see *secondary drive*)

action language punishment use of culturally standardized body postures to indicate disapproval of behavior

action language reward use of culturally standardized body postures to indicate approval of behavior

adapt to be possessed of a genetic heritage that allows survival in a given environment

adaptation a biological character or cluster of characters possessed by a population of animals, selected by the natural environment, that increases the chances of survival for a population

affinal refers to patterns of kinship behavior based on a social recognition of relationships established through marriage

age-grade categories of people recognized in a culture as being at the same point in the life cycle

age-set a social group based on the principle of recruitment of persons of the same age, without regard to their kinship relations

alchera a native language term used by the Arunta of Central Australia to designate the mythical past and its events

alimentary canal a tube or passage used in the digestion and the absorption of food, beginning in most animals at the mouth and ending at the anus

anaclitic characterized by an extreme dependence, in which all psychological functions are suppressed or are secondary to drives

anal sphincters the circular band of muscles that encircle the opening at the lower end of the colon, through which wastes are excreted

anatomy the morphology or body structure of an organism

anthropology a science concerned with the comparative study of humans and their physical and cultural characteristics

antibody a specific substance produced by an organism in response to the introduction of a particular antigen and capable of uniting with that antigen

antigen any protein substance that, when introduced into the body, will stimulate the formation of specific antibodies

ape a common name for the members of the *Pongidae* family

apocryphal a false or spurious account

arboreal tree-living

archaeological the remains, usually artifacts and often bones, left by humans at their living and working sites

Archeozoic a geologic era that began some 1,500,000,000 years ago and ended approximately 925,000,000 years before the present

artifact objects purposely shaped by animals, especially man, to alter or deal with a natural environment

Arunta a native society of Central Australia

ascribed status automatic assignment of a status in a society

Ashanti a native society of West Africa

Australopithecine a genus of fossil *hominids* containing two, or possibly three, species, *A. africanus, A. robustus,* and *A. afarensis,* which existed from the middle Pliocene to the middle Pleistocene epoch

autism a psychological state characterized by extreme emotional and social withdrawal and absorption in fantasies

avoidance conditioning a form of operant conditioning in which introduction of a harmful stimulus is avoided by a correct response by the subject (see *escape conditioning*)

avunculocal family kin group a type of extended family kin group in which unmarried males leave their households to reside with a mother's brother and then after marriage bring their wives to reside in their mother's brother's household

baboon a common name for a large, ground-dwelling monkey of the genus *Papio*

bayi the native language term used by the Ashanti to denote a special form of witchcraft that a mother can use to discipline unruly children

behavior the total movement activity of an animal

behavior kind a concept that refers to ethnographic records of well-identified adults behaving repeatedly in ways that can be counted and classified

Bemba a native society of East Africa

bilateral kin group a type of consanguineal kin group in which children are said to be equally related to and descended from their father and mother and the ancestors of their father and mother

biology   the nature—that is, the structure and functioning—of living organisms

bipedalism   locomotion using two feet

Botocudo   a native society of the Amazon River Basin

brachiation   locomotion using the arms

brainstem reticular system   a network of intercellular fibers forming the core of the brainstem which reach the brain cortex and which appear to be involved in the transmission of visceral, auditory, visual, and other nerve impulses

brono   a native language term used by the Ashanti to refer to a subdivision or "ward" of an established village, occupied by members of the same matrilineage

capacities   genetically based patterns of behavior brought into operation at particular stages of growth and development only when elicited through specific combinations of physical, cultural, and social circumstances

carnivores   an order of flesh-eating animals that includes dogs and cats

caste   an endogamous social group linked to a specific occupation

catarrhini   the group of primates which includes humans, apes, and Old World monkeys

Cheyenne   a native North American Indian society

chimpanzee   a common name for a member of the ape family which is smaller and more arboreal than the gorilla

chordata   the phylum of animals which at some time in their lives have a notochord, or rodlike cord of cells, that forms the chief supporting structure of the body; in humans the notochord appears during embryonic development

churinga   a personal totem symbol used by the Arunta of Central Australia at the time of a boy's initiation into his father's patrilineal descent group

ciliary muscles   the muscle in a portion of the eyeball that affects adjustment of the thickness of the lens

clan   a type of unilineal kinship group that is based on a working compromise that some affines, or relatives by marriage, are to be included, while some consanguineal relatives are to be excluded; a clan may be a greatly enlarged lineage or a grouping of a number of lineages which trace their descent from the same known or often mythical ancestor

class   a group of persons acting on the basis of their awareness of common or shared status-roles

classic conditioning   the type of conditioning in which a conditioned stimulus and an unconditioned stimulus are used, or paired, together (see *respondent conditioning* and *operant conditioning*)

cognition   an idea or a thought

cognitive   refers to the process of thinking

colon   the part of the large intestine extending from its beginning at the cecum to the rectum

concept   an idea of something, formed by mentally combining all of its features

configuration of culture   a concept used in cultural anthropology studies to denote a grouping of patterns of culture with similar forms, functions, or meanings; a whole category of culture

consanguineal   patterns of kinship behavior based on social recognition of common biological descent; all those relatives whose connecting links are one of common ancestry

contagion   the spread of disease by direct or indirect contact

contextual analysis   a methodological procedure and a theoretical assumption used in anthropology that notes each aspect of culture must be viewed and studied in terms of its interdependence with other aspects of culture

cranial capacity   a measurement of the volume or space filled by the contents of the skull

Cretaceous   a geologic epoch that began approximately 120 million years before the present and lasted until some 60 million years ago

critical events   a hypothesis that there are specific events occurring during the development of human infants and children that influence similar events during adult life

critical periods   a hypothesis that there are times in the development of animals during which the individual is most receptive to learning from particular kinds of experience

cross-cousin   a cousin whose related parents are siblings of different sex—that is, the children of *Ego's* mother's brother or father's sister (see *parallel cousin*)

cultural charter   patterns of culture that detail the work to be undertaken in a society, the ways tasks are to be performed, and the recruitment of persons to such tasks

cultural ecology   the mutual relationships between humans and their surrounding environments that are shaped and directed by the products of learned, shared, patterned, and transmitted behavior *(see ecology)*

cultural environment   the surroundings of humans, including the products of learned, shared, patterned and transmitted behavior (see *natural environment*)

cultural transmission   the process of socialization

culture   explicit and implicit patterns of learned behavior that comprise the distinctive achievements of human groups; culture consists of traditional ideas and their related values, which are the products of action and also are conditioning elements for further action; culture is seen in both artifacts and patterned behavior that is widely shared in a society and is transmitted from one generation to the next

culture-bound   studies and conclusions limited because research has been conducted within only one culture, or a few closely related cultures (see *transcultural*)

culture-fair   description of a psychological test that is free of culturally specific or limiting items

cumulative evolutionary adaptations   the biological inheritance of genetic modifications that have occurred in a population over a long period

curare   a substance derived from tropical plants of the genus *Strychnos*, used in medicine and research for arresting the action of motor nerves; also used by some South American Indians as a hunting poison

Dahomean   a native society of West Africa

deoxyribonucleic acid (DNA)   any of the class of nucleic acids that contains deoxyribose, found mainly in the nuclei of cells; with ribonucleic acid (RNA), a vehicle for the transmission of genetic information

diachronic   changes in the facts of a system through time (see *synchronic*)

Dobu   a native society of Melanesia

drive   an aroused state in an organism in which behavior tends to be oriented toward reducing stimuli that are noxious or to remove a condition of deprivation

duolocal family kin group   a type of extended family kin group in which the husband and father and wife and mother do not regularly reside with one another but remain as members of their own nuclear families, with children usually residing with their mother

Dusun   a native society of northern Borneo

ecology   the mutal relationships of different organisms and the environments in which they live

eight-class system   among the Arunta of the northern part of the Central Australian desert, an individual must learn that there are eight groups of important persons, consisting of all the members of the two Arunta moieties, two generational groups, and all first and all second cross-cousins in each of the two moieties, that define the locations of possible marriage partners and set rules for proper social behavior outside of the nuclear family, local group, patrilineal descent group, and clan (see *four-class system*)

electroencephalogram   a graphic record made by a special machine that shows the electrical activity of the brain

emotion   visceral changes that result from an animal's response to an experience; emotion is the physiological form in which an animal experiences the consequences of reflection

enculturation   the process of transmitting a particular culture (see *socialization*)

endogamy   a rule of marriage that requires an individual to take a husband or wife from the local or kin groups to which they belong (see *exogamy*)

environment   the total surroundings of an organism (see *natural environment* and *cultural environment*)

enzyme   any one of a variety of complex organic substances originating from living cells capable of certain chemical changes in organic substances by catalytic action, as in digestion.

Eocene   a geologic epoch that began about 55 million years before the present and ended approximately 35 million years ago

escape conditioning   a form of operant conditioning in which a harmful stimulus is removed after a "correct" response by the subject (see *avoidance conditioning*)

ethnocentrism   a tendency to regard the ways of one's own culture and society as inherently superior and to judge all of the ways of other cultures in terms of a local culture

ethnographic   a written record setting forth the details and interrelations of the parts of a culture

ethnographic present   a descriptive account of a culture written as though the people being described all live today as they once did in the past; a literary device

ethology   the scientific study of animal learning and behavior

evolution   biological descent with cumulative adaptive changes in the genetic and behavioral features of whole populations of animals

exogamy   a rule of marriage that requires an individual to take a wife or husband from outside of the local or kin groups to which they belong (see *endogamy*)

extended family kin group   a type of kin group created when two or more nuclear family kin groups are linked together through either a special form of parent-child or brother-sister kin relationship

extrapolate   to infer an unknown entity or quantity from something already known

feral   existing in a natural state; having reverted to a natural conditon

fie   the native language term for the Ashanti dwelling group

focal value   a concept abstracted through relating statements made by persons in a culture concerning the worth of conduct and cultural goals and the kinds of behavior such persons regularly use

four-class system   among the Arunta of the southern part of the Central Australian desert, an individual must learn that there are four groups of important persons, consisting of all the members of the two Arunta moieties and two generational groups, that define the locations of possible marriage partners and set rules for proper social behavior outside of the nuclear family, local group, patrilineal descent group, and clan (see *eight-class system*)

fraternal polyandry   the marriage of two or more brothers to one woman at the same time

free soiling   a *Homo sapiens* species-characteristic behavior form in which the infant freely releases accumulated bowel and bladder wastes

Galton's question   a methodological caution to ensure that in making transcultural comparisons the cultures chosen for study have no known history of cultural contact, borrowing, or common language and physical origins

genotype   the genetic makeup of an organism: contrasts with *phenotype,* or the appearance of an organism imparted by its genotype.

glycogen   a polysaccharide $(C_6H_{10}O_5)$ that makes up the principal carbohydrate storage material in animals

gorilla   a common name for the largest member of the ape family

gracile   light, slender, or thin in appearance

grammatical system of language   a stock of morphemes and the arrangements in which they occur

holistic   an approach to the study of culture based on the assumption that every part of culture is interrelated with every other part

hominid   the family that includes all species of *Homo* as well as all of the *Australopithecines*

hominoid   the superfamily that includes humans and apes

Homo   the genus to which modern humans, *Homo sapiens,* belongs

Homo sapiens   the only living species of the genus *Homo*

hormone   any one of a number of internally secreted compounds, such as insulin or thyroxine, formed in the endocrine glands, that affect the functions of specific organs or tissues

hyperkeratosis   a thickening of the horny layer of the skin

ideology   all of the cultural beliefs or values developed and used in a society

imprinting   a process of strong, often irreversible, social attachment to stimuli learned early in life in a specified period of limited duration

inarticulate experience   experience involving the generational transmission of learned behavior without the use of sounds, particularly sounds formed into language

incest taboo   a social rule prohibiting close relatives from having sexual intercourse; the kinds of relatives included or excluded as sexual partners vary from culture to culture

infantilization   the biological process through which adult *Homo sapiens* exhibit specific body characteristics typical of the infant ape (see *neoteny*)

inkata   a native language term used by the Arunta of Central Australia to designate the senior male in a patrilineal descent group

innervate   to communicate or transport nervous energy or impulses

instinct   a term and concept used in the social sciences until the 1940s; the concept of *species-characteristic behavior* now has largely replaced *instinct* in studies of human behavior

instrumental   movements by an organism directed at attaining a specific goal or reinforcement

intrauterine   within the uterus

intrinsic reward   approval for behavior arising in the context of specific situations

intrinsic situational punishment   social situations that confront an individual with implied disapproval of behavior

iris   a part of the anatomy of the eye which is the contracting, circular diaphragm forming the colored part of the eye and with a circular opening, or pupil, at its center.

Jurassic   a geologic epoch that began about 180 million years before the present and ended approximately 120 million years ago

kinaesthesia   the style of movement imparted through the stresses in muscles, tendons, and joints of the body

kindred   a local group that is comprised of bilateral relatives—that is, all persons related to a specific individual

kin group   any social grouping based on recognition of kinship ties and regular use of kinship terms

kinship   ways of defining the social, rather than biological, relationships leading to a continuity between generations and maintenance of particular features of social living

kra   a native language term used by the Ashanti to refer to an aspect of the self inherited directly from the father

language   a complex set of verbal habits that is organized into three central sub-systems (grammatical, phonological, morphophonemic) and two peripheral subsystems (semantic, phonetic); all human languages possess all five subsystems

larynx   the air passage and vocal organ between the tongue and trachea

law of effect   the principle that asserts that the response of an organism to a stimulus is automatically strengthened if it is followed by a reward or automatically extinguished if followed by a punishment (also termed the *principle of reinforcement*)

learning   any permanent modification of behavior by an animal based on reinforced or rewarded experience

lexical   refers to the words or vocabulary used in a language

lineage   a type of unilineal, consanguineal kin group that traces descent from a known, common ancestor who lived about five or six generations before *Ego*'s generation.

local group   a collection of nuclear families

locomotion   the power to move from place to place

locus   a place or locality

mammal   a class of vertebrates

material reward   a tangible remuneration as an incentive for repetition of approved forms of behavior

matrilateral family kin group   a type of extended family kin group based on close, nonsexual relationships between a brother and sister, in which the wife, her husband, and their children reside together but do not interact socially as a nuclear family

matrilineage   a type of unilineal, consanguineal kin group that traces its descent from a known, common female ancestor who lived about five or six generations before *Ego*'s generation

matrilineal kin group   a type of unilineal, consanguineal kin group in which *Ego*'s descent is traced exclusively through the mother and mother's female ancestors

mbanbiuma   a native language term used by the Arunta of Central Australia to designate a special ritual concerned with increases in the numbers of totem animals and plants

Mesozoic   a geologic era that began approximately 220 million years ago and ended about 60 million years before the present

metabolic   the sum of the physical and chemical processes in an organism by which protoplasm is produced and maintained and by means of which energy is made available for behavior

Miocene   a geologic epoch that began some 25 million years before the present and ended approximately 12 million years ago

mmusuaban   a native language term used by the *Ashanti* to refer to a matrilineal clan

mogya   a native language term used by the *Ashanti* to denote the essence of their biological heritage from their mother and their mother's female ancestors

moiety   a unilineal kin group; usually a society is divided into two so that each individual is a member of one or the other; moieties are also based on residence and choice

monkey   a common name for a grade of *Anthropoidea* whose members all possess tails

morpheme   a minimal unit of language, comprised of one or more phonemes, that carries a unitary cultural and social meaning for both speakers and hearers (see *phoneme*)

morphophonemic system of language   a code uniting the grammatical and phonological subsystems of language

motor pattern   an activity skill, such as walking, that requires fine coordination of body parts

nana   a native language term used by the Ashanti as a designation for "grandparent" as well as for senior political and religious leaders

natural environment   the surroundings of an organism that are unshaped or altered by forms of cultural behavior

natural selection   genetic selection occurring without direction or plan by anyone

Neanderthals   a generic name used for a group, or taxon, of fossil humans; the earliest forms of the species *Homo sapiens*

neoteny   in *Homo sapiens*, the phenomenon of being a fully mature animal while exhibiting many of the body characteristics of the infant ape (see *infantilization*)

neurophysiological   the normal functioning of the nervous system

nonseasonal sexuality   the regular and continuous sexual interest of the *Homo sapiens* male in the *Homo sapiens* female

ntoro   a native language term used by the Ashanti to denote the essence of spirituality believed inherited from the father and father's male ancestors

nuclear family   a family kin grouping comprised of a married man and woman and their children and characterized by eight special social relationships based on sex and descent

nucleic acid   a chemical compound vital for all life, comprised of oxygen, hydrogen, nitrogen, carbon, and phosphorus

Nuer   a native society of the Nilotic Sudan

nuture   to promote the physical and emotional development of an infant or child by providing food, support, care, protection, comfort and consolation. Nurture involves parents, their surrogates, or unrelated adults providing care and comfort to a dependent child

Numbakulla   a native language term used by the Arunta of Central Australia to refer to a founding hero ancestor of Arunta society

Oligocene   a geologic epoch that began approximately 35 million years ago and ended about 25 million years before the present

Onyankopon   a native language term used by the Ashanti to refer to the creator god

operant conditioning   the type of conditioning in which the subject's responses are instrumental in obtaining reinforcements

optic nerve   either one of the second pair of cranial nerves consisting of sensory tracts that conduct impulses from the retina to the brain

Ordovician   a geologic epoch that began approximately 500 million years before the present and lasted until approximately 450 million years ago

organic bridgeheads   a term used in this text for specific links between human biology and culture in the process of socialization

organic emphasis of hearing   an accentuation of the sense of hearing in *Homo sapiens* as the consequence of primate evolutionary adaptations

organic emphasis of sight   an accentuation of the sense of sight in *Homo sapiens* as the consequence of primate evolutionary adaptations

organic repression of smell   a limitation of the sense of smell in *Homo sapiens* as the consequence of primate evolutionary adaptations

organism   a form of life consisting of interdependent parts that together maintain life processes

ostracoderm   any one of numerous living and fossil, small salt and fresh water crustaceans having bodies covered by a hinged bivalve shell

palate   the roof of the mouth; often termed as either the *hard* (the forward portion) or the *soft* (the back portion) palate

Paleocene   a geologic epoch that began some 60 million years ago and ended approximately 55 million years before the present

Papago   a native North American Indian society

parallel cousin   a cousin whose related parents are siblings of the same sex—that is, the children of *Ego*'s mother's sister or father's brother (see *cross-cousin*)

patrilineage   a type of unilineal, consanguineal kin group that traces its descent from a known, common male ancestor who lived about five or six generations before *Ego*'s generation

patrilineal kin group   a type of unilineal, consanguineal kin group in which *Ego*'s descent is traced exclusively through the father and father's male ancestors

pellagra   a disease caused by a deficiency of niacin in the diet

pepsinogen   a *zymogen* from gastric cells that changes into an enzyme because of some internal change in an organism

pharynx   the tube or cavity that connects the mouth and nasal passages with the esophagus

phenotype   the external morphological appearance of an organism, imparted by its *genotype*

phone   a speech sound

phoneme   the smallest unit of sound recognized and used by speakers of a language (see *morpheme*)

phonetic system of langauge   the ways in which sequences of phonemes are converted into sound waves by the articulation of a speaker and are decoded from speech by a hearer

phonological system of language   a stock of phonemes and the arrangements in which they occur

phratries   unilineal kin groups consisting of two or more clans that recognize a special bond of concern as clans, particularly with reference to other phratries in a society

phylogenetic reductionism   the assumption that the behavior of all individuals in a species and that of all species occurs according to the same set of biological laws

physical punishment   the use of blows and social isolation to elicit desired forms of behavior

physiology   the normal organic functioning of an animal

Pithecanthropian   a term used for a group of *hominids,* now usually considered to be a single species termed *Homo erectus,* that was directly ancestral to *Homo sapiens*

placoid   platelike scales or skin surface

platyrrhine   broad-nosed; a term used to describe all of the New World monkeys

pleasure principle   the tendency to satisfy basic id impulses

Pleistocene   a geologic epoch that began approximately 2 million years before the present and ended approximately 15,000 years ago

Pliocene   a geologic epoch that began approximately 12 million years ago and ended about 2 million years before the present

polyandrous family kin group   a type of extension of the nuclear family kin group in which a woman is wife and mother in two or more nuclear families—that is, a woman is married to two or more men at the same time

polygamous family kin group   a type of extension of the nuclear family kin group in which two or more nuclear families are joined through sharing one husband and father or one wife and mother

polygynous family kin group   a type of extension of the nuclear family kin group in which a man is husband and father in two or more nuclear families—that is, a man is married to two or more women at the same time

pongidae   the family of primates that includes the gibbon, gorilla, orangutan, and chimpanzee, as well as many fossil forms

postulate   a proposition assumed to be true and used in the proof of other propositions

primate   the order of mammals to which *Homo sapiens* belongs

process of socialization   abstract statements of empirical reference concerning the transmission of human culture (see *socialization* and *socialization process*)

propensity   a natural inclination or tendency

psychoanalysis   a method of treating illness, developed by Sigmund Freud, that stresses insight on the part of the patients into their unconscious conflicts

psychology   a science concerned with study of human behavior and mental phenomena

puberty   a series of gradual biological changes involving sexual maturation

pyloric valve   the valve between the opening from the stomach to the duodenum

ramage   a bilaterally extended kinship group that centers upon a particular *Ego*

reality principle   the action of the ego in attempts to identify and eliminate potentially painful stimuli

reason   the capacity to form conclusions, make judgments, or draw inferences

reflection   the capacity to go beyond observed properties of particular objects or events to draw inferences about unobserved properties of such objects or events on the basis of past or present experiences

reflexes   relatively fixed or stereotyped responses to stimuli, usually involving only a specific body part, that can be modified through experiences (see *taxes*)

remuneration   to give, bestow, or compensate

repetition-compulsion   behavior forms that are unusually resistant to elimination by adverse stimuli

respondent conditioning   an unlearned response to a specific stimulus; the conceptual opposite of operant conditioning (see *classic conditioning*)

retina   the innermost coat of cells on the back part of the eyeball that receives visual images

reward and punishment   elements such as food, water, or electrical shock experienced by an organism that affects its behavior

ribonucleic acid (RNA)   any of the class of nucleic acids that contain ribose, found mainly in the cytoplasm of cells; with deoxyribonucleic acid (DNA) a vehicle for transmission of genetic information

rickets   a childhood disease characterized by softening and deformities of the bones as the consequence of malnutrition

role   the precise ways rights and duties associated with a polar social position, or status, are put into operation (see *status*)

secondary drive   a drive that develops as a consequence of positive reinforcement of stimuli arising from an organism's environments (see *acquired drive*)

semantic system of language   the association of various morphemes, combinations of morphemes, and arrangements of morphemes with things and situations, or kinds of things and situations

shaman   an individual who specializes in dealing with the supernatural as a healer and an intermediary

shaping   modification of behavior through reinforcement of successive and larger steps that lead to the behavior desired by the experimenter

skill   competent performance of a task (see *ability* and *capacities*)

social identity   social categories or kinds or persons recognized in a society

socialization   the process of transmission of human culture

socialization process   abstract statements of empirical reference concerning the transmission of human culture (see *socialization* and *process of socialization*)

sociology   a science concerned with study of the structure and functioning of human social groups

soft palate   the part of the palate near the uvula (see *palate*)

somatic   pertaining to body cells

sororal polygyny   the marriage of two or more sisters to one man at the same time

space of recognition   an awareness by an animal of its environment that is limited, or extended, by its sensory and brain structures and their capacities

spear thrower   a device used to propel or add extra thrust to a spear

species-characteristic behavior   all the forms of behavior by an animal, having a physical-chemical basis, that are exhibited widely in a species and generally subject to a minimum of modification through experience

sphincter   a circular band of "voluntary" or "involuntary" muscle that encircles a body opening or one of the body's hollow organs

status   a polar position in a pattern of reciprocal social behavior (see *role*)

status relationship   a reciprocal and doubly contingent right-duty pair or set widely known and used in a society

stereoscopic vision   sight in which each eye sees an object from slightly different points of view producing a single image of the object with the appearance of depth or relief

stimulus   any form of environmental energy capable of affecting an organism

stimulus-response reinforcement learning   the association and reinforcement of any number of stimulus-response connections stemming from reduction of body needs

sunsum   a native language term used by the Ashanti to refer to an aspect of the self inherited directly from the father

susu   a native language term used to refer to the matrilateral family kin group among the Dobu of Melanesia

symbolic   something that is used for or regarded as representing something else, such as an object representing an idea

symbolic interaction   a mutual exchange of information between animals through the use of signs that stand for or represent experience

synchronic   having reference to the facts of a system at one particular time and without regard to the history of such facts (see *diachronic*)

tactile pad   a fleshy portion of the anatomy very sensitive to touch; in *Homo sapiens* each fingertip has a tactile pad

taro   either one of two varieties of stemless plants cultivated in tropic regions of the world

taxes (singular, **taxis**)   continuous stereotyped movements of an organism, usually involving the whole body toward a particular direction, as a response to an external stimulus; taxes are generally not modifiable through experience

taxon (plural, **taxa**)   a group of animals related by descent from a common ancestor

taxonomy   the classification of plants or animals in a way that places them in groups according to their structural relationships and the ordering of such groups into a ranked set; the ranked set used in this text, which is a conventional one in evolutionary studies, is:

kingdom
  phylum
subphylum
  class
    subclass
     order
      suborder
       superfamily
       family
        subfamily
         genus
          species

technology the subsystem of culture that enables man to produce from the natural environment the artifacts that make it possible to survive through culturally adapting to a local setting

teleological a kind of reasoning that explains events in terms of their contributions to the achievement of the goals of a larger plan or design

theme a postulate or positon, declared or implied, and usually controlling behavior or stimulating activity, that is tacitly approved or openly promoted in a society

tool an object used to perform or to make easy a mechanical operation, which is directed toward changing the natural environment to facilitate survival

transcultural statements derived from research concerned with the universally human, or general, statements true of all human cultures, rather than one or a few cultures (see *culture-bound*)

transtemporal a concern in research with the nature of events or processes as they have existed through the long span of historic and prehistoric time

tree shrew an order of squirrellike, generally arboreal animals, classified either as a separate primate suborder *Tupaiodea)* or as members of the lemur suborder of the primates

trial and error the elimination of "wrong moves" and the consolidation of "right moves" as an organism modifies its behavior through experience

Triassic a geologic epoch that began approximately 220 million years before the present and ended approximately 180 million years ago

urethral sphincters the circular band of muscles that encircle the membranous tube that extends from the urinary bladder to the outside of the body

uxorilocal family kin group a type of extended family kin group in which the groom is required to leave his paternal household and reside with his bride, either in or close by the household of the bride's parents (may also be termed a *matrilocal family kin group*)

verbal punishment uses of speech to convey disapproval of behavior

verbal reward uses of speech to elicit desired behavior or to approve and encourage repetition of approved behavior

vertebrate the subphylum which contains all animals with backbones, such as birds, fish, reptiles, and mammals

vibrissa hair with nerve endings at the base that can serve as a sense detector in touching objects

virilocal family kin group a type of extended family kin group in which the bride is required to reside with the groom either in or close by the household of the groom's parents (may also be called a *patrilocal family kin group*)

visceral the organs in the cavities of the body, particularly those in the abdominal cavity

xenophobia a morbid and unreasonable fear of strangers, particularly strangers from other cultures

yafunu a native language term used by the Ashanti to refer to the segment or part of the matrilineage residing together as a *fie*, or dwelling group

yoga any one of the methods or exercises through which freedom of the self is sought from its nonexternal and impermanent states

Zinjanthropus an *Australopithecine* fossil form discovered in Tanzania, East Africa, in 1959

Zuni a native North American Indian society

INDEX

nuclear family as basic unit of culture, 200
parent surrogates among, 201–02
personal totem symbols (*churinga*), 206
ritual capture following female initiation rituals, 285
technology, 199
totem centers, 204
totem spirit as father among, 204
use of magic for internal discipline, 209
use of sorcery for internal discipline, 209
virilocal extended family, 200
Ashanti of West Africa
abusua (matrilineal kin group), 218–19
and Arunta of Australia, configurations of kinship and kin groups of, contrasts between, 222
bayi (special form of witchcraft), 215
brono (neighborhood wards), 220
economic organization, 216
fie as dwelling unit, 212–13
history, 211–12
importance of grandparents in culture, 217
kinship, kin groups, and enculturation of, 212–21
kinship relations, 212–17
kinship terms, 214
kra (life force), 220
matrilineal kin groups, 212, 220
mmusuaban (matrilineal clan), 220
mythology of
abosom (god), 220
Onyankopon (Ashanti creator god), 220
notoro (patrilineal kin group), 220
parent surrogates, 214–15
patrilineal kin group (*notoro*), 220
sibling relationships, 217–18
social mobility, 221
sunsum (personality), 220
"talking drums," 218
technology, 211–12
themes, 332
village organization, 219–20
yafunu (maximal matrilineage), 220
Australopithecus, 9–11
communication, 13
conjectural drawings, 10
use of tools, 11
Autism, 161–62
Bettleheim, B., studies of, 161
deficient socialization in, 162
Kanner, L., studies of, 161
London Institute of Psychiatry, study of, 161
roots of, as a functional disturbance, 161
roots of, as a genetic malfunction, 161–62
Autistic children; *see also* Children, autistic
Autonomic nervous system, 54–56
Avis, V., 13
Ayers, B., relationship between social organization and shelter floor plan, 319, 320, 326–27, 341
Aztec, cannibalism as a consequence of population growth, 119

Babbling and language learning, 371
Bacon, M., 419
Baer, D., 134
Bales, R., 198
Bali, 123, 124
Bandura, A., 97, 98–99, 107
Banton, M., 259
Barker, R., 105
Barry, H., III, 238, 419; relationship between child training and art, 339–40
Bateson, G., 97, 398, 402, 405, 406
Bayi (special form of Ashanti witchcraft), 215
Behavior, human
and biology, relationship between, operant conditioning and, 113–50
childhood, attitude toward in Papago culture, 86–87
deviant, relationship to social class, 291

measures of in operant conditioning, 134–38
sexual
critical periods hypothesis in, 179, 182–84
development of, critical periods in, isolated and motherless monkeys in study of, 183–84
social
critical periods hypothesis in, 179–80
development of, critical periods in, isolated and motherless monkeys in study of, 182–84
species-characteristic, 35–51
definition, 36
in humans, 37–51
speech, dependence on in language learning research, 370–71
Behavior kind data, collection and use of, 87
Behaviorism, Thorndike-Hull, 75–80
Bemba, adaptation to chronic threat of hunger, 120–21
Benedict, R., vi
Bettelheim, B., 41, 58, 160, 161, 170
basis of feral child myths, 160
effect of Nazi death camps on enculturation process, 170
human apparatuses for relating to reality, 41
infant inner life, 58
roots of autism, 161
Bijou, S., 134
Biological and cultural modes of transmission in socialization process, 125
Biological isolation, degrees of, 166
Biology, human
and culture, 113–32
and culture, interplay of in socialization process, as a cybernetic interrelationship, [C ⟷ B], established through the course of human evolution, 27–28, 51
emergence of human abilities through, 130
and culture, organic links between, 35–70
cultural structuring of features of, 121–29
and human behavior, relationship between, operant conditioning and, 113–53
Bipedalism, 6–7
effect on "space of recognition," 7
Birdwhistell, R., x
Bladder
control of, enculturation of in Arapesh culture, 126
Blauvelt, H., 39
Blood pressure changes in operant conditioning of rats, 139
"Blood rite" in male initiation rituals of Arunta, 281
Bloom, B., age of development of intelligence, 47
Blount, B., 385, 386
Blushing, enculturation of, 123
Boas, F., vi
relationship of grammatical structure to thought, 365–66
Bock, P., 231
Body, size of in language, 355–57
Body movements, enculturation of, 123
Body needs, energy for learning derived from, 77–78
Bolton, C., 419
Boram, C., 242
Bowel control, enculturation of in Arapesh culture, 126
Bowels, constipation or looseness of, enculturation of, 121–22
Brachiation
in early primates, 6
effect on "space of recognition," 6
Brain, size of human
change in, possible relationship to cultural development, 11–12
in language, 355–56
relationship to use of tools, 12
Brain case, size of, relation to size of human face, 47
Brain wave patterns
changes of in operant conditioning of monkeys, 140